READY-TO-WEAR

READY-TO-WORK

D0923918

A book in the series

Comparative and International Working-Class History

GENERAL EDITORS:

Andrew Gordon / *Harvard University*   Daniel James / *Duke University*

Alexander Keyssar / *Duke University*

READY-TO-WEAR

READY-TO-WORK

A CENTURY OF INDUSTRY AND IMMIGRANTS

IN PARIS AND NEW YORK

NANCY L. GREEN

DUKE UNIVERSITY PRESS

DURHAM & LONDON

1997

© 1997 Duke University Press

All rights reserved

Printed in the United States of America

on acid-free paper ∞

Typeset in Bodoni Book with Miehle Condensed display

by Keystone Typesetting, Inc.

Library of Congress Cataloging-in-Publication

Data appear on the last printed page

of this book.

In

memory

of my

mother

CONTENTS

ACKNOWLEDGMENTS

Academics are homeworkers too, albeit privileged ones. We reflect and write at home, alone in front of blank pieces of paper (yes, some of us still cherish the pen and pencil) and screens. But we also fan out to the archives and libraries and create our own networks. No project this long could have taken place without incurring many intellectual, material, and moral debts among colleagues, friends, and students.

The first week I got to New York in 1984, on a German Marshall Fund Research Fellowship, I was lucky to be warmly welcomed into the small circle of garment industry scholars by Roger Waldinger, with whom I have kept up discussion (and sometimes disagreements) over all these years. Bob Lazar, at the ILGWU Archives—then still down on Seventh Avenue—shared his knowledge of the collection and suggested files I never would have found on my own.

Back in Paris, I attacked the Archives nationales and found that a twentieth-century project was not quite as easy as sticking to the period before World War I. But I learned, like so many others, the fears and joys of the terms "dérogations" and "à titre exceptionnel." With a small group of sociologists, a garment industry study group "Travail et quartier" was formed, funded by grants from

the Ministère de la culture (via the Mission recherche expérimentation—MIRE) and the Ministère de l'équipement, du logement, de
l'aménagement du territoire et des transports (MELATT). I learned
much about the contemporary Sentier thanks to Annie Benveniste,
Jeanne Brody, Kenan Ozturk, Yinh Phong Tan, Sandrine Tasmadjian, and Agnès Vince, while they learned its history. Above all, the
stimulating intellectual environment of the Ecole des Hautes Etudes
en Sciences Sociales has been a privilege and a pleasure.

Then came the too-long years of writing. Back and forth, between
American and French libraries, I had the good fortune to spend two
semesters at the Charles Warren Center for Studies in American
History at Harvard, where Bernard Bailyn, Susan Hunt, and the
Center's "fellows" and "sisters"—Deb Coon, Phil Ethington, Janice
Knight, Peter Mancall, Mary Odem, Lisa Wilson—provided very
much appreciated intellectual and moral support.

People too numerous to mention have read bits of this manuscript
along the way; others have read substantial chunks. I thank them all
and especially: Alex Keyssar, who has given ever-critical support to
this project from early on and has saved me from many Gallicisms
along the way; the two no-longer-anonymous readers for Duke University Press, John Merriman and Don Reid; Laura Frader, Donna
Gabaccia, Jan Goldstein, and Roger Waldinger; as well as my
French *doctorat d'Etat* committee, who read the thousand-page
French version: Michelle Perrot, Louis Bergeron, Jean Heffer, Yves
Lequin, and Emile Témime. Thanks also go to Robert H. Green, who
has fielded so many questions throughout the years.

Portions of this research have appeared in earlier forms in various
publications over the last several years: "Immigrant Labor in the
Garment Industries of New York and Paris: Variations on a Structure," *Comparative Social Research* 9 (1986): pp. 231–43. "Juifs et
noirs aux Etats-Unis: La rupture d'une 'alliance naturelle,'" *Annales, E.S.C.* 42, no. 2 (Mar.–Apr. 1987): pp. 445–64; "Sweatshop
Migrations: The Garment Industry between Home and Shop," in *The
Landscape of Modernity,* ed. David Ward and Olivier Zunz (New
York: Russell Sage Foundation, 1992), pp. 213–32; "La main-
d'oeuvre immigrée et l'industrie du vêtement: Au-delà de la culture
et du capital," *Sociologie du travail* 32, no. 2 (Spring 1994):
pp. 165–84; "Art and Industry: The Language of Modernization in
the Production of Fashion," *French Historical Studies* 18, no. 3

(Spring 1994): pp. 722–48; "Classe et ethnicité, des catégories caduques de l'histoire sociale?" in *Les Formes de l'expérience: Une autre histoire sociale,* ed. Bernard Lepetit (Paris: Albin Michel, 1995), pp. 165–86; and "Women and Immigrants in the Sweatshops: Categories of Labor Segmentation Revisited," *Comparative Studies in Society and History* 38, no. 3 (July 1996): pp. 411–33. I thank the journals and their publishers for permission to reuse the materials here.

Two important last words of thanks, first to a building: the Bibliothèque nationale. As many colleagues know, it has served as intellectual fount as well as *lieu de sociabilité* for American academics in Paris. It has been a place where I've researched, written, checked footnotes, and kept up with American and French colleagues for the many years I have lived in Paris. We will all miss the rue Richelieu.

Finally, my deepest thanks go to Pierre Bouvier. Of course. The Franco-American comparison started at home.

Acknowledgments

xi

INTRODUCTION

Apparel, One of the Last Urban Industries

Is women's wear frivolous or functional? Clothes protect the body from the elements and from the wandering eye. They add a bit of art to the quotidian, sometimes subtly, at times controversially. They provide protection, modesty, and adornment along with that elusive, sociopsychological quality, appearance.[1] Yet clothes serve one other, less heralded but nonetheless important, purpose. They provide jobs. The women's apparel industry is one of the last manufacturing sectors left in the finance- and service-centered "global" cities of today. From Jews to Puerto Ricans, Italians to Chinese and Turks, the sewing machines have offered work to the immigrants and women of New York and Paris for the last century.

New York and Paris have both been heralded as fashion capitals—of the United States, of the world. Seventh Avenue and the Sentier, their respective garment districts, were both centers of clothing and design even before the takeoff of the ready-to-wear revolution in the late nineteenth century. The concentration of the industry in these cities occurred largely because they were manufacturing and financial capitals, cosmopolitan cities that have attracted fashion extremes and the immigrants who helped produce them. The women's apparel business has been a textbook case in the economics of agglomeration. Close to rapidly shifting fashion fads, able to copy the latest trends while adding that little je ne sais quoi of difference, the industry's centralized locations abet quick communication about design changes.[2] The nearness to museums and the beauty of the city, not to mention its women, was how one Parisian admirer accounted for the symbiosis between fashion and the French capital.[3] More prosaically, nearby sewing-machine repairmen, buttonhole specialists, or accessory suppliers expedite manufacture and ease last-minute crises, while a critical mass of wholesalers makes the trip to the garment districts worthwhile for buyers. Thus, while Paris and New York increasingly fit into the twentieth-century logic of urban segregation—commerce within, manufacture relegated to the outlying areas—women's apparel manufacture continues to hover around the urban hub.

Already in 1855, clothing was by far New York City's largest industry, occupying one-third of all those working in manufacture. Similarly, the garment trades in Paris employed the greatest number of Parisian workers in 1847.[4] By 1900, apparel "fed" some 134,308 dressmakers, tailors, and factory garment workers in New York City, over double that of the 57,039 carpenters, joiners, painters, and glaziers, and accounted for one-quarter of the manufacturing jobs. By 1920, when factory garment workers were singled out, they alone represented 135,682 jobs, while the women's-wear custom-made trade had begun its inexorable decline.[5] The number of operatives in "apparel and other fabricated textile products" climbed to 228,857 in 1950, over double those in printing and publishing, before beginning to decline to 180,352 workers in the entire metropolitan area in 1960, 131,962 in 1970; and 98,939 in 1980.[6] Even shrunk to only 83,000 jobs in 1993, garment still represented the largest manufacturing sector in the city.[7] "Tattered and torn," as Roger Waldinger has put it, "the garment industry hangs on."[8]

Similarly, *travail des étoffes* reigned in Paris at the turn of the century. With 290,340 jobs in 1906, it was well over double the next manufacturing category (*métaux ordinaires*) and represented 38.5 percent of all manufacturing jobs. By 1926 the industry had slipped to 192,853 jobs, with metalwork catching up, and in 1931 the transformation of metals had slightly bypassed that of clothes. By 1946, clothing jobs had plummeted to 85,461, due to the deportation of many Jewish garment workers, increasing standardization in the industry, as well as a new counting system. In 1962, the garment industry was the third largest, employing over 90,000 people, roughly one-quarter of all of the *industries mécaniques.*[9] Yet even as most sectors of the increasingly standardized French garment industry suffered job losses between 1975 and 1987, apparel work in the Paris region declined less than elsewhere.[10] With an estimated 40,000 people on some 2,000 payrolls, women's ready-to-wear was still the second-largest employer in the Paris area in 1993 (after printing and publishing).[11]

The Meaning of Light Industry, or Flexibility Revisited

Heavy industries are stationary, mechanized, concentrated; ours is mobile, labor-intensive, competitive.[12]

Garment manufacture has thus been an important presence in the modern city. Yet, curiously, it has had a very small role in the history of industrialization. Three things stand out from a transcontinental review of card catalogues and computer databases: (1) Clothes have in general attracted much more interest for their form than for their fabrication; studies of costumes and changing styles abound, and most sociological treatments of fashion have stressed consumption over production. (2) The industry per se has attracted much more attention in New York than in Paris. (3) None of the stories has been truly integrated into a reflection on the history of the Industrial Revolution. The first finding seems obvious. That is why fashion appeals in the first place. The second remains almost inexplicable: Why has the important and prestigious Parisian fashion industry aroused so relatively little historical interest?[13] Undoubtedly, the first point explains the second; so fascinated by *la mode,* the French have been less interested in its mode of production.

But the third proposition is more intriguing still. Until recently, the history of industrialization defined itself as the history of heavy industry, relegating light industry to the explanatory margins. With its concentration of men and machines, of steam and smoke, mining and metallurgy, textiles and railroads captured the economic and historical imagination for the greater part of the last century and a half. Yet heavy industry never entirely tamed its light counterpart. Light industry, with its low capital needs and relatively low-cost, low-bulk technology, found its place within the urban economy (and urban history) if not within the mainstream history of the Industrial Revolution.[14] As Louis Bergeron has argued, we need to extract the term "industrialization" from a conceptual or verbal monolithism.[15] We need to consider the small garment factories alongside the strip mines, homework as well as assembly lines, in order to redefine the multiple paths of twentieth-century urban industrialization and re-evaluate our ideas about full employment and steady hours inherited from a nineteenth-century factory model.

Raphael Samuel was among the first to remind us of the hand technology beside the steam power, and the debate over protoindustrialization has shown that there were alternate, nonlinear paths to the factory floor.[16] More recently, the "flexible specialists" have sought to deconstruct the notion of an inevitable assembly-line model altogether.[17] There is no better sector than the garment industry to address these issues. While Philip Scranton has challenged the heavy industrial paradigm from within—by finding the flexibility within the textile industry and in batch processing[18]—I would argue that this mass-production industry without mass-production methods challenges the paradigm from without. The garment industry was not marginal to the urban economies and should not be so to the history of industrialization. And, unlike Samuel's example or the nineteenth-century protoindustrialization debate, women's wear is striking in its very staying power. Its small shops and homeworkers persisted in spite of Taylor, in spite of Ford. It was an example of "flexible specialization" before the term was coined and of an "informal economy" before the notion was repatriated from the Third World.[19]

For a long time, the garment industry was castigated as archaic. Karl Marx predicted that the sewing machine would convert garment making into a proper factory system.[20] Indeed, only the sewing machine, a model of technological diffusion, has usually merited note in the often technologically centered histories of industrialization. As Alfred Chandler said about the industry:

Ready-to-Wear and Ready-to-Work

The improvements in the sewing machine brought the factory into the production of shoes and clothes. By the 1870s, the one remaining vestige of the older putting-out system was in the making of clothing in or near some of the largest cities.[21]

Thirty years later the "vestige" was still there and still labeled backward. The United States Industrial Commission described the garment industry as an "antiquated," "primitive mode of production" at the turn of the century.[22] In the late 1930s, this meant that "the largest industry of America's financial center harks back to an era of small-scale capitalism."[23] The fashion business is "somewhat of an anachronism" summarized a report in the late 1950s.[24]

Images of homework—the "factory at home" (*l'usine chez soi*) or production-in-bits (*la production en miettes*)—as Michelle Perrot and Alain Faure have called it, and those of garment manufacture in general, have been undergoing change, however. Philippe Vigier called attention to the double myth of light industry, with its dark legend and rosy one. The former harps on an outmoded, precapitalist past; the latter vaunts the virtues of a new "third state" between capital and labor.[25] From contemptible anachronism to contemporary adulation, the garment industry has dramatically changed status in the eyes of the new economic historians studying flexible specialization and the sociologists studying ethnic entrepreneurs.

Charles Sabel, Jonathan Zeitlin, and Michael Piore have postulated a theory of "flexible specialization" which can provide an alternative explanation for past economic history as well as a prescription for the future. They argue provocatively that the outcome of mass production was not as inevitable as once thought in the light of its successes from the 1920s to the 1970s. In a similar vein, Alain Cottereau has proposed a stimulating reading of the "dispersed workshop" (*fabrique éclatée*) of the British and French shoe industries to reflect on alternative "possibilities of development."[26] In reaction to the rigidities on the assembly line and in the union rulebooks, a more flexible organization of production implies more cooperation within firms as well as a wider notion of "community" among competitors within industrial districts. The argument is both historic and historiographic, and is itself grounded in the 1980s recession that challenged previous models of economic success.

In this new view, the women's garment industry has shifted dramatically from archaic to avant-garde. Reinterpreted as a proud rebel from the mass production model, the manufacture of fashion, particularly in its Benetton version, has been hailed as one of the harbingers of the new second industrial revolution. Views of the *système Sentier* in Paris have shifted in some circles from a negative one of tax fraud and undocumented workers to that of a model of flexibility that will solve our post-Fordist woes.[27] Yet neither image does the apparel industry historical justice. If the century-long endurance of the garment-producing form of flexibility is an important corrective to smokestack-filled narratives of industrial development, the content and context of that flexibility need to be examined. What we have to ask is, flexibility for whom?

Interest in flexibility has shifted the analysis from labor markets to capital deployment. The characteristics of the secondary labor market so well analyzed and seemingly criticized by Michael Piore in his earlier and important *Birds of Passage* have now become keys to entrepreneurial success. In the more macroanalytical approach of his and Charles Sabel's *The Second Industrial Divide*, the equilibrating effect of flexibility is seen as the remedy to the ossification of standardization that defines the now-castigated primary sector. Yet I would argue that two important qualifications need to be added to this optimistic view. For one, the term "flexibility" itself has entered the language of political economy to describe what in fact are two different levels of activity: the global level of an economic sector and the firm level of work organization. For the industrial sector, flexibility may successfully juggle supply and demand. However, at the individual firm level, this implies both individual successes and failures. Analyses of flexibility have thus far emphasized the former to the latter, incorporating an implicit social Darwinism.

Second, then, in proposing a labor rather than an entrepreneurial history of flexibility, I will examine the social consequences of what may simply be one of the most transparent cases of fluctuating demand. From pleats to shoulder pads, the extreme variability inherent in the fashion business has to this day meant high levels of turnover, seasonal unemployment, and poor working conditions, which seem to be a common corollary to the highly competitive contracting-out system. What does this mean for labor recruitment?

Ready-to-Wear and Ready-to-Work

The migration "laws" first elaborated by E. G. Ravenstein were full of aquatic imagery: he spoke of "currents of migration," with their "eddies" and their "shallows." Gradual movement became a veritable rush as the "cistern of water after the tap has been turned on" became a "spilling over" from overpopulated countries.[28] The language of migration, in English as in French, has been replete with waves/*vagues,* flows/*flux,* tides/*marées humaines,* and streams ever since the late nineteenth century. It is a language useful for its dynamic quality (which I will continue to borrow) of movement. But it can also imply an inevitability of which we must beware. Did immigrants just float into the garment industry unwittingly?

There are two recurring founding myths about the peopling of the garment shops: the Jewish tailor and the nimble-thimbled woman. The clothing-industry labor force has indeed had more than its generous share of "Wandering Jews" and skilled women. But in addition to Eastern European Jews and native seamstresses, other men along with battalions of immigrant women from around the world have come in "waves" to the sewing machines, out of choice, out of skill, or out of necessity. Italians, blacks, Puerto Ricans, Dominicans, Chinese, and Koreans in New York; Armenians, Turkish Jews, Italians, North African Jews, (largely Serbian) Yugoslavs, Turks, Southeast Asian Chinese, and Pakistanis in Paris have also found jobs making skirts and blouses, dresses and slacks, over the last century. The industry has been (in)famous for its multiethnic labor force and has been a microcosm of a good part of each city's immigration history. Even though there are nonimmigrants in garment work, and all immigrants do not end up sewing, the apparel industry is an important example of immigrant networks in action.

Here, too, an image has shifted considerably, that of the garment shop entrepreneur. From exploiter of men and women in grim turn-of-the-century sweatshops, he (more likely than she) has become the hero of a new era. Mobilizing kith and kin within the immigrant neighborhood, the ethnic businessman is the modern job-giver within what Alejandro Portes has called the "ethnic enclaves." In his study of the New York case, Roger Waldinger has well shown how this works for the garment industry. "Birds of passage," men or women, have not just been sucked by happenstance or against their will into the vortex of an anonymous secondary labor market.[29] They have most likely been hired by fathers or brothers, found work through mothers or sisters, or been employed thanks to someone with a familiar face or accent from home.

Yet, according to one estimate, only 5 percent of garment workers become garment bosses.[30] Like flexibility, the ethnic entrepreneurs (who practice it) are only part of the story. The saga of labor must complement the tale of capital. The opportunity structure importantly stressed by Waldinger (in criticizing cultural explanations of immigrant entrepreneurial success) works for the machine operators as it does for their employers. Easy-to-learn skills are as important as low-capital start-ups in explaining the plethora of immigrant garment firms and their appeal to the newly arrived.

I would like to take the perspective one step beyond the immigrant networks. The study of ethnic entrepreneurs, like immigrant communities in general, has made important historiographic strides in recent years. The focus on foreigners and their families has been an important corrective to the color-blind or accent-mute studies of the working classes.[31] However, the majority of migration studies have taken on immigrant groups one by one. In so doing, an important dynamic has been overlooked: how immigrants relate to one another at the intersection of successive "waves." It seems that cities more than industries have attracted interest in this aspect of population change.[32] By studying ethnic succession through the looking glass of one industry, I propose to examine the interactive nature of a multiethnic labor environment.[33] Different immigrants have replaced one another over time, while at any given time, the comings and goings of newcomers have meant a cacophony of accents in the garment districts. In looking at the different paths to the sewing machines, I will explore conflict and consensus, notions of class and notions of ethnicity, as interpreted on Seventh Avenue and in the Sentier.

Comparative History and Poststructural Structuralism

Finally, this book is not only a reflection on flexibility and stability and on the ebb and flow of immigrant groups. It is also intended to chart new methodological territory. There have been calls for comparative history ever since the turn of the century, although it seems the more frequent the calls, the greater the proof that they have been ignored.[34] The repeating history of immigrant garment workers offers a doubly comparative analysis, that of one industry in two places and of different immigrant groups in one industry. The comparison is spatial, ethnic, and temporal, covering a century.

This study is thus, among other things, an exercise in comparative economic history, one which, along the lines of Claude Lévi-Strauss's call for "*niveaux significatifs,*" has sought the significant level for comparison.[35] An intermediary level of analysis focusing on one industrial sector in two cities seems particularly conducive to analyzing different rhythms of economic development in a more "controlled" manner than attacking "industrialization" at the level of the nation-state.[36] Furthermore, I have included what I would call an interactive comparative method, not only constructing the comparison and analyzing the differences from the historian's point of view but also examining the asymmetric visions about style and standardization perceived by garment industrialists and analysts on both sides of the Atlantic.

This is a tale of one industry in two cities and also a tale of Jews and Chinese, blacks and whites, Turks and Armenians. Some immigration historians have also taken up the call for comparison, but they, too, have been little heeded.[37] Yet immigrant studies should by their very nature be comparative. The immigrant embodies a host of comparisons: from country of origin to country of settlement; along divergent paths toward various destinations; converging from different regions toward one city. The comparison of different groups across time and space which I propose here suggests that a new approach to immigration history can shift the focus beyond the single-group community study, important as it is. How else can we ask broader questions of similarity and difference, of variations on a theme? What, in the migration experience, may be common to all immigrants? What, in addition to the obvious factors of culture and accent, synagogue and parish, differentiate them on the shop floor or in the union halls? The century-long perspective is as necessary to evaluate the different voices and the no-less apparent similarities within the labor force as it is to understand the economics of garment making.

The *longue durée* here does not mean immobility and stasis. On the contrary, it is only over time that we can see the important differences within the structure, while recognizing the structure nonetheless, in what I call a "poststructural structuralist" approach.[38] The debate over structure versus agency presents a false dichotomy. Jews, Italians, Turks, and Chinese have all sworn at broken needles and snagged bobbins in similar veins but in different languages. As we will see, it depends on the moment as to whether it is the bobbin itself or the linguistic variant of its name which is more important.

The book has two parts. The first examines the industry in comparative perspective. The second focuses on work, the labor force, and relations among workers. Chapter 1 addresses the fashion dialectic of imitation and differentiation and its implications for mass production. It describes the general history of the democratization of clothing demand and the widening of supply through an increased division of labor and the mid-nineteenth-century introduction of the sewing machine. The next two chapters (2 and 3) discuss the specific developments of the women's apparel industry in New York and Paris from the "takeoff" of the women's ready-to-wear revolution in the late nineteenth century to the present. Each city's garment industry has its own narrative, punctuated differently by the two world wars. Chapter 4 more explicitly compares those differences with regard to markets, rhythms of development, labor movements, and labor legislation, while giving expression to the different definitions of style and attitudes toward industrialization.

The much-heralded "return of the sweatshop" (chapter 5) is examined in the context of flexibility at work. Three particular traits have characterized garment labor conditions in both cities over the last century: the little skill needed for most operating jobs, high seasonality, and extensive contracting and subcontracting. These are not, as some sociologists and economists have argued, simply a response to the contemporary recession of the industry. They have recurred during times of expansion as of decline. They clearly situate the garment industry within the secondary labor market, in which women and immigrants bear the brunt of variability and poor conditions. The next two chapters examine the images of innate and imported skill attributed to these workers and question whether gender and ethnicity are the best ways of understanding the labor force and whether "cheap labor" is not a more useful category of analysis (chapter 6). Similarly, the cultural stereotypes most often attributed to different immigrants contradict themselves more than they enlighten. Industrial structure rather than cultural characteristics explains why immigrants were attracted to the industry. Yet political upheaval and poverty at home and immigration policies in the United States and France explain who came to which machines and when (chapter 7).

Finally, an examination of conflict and cooperation, perceptions of ethnicity and those of class, shows clearly how "poststructural" options have varied within the industrial structure. Jewish-American women, Italians, blacks, Hispanics, and Chinese have perceived themselves both as garment workers and as specific actors within the International Ladies' Garment Workers' Union (chapter 8). In Paris (chapter 9), native-immigrant relations overlaid at times by gender ones and more importantly by rising xenophobia in the 1930s raise other questions about harmony and discord in an industrial context. The reciprocal visions of Polish and Tunisian Jews, of Serbian Yugoslavs and Turks, or of Turks and Chinese show how notions of economics and ethnicity, of both structure and agency, coexist within intergroup relations.

In one respect, Italian, Puerto Rican, Chinese, or Mauritian needleworkers have distinctive interests and identities. In other respects, they have a great deal in common. In the end, this dual-city, century-long, multiethnic study leads me to conclude with further suggestions for a poststructural structuralist approach. It can be a way of analyzing structures and ruptures, similarities and differences within the modern world. It is attentive to the ways in which *vêtements* and garments, *sous-traitance* and contracting, culture and structure speak to each other and have been inflected on the Left and Right banks of the Atlantic.

I

FASHION

AS

INDUSTRY

1

FASHION AND FLEXIBILITY

The Garment Industry between

Haute Couture and

Jeans

ashion expresses the "antagonistic tendencies of life," wrote Georg Simmel in his now-classic article of 1904.[1] It reflects both uniformity and differentiation, imitation and demarcation, social obedience and individual expression. People express their individuality through fashion yet are also slaves to it. *La mode,* Simmel argued, represents an important equilibrium through which individuals manifest their differences via generally well-defined social signs. Fashion is ultimately a description of both dependence and freedom.

This contradiction does not simply affect the individual. It underlies the very functioning of the industry which produces fashion. Torn between art and industry, marketing individualism for the masses, the women's apparel industry is a prime example of one of the central tensions of mass production, that between flexibility and standardization. How to provide differentiation within industrial production? How to adapt or create changing styles while producing for the masses? This tension is crucial for understanding both the emergence of the garment industry, its particular structure, and its labor force. The garment industry is perhaps simply the most transparent example of that most basic of capitalism's dilemmas, the adjustment of supply to demand. The making of fashion can provide us with a way of thinking about this delicate industrial balancing act.

We can first turn to the basic functions of clothing and some of its contradictory representations before examining the emergence of the ready-made industry over the last century. It is a story of concentration and standardization but also one of flexibility and specialization. It is to this day a tale of hectic seasons in the urban industrial environment.

From Chastity to Social Sign: Clothing and Its Functions

The three basic functions of clothing were perhaps best summarized by Roland Barthes: clothes provide *"protection, pudeur, parure"* (protection, modesty, and adornment).[2] They are utilitarian, chaste, and pretty. In other words, garments are functional, fashionable, and furnish the figleaf.

Protection from the elements has attracted the least attention among modern authors, even though a wartime treatise in occupied France suggested that clothing be reconceptualized as an emergency heating system (*chauffage de crise*). Jeanne Lanvin even named one of her wartime quilted outfits "I replace central heating" (*"Je remplace le chauffage central"*).[3]

The garment's chastity function has also received little attention per se (interest having been shed along with the garments themselves?), although its closely linked obverse—style as sexuality— has been studied.[4] Yet, French swimwear makers notwithstanding, the covering function has had religious and societal implications deeply ingrained in the Judeo-Christian *imaginaire* from the Adam and Eve myth through the present.[5] As one French clothier wrote in 1931:

Clothing . . . separates man and beast. . . . As soon as modesty appears . . . so does the shirt. The shirt thus marks the advent of moral progress, the birth of a new emotion which would be a powerful aid to the development of civilization.[6]

Beyond chastity, however, the covering function has had a more general, civilizing function. The shirt, like the fork so well analyzed by Norbert Elias, is one of the quintessential signs of civilization (an argument that would in fact be used to sell clothing to the colonies). However, like the fork, the shirt must also be understood as an evolving historical phenomenon, not a given. Not only being dressed but being properly dressed is part of the "civility of manners." Analyses of clothing by class, country, and time period provide variations on the theme of civilization.[7]

As Simmel, Veblen, Barthes, and Bourdieu have all shown, clothing has gone beyond a "simple" civilizing function to become a complex social sign, distinguishing strata within Western civilization. Fashion is a sign of class and one of "distinction," just as it is a mode of sexuality as well as *sociabilité*. These signs were codified until as little as two centuries ago by sumptuary laws. However, since their demise and the rise of sociologists, the latter have largely interpreted the unwritten laws that help us understand fashion patterns and their meaning for civilization.[8]

Since the late nineteenth century, such analyses have revolved around the notions of consumption and class. Thorstein Veblen was the first to emphasize the relation of fashion to consumption rather than to any absolute idea of beauty. Yet, what he was describing for the leisure class in 1899 was already on its way to becoming a phenomenon of mass consumption. In an early article later elaborated in his well-known book *Système de la Mode* (1967), Roland Barthes used Saussure's categories to analyze fashion as a veritable language. *Vêtement* (clothing) is analogous to *langue* (language), and *habillement* (garments) to *parole* (speech).[9] "Costume" is the social group's normative system of dress, while *habillement* is the individual's choice of garb, and *vêtement* the combination of the two. For Barthes, then, *vêtement* (a *"fait social total"*) is a combination of the social ("costume") and the individual (*habillement*), the synthesis, one could say, of Simmel's dialectic. Barthes also recognized class as a factor in the crucial relationship between *être* and *paraître*, being and appearance. Pierre Bourdieu pushed the notion even further, including clothing among the signs of distinction.[10]

In addition to covering and civilizing, to representing consumption or class, clothes have even become, more recently, metaphors for the political, in a debate over democracy versus demagogy. Whereas for Simmel fashion was a way of looking at the limits of individual expression, other writers have used the fashion paradigm to explore expanding freedom within society. For the eighteenth

Fashion and Flexibility

century, Daniel Roche, while judiciously describing fashion as "an equilibrium point between the collective and individual," explained the emergence of a "culture of appearance" in the context of rebellion against the Court: the "reign of diversity and change" emerged as a form of freedom.[11] Ranging more globally from the fourteenth century to the present, Gilles Lipovetsky has elevated fashion to represent the empire of the individual. He argues that clothing is the very expression of the symbiosis of democracy and individualism. While also allowing that "fashion always combines individualism and conformity," Lipovetsky dismisses Simmel, Tarde, and Bourdieu from the outset. He insists on the differentiating function to the exclusion of the imitative function, emphasizing the individual nature of the democratic clothing process.[12]

Yet, fashion is also socially constructed. Jean Baudrillard has criticized *la mode* as a modern mode of servitude, replete with false consciousness. In his view, consumption and fashion provide only illusory independence. The commercialization of personalization—through clothes, apartments, and other objects—only gives the appearance of differentiation by perfecting the "PPDM" or *"plus petite différence marginale"* (smallest marginal difference). Individual choice is more apparent than real, given the "monopolistic production of difference."[13] The ultimate key, as Stuart and Elizabeth Ewen have pointed out, may be the way in which the garment industry has been able "to produce and distribute standardized-goods, laced with the lingo of individual choice and self-expression."[14]

Representations of fashion remain stubbornly contradictory. Fashion is both freedom and dependence; it is chaos and movement, yet also order and a "universe of discourse" providing a repertoire of choices that "nurtures and shapes a body of common sensitivity and taste."[15] Who creates fashion? Is it capricious and unpredictable, emerging from below, or manipulated by textile manufacturers and clothing designers planning obsolescence from above? Does it come from the invisible hand of the market or the visible hand of managers, manufacturers, and designers? There are those à la Lipovetsky who believe in an ultraliberal theory of fashion development, and others who hold to a conspiracy theory of style: "there must be some secret group of capitalists who, on the sly, decide that women will wear this or that style this year."[16]

Ultimately, however, Simmel's definition of tension between differentiation and uniformity has ceded to popular usage in which fashion is a metaphor for constant change. The representations of *la mode* are generally heavily weighted in favor of the "lingo of individual choice." Yet to celebrate only individualism (or only uniformity) is to amputate the Simmelian dialectic. Both elements of the definition are necessary for understanding the functioning of fashion, just as both flexibility and standardization are necessary for understanding the apparel industry. And the two are related. Regardless of who dictates fashion, fashion dictates production insofar as it incarnates demand. The manufacturer must find the equilibrium between mass production and individual needs, between supply and fluctuating demand.

Fashion, a Production Problem

To paraphrase Simmel, then, the apparel industry illustrates the antagonistic tendencies of production. Rationalization and change are the twin imperatives of the modern economy. Production has to accommodate the two without becoming impaled on one or the other.

Beyond fashion, its industry has also been represented by contradictory images. The garment industry has been called a textbook case of capitalism, but not in its most flattering light: "a beehive gone berserk because it is probably the most unrestrained example of free enterprise found outside of an economic text." Even worse, this unbridled capitalism can lead to anarchy: "deplorable industrial chaos"; "offensively inefficient."[17]

For some, the disorder has been seen as deceptive, simply the visible manifestation of a functioning flexibility. Michael Piore and Charles Sabel have minimized the chaos and maximized the conscious control in their interpretation of the garment industry as a model for the future. The garment industry for them is a harmonious, multiethnic "community," which, through its elaborate contracting and subcontracting system, is a model of flexibility.[18]

Yet such a view ignores the opposite tendency of standardization of style and production methods. The history of the industry comprises both standardization and flexibility, due to the contradictory imperatives of fashion. As Simmel described it, fashion carries within it the seeds of its own demise. As it spreads, "it gradually goes to its doom."[19] The democratization and speed-up of fashion-as-change leads to a rationalizing imperative that, in its attempt to regulate supply and demand, undercuts the very notion of fashion as distinctiveness. Already at the turn of the century, Simmel recognized the duel that flexibility would have to fight against the imperative of standardization:

The polar oscillations, which modern economics in many instances knows how to avoid and from which it is visibly striving towards entirely new economic orders and forms, still hold sway in the field immediately subject to fashion. The element of feverish change is so essential here that fashion stands, as it were, in a logical contrast to the tendencies for development in modern economics.[20]

If globally flexible in relation to other industries, the garment industry, we will see, is itself divided into more standardized and more variable parts, just as its labor force is divided into more stable and more fluctuating portions. Men's wear and women's wear, factory workers and homeworkers, are distinct components of this manifold structure.

Fashion is thus not just fantasy or social signifier. It is a specific production problem (of "hyper-innovation," as economist Bernard Smith has called it),[21] an extreme example of the more general problem of fluctuating demand. The challenge to the ready-made industry has been to mass-produce imitation while promoting differentiation and "distinction." The production of fashion has led to a complex system of contracting and subcontracting. The history of this branch is perhaps indeed a textbook case of the interplay between supply and demand.

The Rise of the Ready-Made

The nineteenth century has been called the century of the "democratization of goods." By the end of the century, clothes, like furniture, had become widely distributed mass-consumer items. Yet a look at the rise of the garment industry will not help resolve the economic historian's eternal dilemma: Which came first, supply or demand?[22] The ready-to-wear revolution occurred thanks to both a democratization of demand—"the spread of fashion"—and a democratization of supply, the combined effects of the democratic and industrial revolutions. While the Industrial Revolution brought us textiles and railroads, new methods of production and transportation, the democratic revolutions brought about new modes of manners. In France, just as local languages and cultures were being integrated into a nineteenth-century "French" norm, the (revived) nineteenth-century regional and class costumes were starting their long trek toward the standardization of jeans. For the United States, Claudia Kidwell and Margaret Christman have described the "democratization of clothing" as the transformation of clothing "made for somebody" to clothing "made for anybody" into "clothing made for everybody."[23] On both sides of the Atlantic, changing use patterns of garments were inextricably intertwined with changing production methods.

I will first draw a brief composite picture of the growth of the ready-made industry over the last two centuries before analyzing the democratization of demand and supply. The American and French documents suggest a remarkable similarity in the broad outlines of the industry's development. From the handheld needle to the sewing machine, from changing demand to descriptions of sweatshops, certain basic elements constitute the garment industrial revolution in both New York and Paris. While the nineteenth century saw the rise of standardization in opposition to individually tailored clothes, the late twentieth century has seen the expansion of differentiation within mass production. A general understanding of these trends and their impact on production must necessarily precede the separate histories of the French and American industries, which will be addressed in the next two chapters.

Where did clothes come from before we started buying them "off the rack"? The answer depends on class. Clothing was made at home by and for the poor, while skilled tailors and seamstresses fitted out the rich. But not all clothing was "made." Secondhand clothing was the first mode of purchasing prefabricated garments—"off the cart," so to speak. At the same time, clothing circulated between the classes, as aristocrats shed last year's models, benefiting their servants. Daniel Roche has spoken of a new "clothing practice" that developed in the eighteenth century as the garment budget of the bourgeoisie greatly increased and new styles were disseminated via domestics. Theft was another method of spreading clothing manners across classes in the early modern period.[24]

While for another good century and a half the upper classes continued to have most of their clothes individually tailored, ready-made clothing first came to ordinary men's wear in the 1820s in France and the United States. Tailors and sailors both contributed to its emergence. On the supply side, tailors began using their slack time to make up garments ahead of time. On the demand side, sailors provided one of the initial clientele for prefabricated outfits. Already in the eighteenth century, with little time to wait on shore to be measured and fitted, they were perfect clients for an incipient cash (or credit)-and-carry system. Other important markets quickly developed: "Negro clothing" and the Western trade for the Gold Rush in the United States, clothing for the colonized in newly acquired French territories.

By the 1830s and 1840s, merchant tailors (often custom tailors by origin) began to farm out sewing, while they still designed, cut, and sold the finished goods. Farmers' and sailors' wives made the cheaper grades, while skilled tailors still made the more expensive outfits. Conflicts between custom tailors and ready-made tailors soon emerged, and bitter debates erupted, particularly in France, over the merits of the new mode of production and soon over its technological implement: the sewing machine. The sewing machine, as we will see, vastly aided, but did not create, the epistemological shift. However, with its increasingly generalized diffusion on both sides of the Atlantic from the late 1850s on, the sewing machine became an important tool in spreading the concept and production of ready-made goods.

At the same time, new distribution methods gave an important impetus to the industry in both rural and urban areas: mail-order sales for the provinces; department stores for the cities. Advertising stressed the facility of buying ready-made goods—fewer fittings, a surer final product—as well as, particularly in the United States, the democratic nature of the goods. One American manufacturer, Simmons, advertised that ready-made goods were for everyone from farmers to travelers, from mourners to children, and from firemen to whalemen. If the department stores were called "palaces," they nonetheless stressed that access was free (*libre*), with no obligation to buy such as that assumed upon entering the small tailor's shop.[25]

Manufactured womens' wear was slower to develop than men's, due to style changes and the fact that more women made their own clothes. Yet by the time of the Civil War in the United States and somewhat later in France, women were purchasing ready-made cloaks. In the last decades of the century, ready-made goods became more diversified: tailored suits for women, shirtwaists, and skirts. But if before World War I, increasing numbers of French and American women were willing to buy ready-made skirts and blouses, they were still having their dresses made to order. This changed in the interwar period as the ready-made dress business took off in the United States; the same phenomenon occurred in France after World War II. The shift to pants after the war and then to the ubiquitous jeans of the 1970s continued the trend begun with cloaks. Except perhaps for the once(?)-in-a-lifetime wedding gown, who would even think of going to a dressmaker today?

The change in clothing patterns and production is surely easier to describe than to explain. What caused this shift from the measured and modeled to the prefabricated, from the ruffles and bustles of the eighteenth century to the Mondrian geometry and plain jeans of the twentieth? How did homemade goods give way to factory-made and again home (industrial)-made ones, while notions about the quality of homemade goods changed as well: from ordinary to fine (in contrast to rough ready-made) to shabby (in contrast to better ready-made) and ultimately to the idea that "handmade" is artisanal and expensive? To answer these questions, we can separate the clothing revolution into two separate but interrelated parts: the democratization of demand and that of supply.

The Democratization of Demand

Revolution, war, and women all contributed to the changing nature of nineteenth-century clothing demand. The democratization of demand can be examined from two perspectives: first, from a theoretical standpoint, in which the timing and meaning of that democratization have been debated, and second, from the identification of the specific markets which fed the increased demand.

Each historian has his or her chosen century for the start of the sartorial revolution, their period of predilection the focus of historical hiatus.[26] While most American histories of the garment industry begin with the sailors, French historiography has been more concerned with older trends. At the same time, American historians seem to stress emerging markets, while French historians have had a greater tendency to look at the intellectual origins of changing demand.

Daniel Roche, in his important work pushing back our conceptions of the modern development of clothing a good century, dates the fashion revolution to the eighteenth century.[27] In his analysis, the story of changing clothing habits is a veritable parable for the rise of the bourgeoisie, almost a cause for revolution itself. The bourgeoisie's revolt against the fetters and feathers of the aristocracy was a sartorial as well as political statement, as they introduced (non–Court-approved) variability into clothing. In this view, the eighteenth-century bourgeois revolution was one of differentiation, as new social signs distinguished the bourgeoisie from the aristocracy while also serving to identify the bourgeoisie itself as a group.

While Roche's point is well taken, for most historians of clothing the democratic revolutions were the cause more than the effect of sartorial change. In this respect, the French Revolution was the starting point for the democratization of clothing. The nineteenth-century clothing revolution, in contrast to that of the eighteenth, was a revolution of imitation. Democrats and aristocrats respectively praised and blamed the revolutionary movements of 1789, 1848, and 1871 for having democratized the *goût du luxe*. Philippe Perrot has spoken of a "veritable euphoria of buying" which he dates to the Second Empire. The petite bourgeoisie began emulating bourgeois lifestyles and purchasing patterns, while workers began to dress up on Sundays.[28] Mass consumption ultimately permitted mass emulation, and, as Rosalind Williams has argued, by the late nineteenth century the working class's "dream world" of bourgeois consumption paralleled the bourgeoisie's "dream world" of aristocratic forms.[29]

In this light, egalitarianism rather than individualism explains the democratization of clothing. Emulation rather than differentiation is more pertinent for understanding fashion in the era of mass consumption. The working classes and the petite bourgeoisie enter the historical clothing scene in the late nineteenth century, not to overthrow their sartorial models—as their bourgeois revolutionary predecessors did a century earlier—but rather to imitate them.

The growth of ready-made goods in the nineteenth century corresponded to several new markets—first among men, then among women. What began as inexpensive clothing for sailors soon became a mass item for soldiers. War was an important stimulus to demand, just as it gave an important impetus to the reorganization of supply. Ready-made clothing soon spread to civilian markets, indeed performing a civilizing function. "Democratic" demand did not simply emerge from below. The democratization of goods also implied a moralizing mission for the masses. Workers and petits bourgeois at home; natives in the French colonies (the "figleaf" function); slaves in the American South; and immigrants in America were among the first to benefit from access to new clothing. While hygienists argued that cheap ready-made garments were safer than microbe-infested secondhand clothes, social reformers and manufacturers envisaged the progressive *embourgeoisement* of the lower classes in France, the covering and "Frenchification" of the colonized, and the Americanization of immigrants in the United States. Henry Ford's Melting Pot ritual, circa 1916, well symbolized the importance of standardized clothing for the assimilation process. In a ceremony for students graduating from his English classes, the immigrants walked up to a giant cauldron in their native costumes only to emerge dressed in identical "American" outfits, with a United States flag in hand.[30]

In order to make this civilizing process work, ready-made goods had to be redefined as respectable. New forms of distribution and advertising played a crucial role. By spreading the notion of store-bought style for the masses, they helped concretize the idea of a democratization of fashion, thus having a performative effect on that democratization itself. The petite bourgeoisie and eventually workers were encouraged to frequent department stores rather than secondhand clothing dealers. The department store experience has even been described as "mental orthopedics," teaching the workers respectability and a new civility of manners.[31] The stores, their catalogues, pattern books, fashion magazines, and "taste professionals" spread the idea that art through clothing was possible for everyone.[32]

Fashion and Flexibility

If increased demand for ready-made goods first came from/was aimed at the male market, by the end of the century women had clearly become the new motor behind garment-industry growth. Changing gender relations and a major fashion shift, "a sexual dimorphism of appearance," accompanied it. Sexual dissymmetry became a striking feature of nineteenth-century dressing patterns. In prerevolutionary France, men at Court vied with women for smooth leg lines. However, the Revolution and the "rise of the bourgeoisie" eventually meant a shift to basic black for men: the business suit popularized by "the bourgeois king," Louis-Philippe himself. Clad henceforth in sober costumes not only in democratic rebellion but for class identification, men gave up their natural animal flashiness in what John Carl Flügel called "the great male renunciation."[33] The fashion-as-fanciful function of clothing was henceforth left to the female.

The rise of the middle classes in the nineteenth century led to a division of labor within the family that was reflected in what people wore. As men monopolized the public sphere and their wives were relegated to the private one, the leisure women of the bourgeoisie increasingly became the social "windows" of their husbands' wealth. The causality of the resultant fashion split is not absolutely clear. One nineteenth-century bourgeois blamed it on the women, who "admit us to their receptions . . . only in the black suit, because rigged out this way, we are frankly ugly, and we serve as a foil to set off their beauty."[34] But, as Simmel more astutely suggested, women's enslavement to fashion is due to their weaker position in society. Fashion is "the valve through which woman's craving for some measure of conspicuousness and individual prominence finds vent, when its satisfaction is denied her in other fields." It functions in indirect relation to access to power.[35]

More importantly for the ready-made industry, however, working women took part in the clothing revolution more through changing active than through shifting representational roles. Pockets symbolized that change. As women entered the paid labor market in increasingly large numbers by the late nineteenth century, an industrious lower-middle class of female employees and shopkeepers all had both a little more disposable income and more clothing needs to spend it on. With the growing separation between home and work, the woman wage-earner needed a place to hold the key for her now-locked door.[36] Women became consumers out of necessity as well as desire, and their collective buying power became a tremendous spur to the growth of the ready-made industry.

As use patterns changed, so did styles. In addition to pockets, a more general masculinization and a constant trend toward simplification went hand in hand with the increasing standardization of production. The first women's ready-made garments were cloaks and coats, ample items which were closest to masculine models. In French the term *tailleur* itself underwent significant change. Previously designating the (male) makers of men's clothing, as tailors increasingly began to make women's clothing, the term had to be qualified as *tailleur pour hommes* or *tailleur pour dames.* Ultimately the term designating the maker came to refer to the object itself as the suit became adapted to the female form.[37]

The masculinization of certain feminine styles encouraged the transfer of ready-made techniques to women's wear. Some unhappy fashion observers perceived the trend with horror as tending to englobe the sexes in a "common ugliness." As bicycling and the automobile brought about new forms of leisure and leisure garments, "the peddling female" was condemned for debasing good taste and femininity, while more generally the "invasion" of sports clothes, "practical but ugly," was denounced.[38] But if Betty Bloomer was ahead of her time in pushing pants in the aim of dress reform in mid-nineteenth-century America, trousers became acceptable at the end of the century, if only under certain circumstances. A French police prefect forbid women from wearing pants *unless* cycling.[39]

The demise of the corset was the other great symbol of changing styles in conjunction with changing gender roles. One enthusiastic female commentator dated clothing liberty for women to the French Revolution: "Civil rights for men, corporal freedom for women, voilà the two great conquests of the Revolution." A male observer agreed, adding that the elimination of the corset was comparable to the fall of the Bastille. However, it ultimately took until World War I, the recruitment of women into the factories, and restrictions on metal wiring to kill the corset.[40]

There has been some debate as to the effect of the twentieth-century wars on women's styles. In one respect, government inter-

Fashion and Flexibility

ference in rationing fabric and other needed materials loosened the corsets and limited the pleats. Over the long term, however, the question remains whether the wars had more lasting, diffuse effects on style change. Women's massive entry into the factories clearly contributed to the demise of the corset and the donning of pants. But while some writers see a direct cause and effect between war and fashion, others argue more convincingly that the world wars, in this as in other matters, mostly furthered trends already in motion.[41] Even when frivolity in clothes and manners succeeded wartime restrictions, the long-term pattern was becoming clear: the continued tendency toward simplification and standardization was crucial to the ready-made revolution.

Coco Chanel on one side of the Atlantic, and ultimately "suburbia" on the other, furthered the trend toward simplification and masculinization. The straight-line look introduced in France in the interwar years and the suburban housedress in the United States both lent themselves to factory production. In the American case, the disappearance of domestic help and the appearance of the television after the Second World War both helped create a more home-centered culture, with new demands for casual clothing. The trend has been seemingly inexorable ever since: from housedresses to slacks to jeans to jogging pants, the twentieth century has decidedly shifted away from nineteenth-century dress dissymmetry. French styles have remained more "feminine," but nobody (I hope) would dream of reinventing bustles. Variations on the straight line seem here to stay, with the production implications they represent.

Both at work and at home, women and their clothing needs have thus changed dramatically from the early nineteenth century, importantly abetting the rise of the garment industry. Yet increasing demand has been in some ways a thankless task for women. Even as the desire for/acceptance of simplification and standardization have proceeded apace, and in spite of numerous paeans to the female consumer, women have continued to come under attack for the inconstancy of their demand. While in eighteenth-century France, members of the Court could be blamed for the sometimes inscrutable dictates of fashion, the nineteenth century's "democratization of clothing" also led to a democratization of blame . . . onto women. Women as consumers are both hailed and feared. Their purchasing power stimulates demand, but they are also blamed for making or

Ready-to-Wear and Ready-to-Work

breaking a season. Their "tyrannical" whims have been lamented by manufacturers and industrial reporters alike as leading to a "capricious despotism" of fashion over which "man has no say."[42] Women, inconstancy, and whimsical capriciousness have become metaphors for the variability of demand. Expanded and democratized, demand is still an often inscrutable production problem.

The Democratization of Supply

Pure demand—from the client's mouth to the manufacturer's ear—rarely exists. Demand comes from below, just as it can be created from above. Textile makers, clothing manufacturers, and designers propose and impose colors, styles, and shapes, often fashioning the female body in their image. "Taste professionals," retailers, and advertisers have all run interference between supply and demand. Most importantly, however, garments had to be producible in mass quantities at reasonable prices in order for the ready-made revolution to take place. Simplification of lines corresponded to changing demand and changing use patterns, but it was also a necessary condition for the industrialization of clothing production. Yet, here, too, fashion had its dialectical part to play. The lower classes could pursue the imitative function only insofar as clothes were available in their price range. But even the bourgeoisie was not impervious to the sirens of cheaper clothes, changed more often. "The more an article becomes subject to rapid changes of fashion," wrote Simmel, "the greater the demand for *cheap* products of its kind."[43] The democratization of demand implied a democratization of supply. Three important steps were necessary for the expansion of supply to take place: war, the reorganization of the work process, and new technology.

War and Clothes

Just as war played an important role more generally in the development of mass production techniques,[44] its impact on the garment industry was no exception. In addition to quite prosaically providing a large demand in the form of uniforms, the Crimean and

Fashion and Flexibility

Franco-Prussian Wars for France, the Civil and Spanish-American Wars in the United States, all helped stimulate the development of mass clothing production—through standardization of sizes, the concentration of the labor force, and as a more general stimulus to production.

Uniforms are the ultimate expression of fashion in the Simmelian sense. They distinguish one from the Other/enemy while permitting a codified sign of belonging to the group/nation. Their purpose is to create an enforced egalitarianism (although divided by rank, via small but symbolically important shoulder and lapel signs) in order to reinforce a homogenized (esprit de) corps. Yet military uniforms were also the harbingers of an important breakthrough in garment production: standardized sizing. Uniforms emerged with the development of the modern army in the early modern period. By the eighteenth century, the standardization of certain parts of the outfit allowed small, medium, and large uniforms to be made up in advance and in the absence of specific body measurements.[45]

The mass measurement of soldiers in the nineteenth century helped support a notion which most tailors already intuitively understood: that the human form, for all its amazing diversity, could be categorized. The chests and heights of over one million military conscripts were measured during the American Civil War. (Large numbers of women were measured at women's schools, starting with Vassar College in 1884.) The new science of anthropometrics and increasing experimentation with patterns furthered the conceptual shift away from personally measured garments. The idea that garments could be made en masse—for anonymous bodies, according to a limited set of predetermined sizes—began to take hold. Furthermore, as increasing improvements showed, ready-made garments no longer had to be the loose-fitting smocks and jackets nor the poor fits of the early made-up goods. "It used to be said of an unpopular man, as a parting shot, after the vocabulary of vituperation had been exhausted, 'and his clothes don't fit!' "[46] With the growing sophistication of sizing, ready-made goods that fit came to be available for all shapes and weights. The fundamental technical basis of the nineteenth-century clothing revolution was put into action: serial production.

The modern army also led to the setting up of military workshops that were the first ready-made shops concentrating large numbers of workers under one roof. The earliest ones in France came into being between 1830 and 1848 in order to outfit the National Guard. Orders for uniforms were so great that production spread from military to civilian workshops while more efficient methods were sought to increase productivity. Larger establishments and an increased division of labor resulted. Although military workshops were not alone in this (prisons and convents were other loci of clothing workshop concentration), they were one of the most important preludes to the modern ready-to-wear factories.

Even less well studied is the way in which wars have stimulated production by affecting civilian markets, beyond pants for women. Although armed conflict can severely hurt the civilian clothing trade, war contracts and subsidized government orders for men's wear have often compensated for civilian clothing losses while in the long run stimulating them. When the Civil War cut off Northern ready-made manufacturers from their Southern black and poor-white market, this stimulated production geared to a Northern market instead. World War I ultimately helped promote American women's wear when the hostilities prevented the United States from importing both goods and, more importantly, the French patterns which were routinely copied for the American market. Similarly, the embargo against Japan during World War II, which cut off silk imports, was a boon for domestic nylon and rayon manufacturers.

The Reorganization of Work

Wars thus stimulated production, standardization, and concentration of the labor force. A crucial corollary to these changes was the reorganization of work. The division of labor which proceeded apace over the nineteenth century was not entirely new. Even in the Old Regime, master tailors had their journeymen and apprentices help them get the dresses to the balls on time. The breaking down of garment making into its component parts was dependent upon neither mechanization nor concentration. The military and then civilian workshops essentially implemented on a large scale that which many tailors already practiced.

Garment making, for one body or for many, basically involves three processes: cutting, sewing, and pressing. Cutting and pressing, at the beginning and end of the process, require particular skill: proper cutting ensures that the parts will fit together and that cloth wastage is minimized; the final pressing, if poorly done, can ruin a finished garment. Cutting and pressing can basically be done by only one person at a time. Sewing, however, can be and was increasingly broken down into various tasks, based on a separation of the garment parts. As a result, by 1840, the price of a ready-made coat was about one-half that of a custom-made one in New York.[47] By the end of the century, sleeves, cuffs, and pockets were being prepared independently, before final assembly. "Ready-made" thus became doubly so, both with regard to the whole and the parts. The sleeve became to the shirt what the shirt had become to the wearer: made up ahead of time for an anonymous end-user.

The division of labor was increasingly refined over the nineteenth century, with different groups being attributed its "invention." German tailors increased the division of labor in men's wear in the mid-nineteenth-century United States via the "family system," giving work to their wives and then to women in surrounding areas. Russian Jews were attributed the paternity of the (criticized) "task-system" or "section-work," which greatly increased production of women's wear from 8 to 10 up to 20 to 24 coats per day in late-nineteenth-century Paris, New York, and London. But at the same time, Boston tailors introduced their "factory-system" or "Boston system," involving a minute division of labor that could produce from 50 to 200 garments per day.

An International Labour Office (ILO) study in 1964 showed that contemporary methods were not that different from those in 1900. Under the bundle system, each worker (working on one or two parts of the garment) gets a package with 10, 20, or 50 parts to assemble; everyone works at their own speed, but much time is lost in handling and stocking the bundles. With a more assembly-line approach, the garment rather than a bundle moves along, via conveyor belts or the workers themselves, with the latter specializing in various tasks; the more rationalized movement greatly reduces time in handling and therefore manufacture, but it also implies a synchronization and lack of flexibility that can only be used for mass-produced articles; and absenteeism throws the mechanism off. Finally, the "progressive bundle" combines the two methods, with machines grouped in sections, and workers working jointly on bundles, with better movement of goods. The ILO concluded, however, that it is difficult to measure the relative productivity of each method.[48]

It could be argued that, from the family system to the progressive bundle, these are discrete historical methods of organization with differential results of efficiency and productivity. Yet, at a more general level of analysis, we can see these different methods as variations on the theme of dividing and conquering the garment. The process has been limited not essentially by technology or garment flow but by fashion-as-change. Section work, hailed as the adaptation of mass-production, assembly-line techniques to clothing, has only been most successful in those periods when styles have been simplest and relatively repeatable.[49]

Thus, as measurement was separated from the individual body, so production became separate from a single needleworker. The new work order had several important implications for working conditions and for the composition of the labor force. For one thing, needleworkers were renamed. "To tailor" (*tailler*) means to fit (closely) in English, to cut (finely) in French. This could no longer designate the new methods or their implementers. The "tailor" became a "garment worker" (*ouvrier du vêtement*) and sewing-machine workers became "operators" or *mécanicien(ne)s*. Secondly, the separation of tasks and the putting out of the sewing function became the premises for the contracting system that became a pivotal characteristic of the urban garment industry to this day. Finally, due in large part to this reorganization of work, the growth in supply of garments proceeded apace with an expansion of the supply of laborers: a new labor force of women and immigrants heralded the demise of the tailor and his tape measure.

The War of the Sewing Machines

The needle will soon be consigned to oblivion, like the wheel, the loom, and the knitting-needles. The working woman will now work fewer hours, and receive greater remuneration. People will . . . dress better, change oftener, and altogether grow better looking.—*New York Tribune*, ca. 1859[50]

Technological innovation furthered the process of relative standardization, division of labor, and the lowering of prices. As Adam Smith noted early on, the division of labor more often precedes new technology than the other way around. The sewing machine was no exception. It followed but then accelerated these changing trends and raised productivity by both encouraging a still greater division of labor and increasing the number of stitches per minute.

The story of the machine's invention and distribution is complicated, replete with the usual ambiguities in the attribution of invention, tinged in this case by national pride. Who invented the sewing machine? Singer, say the Americans (son of an immigrant, no less, admit some; of a German immigrant, specify others; a Jewish-German immigrant, insist others, apparently incorrectly). Thimonnier, counter the French.[51] Popular accounts in particular tend to stress compatriots in claiming fame. The invention of the sewing machine has been described as a typical American success story of the self-made man: "At the age of 38, [Singer] borrowed $40 and began tinkering with what would become the first sewing machine that could be easily used by a homemaker. Introduced in 1850, it was an immediate success."[52] But there is also a French version, of revolution and ingenuity: "[The sewing machine] is a veritable revolution, the point of departure of which is a French invention."[53] The question, as with any new technology or scientific discovery, is that of defining invention and pinpointing which "first" is being accredited.

Barthélemy Thimonnier comes first chronologically (unless you count the Englishmen Weisenthal in 1755 and Thomas Saint thirty years later who, respectively, thought up devices for embroidering and for sewing leather). In 1829, Thimonnier invented and a year later patented a machine with the first working chain-stitch that had any practical application. A year after Thimonnier's patent, eighty of the machines were set up in a military workshop. However, as his in-house biographer, Marcel Doyen, emphasizes throughout his rather romanticized tale, the former poor (in wealth and luck) tailor was constantly plagued by bad fortune.[54] His machine was introduced at a time of political and labor unrest in France. Following the Revolution of 1830, the silk *canuts'* revolt in Lyon and other workers' uprisings were outbursts against machinism and changing labor processes. In February 1831, some two hundred angry young tailors broke into Thimonnier's workshop saying they wanted work and threatening to destroy the machines, which they called "arm-breakers" (*casse-bras*). In some versions, although not others, they actually did smash the machines.[55] The truth is perhaps less important than the fact that this incident became the violent symbol of rejection of the new devices. The National Guard defended the machines and arrested some seventy-five of the (potential) Luddites, whose defense in court was that they simply wanted to admire the terrific new machines up close. Thimonnier "fled" to England (then or later, depending on the account), improved on his machine, and received first an English and then an American patent for it in 1849. According to one analysis, Thimonnier's "first" was thus his perseverance. "Le sieur B. Thimonnier tailleur" of the early patents became "le sieur B. Thimonnier mécanicien" in subsequent ones.[56]

Doyen speaks of the American Walter Hunt as having "reinvented" one of the Frenchman's ideas, but he bears no grudge, for he later defends Hunt against Elias Howe's usurpation of pride of place.[57] Hunt developed a double-threading machine in 1834, but it was Howe who received the patent (and later the postage stamp commemoration) for an improved device in 1846. Two key aspects of the new machine were the lockstitch, which prevented the stitching from ripping out, and continuous threading from spools. However, disappointed that his invention did not get greater recognition in his home country, Howe, like Thimonnier, moved to England (symbol of the Industrial Revolution and magnet for disgruntled inventors) for several years, in hopes of finding greater acceptance there. In the meantime, others became interested in refining the sewing machine idea, and between 1849 and 1854, a veritable avalanche of patents began. By 1863, 607 had been issued in the United States alone.

Isaac Merritt Singer, somewhat of a wandering minstrel—or strolling player—but a machinist as well (like Hunt and Howe, rather than a tailor, like Thimonnier), also stood on the shoulders of his predecessors. As a result, though, Howe sued him. Singer's first model, patented in February 1854, incorporated Howe's lockstitch and continuous-threading device. But in addition, Singer added the treadle, an important improvement. The (wo)man-powered machines could now be activated by foot, thus freeing both hands to guide the cloth. Two other major sewing machine companies were set up around the same time, the Wheeler and Wilson Manufacturing Company, Singer's strongest competitor for many years, and the Grover and Baker Sewing Machine Company, founded by two Boston tailors.

Fashion and Flexibility

However, it is the Singer Manufacturing Company which became a legend (along with Singer's two wives, at least three mistresses, and twenty-four children; he, too, ended up in England).[58]

One author, who opts for Singer's paternity for the sewing machine invention, argues that Singer's concept has stood the test of time.[59] Indeed, new technology needs successful diffusion to ratify the creative function, the attribution of invention often read backward from successful application and distribution. Many "firsts" were involved, however, not the least being Singer's novel commercial techniques. Lawyers and businessmen as much as the inventors themselves were crucial in transforming the sewing machine market and defining new uses for the machines. Appealing showrooms with attractive female demonstrators, newspaper advertisements, and "schools" helped disseminate information about the machines. For some, Singer's (or his partner, Edward Clark's) real "first" and cause for success was his use of the installment plan to mass-market the machines. The commercial takeoff of the sewing machines grew in the last third of the nineteenth century.[60]

The Singer Manufacturing Company became one of the first American multinationals. As early as 1855, the French government contemplated introducing machines into its military workshops on a large scale; it brought over an American seamstress along with one of Singer's machines in order to demonstrate it. She was so successful that the French offered her a full-time job and apparently considered importing not only more of the machines but also American women to operate them. The sewing machine spread in France after 1870, where it was often just called "la Singer." Isaac Merritt Singer has had the great posthumous honor of being called the "Napoleon of the sewing machine."[61]

The sewing machine was not accepted without a struggle. It was accused of throwing tailors and seamstresses out of work. Hygienists and doctors considered it dangerous to the health, and custom workers blamed it for lowering standards and fueling the entire shift to inferior ready-made goods.[62] The early machines were indeed cumbersome to use and produced rather poor-quality clothes. However, the machines improved, and so did their reputation, ultimately leading to a reversal in definitions of sewing beauty. As machine work gained in favor, it was the uneven stitch of the average tailor or seamstress that ultimately came to be seen as shoddy. Precision created new ideas about beauty: "It is impossible for hand work to approach the beauty and precision of machine work," wrote an early admirer.[63]

Even more important, the attraction of the sewing machine, and the reason that it became the basic tool and veritable symbol of the garment industry until today, resides in its flexibility, a flexibility of place. Like much technology, it encouraged a concentration of the workforce insofar as clothing capitalists gathered machines and workers under one roof, even if most of the early workers had to buy or rent the machines and

hire a pushcart at a quarter, get the machine into the pushcart, trundle the load up to my new job, drag the machine up three or four flights of stairs, put it together, oil it, clean it, supply it with all sorts of gadgets and tools, including needles.[64]

(Some employers even rented out the chairs.) However, although the number of clothing establishments did initially decrease (by 11 percent between 1850 and 1860 in the United States) and capital investment increased (doubling during that same period),[65] the new technology was also amenable to small-scale usage. Sewing technology was "light" enough to be used in a variety of places, from factory to contractor's workshop to home. As supply spread, so did the places of its production.

Technologies Old and New

From the first hand-powered machines, which sewed 20 stitches per minute, to the steam-powered ones of the 1870s and the electrically powered ones doing up to 200 stitches per minute at the turn of the century, the sewing machine has been constantly perfected to increase speed, safety, and flexibility. Greater speed has required better lubrication and cooling techniques (ventilated needles) to keep down the heat produced by the needle's motion. By the 1950s some machines sewed up to 4,500 stitches per minute, and more recent machines now go as fast as 8,000 per minute or more. Computer-aided machines can now preprogram specific sewing tasks as well.

Buttonhole, cloth-spreading, and other specialized machines were invented and quickly adopted. A machine-made buttonhole in

1900 took five seconds to make, compared to ten minutes by hand. Steam pressers replaced the old flatiron by the end of the nineteenth century. The band-knife machine, first introduced in England in 1860, replaced the shears or knives previously used to cut material and allowed several thicknesses of cloth to be cut through at one time. Although harder to handle and heavier to operate, these machines spread quickly from the 1870s on. The electric cutting knife of the twentieth century "smoothly, accurately, and easily slices its way through 300 plies of cloth as if it were cutting through cheese."[66]

The newest technology has also been literally at the cutting edge of production. Computerized layout and grading programs, which maximize cloth use while grading and cutting patterns from an original set to all sizes, along with computer-controlled laser-beam cutters, have increased productivity and efficiency at the most skilled end of production. As hailed by new technology enthusiasts, the (so-far prohibitively expensive) tailor shop of the future may permit the return of the individualized garment. If you are willing to be measured by a laser beam, you may soon be able to choose your own cloth and pattern, while the computer does the rest.[67]

The new technologies have brought with them new problems: sewing machines so fast that fabrics can catch on fire (especially new, lower-combustion, synthetic ones); cutting apparatuses so perfected that a slip of the hand can ruin three hundred pieces of fabric at one time. And the greater the repetitive motion and the speed, the greater the fatigue and strain on twentieth-century workers.

However, all of the new technologies, from Singer's sewing machine to the latest laser-cutting devices, have increased productivity and helped expand supply basically due to two factors: greater speed and less cloth wastage. It is estimated that the sewing machine globally increased productivity ten- or elevenfold when it was introduced in the United States, and that by the end of the century in France, a ready-made garment could be made in approximately one-third to one-half of the time needed to make an individually tailored one.[68] The newest machines today allow flexibility within standardization by rationalizing different parts of the sewing process and programming zigzags when they are in, straight seams when they are out.

Nonetheless, several factors continue to limit any absolute automation of the garment industry. While computer-aided machines can adapt to changing styles, they are still too expensive for most small contractor shops. "Too much technology hinders subcontracting," found one recent French reporter.[69] Changing styles and production runs still limit capital investment. Furthermore, even while the most spectacular changes have occurred at the more highly skilled end of the trade, sewing seams still needs to be done by an operative. And stitch-per-minute figures alone are misleading. Speed in sewing is only one part of the production process (37 percent of total work time, according to one study[70]). Cutting and pressing, and especially cloth handling, and preparation and movement of goods, are time-consuming activities that ergonomists keep trying to rationalize.

Standardization and Flexibility within the Industry

Garment manufacture has thus been increasingly industrialized over the last century, albeit within the limits of fashion's double imperative of imitation and change. This has implied a reconceptualization of both art and industry to permit mass production and a constant readjustment of production into more standardized and variable portions. At one extreme is haute couture, which emerged at the end of the nineteenth century, taking the notion of art-in-clothing onto itself just as the made-to-measure crowd was declining. At the other extreme are jeans, serially produced in larger factories according to a limited set of styles and sizes.[71] Yet, within the ready-made sector itself, work clothes change less than street clothes, men's wear remains more standardizable than women's wear, underwear is less volatile than outerwear.[72] And, within women's outerwear, certain lines are more fashion-conscious than others. In each case production methods vary. The more standardized a sector, the larger and more automated the production units, and the more often located outside of the urban core.

In one example, two researchers claimed that two sectors of women's outerwear were so different in fashion content, relative standardization, and production methods that they should be considered separate industries altogether. Housedresses and street dresses were marketed for different uses (private and public), made with different fabrics (the latter known as the "silk dress" trade long after silk was replaced by synthetic materials), and even priced differently: cheap housedresses by the dozen as distinct from the more expensive "regular or unit-priced" street dresses. Writing in the early 1940s, Drake and Glasser described the latter as "archaic," the former as "industrial" in nature.[73]

In spite of the "smallest marginal difference" between five-pocket Levi's and an ordinary pair of Wranglers, nothing could be more standardized than blue jeans or more variable than the stylish blouses that top them off. Yet two tendencies still work at cross-purposes within these models: the search for the distinctive jean and the production of enough of the same blouses for them to be low-priced and profitable.

Serviceable yet stylish, the garment industry has thus evolved as a complex structure of different-sized production units. From the Belle Jardinière's large factory in Lille to Turkish subcontractors in Paris, from Levi's thousands of employees to the tiny Chinese sweatshops in New York City, the industry has remained, over time and place, in what looks like perpetual transition. Emile Levasseur commented at the end of the nineteenth century: "While industrial concentration was gaining ground, small-scale manufacture was not expelled; it was displaced. . . ."[74] A century later, the situation in the garment industry has not changed greatly. For all the standardization and industrialization, elements of fashion—proposed or imposed—remain stubbornly volatile. And the industry still embodies the production tensions of standardization and flexibility.

Theories of "Takeoff" and the Meaning of Ready-Made

The nineteenth century thus saw an epistemological shift in garment production from a sell-and-make operation to a make-and-sell one, from the making of whole garments to parts, from custom-made to ready-made, from handheld needles to machine-driven ones, from tailors to garment workers, and, as we will see, from men to women and immigrant workers. The emergence of this *"bloc socio-technologique,"* as Pierre Bouvier has stressed the sociological along with the material, calls for two final remarks.[75] First of all, the meaning of ready-made is in some ways a historiographic and sociological construct. Fashion and its industry have been constantly reinvented by both actors and observers. Secondly, the development of the women's garment industry was not simply a linear one of progress. Its growth, as we will see in the next two chapters, was accompanied by conflict and self-questioning.

The dating of the "takeoff" of the garment industry, like that of the sewing machine, implies a defining of "newness." Daniel Roche and Philippe Perrot have stressed different centuries (and different classes) with regard to clothing habits. Roche has emphasized the increased circulation of clothing by the bourgeoisie (and their domestics) in a story of eighteenth-century acceleration of change, while Perrot has stressed department stores as the harbingers of new clothing manners among the petite bourgeoisie of the Second Empire. Both versions echo Veblen's description of mass consumption, which he, however, dates to the turn of the twentieth century. Manufacturers themselves have repeatedly seen *their* era as that of the speeding-up of clothing change. Already before World War I, manufacturers complained that the tendency toward increased style variation completely disorganized "whatever regularity there has been in an already irregular business."[76] Interwar observers claimed that the 1920s instilled a new idea of clothing obsolescence, and only then was the "fashion industry" born. Fashion designers today argue that the 1970s invented true democratization in clothing, i.e., "style" and frenetic clothes replacement.[77]

Still others have denied newness altogether. In 1902, the French art critic Arsène Alexandre contested the idea that fashion was a contemporary phenomenon for the simple reason, he proudly asserted, that the French had always had style, "by aptitude of race and from a long tradition."[78] But he did recognize a new sense of newness, attributing it to a modern emphasis on the notion of "personality." A good sixty-five years before Baudrillard, he argued that *la mode* only appears to be new: "we imitate each other with the profound conviction that we are completely different from each other."[79]

There is a parallel debate on the dating of the ready-to-wear revolution itself. At least three moments lay claim to invention. A strong argument may be made for the 1840s to 1860s, when military then civilian workshops in both countries began using sewing machines to produce men's wear on a large scale. The term "confec-

Fashion and Flexibility

tion" became used to distinguish the new mode of production from individually tailored garment-making. When the origin in ready-made goods is (generically) dated to the mid nineteenth century, it actually refers to men's wear and should be specified as such.

The second ready-made "takeoff" dates to the late nineteenth century, with the widespread adaptation of those methods to women's wear. As we have seen, this implied not only a transfer of techniques from one domain to another, but a transformation of *mentalités* concerning the artistic or feminine content of women's clothing. The growth in women's ready-made goods in the last decades of the nineteenth century corresponds more generally to (one of) the takeoff(s) in the consumer revolution. The term "ready-to-wear" was introduced in the Montgomery Ward catalogue in 1895.[80]

Most recently, however, industrial observers, social actors, and sociologists have described the 1960s and 1970s as *the* crucial moment of change. One study has gone so far as to reject any long-term or historical perspective altogether.[81] The French even changed their terminology to reflect this newness by consciously outmoding the word *confection* and replacing it with *prêt-à-porter*, a direct translation of the American term. As with many imported terms, it began surrounded by quotation marks but gradually entered the language without its typographical crutch.[82]

There is thus a constant reinventing of the notion of takeoff, both by historians and contemporaries. Just as early-nineteenth-century commentators lamented that, with the increasing demise of distinctive clothing for distinctive classes, you could no longer tell what *état* (class) someone belonged to, some late-twentieth-century observers complain that the current uniformization of clothing means that you can no longer tell what *état* (nation) a person is from. Garment manufacturers from the nineteenth century to the present have repeatedly wrung their hands in despair over changing demand, claiming that it is worse than ever before. A historical perspective on the constant rediscovery of discovery may relativize the presentist perspective of each period's triumphalism or despair. Nonetheless, by focusing on ready-made women's wear in particular, I am clearly favoring the 1880s and 1890s in the "takeoff" debate, choosing to pinpoint the diachronic dimension of change to the first major spread of ready-made goods to middle- and lower-class women. Furthermore, the narrative that I have outlined here, and

Ready-to-Wear and Ready-to-Work

which lays the foundation for an understanding of the garment labor force, draws upon those structural elements which were similar in New York and Paris. However, as the succeeding stories will show, the ready-made revolution was also affected by the spatial dimension of difference.

2

SEVENTH AVENUE

Seventh Avenue is called "the Market," but it has also been called a "jungle." The term has been used as a metaphor for the American garment industry in general and, more correctly, for the women's-wear industry in particular. It is in fact the epitome of that portion of the women's apparel industry which is most variable. The story of the growth and decline of the New York garment industry illustrates the difficult adaptation to the double imperatives of the production of fashion.

Various aspects of the history of the city's apparel industry have been told elsewhere.[1] What I would like to emphasize here is how that story illustrates the "antagonistic tendencies" of garment making. On the one hand, this can be seen in the geography of women's wear and how the New York market developed as a result of a sorting out of the more and less standardized elements of the trade. On the other hand, the history of the industry is connected to its particular labor force and to the union that has represented it since 1900. Indeed, from the perspective of the International Ladies' Garment Workers' Union (ILGWU), its history is the history of the industry itself. More important for our purposes, that labor history can itself be seen as an example of tensions between standardization and flexibility, or the problem of regulating labor relations in a context of "industrial chaos."

Democratization of Demand, Growth of Supply

War, as we have seen, provided the first important stimulus for the ready-made industry. One of the earliest clothing manufactories in the United States was the United States Army Clothing Establishment, set up in Philadelphia at the beginning of the War of 1812. It continued to operate after the war ended, distributing bundles of cut pieces, thread, and buttons to "widows and other meritorious females" for assembly. By the late 1840s, several large firms in New York were doing a brisk business. In a separation of functions that would hold true for over a century, Lewis and Hanford employed 75 inside cutters and 4,000 outside sewers; Brooks Brothers had 78 "insiders" and 1,500 "outsiders."[2] While the Civil War gave the real push to men's ready-made garments in the United States, internal migration also stimulated mass production as the adventuresome set off on the trek westward. From the California gold rush of 1848 to the expansion of the railroads and the settlement of the West in the 1870s and 1880s, the frontier also favored the expansion of premade clothing.

Women's wear first appeared as a separate item in the United States Census in 1860, the same year that a unique and short-lived article made a spectacular appearance. The hoopskirt combined extreme fashion (change) and industrial methods. Bradley and Carey's Hoop Skirt Works on West Twentieth Street in New York City employed sixteen hundred young women converting "steel rods into finished skirts," in what was perhaps the closest that garment manufacture ever came to heavy industry.[3] But hoopskirts went out of fashion, as did the large factory mode of production. The real takeoff in women's ready-made garments did not occur, as in France, until the last decades of the nineteenth century and would be marked by small, medium, and larger production units, rarely the size of the Hoop Skirt Works.

Ready-made clothes spread across the nation and across classes.

As the variety of goods increased, the market expanded. First there were women's cloaks, then ready-made tailored women's suits became popular in the 1880s and 1890s. Shirtwaists became the rage in the 1890s and gained an even greater market share after 1900 as their styles became more diversified. By the First World War, almost all Americans were wearing some garment that had been made up without multiple fittings. Shirtwaist makers had begun to make dresses, which became the growth sector of the ready-made market in the 1920s. Then, as we have seen, pants for women—the ultimate adaptation of men's-wear techniques—took off and have marked the period since World War II.

The importance of these shifting fashions is not simply to chart the history of the variability of whims. Changing use patterns of clothing, reflecting transformations in the sociological status of women, standardization of production, and democratization of supply allowed the American women's apparel industry to expand. Like their French counterparts, American women sought both freedom and constraint in their conversion to ready-made goods: freedom from fittings or from sewing, even if it meant greater constraint in their choices of style and size.

The growth of the garment industry in the United States (men's wear and women's wear combined) from 1870 to 1900 was spectacular. Capital investment tripled from $54 to $169 million. Product value did almost as well, increasing from $162 to $437 million. At the same time, the average number of wage earners almost doubled, from 120,000 to 206,000, men's employment increasing from 49,000 to 75,000, women's rising more dramatically from 69,000 to 127,000, and employment of children under sixteen from 1,600 to 3,800. Significantly, however, the number of establishments counted in the United States Census of Manufacture declined over that same period, from 9,700 to 8,600, as initial growth of ready-made methods corresponded to a certain concentration of production.[4]

New York State's predominance in the industry was clear by 1900: roughly one-half of the nation's clothing establishments, capital, and product value were located there. The state had 90,000 garment workers, out of the nationwide total of 206,000. Women slightly outnumbered men in New York (45,687 to 44,199), but the number of men sewing there was particularly striking. New York's male garment workers constituted half of the total American figure, whereas the New York women represented only one-third of all female garment workers in the United States. The New York industry, even more so than elsewhere, showed that not all needleworkers were women. Furthermore, only 633 children garment workers were counted in New York State, out of a nationwide total of 3,814.[5]

The women's clothing industry alone contributed significantly to the growth in garment production. From 1869 to 1899, invested capital increased fourteen-fold (from $3.5 to $48 million), product value twelve-fold (from $13 to $159 million), while the workforce increased seven times over (from 12,000 to 84,000 wage earners) in the United States.[6] At the upper end of the market, even department stores such as Bergdorf Goodman, whose reputation had been established from custom-made clothes, began selling ready-made goods in the 1920s. From 1929 on, their custom salon, maintained for its prestige, became less and less profitable. The Great Depression, like smaller ones before it (1893–96, 1907–8), only accentuated the shift toward ready-to-wear garments as women sought cheaper clothing. And even the garment-workers' union got into the act to promote ready-made garments and convince American women that they should drop the decidedly unmodern practice of making their own housedresses.[7]

While the trend toward ready-made dresses began to toll the final bell for the vast majority of custom dressmakers,[8] it also meant a shift in the labor force within the ready-made sector. Since dresses are easier to make than suits, somewhat less-skilled newer immigrant and second-generation women dressmakers soon outnumbered the (more-skilled) male immigrant cloak-makers who had reigned over women's coats and suits in the 1890s and continued to dominate within the union. By 1919, while the New York Cloakmakers' Joint Board was still the most powerful district board within the ILGWU, the thirty thousand members of the Ladies' Waist and Dress Makers' Union, Local 25, in New York City, was the largest single local, comprising nearly one-quarter of the union's total membership. The increasing importance of dresses finally led to a separate Dress Makers' Union, Local 22, in 1920. But, as Alice Kessler-Harris has pointed out, the separation of sectors also served to split up a feisty female leadership.[9]

Seventh Avenue

The Geography of Garment Making: Concentration, Decentralization, Clustering

By the late nineteenth century, New York City had become the fashion capital of America. The growth of ready-made garments had led, among other things, to a relative centralization of production as sewing migrated from the local tailor shop and rural outworker to urban factories and shops. By 1890, 44 percent of all ready-made clothes in the United States was produced in New York City, but 53.3 percent of all *women's* garment industry workers worked there (in 1899). In 1904, the latter figure rose to 65 percent, dropping back to a still healthy 57.3 percent in 1925.[10] New York's position was even more marked in terms of product value: 65 percent of the total value of American-made women's wear came from the city in 1899 and 78 percent in 1925, far exceeding the role played by any other city.[11]

Nevertheless, as ready-to-wear spread, so did the decentralization of production. Standardization of production carried within it the seeds of dispersion: to areas of greater space and, especially, lower labor costs. Those items that were best able to be mass produced gradually moved away from the highly skilled, greatly cramped, relatively expensive New York labor market. Men's wear rather than women's wear, work clothes rather than fashion items, underwear rather than outerwear were best able to take advantage of production in larger factories. A veritable exodus of men's wear occurred in the 1920s, with Chicago and Rochester becoming the centers of men's wear manufacture on a large scale. The men's apparel that did stay in New York City remained located in smaller contracting shops. By 1890, only 27.4 percent of the nation's ready-made men's wear was produced in New York City.[12] At the same time, the more standardized women's housedresses, uniforms, and aprons also moved away from the center of the city, while movement to the outlying boroughs of New York City constituted a microcosm of this centrifugal motion.[13] The smallest shops and the highest-priced dress lines remained closest to the fashion core.

Thus, well before the current trend in overseas manufacturing, and after the initial period of ready-to-wear growth and concentration in New York City, the geographic implications of more standardized garment production resulted in a spin-off from the fashion centers. To the outlying boroughs and suburbs of Manhattan, across the river to New Jersey, to Pennsylvania, to upstate New York and beyond, the garment industry then shifted westward, to the Midwest, and then on to the Southwest and West, before going offshore, to Puerto Rico or the Dominican Republic, but also to Asia, in what has been called the "extended work-bench."[14]

Nevertheless, two significant factors have limited an absolute dispersal of garment production: the advantages of geographic concentration and the imperatives of fashion. The city's very reputation has served as a powerful stimulus along with its noted concentration of skilled labor (higher productivity compensating higher wages) and skilled management. Concentration itself has acted as a positive magnet, offsetting the much-decried congestion that is its corollary.[15] Although workers moving dress racks of samples and merchandise at a snail's pace through the streets may be aggravating to taxi drivers, they symbolize the raison d'être of a centralized location. Furthermore, fashion (as change) itself has limited the centrifugal movement and reinforced the urban industry. Housedresses left, but silk dresses stayed. More style-oriented, made of more expensive material, needing greater skill and supervision, these were the goods that made Seventh Avenue's reputation in the interwar period.[16] High-fashioned women's garments have kept manufacturers together in the urban center, bemoaning the inscrutability of female whims and the impossibility of foreseeing fashion trends, yet clinging together in order to defy and define those trends.

Strikes and Unions

Space was not the only factor in the successive movements away from Manhattan. Labor costs and union avoidance were paramount in the setting up of "runaway" shops. New York labor is relatively expensive, and the precocious development of the garment unions made it all the more so. An inexpensive and noncombative labor force has been as much a clothing industry imperative as the desire to standardize production.[17] At the same time, clothing manufacturers looked with a dim eye on protective labor and housing legislation that affected garment work in both home and shop. The New York Factory Law of 1886, revised in 1897, set standards for the large shops, with a 1904 amendment still trying to enforce better lighting for workrooms, halls, and stairways "deemed necessary in the interest of public morality."[18] The 1892 New York State tenement law sought to eradicate sweatshop conditions by limiting homework. Such work was restricted to the family only, and laws of 1899, 1901, and 1903 strengthened requirements on licensing.

In this respect, the New York garment landscape has been shaped by two competing tendencies. Progressive reformers, labor leaders, and state legislators pushed through laws to better conditions within that environment, while manufacturers threatened that too many constraints would make the landscape disappear altogether. But the garment unions persisted, waging their own battle for a regulation of working conditions in the face of the vagaries of oscillatory production patterns.

A burning factory, sweatshops, homework, seasonality, and cutthroat competition all form part of the industrial image crystallized in the turn-of-the-century depictions by labor activists and reformers. Between "inside shops" that concentrated production and a greater regulation of working conditions and "outside (contracting) shops" subject to the worst effects of seasonal production, labor leaders and social progressives clearly preferred the former, while manufacturers argued that they needed both in order to respond to fashion demands. The tensions of trying to produce enough of the same line at any given moment while responding to seasonal trends and consequent production shifts were reflected in tensions between capital and labor. As the union tells it, the tale is a heroic one, of strikes and of a language of class struggle in the early days, of peace treaties and innovative collective bargaining soon after.

One of the earliest strikes occurred in July 1883, when several inside shops struck over working conditions. The "emigrants' strike," as the newspapers called it, involved about as many women as men (meeting, as with most of the early strikes, in separate halls). Garment workers were caught up in the general strike movement that swept the country in the mid-1880s, and they continued to protest into the first decades of the new century. But what has been called a general uprising against industrialism was, for garment workers, a protest against conditions in both the larger inside shops and the smaller contractors' shops. As one observer commented, "Clothing workers had been striking almost continually since the 1890s.

In fact, in some years it appears to have been their main outdoor activity."[19]

A general strike broke out in the cloak trade in New York on August 15, 1885, and more frequent "seasonal" shop strikes mirrored the uneven cycles of work. They occurred frequently at the beginning of the season when rates were being set, and a certain ritual set in. Workers stopped work and headed out in protest for a picnic in "Cendele" (Central Park) or the Market Street docks area. Employers had to seek them out there to negotiate; a shared keg of beer often marked the settlement of the dispute.[20]

Beyond bread-and-butter issues, the early strikes already reflected a critique of the industrial structure itself. As early as 1886, workers expressed dissatisfaction with the outside contracting system when 3,000 inside–New York cloak-makers joined 1,500 outside cloak-makers striking against their contractors.[21] In 1894, workers struck not just for higher wages or fewer hours but against flexibility itself with the following demands: (1) payments should be weekly instead of by piece rates; (2) hours should be fixed (nine-hour days in "inside" shops, ten-hour days in "outside" shops); (3) homework and night work should be abolished; (4) wages should be paid weekly in a timely fashion (on Saturdays for inside shops, on Monday for outside workers); (5) firms should cut their own garments and have them made up by their contractors alone, not by "secondhand" manufacturers; (6) "only union men" [sic] should be employed; (7) the union should have the right to "control" its members at any time; (8) no workers should be discharged without sufficient cause; and (9) there should be only one helper for every ten operators.[22]

Just as the seasonal trade engendered seasonal strikes, it also engendered seasonal unionism. After several short-lived attempts, a cloak-makers' union was set up in late 1889–90 at 92 Hester Street with the help of the United Hebrew Trades. By May 1890, the Operators' and Cloak Makers' Union Local no. 1 had a membership of over three thousand. But the early efforts at organizing women's garment workers were plagued not only by industrial seasonality but also by institutional, political, and personal infighting. Jurisdictional skirmishes and ideological battles between the Knights of Labor and the American Federation of Labor (AFL), disputes between anarchists and socialists, between those for and against the

Seventh Avenue

popular Joseph Barondess, and between those favorable to the Socialist Labor Party and those fed up with its leader Daniel De Leon, all envenomed efforts at unification throughout the 1890s. And, as the leftist historian Jack Hardy stressed, rank-and-file opposition to union leadership began as early as efforts at unionization itself.[23]

Men's-wear and women's-wear workers organized separately, largely due to their different production methods. A national union for men's-wear workers, the United Garment Workers (UGW), was founded in 1891, affiliated with the AFL. It mainly represented the more skilled craftsmen of the trade—the cutters—and was especially predominant in the most well-organized, standardized overall sector. The executive officers were mostly American-born.

However, the more foreign-born and less skilled workers in the relatively more erratic ready-made sectors of men's-wear manufacture felt ill at ease within the United Garment Workers. In 1892, several immigrant locals in New York—mostly Jewish and German—formed District Council no. 7, which included the United Brotherhood of Tailors local (of coat tailors), two vest-makers' locals, a pants-makers' local in New York, and one in Brooklyn, as well as a Brooklyn local of German tailors. When the UGW gave little support to the 1911–12 general tailors' strike in New York, a serious rift began. After a bitter struggle, the largely Jewish immigrant dissident tailors' and cutters' locals from New York, Chicago, Baltimore, and Boston set up their own national union in 1914, the Amalgamated Clothing Workers of America (ACWA). The English Jewish leader of the AFL, Samuel Gompers, complained that this was religious separatism at its worst.[24] But by 1920, under the firm helm of Sidney Hillman, the ACWA became the primary representative of men's garment workers in the country, with nearly 170,000 members nationwide. It was finally admitted to the AFL in 1933.[25]

The ILGWU and the Search for Industrial Stability

The International Ladies' Garment Workers' Union (ILGWU) was founded in 1900 directly under the aegis of the AFL. The union organized its first general strike in July 1901, in which it sought to sign contracts not only with the small contractors but with the large manufacturers as well. Its aim from the beginning was to make the latter more responsible for conditions in this "curiously disorganized trade."[26] The early period of industrial warfare set the terms for subsequent industrial relations, not simply as a variation on the clash between bosses' and workers' interests but as a rivalry over competing paradigms of flexibility and regulation. The conflict over standards became a veritable union leitmotiv: "To bring order out of chaos."[27]

In the first years of the century, global ILGWU membership fluctuated around 2,000. In 1908 there was a first major increase to over 7,800 members, but this was little compared to the impact of the strike movements of 1909–10. Membership jumped to over 58,000 in 1909, and to over 84,600 in 1912. According to the Immigration Commission in 1911, almost 36 percent of all of the clothing workers and 80 percent of the cutters in New York were organized.[28]

The pre–World War I period is marked in American women's garment-industry memory by four major events: two strikes, a collective agreement, and a tragic fire. The "Uprising of the 20,000," "The Great Revolt," the Protocol of Peace, and the Triangle Fire all reveal the disgruntlement over chaotic labor conditions, attempts at industrial regulation, and the continued impunity of many of the early clothing manufacturers.

Women led the way in fighting for better conditions, often over (male) union hesitation. In a legendary speech, on November 22, 1909, Clara Lemlich intervened from the floor in Yiddish at the overflow meeting at Cooper Union that had been called by the Waist and Dress Makers' Union, Local 25. While the ILGWU and the New York Women's Trade Union League (WTUL) leaders hesitated over the next step to take, Lemlich got directly to the point:

I am a working girl, one of those who are on strike against intolerable conditions. I am tired of listening to speakers who talk in general terms. What we are here for is to decide whether we shall or shall not strike. I offer a resolution that a general strike be declared—now.[29]

As the crowd rose to its feet, applauding wildly, the chairman asked the audience to pledge the old Jewish oath: "If I turn traitor to the cause I now pledge, may this hand wither from the arm I now raise." Lemlich had sparked what was called "the girls' strike" and became known as the "Uprising of 20,000." It became a legend, symbolic of the spontaneous, female, and largely, but not exclusively, Jewish nature of many of the early actions.[30]

The 1909–10 strike, in a branch where 80 percent of the workers were women, 55 percent of the women Jewish, 35 percent Italian, and 7 percent native-born Americans,[31] had begun over the issue of whether the company union at the Triangle Shirtwaist Company (the Triangle Employees Benevolent Association) would distribute ten dollars in aid to needy families as the Jewish high holidays approached. The company refused, and the (mostly Jewish) workers at Triangle turned to the umbrella organization of United Hebrew Trades for help. Neither the ILGWU nor the WTUL were prepared, but they became active organizers as the strike spread beyond ethnic issues and became a symbol for labor demands in general and for women's activism in particular. According to one estimate that counted as many as 30,000 strikers, 21,000 of them were Jewish women, 2,000 Italian women, 1,000 American women, and 6,000 men.[32] It was a dirty fight, "marked by assaults of gorillas, ill-treatment of police, hunger and heroism of the embattled workers."[33] The company used prostitutes to taunt the strikers, thugs to beat them up, and the police to bully them. Hundreds of people were arrested, including Mary Dreier, the middle-class president of the WTUL. The strike itself was only moderately successful. Many small manufacturers signed separate contracts, while many of the larger manufacturers never signed at all and refused to recognize the union.

The waist-makers' strike paved the way for some 50 to 60,000 (mostly male) cloak-makers who followed their example several months later. The "Great Revolt" of the summer of 1910 was better planned and more successful in attempting to curtail "deplorable industrial chaos."[34] The employers finally settled, thanks to effective mediation by A. Lincoln Filene and Louis D. Brandeis. A "Protocol of Peace" was signed on September 2, 1910, by the ILGWU and the Cloak, Suit, and Skirt Manufacturers' Protective Association.

The Protocol's very name was testimony to the depths of the strife just ended. The agreement called for a 50-hour week (five 9-hour days plus 5 hours on the sixth day), the abolition of homework, minimum-wage scales, and a "preferential shop" (in which "union men" [sic] were preferred). A Joint Board of Sanitary Control, a

Board of Arbitration for major disputes, and a Committee of Grievances for smaller problems were set up. Similar protocols were signed shortly thereafter for the dress-and-waist, housedress, and other garment specialties. By early 1912, the ILGWU's New York Joint Board of Cloak, Suit, and Skirt Makers' Unions had signed contracts with 1,796 out of 1,829 New York shops.[35]

The garment industry led the way in collective bargaining. The Protocol of Peace was more than a truce. For its architects and defenders, it heralded a new philosophy of common interests between employers and employees to end class warfare. "Protocolism" was seen as leading the way to true industrial democracy, as a way of "replac[ing] the chaos and confusion of unregulated competition with a system of law and order."[36] The Protocol marked the growing acceptance, on the part of American labor and capital alike, of the idea that negotiations and bargaining could replace conflict. In men's wear, Sidney Hillman, a former Bundist, now leader of the ACWA, had also changed his tune. He too had become convinced of the "tremendous waste" inherent in the strike as "the weapon of the jungle."[37] The consequent organization of labor relations, to combat the anarchy of unplanned strikes, was concretized at the federal level by the creation of a Department of Labor in 1913. Although a minority of left-wing dissenters (workers along with intellectuals, such as Isaac Hourwich, within the ILGWU) denounced the new tactics as collaborationist and deplored that the right to strike was forfeited in favor of an apparatus of arbitration and conciliation,[38] by all accounts (and particularly those of the union), a new era of American labor relations had begun, led in large part by the garment-industry unions.

The Protocol was hailed with excitement. But enthusiasm soon turned to disappointment. The popularity of protocolism lasted until the next depression, of 1913–14, when manufacturers turned more and more to contracting outside the union shops. In addition to economic conditions, the arbitration and grievance machinery itself furthered the Protocol's demise. As Louis Levine, early historian of the ILGWU, pointed out, it did not provide sufficient outlet for workers' complaints. He also blamed the newer immigrant employers for not understanding the American context, for resisting workers' demands, and for being "out of harmony" with the spirit of the agreement.[39] The terms of the Protocol were never fully enforced (it

Seventh Avenue

was formally ended after a 1916 lockout), and its attempts to regulate the industry led to the reinvention of flexibility in other forms.

The Triangle Shirtwaist Company fire in 1911, one of the worst industrial accidents of the century in New York City, became a lasting symbol of manufacturers' methods. The incident has remained engraved in garment-industry and indeed municipal memory as a sign of early-twentieth-century conditions—forever abolished? On March 25, a cigarette fell on some clothing remnants, igniting a terrible fire that spread throughout the ten-story building, along the wooden stairways. Many of the girls working inside were trapped in their workrooms, where the doors were locked from the outside for fear of theft. The fire department ladders did not even reach as far as the upper floors, where the manufacturing company was located, and 146 girls died in the fire, most of them by jumping, in flames, to their death. The widely reported, horrible image of the tragedy stirred public opinion and led to a state investigation into factory conditions.[40] The locked doors and crowded workshops, emblematic of working conditions in the garment trades, were condemned, and union membership rose.

Between the Wars

After the depression of 1913–14, World War I brought relative prosperity to the garment industry as well as a further increase in union membership. With men drafted for the war effort and immigration halted due to the war, a labor shortage occurred just as orders increased. The government needed everything from mattress sacks to overcoats. From 1913 to 1917, ILGWU membership fluctuated between 72,000 and 85,000, and the war ended in 1918 with a high of over 129,000 members. Thereafter, however, the union started a seemingly precipitous decline. By 1927, there were only 28,000 workers enrolled, and although over 10,000 more joined within the next couple of years, the onset of the Depression brought the ILGWU to its interwar low of 23,800 members in 1931.[41]

Sluggish union membership in the 1920s can be attributed to several factors: slowed industrial growth; expansion of the jobber-submanufacture system; and internecine fighting within the union.

By 1910, the fast increase of women's wear had peaked. After the post-armistice business-boom turned into a depression, the industry continued to grow again, but at a considerably slower pace than before the war. The years 1927 to 1929 were perceived as a key period of "violent expansion" after a long cycle of inactivity, but it was a boom before the fall. Sweatshops returned during the Depression, and union headquarters were reduced to a ramshackle office without a phone and often with no light.[42]

The jobber-submanufacturing system has been described and decried as one of the major "inventions" of the interwar period, as the manufacturer, contractor, and homeworker of the prewar period were replaced by jobber and submanufacturer. While contracting had developed during the initial growth of the industry, production had moved back inside in the 1890s. That is, while small-, medium-, and large-sized production units all continued to coexist, there was a relative shift toward greater concentration at the turn of the century as a result of the growing standardization of production and attempts to regulate homework. In 1913, 56 percent of dress and waist workers were employed in factories of more than 75 workers, and 27 percent worked in factories of 100 to 200 employees. (Coat factories remained smaller, however.) It was during this period of relative concentration that the ILGWU was founded and union organizing made its greatest initial gains.[43] However, even within this context of consolidation, inside contracting allowed manufacturers to shift the burden of labor organization on to contractors who organized their own labor force within the factory premises.

After World War I, several factors led to a shift back toward greater decentralization outside the factory walls. With stagnation after 1915, inside manufacturers became cautious about too great a fixed investment and reverted to the "new" jobber-contractor system. At the same time, a perceived notion of the "growing importance of style" stimulated the need for flexible shops able to produce short runs quickly. Furthermore, as factory conditions increasingly became the focus of criticism and conflict (particularly after the Triangle fire), state efforts to regulate conditions in the inside shops, prewar strikes, and the emergence of the ILGWU all spurred on the shift toward the use of outside shops.[44]

The main difference in the interwar period, beyond that of terminology, was in the separation of production from sales. The jobbers' main function was to supply the retailer directly, with quick deliveries. To do so, they contracted out the sewing to submanufacturers (who cut and sewed) or contractors (who only sewed). But jobbers were above all blamed with imposing cutthroat competition on the contractors. During a particularly nasty price war in New York City in the 1920s, 200 jobbers pitted some 1,200 contractors against each other.[45]

Although the jobber system was perceived as a new phenomenon, designed to avoid labor legislation and union-imposed conditions, it could be argued that its novelty was more apparent than real. As one of the garment-union newspapers wrote, "sub-manufacturer" was merely a new name for contractors, a subterfuge to evade post-Protocol controls on contracting.[46] The shifts from contracting to concentration and then to the jobbers were visible moments of historical change. Yet they can also be seen as part of a more long-term variation on the theme of contracting.

Given the importance of the quick turnover of high-fashion goods there, the jobber system was more extensive in New York than elsewhere. It was defended by the manufacturers, damned by the unions. In her 1930 study, Mabel Magee went so far as to say that "both workers and employers feel that in the submanufacturing system lies the secret of New York's supremacy," and that, if regulated, it would drive manufacturers out of town.[47] This then became the union's dilemma: to better conditions without making the New York labor market so regulated or so expensive that manufacturers would (continue to) send production elsewhere. The very flexibility of the industrial structure and the persistent possibility of contracting work away created a continued menace with regard to jobs, just as it tended to create poor conditions within those jobs that remained within the urban core.

The union struck back with strikes. An important three-month waist- and dress makers' strike in 1919 led to the walkout of 35,000 Italian, Jewish, American, and African American strikers from 860 shops. A cloak-makers' strike in 1926 ended in defeat, but another cloak-makers' strike in 1929 was more successful. On February 4, 1930, a general strike began, the first industry-wide movement in seven years. It both strengthened the union and eliminated the Communist influence. But the most important interwar strike was the

Ready-to-Wear and Ready-to-Work

walkout of 70,000 dressmakers from both New York City and out-of-town shops in August 1933 in order to enforce the new labor codes.

Yet none of these strikes captured industrial history's imagination like the early ones. Perhaps the heroic memory of the early strikes was kept alive all the more so as the union changed tactics in the interwar period. Its increasing recourse to collective bargaining meant that allies and enemies had shifted within the ongoing war between regulation and flexibility. From a struggle of workers against employers, the debate and dispute were transformed into an alliance of the organized employers' associations and labor unions against unorganized employers and their nonunion workers.

The subsequent history of industrial relations, like that of the industry itself, became one of "stability versus flexibility."[48] As J. B. S. Hardman, director of the ACWA educational program, later put it, the needle-unions' aim was "to bring about a measure of stabilization in the industry and thus assure that competition for buyers would not be carried on at the expense of the workers." He added, rather optimistically, that "intelligent employers appreciated the unions' efforts to instill order in this basically chaotic branch of American free private enterprise."[49] While the ILGWU pioneered efforts to assure job security,[50] it claimed that it had stabilized the industry itself:

In the coat and suit industry of New York, we are proud to state, our Union not only has contributed to industrial stability and the elimination of economic chaos,—it has been the chief factor of such stability and control. For more than twenty-five years it has kept up collective relations with employers' associations and this has resulted not alone in enhancing the prestige of the Union in the industry, but likewise in solidifying the collective responsibility of the manufacturers' groups.[51]

This triumphalism was particularly understandable in 1937, in the euphoric aftermath of the New Deal, itself replete with a language of order and enlightenment.[52] But it also underlay the new spirit of union organizing.

The union sought to regulate conditions within the trade as it sought better to control conditions within the union and to define the repertory of union activity. Not everyone agreed with the change of strategy. As one dispirited observer commented wryly on the more general shift toward collective bargaining: "The Jewish radical,

Seventh Avenue

once he gets tired, gets awfully tired."[53] More seriously, disgruntled members provided a ripe terrain for Communists and other "rank-and-file" opponents in the 1920s.

Internecine struggles seriously gnawed at the union's attempts to regulate either itself or the industry. On the one hand, the political struggle against Communist influence within the union became a pervasive subtext to union activities in the 1920s. On the other hand, the major organizational dispute within American labor in the twentieth century—that between the American Federation of Labor and the Committee and later Congress of Industrial Organization—affected the women's-wear industry in a particular manner, due to its very composite structure.

The fierce fighting between Socialists and Communists that marked the garment unions in the 1920s has been called the "civil war in the needle trades."[54] After the left-wing split from the Socialist Party in 1919, leading to a workers' party and a new trade union under William Z. Foster, two predominantly New York (and also Russian Jewish) unions—the International Ladies' Garment Workers' Union and the International Furworkers' Union[55]—became particularly influenced by Communism. Left opposition within the ILGWU began with the "Current Events Committee" of 1917, a group of young women in Local 25 (Ladies' Waist and Dress Makers' Union) who became enthused by the Russian Revolution and wanted to make the union more than "a mere question of bundles."[56] Four years later, a successor group affiliated with the Communist-backed Trade Union Educational League (TUEL). As J. B. S. Hardman later wrote, "a progressive hardening of democratic arteries in some unions' management" had led to pent-up discontent.[57] The AFL, in spite of past disagreements with the ILGWU, lent support to its Socialist leaders. But, in 1925, feeding on rank-and-file discontent, Communists gained control of the executive boards of Locals 2 (cloak operators, formerly Locals 1 and 17), 9 (cloak finishers), and 22 (the large dressmakers' local), jointly comprising 70 percent of the New York membership. The Socialists in the ILGWU fought back, with somewhat undemocratic bureaucratic maneuverings, and, in December 1926, after the unsuccessful cloak-makers' strike (whose lack of success they blamed on the opposition), they expelled the three locals dominated by the left-wing opposition.[58]

The Communists then shifted strategy. Abandoning the TUEL

tactic of "boring from within," they set up a dual union in 1928. A mass meeting held at Bronx Stadium on August 8, 1928, attracted some 15,000 dissidents, and a separate national union—the Needle Trades Workers' Industrial Union (NTWIU)—was launched. By 1934, it had recruited some 25,000 members.[59] This split temporarily freed the ILGWU from internal criticism, while some of those previously expelled, such as Charles Zimmerman, leader of the Progressive Group and the Left Wing Group, and manager of the powerful Dress Makers' Union, Local 22, ultimately returned to the fold. The "left hysteria," as the union called it, was over, but the ILGWU had lost some of its punch.[60] The idealism of the early years was buried in the battles engaged against the Communist opposition.

As the union moved politically to the right during the interwar period, it definitively joined the mainstream of the American labor movement, with its two-pronged emphasis on collective bargaining and benefits. Its new president, David Dubinsky, who would reign over the union for the next thirty years (from 1932 to 1966), was right for the job. (In France, the ILGWU is often known simply as "le syndicat de Dubinsky.") What Singer was to the sewing machine, Dubinsky was to the union, a charismatic character with a perfect "origins" story. Always represented as a man of humble and radical beginnings—who had led one of his first strikes in his father's own bakery in czarist Russia, was later arrested, sent to Siberia, and escaped[61]—he and the ILGWU as a whole remained staunchly anti-Communist from the 1920s on and became important partners in the AFL's effort to thwart Communism in the rebuilding of "free trade unionism" in postwar Europe.[62]

Nonetheless, from the AFL perspective, both the industrial-based ILGWU and the (even more so) ACWA remained left-wing thorns in the side of the reformist, craft-based federation. Sidney Hillman (of the ACWA) and David Dubinsky participated in the initial organizing meeting of the Committee for Industrial Organization (CIO) in 1935, which challenged AFL hegemony within the American labor movement. Given the more relatively standardized and "industrial" nature of men's-wear manufacture, it is not surprising that the ACWA was more attracted to the new industrial unionism and more committed to its founding.[63]

The ILGWU, on the other hand, had a somewhat more ambiguous relationship to the CIO, undoubtedly due in part to its own more

Seventh Avenue

heterogeneous industrial makeup. The General Executive Board voted by 12 to 10 to affiliate with the Committee in 1935, thus leading to the garment union's suspension from the AFL in 1936, along with nine other unions who had joined the CIO. But as the CIO moved toward dual unionism, and the ILGWU became increasingly unhappy with CIO leader John L. Lewis, the ILGWU maintained a separate stance. From 1938 to 1940, it remained unaffiliated with either the AFL or the CIO (now Congress of Industrial Organization). In 1940, the ILGWU rejoined the AFL (while the ACWA remained in the CIO), but, still critical of the atmosphere of civil war within the labor movement, Dubinsky continued to reproach the AFL from within and work toward reconciliation of the two federations. The ILGWU was instrumental in their merger in 1955.[64]

Political strife was not the only problem plaguing the union. The union was also criticized from within both by women who wanted the ILGWU to have more "soul" and by immigrant groups wanting their own language sections, as we will see below. Furthermore, the ILGWU and the ACWA began to fight each other over which union should organize which shops. Their jurisdictional battles reflected the ways in which the expansion of women's ready-made clothing was in many sectors predicated on an increasing masculinization of women's styles, accompanied by further standardization of production. The ILGWU Cloak Joint Board complained of the ACWA's "militant attacks," "pressure tactics," and even their "hired agents" who threatened "direct physical attack" in order to "capture" some of their women's skirt and suit shops. Certain men's manufacturing firms, already organized by the ACWA, were branching out into fields traditionally under the ILGWU umbrella.[65] The later rise of sportswear only exacerbated the problem of defining men's or women's clothing and consequent union territory.

All in all, the 1920s were at best a period of "fitful but cumulative progress" in labor conditions and wages brought to an abrupt halt by the Depression.[66] Since the turn of the century, labor agreements had brought the average working week from 56 to 60 hours down to 50 after the Protocol of Peace and finally to a theoretical 40 hours by 1928, even if, in the contractors' shops and during the busy season, the workweek could still expand upwards toward 80 hours to fill an urgent order. The Depression of the early 1930s shattered what wage-and-hour standards had been agreed upon through two decades of union activity. Homework and sweatshops reemerged; hourly wages gave way to piece rates once more. Skilled workers shifted to less skilled lines, while part-time employment and work sharing only partially mitigated unemployment: "The industry itself continued to leak out of the central markets to distant hideaways beyond the reach of the reviving ILGWU."[67]

The federal government and the labor unions tried to alleviate the effects of the Depression. In 1933, the National Industrial Recovery Act (NIRA) was passed, enabling the National Recovery Administration (NRA) to establish a series of codes described by the ILGWU as an "instrument of stability."[68] Close to the protocol mentality and to existing collective-bargaining agreements, the garment-industry codes "fitted this particular trade like one of its own cloaks," commented the *New York Times.*[69] The garment industries were indeed those which most benefited from the new laws. Contractor limitation and jobber responsibility for conditions in the contractors' shops, called for unsuccessfully in the 1920s, were now inscribed in the cloak-makers' code.[70] (The dressmakers' code only called for contractor registration; limitation of their number was not won until 1936.) Homework was once again regulated, and 94 percent of men's-wear homeworkers were taken into factories after the code was adopted.[71]

However, this new deal was as short-lived if not more so than the Protocol had been in its day. The Supreme Court declared the codes unconstitutional in May 1935. Standards declined again and old issues resurfaced. Homework reappeared; a 1936 study found that 194 New York manufacturers were sending work out to 1,661 homeworkers in sixteen states and Puerto Rico.[72] Other attempts were made at the industry, state, and federal levels to control conditions. An industry-run National Coat and Suit Recovery Board was set up in 1935 to try to police contracting competition, although the more volatile dressmakers' sector was not able to maintain a board.[73] A 1935 New York State law set up a mechanism for strictly controlling industrial homework in view of eliminating it entirely. In 1938, the federal Fair Labor Standards Act (FLSA), known as the "Wage and Hour Law," set minimum standards for factories and homework alike. The forty-hour workweek was passed, to take effect in 1940.

Seventh Avenue

But if some saw the FLSA as a victory for greater stability, the law was replete with exceptions written into it. Others argued that it was, in any case, too difficult to enforce.[74]

Nonetheless, as in the earlier period of regulation, the years 1936 to 1940 saw a greater relative consolidation of big inside shops and a decrease (by 26 percent) in the number of contracting shops.[75] In 1945, further restrictions were extended to all other industries, and it was estimated that between 1935 and 1955 the number of home-workers in New York State had dropped from 500,000 (in all fields) to less than 5,000.[76]

The 1930s were difficult ones for the workers, but they were prosperous ones for the union. When David Dubinsky became president of the ILGWU in 1932, the union's membership was only 40,000 (up from the previous year's low of 23,800, but nothing close to the 1918 high of 129,000), largely as a result of the political infighting. During the 1933 strike, thanks to the NIRA, membership jumped to almost 200,000 and rose steadily thereafter to almost a quarter of a million members in 1940. By 1934, the ILGWU had become the third-largest union in the AFL. It offered its members everything from health care to group singing to its own newspaper (*Justice*) and greatly expanded its social welfare programs during the 1930s. Health insurance, housing, and unemployment benefits were provided to union members. A Union Health Center had been set up as early as 1914 (the first in the country), and the ILGWU joined with other unions in 1924 to create the International Union Bank. The ILGWU rented, as of 1915, and later purchased, a summer resort called Unity House for its members' use. Like the ACWA, the union was a pioneer in educational and cultural activities. The ILGWU even produced a play that went to Broadway and was performed at the White House: *Pins and Needles* ran from 1937 to 1940, setting a record for long-running musicals.

By the mid-1930s, the garment manufacturers were themselves increasingly well organized. In men's wear, the New York Clothing Manufacturers' Exchange, Inc., grouped together twenty-one members in 1933 to counter the ACWA. Mirroring the more complex organization of women's wear, the cloak, suit, and skirt trade had three employers' organizations: an inside manufacturers' organization, a jobbers' association, and a contractors' association. The dressmakers followed suit. But regulation of the industry kept con-

Ready-to-Wear and Ready-to-Work

fronting two dissenting arguments: that rules imposed on one sector (factories) could lead to greater abuses elsewhere (homework); that total regulation would simply lead the manufacturers to move away.

World War II and Beyond: Prosperity and Decline

World War II ended the Depression and finally stabilized production. Garment manufacturers lobbied for military contracts. War orders were sufficiently important to cause a minor skirmish between the women's wear and men's wear sectors. Dubinsky charged Sidney Hillman of unfairly arranging for his shops to get contracts from the War Production Board. Dubinsky argued a bit petulantly that the sewing machine was a highly versatile instrument that the women's-wear manufacturers could use just as well as the men's-wear makers to help the war effort. Some ILGWU shops got orders for lighter military products and accessories, and about 10 percent of the women's garment industry workforce set about making cartridge belts, mosquito nets, tents, etc.[77]

In fact, the women's-wear sector in the United States ultimately did not suffer too greatly during the war. The initial lag in consumer demand was soon reversed due to the "unprecedented prosperity which the war had brought to American industry"[78] and the large number of women drawn into the labor market. While consumer demand increased, supply also became more productive. Limitations on fabrics affected style and its variety. (In what may not have been the worst of secondary effects, two-color shoes were banned—due to restrictions on dyes—and girdles became scarce—as elastic was directed toward the war effort.[79]) The simplification of styles made garments easier to make. The war flattened seasonal production oscillations, and there were even labor shortages. By 1942, the women's garment industry was working at full capacity.[80]

At the end of the war, industry pessimists predicted gloom. But by 1946, prosperity and full employment had returned. Labor was quiescent and business good. Industrial employment peaked in 1948. By the early 1960s, Seventh Avenue was the undisputed American capital of fashion dresses. While over two-thirds of the dozen-priced dresses—retailing for $2.94 to $5.84 (of which the total wholesale value was some $321 million in 1961)—were produced in large quantities in assembly-line methods outside of Manhattan, the New York garment center produced over 70 percent of the unit-priced dresses (whose wholesale value was $1.255 billion in 1961), in whose image the entire industry basked.[81]

In the same period, global ILGWU membership rose to 300,000 in 1942 and reached over 430,000 in 1950, with approximately 200,000 in New York alone in 1958. Nationwide enrollment vacillated around 450,000 through the 1960s. The return to postwar "normalcy" also meant a return to seasonality, high firm mortality, unemployment, and runaway shops. In March 1958, the ILGWU organized the first general women's garment industry strike in twenty-five years, the largest in its history.[82] Given the high turnover of workers, membership drives had to remain vigilant, however. While some 185,000 new members joined the ILGWU in 1956–58, there had been a net membership loss of some 2,000, indicating an overall departure of 187,000.[83] But the union was becoming big business. It ran a training institute for its organizers, owned buildings, and had an impressive number of its own employees. Dubinsky and other leaders were active in state and national politics. And most important, the union handled those welfare functions not covered by any federal or state plan. Fringe benefits became a critical component of the union's functioning and of its appeal. Given the decentralized nature of production, the union's role in collecting employers' payments and employees' deductions, and in disbursing health, vacation, welfare, retirement, and death benefits was particularly important.

Since World War II, there have actually been two histories of the garment industry, to which we can now turn. There is a fashion history, generally upbeat in tone, emphasizing the takeoff of a specifically American style. The industrial history is more mixed and depends on the geographic perspective—whining from the East, grinning in the West.

American Style and Sportswear

American dependence on French fashion had once again been punctuated by war. Concomitant with frustration at being cut off from French styles were repeated calls for greater self-reliance, not only on behalf of abstract Emersonian values, but in order to complete America's moral and material independence from the Old World. After disruptions in international commerce and penury on the Continent had halted the regular transmission of fashions westward across the Atlantic during the First World War, Paris had regained its predominance as fashion capital of the world. However, the inexorable move toward ready-made goods in American female fashions put greater pressure on French couturiers. When World War II broke out, one American observer noted, "Nothing did more to liberate American fashion from the domination of Paris than Germany's conquest of France in 1940."[84]

More important, perhaps, World War II furthered the progressive shift in American women's clothes. Simplicity and comfort became the watchwords of American "style." Again there was a perceived notion of a new fashion awareness, fed by the general postwar increase in the standard of living and the further development of mass communications helping to disseminate the new vogues. An adventuresome group of designers (including Frank Adams, Chuck Howard, John Norman, Frank Smith, Pembroke Squires, and John Weitz) helped create a specifically American look in the 1950s and 1960s. Using simpler shapes, new fabrics, more lively designs, and new mass-marketing techniques, they began to compete successfully with the more serious Paris styles.

The most specific shift came with the growth of sportswear. While the New York designers had been trying to compete with transatlantic styles, a new menace appeared from the West: the rise of sportswear and the growth of production in California. Coats, suits, and dresses, the more skilled ends of the trade which had formed the core of the New York industry, began to feel the crunch of suburban styles.

Representations of Decline

While total United States employment in the apparel industry rose in the postwar period, there was a sharp loss of jobs in New York. Statewide employment declined by one-quarter of a million from 1948 (424,000) to 1980 (170,000). New York's share of nationwide garment jobs fell from 36 percent to 13 percent. Other eastern states (New Jersey, Pennsylvania) were similarly affected, while the western states, especially California, and some southern states, such as North Carolina, benefited from the locational shift in the industry.[85] In New York City, the total garment-industry labor force (manufacturing and sales) declined by 45.3 percent from 1950 (316,843) to 1970 (173,304), with a loss of 50.7 percent (5,233) of establishments between 1958 and 1977.[86] By 1987, the industry accounted for only 105,000 jobs in New York City, although it was still the largest manufacturing industry in the city.[87]

The specter of decline has become an incessant plaint since the 1960s. Yet decline is both dire reality and comparative construct. It was already a subtheme of industrial reports in the 1930s. Indeed, each period seems to reinvent decline, attributing its causes to present concerns, ignoring past precedents, and reinterpreting the very nature of the industry in the light of contemporaneous understanding.

As we have seen, growth began slowing in the early 1920s with the relocation of men's wear and other standardized goods. The first definition of decline is thus a result of the centrifugal motion described above. Mabel Magee set a pessimistic tone as early as 1930, attributing the declining number of wage earners ever since 1919 to increased productivity and changing women's styles.[88] The shift from suits to easier-to-make dresses in the interwar period was accompanied by a concentration on fewer designs, a phenomenon that was repeated during the Depression and the Second World War, each time giving a further boost to the ready-made concept and realization.

The Depression itself, interestingly enough, does not appear as a major factor in perceptions of the garment industry's decline. (Indeed, light manufacturing was generally affected much less than heavy industry.) A 1942 report (based on 1939 data), undertaken specifically because of popular concern that the industry was migrating out of the city, did not explicitly lay the blame on general economic conditions. Leonard Drake and Carrie Glasser in fact tried to be optimistic, explaining that decline is not an absolute fact, but a relative concept.[89] Yes, the garment industry had lost jobs, but it still remained the most important industry within the city. And while work had gone to other parts of the country, New York still had the largest national concentration of clothing workers. Over a decade later, Roy Helfgott also tried to calm pessimism about decline, in his case by redefining the pertinent geographic unit. The "New York Production Area"—that area within overnight trucking distance from the garment center, i.e., New York, New Jersey, Connecticut, Massachusetts, and Pennsylvania together—had not done so badly, jointly maintaining its roughly 70 percent of women's outerwear production in 1947 and 1954.[90]

Explanations for decline thus also depend on geographic perspective. Job "loss" occurred due to exodus to other areas (including a continued decentralization within the New York area itself), but it was also initially due to the fact that other parts of the country (and then the world) had begun significant garment production sites of their own. Even if the New York–New Jersey Standard Metropolitan Area had had an absolute job increase (of 1.8 percent) in the period from 1947 to 1954 (while Chicago had lost 20.1 percent), the total United States garment workforce had increased by 7.8 percent during that period, and the Los Angeles region had made a spectacular gain of 30.5 percent.[91] New York had lost its hegemony but not its major role.

The relative job shrinkage in women's wear in the early postwar period was explained by technology and sociology. The growing use of rayon abetted the encroachment of housedresses into the silk street dresses that were New York City's specialty. Housedress manufacturers around the country began to upgrade their (more standardized) output as it became more acceptable to wear more casual dresses out of the house. Although one industry analyst attributed greater simplification in styling to the Depression, when people had fewer jobs, thus fewer places to go and less money to spend on clothes,[92] as we have seen, style simplification was a long-term trend inherent in the very notion of ready-made goods. As increased informality blossomed in the postwar period, and department stores and discount chains grew in size and power, furthering standardization and more decentralized production, the more casual West Coast began to dominate the newly rising sportswear industry. The film industry also played an important role in popularizing new styles. By 1963, as one fashion observer put it, "Los Angeles, once known primarily for bizarre sun clothes, now manufactures almost every variety of outerwear."[93]

Other factors, indigenous to the East Coast, also explained New York's decline. Other states offered lower rents and sometimes tax inducements.[94] Trucking companies lowered transportation costs to encourage business and provided credit to help out-of-town contractors set up shop. And, as always, relatively high labor costs and union interference prompted many manufacturers to flee the city. However, all of these explanations and historic, geographic, or fiscal comparisons seem to pale before the menace from abroad, which has federated industry ire in recent decades.

Fear of Imports

"Garment Industry in a New Squeeze," announced the *New York Times* in 1987. ". . . [What] some industry veterans describe as the toughest business climate they have encountered in years" renewed the language of doom and gloom. The number of manufacturers belonging to the New York Skirt and Sportswear Association had decreased from 297 members in the 1960s to 189 in 1979, and to 72 in 1987. Jay Mazur, of the ILGWU, estimated that about 200,000 union jobs had been lost from 1985 to 1987 alone. Eli Elias, of the manufacturers' association, put that number at about 700,000 lost union and nonunion jobs since 1960.[95]

Imports "of epidemic proportions" have been blamed as the crucial new factor explaining decline and its response: the contemporary recourse to immigrant labor in a search for ever-lower labor costs at home to combat even lower labor costs abroad.[96] But imports are not an entirely new phenomenon either. As early as the 1934 ILGWU convention, a resolution was introduced against Japanese textile goods flooding the American market. The issue became more serious in the 1950s, and imported goods grew from $0.3 to $6.4 billion (an over twenty-fold increase) from 1960 to 1980. Those sectors most severely hurt were men's shirts, women's blouses and skirts, and children's wear. Imports of women's apparel alone grew from 10 percent in 1962 to 27 percent in 1972 to 70 percent in 1982.[97] The early culprits were Japan, Hong Kong, Taiwan, and South Korea, where lower wage costs more than compensated for lower productivity and added freight and tariff costs. As the International Labour Office put it in 1980, the fact that garment exporting countries had become importing ones was a sign of a reordering of garment production among the different regions of the world.[98]

Ready-to-Wear and Ready-to-Work

According to José De La Torre's business study, the result of this competition led to four structural changes in the period from 1961 to 1972, which I would call avoidance, concentration, emulation, and decentralization: (1) manufacturers avoided confrontation by focusing on those garment lines least affected by imports, namely the higher-priced, more fashion-sensitive goods; (2) there was a move toward somewhat fewer but larger firms in those sectors where foreign competition is greatest, that is among the more standardized lines; (3) there was an if-you-can't-beat-'em-join-'em response of shifting certain operations to lower wage locations, notably to Southeast Asia; and (4) the garment division of labor was further decentralized by exporting semifinished goods for labor-intensive sewing overseas.[99]

Yet import increase is a relative as well as an absolute concept. From 1960 to 1980, the value of clothes imported to the United States increased over twenty-fold. However, as compared to all goods, clothing only rose from 2 to 2.7 percent of total imports.[100] In a period of greatly expanding consumer power, with postwar pent-up demand for other consumer durables, a generally rising standard of living, and a greater variety of consumer goods to choose from, clothing became a relatively less important item in the shopper's world as imports grew across the board.

In many ways, the emphasis on imports as a popular explanation for current decline, while clearly right, nonetheless ignores the composite and comparative elements that have also gone into a constructed notion of decline. Yes, both dramatic job loss and huge increases in imports have occurred. But in both respects these trends have comparative dimensions and historic precedents. At one level, the garment industry is participating in more global trends. With worldwide growth in clothing production (due to the very light technology and easy set-up requirements that led to its growth to begin with), even *if* New York output had remained constant, it would have declined as a portion of worldwide manufacture.

Moreover, certain sectors have been much less affected than others. Whereas overall manufacturing establishments declined by 41.9 percent in Manhattan from 1958 to 1977, and the garment industry as a whole lost 50.7 percent of its firms, the women's-wear sector "only" declined by 27.8 percent. Similarly, there was a general 43 percent decline of production workers over the period, but

Seventh Avenue

only a 37.8 percent decline in the labor-intensive garment industry and a "mere" 21.4 percent loss in the women's-wear sector. At the same time, total value added in manufacturing more than doubled in Manhattan from 1958 to 1977. The garment industry as a whole did somewhat less well (increasing from $1.6 to $2.8 billion), while women's wear doubled its value from $735 million to $1.5 billion.[101] Indeed, certain comparisons eliminate the notion of decline altogether. Already in 1939, dress sales far exceeded dress employment in New York City. Then and now "decline" may have correctly described production, but it has not always pertained to product value.

This is not to say that terms such as "squeeze," "exodus," or "epidemic" are not appropriate or scary perspectives. Decline has indeed occurred, as attested to by job loss and bankruptcies. But it is a decline that corresponds to a logic that has been in place ever since the early period of growth: standardization, the search for lower labor costs and fewer union rules, be they across the river or across an ocean. The focus on imports as a primary cause for decline has allowed manufacturers, union leaders, and employees to join in a corporatist lament. The battle against the foreign "other"—in this case clothes—overrides different strategies among those categories and notably the manufacturers' own role, ever since the beginning of the industry. Garment bosses have been "exporting" parts of the production process from inside to outside to offshore shops since early in the century. Spinning off more standardized portions of production, concentrating on the more volatile segment of the industry, the urban women's apparel business has held on to that which it does best in the tug-of-war between imitation and differentiation. In so doing, it has shown the adaptability of light industry to the possibilities of the city, largely in the form of immigrant shops filling last-minute orders. While the steel mills have brought desolation elsewhere, the garment industry is still in the Big Apple.

Finally, if decline is both absolute and relative, the tension between chaos and organization has nonetheless remained constant. A major study completed in 1982 by the New York State Department of Labor decried illegal conditions and disorganization within the industry. The report concluded that better regulation was necessary: registering and licensing contracting shops, enforcing minimum-wage laws and better record-keeping. The responses to the Industrial Commissioner's recommendations are telling. The ILGWU submitted a letter supporting the report and its call for regulation. The contractors' association politely rejected the conclusions, arguing that the recommendations would only cause manufacturers to send work out of town. The manufacturers' association Federation of Apparel Manufacturers simply sent an insulting telegram. It deemed the report's conclusions "astonishingly biased, inaccurate and undocumented."[102] Like explanations of decline, representations of remedies can be relative. And the historian has a sense of déjà vu.

A poststructural structuralism can be temporal as well as spatial. The New York story of garment making provides a geographic variant on the general industrial structure outlined in chapter 1, while important events mark the century: the strikes of 1909–10 and the Protocol of Peace, the National Industrial Recovery era of the 1930s, the growth in imports since the 1970s and 1980s. Events lived, perceived, and remembered, periods of hope over stability and despair over chaos, have coexisted with a more general sense of repetition in the *longue durée* of contracting. The present decline is real, and no amount of postmodern relativism will give workers back their jobs. What I have shown here are the century-long trends that perhaps the historians can see best along with the chronological shifts that historical actors perceive acutely.

3
THE SENTIER

The French Revolution was, among other things, a color war (a *"conflit chromatique,"* as clothing historian Philippe Perrot has called it).[1] Pants, not tea leaves, became the symbol of revolutionary ardor. This alone augurs a different sort of narrative for the Parisian garment industry. Parisian garment history is situated within the history of French labor and politics to a greater extent than the more self-contained New York story.[2] From the French Revolution to World War II, the underlying tensions between art and industry, between flexibility and standardization, have been the same, but these issues have been expressed through discussions over everything from revolutionary clothing to the meaning of male and female demand, from Socialism and Communism to Aryanization.

Sans-culottes: Actors and Sartorial Signifiers

Revolutionary adversaries showed their colors through dress: the red, blue, and white of the revolutionary cockade, the green and yellow of the royalists, or the black and green collars of the *jeunesse dorée.* Revolutionary "fashion" was like all fashion: a symbol of distinction, distinguishing one social group from another, but also heralding belonging to the group. The French Revolution was also a revolution about cultural meaning.[3] With regard to garments, it was a war over forms and the meaning of clothing. It represented the right to greater flexibility of demand and ultimately paved the way for greater simplicity of style.

As Daniel Roche has masterfully shown, the right to fashion began to take form in the eighteenth century, one more indicator of change leading to the Revolution itself.[4] The opening ceremony of the Estates-General, on May 5, 1789, was one of the last visible expressions of a population divided deeply not just by estate but by clothing. The clergy was convened in its ecclesiastic robes, the noble Second Estate in aristocratic black silk breeches, white stockings, and befeathered hats, and the Third Estate ordered to wear plain black cloth suits and stockings and simple three-cornered hats. This imposed "sartorial apartheid," as Aileen Ribeiro has called it, led to protests for freedom in fashion. Mirabeau objected to the dress code, arguing that the deputies of the Third Estate should be able to wear lace if they so desired. By October, a revolutionary text had decreed that freedom of clothing was one of the fundamental individual rights. Gender restrictions, however, still forbade women to dress as men.[5]

To be sure, clothing and other divisions also existed *within* the prerevolutionary estates. The revolutionary aristocrat Philippe, Duke of Orléans, soon to be Philippe-Egalité, had led the way with more sporting styles influenced by the English, which his more formally dressed detractors dubbed Anglomania. The Church was also split between the rich red and purple silks of the hierarchy and the black frocks of the parish priests.

But they were the dress divisions within the Third Estate that soon made history and consecrated not only freedom of fashion but freedom of movement. While some revolutionary fashion-plates sported Bastille buckles (in the shape of the demolished towers) or the tricolor ribbon, the loose-fitting pants of the workers, rather than the dark lawyers' coats, came to symbolize the Revolution. The baggy trousers that symbolically defied the tight knee-breeches of the aristocracy gave a sartorial name to the revolutionary actors and were a social sign elevated to a "symbolic form of political practice."[6]

They heralded not only new forms of clothing but new modes of its

The Sentier

production. The 1664 bylaws (*statuts*) of the secondhand clothing dealers had already evoked the relationship between freedom from form-fitting garments and the advent of ready-made ones. The *fripiers* were legally permitted to "make all sorts of new clothes, *à l'aventure* and without measurement."[7] To depart from Old Regime measurement was in itself an adventuresome revolution of manners and manufacture. The wide tricolor striped pants of the *sans-culottes* so abundant in the revolutionary iconography may have been a relatively brief fashion phenomenon, but *sans-mesure* was not. In this the political revolution helped prepare the way for the cultural revolt against *sur-mesure* which would be crucial to the nineteenth-century ready-made revolution. The Restoration(s) would restore aristocratic fashion, but in clothing as in other domains, the Revolution had both crystallized eighteenth-century trends and presaged nineteenth-century change. Relative simplification of style and an expanding demand freed from the conventions of estate slowly became the motors of clothing change. While Daniel Roche has hailed the Enlightenment for, among other things, bringing underwear to the masses ("la grande conquête des Lumières: celle du linge"[8]), the nineteenth century would democratize outerwear.

Creating Demand: The Civilizing Mission

The nineteenth-century revolutions affected not just the political realm but civil society down to the way people dressed. However, not everyone appreciated the leveling of taste. Midcentury, Balzac complained about the "confusion of rank," and Baudelaire commented that "a desolate uniformity of dress bears witness to equality."[9] Many late-nineteenth-century commentators continued to deplore the "democratization of luxury." Indeed, representations of the democratization of demand took a different form in France than in the United States. "Clothing for everyone" was not an argument that would sell well in France. The notion of fashion remained more closely linked to differentiation than to imitation, while being conceptualized along gender lines. Men's wear was imbued with a moralizing mission that could cross borders; women's wear remained characterized as inscrutable, beyond the means of (male) manufacturers to "know" with any great certainty.

With the growth of men's ready-made clothing in France, discussions about the industry attributed it with a double civilizing duty. First of all, cheap ready-made clothes helped transform "peasants into Frenchmen" and urban workers into respectable Sunday strollers. Hygienists argued that new clothes were healthier than old ones, "flushing out the pathogenic germ from every corner of the social body."[10] More generally, as one early enthusiast argued, the promotion of better clothes aided the fight against alcoholism and helped "moralize the masses." By providing jobs for women, children, the elderly, and the invalid, the industry would "reform these masses" through work as well.[11] Although secondhand goods and the Marché du Temple continued to be popular well into the twentieth century, their decline was inversely proportional to the success of ready-made clothing. The moral universe of the department-store world of consumption spread the clothing mission to the middle classes. Second, ready-made goods helped civilize the colonial masses. The manufacturer and wholesaler Lémann was practically lyrical on the subject. Excited about a recent order from an African prince, he foresaw a great future for the industry in covering the colonial natives. Writing midcentury, he fervently predicted "a limitless horizon" for the ready-made trade.[12]

Female demand, however, was more difficult to channel. Women were frequently castigated by manufacturers and industrial observers for their enigmatic instinct: "in this regard, woman abstains from reason . . . She likes or she doesn't like."[13] The female artistic sense was seen as that which gave the industry its aura, but also as that "excessive individualization of the clientele" which radically separated men's wear from women's wear and interfered with the industrialization of the latter. Pierre Du Maroussem, social investigator for the Office du Travail, worried in 1896 that this problem would in fact be a serious barrier to the expansion of the ready-made business.[14]

In the French context perhaps even more so than in the American one, women and (male) workers thus had different places in the manufacturers' *imaginaire*. While the male, working-class, petit bourgeois, and colonial ready-made markets were perceived as forming a staple of increasing need, the expansion of women's wear was accompanied by less sanguine pronouncements about the nature of demand. Women were continually blamed for its vicissitudes. Workers and women, the main clients of the growing nineteenth-

The Sentier

century clothing industry, clearly represented the two sides of the fashion paradox: standardization and flexibility.

The Geography of Supply

The first *maison de confection* for men's wear in Paris opened in 1828, and cloth merchants soon began setting up shops in which skilled (male) cutters prepared piece goods that were given out to male and female pieceworkers (*apiéceurs*) to make up in their homes. Ready-made clothing progressed steadily during the July Monarchy (1830–48); by 1847, 233 male Parisian *confectionneurs* employed over 7,000 workers, and *confection* accounted for one-third of all men's clothing sales in the capital. By 1860, half of all men's wear was ready-made.[15] By 1904, two-thirds of the men in France were dressed "off the rack."[16]

The Belle Jardinière, the Parisian department store that built its reputation on men's wear, reflected the geographic interplay between more standardized and flexible production. In 1855, it employed some fifty cutters in its Pont Neuf building, furnishing goods to a veritable army of 2,000 homeworkers who created a constant flow of movement in the neighborhood as they picked up and returned work. While custom-made garments still accounted for 10 percent of its sales in 1866, the Belle Jardinière set up a large factory in Lille that year to make workers' shirts and overalls; a smaller clothing manufactory was set up in Paris in 1889.[17] By 1900, and particularly after 1920, in Paris as in New York, more standardized men's wear manufacturers were foresaking the urban center for larger production units in the provinces: to the North (Lille, Amiens), to be close to the textile industry; and to Lyon, former silk capital of France.[18] Yet Paris remained the center of women's wear, with its myriad of dressmaking and ready-made shops. The geography of men's wear and women's wear differed.

In France as in the United States, women's wear was slower to join the ready-made wagon. While the 233 male *confectionneurs* had over 7,000 employees in Paris midcentury, practically the same number of female *confectionneuses* and *couturières/confectionneuses* (225) employed only 1,300 workers.[19] Ready-made lingerie preceded ready-made dresses, but by the 1840s, more standardized

Ready-to-Wear and Ready-to-Work

techniques were increasingly being applied to outerwear. This involved the transfer of ownership and control of production from
women to men; the proliferating larger shops run by older women
were in fact subcontracting shops for male manufacturers. And,
as in tailoring, the rise of ready-made goods, however beneficial
for the female consumer, corresponded to de-skilling of the female
dressmaker.[20]

However, the shift toward *confection* for women's wear was a
longer process in France than it was in the United States. Intermediary categories of production emerged in the nineteenth century and
held on into the twentieth. Not only was the French garment industry
at the turn of the century divided into very distinct *couture* and *confection* categories, but each had their own subdivisions. *Grande couture* (or *haute*), *moyenne*, and *petite couture* persisted side by side.
Haute couture was dominated by men; *moyenne couture* consisted
largely of dresses made on order (by women) for upper- and middle-
class clients; and *petite couture* served petit bourgeois and working-
class women who brought their own cloth to be made up. *Confection*,
at first largely confined to women's coats, as in the United States, was
produced in either wholesalers' (*maisons de gros*) or retailers' (*maisons de détail*) workshops, the latter set up by the department stores.

The Paris garment district, the Sentier, initially developed quite
differently from Seventh Avenue. Its origins were more commercial
in nature, and it was more closely tied to nearby department-store
manufacturers. The Compagnie des Indes set up its headquarters in
the Sentier in the eighteenth century in order to import Indian cot-
tons. These textiles were at first only intended for reexport to protect
French textile manufacturers and *teinturiers* from competition. But a
"bataille des Indiennes" ensued, in which even Mme de Pompadour
clandestinely ordered the cloth to cover her furniture.[21] A decree
finally ordered that the prints could be used by the nobility only;
anyone else caught with them could be fined. More important, the
Indian print business brought other cloth merchants to the neighborhood. The provincial origins of the early textile representatives gave
a certain "immigrant" character to the Sentier, which became a
"typical example of a transitional neighborhood [*quartier médiateur*]
which helped newcomers settle in to the city."[22] Thus commerce,
textiles, and provincial migrants, rather than manufacturing and
foreign immigrants, as in New York, gave the area its identity and

The Sentier

were the primary force behind the early concentration of the garment industry in this district.

Department stores also played an important role. In Paris, like New York, they helped stimulate demand for ready-made apparel. But in Paris they helped shape supply as well. Unlike in the United States, where department stores had workrooms only until the 1870s depression "persuaded them to leave the risks of manufacturing to others," the Parisian department stores became important manufacturers.[23] The Bon Marché and Galeries Lafayette, among others, did for women's wear what the precocious Belle Jardinière had done for men's wear: set up some of the largest garment workshops in town. This did not, however, mean the immediate demise of the local *couturières.* By facilitating access to fabrics and accessories, the new commercial emporia gave added business to private dressmakers, whose number in Paris climbed from 158 in 1850 to 494 in 1863 and up to 1,636 in 1896.[24]

The stores went into the manufacturing business because they were tired of depending on independent shops and homeworkers who filled orders for a multitude of retail and wholesale clients. Conceived of to ensure production quality and quantity, the large, department-store workshops soon reached the limits of their usefulness, however. By the interwar period, the large manufacturing units succumbed to the rigidities involved in managing units within a context of fluctuating demand. Strikes and threats of strikes also helped lead to their dismemberment in the 1920s and especially 1930s. The closing of these inside shops and the consequent increase in contracting testified once again to the difficulties of standardizing either demand or supply.

The Export Market

In marked contrast to the American market, Paris produced not just for Parisians and the provinces, but largely for export. Two distinct foreign markets, corresponding to the two main segments of the industry, had evolved by the end of the century. At one end, English, American, Dutch, Swiss, Belgian, Italian, German, and Canadian buyers came to Paris to purchase haute couture cloth patterns (*modèles*) and the right to reproduce them. At the other end of the spectrum, the expanding colonial market formed an important outlet for ready-made garments.

The haute couture pattern market was important both for the prestige and the francs it garnered. It was not, however, without its problems. Pattern sales implied a loss of potential exports of clothes themselves. The resale of patterns abroad and their indiscriminate reproduction by ready-made manufacturers there exasperated French clothiers. A Comité de défense des chambres syndicales de la couture, des dentelles et des broderies in 1896 tried to prevent the stealing and copying of patterns by deciding not to sell to foreigners before certain dates. A Syndicat de la protection artistique des industries saisonnières was created in the interwar period to prevent the illegal copying of patterns within France. (It was forbidden to sell haute couture patterns to French ready-made manufacturers.) Defenders of French fashion, as an ideal and as a market, railed against the dissipation of French genius through counterfeiting at home or abroad.[25] But the export pattern market remained important throughout the interwar period.

It was largely thanks to the colonial market, however, that, by 1925, the garment trades represented the second-largest sector of French exports. Before World War I, French exports of ready-made garments alone had reached over 252.6 million francs (compared to only 10 million francs worth of imports). At the same time, France had exported 160.6 million francs of custom-made dresses and coats while importing a mere 3.8 million francs' worth. In 1926, total garment imports cost France 11.5 million francs, while exports had risen to a value of 1,970.6 million francs. Although these figures shifted slightly over the decade, with imports reaching 18.9 million in 1929 and exports declining to 1,434.6 million francs, clothing remained an important sector for the French balance of payments.[26]

War and Labor Laws

Given the export market, the French garment industry, like the country itself, suffered from both world wars to a much greater extent than the United States. Besides cutting off French patterns from the rest of the world, as it dragged on in the trenches, the "war to end all wars" worried French observers who drew up lists of export figures divided into columns of enemy countries, allied countries, and neutral ones. One confidential report accused the Germans of dumping flannel underwear on the world market during the war.[27]

Although the First World War did temporarily threaten French hegemony on the world clothing market, in certain respects it was beneficial. Initial reports were relieved that foreign counterfeiters had been chased out of the country thanks to the war. (German and Austrian *couture* houses that had set up shop in Paris under French-sounding names were eliminated in a minipurge of "firms suspected of enemy nationality."[28]) More important, the war gave a major push to both domestic demand and labor relations. It stimulated demand on the part of female factory workers recruited to (wo)man military and industrial plants who now had greater clothing needs, more cash at their disposal, and less time to make their own outfits. At the upper end of the market, the better grades of ready-made garments benefited from family budget restrictions to the detriment of *couture* houses.

The war also brought important labor legislation to the predominantly female trades. Under the double impact of war and strikes, the state and the manufacturers gave greater recognition to women's role in the polity, or at least the economy. Labor inspector Gabrielle Letellier's series of articles in the 1920s is in itself an interesting episode in the historiography of the French garment industry and of French labor law. She began with a somewhat wistful tone of reproach, criticizing interwar needleworkers for not realizing how good they had it, lacking historical consciousness about prewar conditions.[29] Speaking like a true civil servant, Letellier attributed the shorter hours and higher salaries since the late nineteenth century to the state's foresightful laws. But she also praised the unions and mutual-aid organizations for defending the workers as well as the manufacturers for having adopted a more conciliatory attitude. However, for Letellier, it was the war that had hastened the entire process in two important ways. It had taught (or forced) the bosses to be more responsive to workers' demands in order to meet wartime production schedules. And it had been the necessary if not sufficient condition for the passage of the 1917 law implementing the English week. Letellier was optimistic. The *semaine anglaise*, giving workers Saturday afternoons off, was a triumph for the woman worker.

Letellier was also unequivocal with regard to the November 2,

1892, law. It had been insufficient. Hailed at the time as a major advance for limiting working hours for women and children in factories, mines, quarries, and workshops, and prohibiting night work, the law also imposed a weekly day of rest and set up hygiene and safety regulations. A complementary decree of July 15, 1893, specified a certain number of important exemptions (*dérogations*) to the law. In 1900, hours limitations were extended to men. Before the law was amended once again in April 1904, a heated discussion over exemptions became a veritable debate over the extent to which the industry could be stabilized in the face of the flexibility demanded by the employers.[30]

Within a decade of its passage, the 1892 law began to be criticized for ineffectiveness. Legal commentators noted that the law was internally contradictory.[31] The *dérogations* in effect allowed for a certain amount of legal cheating. Owners hid workers in closets and dressing rooms when the labor inspectors came to call or gave workers clothes to take home rather than have them work overtime on the premises. Inspectors complained about the frequent abuse of the exemptions, and the archives evoke the image of a cat-and-mouse game, with (mostly female) labor inspectors climbing stairs late at night and early Sunday mornings trying to catch violators and avoid complicitous concierges who could give advance warning. They nevertheless often only found the *patronne* in a nightshirt, yawning disingenuously as she opened the door, pretending to wipe the sleep from her eyes.[32]

Furthermore, family workshops had been exempted from the law's purview, the home considered an inviolable sphere of privacy. This left over one million women untouched by the legislation and most significantly limited its effect in the garment industry where homework was rampant, while small immigrant workshops seem to have remained particularly invisible to the eye of most inspectors.[33] Many observers also pointed out that factory legislation only increased the recourse to unregulated homework. The law thus undermined itself but was also, like laws everywhere, dependent upon the enforcement means at its disposal.

Letellier argued along these lines that conditions for garment workers had improved only slowly in the prewar period. It had taken fighting on the battlefront and labor unrest on the home front for the 1915, 1917, and 1919 laws to be passed establishing, respectively: a minimum wage for female homeworkers, the *semaine anglaise*, and

The Sentier

the eight-hour day. The laws of 1917 for the English week and 1919 for the eight-hour day were only passed under duress, after strikes by the *midinettes*.[34] The "eight-hour" agreement that was finally signed for the garment trades recognized the specific nature of the industry. A forty-eight-hour week (nine hours a day for five days, plus three hours on Saturday) was legislated that was still subject to the principle of *dérogations;* a *décret* of December 12 provided explicit exemptions for the busy season.

The structure of the industry remained rebellious to regulation. The holes in the 1892 legislation, like the exemptions written into the wartime laws, were yet another sign of the struggle between rigidity and flexibility. While workers, unions, and the state sought greater protection and standards for labor conditions, the garment industry remained reticent to restrictive rules. This forced the legislators to incorporate exemptions into the law. The fact that the garment industry, where some one-third of women in manufacturing were employed, took the brunt of these exemptions[35] showed the weakness in the law and the strength of seasonality. By the interwar period, legal limitations on the workday and the workweek still could not even out the bumps of a highly uneven annual workload.

If it was in the interest of a labor inspector to defend her work and her employer (the state), the view from labor in the interwar period was, not surprisingly, less rosy. By 1921, the eight-hour day and the English week had disappeared from many of the garment shops. Well-known female union activist Jeanne Bouvier railed in her memoirs about the ineffectiveness of the minimum-wage law, harshly criticizing the Confédération générale du travail for not doing more to ensure its enforcement.[36] In 1937, when the homework problem had only become that much greater due to immigration and depression, the Ministry of Labor answered one researcher that no one was interested in the issue anymore.[37] The interwar story of the garment trades sheds a less-optimistic light on the evaluation of either prewar or wartime gains.

Between the Wars: Fashion, Production, and Politics

The interwar history of the Parisian garment industry was affected by three phenomena: changes in fashion, related changes in the labor force, and the rather tumultuous story of intralabor relations. As in New York, it was yet another period of takeoff for women's wear, even as employment figures leveled off. However, the side effects of the Russian Revolution were even more dramatic on needleworkers in France than in the United States. While the civil war in the needle trades was a *cause célèbre* in the New York of the 1920s, the national split between the Socialist and Communist Parties had an even more debilitating effect on garment-union organizing in France.

Fashion and Labor

Jobs in the garment industry declined by as much as 25 percent in the interwar period for reasons both conjunctural and cultural.[38] Massive layoffs occurred in the immediate postwar period (1920–21) as military workshops closed. But the longer-term cause was the streamlining of women's fashions, also partly due to the war. Besides the demise of the corset, finally done in by the exigencies of factory work during World War I, embroidery and feathers also fell out of fashion after the war, and hats became simplified. Worse yet, as some commentators noted, some girls were going out of the house bareheaded. Sports and cars were to blame, the latter because they left no place for "cumbersome clothes or voluminous hats." The car had taken the place of the woman as drab bourgeois man's status window onto the world.[39]

Changing fashion did not just affect the silhouette; it streamlined production as well. Middle levels of production were disappearing. *Moyenne couture* began losing out to *petite*, while many women started abandoning their local *couturières* altogether for ready-made goods. Parisian department stores and new women's specialty shops added important markets to the continued strong sales of ready-made goods to the colonies and the provinces. Prefabricated goods had themselves changed, becoming more elegant. Advances in the chemical industry permitted better coloring of less expensive fabrics, diminishing the divide between *couture* and *confection*.

Although post–World War II observers would claim that their epoch had invented pretty ready-to-wear, interwar commentators (Letellier again) hailed the important changes that they perceived

The Sentier

compared to the period before the First World War: new items (the shift from suits, skirts, and blouses to dresses, as in the United States); better quality; more style. The straight-line dress then in fashion helped women become accustomed to looser-fitting, less "tailored" clothes. Ready-made garments themselves became differentiated into at least three categories: *la très belle confection, articles moins soignés* (or *confection courante*), and *la confection ordinaire.*[40]

In addition to these more long-term, structural changes, the Depression gave a decisive push to the domestic market. While the shock waves of the New York stock market crash of 1929 took a few years to reach Depression levels in France (hardest hit from April 1932 to 1937), they had an immediate effect on the Parisian garment industry. *Les riches américaines* left Paris at once, canceling orders and leaving garments unpaid at their dressmakers'. The crisis then spread downward. There was a domestic shift from *petite couture* toward *confection* (a *déclassement de la clientèle*), and the ready-made business lost important foreign sales in the 1930s as all of the industrial countries became more protectionist. By contrast, the 1920s became remembered as a golden age of exports. An increase in French exports in 1936 was due uniquely to colonial sales.[41]

Strikes: The Making of the Militant Midinette

While New York garment industrial warfare peaked before World War I and then diminished under the combined impact of war, postwar prosperity, and collective bargaining, Paris strike activity surged during the war. French workers protested the war and their wages simultaneously, and continued to voice their grievances loudly into the interwar period. In Paris, as in New York, women were prominent both in the industry and on the picket lines.

The first general strike of Parisian tailors and seamstresses in 1901 involved some 700 workers demanding, among other things, an end to piecework and the establishment of fixed wage schedules (*tarifs*).[42] But the major Parisian garment industry strikes which "made history" were those of 1917 and 1919. The 1917 strike began on May 11 when two workers walked out at the Maison Jenny (*couture de luxe*) on the Champs Elysées. By mid-June, 42,000 people were on strike (30,000 women and 12,000 men) in a wide variety of sectors from banks to the food industry. The 25,000 *midinettes* from all clothing specialties (hats to corsets, women's wear to men's wear, dressmakers—often in the lead—to ready-made workers) were in the forefront on the streets and in the journalists' accounts as they demanded more money (a wartime cost-of-living raise), less work, and an end to the war, chanting: "Our twenty *sous!* The English week! Give us back our 'boys.'"[43] They did not get their men back right away, but they did win the English week (Saturday afternoons off, fifty-four hours pay for fifty hours work), voted into law that September. And the strike stuck in popular memory and in garment industry folklore as a tremendous success. With regard to the 1917 strike, at least, Letellier's vision is supported by the view from below.

Agitation continued in March 1918 and again in September and October of that year. The 1919 strike began a month after the (March 25) law on collective bargaining and one day after the (April 23) eight-hour law were signed. By May 1, over 55,000 garment workers were on strike. Two people died and five hundred were wounded in a clash which pitted workers against employers and police over the definition of collective bargaining. The workers rejected the idea of separate shop agreements, insisting on a clearly defined *convention collective* for each specialty. The strike ended with an increase in salary and a redefined English week (forty-eight hours pay for forty-four hours work). The *pompiers,* the skilled finishers who had begun the strike, did not get the shortened week, but they did get a promise that piecework would be abolished in the workshops.

Finally, the important, if less successful, strike of 1923 also helped consecrate the militant *midinette* in Parisian memory. The well-publicized image of the *cousettes,* as they were also called, marching down the Champs Elysées to press their demands impressed itself on contemporary observers as another example of the feminization of workers' protest. The women's public marches (*cortèges*) served as symbolic statements of protest, as they marched along well-recognized public routes beyond the garment industry neighborhoods. The laughter, gaiety, and enthusiasm of the women's processions were widely reported in the press: "Are the laughter and songs not part of the *cousette*'s battle ammunition?" asked *L'Humanité* of April 6, 1923. But a counterimage was also evoked, contrasting

The Sentier

that laughter to the female needleworker's harsh lot. An article in *Le Populaire* of April 21, 1923, complained that the police were using a particular vision of femininity as an excuse for their own repression. According to the Socialist newspaper, it was unlikely that the police had, as they argued in self-defense, been poked by hairpins. "Monsieur Naudin is behind the times. Hairpins are out of style."[44]

The garment industry strikes cannot be isolated from the other strikes that marked the war and postwar periods in France.[45] Like workers in other trades, needleworkers struck first and foremost for increased wages and decreased working hours. What is perhaps specific to the garment industry strikes is the way in which wage-and-hour demands were often accompanied by demands for regularization of the trade. And particular incidents could lead to shop walkouts in protest against an insufferable supervisor, in defense of a fired coworker, or in demand of generally better treatment and greater dignity in shop-floor relations.

All of these grievances had to do with bettering conditions within the industrial structure. Yet other demands questioned the way in which the industry itself was structured. Parisian garment workers continued to demand the abolition of homework and piecework in an effort to regulate the volume and pay schedule of the workload. The 1923 strikers asked for a limitation to seasonal unemployment, which was optimistically written into the signed agreement: the employers agreed to limit the off-season to thirty days per year (fifteen days per season). But as one female union leader asked skeptically, how were they going to do it?[46] A last interwar seamstress strike, in the middle of the Depression in 1934–35, and in the context of barely twenty-five-hour weeks, successfully won a shift back to hourly instead of piece wages. It was only temporary.

The history of strikes is like the history of labor legislation. There is a progressive version which calculates their successes or failures, emphasizing, since the historiography of the 1960s, the former. Yet perhaps another reading of strikes is now in order. For one, their repetition over time with recurrent demands, even if successful, implies a certain long-term failure. In the case of the garment industry in particular, the strike history shows the difficulty of regulating working conditions within a constantly fluctuating industrial structure. By fits and starts, better conditions were wrested from employers. But the movement was neither linear nor cumulative and

Ready-to-Wear and Ready-to-Work

often wiped out in the next off-season or cyclical downturn. Signed agreements, like passed laws, still depended on industrial—and seasonal—health. If shops became better regulated, homework still allowed invisible abuse of the laws and agreements. And neither strikes nor laws—both expressing the desire for stability over volatility in the workplace—were able to abolish seasonality.

Socialism, Communism, and the Needle Trades

Nor could twentieth-century Socialists or Communists eradicate variability in demand and production. The 1923 strike was ultimately a failure not only because the manufacturers could not will away the *morte-saison*. It was also a failure due to union strife, which characterized all of French labor history from the early 1920s to the mid-1930s. During the strike two different unions tried to negotiate separately on behalf of the garment workers, while the employers finally signed an agreement with two other, independent, women's unions who had come to the fore to defend the *cousettes'* cause.[47] The history of the garment-workers' unions in interwar France is, like all French labor history, marked by their politicization and split along ideological, rather than craft or industrial, lines, as in the United States.

The first national federation of garment workers in France, the Fédération nationale des travailleurs de l'habillement, was founded by *ouvriers tailleurs* in Nîmes in 1893. In 1910, its headquarters were transferred to Paris. Although 80 percent of the garment workers were women, only 20 percent of the union members were. Before the war, the union in any case had only some 4,000 members. With each strike, the numbers swelled, to 7,000 in 1917, to 26,000 in 1919, and to 56,000 in 1920.[48]

By 1921, however, membership had dropped dramatically, down to 7,000 in the first half of 1921.[49] The postwar depression and the failure of the spring 1920 strike movement accounted for the decrease. So did tensions already apparent within the movement. Dissensions within the garment workers' union initially turned in part around different interpretations of that membership loss. More fundamentally, the garment-workers' division into competing Confédération générale du travail (CGT, reformist) and Confédération

The Sentier

générale du travail unitaire (CGTU, Communist) unions was but an epiphenomenon within the larger political split within the French left subsequent to the Congrès de Tours. Nonetheless, the divisions within the garment-workers' union had their own dynamic. The issues centered around: the Federation's secretary; dissatisfaction with reformist politics; and perhaps, as we will explore below, some ethnic differences. Underlying these disputes were different evaluations about ways of dealing with the industry's particular structure.

Pierre Dumas, the Federation's powerful prewar secretary, began to come under criticism during World War I. The left wing of the union protested his stand against Zimmerwald and the Russian Revolution and urged him to back the forty-four-hour week instead of a forty-eight-hour one. His leadership of the wartime strikes seemed dispirited, and he was increasingly reproached for a general lack of activism.[50] (He also turned out to be no friend of the immigrants and later joined Georges Valois' fascist movement.)

While the initial grumblings from within focused on Dumas as an individual, his resignation in September 1920 (replaced by Gaston Ringenbach) led to only a short respite in fractional in-fighting. The Seine and Limoges sections, which had led the battle against Dumas, created a subcommittee to radicalize the union from within. They argued that the drop in membership was due to lack of militancy, whereas the Federation's defenders contended that it was simply caused by unemployment. In 1921, the Syndicat de l'habillement de la Seine, under the leadership of Fernand Bellugue and along with seven other union sections, joined the Comités syndicalistes révolutionnaires (CSR) which were forming throughout the CGT. By December, twenty-nine out of a total of seventy-nine unions in the garment federation had joined the *minoritaires* rump group. By January of the following year, after reciprocal accusations of self-exclusion (the Federation to the CSR) and of being excluded (the CSR response to the Federation), the divorce was consummated.[51]

Henceforth two garment unions vied for the garment workers. The more reformist *confédérés*, who remained affiliated with the CGT, carried on the Fédération d'industries des travailleurs de l'habillement, while the *unitaires*, affiliated with the CGTU, constituted the Fédération (or Syndicat) unitaire du vêtement. Both groups initially claimed to be faithful to the precepts of revolutionary syndicalism, citing the 1906 Charter of Amiens on the separation of unions from the political sphere. (In June of 1921, Bellugue flatly denied Ringenbach's accusation that he had gone to Moscow for his orders.) However, by 1923, Ringenbach admitted that his—CGT—union was more revolutionary in aims than in means.[52] And that same year, the Syndicat unitaire of Bellugue voted 50 to 10 to join the Moscow-based Internationale syndicale rouge, over the objections of those who said it would contradict the Charter of Amiens.[53] The CGT thus moved away from the spirit of revolutionary syndicalism toward a de facto reformism, while the CGTU moved away from the 1906 Charter via political alliance with the Communists.

In terms of union strategy, the split also represented two different attitudes toward labor activism: emphasis on collective bargaining (CGT) versus the strike (CGTU). Beyond that, however, at least three other issues seem to have been at stake. First, the split also echoed a division between Paris and the provinces. The Federation claimed it had the provinces on its side and dismissed the Parisian dissidents as unrepresentative. Second, the difference between the two unions perhaps also reflected distinctions between different categories of garment workers. The core of the Federation's supporters, according to its newspaper, *L'Ouvrier de l'habillement,* were *ouvriers apiéceurs,* that intermediary category between wage worker and independent worker. The *unitaires* at first refused to admit *apiéceurs* to their union, on the grounds that the latter were bosses rather than workers. (Bellugue changed his mind later, however, in a bid for increased membership.) Finally, there is some evidence that an ethnic divide also underlay the CGT-CGTU split. There were more radicalized Jewish immigrants among the Paris *unitaires* who both wanted greater control over some specific tactics (propaganda in Yiddish) and were disappointed with the CGT's reformist strategy. The Fédération unitaire du vêtement merged with the CGTU textile union in 1924, but its fortunes, along with those of the CGTU in general, declined. By 1925, only eleven unions were still affiliated with the Fédération unitaire. At the end of the decade, a Ministry of Interior report took note of the Fédération unitaire's declining membership, but nonetheless qualified the union as an *"influence morale."*[54]

In December 1935, the two garment unions merged, as did most

The Sentier

other CGT-CGTU union couples in France. Combined union membership surged to 80 to 100,000 after the merger and in the euphoria of the Popular Front era.[55] The garment workers joined in the general excitement, although as one homeworking participant later reminisced, it was not easy to occupy your workplace when it was your bedroom, dining room, and living room at once. Yet, he added, "everyone" (well, thousands of garment workers) did go on strike, streaming to the Bourse de Travail and surrounding cafés.[56] By 1938, the (reunited) CGT garment-workers' union counted some 57,000 members.[57]

Homework, Piecework, and the Façonnier Question

Many of the issues debated by the unions and the manufacturers in the interwar period reflected the renewed expansion of contracting and homeworking, while they also echoed prewar concerns. The forty-hour law passed in 1936 (effective April 1, 1937, for the garment trades) once again brought employers' demands for flexibility up against employees' demands (backed now not only by the union but by the state) for greater regularity of working conditions. In a militant speech at the 1937 conference of the National Federation of Men's Wear Manufacturers, Maurice Olivier, introduced as president of several employers' organizations and as "father of nine children (applause)," argued against the forty-hour law and for a wide system of exemptions: "that we should add to the law *all of the flexibility [assouplissements] necessary.*"[58] He and others argued that the law would raise prices, making garments too expensive, leading to a drop in the quantity of better goods, and an overall drop in quality. Another delegate, Georges Lainel, made the dire prediction that the consequence would be not only unemployment, but worse yet a decline of good taste.[59]

The interwar unions were more concerned with workers' unemployment than with consumers' good taste. In this respect they subsequently had their own concerns about the side effects of the forty-hour law. At the garment union congress of 1937, delegates noted that homework was again on the rise, especially insofar as the department stores were closing their inside manufacturing shops and giving all sewing to outside workers; the Louvre department store was even selling off its sewing machines cheaply to encourage workers to work at home.[60] The legislating of working conditions presented a double bind for garment-industry workers and their representatives. In theory, the eight-hour day and the forty-hour week could mitigate seasonal highs and lows by limiting overwork during the full season and underwork during the slow season.[61] In practice, however, the laws had the effect of moving production out from under the eye of labor inspectors away from the shop and into the home.

The labor movement's attitude toward homework was both firm yet ultimately weak. Until 1936 (when the union backed the inclusion of homeworkers under the social insurance laws), the Fédération de l'habillement consistently argued that homework must simply be abolished. Only in the workshop could conditions and workflow be adequately regulated. However, as one contemporary observer noted, by pressing (unsuccessfully) for the abolition of homework, the union never addressed possible measures for bettering the homeworkers' lot.[62] And, significantly, only women and immigrants within the union seem to have complained. Noted labor leader Jeanne Bouvier ultimately broke with the union over its lack of vigor on women's issues.[63] Albert Matline, Jewish immigrant, secretary of the hat and capmakers' union, and voice of historical consciousness about homework, chastised the union delegates in 1948 for acting as though homework were a new problem. He reminded them of its long history and went so far as to suggest that the CGT had failed in not addressing the issue earlier.[64]

One of the most interesting debates of the interwar period turned around the status of the *façonnier*.[65] Descendant of the nineteenth-century *apiéceur* (literally pieceworker) and turn-of-the-century *entrepreneur* (literally intermediary), the interwar *façonnier* (he who fashions) was also a product of his time. As employers sought to avoid paying into social insurance funds for homeworkers, they encouraged if not obliged their workers to register as independent artisans. And, given increasing restrictions on work possibilities for immigrants during the 1930s, going independent was the only way that many of them could work.[66] Yet like his or her predecessors, the *façonnier* was as important to the organization of the industry as he

The Sentier

or she was symbolic of a fundamental ambiguity regarding industrial relations. Independent because working at home, setting one's own hours and conditions, often working for more than one employer and giving work in turn to kin or neighbors, the *façonnier* was also an employee in the sense of being ultimately bound by the jobbers' or manufacturers' demands for finishing the work at a certain time, to certain specifications, at a (more or less) agreed-upon price.

This situation led at times to shifting alliances and even "bosses" strikes. In 1922, for example, three *entrepreneurs-culottiers* went on strike against the *maître-tailleurs* for whom they worked, insisting on higher rates. The police estimated that there were 300 such *petits entrepreneurs* in Paris, working at home and employing some 2,000 men and women to fill orders for 150 master tailors (*grands patrons*). About fifty workers joined the *entrepreneurs*, their immediate bosses, in striking against the ultimate employers, the *maître-tailleurs*. The *entrepreneurs* turned to the union for support. It is unclear how the latter responded, but the strike was apparently a failure.[67]

The class definition of the *apiéceurs, entrepreneurs,* or *façonniers* (the three terms continued to be used interchangeably) was a difficult one for the interwar unions. A January 30, 1921, general meeting of all sections of the Syndicat de l'habillement in Paris took up the "delicate question" of the *apiéceurs.* Were they exploited or exploiters? Should a distinction be made between those who had only one or two people working for them and those who had more and were therefore real "entrepreneurs" who thus could not "take their place among us"? At the 1937 meeting, a union report on homework complained that the language used by the bosses was inexact if not mystifying; by calling homeworkers *façonniers* or artisans, they sought to transfer responsibility onto their workers.[68]

The *façonnier* debate was a problem of language and of class ideology. But it also has to be understood both within the general structure of the industry and the specific context of the 1930s. On the one hand, the ambiguous definition and changing language illuminates one of the key problems of the subcontracting structure: shifting responsibilities, shifting statuses, and shifting boundaries between worker and employer. On the other hand, it is not surprising that the debate became more heated within the context of the economic crisis of the 1930s. And, at the same time, as we will see, the *façonnier* issue was also an immigrant one.

As legal opportunities for salaried immigrant employment were successively reduced during the 1930s due to rising xenophobia, the multifaceted garment industry remained an amenable source of activity for Jewish immigrants in particular. However, as employee or employer, the Polish Jewish tailor's niche within the industry was seriously threatened by the war. World War II represented a rupture for the French garment industry in many ways, and the contrast with American wartime prosperity could not be greater: penury of raw materials, German requisitions, economic restructuring, and Aryanization of Jewish firms.

As raw materials and finished goods were shipped to Germany for the war effort, penury in occupied France even affected style. Wool went to clothe German soldiers, and French skirts got shorter. As leather followed the same route to Germany, wooden-soled shoes became the uncomfortable substitute. Pétain received letters of complaint from women disgusted with the new synthetics, which could shrink to surprising proportions after the first washing or a good downpour! There was even a lack of silk, as the Germans bought up fancy silk goods, not exactly for immediate war needs, but as a testimony to inimitable French style. Privations in other domains also affected clothing fashion. As automobiles became a rare luxury, and the bicycle and *métro* the obligatory modes of transportation for all classes, fashion magazines counseled women on how to dress appropriately. Split skirts and pants became popular for "the peddling female," even if this clashed somewhat with the Vichy ideology of wholesome femininity. Cold apartments led to the layered look, and the *couturiers* proposed new lines with extra padding.

The haute couture sector got by, due to an active collaboration on the part of some (Mary Rueff, Jacques Fath) and a more preventive collaboration on the part of others.[69] The *couturier* Lucien Lelong, appointed head of the haute couture group within the wartime Comité d'organisation du vêtement (COV), tried to defend the French art against a German takeover. In the end, no *couturier* houses were "concentrated" (see below).

The ready-made sector had a different problem. Besides making do with limited fabric and other raw materials, some firms were directly enrolled in the war effort. The Belle Jardinière (men's wear), for example, got through the war by filling German orders. But after the war and a change in management, it turned to making uniforms and suits for the American troops in 1945, for the Ministry of Prisoners in 1946, and for various French administrative offices.[70]

More globally, the ready-made industry was hit frontally during the war by economic concentration. The restructuring corresponded to at least three aspects of economic theory and practice which affected almost all sectors, but light industry more so than heavy. It originated in a prewar critique against overproduction and thus the perceived necessity, under any circumstances, for a "weeding out." It was implemented under the duress of wartime restrictions, which created a de facto situation of scarce raw materials and scaled-down production. But it also corresponded to a rationalizing and centralizing ideology, both on the part of the Germans and within the Vichy National Revolution, stressing the need for economic planning.[71]

Those who were "concentrated" first, however, were Jewish firms. The language, like the policy, became in one way bolder over time: aimed first at *"entreprises présumées israélites"* then at *"entreprises israélites"* and then at the less flattering (in French terminology) *"entreprises juives."* But, in other ways, it was more euphemistic: owners had "disappeared," firms were "sleeping" (*en sommeil*).[72] Racial ideology mixed with economic theory to implement the "concentration" policy and allow the survival of Aryan firms.[73]

The story of Aryanization, like that of occupied and Vichy France in general, is one of a mixture of German and French control. The latter was sometimes instituted by the Germans in order to legitimate their own activities, but the French organizations often pursued their own raison d'être. It was one thing to have French Aryans take over Jewish firms. The French ministry was less anxious for Germans to do so.[74] In a first stage the French government simply applied the German orders. From mid-1941 on, however, the Vichy government began to react to what it saw as a Germanization of the French economy. Thus, in part in order to defend its own interests, the regime began promoting its own state anti-Semitism. As Henry Rousso has commented, "The French and the Germans fought each other for legitimacy" in this domain.[75]

As early as May 20, 1940, a German order initiated the appointment of *administrateurs provisoires* (trustees) to handle the sale or closure of all firms delicately described as *"privées de leurs di-*

rigeants" (deprived of their owners). This was transformed into a French law on September 10, three weeks before Vichy promulgated the first Statut des Juifs (on October 3) prohibiting Jews from certain sectors of the economy. On October 18, another German order specifically provided for placing all Jewish firms under trusteeship. Jewish firms were defined as those whose owners, presidents, or over one-third of the shareholders or associates were Jewish; the *administrateurs provisoires* had to provide a certificate proving their Aryan origins.[76] At first, the occupying forces controlled the trustee appointments themselves. However, on December 9, 1940, a Service de contrôle des administrateurs provisoires (SCAP) was set up within the French Ministère de la production industrielle as the French attempted to regain control of what was, after all, "French" patrimony. On June 19, 1941, the SCAP was transferred to the recently created Commissariat général aux questions juives (CGQJ).

Within the French Ministère de la production industrielle, the Direction des textiles et des cuirs and, more specifically, the Sous-direction du vêtement, dealt with everything from approving exports and imports to organizing the distribution of raw materials to assuring the production and distribution of finished goods: work clothes for French workers sent to Germany, civilian clothes for returning French prisoners, uniforms for civil servants, even providing enough *espadrilles* for wholesale bakery and pastry workers.[77] The Comité d'organisation du vêtement (COV) was one of many such committees set up in all economic sectors in order to regulate and reorganize industrial production. A sub-, yet separate, group within the Comité d'organisation de l'industrie textile, the COV was in turn divided into seven groups.[78]

The *comités d'organisation* (COS) had a somewhat ambiguous role. On the one hand they served as official organizations, providing informational lists to the police and to the Ministry of Industry with regard to distributing raw materials and requisitioning goods. Yet at the same time, they often acted as manufacturers' associations (from which prewar organizations many of their members came) with their own, corporatist, interests to defend. This could even lead to conflicts between the COV and the SCAP, such as in March 1942, when the two clashed over some trusteeship appointments, with the SCAP virtually taking the side of the Jews! Responding angrily to a COV protest, the SCAP argued that the COV's candidates were not neces-

The Sentier

sarily any better than the SCAP's, and that, furthermore, the SCAP suspected the COV's trustees would only use their influence to retaliate against former Jewish competitors.[79]

Joseph Billig has emphasized that liquidation rather than sale was the first choice for Jewish firms, although the initial plan after the mass roundup of the Jews in 1942 was to sell the firms; only subsequently were they simply closed, in large part for lack of buyers.[80] The *comités d'organisation* seemed to prefer closings to takeovers in order to eliminate competition.[81] In general, "concentration" was favored in order to "perfect the organization" of the profession.[82] The number of garment-industry firms "concentrated" as of December 31, 1943, were as follows (the percentages in parentheses reflect the number of those closed in relation to the existing firms in the Occupied Zone at the time that concentration went into effect): haute couture and custom-made: 0; men's ready-made: 326 (33.1 percent); women's ready-made: 280 (22.7 percent); white goods: 488 (18.8 percent); furs: not indicated; accessories: 129 (9.0 percent); textile trade: 0; total 1,223.[83] As a result, 7,923 employees (1,336 men and 6,587 women) were "freed" (*libérés*) [*sic*], and it was later specified that nine-tenths of the closed/concentrated women's-wear businesses had been Jewish firms.[84] According to another estimate, the industry's labor force had dropped 45 percent during the war, from 478,000 in 1938 to 250,000 in 1944.[85]

Not all Jewish garment firms were eliminated during the war. Some Jews were able to slip through the Aryanization process thanks to friendly *administrateurs provisoires* or because they were considered "economically useful." The Gestapo itself protected certain workers needed to help fill orders for sweaters, gloves, etc. Some 3,000 safe passes were given to immigrant fur-workers, and at one point there was talk of releasing knitwear workers from the Drancy concentration camp in order to replace striking workers.[86]

Furthermore, a small but determined minority of Jewish resisters struck back. With the invasion of the USSR and increased German demands on production, the Jewish Communist resistance (liberated from the Soviet-German Pact) along with the Bundists called for boycotts, strikes, slowdowns, and sabotage. In addition to an estimated production loss of 160,000 gloves and 375,000 sweaters, glove fingers were shortened, thumbs sewn onto the wrong side, sweater head holes made too small, and furs slit on the inside.

Machines were broken or put out of commission by introducing sand, and clothes were stolen for the Jewish resistance. Work stoppages occurred in May 1943 in solidarity with the Warsaw ghetto uprising, and even fire bombs were occasionally set in shops.[87]

On the whole, however, resistance did not stop the COS and the SCAP from functioning and ultimately prefiguring postwar discussions about industrial modernization. Two different economic visions underlay the conflicts between the French, German, SCAP, and COV interests. The *comités d'organisation,* who wanted their own members and allies to be the first to benefit from the reorganization, had a more microanalytical and corporatist perspective, while other, more general arguments emphasizing centralization and concentration appealed to the good of the industry as a whole. Thus, when the COV argued professional competence in support of its candidates, the SCAP accused it of base competitive motives and appealed to a more macroanalytical level of industrial needs.[88]

Nonetheless, both organizations situated their actions within a more general reordering of the industry.[89] As early as October 1941, the women's ready-made section of the Comité d'organisation proposed setting up a study to reinvigorate the profession. And there was talk of finally allowing French ready-made manufacturers to purchase haute couture designs for adaptation.[90] France came out of the war with its important ready-made industry seriously weakened but more or less intact. Like New York, Paris now produced only 39.4 percent of all French garments in 1945, but it still made 74.4 percent of women's wear.[91] The stage was set for serious reflections on the meaning of "modernization."

The Invention of "Ready-to-Wear"

Concern over the "modernization" of French industry was not a new theme. Garment manufacturers since the nineteenth century had worried about France's place on the world market and about how to increase productivity without losing artistic content. Mid-nineteenth-century observers, such as the Comte Léon de Laborde, had worried about the foreign menace in the context of nineteenth-century industrialization, criticizing English, German, and other products for their lack of good taste. By the turn of the century,

German competition had become a veritable obsession for military men and manufacturers alike. The cheaper price of German ready-made goods gave pause for reflection, inspiring declarations about the need to reorganize the French industry. Industrialists and industry observers began to admit, with somewhat bitter resignation, that elegance was perhaps not enough to ensure sufficient sales. Investigators went abroad to study other countries' art schools, and American methods of productivity were (already) studied.[92]

Worry about foreign competition in the women's ready-made sector abated somewhat during the interwar revival but was heightened again during World War II, prefiguring postwar concerns. In March 1942, Jarillot of the Sous-Direction du vêtement anticipated worry about postwar competition. Already "Vienna, Berlin, Hamburg, Frankfurt, etc. are buying their patterns on the German market and from other Axis countries." "What will happen with this competition the day that the situation returns to normal?"[93] One of the suggestions, ultimately implemented, was finally to allow French *confectionneurs* to purchase patterns from the *haute couturiers*.

Even before the end of the war, garment industry specialists lamented the comparative state of the French industry. In April of 1943, the Centre d'études techniques des industries de l'habillement (CETIH) was created explicitly to modernize the industry. Jean Allilaire, in a fifteen-page report dated December 1, 1944, and again in a 1947 book, pleaded for a tempered industrialization of women's wear in France. He stressed the importance of modernization, defined as better machinery, greater productivity, and a certain standardization of production. He criticized the outdated French equipment and pleaded for a rationalization of the labor process and a renewal of both management and skilled labor.[94] At the end of the war, approximately 80 percent of the garment-industry machinery was over twenty years old. New machines were imported from Germany and England, and the Marshall Plan allocated up to $900,000 to $1,000,000 of credit per year to purchase new material.[95]

One definition of modernization was Americanization. Production directors went to the United States to study industrial methods, and, in 1956, a French group of garment manufacturers headed by Albert Lempereur was invited by the American government. "They discover with astonishment not only good quality ready-to-wear but above all an efficient system of merchandising."[96] The American model, however, was as much revered as feared. The postwar CGT took up a general stance against American expansion, and if the 1946 Congress of the Fédération de l'habillement et de la chapellerie was optimistic about postwar prospects for the industry—"The country must be clothed"—by the 1948 Congress, pessimism reigned: "our industries [are] in mortal danger." The "false philanthropy" of the Marshall Plan was harshly criticized, although some of the most critical anti-American phrases against the "dangerous American competition" were crossed out or toned down in the final draft.[97] The Marshall Plan was blamed for unemployment as well as the loss of good taste. The 1950 Congress bemoaned the fact that women's ready-made goods were down to 70 percent of prewar figures, and that all fields—from haute couture to Boussac's underwear monopoly—were in difficulty. The Plan's imposition of American war surplus goods was also criticized, along with, more generally, the AFL and "Irwin Braun" 's [sic] financing of the Force ouvrière (FO) splitting off from the CGT in 1947.[98]

There was, however, another response to "modernization": the (re)-invention of newness. Christian Dior led the way in February 1947 with his "New Look."[99] The longer skirts and softer lines were explicitly meant to counter the privations "of the dark years." Other haute couturiers descended into the ready-to-wear arena. Coco Chanel came out of retirement in 1954 with her simple, youthful lines, saying that she was now going to make clothes not just for the few but for thousands. Jacques Fath and Pierre Balmain started designing ready-to-wear for both the French and American markets, while André Courrèges and Pierre Cardin, and soon dedicated ready-to-wear manufacturers such as Daniel Hechter and Cacharel, started conceiving more youthful and audacious styles for the young.

To mark the sense of newness, the term *prêt-à-porter* was translated directly from "ready-to-wear." First used by Jean-Claude Weill in 1948, the neologism (which elicited serious reservations from some linguistic critics[100]) was meant to be performative: to change the image of *confection*. The first *prêt-à-porter* salon was held in 1957, and soon one more "takeoff" of the ready-made clothing industry was hailed. Concomitant with this new construction of style was the usual disparagement of previous fashions. As one labor leader later described interwar *confection*, it was "very low quality," "quite ugly," which, of course, is how the *confectionneurs* of the interwar period had characterized pre–World War I goods. As "style" was reinvented in the 1960s, there was an important sense of a "completely new" French apparel industry.[101]

The change of terms also meant a shift in both consumers and producers. The 1960s are also represented as a (if not the) new period of mass consumption: "It was the beginning of rapid style change and excessive consumption."[102] As postwar penury turned into prosperity, the garment industry shifted its sights from the petite bourgeoise to the bourgeoise. It was she who was now blamed as the cause of continued variability in women's wear, it was she whose individualism was preventing greater productivity, it was she who was still stubbornly having her dresses made up at her neighborhood *couturière*'s. But it was also she who became the motor behind this new period of apparel growth.

In terms of production, the upgrading of *confection* to *prêt-à-porter* meant a certain downgrading of haute couture: Dior was embarrassed, at first signing his *prêt-à-porter* line as the anonymous Monsieur X.[103] It also meant the virtual elimination of *petite couture*. Whereas there were still some 45,000 dressmakers in France in 1970 according to one estimate, by 1985 there were only 6,000.[104] If ready-to-wear offered less choice, it meant a more even quality of goods and freedom from fittings that often included "disparaging comments about my body."[105] Ironically, however, the different levels collapsed within the term *prêt-à-porter*, which can now refer to anything from Cardin to basement bargains at Tati.[106]

The Sentier and "le système Sentier" came to represent this newness. Indeed, as apartments and bakeries, cafés and groceries have vacated the area since the 1960s, workshops and showrooms have taken their place. Generally dated to the 1960s, this new *système* is defined as or linked to two elements: the arrival of the North African Jews, to whom we will return, and the speeding up of production. Speed has become the exhausting alter ego of newness, marked by a constant pressure to create new models, to continually restock during the season, and thus to maintain frantic production schedules. Clients are blamed but so are the retailers, who demand quick turnover and refuse to keep large inventories.

Finally, the modernization issue has come full circle with renewed concern about the French industry's place on the world market. "Democratization" affected not only the French bourgeoisie's representations and fears. As a worldwide phenomenon, Allilaire lamented its effect on French exports as new clients increasingly preferred cheaper, mediocre goods. In his immediate postwar report, he therefore once again stressed the importance of both invisible and colonial exports. Lingerie, for example, taken back home by travelers, accounted for approximately 35 percent of total sales. Nevertheless, the colonial market, he felt, held out the best hope for expansion. The 60 million inhabitants of the French colonies "that civilization strives to clothe" represented a growing population compared to the 40 million on the "old continent" with their notoriously sluggish demographic growth.[107] Yet decolonization would affect French clothing exports in the 1960s and 1970s just as massive imports began to encroach on the French market in the 1970s.

The Commissariat général au plan saw the postwar problem of reorganizing the industry as one of a necessary rationalization within the constraints, one could say, of flexibility. Arguing for financial concentration and vertical as well as horizontal integration, the Commissariat argued in 1971 that, "without trying to normalize or rationalize excessively," it was necessary to create larger units either through internal growth or mergers. The Commissioner's report tried to remain hopeful in spite of

the difficulties and obstacles that exist due not only to the individualism of the French temperament, but due to the fact that many garment firms have maintained a legal status that is no longer consonant with the needs of modern industry.[108]

So, the female client was not alone in her individualism as an obstruction to greater industrial rationalization. The myriad of garment manufacturers themselves also stood stubbornly in the way of greater concentration.

Such was the interpretation in 1971, before flexibility and the entrepreneur-as-economic-hero made a comeback in recent industrial analyses. The Commissioner's report, however, is a fitting testimony to the French expression of the tensions between standardization and flexibility in the garment trade. Foreign and domestic demand; workers, the colonized, and women; large department store factories and contractors' workshops have all incarnated the different sides of the garment-industry dialectic in Paris over the last century. The interplay between concentration and dispersion has

The Sentier

been constant, with only the *façonnier* explicitly conceptualized as an ambiguous intermediary symbol of the productive structure. In this respect the Parisian story sounds in many ways like the New York one. The basic plots are indeed strikingly similar.

Nonetheless, modernization worries, artistic belief, and the slower appearance of the ready-made dress give the Parisian industry its own concerns and its own chronology. World War I, the Congrès of Tours which split the French left, and World War II were ruptures of national importance each of which had an important impact on the Sentier. The labor legislation, competing unions, and "concentration" and Aryanization that these events produced reverberated to the realm of garment production. The city's industrial history is also a national political one.

With this in mind, we can turn to a closer comparative reading of garment making in two cities to see how a Singer in Paris and one in New York can produce variations on the theme of fashion.

Ready-to-Wear and Ready-to-Work

4

BERMUDA SHORTS IN COMPARATIVE PERSPECTIVE

W hy do Bermuda shorts look different in Paris and New York? Unknown for many years in the French capital, they made a surprising appearance in the early 1990s. The baggy sportswear was miraculously transformed into office and even evening wear, causing even the most casual American observer in Paris to wonder about the mechanisms of cultural exchange. A poststructural structuralism has to ask how a single garment, like a single industry, may vary from one side of the ocean to the other. It means exploring and respecting the differences while understanding the similarities. Various comparative questions are possible, each carrying within it the seeds of its own response. John Stuart Mill referred to two methods of comparison: the method of accord and the method of difference.[1] After having sketched the global outlines of industrial growth as well as the specific narratives for New York and Paris, I will now address the industrial comparison frontally in order to identify more clearly those elements of demand and supply, of union and state intervention which distinguish the two industries. This means a focus on difference, both to demonstrate and explain it, but it will not preclude a return to "accord" later.

Two specific types of comparison are possible. I have already alluded to the temporal one. Garment bosses and garment workers have been complaining about the uneven pace of production ever since the nineteenth century. They swear, each year, that the change of seasons is worse than ever before, while they herald newness time and again. Temporal comparisons by garment practitioners, imagining the past in function of the present, merit a study in themselves. They would fit into the general genre of the constant renewal of discovery.

Spatial comparisons, however, are those that interest me here. In their most obvious form, they have to do with mundane matters of competition. They are thus not just an academic construct. French garment manufacturers have been wary of growing American industrial strength since the nineteenth century, while American designers have been anxious about creating a distinctive American style since the early twentieth. Such comparisons, by manufacturers and industrial reporters, reveal transatlantic understandings of the garment "other" which fall into the realm of what I call reciprocal visions.

I will begin with those reciprocal visions and the way in which French and American clothing manufacturers and industry analysts have understood and constructed the differences between the industries. I will then explore the ways in which these different perceptions of demand have been reflected in and reflective of different rhythms of development: How can we understand the persistence of the Parisian *couturière?* Two separate issues can then be addressed: how the unions and how the state have affected and reflected similarity and difference in the Paris and New York ready-to-wear businesses.

Reciprocal Visions: The French View of American Style

Already in 1857, the Comte Léon de Laborde ominously warned French manufacturers about the growing potential of American competition in the field of industrial art:

Beware the long strides of these Know-nothings, the giant steps of these new initiates. To be a novice in the arts and to have a passionate intelligence for them, to be part of the industrial movement and at the head of this most redoubtable manufacturing army, and to undertake to use this strength in the service of the arts, means combining two actions which will have the effect of a lever on Archimedes' fulcrum.

In the current state of our arts and our industry, this danger is real, since it is easy for the enemy to wear down a troop that is scattered. Tighten our ranks. Let the rules of good taste, like the rules of discipline, allow us to hold off these assailants.[2]

The count, nostalgic for the Old Regime and worried about declining standards of taste, was perhaps more pessimistic than most. But cultural attitudes, then as now, underlay competitive worries. Attitudes about art, industry, and women have been brought to bear in explaining differences in Parisian and New York fashion and industrial history.[3]

While a general concern over the relationship of art to industry was expressed everywhere that new methods challenged the art of the unique, each country also had its specific worries.[4] Long convinced of the strength of their good taste, French observers and manufacturers from the nineteenth century on had to reconceptualize their art in the face of growing industrialization and increased competition. As ready-made industries developed in most of the late-nineteenth-century industrialized or industrializing countries (England, Germany, the United States), French garment manufacturers worried about their place in the world market and about how to increase productivity.

Wishes for industrial reorganization in the garment trade were nonetheless accompanied by solemn promises that there was no question of lowering standards even as "individualism" began to be evoked almost nostalgically. Jean Allilaire, in his post–World War II recommendations for the French industry, lamented that a uniformity of manners was emerging, a "depressing tendency" that French clothiers (*couturiers* and *confectionneurs* alike) should combat. However, like it or not, he also recognized that individualism, like art, had its limitations and that the production process had to be revamped. He repeated that while a "judicious standardization [*normalisation*] of certain elements of the garment" was necessary, a rationalization of production did not mean a pure standardization. The French garment industry would have to weave its way between

Bermuda Shorts

an imperative of *normalisation* without succumbing to the evils of *uniformisation*.[5]

In analyzing the needs and prospects of the French garment industry, French observers often had a double discourse. Self-criticism and calls for greater industrialization were aimed at the French audience in order to stimulate greater productivity and maintain competitivity. However, to the outside world, manufacturers and "taste professionals"[6] proudly placed French elegance first and foremost. This dialogue/monologue with the competition was in fact constructed as a comparative question. Within a universalist discourse concerning French sartorial leadership was a reflection on taste in the age of mass production and a comparative evaluation of it worldwide.

In conceptualizing the competition, French fashion analysts often utilized a language of differing (and hierarchical) national characteristics. French goods have been proudly hailed as a reflection of the French character itself: "the good taste and creative power particular to our race."[7] De Laborde positively glowed over the innate elegance of the French spirit. A century later the certainty remained that if there were perhaps pretty styles elsewhere, "nowhere has anyone succeeded in combining in a dress these [French] qualities of psychology and technique."[8] The combination of artistic sense and industrial technique has been acclaimed as a French specialty that no other country has mastered. As prolific art critic Arsène Alexandre said, how can you argue with five centuries of good taste?[9]

Unabashed pride in French goods rested on the identification of those goods with a national character imbued with artistic sense. This was precisely what was lacking in competitors' goods. Disdain (if not pity) for other countries' clothes has similarly been explained in terms of national character. The lawyer Edouard Debect, in his lyrical doctoral thesis on the subject, developed a veritable climatic theory of style:

The style of the Englishman is too sober, that of the German too heavy, that of the Spaniard and the Italian too bright with color, the harmony too keen: the influence of climate and ethnographic conditions no doubt. In between these cold countries and these blazing ones, France offers its own properties, which are the cause of its success.[10]

Ready-to-Wear and Ready-to-Work

Others were less flattering in their comparative characterizations of competitors and their clothing. German imitations of French styles were described as but "mutilated" (*tronquées*) copies, and German children's wear was considered limited because "this type of ready-made goods demands taste, inventiveness and lightness."[11] English garments found no more favor, their fabrics and forms boringly repetitive:

English ready-made, which constantly transforms the same cloth, according to one style which is practically invariable, only hurts Parisian ready-made when the current fashion is simple lines.[12]

As the traditional nineteenth-century economic rivals were overtaken by another, the alignment of French artistry against American industrialism became a staple of the industrial language. By the end of the nineteenth century, concern over American industrialization led to an in-depth investigation of the American worker by Emile Levasseur for the Académie des sciences morales et politiques. Like Tocqueville before him, Levasseur was particularly impressed by the democracy (even the "*luxe démocratique*") which he discovered, down to clothing styles. Levasseur recounted how, on a Sunday stroll through Central Park, he was fooled into mistaking workers in their Sunday best for the bourgeoisie (a bit shabby, it is true). He observed that the American woman worker was perhaps not quite as successful as her husband in imitating her bourgeois counterpart, although he admitted that perhaps a female eye might have picked up the more subtle American class distinctions. Citing an "*indiscrète*" corset survey and commenting that he himself had seen little underwear on outdoor laundry lines, the wily investigator speculated that American class differences may not be visible on a walk through the park.[13]

Levasseur's observations on clothing in America are particularly interesting in the context of his more general comments implicitly comparing French and American taste. Impressed with the American democracy apparent in outerwear if not underwear, Levasseur was a great enthusiast for American manufacturing methods: faster, cheaper, producing greater quantities. But, in spite of the fact that American workers worked harder than the French, he found their goods to be of inferior quality. The weapons, furniture, saddles, and draperies that he saw all lacked taste, finish, and artistic sense: "In America, variety is the exception and good taste even more so."[14]

Bermuda Shorts

The question for many observers was why? Why do Americans have no (or bad) taste? For Levasseur, uniform taste resulted from a classless society. The standardization of clothing manufacture was thus not simply a result of poor taste but of the democratic process itself. Half a century later, Allilaire placed the motor behind mediocrity squarely within the American spirit: "The standardized manners of our American friends have easily accommodated themselves to the needs of modern manufacture."[15] Other writers, in the productivity studies of the late 1940s and early 1950s, more generally criticized the American way of life and a standardization of lifestyles abetted by radio, television, newspapers, and advertising.[16]

Whatever the explanation, two elements are clear. First, democratization has been criticized for its leveling aesthetic practice, a view virtually unknown in American garment discourse. Second, the French analysis of American clothing manners has served to explain if not justify the difference between French and foreign firms. In what I would call a cultural language of production, national characteristics become an explanatory device for understanding the relative problems of French industry on the world market. The construction of the comparison helps explain the competition. The taste gap elucidates the productivity gap.

Furthermore, in this taste battle between nations, women have been assigned a particular role. The individuals over whom (male) manufacturers are competing are women. They are represented in garment discourse not only as producers and especially as consumers, but as representatives of national character in a war of the wearers. The garment industrialists' image of French and foreign women has become another explanation for competitive differences in the marketplace. Thus German, English, and American women have been described as lacking individualism, as being less skilled workers and less discerning shoppers. In the early 1950s, the overwhelming success of ready-to-wear in the United States was attributed by one French observer to lack of inspiration on the part of "l'Américaine."[17]

By contrast, the French woman has been lauded. She incarnates the positive artistic and individualistic aspects of the French garment industry, a veritable symbol of national identity. If Paris is the "capital of elegance," it is because it is a "paradise of women."[18]

Nevertheless, the image of the French woman has remained ambiguous. Her good taste has been praised as fundamental to the production of elegance. But the productivity worry remains: Is this sufficient to sell enough clothes?

One French observer in the United States concluded that, in order to conquer other markets, the French simply had to adapt, in spite of what they might think of other women. In an in-depth analysis of "la consommatrice américaine" in 1960, the French commercial counselor in New York described a "certain uniformization" which allowed women of different socioeconomic categories and ages to dress alike and to dress stylishly. But, he observed, the American notion of style differs from that of the French. Comfort, practicality, and simplicity were the new values of the American suburbanite. As a result "the quality may appear mediocre to a European," but it had its own logic. He noted the growth of sportswear for women and their wearing of men's clothing. He was particularly horrified by the "unaesthetic" Bermuda shorts "that no French woman would ever think of wearing."[19] His suggestions were practical. The French had to adapt exports to American sizing, commercial techniques, and even "style" if they wanted to sell there. Nonetheless, he too stressed that the French had to maintain their "originality," which the American public expected in French goods.[20]

French garment discourse has thus set up a certain dichotomy between art and industry paralleled by the difference between the French and American industries. Art and aesthetics remain the universal values to which the industry should appeal, even though competitive concerns over productivity often undercut that certainty. Such pronouncements may in fact be meant to be performative: stressing the continued importance of differentiation in clothing allows mass production without too great a compromise.

Yet at the same time, the "modernization" fear has haunted the manufacturers. French analysts have combined both disdain and admiration for American methods and style.[21] As one contemporary Parisian ready-to-wear consultant expressed the dilemma in her book entitled *Raison et passion,* it is necessary to combine fantasy and reason, the flighty and the serious, and creative dynamics with the reality of industrial constraints. In sum, argues Françoise

Bermuda Shorts

Vincent-Ricard, the French need to integrate American productivity ratios with a "suitable aesthetic."[22] Economic necessity? A measured artistic defeatism, including ultimate acceptance of Bermuda shorts, as the early 1990s have shown? The French view of the American industry has been both shaped by cultural beliefs and undermined by economic worries. The opposite is true on the other side of the Atlantic.

Reciprocal Visions: The View from the Left Bank (of the Atlantic)

To a great extent American garment-industry practitioners and observers have agreed with the French *imaginaire* of the art/industry dichotomy: French expertise in the former, American prowess in the latter.[23] The American construction of a comparative garment-industry vision has on the one hand admitted the French monopoly on aura. But on the other hand, it has gone beyond that admission to celebrate American industrialism and democracy and even gone so far, in some cases, as to disdain French fashion. Within a general acceptance of French stylistic superiority, American industrialists and industry analysts have taken different tacks, one more defensive, the other offensive.

As early as 1922, American decorative-art critic Charles Richards wrote a book whose title echoed that of De Laborde's sixty-five years earlier: *Art in Industry*.[24] Richards too was concerned about the relation between the two and looked to France as a model. He, along with other American investigators of fashion and the apparel industry, suggested reasons for Parisian supremacy that echo those of their French colleagues, namely the presence of: art collections; skilled Parisian seamstresses "who have sewing skill in their fingertips"; demimondaines and nouveaux riches unafraid to try out new ideas (including foreign women "who will dress while in Paris in apparel that they wouldn't possibly think of wearing at home"); or simply "atmosphere."[25]

At the same time, Richards was on the defensive, worried about a French cultural imperialism. He complained that New York designers constantly copied French styles and even put French-sounding labels on clothes made in the United States. He pleaded for the development of American designers and for American independence vis-à-vis French style. Acknowledging French supremacy in the industrial arts, Richards concluded his study with a perhaps disingenuous but forlorn comment on American world superiority:

This country finds itself unexpectedly today the richest country in the world. Economic leadership is forced upon it and such dominance brings with it the demand for leadership in many other directions. In many fields we are sadly unprepared for such world ascendancy and in none is this more true than in the field of art. We represent a strong national life with marked individual force and characteristics, but it is a national life that has been absorbed in the conquest of material things and the gaining of material comforts. It has not yet paused to concern itself seriously with interest in art or beauty.[26]

In a reverse echo of De Laborde's earlier plaint, Richards encouraged American examination of European art schools in order better to develop applied-art programs in the United States.[27]

Defense of the American garment industry has focused on two elements: serial production and industrial prowess; and a defense of democracy itself. Apparel-industry historians Claudia B. Kidwell and Margaret C. Christman have argued that the mass production of clothing is "a unique American success story." Richards, too, stressed "our genius of quantity production." This, for him, was the true mastery behind American industry: "Whether we borrow, or whether we create, the art that will minister to American needs will be the art of the machine."[28] Another commentator expressed it somewhat more crudely in terms of American material motivations, stating that there are three different definitions of fashion: that of the Frenchman—"a constantly repeated attempt to reform nature"; that of the Englishman—"that by which the fantastic becomes for a moment universal" (writing in the early 1960s); and that of the American—"Fashion is a racket to sell clothes."[29]

Beyond the balance-sheet view, however, the defense of quantity production has been elevated to a defense of democracy. Contrary to Levasseur's and others' more pessimistic evaluations about the effects of democracy on American clothing habits, American observers have celebrated Seventh Avenue's concept of fashion for the many:

Bermuda Shorts

Only through quantity production and the machine can the needs of modern democracy be met. Consequently, our problem in artistic expression is to master the machine and in so doing to create art for the people.[30]

French styles have been described, by contrast, as elitist: "Paris still operates on the old idea of fashion for the few"; "sandals with Louis-the-umteenth heels" have been mocked.[31] The success of the American apparel industry has become a veritable mission of "translating high fashion into mass fashion."[32] As Kidwell and Christman expressed it (in what the French would consider an oxymoron), "average Americans became the best dressed average people in the world." In this context, the American garment industry has had its own, internal, civilizing mission: "the common quality of American dress served to obliterate ethnic origins and blur social distinctions."[33]

In addition to the defense of mass production and democracy, American manufacturers and commentators have launched veritable offensives around the notion of a genuine American style. The American "revolt" began even before World War I as some fashion plates began to criticize the "tyranny" of foreign fashions with calls for "a new war of independence" for American women. A 1912 contest launched by the *New York Times* to design an "American" dress and hat was encouraged, among other things, as a patriotic imperative. Campaigns to create a specifically American style have recurred since the beginning of the century: from 1907 to 1914 (the *American Dressmaker* magazine was founded in 1910 explicitly to counter *The French Dressmaker*); in 1932, when Lord and Taylor "made history" by advertising American-designed dresses; and in 1947, when a group of American designers formed the Guild of New York Dress Designers. Since World War II, the rise of sportswear has consecrated an American "style." As one observer of Seventh Avenue wrote in 1953,

Though we may still look back with a certain nostalgia toward France, though we may still be ready to accept an idea which she suggests, we are no longer her slave. We have in a sense once more asserted American independence.[34]

Never mind that American commentators are sometimes comparing apples and oranges—French haute couture (or their image of that

Ready-to-Wear and Ready-to-Work

most visible portion of French production) to American ready-to-wear—making it all the easier to criticize the elite nature of French apparel for the few and to celebrate the democratic nature of American production for the many. In this view, the elite/democratic dichotomy is constructed in favor of American goods.

What is specific to American taste? It is defined and defended by American industrial discourse (as the French commercial attaché had learned) as the American woman's insistence on comfort, practicality, and wearability. All of which also include a redefinition of style. To argue the point of a specific American style, Paul Nystrom, Professor of Marketing at Columbia University's Business School, provided a long list of American "fashions," from women's athletic underwear and athletic clothing, rubber-soled shoes, and jersey garments to the Gibson waist, the jumper, and the corsetless flapper figure.[35] Others have defined style comparatively. Clothes are not cars, after all, went one argument, in the *Women's Wear Daily* in 1925:

While it might be possible to turn out garments in the same manner as Ford turns out automobiles, it would be impossible to sell them because the American woman demands the maximum of style.[36]

And there were always those even worse off: "We are still far from standardized clothing along the lines of the British 'utility' types."[37] In comparison to cars or to the British, Americans are thus very stylish indeed. In this explanation, British goods are to American goods what American (and British of course) items are to the French. The comparative vision shows standardization and style to be relative concepts.

Finally, the logic of American superiority, a mirror image to that of the French, is also at times accompanied by denigration of the competition as unwearable or pretentious. One observer complained that Paris fashions are simply too hard to get into; they assume that the wearer has a maid. "The clothes that come from Paris are made to be shown, not worn. Once the girl squeezes into the dress, nobody cares whether or not she can sit down."[38] Some fashion observers have pointed out historic French fashion errors. Nystrom noted that French creators had been wrong at times: in their persistent but failing efforts to bring back ostrich feathers; in a long, lost war against shortening skirts in 1921–22. He added that many

Bermuda Shorts

so-called Parisian styles actually originated elsewhere, but were (only) adopted and reissued there.[39] After all, many of the great French couturiers were not even French, starting with the Englishman Charles Frederick Worth. The severest critic, Bernard Roshco, went so far as to dispute the French art/industry *imaginaire* altogether: "Paris couture is built on daring originality, painstaking attention to detail, arrogant pretentiousness, and calculated hokum."[40]

Beyond specific jabs, the reciprocal visions and competitive language of American and French clothiers stress the differences between the two industries all the while trying to imitate that which the other does best. American discourse has alternated between slavish awe of and themes of domination by French fashion; and proclamations of self-reliance and independence. French language has been permeated by pride in the individual and that French cachet of style but also infused with worries about "modernization" and, after all, sales.

There are thus mirrorlike similarities in their contradictions. But there is also a fundamentally different discourse at work in the American and French imagining of garment-industry "fashion." Democracy, for one, is interpreted differently on both sides of the Atlantic. Celebrated in American industrial discourse, it is also a rationale for the industrialization of art and its mass-consumer derivative, clothing. There are no worries about the "*démocratisation du luxe*" in New York. French clothiers, however, more Jacobin than Jacksonian in their view of democracy, rarely market clothing explicitly *for* the masses (even if aimed at them). However many items are made identically to be sold off the rack, the discourse is one of the individual rather than the mass, of differentiation rather than imitation.[41] These differences are largely explained in cultural terms, with forms of fashion rather than production methods the focus of most of this competitive and comparative literature. Yet production rather than fashion may provide a different comparative category. A more historical perspective can help go beyond practitioners' perceptions of changing fads by asking how these different representations of demand correspond to different rhythms of development in the two trades.

Ready-to-Wear and Ready-to-Work

The construction of these reciprocal visions functions to explain different artistic and/or economic successes or failures on the world market. They also correspond to a certain reality: production for different markets and different rhythms of development within the overall pattern of ready-to-wear growth. Our two protagonists have become rivals in the twentieth century, although perhaps not to the extent that their mutual saber-rattling would lead us to believe. Both industries have been concerned about encroachment on their domestic markets, although not in the same periods or over the same issues. While the art/industry division of labor has run through both garment *imaginaires* over the *longue durée,* specific moments of import worries have activated those concerns. New York rejection of Parisian style flared in 1912 and again in the interwar period, as we have seen, while Parisian concern over American jeans and the importation of other standardized sportswear has been most prevalent in the last twenty years.

Beyond domestic competition, both industries have also constructed their competition in terms of contest over global markets. Nonetheless, for most of the last century, the Paris and New York ready-to-wear industries have in fact been manufacturing largely for different markets: New York makes goods mostly for the United States, while Paris has produced for Parisians but also for the rest of the world. For the period from 1955 to 1962, for example, a telling set of comparative statistics was drawn up by the OECD. France's clothing exports exceeded imports by $1 million in 1955, that figure jumping to $153.4 million in 1960 and back to a still healthy $132.4 million in 1962. During the same period, the United States ran a constant clothing deficit. Imports exceeded exports by $31.3 million in 1955, by $196.6 million in 1960, and by $275.5 million in 1962.[42]

Producing in large part for the domestic market, it is no wonder that American manufacturers have been more concerned with constructing a defensive definition of American style, while French clothiers have focused more on an offensive definition of an exportable French style. The reciprocal visions are both discursive attempts at performative stimuli to economic competition and reflec-

Bermuda Shorts

tions of different market shares. I would suggest further that comparative garment-history growth also reflects different interpretations of the relative forces of supply and demand. Producing for export, the Parisian language has been outwardly focused, emphasizing the superiority of (tasteful) supply. Producing first and foremost for the domestic market, New York manufacturers have been more protective, constructing an American style grounded in perceived democratic domestic demand.

The Persistence of the Neighborhood Couturière, or Different Rhythms of Growth

The reciprocal visions constructed to justify and stimulate production also reflect different rhythms of development. Although the ready-made women's-garment industry took off everywhere in the industrializing West in the late nineteenth century, and the general tendency of that linear development has been the same over the last century, the Paris and New York industries grew at different paces. Parisian *confectionneurs* in all periods have hailed the steady progress of their trade. But in comparison to New York City, there was a *relative* lag in the development of their business. This too shows how standardization can be a relative concept. Increasing standardization occurred everywhere that ready-made garments were introduced, but French women's clothes became more standardized somewhat less quickly than did American ones. (In analytic terms, structure and its variants are intertwined.)

A single set of comparative figures is revealing. At the end of the 1860s, ready-made goods comprised approximately 25 percent of American garment production; by 1890, they accounted for 60 percent of production; and by 1951, over 90 percent of Americans were buying their clothes "off the rack." By contrast, in 1950, only two-thirds of all French garments were ready-made.[43] While by the First World War, American women had largely adopted a wide range of ready-made garments, French women, who had long been buying ready-made underwear and now skirts and blouses, were reticent to buy ready-made dresses. They were still going to their neighborhood dressmakers through the interwar years and beyond the Second World War. Paradoxically, then, while producing for export and civilizing while clothing the world, the growing Parisian ready-to-wear industry had certain limitations. The local *couturière* persisted.

The question is, however, whether the Parisian woman's innate individualism is the sole cause for this variation on the theme of ready-to-wear growth. How, in other words, can we understand the "lag"? Worry over French lag is not just an economic historian's construct; French industrialists and analysts' worries about "modernization" reflect the notion of a more productive "other." Are their cultural visions the only available explanatory factors? Whitney Walton has argued that the notion of good taste and thus the power of the French consumer explains the longer French attachment to small-scale, handmade production in general.[44] While this concords with French industrial discourse and is indeed an important factor in the relative lag of French ready-to-wear, we still need to ask whether demand is the only reason.

Recent French economic historiography has in fact argued that we need to turn the tables on perceptions of "lag," which is, after all, a relative and comparative concept. In a polemic with David Landes's classic explanation of the weaknesses inherent in the French family firm, economists and social historians have emphasized the strength and virtues of *la petite enterprise* in France. "Light industry is not a relic but rather a full-fledged component of French industrial society."[45] The French simply developed along a different path. In this respect, the Paris garment industry could be seen as but a variation on a larger theme of Parisian urban development.

However, the small-scale character of the garment industry, as we have seen, goes beyond one city's boundaries. It is not merely a function of a general Parisian phenomenon. It has another context, which is that of the urban needs of the fashion industry as expressed in both New York and Paris. The "lag" question is not simply why one garment industry is smaller or less standardized than another, but how two basically similar small-scale industries have differed. The reasons for the slower acceptance of ready-made goods in France or their faster acceptance in the United States may be cultural, but there are at least two other factors that may be taken into account: the clothing equivalent of patent law; and the effects of both world wars on the Parisian economy.

French design protection has a long history dating back to Louis XVI if not Colbert and reconfirmed during the Revolution. A peculiarity of the functioning of the haute couture sector in France from the late nineteenth century until after World War II meant that, although the *haute couturiers* sold their models to French *petite* and especially *moyenne couturières* as well as to foreign *confectionneurs,* they were forbidden (as a protectionist measure) to sell their models to French *confectionneurs.* Thus, consistent disdain for *confection* in France, coupled with "indiscriminate" sales to foreign buyers, meant that the latest fashion could be reproduced thousands of times over in the United States before the French ready-made manufacturers had seen them:

> We know what skill, ingenuity and care the American genius exhibits in imitating and reproducing others. Fashion does not escape this law. The models are reproduced in the United States as perfectly as the machine permits.[46]

This helped the competition abroad while stifling it at home.

Perfectly consistent with a notion of protecting their own art while dismissing industrial goods produced abroad, this practice helped the survival of the intermediary category of producers in Paris—the *petite* and *moyenne couturières*—while slowing the growth of ready-to-wear. With style piracy a criminal offense in France up through the Second World War, Parisian dressmakers were able to maintain their monopoly on the social construction and actual production of differentiation within France while the rights to imitation were being sold abroad.

By contrast, style copying has by and large been considered legitimate in the United States except in specific instances of copyright protection. When the Fashion Originators' Guild and the Millinery Creators' Guild tried to boycott firms accused of pirating styles in the early 1940s, the United States Supreme Court declared the boycott illegal.[47] Design protection laws have thus reflected differing attitudes about differentiation and imitation while at the same time abetting them—sometimes to the exasperation of the *confectionneurs* or designers involved.

The experience of war also affected the American and French economies differently, down to the New York and Parisian garment industries. On the one hand, both world wars globally encouraged long-term trends toward greater style simplification and, during World War II, experimentation with chemicals and easier-to-handle

Ready-to-Wear and Ready-to-Work

new fabrics. On the other hand, the two wars had another, very different, effect on both countries and their respective industries. While prosperity occurred on one side of the Atlantic, there was penury across the ocean.

Both wars were a disaster for the French economy and society. From the perspective of the garment industry alone, the world wars interfered with the usual dissemination of fashions from Paris outward, and although the city recovered its supremacy as fashion capital of the world in the interwar period, certain factors already presaged change. A good portion of the Parisian garment labor force was deported during the second war, and in spite of efforts at "concentration," the Parisian industry came out of World War II with a particularly heightened sense of the need for change and renewed calls for "modernization." In this respect, the war slowed the pace of French ready-to-wear development, while for the New York industry it meant prosperous times. Even if wages did not entirely keep up with the cost of living and if a sense of decline already beset it, the New York industry's part in the strong wartime economy was a powerful springboard for postwar productivity. The wars, as recent historiographers have argued, were as much catalysts as causes. Yet while abetting the general push toward ready-made clothes, the "culture of war"—both times—punctuated the two stories strikingly differently and can account for some of the differences in rates of growth.[48]

Bermuda shorts, domestic and foreign markets, the persistence of the Parisian *couturière,* and the experience of war are but one way of describing the differences between Paris and New York. The comparative history can also be inscribed in another context that moves beyond the industry alone. Not surprisingly, social movements and social legislation—the unions and the state—have also participated in a construction of difference of these garment trades while, at the same time, reflecting larger variations across national boundaries.

Labor Unions and Industrial (Dis)Organization

When the International Ladies' Garment Workers' Union jingle became a nationwide hit in the late 1970s, no one would have suggested comparing (as similar) the powerful American union to its weaker French counterparts. Where the American women's garment-workers' union became not only a recognized label but a household word—affectionately called the "ILG" in New York—the Fédération de l'habillement has never had the strength or the visibility of the New York–based union. One of the uncontrovertible differences between the two unions has been the greater ability of the ILGWU to organize workers across garment neighborhoods in the interstices of the New York City landscape and to become a highly visible part of that landscape. In marked contrast, the Fédération de l'habillement has always taken a media backseat to that of garment strikers—be they the *cousettes* of the interwar years or the undocumented immigrant workers more recently. How can we understand this difference in garment labor movements?

An early view of the differences between the unions was given by John Dyche, General Secretary and Treasurer of the ILGWU, when he passed through Paris after the International Congress of Needleworkers in Vienna in July 1913. Commenting on the American labor movement's view of its European counterparts, he expressed his own—labor—version of the art/industry dichotomy:

The Germans are too slow, much too slow. You, the French, you are too crazy. You're not practical; you are artists.

For us, it's now, right away, that we want to better conditions. And we work at it more vigorously than you. Tomorrow doesn't interest us.[49]

The "artistic" nature of the French labor movement had a somber corollary: the relative weakness of the French garment union. Even the French unionists bemoaned this fact—all the more bitterly given the prestige of the industry for which they labored.[50]

These perceptions corresponded to different rhetoric and to different strategies. The ILGWU, as we have seen, was one of the pioneers of collective bargaining in the United States, with its Protocol of Peace in 1910. Its discourse soon reflected this search for stability. Although the ILGWU's first constitution in 1900 used a fiery language of class struggle, the tone changed markedly within a decade as industrial peace became the union's slogan. No longer would the ILGWU rail against "capitalist exploitation," as the French unions did again and again. A major theme at the 1936 merger meeting between the Confédération générale du travail (CGT) and the Confédération générale du travail unitaire (CGTU), such language was

Ready-to-Wear and Ready-to-Work

inconceivable by that date in the ILGWU. As a general matter, once the ILGWU turned to collective bargaining, general industry-wide strikes became rare if not discouraged in the 1920s. In Paris, however, although employer-employee agreements likewise began to be signed after World War I strikes in the postwar decade attested to a continued combativity not resolved through collective bargaining alone; strikes acted, among other things, as important leverage for bargaining.

Is it simply then a question of the usual stereotype differentiating the French and American labor movements: romantic revolutionary activity on the part of the former, reformist politics of the latter?[51] In this respect, the ILGWU seems largely to have mirrored, if not led, the American labor movement's twentieth-century search for stability through collective bargaining, whereas the French garment unions reflected the more fractured and rebellious nature of the French labor movement.

In their collective book on working-class formation in the nineteenth century, Ira Katznelson and Aristide Zolberg noted both economic and political variables that can account for the different paths taken by the American, French, and German labor movements. France (and a *fortiori* Paris, as we have seen) remained a country of small- and medium-sized entrepreneurs well into the twentieth century, while massive industrialization and urbanization occurred more quickly in the United States. Political scientists have characterized the French state as strong, the American state as weak. All of these differences explain how a more embattled artisanal class transformed its corporatist language into a fiery class-conscious one in France, while the United States effected the transition with a less combative labor movement.[52] Of course both of these images, and explanatory devices, have been nuanced in important ways by those trying to answer Sombart's poorly posed question: Why is there no socialism in the United States?[53] Yes, Sombart, there was (some) socialism in the United States; no, Sorel, not all French workers were committed to the general strike.[54]

I would suggest, however, that another level of analysis can shed different light on the question. The answer may lie less in national-level schemas than in industrial-sector studies.[55] If we return to the postulate that the garment industry, in its broad outlines, is globally more similar across space than different, in spite of varying rhythms

Bermuda Shorts

of development and different perceptions of the industrial "other," a single-industry study, with two very different labor movements, must question national-level analyses that explain industrial relations largely in terms of economic development.

How is it that an industry basically similar in structure led to such unlike organizational forms in Paris and New York? Admittedly, if we remagnify the small differences, perhaps the premise of similarity is faulty. It is true that the relatively slower pace of ready-to-wear expansion in Paris may be partially to blame. Indeed, the early history of the French garment labor federations was marked by disputes between tailors and *confectionneurs* over the very nature of the industry. Conflicts between custom tailors and ready-made garment workers persisted through the end of the nineteenth century, marked by resentment and disdain of the former for *la confection,* "this evil which harms the worker."[56] The ILGWU, by contrast, was founded concomitantly with the rise of ready-to-wear and was a union of ready-made workers from the beginning; it did not have to defend against or appease made-to-measure tailors within its ranks.[57] Timing may thus be a key to different developments. The ILGWU was created in that period when the move to larger factories in New York City was most prominent.[58] This does not, however, explain why the French unions were not more successful in organizing the large Printemps or Galeries Lafayette workshops, nor how the ILGWU reconstructed its predominance even after the industrial norm reverted to jobbing and subcontracting.

If we return to the notion of transatlantic similarity, the more precise comparative question is how, under conditions of relatively small, scattered manufacturing shops, was the New York–based union able to forge a strong institutional presence, whereas the Fédérations de l'habillement, while supporting several important strike activities, never had the same organizational impact? These different outcomes show that (1) neither technology nor industrial development necessarily explain patterns of industrial relations, (2) nor do national explanations that ascribe small-scale industrial characteristics to France alone. That is, in the context of a similarity of structure across time and space, neither different perceptions of fashion, different markets, different rhythms of growth nor different timing of union development seem adequate to explain the different forms of labor organizing spawned in each city.

We have to look elsewhere and reexamine the political sphere. It is not simply a question of some vague political culture—reformist or revolutionary—reflected in each union, but more concretely each union's relation to the political realm. Two specific, historic factors seem more pertinent in understanding the different paths taken by the garment unions: their confrontation with Communism and, more generally, their relationship to the welfare state.

The garment unions' experiences with the Communist "opposition" (as it is called in ILGWU history) or "split" (as it is called in French historiography) had significant consequences for the two unions. The terminology alone makes the different outcomes transparent. In the case of the ILGWU, this was part of a particularly New York City story of industrial radicalism, which touched only a few other AFL unions, and which, by the 1930s, had led to the fairly successful routing of the Communists from the union. Then and henceforth described as an "opposition" that had been ousted, the small Communist Needle Trades Workers' Industrial Union never represented a serious full-fledged threat to the ILGWU.

In France, however, the national-level political divorce between Socialists and Communists at the Congrès de Tours in 1920 went well beyond industrial oppositional politics and had major repercussions in almost all unions. In the 1920s, this meant the creation of the CGTU parallel to and initially more combative than the old CGT. The political nature of competing union formations continued into the postwar period. After World War II, a "free trade union" CGT-FO (Force ouvrière) split off from the reunited CGT. Ironically, perhaps (but not incomprehensibly), this break—to the right this time—was effected with the AFL's and David Dubinsky's help and encouragement. Rival national federations in France along political lines have persisted to this day, with CFDT (Confédération française démocratique du travail) and CGT unions still competing for garment-workers' votes, membership, and attention. Ideological differences, mirroring larger French politics, have contributed to a relative institutional weakness of the multiple French unions in an already splintered trade.[59]

The state has also played a contrasting role in labor relations in France and the United States. The preferred American strategy of collective bargaining has, with the exception of the New Deal period, explicitly refused government intervention; the American

Bermuda Shorts

Federation of Labor had espoused a policy of "voluntarism" in which unions regulate labor problems without interference from the state. French unions, however, have in all sectors traditionally considered the state to be an important part of the regulatory mechanism. Furthermore, they have emphasized industry-wide *conventions collectives* and legislation rather than American-style firm-level negotiations.

Beyond the state's role as potential arbitrator, its role as welfare provider has had an important but too-little-explored impact on labor organizing down to the garment unions. The American union has been especially strong where the state has been weak with regard to providing medical and retirement programs. By providing the health and insurance benefits that the United States system does not, the ILGWU has stepped in where the state still fears to tread. In this view, the early founding of an ILGWU Health Center in New York City (in 1914) was perhaps more than just a precocious expression of union welfare-ism. It can be taken as a symbol for that which would become one of the American union's greatest strengths: "benefits." A 1980s survey found that, even before fighting for wages-and-hours standards, benefits were the main reason given by a majority of the members for belonging to the ILGWU. In a trade marked by small shops offering little health-and-welfare benefits of their own, such support is crucial. In France, such a role has been unnecessary, since the more comprehensive French social-security system was established after World War II.

By temperament, rhetoric, and strategy, the ILGWU and the Fédérations de l'habillement could not seem more different, while the urban industrial settings of small shops of immigrant workers remain stubbornly alike. Clearly, other comparisons could yield other conclusions. If the ILGWU has been reformist compared to the French labor unions, it was, after all, a constant prod from the left vis-à-vis the American Federation of Labor for much of the first half of the century. French garment strikers, more militant in the inter-war period by comparison with American garment workers, have never been as successful as the French printers in their claims. Ultimately, the comparative images are themselves contradictory: an American union that is strong yet not militant, a French union that is weak but feisty. The differences, however, reflect more on their specific political environments than on the nature of the industry.

Ready-to-Wear and Ready-to-Work

Finally, then, how do the states differ in their relationship to the industry per se? A lively debate has begun over protective legislation in a comparative perspective, attempting, it seems, to attribute kudos to that country deemed more progressive. Were they the European countries, early implementers of a protowelfare state, or the United States, as Theda Skocpol has recently argued, contrary to previous opinion?[60] The answer seems to depend on how the question is posed, how "progressive" is defined, what aspect of the welfare state is compared, and for which countries.

First of all, different temporal perspectives can yield different appreciations of laws and their effects. The older American historiography of labor legislation saw the turn-of-the-century reformers' successes in a progressive light, corresponding to the actors' self-designation. Along a temporal span of comparison, things did keep getting better. But more recent historiography has questioned the linear nature of improvement by querying the intent of the reformers, redefining what welfare is or should be, and in some cases turning to a spatial comparison to make the point.[61]

The answers may differ depending on the units and criteria being compared. In contrasting German and French social policies, Allan Mitchell describes a rather classic French lag, consistent with his earlier work.[62] But, comparing France and England, Susan Pedersen is more guardedly optimistic about relative French "successes." While France may have lagged behind Germany and Britain with regard to social insurance, the Hexagon was a veritable pioneer with regard to family allowances, which she postulates as fundamental to the welfare state itself.[63] In comparing France, Germany, Great Britain, and the United States, Seth Koven and Sonya Michel have distinguished between strong states and weak states, arguing that the stronger French and German states ultimately provided more in terms of protection than the weaker British and American ones.[64] Similarly, with regard to France and the United States alone, Alisa Klaus and Jane Jenson have each pointed to the relative merits of the French conceptualization and practice of protective legislation. Klaus concludes: "The irony, of course, is that although women seem to have wielded greater power in the United States, in many ways the French state treated motherhood with much greater respect."[65]

Bermuda Shorts

From many recent feminist perspectives, however, the evaluation of late-nineteenth-century reform, whether in France or the United States, has been harsh. The labor laws that began to be passed around the turn of the century have been reinterpreted as a willful attempt to set up a dual labor market, with "protected" women shunted into the secondary sector. Mary Lynn Stewart has most forcefully argued that the 1892 French law limiting hours for women and children was based on a different logic than appeals for universal, non-sex-specific labor protection, and that it should not be integrated into a progressive history of the latter. Instead of protecting women, the 1892 law actually aimed to protect men's jobs from female competition.[66] Similar arguments have been made for the American case.[67]

The differences in fact and interpretation can be seen most strikingly with regard to that which had the most potential impact on garment work: homework legislation. American and French homework laws differed in one important respect. Laws to abolish homework were passed in the United States. Only lip service was paid to the idea of regulating it in France. This contrast has generally been explained as cultural. However, the homework debate can be seen from at least three different perspectives. First, a comparison of homework proponents and opponents on both sides of the Atlantic shows a certain similarity in the arguments of those for and of those against, no matter where they live. Nonetheless, the different legislative outcomes show which attitudes toward homework "won out" in each country. Yet, third, we can also ask whether looking at effect rather than intent does not bring us back to greater similarities over time.

General mores everywhere stressed belief in the sanctity of the home and in "sacred motherhood" or the *femme au foyer*. In both New York and Paris, proponents of homework argued that it saves the home, while critics said that it destroys it. Homework generated an important discussion centered on female labor, infused with a moral vision of family life and an interpretation of gender roles. Early defenders often framed the debate in terms of a defense of the (male) private sphere in which the state should not interfere. "A man's dwelling house is his castle" went the argument in the United States; the *"droits du père de famille"* were considered inviolable in France.[68]

Homework opponents on both sides of the Atlantic, however, criticized not only the "*confusion des espaces*" or the "*'pollution' de l'espace domestique*" that homework produced, but argued that *it* (rather than the state) interfered with male prerogative. A normative division of labor within the family meant the man's right to a hot meal prepared by his wife. French reformers and American social feminists alike argued that homework hurt the home, and if mothers had to work, they should do it in the factory. Labor leaders in both countries also argued for organization in all senses of the term: by organizing (concentrating) the labor process, the better the chances of organizing (unionizing) labor (and better protecting—male—factory workers from unfair competition). Homework was bad for the homeworker but also bad for the shop worker. In defending women and the home against homework, critics of homework in New York and Paris argued for women's difference and the need to protect them. Ultimately discourses both for and against homework in Paris and New York were based on common notions about the sanctity of the home, husbands, children, soup. They have differed only, but importantly, on how best to preserve that sanctity.[69]

Beyond the similarities in the pros and cons, there was a different emphasis in the language of reform and, more importantly, a different legislative outcome in each country. In the United States, reformers sought to protect mothers by separating work *from* the home and eliminating homework that soiled the image of a home-sweet-home. In France, the reformers who got the upper hand sought to defend mothers by allowing them to work *at* home, seen as the proper place for them. Furthermore, anxious on moral and military grounds about the slow population growth, French Catholics and pro-natalists were more reticent to send women to the factory.

The language is particularly revealing. Homework supporters in France infused their arguments with an emphasis on individual liberty and privacy, whereas early American legislators more generally grounded their arguments on the notion of freedom of contract. American supporters of homework argued successfully in the case of *In re Jacobs* in 1885 to strike down an 1884 bill prohibiting cigar manufacture in tenements on the basis of the male independent artisan's right to contract. Restrictions on homework (rather than homework itself) were considered an invasion of privacy in France, a limitation to individual liberties and an interference into the male

Bermuda Shorts

[sic] domain of the home.[70] As for women, increasingly envisaged in both countries as the only sex of homeworkers, French reformers of the late nineteenth century continued to be more explicitly concerned with the larger issue of how to regulate working conditions without interfering with individual freedom, while American opponents of homework became more critical of the home atmosphere violated by industrial homework.

A closer look at the French and New York laws provides a more complicated picture than one of simple difference across national boundaries.[71] A New York State law of 1892 set up a licensing procedure for family homework that was reinforced in 1899. In 1911, the State Factory Investigating Commission Report suggested complete abolition of tenement work, but then (only) recommended reinforcement of existing licensing laws.

In 1892, the same year as the initial New York legislation, an hours law was passed in France to protect women and children by limiting female and child factory labor to eleven hours per day and banning night work for them. The law specifically exempted much seasonal work, including the garment industry, and more generally excluded both the home and men (the latter were viewed as independent citizens whose working day was governed by the notion of *liberté du travail*).[72] Although hours limitations were extended to men in 1900, homework was still exempted on the grounds that any such legislation was an invasion into the private domain of the family. A French health-and-safety law pertaining to mechanized shops only was passed in 1893. The first legislation directly concerning homework was not passed until 1915, in the context of war and increased demand for military uniforms. A minimum wage for female homeworkers was voted, to regulate rather than abolish homework. The 1915 law further stipulated that prices for each garment had to be clearly posted and that all contractors had to keep a register of their homeworkers. (The law was only extended to male homeworkers on December 14, 1928.) It also, however, had very few sanctions written into it. The French did not institute a general registration system for homeworkers until 1957.

In the meantime, American efforts to regulate homework continued apace (albeit a very slow pace). The United States Women's Bureau (a fact-finding agency within the Department of Labor) itself had mixed attitudes about homework: calling for a family wage for men and mother's primary responsibility for childcare but also decent labor conditions for working women.[73] Things finally came to a head with the National Recovery Administration (NRA) codes which banned homework and reemphasized the notion of a family wage for men to support the whole family. Although the federal codes were subsequently deemed unconstitutional, a New York State law of 1935 strengthened homework licensing requirements, leading to a more general ban in 1945.

Two conclusions may be drawn from this legislative history. One emphasizes the difference between the French and New York law, to the benefit of the latter for its "abolition" and not just reform of homework. Another conclusion, however, looks more generally at the relation between the state and reform. Here there are two camps. The optimists have argued that the state helped improve working conditions. The pessimists have challenged the ideology behind the laws, pointing out that they only served to marginalize those whom they were pretending to protect. This criticism has focused on intent (the gender analysis drawing strikingly similar conclusions both sides of the Atlantic): the progressive reformers were not so progressive after all; homework legislation, like factory legislation, only restricted women's choices. Jane Jenson has explicitly disagreed with the pessimistic critique, arguing that the shortening of women's hours must be situated within a more general move toward shorter hours for all; French notions of gender at least conceptualized the working woman and passed legislation specifically for her (in 1892), whereas she was practically invisible at the federal legislative level in the United States.[74] Does the legislation construct gendered notions about work or vice versa? Was protective legislation for women a first step toward regulating general labor conditions, or did it in fact intend to keep women in a secondary labor market?

I would emphasize that for the garment industry in particular, we must look beyond intent to effect. As Eileen Boris shows for the American case, chronic underfunding of labor inspection undermined enforcement again and again; and in the context of state-level rather than federal legislation, New York City manufacturers could simply send homework across its narrow border out of state. In this respect, Miriam Cohen and Michael Hanagan's comparative study of American and French homework legislation has stressed the global similarities in the rhythms of the laws in France and the United

Bermuda Shorts

States. They have looked less at intent than at effect in placing the two countries' early efforts within the broader context of the era of rising protective legislation. They see abolition and regulation as two tactics of a similar reform impulse, in which both countries ultimately tried to regulate homework at a certain stage of capitalism and under pressure from reformers. Yet, in spite of attempts to either abolish or reform it, as they well remind us, neither country made any real progress until the New Deal and Popular Front eras.[75]

In both countries, labor bureau reports are legion lamenting the lack of adequate resources for enforcement. Most commentators on the 1892 laws in both France and New York observed that they were never properly implemented. This was true even beyond the heroic 1930s. Shortly after the National Recovery codes were passed, the ILGWU was still complaining about homework in 1937. And even after the 1938 federal Fair Labor Standards Act was initially hailed as an important stabilizing force in labor conditions, two union investigators argued in 1941 that the net effect of that law was only to increase homework as a way of evading wage-and-hours provisions.[76] Homework began to reappear after the war and has grown again in recent years.

The return to homework in certain industries became official in the United States in the 1970s, while it had never been abolished or adequately regulated in France. In the 1980s Reaganian atmosphere of deregulation, a move to overturn earlier bans was ultimately successful, thanks to arguments once again couched in terms of freedom versus constraint, with advocates of free enterprise countering defenders of workers' rights and New Deal laws. The ban on homework in five industries—gloves and mittens, buttons and buckles, embroidery, handkerchiefs, and jewelry—was lifted. However, the ILGWU has thus far been able to battle successfully the Department of Labor to prevent the reinstatement of legal wage homework (other than for the elderly and disabled) for women's apparel. Those who uphold the ban have called anything less a return to the Dark Ages of worker exploitation; those who want to remove the ban and re-legalize homework use the language of "rights": women's rights, mothers' rights, the rights of the disabled.[77]

Attempts to regulate or eliminate homework have consistently confronted needs of seasonal production. Differences in laws and intent may look more similar at the level of (poor) application and

Ready-to-Wear and Ready-to-Work

effectiveness over time. Legislators and their historians need to chart the similar stories of non-enforcement in a flexible economic environment. As we will see below, the differences between the two cities pale further when we look at immigrant workshops and sub-contracting in general. While New York law restricted homework, small-family workshops remained legion. In Paris, immigrant work-shops were abundant, too, alongside the female homeworkers and no less persistent neighborhood *couturières*. How different, ulti-mately, were the functioning of family and immigrant workshops and homework?

The comparative vision is most often read as difference, a differ-ence not difficult to document. Images of competition and reflections on fashion and taste have at times been at distinct odds from Paris to New York. Discrete markets, varied rhythms of growth, variable union strength, and homework legislation provide important chrono-logical and spatial variations on the garment story. The variants are all the more important in a poststructural analysis. This does not mean, however, that we cannot return to comparison as similarity, with a closer look at labor conditions and at the women and immi-grants working the sewing machines.

Bermuda Shorts

"Oh dear! How antiquated!!!" "Oh my! How foolishly new...." Late eighteenth-century French caricature. (*Cabinet des estampes, Bibliothèque nationale*)

Hoop skirts, a brief fashion flame of the early 1860s, were one of the early ready-made items made under factory conditions. (*Courtesy of Fairchild Publications*)

Advertisement for a ready-made linens-goods factory in Paris, 1872. *(Cabinet des estampes, Bibliothèque nationale)*

(Above) "It's fun to be a man!" reads the caption of this 1872 caricature by Grévin in *Les Parisiennes*. But if cross-dressing was still formally illegal, the masculinization of women's styles was proceeding apace by the turn of the century.

(Left) In this 1913 edition of the *Journal des Dames et des Modes*, a fashion plate by Bernard de Monvel Boutet shows the evolution of the woman's suit. The commentator, however, was still skeptical of this trend. *(Both images Courtesy of the Bibliothèque nationale)*

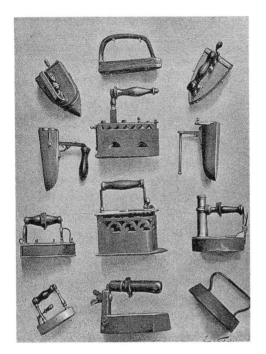

Irons exhibited at the International Exhibition of 1900 held in Paris. *(Courtesy of the Bibliothèque historique de la ville de Paris)*

Thimonnier's sewing machine: 1830, 1845, and 1848 patent models. *(Courtesy of the Bibliothèque historique de la ville de Paris)*

LA SEMAINE ANGLAISE

A L'ATELIER   **LE SAMEDI APRÈS-MIDI**   **LE DIMANCHE EN FAMILLE**

Que de tableaux charmants, que de ravissantes perspectives de vie heureuse nous présage l'acquisition de la Semaine Anglaise !

Mais il faut la conquérir. Le pourrons-nous? Certainement, pourvu que nous ne comptions que sur nous-mêmes

La voilà l'œuvre immédiate à entreprendre ! La voilà l'action persévérante qui s'offre à nous !

Hardi ! les travailleurs de toutes corporations pour la conquête de la Semaine Anglaise !

Elle nous donnera un jour entier de re-

pos hebdomadaire ; elle nous incitera à vouloir abréger le nombre journalier de nos heures de travail ; elle nous donnera le temps de mieux vivre.

Pour nos familles et pour nous-mêmes, conquérons donc la Semaine Anglaise !

(Above) Poster of the 1912 Confédération générale du travail (CGT) union in favor of the English-style week that gave women Saturday afternoons off (to clean the house!) in addition to the Sunday day of rest. *(Courtesy of the Bibliothèque nationale)*

(Right) The cover of a lively historical and informative brochure published on the 60th anniversary of the founding of ILGWU cutters' Local 10. *(Courtesy of UNITE)*

Skirts in comparative perspective: Paris style (top), and New York style. *(Drawing in Murray Sices, Seventh Avenue. Courtesy of Fairchild Publications)*

II

THE

SOCIAL

CONSEQUENCES

OF

FLEXIBILITY

5

THE SWEATSHOP AS WORKPLACE AND METAPHOR

A t the turn of the century, the Frenchman Emile Levasseur, like many social investigators before and since, climbed the dark, dank hallway of a New York tenement in order to examine a garment workshop firsthand:

Visit to the "Sveating [sic] system." . . . They were situated in the South-East portion of the city, in dilapidated-looking buildings; the wooden steps shook, narrow and nauseating toilets were in the stairway, medium-sized rooms where some twenty workers worked like demons, cutting, placing buttons, ironing, each according to his specialty. The windows were open and, although it was very hot, the temperature was not stifling; but the spectacle of such feverish activity, of all of those hands following the movement of the machines made me think of one of the circles of hell in Dante.[1]

While Levasseur's vision has been analyzed as more literary romanticization than social realism,[2] the sweatshop which he and others discovered has come to symbolize recurrent labor conditions in the garment industry. I would like to reexamine that imagery by turning now from industrial structure to shop floor and exploring working conditions in the various places of garment manufacture. Economic history can be written without the workers, but it should not be.

The garment industry has recently been rediscovered as an example of flexible specialization. Its light industrial structure—like nineteenth-century cutlery works or contemporary American mini-mills—is another example of an artful balancing act between rigid forms of production and volatile demand. This success is furthermore underwritten by a moral order in which unspoken codes of conduct bind the flexible specialists to one another. Jonathan Zeitlin and Peter Totterdill have perhaps most explicitly characterized the optimistic view, for the British case, heralding garment production flexibility as a successful model that will save the industry from extinction.[3]

Nonetheless, there is a competing and much more pessimistic image of the industry which even today echoes Levasseur's vision of yesteryear. The sweatshop as workplace and metaphor poses a problem for the theorizing of flexible specialization. To what extent are they linked? To what extent does the former characterize some aspect of the latter?

The economics and politics of flexibility—from the viewpoint of capital—can be summarized by three basic elements: the avoidance of fixed costs, a fixed labor force, and fixed rules. Flexibility permits the adjustment of supply to demand by cutting the risk of long-term investment, adjusting the labor force to production needs, and limiting rigidities due to union and legal restrictions that regulate wages, benefits, social welfare payments, and working conditions. At a systemic level of analysis, the flexible model has an inherent beauty. However, managing variability does not mean that it disappears. Responsibility and costs are shifted elsewhere.

By looking at what I would call the social consequences of flexible specialization, I will argue that the view from below offers a different perspective than the macroeconomic one. We can return to what Michael Piore analyzed earlier as those factors contributing to a secondary labor market: poor conditions, long hours, low pay.[4] The organization of labor in the garment industry, often characterized by a particularly extreme form of flexibility, creates both an image and a reality of a secondary labor market, which have an important effect on labor recruitment.

One hundred years of sewing, in comparative perspective, can be summarized by three *s*'s: skill, "seasonality," and subcontracting; that is, low skill needs (to which we will return in the next chapter); high seasonal fluctuations; and pervasive subcontracting. We have seen how the garment industry, from men's shirts to women's blouses, is comprised of different production units and how the women's-wear sector alone is a microcosm of the tensions between art and industry, flexibility and standardization. While a reorganization of work, an increased division of labor, deskilling, and the introduction of new technology form the history of much of the Industrial Revolution, two particular features have defined garment making since the nineteenth century: its flexibility of time and its flexibility of space. Seasonality and subcontracting emerge as leitmotivs from a composite picture of industrial sewing in the articles and archives, industrial surveys and memoirs of Paris and New York. The transatlantic comparison only reinforces the diachronic repetition. While labor legislation and generally better sanitary conditions have eliminated a certain amount of the dirt and dust since 1880, the theme of poor conditions remains. They seem to be constitutive of the industry and provide a cautionary tale about the understanding of flexibility, past and present.

Timing: Seasonal Production and Seasonal Unemployment

"Oh, that eternal repetition—slack, busy; busy, slack!"

"For the Sentier, it's cyclical hysteria: periods of devastating lulls alternating with weeks of frenzied activity."[5]

The first and foremost characteristic of the women's apparel industry is its highly seasonal character, itself a disincentive to heavy investment in fixed capital and labor costs. Seasonal fluctuation in garment production comes from both the functional and the fashionable. Changes in climate (literal seasons) cause us to don swimsuits in summer and turtlenecks in winter. Beyond that, however, fashion intervenes, adding a powerful figurative dimension to the notion of seasons. Turtlenecks are not always "in."

Depending on the specialty, the slow season can last up to four or five months a year. Some garments are more (literally) seasonal than others: rainwear, swimwear, furs. But even in ordinary outerwear,

Sweatshop as Workplace and Metaphor

dressier items worn in public tend to be more (figuratively) sea-sonal than garments worn around the house. Women's wear is more seasonal than men's. General economic conditions—appropriately called the economic "climate"—can also exacerbate seasonality, especially when retailers wait until the last minute to order. The International Labour Office (ILO) defined four different types of fluctuations as having an impact on the garment industry: long-term structural economic change; cyclical economic fluctuations (reces-sions, upturns); seasonal swings; and sectoral variations. Sociologist Carol Smith has suggested that we simply speak of regular and irregular seasonality.[6] The climatic season for swimwear is a known factor, but the latest fashion cut, a rainy summer, or a weak economy is not.

Dips in employment follow accordingly. Seasonal unemployment, a corollary to this form of flexibility, has been endemic to the gar-ment trade and images of it since before the advent of ready-made goods. The "slack," "slow," or "dull" season, as it is called in En-glish, sounds yet more ominous in French. *La morte-saison* or simply *la morte* (death) even moved into Parisian Yiddish to describe the downturn. As we know, a nineteenth-century model of full employ-ment never really existed. As Alex Keyssar has persuasively shown, people were frequently out of work and in between jobs. What made the unemployment invisible was the workers' continued connection to the countryside, enabling them to tide themselves over during the slow season. Yet even within occupations where employment was ongoing from one year to the next, pockets of precariousness were sometimes built into the yearly rhythm. Seasonal trades often af-fected women even more than men. With the mass migrations of the end of the nineteenth century, the new urban immigrants—male and female—were even more vulnerable.[7]

In the garment industry, the complaint about the slack season is an ever recurring one, although most garment professionals usually decry their period as a contemporary calamity, worse than ever before. Before the growth of ready-made goods, women's-wear tai-lors complained of the cyclical nature of balls and weddings. Early clothing capitalists criticized seasonal ups and downs as one of the worst evils of the trade. In the spring of 1916, American clothiers complained that an increased tendency toward style changes, since the fall season of 1914, meant "complete disorganization of whatever regularity there has been in an already irregular business."[8] Half a century later, at the first Technical Tripartite Meeting on the garment industry organized by the ILO, even though general prosperity meant that seasonal perturbations were relatively better than before World War II, they were nonetheless still considered enough of a constituent curse to be one of the three major axes of the commission's work. As American labor delegate (International Ladies' Garment Workers' Union [ILGWU] member) Lazare Teper pointed out, even in relatively good times, women's outerwear still suffers from seasonal instability more than most other goods. When a second tripartite meeting was held sixteen years later, seasonal fluctuations were still considered "a serious problem" and growing. Nothing much had changed by the 1995 meeting.[9] Today's ever-changing styles give even more urgent meaning to seasonal turbulence. Once again, current practitioners pronounce the hectic pace of change as unprecedented.

Yet while (almost) everyone publicly laments the ups and downs of production time, analyses have differed over who is to blame and what is to be done. The customer, and particularly women's whims, have traditionally been blamed for fashion's inscrutability and instability. Consumers' leagues in New York and Paris formally blamed demand itself and tried to convince customers to change their buying habits in order to make their purchases during the slow months. One of the more dramatic attempts along these lines was a Musée des horreurs économiques set up in Paris in 1908, similar to other *salons de la misère*. Aimed at raising buyers' consciousness to the conditions of production, the exhibit led viewers through a display depicting the grim conditions of garment making. At the end, the visitor was confronted with a big sign asking, Who is to blame? The answer was found in a large mirror: the consumer.[10]

Ready-made goods were initially conceptualized as a remedy for seasonal oscillations. In a first stage, they were made up during the tailors' slack period, giving workers relief from *la morte*. As ready-to-wear became a separate industry, it was conceived of as more orderly and less dependent on seasonal orders precisely because of its prefabricated nature. And to the extent that seasonal fluctuations were blamed on (female) capriciousness, the advance production of garments was seen as giving (male) manufacturers more control over such fashions and passions. Marx predicted that steam power would lead to factory production that would eliminate the "murderous, meaningless caprices of fashion."[11]

However, as a method of regularizing the rhythm of production, the ready-made industry failed. It soon developed the same bad habits as the tailoring trades, waiting until the last minute to create new styles. Ready-made methods shifted from being a "regulatory agent" to accentuating the "fits and starts and the periodic overwork." The trade thus remained "condemned twice a year to unemployment and twice a year to overproduction."[12] Neither regulating demand nor regulating production seemed to work. Customers kept their bad habits, and ready-made manufacturers acquired them. Retailers have only exacerbated the problem with last-minute ordering practices.

Manufacturers and labor unions have sought relief in two different ways: dovetailing and work sharing. Firms have sometimes tried dovetailing winter goods with summer ones. The ILGWU even suggested at one point that if you cannot beat the seasons then join them: export to the Southern Hemisphere, where the seasons are the reverse of ours.[13] More frequently, producers have tried switching from expensive to cheap dresses or preparing more standard items during the slack season. However, switchable skills or sewing machine attachments do not always match. Versatility can be checked by specialization. Unions have also tried to combat the oscillation of production by pressing for the elimination of overtime, insisting on extra money for it, and urging contractual limits on seasonal unemployment. In France, global solutions were sought for the garment workers' *veillées* by proponents of the eight-hour day and later the forty-hour week. The hardworking *midinettes'* lot became part of the larger issue of regulating working hours as a whole.

In the United States, the issue was addressed more specifically within the industrial-level collective bargaining procedure. The historic agreements signed after the 1909–10 strikes in New York included a provision for employers to divide the work equitably among workers during slack periods. The ILGWU was a pioneer in work sharing but continued to needle the employers to even out production schedules. The Committee on Resolutions stressed in 1922 that

We will insist on a shorter workday until such time when even the ladies' garment industry will recognize our rights to work normally and regularly throughout the year as human beings ought to work.[14]

A 1924 resolution was even more forceful:

The present disgraceful system of uncertainty, of frequent job changing, of daily job hunting, of repeated privations, misery, and despondency in the homes of the families of our great membership must be abolished.[15]

However, two paragraphs later, the committee admitted that the enforcement of guaranteed employment was a pious wish. Shortly after the 1933–34 National Recovery Administration codes were overturned, the ILGWU again complained about the "chiselers," who tried to continue their "old, nefarious ways and methods."[16]

Workers were supposed to expect the *morte-saison* and prepare for it. Work sharing could not eliminate seasonal fluctuations. In fact, any implementation of the former only acknowledged the irradicability of the latter. The sources emit a resigned sense of inevitability. In one early discussion about the setting up of a workers' fund, it was argued that payments could only be made in the event of unemployment beyond the *regular* slow season.[17] Commentators remarked that you cannot transform human nature—an instinctive desire for change—any more than you can alter the climate. As one French Ministry of Labor study observed, "The bosses hated the effects of downtime, the workers suffered it; all accepted it as an inevitable evil . . ."[18]

Only a minority of mostly entrepreneurial voices have admitted the virtues of seasonal fluctuations. Rush orders may be the bane of the industry's organization, but they are also the boon to its existence, the essential motor of ever-changing demand behind clothing and capital renewal. Even the effects on labor may not be so drastic in this view: the downtime gives women opportunity to catch up on their responsibilities at home. And, as one worker described it, in spite of laws or rules, workers would often sneak into union shops after hours when needed to work overtime and be paid double.[19]

Yet when workers in one turn-of-the-century New York shop went on strike to install a clock, they did so to protest against erratic hours.[20] Half a century later, the ILO study on seasonal fluctuations suggested several measures to reduce seasonal and intermittent un-

Sweatshop as Workplace and Metaphor

employment, from the most general to the more specific: increase consumption and thus clothing purchases; implement greater production planning; constitute inventories; manufacture complementary goods; simplify, standardize, and specialize production. However, recognizing the perhaps utopian nature of a call to eliminate variability in production, the commission concluded with a series of suggestions designed to attenuate their effects: contractor registration; work sharing; homework regulation; labor laws; unemployment insurance, etc.[21]

Labor laws and union rules have sought to regulate excessive hours. Unemployment insurance has come to cover the gap between seasons.[22] Yet fashion fluctuation and the extremes of overtime and no-time work have remained. The recurrent image abets the fact by relegating the industry to the secondary labor market. Long hours to fill an order are the modern equivalent of getting the gown to the ball on time.

Space: The Multiple Places of Production

If seasonality is the temporal expression of flexibility, subcontracting is its spatial manifestation. While seasonal unemployment essentially shifts the burden of the slack season onto the worker, contracting shifts risk as well as costs, of equipment and upkeep, onto the contractor or homeworker.

Garments can be made just about anywhere. The division of sewing labor, the separation of the stages of production, the light weight and low cost of garment technology, and the relatively little space needed to set up a garment shop have allowed a division of sewing space. Industrial garment making has thus sprouted and survived in the interstices of the modern urban environment, proving, in contrast to other forms of industrialization, that a division of labor does not necessarily imply a concentration of same. Garments have been made in tenements, loft buildings, high rises, and suburban homes. Machines have been set up in living rooms, bedrooms, dining rooms, attics, and garages in a creatively flexible use of space.[23] In what can be called the dispersed assembly line, home, workshop, and factory have coexisted as varied loci of production. While each has had its period of historical prominence, all three have persisted over the century, and the three uses of space are interrelated. Manufacturing space, like the latest trend in sizing, can be classified as small, medium, and large.

Factory

As we have seen, prior to World War I, the factory seemed to be gaining ground in women's-wear production both in New York and Paris, as Marx had predicted.[24] Early ready-made enthusiasts envisioned garment making along the classic lines of the Industrial Revolution and began concentrating capital and workers under one roof in order to save time in transportation and to ensure better supervision. The infamous Triangle Shirtwaist factory in New York employed some five hundred young immigrant women prior to the fire. The "manufacturer" (*manufacturier* or *fabricant* in French), who organized everything from designing to cutting to sewing to selling, could even be a department store. Galeries Lafayette in Paris had over nine hundred workers sewing at four sites in Paris in 1911.

However, even the most successful large production units had their limits. Too great a fixed investment was risky in the face of regular and irregular seasonality. Labor unrest—by "class-conscious flappers" and *midinettes*—also encouraged New York manufacturers and Parisian department stores to redefine the economics of concentration. The early clothing capitalists kept the core of production inside the plant and relegated seasonal fluctuations to outside contractors and homeworkers. Ultimately, however, this gave way to another type of spatial division that was not simply seasonal. The different stages of making and marketing clothes were themselves disaggregated. Sewing became increasingly separated from design, cutting, and sales.

In the United States, two linguistic innovations marked this shift. First, the terms "inside" and "outside" shops came to represent the big and the small, the standard and the variable, the manufacturers' core production plant and the shoestring-contractors' sewing shops. Before World War I, the term "manufacturer" meant one who assumed all functions within the industry, from conceptualizing a garment to selling it, even if the sewing was increasingly subcontracted out. By the interwar period, this separation of functions became formalized with the appearance of jobbers, who sometimes cut but never sewed. Jobbers[25] served as intermediaries between the factories and the firms that cut and their subcontractors who sewed, but they also began setting up their own cutting facilities. At this point, the term "manufacturer" itself underwent change. As jobbers began to cut and manufacturers sewed less and less, the two terms merged, although not before some hostile words were exchanged with the manufacturers calling the upstart jobbers "worms" and "parasites." Both "jobber" and "manufacturer" ultimately came to designate the clothing capitalists who put up the money, arrange for design and cutting, send out the sewing, and then ship the finished goods to market. By the interwar period, at the height of the jobber-contractor system, only about 20 percent of New York–made dresses were still made in inside shops.[26] The linguistic irony is that in most cases the manufacturer no longer manufactures; the contractor, *entrepreneur*, or *façonnier* does. As an article in *Le Monde* characterized the clothier Alain Manoukian in 1987: "He creates, he sells, but above all he does not manufacture. Result: one of the rare French textile successes."[27]

Contracting and Subcontracting: Beyond (Below?) the Secondary Labor Market

The New York State Governor's Commission was explicit: the small shop "permits greater elasticity and flexibility of employment."[28] Contracting, prevalent in the nineteenth century and having a renaissance today, had its heyday in the interwar period. "With $2,500, a few customers, and a colossal amount of nerve, almost anyone can go into the dress business," commented a 1930s magazine article.[29] While large production sites continued to exist (although increasingly moving away from Manhattan and Paris), the women's-wear firms of the urban centers shrunk in size as sewing shifted to the contractors' shops.[30] Contracting became and has remained the most emblematic symbol of variable production, where supply must meet ever-changing demand. The contractors' shops have come to represent women's wear, ready-to-wear, the garment industry, and flexible specialization in increasing claims of generality. Here is where current controversy over the "return of the sweatshop" lies. And here is where most of the immigrants work.

The advantages of contracting are many. As a system, it provides overall flexibility. For manufacturers, it shifts certain risks, costs, and responsibilities onto the contractor. Modern contracting has historically been a means of avoiding the rigidities inherent in labor legislation and unionization. And contracting has always been more prevalent in women's wear than in more standardized production. In 1958, for example, jobbers and subcontractors employed 67 percent of all workers in the women's outerwear sector across the United States, while accounting for "only" 45 percent of employment in men's and boys' apparel and 38 percent in women's and children's underwear.[31] Contracting provides opportunities for newcomers. The low start-up costs make entry into business easy, and contractors are most often immigrants who hire other immigrants. A readily available community labor pool has helped foster contracting from the Lower East Side of New York to the Pletzl of Paris at the turn of the century to both cities' Chinatowns today. In their most positive light, contracting shops have also been called "social shops," emphasizing their familial, ethnic, or simply more congenial character as compared to factories.[32]

Contractors come by various names and in various forms. The changing work organization, both in bespoke tailoring and ready-made manufacturing, was symbolized in French by the new category of *apiéceur*, first consecrated in a dictionary of 1836. These "proletarianized tailors" comprised a category as fluctuating in composition as in name (and even in spelling—two *p*'s mid-nineteenth century, only one later on). Later called *façonniers* and *entrepreneurs*, the *apiéceurs* were often both worker and boss, organizer of labor and laborers themselves, at the crux of a constantly changing yet strikingly persistent network of outwork, subcontracting, and homework. Levasseur distinguished between those who had shops of more than twenty workers and the *sous-entrepreneurs* employing less. Mirjana Morokvasic has calculated that 96 percent of the Parisian garment shops today have fewer than 20 employees. New York contractors in the 1940s often had between 35 and 40, similar to the Chinatown shops today.[33] However, contractors may or may not have a physical shop of their own; they may simply distribute work to a scattered (home) work force. Some contractors cut, most do not.

Sweatshop as Workplace and Metaphor

They may work for only one but usually work for more than one jobber or manufacturer. One recent study found up to six levels of subcontracting.[34]

Regardless of their size or setup, contractors are especially characterized by their low-margin operations. It takes little capital to set up a sewing shop and could be done for as little as $50 in 1900, $2,000 to $3,000 in 1924, $10,000 in 1942, and $15,000 to $25,000 in 1959 in New York City. In the early 1980s, a 25- to 30-person shop could be started with $25,000 in New York's Chinatown. In Paris, a contractor needs a minimum of 50,000 francs to set up a SARL (société à responsabilité limité, limited liability company) but more likely about 150,000 francs to go into business.[35] He or she who underbids the next contractor then gets the work.

However, business closings are rampant. Low capital correlates with high turnover. The dress manufacturer, engaged in a "razor-edged" struggle of survival and "known to doctors for his 'dress stomach' and his frequent nervous breakdowns," has been estimated to have an average business life of five to seven years. Firm births and firm deaths, a high "firm mortality" and "entrepreneurial turbulence" affect manufacturers, contractors, and workers alike.[36] A study of 927 New York contract shops existing in 1926 showed that 68.2 percent of them had closed within three years. In the early 1980s, the Chinese Garment Makers' Association estimated that one-third of the firms fold each year.[37] Contemporary figures for Paris range from 13 percent of contractors' failures yearly to an estimate that two-thirds of all new firms close within three years. Newspaper articles tell grim stories of contractors disappearing without paying their workers.[38]

There have been two basically contrasting images of the contracting system and the contractor. "Whoever says 'entrepreneur' generally says exploiter," commented one turn-of-the-century observer in France.[39] More crudely, contractors were compared to the ubiquitous cockroaches in New York City and were criticized for buying labor on the "pig market" (khazer mark in Yiddish).[40] An ILGWU report described the interwar contractors as "irresponsible beggar employers," adventurers, and parasites. Jesse Carpenter, in his book on collective bargaining, preferred "industrial termites" as his insect metaphor.[41] The contractor has been blamed for everything from maintaining a backward ("primitive") mode of production

Ready-to-Wear and Ready-to-Work

to preventing assimilation by maintaining and encouraging ethnic ghettos. A 1913 *Forverts* article argued that workers felt more dignified, "somewhat higher *spiritually*" in a big factory rather than at the mercy of the "one-cent" soul of the hated small-time boss.[42]

However, contracting has also had its advocates. Contractors defended themselves and refuted the image of oppressors: "We work harder than you. We earn sometimes less than you, in any case never more than you. We suffer from the hands of the manufacturers, what kind of exploiters are we?"[43] Jobbers and contractors alike have stressed the latters' independence. And workers too have been described as freer in the neighborhood shop context. In yet another *Forverts* article the same year, the contractor's shop was described favorably: discipline is less rigorous than in the factory; workers can go home for lunch; they don't have to be squeezed onto public transportation to get to work; and "the workman feels more at liberty" in the outside shop.[44] The immigrant contractor's shop can be, in short, a "cultural cushion" for employment.[45]

Yet at the same time, the Industrial Commission reported at the turn of the century that "The contract system possesses as one of its advantages, not merely the cheaper cost of manufacture, but also the shifting of legal responsibility from the manufacturer to the middleman."[46] According to one estimate, the contractor's labor costs represent approximately 75 percent of the price received for the made-up goods.[47] A 1958 OECD study showed that salaries represented only 11.3 percent of expenses in the American dress industry, *excluding* subcontractors, yet comprised 68.8 percent of the latters' costs.[48] By managing the labor supply, contractors manage economic as well as social flexibility. As William Reddy has forcefully argued, contracting relationships in general are never engaged among equals. What he calls asymmetric exchange relationships displace costs and risks onto weaker bargainers.[49]

Is contemporary contracting a new phenomenon, as Alejandro Portes and Manuel Castells have argued, implying that it is thus immune to the ills of its predecessors? "An old form in a new setting is, in fact, new."[50] The accounts past and present are too similar to be dismissed lightly. The long-term study shows what I would call an "intermittent continuity" in which Jewish-immigrant workshops in turn-of-the-century Paris and Chinese shops in lower Manhattan today have been described in details too much alike to be mere

Sweatshop as Workplace and Metaphor

literary convention. With variations, contracting keeps reappearing in an industry caught between the Scylla of standardized production and the Charybdis of flexible demand. Collective-bargaining agreements and labor legislation have ameliorated conditions, but contracting has permitted stubbornly recurrent pockets of evasion. The question remains as to whether volatile flexibility can exist without cutthroat competition, high turnover, and poor working conditions.

Contracting thus needs to be reconceptualized, between the literary excesses of the critics of exploitation and the optimism of some contemporary social scientists. Its long and persistent history gives lie to Marx as well as to protoindustrial imaging of outwork as a transitional stage of production doomed to disappear. Merciless competition also fits poorly with the notion of "trust relationships" described by Sabel, Zeitlin, and Totterdill as necessary for the industrial-district model of flexible specialization.[51] Furthermore, is there not a functional continuity between contracting shops and that ultimate locus of even more flexible production, homework?

Homework

"There were thread and cloth all over the apartment; the work came first, and room for living was wherever you could find it."[52]

An ILO resolution of 1964 argued that homework is not only bad for the workers but bad for the industry's reputation. Homework and subcontracting have been subsumed to the same function, as an ILGWU study of "Garment Workers of Other Lands" asserted:

In some countries, notably France, the development of large scale factory production of clothing has been checked by the persistence of homework, which exists for the same reason that the contracting system is found in England and the United States: it affords a cheap labor supply and is easily adjustable to market and seasonal requirements, and the cheapness of the sewing machine makes large investment of capital superfluous.[53]

The 1980 ILO report included homework as a category of subcontracting.[54]

As the contractor is to the manufacturer or jobber, so the homeworker is to the contractor: an elastic labor force, expandable and contractible according to the weather or the latest fad. The homeworker pays the overhead and usually for the sewing machine, and is the least-paid operator in the industry. Eating, sleeping, and working in the same place, the homeworker bears the brunt of the most flexible portion of production. Manufacturers, jobbers, and contractors can avoid social legislation, unionization, and benefits payments in the process. Economist Joseph Klatzmann has called homework a *"concurrence parfaite,"* a perfect labor market.[55]

Homework persisted and thrived in the transition from one *bloc socio-technologique* to another.[56] As demand grew, nineteenth-century tailors enrolled the help of their families for the least-skilled portions of the work. When wives and children became insufficient, a more elaborate putting-out system developed that spread rapidly with the growth of ready-made clothes. Yet even after the rise of garment factories, firms such as the Belle Jardinière kept a fluctuating population of homeworkers in what Marx called the "external department of the manufactories."[57] Native women (in Paris) and immigrant men and women in both Paris and New York have chosen homework as an entrée to the labor market.

By their nature, homeworkers are difficult to count. New York State licensing laws (of 1892 and 1899) helped the Commissioner of Labor keep track, although he kept complaining that he did not have enough inspectors to do so properly. Approximately 50,000 homeworkers were registered in New York City at the turn of the century, most of whom worked in the garment trade (cigar making was the other most frequent occupation). But the number kept falling, down to approximately 20,000 in 1913. By the late 1920s, the Labor Commissioner patted himself on the back for the declining numbers while admitting other explanations for the steady decrease: the immigration restriction laws; labor troubles; poor business.[58] Yet, not all homeworkers were registered. The New York State Factory Investigating Commission estimated that there were 125,000 homeworkers in greater New York City in 1913. In the 1920s, approximately 20 percent of the women's garment firms sent their work out of state, beyond the control of the New York labor inspectors. With the Depression, homework increased until the National Recovery codes of 1933–34 prohibited it in certain specialties altogether. As we have

Sweatshop as Workplace and Metaphor

seen, these laws severely curtailed but did not eliminate homework entirely, even when the New York state regulatory system took over after the codes were deemed unconstitutional.[59]

In France, where homework was never forcefully regulated, and where restrictive hours legislation in the factory even contributed to its spread, there are only global assessments of the numbers of homeworkers. One author estimated that there were as many as 1.5 million homeworkers in France before World War I, of which 850,000 worked in the garment industry. A late-1930s labor inspector guessed that there were still one million female homeworkers. There are no good figures for Paris alone.[60]

Homework is periodically proclaimed eradicated and just as frequently (re)discovered. In both Paris and New York there was a recrudescence of homework after World War II as a quick way of getting back to work. One source estimated that one-half of the women's ready-made goods were being made at home in France in 1950, with approximately 20,000 homeworkers in the Paris area alone.[61] In 1962, the New York State Department of Labor abolished its special homework unit due to its "apparent success" in policing homework and enforcing sanctions.[62] But in both cities the phenomenon finally decreased due less to legislation than to the long postwar boom. Nonetheless, like contracting and the sweatshop, homework has made a comeback in the last twenty years, from garment making to insurance-claim processing. Homeworkers constitute an estimated 10 to 20 percent of the current garment workers in Paris; there are perhaps 17 to 18,000 in the Paris area.[63] There have been similar estimates of 20 percent for New York City or 30,000 homeworkers in the city.[64]

Like seasonal fluctuations and contracting, there are several definitions of homework and just as many opinions about it. Ruth Shallcross emphasized in the beginning of her 1938 book on *Industrial Homework* that it can be bad or good, depending on who is doing it and under what conditions. Although she admitted that most homework took place on the "margin of employability," she objected to automatically defining homework as sweating and argued for the importance of distinguishing between desirable and undesirable conditions.[65] If the piece-goods-amidst-pots-pans-and-debris image has often been oversimplified, other representations have been more complex. Homework has multiple meanings in relation to space, skill, and the ownership of the means of production. And, like the contractor, the homeworker has represented both freedom and constraint.

The term "homework" designates a specific location of production, although a spatial definition is not sufficient. Housework is not homework, although Singer cleverly advertised his machines for both the homemaker and the homeworker. The term homework has generally been reserved for industrial production for the market as distinct from domestic production for home use. However, garment homework alone can cover a range of skills, from cutting off the last threads to fine hand finishing, from straight seam work and garment assembly to custom tailoring. Strictly speaking, dressmakers and tailors are often also homeworkers.[66] But too wide a definition of homework worried reformers, who did not intend to regulate individual dressmakers out of business.

At the turn of the century, many observers on both sides of the Atlantic thought that homework, "archaic" like the garment industry itself, was destined to disappear. But some of the French synonyms for it were telling. The early social investigator Le Play called it "*la fabrique collective*"; political economists Charles Gide and Charles Benoist respectively used the terms "*la manufacture à domicile*" and "*la fabrique dispersée.*"[67] Inherent in these terms is the notion that homework is a fundamental part of the industrial system and cannot be conceptualized as an occasional or marginal factor of production.[68]

Even defined as industrial, labor-intensive, low skilled, low paid, and unstable, homework is still subject to multiple representations. Images of homework are images of gender roles. The debate on homework is also a debate about the advantages and disadvantages of a flexible organization of work.[69] The boundaries between categories are themselves flexible.[70] Shopworkers can turn into homeworkers at night, when they take extra work home to finish. Homeworkers may be employed or self-employed. While some work alone, others employ family members or boarders. As many labor inspectors have complained, homework often means child labor as well.

At the same time, homework importantly provides work for some people who would otherwise be excluded from the labor market. Women with children, an unemployed husband, or a sick parent, or those whose cultural traditions make it "normal," have often turned

Sweatshop as Workplace and Metaphor

to homework to contribute to the family budget. Women's seasonal employment can offset male seasonal unemployment. Similarly, immigrants often work at home or in "social shops" to maintain ethnic or religious customs or simply to speak their own language. For all of these workers, informal recruitment networks aid the job search, and learning the trade from relatives or friends eases labor initiation rites. This is flexibility at its best.

Yet, finally, homework is subject to contradictory representations of freedom and constraint. Homework proponents from the late nineteenth century to the present have emphasized choice as an inalienable right, underscored by a language of liberty. Regulation interferes with personal choice and the use of private property, and women should be free to stay in the home. To the extent that individual choice has been championed for entire groups, women's rights (and an early defense of the rights of the disabled) have in such cases been opposed to a more general definition of workers' rights.[71]

Female homeworkers themselves have at times been adamant about their rights/need for the work, speaking with their hands.[72] New York and Parisian labor inspectors constantly complained about reticent compliance, locked doors, and the kicking, biting, scratching (and even blood poisoning) which they sometimes risked in the battle over the bundles, testimony to women's insistence in holding on to their work. Indeed, one American inspector lamented that "a New York factory inspector must have the abilities of the fabled French detectives in the popular novels" in order to investigate behind the scenes/doors of the garment trade.[73] Homeworkers have appreciated the sense of liberty and independence that working at home provides.[74]

In contrast to a language of freedom, flexibility, and individual rights are the constraints. Delegates to a French garment workers' congress of 1912 explicitly questioned the language of liberty. Bosses' demands, unreasonable deadlines, and the imperatives of piecework (the more you do the more you earn)—voilà, the invisible supervisors regulate the homeworkers' day.[75]

Ultimately, homework is almost a caricature of flexibility, both in its functioning and its representation. Even among homeworkers, there is a more stable and a more variable group, those who get work regularly and those who work less frequently. The discourse on homework has been multivocal over time, representing different agendas and ranging from idylls of the happy housewife or industrious immigrant combining home and work to denunciations of the horrors of the industrial revolution brought home. From the turn-of-the-century Italian homeworker in New York balancing twenty pairs of pants on her head to the Jewish immigrant shlepping his *toilette* (of piece goods) in the Paris *métro* to the Chinese worker taking a duffle bag full of work home today, the privacy of homework and the labor consequences of fluctuating demand are also visible on the street.

The "Return" of the Sweatshop?

When a foreman is in back of you, watching what you are doing—and God forbid you do just a little bit, he start screaming, he start yelling. . . . That's a sweatshop.[76]

The sweatshop has often summarized the worst of the seasonal unemployment, contracting, and homework paradigm all at once. It is a vivid vision that has been attributed to factory, shop, and home alike and has been used to denounce poor working conditions ever since the nineteenth century. Then and now, the term "sweating system" has been an emotional one, implying cramped space; long hours; low wages; child, female, and immigrant labor; exploitative middlemen; and/or germs.

The American vision of the tenement was not that different from Levasseur's view above:

[T]enements were converted into workshops, and here men, women, and children toiled in unventilated and badly lighted rooms. They worked early and late for starvation wages, often sleeping at night on the "bundles" to save time.[77]

The classic description of the sweatshop, whether in English or French, whether situated in New York or Paris (or elsewhere), is almost formulaic. A dingy, narrow stairway leads up to a dirty interior, where living and working space are intermixed. Kitchen utensils, piles of garments or piece goods, and a sick child, aged mother, or sickly husband huddled in a corner often complete the picture of the home turned shop. But the workshop too has filthy walls, poor

Sweatshop as Workplace and Metaphor

lighting, and bad ventilation, and it becomes "home" to newly arrived immigrants who stretch out on unsewn stacks of cloth or on
cutting tables at night.[78]

The literary vision leaves room for multiple definitions. As Judith
Coffin and Eileen Boris have shown, these images were part and
parcel of the reformers' view of a moral order and a gendered work
place.[79] However, beyond the exaggerated form that the moral ordering took lay a multiform criticism of conditions which the term
"sweatshop" summarized. "Sweating" as a metaphor for toiling and
severe exertion dates back to the fifteenth century, but the term took
on its modern meaning in the nineteenth century to describe conditions in the tailoring and ready-made shoe trades. At first sweating
referred to those working outside of corporate norms and exploiting
themselves. By the late nineteenth century, however, London social
investigators Charles Booth and the Webbs had set the literary stage
for descriptions which combined two essential elements: hard or
excessive work and the system of contracting—that is, the sweating
of others.[80]

The term became as widespread as both the conditions themselves and the growth of reformers' literature in the late nineteenth
century. Legislation against sweating conditions was passed from
Great Britain to New Zealand, and from Massachusetts to Illinois.
But no country wants to take credit for their derivation. The *Oxford
English Dictionary* attributes the origin of the term "sweatshop" (as
distinct from sweating) to the United States (in 1892). A French
commentator at the turn of the century complained that "sweating
system" was an inappropriate Anglicism. But the French never developed an indigenous word for it, speaking of *le sweating,* or, as
Levasseur perhaps understood it from an immigrant practitioner,
sveating. The New York State factory inspectors defined the sweatshop as a "foreign method of working" in contrast to the clean, neat
"American idea of doing business."[81]

The classic descriptions of the sweating system come from the
period before World War I. As one critical (Communist) observer
commented later, in spite of turn-of-the-century labor legislation
and the New Deal codes, "During the course of twenty years the
needle trades have completed a cycle—from sweatshop back to
sweatshop."[82] The Depression only gave it more scope. Debate cur-

rently exists as to whether or not the sweatshop has returned, in spite of union pressure and labor and housing legislation.

There are several indicators of continuity within change. In the late nineteenth century, cloth particles and dust, poisonous gases from irons, and steam from the pressing machines chronically led to tuberculosis (the "tailor's disease"). Today's workers suffer from bronchitis and asthma. Health and labor officials have tried to regulate dust and air, and the Triangle Shirtwaist factory fire in Manhattan in 1911 was a powerful stimulus to reinforce fire safety controls and better factory conditions. However, air standards have only been as successful as garment-industry regulations in general. New chemicals used to treat some fabrics have added new fire hazards. Even today, some garment workers call their factories and workshops a "death trap."[83]

To be sure, as Coffin has persuasively shown, the early *misérabiliste* descriptions of sweatshops that emphasized the dirt, dust, and disease were part of the reformers' rhetoric of pathology, a repulsive, morbid vision designed to combat the sentimentalist vision of the fairy fingers of the imagined seamstress. Behind their critique, the social scientists were arguing for order versus chaos, productive rather than unproductive, and male rather than female work.[84]

Yet the image has held on:

Today's sweatshops are physically not very different from those of the turn of the century: ventilation is poor; piles of fabric sit near boilers and gas burners; there are no fire exits.[85]

Newspaper reports speak today of squalid conditions in deteriorating factory buildings where illegal immigrants work ten to eleven hours a day without overtime and for less than the minimum wage. Chinese-Cambodians in Paris are reportedly working eighty hours a week during the season. Turks complain about how they have to wait for work, often in vain, and then, when the piece goods arrive, they have to work all night to finish assembling the garments for the next day: "It's like a prison."[86] Senator Leichter described the contemporary contractors' shops as sweatshops in his widely reported 1979–82 investigation into the New York garment industry. Drawing on an ILGWU evaluation, he estimated that there were approximately

Sweatshop as Workplace and Metaphor

3,000 sweatshops in Chinatown, the South Bronx, North Manhattan, and other boroughs of New York, employing some 50,000 people, up from less than 200 garment sweatshops, mostly in Chinatown, a decade earlier. Subsequent newspaper and magazine articles have repeated these numbers.[87]

The evidence seems in some ways contradictory. The union itself has a double language: stressing its past successes in a linear interpretation of betterment, yet at the front lines of those criticizing contemporary sweatshops. On the one hand, the labor history of the industry as constructed through the union records contrasts the sweatshops of the 1900s to the subsequent amelioration of conditions, thanks to union efforts and especially the legendary 1909–10 strikes. Louis Levine's early triumphal history of the union, published in 1924, set the tone for succeeding accounts: thanks to the ILGWU, the garment industry had evolved "from the early sweatshop to the present status of industrial citizenship."[88] As union leader Pauline Newman stressed in 1965, from the perspective of over half a century of union struggles:

I would like to tell the younger generation here . . . that my generation had the privilege, the great honor to fight and bleed in order to improve the conditions under which you work today. We worked 80 hours a week—I did anyway—in the Triangle Waist Company. You work 35. It took my generation to change conditions to those under which we work today. (Applause)[89]

Yet while hailing its past successes, the union has another discourse, renewing that of the earlier period: castigating current conditions in the workshops as anathema to everything for which the union stands. The two discourses are not contradictory. They are linked by the notion of return, which bridges the gap between memory and history. The ILGWU speaks of the return and reemergence of the sweatshop, a theme which does not conflict with its own representation of having brought about important, indeed heroic improvements. In the general press as well, the language of return has been prevalent: "96 Cents an Hour: The Sweatshop Is Reborn."[90]

Roger Waldinger and Michael Lapp have questioned this view of return as overstated. As they have rightly pointed out, Leichter's figure has been repeated over and again without apparent verification. However, the difference of interpretation seems to be in part a difference of definitions. Waldinger and Lapp define sweatshops according to the OECD definition as illegal or concealed employment, which they argue is much less widespread than commonly believed, while Leichter englobes hazardous and unsanitary working conditions, illegal practices, and health or safety violations in his use of the term.[91]

Beyond differing definitions, an important historiographic issue lies between the divergent views. Among other things, the sweatshop symbolizes a problem of analysis: continuity versus rupture; and the relationship of the sweatshop image to flexible specialization. Indeed, return is not continuity. There have been periods in which workshop or homework conditions have been better than others, periods of greater or lesser regulatory compliance, and periods of more or less public interest in exploring and exposing working conditions. Is the twentieth-century use of a late-nineteenth-century term simply a reformer's ploy, or does it imply a continuity of form and indeed of content? To what extent does the very repetition of the imagery over time reveal certain conditions structural to flexible specialization or merely testimony to the poverty or obstinacy of the reformers' vision?

Michael Piore and Charles Sabel have explicitly rejected the idea that flexible specialization leads to sweating:

Sweating, to underscore the point, is the generic response of embattled firms—whether mass or small producers—that cannot innovate. It is not a strategy peculiar to endangered flexible specialists.[92]

Obviously all flexible specialists are not sweaters. However, the concepts have too many characteristics in common for the parallel to be entirely dismissed. Flexibility in the garment industry has most often meant contracting within a context of cutthroat competition at all levels—between New York or Paris and Taiwan, between New York and Paris, among contractors in each city, and also among workers for scarce jobs during the off-season—which lowers wages and working standards. Flexibility, competition, and speed all seem to favor poor working conditions.

If dirt, dust, fire hazards, and excessive hours have thus permeated the definition of garment industry conditions to this day, I would argue that they have done so due to their very evocative power. Reformers past and present have indeed been bent on moralizing, but they have also aimed at denouncing and changing poor working con-

Sweatshop as Workplace and Metaphor

ditions. If the use of nineteenth-century terminology in the twentieth century is a reformer's literary tactic, it is one serving to criticize twentieth-century practices relative to twentieth-century expectations. Despite or because of its multiple definitions and romanticized imagery, the term "sweatshop" has become a metaphor for bad working conditions in general. Very recent uses of the term have even moved the sweatshop outdoors, to englobe flower farms, asbestos removal, and taxi driving.[93] Cloth particles in the air, long hours, and low pay may be relative concepts over time, but they are absolute problems decried in each period. To dismiss the turn-of-the-century language as an outdated image misses the point about the intended power of that imagery. Both the reality of poor conditions and the mobilization of this gloomy view of industrial sewing help define this sector within the secondary labor market. They also help explain the high percentage of women and immigrants in the trade.

The paradigm that emerged with the development of ready-made goods at the end of the last century has improved over time through hard-won labor legislation, union standards, and a general betterment of living and working standards. However, interpretations depend on comparative perspectives. Women's historians have minimized the union's gains by arguing that the male leaders were misogynous, a grave accusation for an industry in which so many workers are women. Evaluations also depend on the time period highlighted: memory of the Uprising and Great Revolt, reflecting a positive view of labor insurgency and worker agency; the New Deal period in the United States or the Popular Front in France, stressing state regulation; or a long-term history that can yield the contradictory conclusion that although labor conditions have improved generally over time, contracting and many of its evils have also remained stubbornly present. What strikes the historian of the *longue durée* is the persistence of complaints over time and space, of the difficulties induced by seasonality and contracting. The nineteenth-century sweatshop may not have returned to stay, but the invocation of its image tells us something about some of the pitfalls of flexible response to volatile demand. Both structure and its representation can account for the specific labor force drawn to the sewing machines, to which we will now turn.

6

WOMEN, IMMIGRANTS, AND SKILL IN THE GARMENT SHOPS

W ho would work under such conditions and why? Predominantly two types of workers have come to the sweatshops, and each has had distinct reasons for doing so. From the nineteenth to the twentieth century, the ready-to-wear revolution was accompanied by a global shift in the sewing labor force, from men to women and from natives to immigrants. The story is a complicated one, yet one that has most often been told in parallel fashion.[1]

The purpose of this chapter is to confront the two stories, thus questioning the very categorizations of "women" and "immigrants." At the same time, some of the causalities implicit in various explanations of labor in the garment shops may be challenged. Who caused the sweatshops anyway? Immigrants and women, or industrial flexibility? Labor supply or industrial demand? Homework, long hours, and low wages have been attributed to women and immigrants in a sort of *causalité sauvage* that has looked no further than a correlation of the labor force to working conditions in order to explain the latter by virtue of the former. As Mabel Hurd Willett wrote in 1902, the bad conditions in the industry were due to the "masses of helpless people" who congregated there.[2]

We need to examine the representations of skill attributed to women and immigrants along with those elements of choice as well as constraint which have shaped the garment labor force over the years. Changing definitions of skill over time have repeatedly reordered roles. These shifts, only perceptible over the *longue durée*, necessarily bring into question the very notions of "women's work" or "immigrant labor." Either these terms only have meaning for particular tasks at particular times, or they have been constructed by the industry in order to serve its faddish, fashion, and flexible needs.

Women's Work

In the apparel industry—trades are traditionally organized by sex.[3]

Sewing is women's work, as all little girls are supposed to learn. There are two levels of explanation of sewing as women's work: popular discourse—the arts-and-crafts and "pin money" theories of women's work—and the contemporary social scientists' explicit negation of that theory, based on an understanding of patriarchy and gender relations.[4]

From needle to treadle, from housework to homework, from the domestic sphere to the industrial one, women have been lauded as the thimble's best friend for two reasons: skill and need. Their "nimble fingers," their "sense of style" have been part of a panoply of popular explanations linked to a biologically determined notion of women's "natural" sewing talent.[5] This idea has passed from needle to machine and from the female consumer to producer. Women are good at making clothes because they are good at wearing them. The pin money (so aptly termed) theory of women's labor has been used to explain women's participation in the labor market, their need described as (simply) complementary to the male breadwinner's wage, their place assigned to the home. These concepts have buttressed the rationale for lower-paid female industrial homework since the nineteenth century.

Reformers countered that such justification was unfair, that women's wages were a necessary part of the family economy. Women's studies scholars of the last three decades have gone even further in seeking to demystify (before deconstructing) the ideology behind women's work as a result of gendered notions of work.[6] The garment industry is perhaps one of the most transparent examples of capitalism's use of patriarchal schemas to link women's reproductive functions to their productive ones. Outwork and homework find a rationale based on women's need to stay at home with their children and take care of domestic chores. Homework is linked to housework, production to reproduction.

The importance of patriarchy, and indeed very basic forms of paternalism, in shaping women's role in garment production clearly challenges the "fairy fingers" explanation of women's needlework. However, we can go even further by examining the process of labor segmentation diachronically. An important literature has shown how male-defined work became female-defined as a corollary to de-skilling.[7] Although this already implies a notion of contingency in the definition of skill, most scholars have argued that, once crystallized, gender definitions became stabilized. However, the garment industry, as we will see, shows how de-skilling can in fact have different gendered outcomes, when immigrant men are needy and willing to do needlework. Although women have almost always outnumbered men in the garment labor market and have generally held the poorest slots within it, gender roles have never been fixed. As men and women have entered and exited the needle labor force, tasks and travails have been redefined. The fluidity of the definitions is itself a clue to the weakness of conceptual and categorical absolutes.

From Women's Work to Men's Work to Women's Work: The Nineteenth Century

As we have seen, until the eighteenth century, with the exception of upper-class tailored wear, outerwear was largely made in the home, for the family, by women. It was during the "bourgeois century," the nineteenth, that such clothing moved massively from domestic to commodity production, with several attendant changes in the organization of labor. With the professionalization of garment production, the locus of production moved from home to workshop. Male tailors came to dominate the trade.[8]

Nonetheless, women then "re"-entered this branch in two ways: as fancy dressmakers and as lowly finishers. In the first case, a gendered division of labor arose, correlating fitter to fitted. Tailors made men's garments, while dressmakers clothed women.[9] However, in New York as in Paris, many more women came (back) into (commodity) outerwear production as wives, or as hired aides of unmarried journeymen. Merchant-manufacturers began farming out the sewing of the cheaper grades to women. Garment making, controlled by men, now had at least become paid work for women, although wives' and daughters' contribution to the family economy did not necessarily mean they actually saw the coins of their labor. An expanded outwork system, based on patriarchy, was entrenched before any technological changes occurred in the industry. And, as we have seen, homework was neither transitional nor marginal but became a confirmed ally of "industrial" garment manufacture.

The introduction of the sewing machine in the 1850s only reinforced this sexual division of labor and aggravated what Christine Stansell has called the "biological experience of class."[10] While nineteenth-century engravings show the cause of the tailors' bowed legs, as they sat cross-legged by windows, plying their needle, the sewing machine did not improve the hunched position much, and it was said that you could tell a seamstress or a tailor by their posture. At first, the machine—although initially resented and contested by the tailors as a technological threat to their manual skill—became *a male tool,* quickly spreading to military and civilian men's-wear workshops.

However, as the ready-made industry grew, the gender of jobs shifted. Women moved massively into all sectors of the growing labor force, doing everything from cutting and sewing to pressing and finishing, first in men's wear and then in women's wear. In Paris, women had increased from 60 percent midcentury to 90 percent of the clothing labor force by 1901.[11] By 1911, the New York Department of Labor reported unequivocally that custom tailors were men, ready-made homeworkers women.[12] The sewing machine had changed sex. It had become *a female tool.*

True, when the machine first spread in the late 1860s and early 1870s, some French doctors and reformers castigated the new invention as dangerous for women's health. They warned that the double-treadle machine could lead to involuntary masturbation, menstrual difficulties, and possible sterility.[13] The sewing machines have also been accused of causing neurasthenia, neuritis in the arm, and even partial paralysis. (The most common accident to this day is a needle through the finger.) But these worries ultimately took a back seat to Singer's cheery advertisements showing smiling women behind their treadles. The "Singer" was marketed specifically for the female user, at home or in the factory, and came to represent the interrelated spheres of housework and homework.[14] Over the course of the nineteenth century, then, sewing had been redefined from a female home preoccupation to male commodity production—with paid female help—to, massively, industrial work for women.

"The Problem of the Men Workers": 1890–1940

Let us first deal with the problem of the men workers.

I confess this will be a surprise to many old trade unionists who are not familiar with our trade. "What," they will ask, "may mean the problem of the men workers"! . . .

The men in our trade are a small percentage of all the workers. According to Mr. Stone's report, they are sixteen per cent, and the women eighty-four per cent. The field of employment for men is rather limited. In the largest shops and at the best lines of work no men would be taken. It is almost certain that in fifty to sixty per cent of the shops, men are entirely excluded.

When a man is sent down or when he loses his employment through another cause, it almost always takes him many months before he gets a new place of employment. . . .

In many cases, however, the men are weak and timid. . . . They try to show that they would not be strikers. They flatter the employer and the foreman; in other words, they act like traitors. . . .

The remedy, therefore, lies in both the men and the women putting the shoulder to the wheel and working together for a stronger Union and a better and nobler life.[15]

Men had not abandoned needlework, and they "returned" to the field, not as tailors but as garment workers, at the end of the nineteenth century. Indeed, in 1898, the New York State Bureau of Factory Inspectors painted a grim picture of women being "driven from" the manufacture of not only skirts, shirts, ladies' waists, boys' blouses, and feminine underwear, but even that bastion of women's work, ready-made dressmaking.[16] Edith Abbott cited the turn-of-the-century Industrial Commission report estimating that 15,000 to 25,000 girls had lost their jobs, concluding rather mournfully that the development of women's ready-made manufacturing had brought nearly 50,000 men into the trade who would not have been employed in the older system of dressmaking.[17]

In spite of these alarmist voices, men of course never became an absolute majority of needleworkers. However, they did increasingly shift in status from being solely tailors to being ready-to-wear workers too. In order for this to occur, definitions of sewing had to be redefined, albeit not without concern over changing gendered roles. "Alas! That I have lived to see this day when Anshel, the celebrated Reader of Scripture, must become a sewer of shirts like a common woman!" wept Anshel's wife in Sholom Asch's novel *The Mother*.[18] While male and female skill were both redefined downward with the increased division of garment labor, men nevertheless became particularly concentrated in certain specialties, such as the more demanding cloak-and-suit trade and the higher-paid crafts. Men's prowess was now defined as coming not from completing a whole garment but from cutting and pressing. While women took over the bulk of the sewing once defined as male work, men took over certain crafts (especially cutting) which had previously been done by women. As an ILGWU brochure later noted, "The work which men do today and which they pride themselves on as being 'men's work' was originally women's work."[19]

By 1900–10, the absolute and relative number of women in the garment industry began to decline, while men's participation, especially in the expanding women's-wear sector, grew. Although custom tailoring and dressmaking remained more sex-specific occupations in both Paris and New York, as the garment and its destined wearer became increasingly separate, the modesty of measurement no longer inhibited cross-sexed manufacture. The ready-made business developed a more "mixed" labor force. In Paris, where there were 14.2 percent men overall in the global *travail des étoffes* category in 1896, there were proportionately more men in ready-made alone: 20.1 percent men in *confection pour dames et enfants;* and 40.7 percent men in *confection de vêtements tout faits*.[20] While women continued to outnumber men by a huge margin, their relative percentage was declining; from a high of 86.6 percent of the garment labor force (*travail des étoffes*) in 1906, their percentage decreased to 78.7 percent in 1926 and to 74.4 percent in 1936. After a small rally in the immediate postwar period, women "only" accounted for 71.3 percent of the Parisian garment workers in 1962. Furthermore, one (declared) homeworker in five was male, contrary to most assumptions about an all-female occupation.[21]

As men entered factory-made women's wear in the United States in the second half of the nineteenth century, the number of women workers also declined, even more noticeably, from 85 percent in 1860 and 88 percent in 1880 to 66 percent in 1890 and 63 percent in 1905. In New York City, some 41.5 percent of the adult women's ready-wear operatives and pieceworkers were male in 1890.[22] In 1910, men comprised 46 percent of the garment industry factory operatives in New York City, 50 percent in 1920, and 45.8 percent in 1930, although women's share increased sharply during the Depression.[23] Gender segmentation varied by branch. Men constituted 77.7 percent of the higher-skilled women's cloak-and-suit workforce in New York City in 1919, while women were increasingly concentrated in the less skilled but expanding shirtwaist and dress factories.[24]

Between the world wars, women moved into more diversified occupations in both the United States and France. In France, where the garment industry had occupied a high of 27 percent of all women working outside of agriculture in 1906, it only employed 20 percent in 1921 and 15.5 percent in 1936.[25] Some provincial workers were going home to the farm, while some Parisian *grisettes* had gotten used to factory work, and both French- and American-born women were increasingly moving into white-collar jobs. Three other explanations have generally been given for the relative decrease of women in the American garment industry at this time, two of which are pertinent to Paris as well: changing technology, the decline of homework, and immigration. Physical strength or biological difference was the first explanation for the male takeover of the new foot-powered sewing machines in the 1850s, the heavy cutting knife introduced in 1876 (replacing the shears used by women), and the pressing machines of the 1890s (in spite of the fact, as Baum, Hyman, and Michel have pointed out, that any photograph of Eastern European women of the time shows them surely as hefty and probably as strong as men[26]). Second, the turn-of-the-century legal attack by reformers and ultimately the state on homework also contributed

Women, Immigrants, and Skill

to the decrease of women in garment making in New York. (This was not a factor, as we have seen, for France.) Thirdly, however, another "culprit" was designated in the substitution of male for female labor in Paris as in New York, to whom we shall return: the Russian Jew.

Male sewers have been a particularly urban phenomenon, largely due to the presence of immigrants. In 1919, whereas there were approximately 7 women to every male garment worker in New Jersey and Connecticut, and a ratio of 3 to 1 in Pennsylvania, there were only 1.5 women to every male garment worker in New York City.[27] Male (mostly Jewish) immigrant garment workers were especially prevalent in Paris in the interwar period. Foreign-born men (foreigners plus naturalized citizens) comprised 48 percent of all male garment workers in the city.[28]

This is not to say that men pushed women out of the sewing machine field altogether. The point is that, as a category, they had not abandoned needlework and even increased their numbers as the ready-made women's industry expanded. And in order for these changes to take place, definitions of sewing had to be redefined. Male garment workers worried defenders of female industrial work at the turn of the century. Their presence in garment industry history remains to this day a theoretical challenge to explanations based on "women's work" alone.

Back to Women and Back to Men

Ultimately, today, most sewing machine operators remain women, underlying the contemporary researchers' *imaginaire* and reinforcing interest in patriarchy and the discourse on sewing as "women's work." Yet where women have replaced men, this did not occur without grumbling, with employers stereotypically complaining that women are less reliable than men, more prone to absenteeism, and less skilled. In New York, after World War II, as women came to dominate the sewing labor force again and men moved off to retirement for the older generation or greater opportunities in an expanding labor market for others, definitions of skill and gender were reversed once more. Section work, for example, an increased division of labor which at the turn of the century had been blamed for forcing out of the workshops women who could not keep up the pace, accompanied a reinforced feminization of needlework in the post–World War II period. Older male immigrants griped against this labor reorganization and concomitant female incursion into their (redefined) skill.[29]

However, in a final twist to shifting gender roles today, there are women cutters and pressers in New York, and Turkish men at the sewing machines in Paris.[30] The Turks have set up shop with severance pay from the automobile factories and construction companies which had hired them during the economic boom. One estimate is that although 80 percent of the workers in the French garment industry are women, only 56 percent of those in the Sentier are. The other 44 percent are immigrant men. A *lycée* in the nearby Saint-Denis suburb even started sewing classes for boys at the request of Turkish parents there.[31]

How can we fully account for all of these changing roles in the gendered segmentation of labor? Neither pin money, patriarchy, nor inborn skill are sufficient explanations. In spite of the by-now easily dismissable popular claims as to the special nature of sewing as women's work and the more convincing social scientists' emphasis on the close relationship between patriarchy and homework, we see that women's and men's participation in the garment workforce has varied: over time, by craft, by specialty, by geographic area, and, as we will see, by nationality group. As Mabel Willett commented, if you study New York alone, you could conclude that women are not strong enough to work on men's clothing; yet in Chicago, Polish and Bohemian girls worked on the heaviest grades.[32] The long-term and spatially comparative perspective is revealing. "Men's work" and "women's work" are constructed historically (and sometimes geographically). What is male work in a Turkish garment shop in Paris today, is woman's work in a Paris or New York Chinatown shop a couple of *arrondissements* or an ocean away. Furthermore, changes over time do not proceed solely in the direction of de-skilling = feminization. Although men have repeatedly appropriated many of the better jobs, better salaries, and positions of power within the industry and the unions, they have not been only shop managers and manufacturers. They have been treadlers too. The constant redistribution of roles within the industry has only been possible through repeated redefinitions of categories concerning skill, machines, and

Women, Immigrants, and Skill

their operators. Today skill has become redefined as speed, sewing machines have been designated as women's technology, and male garment workers have largely retreated to memory. Yet the history of the industry, with its mixed industrial form of concentrated as well as dispersed labor, is perhaps the best example of how "women's work" could at different times be housework, homework, factory work, and "men's work."

The Immigrant Niche

The Jewish tailor is perhaps as much a stock figure in garment lore as the nimble-fingered seamstress. As an old Jewish joke goes: The father sends his son to Harvard Business School and then calls him in for a heart-to-heart talk. "Son," he says, "now is the time to decide. You have to make choices in life. So, what will it be? Men's wear or women's wear?" Nonetheless, the Jewish tailor can only be but a metaphor for other immigrants in the garment labor market. As we will see at greater length in the next chapters, over the last century sewing machines in New York and Paris have been run by Jews, Italians, blacks, Puerto Ricans, Chinese, Armenians, Serbian Yugoslavs, and Turks, to name a few. Explanations of immigrant labor in the "rag trade," like explanations of women's work, range from popular discourse about skill and need to social-scientific theory. However, immigrant skill is more often represented as imported rather than inborn, and immigrant need is often envisaged as that of the male breadwinner rather than "simply" extra "pin money." Furthermore, these popular images are often contradictory. Economic need, after all, does not necessarily imply prior skill; on the contrary, it can encourage skill acquisition.

Immigrants, like women, have been described as "accept[ing], and even offer[ing] . . . derisive prices [for their work]" due to need.[33] Both groups have been described as having a penchant for homework and informal recruitment patterns. But certain factors are specific to the needs of the newly arrived: the importance of quick access to a first job; the advantages of working among one's own, where traditions may be maintained and language is no barrier. Furthermore, as one recent observer commented: "With 6000 francs monthly, he [the Turkish cutter] earns ten times more than he would in Turkey, where he would surely be unemployed and have the dictatorship on top of it."[34]

Sweatshop investigators from the turn of the century to today have often blamed cutthroat competition, low wages, and poor conditions on the immigrants themselves, correlating dirty shops with unkempt newcomers. Availability has most often been the crux of this supply-side, labor-driven theory of industrial development. As the New York State Department of Labor stated at the turn of the century, the "almost inexhaustible supply of cheap labor" was one of the major reasons for growth of the garment industry.[35] Blaming immigrants for the very form of the industry is both generic and specific. It partakes in a standard complaint that immigrants drive down wages by their low standard of living and by accepting low prices for their work. But such explanations are furthermore often accompanied by racialist assumptions about imported group characteristics.

Social scientists have by and large questioned these "old-world traits" assumptions by arguing implicitly if not explicitly that cultural explanations are not sufficient. Political scientists have stressed political disabilities. Disenfranchised, sometimes illegal residents, immigrants take low-paying, semiclandestine jobs not for pin money but simply to survive. As a New York State labor investigator commented, "The fertile soil of sweatshops is an immigrant community living in fear."[36] Economists have situated the blame in the functioning of the dual labor market, while sociologists have stressed how immigrants use the opportunities of the industry as much as any inherent cultural predisposition to set up shop.[37]

Yet what neither the population explanations nor the scientific theories have sufficiently recognized is how "immigrant work," like "women's work," has been constantly redefined. The immigrant side of the story thus reinforces the point. Sewing is not just women's work nor is it a Jewish or Italian specialty. What was Jewish needle-work in the 1920s in New York or Paris (and still so in 1950s Paris), is Dominican sewing in New York or Turkish subcontracting in Paris today. Repeated waves of immigrants have learned to pedal and treadle, to become sewers, cutters, bosses, or "shleppers." Different tasks and different crafts have corresponded to the needs of different newcomers and the needs of the industry at their time of arrival. As I will explore more fully in the next chapter, ideas attributed to one group have often been carried over to the next in an ever-shifting

Women, Immigrants, and Skill

process of explaining sewing skill. Variety alone attests to something more general than national character or even entrepreneurial opportunity in explaining the immigrant presence in the industry. And the same phenomenon has been repeated from London to Chicago to Los Angeles, with different immigrants still.[38] "Immigrant labor" as a category adds further contingency to a complex model of labor segmentation.

If theories about "immigrant" or "women's" work cannot fully explain the garment labor market, what about "immigrant women," as a category and reality? Just as earlier analyses of women's work have emphasized gender over class or ethnicity, ethnic studies have generally overlooked women in two important ways. On the one hand, the immigrant worker has been largely conceptualized as a young, single male.[39] On the other, ethnic business theorists have been writing more about capital than about labor, more about entrepreneurs than their workers, and, implicitly if not explicitly, more about men than about women.[40] A growing body of literature has begun to put gender back into immigrant studies and ethnicity into gender studies. Can "immigrant women" bridge the epistemological gap between two discrete categories of analysis?

Immigrant Women

That the garment labor force has been constantly redefined over time does not mean that at any given time certain categories of workers have not had specific roles. Immigrant women have consistently filled the bottom rungs of the already low labor hierarchy. Italian embroiderers in turn-of-the-century New York, Puerto Rican women there today, like the Chinese immigrant women in the Paris or New York Chinatowns, are often represented as combining the attributes of skill and need relevant to both parts of their combined identity: inborn skill as women, imported with them via migration; the pin-money need of the married woman or daughter is overlaid by the more general economic need of the immigrant family.

Much of the recent literature on immigrant women and the garment industry can be categorized as one of three genres. As with current labor and social history in general, there are what I would call the pessimists, the optimists, and the functionalists. The first have pointed to the objective oppression of immigrant women work-ers; the second have stressed the latter's responses and agency, in terms of struggles, identity, and community networks. The third have studied the dual labor market.

Annie Phizacklea, for one, has firmly grounded much of her study of immigrant women in a conceptualization of what she calls a "hier-archy of vulnerability" in which unskilled workers, women, and immigrant women, in that order, are subject to low wages and poor working conditions.[41] Others have spoken of the triple oppression of class, gender, and ethnicity or race. Class and gender can make life miserable enough for indigenous female homeworkers. The foreign-ness encountered through migration can make matters even worse.[42]

In a path-breaking study of women in the ILGWU, Alice Kessler-Harris showed how immigrant women attempting to organize along gender and ethnic lines had difficulties in both regards. Middle-class feminists of the Women's Trade Union League did not always understand or sympathize with the working-class immigrant women. But Rose Pesotta, Rose Schneiderman, and others often fared little better with working-class Jewish immigrant men within the union. Women's issues were either ignored or used as a rationale for special "protection" of, often meaning discrimination against, women.[43]

Kessler-Harris's early piece stands at the crossroads of histo-riographic trends. Pessimistic in its understanding of how women were caught between gender and class agendas, it nonetheless led the way in analyzing key moments of immigrant women's agency. Susan Glenn, in her more recent book on Jewish women, has, not surprisingly, written a more celebratory book of the immigrant wom-en's life and labors.[44] While filled with hardship, their lives were also testimony to a determined willfulness. Carefully looking at the gendered division of labor in the turn-of-the-century garment indus-try, Glenn has noted differences between opportunities in New York and Chicago, and how, in spite of a globally sex-segregated craft structure, both men and women could be found behind the sewing machines and in other middle-level skill jobs.

A third approach looks at the distribution of immigrant women within the labor market, studying gender and ethnicity as criteria of labor segmentation, and at how these categories are constructed. In one of the few explicitly comparative studies, Thomas Kessner and Betty Boyd Caroli examined the occupational segregation of Italian and Jewish women at the turn of the century.[45] They found important similarities in gender-related preferences. Single women tended to work outside the home in both groups, while married women were discouraged from doing so.[46] However, more pertinent for them were the ethnic differences they found. Occupational patterns of Jewish women and Italian women more closely resembled those of their male ethnic counterparts than each other. Jewish women, like their husbands and brothers, performed more skilled work, whereas Italian women "specialized" for the most part in less skilled work, like Italian men.

The construction of the comparative study is crucial. By postulating the category "women" as a constant and treating immigrant characteristics as variables, Kessner and Caroli's conclusion that ethnicity is more determinant than gender is not surprising. Studying gender at a more general-level description, Elizabeth Ewen has stressed the fundamentally similar rather than different experiences of these immigrant women qua women.[47] Miriam Cohen has since suggested a more nuanced analysis with regard to different patterns of work and radicalism on the part of Jewish and Italian women. Insofar as Italian men earned much less than Jewish men, this alone may account for different work patterns for women within the family economy. Yet, where there were similar economic circumstances, she argues, there were similar employment patterns.[48]

While immigrant women have often (but not always) stood out numerically on the garment shop floor, they are even more important perhaps "categorically." As a symbol of labor recruitment, they essentially combine a double disability. They point to the ethnicity of gender and the gender of ethnicity. "Women's work" in the New York garment industry since the mid-nineteenth century and to a large extent in Paris today has been largely done by immigrants; the *homo economicus* of migration studies has often been a woman.

The reality and conceptualization of immigrant women at the sewing machines only adds to a sense of contingency in explanations of labor segmentation. Ultimately, I would argue that ethnicity and gender, alone or combined, are important but not sufficient to understand labor-force recruitment. Political disabilities and/or patriarchy are necessary explanations of labor market divisions. "Immigrants," "women," and "immigrant women" share many of the same representations. What is striking is the way in which explanations of their work overlap while within those categories Jewish/Chinese or male/female work has been consistently redefined. Their very interchangeability over time implies other explanations still. Reexamining notions of skill and need, at the heart of any definition of immigrant/women's work, may provide part of the answer.

The Skill of Sewing

Skill is itself a flexible concept, in many ways as much a construct as "women" or "immigrants" in explaining the garment labor force. In his classic study of the garment industry, Jesse Pope commented that, compared to a custom tailor, the Jewish team worker was unskilled. But, compared to other workers, "we shall call him skilled." Or, as others have more generally argued: "Every decade has been one of change in the particular elements which made for skill"; "skill is often an ideological category."[49]

In the sewing trades, skill is a matter of historic period, of craft, of garment type and of raw materials. The manufacturing and epistemological shift from tape measure to presized patterns, from one *bloc socio-technologique* to another, affected the highly skilled tailors along with their less-skilled aides. Workers feared the machine replacing the hand, but new technology was not the sole issue. Workers' organizations assimilated loss of skill to loss of art and joined the two in a criticism of the "spread of shoddy ready-made goods . . . without any worry over questions of taste or quality," which lowered standards and increased exploitation.[50] They more generally castigated the reorganization of work, the increasing division of labor, the putting-out system, and homework as all fragmenting work and demeaning their labor.[51] Nevertheless, the ready-made industry developed its own hierarchy of skill.

Gradations of dexterity and care in ready-to-wear are numerous. There is a full range of skill hierarchy, from stylists to highly skilled cutters to machine operators and less-skilled finishers. The level of skill depends on the craft, the specialty, the fabric, and the general quality of the goods. Cutters are more skilled than machine operators, upper pressers more skilled than under pressers. Coats and suits are more difficult to make than dresses; silk is more delicate than cotton; and high-priced garments need more care than lower-priced lines. Even the category "finishing" can imply different levels of expertise, from simple tacking and basting to homemade, handmade buttonholes.

At the turn of the century, the United States Industrial Commission estimated that it took four or five years to learn to be a qualified tailor but only two or three months to work up the skill and endurance needed for ready-to-wear.[52] Even so, ready-made skill depended on types of garments and even styles. The shift from tight-fitting suits to looser-fitting coats in New York in the 1920s led to de-skilling and abetted increased subcontracting. When fashion shifted to dresses in the same period, the ILGWU lamented that this was hurting the more skilled cloak-and-suit trade, leading to a "migration of workers" among the various branches, which they wistfully regretted not being better able to regulate.[53]

Social investigator Louise Odencrantz estimated that it took about two years to become a skilled cloak-and-suit finisher in the early part of the century. In the 1920s, union historian Louis Levine reported that it took only about three months for "an ordinarily intelligent adult" to become a good enough machine operator to earn a living wage.[54] A 1939 study of seventy-six dress firms showed that the learning period for operators ranged from one week to one year.[55] A 1961 French report estimated that only 3.2 percent of all garment-industry workers were highly skilled, 18 percent were skilled, 16.5 percent were classified as unskilled, 48.9 percent as laborers (*ouvriers* and *manoeuvres spécialisés*), and 13.4 percent as under the age of eighteen (a definition of skill?).[56]

That there are so many different definitions of skill seems confusing. Yet there are basically two different discourses with regard to skill within the apparel industry, discourses which have important consequences for the hiring of immigrants or women. One periodically bemoans the lack of skilled workers. The other admits that most jobs are easily learned on the job. These attitudes are only apparently contradictory and often correspond to different specialties and crafts.

When the post–World War II French and American garment manufacturers lamented the lack of skilled labor, they were mostly concerned with the (more skilled, yet relatively declining) cloak-and-suit sector. Full employment, women workers moving off to other opportunities, the aging (in the United States) or deportation

Ready-to-Wear and Ready-to-Work

(in France) of the prewar generation of immigrant tailors had all decimated the ranks of the highly skilled. After the war, the ILGWU Joint Board of Cloak, Suit, Skirt, and Reefer Makers, along with several manufacturers' trade associations, submitted a joint petition to the Attorney General to allow the immigration of ten thousand skilled tailors beyond the national quotas and the displaced persons laws and as an exception to the 1885 contract labor law. They argued that there was a critical shortage of skilled tailors (in their high end of the clothing trade), given that almost 67 percent of all men in the industry were fifty-five years or older.[57] The American men's-wear manufacturers' association and the ACWA also attempted unsuccessfully to get above-quota admissions of skilled tailors from the camps in 1947. In 1961, they again pleaded with the government for looser immigration laws to admit more European-trained, highly skilled tailors.[58] A clothing manufacturer said in 1953: "A college education is a wonderful thing, but in the garment industry, you need skilled workers with good technical knowledge to supervise."[59]

More recently, social scientists and state employment agency officials have also expressed the importance of sewing skill. One study found that "most basic sewing and stitching jobs listed by New York City employers with the New York State Service require at least one year of experience." Yet the same study recognized the ultimate importance of informal, on-the-job training in immigrant shops.[60] As one New York contractor commented, a nimble worker can become a good operator within two weeks.[61]

For the bulk of the industry's labor force, "skill" means speed and accuracy. "The ability to work at high speed is a skill inadvertently created by de-skilling."[62] The repetitive tasks of the machine operator—80 percent of the garment workers—are relatively easy to learn, and skill comes through practice. Seam sewing is an "imitative" rather than an "initiative" skill, to use Laura Lee Downs's distinction. And it is one which, importantly, is learned more often from older relatives and coworkers than through a formal apprenticeship. Even school-trained beginners need to start at floor-level jobs in order to work up the speed. Changing styles present a constant challenge but one that is usually resolved on the shop floor.[63]

Schools were set up on both sides of the Atlantic to teach industrial garment making. The Central Needle Trades Continuation School was founded in New York City in 1926 and became the High

School of Fashion Industries (HSFI) in 1935. By the 1950s, with new immigration to the United States limited and a skill shortage in the better price lines, the vocational high school joined forces with the ILGWU locals to encourage the children of the older immigrants to "learn a skill and also get your complete academic education at the same time."[64] But in the 1960s, as other job opportunities widened, the school became worried about graduates "defecting" from the needle trades. By the following decade, most students (African Americans, Puerto Ricans, Chinese) had no parental connections to the industry. A 1970 study found that, six months after graduation, 38 percent of the students had gone into manufacturing, 22 percent into the wholesale and retail end of the business, and 20 percent were unemployed (the rest unknown).[65] In 1969, the day school had 1,600 registered students, but the adult evening extension classes had 2,950.[66] The largest adult training program in New York City, it offers training for entry-level jobs or for upgrading skills. (About 750 of the 2,500 students enrolled in the evening program in 1973 were ILGWU members.) Yet, paralleling the fate of the industry, adult evening enrollment had declined to approximately 1,000 in 1983 and roughly 700 by 1995.[67]

"Every kid who comes in here dreams of being a famous designer."[68] Nonetheless, and in spite of their initially close connections, the HSFI has never been a major source for students of the Fashion Institute of Technology (FIT). Founded in September 1944, FIT's aim, then as now, has been to train designers, marketing people, and managers. The college-level institution also offers continuing-education classes for those already in the industry who want to upgrade their skills. Described as the "life-blood of the industry as the apparel industry is the life-blood of the City," FIT had some 12,300 students enrolled in 1995, of which 8,000 were continuing-education, full-time students.[69]

In France, garment skills have been taught through programs in the public vocational high schools. The collèges d'enseignement technique which began to be set up in France in the 1930s issued over half a dozen different diplomas—certificats d'aptitude professionnelle (CAP)—in sewing. The Centre d'etudes techniques des industries de l'habillement (CETIH) was set up in 1943 to further research on garment making. More recently, the Institut français de la mode (IFM) was created in 1985, aiming, like the FIT, to furnish

Ready-to-Wear and Ready-to-Work

high-level designers and managers to the industry. Approximately fifty students enroll there each year to prepare for a master's degree.

Clearly the industry on both sides of the Atlantic has been concerned about labor recruitment, and has joined forces with manufacturers and the unions (in New York) and the government (in France) to further skill training. The question here is how basic entrance to the industry works. Given a division of labor that allows some specialized tasks to be learned in under two weeks, some employers have even argued that training workers to make a whole garment is counterproductive; they only have to be retrained for more industrial methods.[70]

Thus, for machine operators, speed as skill has often been defined as not very skilled after all. Immigrants and their literary representatives have participated in the discourse on (little) skill by complaining bitterly in memoirs and romanticized novels about loss of skill in the New World: "They only do cheap work in this country. Everything must be done in a hurry. In Italy it would take six months to do a pillow," complained one embroiderer. "And here it must be done in three or four hours. Cheap work!"[71] Disappointment was keen for those who had brought skills with them only to find that the meaning of the term had changed. Roger Ikor dramatized this dilemma in his prize-winning novel about a Russian Jewish capmaker in Paris:

Sometimes he surprised himself, fairly naively, at being bored in the workshop. Only yesterday wasn't the least gesture of his trade a constantly renewed source of pleasure? To appreciate from afar a fresh piece of material, to appreciate in advance the suppleness of the cloth, its texture, with a squint in order to carefully judge the color. A cluck of the tongue, a knowing nod of the head, the look of a connoisseur: "Hmm! It would be a jewel, I tell you!" . . .

No: that was in the old days, in the Rakwomirian days. Now Yankel's work was mechanized. He no longer jokes, he no longer smiles at jokes. . . .[72]

But skills were not just "lost." They were imported, transferred, and transformed. Many Italian women with prior experience at the turn of the century only got jobs doing the unskilled tasks of tacking and basting, just as many Puerto Rican women in New York today have had to retool their fine handwork skills in order to do de-skilled section work. Other Italian housewives and farmhands with no such experience also went into finishing. One historian of Local 10, the Cutters' Union, described the Jews who entered the cloak industry in New York in the 1880s as a mixture of Talmudic scholars who learned the trade upon arrival, along with little-educated but already-skilled men's-wear tailors who shifted to women's wear, and physically strong pressers who had been blacksmiths, drivers, and porters in the old country.[73]

How many immigrants came with skills? Just as women are supposed to enter the trade with "innate" skill, so the German family, the Jewish tailor, or the Italian handworker were presumed to have imported theirs, bringing skills from the old country *in der hand,* as the Yiddish expression goes. Even John Bodnar, arguing importantly that an overemphasis on "premigration skills [neglects] the structural transformation which characterized expanding industries and the extent to which a match took place between previously acquired behavior and available opportunities in America," nonetheless makes an exception for the "well-known" transfer of Jewish tailoring skills.[74] But how many immigrants found occupations in the New World consonant with their training in the Old?

If entry declarations can be believed (the immigrant network spread the word as to which answers were best), two-thirds of the five thousand Jewish women who were met in New York by the Council of Jewish Women in 1909–10 said they had been clothing workers in their home country.[75] According to the U.S. Immigration Commission's sample of garment-industry employees in New York City, 63.3 percent of the Russian Jewish (designated as "Russian Hebrew" in the report) men and 66.8 percent of the Southern Italian men had previously worked in clothing manufacture before coming to the United States. Even higher percentages of female immigrant garment workers had prior experience: 90.4 percent of the Russian Jewish women and 90.9 percent of the Southern Italian women had previously worked in sewing, embroidering, lace making, etc.[76]

However, the data is just as often more mixed. A U.S. Department of Labor Bulletin found entirely different results for the cloak, suit, and skirt industry: only 6 percent of the Jewish pressers in New York City had been pressers in Russia; only 4 percent of the cutters had learned their skill in the old country. Previous occupations ranged from carpenters to butchers to brewery workers. Most declared they

Ready-to-Wear and Ready-to-Work

had learned their trade in the shop after coming to the United States.[77] One factory inspector was adamant: "It is certain that they did not work at tailoring in the countries from whence they came." Conditions in the trade were too grim, and only a "powerful influence" could have "guided" the Polish and Russian Jewish immigrants into it.[78] Samuel Joseph, while estimating that almost one-half of the already-skilled Jewish immigrants who came to the United States between 1899 and 1910 had been in the garment trade in Eastern Europe, also pointed out that this meant that as many Jews entered garment work without prior experience.[79] In another study, of 295 Italian women in the garment industry in the United States, 121 had already done industrial-sewing wage work in Italy, another 6 had done hand embroidery, and 6 others had worked in textile manufacture. However, 131 had not worked at all, 20 had previously done farm work, and another 11 had been in domestic and personal service. Among a sample of 24 Turkish men in the contemporary Parisian ready-to-wear business, 19 had indeed been tailors in Turkey, but only 1 of the 14 Turkish women garment-workers had done any professional sewing there.[80]

Then there were those who did not even know how to sew on a button. The great David Dubinsky himself had started out life as a baker in Russia.[81] There were enough new learners in the trade for the term "Columbus tailor" to be coined in New York to name inept greenhorns, while freshly arrived immigrants to the Pletzl of Paris also joined the ranks of sewing machine operators without apparent prior skill. According to one estimate, most Italian women entered the New York garment industry unskilled.[82] The "newness" of the job experience in the United States was apparent in the number of specialized words that were borrowed from the English: bushelers became *bucellatrici;* operators, *operatrici;* pressers, *pressatori, pressatrici;* dressmakers, *dressatrici;* there were no equivalents for these specific occupations in Italian.[83]

"What do I know about machines?" asked a Turkish contractor in Paris today. "I was a shepherd at home, the guy over there was a teacher, and the other one played soccer."[84] Expanding opportunity at the turn of the century, just like particular opportunities in a contracting market today, have drawn tens of thousands to the sewing machines who have never touched a thimble or treadle before. While over the last century tens of thousands of Jewish, Italian,

Puerto Rican, Armenian, or Turkish tailors and seamstresses have indeed brought skills with them from the old country, for many others, the "gnarled fingers" of farm labor had to be retrained. There are Puerto Rican women who were midwives or bookkeepers before moving into the skirt industry in New York today. One woman sewing in Paris was a literature professor in Shanghai; there are Chinese-Cambodians who were teachers and physical therapists; and there are Turks who were farmers, students, or refugees. Many others worked first in the Parisian automobile factories before "recycling" into the apparel industry. As a Moroccan Jew in Paris said recently: "It's a job you can start with nothing."[85]

For many, then, a job behind the sewing machine has meant skill acquisition, rather than skill import or skill loss. True, not everyone has the knack. Later union leader Abraham Bisno complained how "My fingers sweated, my needle screamed," as he learned the trade. But, more typically, as one turn-of-the-century Italian girl said, "it takes only a few minutes to learn." "It's as easy as a hello," commented more recently a Chinese-Cambodian garment worker in Paris.[86] In some cases, "imported" skills may simply have been learned en route: a worker may have had a "vague apprenticeship" in an Armenian orphanage, or learned how to sew in a refugee camp in Thailand, having heard that there were apparel jobs in France.[87] Even many manufacturers and jobbers often basically learn the business while doing.

These different meanings of skill have important implications for labor recruitment. By emphasizing notions of innate or imported needle skills, both the immigrant and women theories of labor minimize acquired skill and underestimate the importance of easy entrance to the vast majority of operating jobs. When asked who first taught them finishing, "many of the women [early Italian homeworkers] laughed." They had just been shown and become proficient on their own. Black and Hispanic female dress operators in the early 1950s found and learned most of their jobs through friends or relatives, just like the Italian and Jewish women earlier in the century. As a French labor organizer put it more recently, "Why did they find themselves in the garment industry? The telephone."[88]

While prior skill has been an important asset for many garment workers, the industry would never have become an immigrant industry without the unskilled immigrants and women who also set to

Ready-to-Wear and Ready-to-Work

work. By redefining "skill" as meaning speed and accuracy for the majority of operatives, the ready-made revolution has held out opportunities for many who have never sewn before in their lives. This understanding of garment skill has helped assign it to the secondary labor market while it has also helped shape workers' notions of access to it.

Choice as Need

There are certain wonderful things about the industry. You don't need English; it doesn't matter what your age, what you look like, or how you dress.[89]

Finally, however, garment work was chosen by vast numbers of women and immigrants because it fit their needs. Low skill abets seasonality and subcontracting in providing flexibility not just to the industry but to workers as well. Industrial flexibility has advantages for mothers with children and immigrants new to the labor market. Flexibility of time and of space, the seasonal fluctuations of production, and the variety of workplaces have often meant jobs close to home, if not at home, and easy access to a needy labor market that speaks one's own language.

Whenever it was suggested that homework be eliminated because of the awful conditions associated with it, a number of priests, welfare workers, sometimes doctors, and often employers supported its continuation. They argued that those who did such work had chosen to do so. To deprive mothers, pregnant women, the infirm, or the elderly of such work would be unfair. Women themselves have historically sought homework. At various stages of the life cycle, homework can be a good solution to the "double day" for those who work for wages and take care of their children at the same time. Seasonal work, if well-timed, can allow convenient breaks during the off-season when children are home from school.[90]

Madeleine Guilbert and Viviane Isambert-Jamati conducted a particularly interesting study of Parisian homeworkers in the early 1950s, analyzing why female homeworkers did the work they did.[91] First of all, they found that only 35 out of 272 respondents said that homework was definitely not their first choice; they took it because they could not find work in a shop (due to bad luck, or being too old or not fast enough). But if these 12.9 percent were the only truly *non volontaires* of the sample, this did not mean that everyone else chose this form of work freely. Another 12.5 percent of the women "chose" it for reasons of health (physical handicap or simply age and fatigue); 27.5 percent took homework in order to stay home with their children or because of other familial considerations. Many of them added, however, that this was not without its own problems: concentrating on complicated dresses while trying to watch the kids; interrupted work time leading to long hours into the night; having to keep children away from the cloth to avoid spills or accidents. Thus, even if over one-half of the homeworkers responded that they had "chosen" homework, they sometimes also used the term "obligation" to explain that choice.

Yet 10.3 percent of the women expressed their work choice as one of independence: freedom from fixed hours; freedom to knock off when they felt like it and make up the work later; freedom from the authority and petty favoritisms, the flatteries and injustices of the shop *camaraderie*. And, an important 36.8 percent answered that working at home was natural (*allait de soi*) for a woman. However, even within this category, almost one in five reflected a certain amount of pressure to conform to that (1950s) model. As one woman said, "If my husband let me, I wouldn't wait: I'd be in a shop tomorrow."[92] Homework was thus definitely a choice, albeit one often flanked by constraint.

For immigrants, as should be clear by now, the garment industry has also often been an important choice. A product and support of the immigrant neighborhood, the apparel industry has provided opportunities for generation after generation of urban newcomers. Ethnic shops permit the maintenance of ethnic or religious traditions. They allow immediate employment in a familiar environment where customs are a comfort rather than a barrier. Language (the tip of the cultural iceberg) may be the determining factor in choice. As the Chinese teacher from Shanghai commented: "Not speaking a word of French, I obviously didn't have a choice," although quickly adding, "But I'm not complaining. It helped me settle in and be strong enough to do something else."[93]

Options and perceptions are necessarily couched in comparative perspective. What may be perceived as upward mobility for previously rural Dominican factory owners in New York can be seen as downward mobility by Chinese owners.[94] Why do most immigrants support the poor conditions and sometimes exploitative environment? Things are better than in their home country; savings can allow them to return home. For Dominican women in the New York garment industry, coming from lower-middle-class backgrounds, the consumer items which they can buy even on their garment salaries lead them to consider themselves middle-class in New York. Furthermore, emigration may be emancipation for some women; many of these women feel that their status in the household has improved as a result of migration and wage earning. When asked why they worked as garment workers in New York's Chinatown, Chinese women responded, in order of importance: (1) the ease of getting a job; (2) the fact that they did not have to take public transportation to get to work; (3) the flexible schedule; (4) their lack of English; (5) the job could be learned in about a week; and (6) they appreciated the social and informal atmosphere of the shop.[95]

Choice, it seems, is often a matter of circumstances, just as it has recently become a matter of historical interpretation. As the historiography has moved away from exploitation to agency, choice has become increasingly viewed and valued. This does not make it a stable category, as the garment industry only too clearly shows. Choice, I would argue, is closely tied to need, itself a function of "skill" and opportunity. Agency, then, is also a question of context.

Gender, Ethnicity, and the Labor Market

Both women and immigrants have been blamed for the sweatshop. In what I would call the desperation wage theory of economics, they have been accused of accepting and thus causing the low wages, undercutting, and poor conditions in the trade. Even sympathetic observers have often basically argued that the viability of the late-twentieth-century garment industry in the Western world rests largely on the availability of immigrant women.[96] Historian John Commons specifically blamed the Russian Jews, while Fabian Socialist Beatrice Webb, in England, explicitly defended the Jews and suggested that women were an even bigger problem in sweating.[97]

Edith Abbott concluded her 1910 analysis of the takeover of the

Women, Immigrants, and Skill

Russian Jewish men with a reflection on garment work as pertaining to women's "peculiar sphere." Given that assumption, she said, "the point of interest is, therefore, not that so many women are employed in the sewing trade, but that so many men have come into the industry as their competitors."[98] She went on to say that the subject needed to be situated in the larger context of the sweating system, homework, and immigrant labor.

Jobs can and do change gender and ethnic attributes. We are confronted with different levels of representation and interpretation. "Women's work" and "immigrant labor" are expressed differently by popular opinion, employers, native women, male and female immigrant workers, and social scientists. Supply-side arguments about innate or imported skill and availability have helped fashion the language of the garment labor market. If the "deft female fingers" or "old-world traits" images can be laid to rest as outdated biological or cultural visions of the sewing masses, other explanations such as patriarchy and women's choices, immigrant bosses and immigrant workers' needs, clearly inform the structure of the industry's labor market and hierarchical relations within it. Yet, we still need to ask, what comes first, women and immigrants, or homework and needlework?

A century-long, historical approach is important. Whereas contemporary analyses have largely explained the presence of immigrant entrepreneurs and immigrant operatives by the current decline of the industry and insisted on the predominance of women workers, other models at other moments have been just as salient: the influx of immigrants during the early period of *growth;* the presence of male operatives in early New York and present-day Paris. Such historical "counter"-examples must make us cautious about ahistorical theories (be they patriarchy or labor segmentation).[99] Temporal comparisons (doubled here by a spatial one) bring into question static definitions of male, female, immigrant work, or skill, for that matter. I am clearly arguing here not for an immobile *longue durée* but for one which emphasizes process and change in the construction and reconstruction of work categories.

Finally, however, categories may be unstable, but they are not totally footloose and fancy-free. Edith Abbott was on the right track in basically calling for a better understanding of garment production in order to explain the changing faces in the contractors' shops. The structure of the industry informs the use of these categories; they are not simply discursively organized but are constructed in order to adapt to the economic need for a cheap, flexible labor force. Women, immigrants, and immigrant women have thus been flexible categories representing . . . flexibility in the workforce. Microlabor markets and internal hierarchies differentiate workers at different times, yet at a more general level, women and immigrants function similarly as an inexpensive yet expansive labor source.

The search for cheaper labor is a continuous one, from natives to immigrants, from older immigrants to newer ones, from men to women, to out-of-town and offshore workers. It is this search which constantly redefines labor recruitment. By shifting the focus from labor supply to industrial demand, from the supposedly inherent characteristics of women or immigrants to an even more intrinsic understanding of the industry's structure, explanations based on gender or ethnicity alone—along with questions of skill as well as choice—need to be placed within a broader context.

Labor divisions and labor segmentation are "contested outcomes" which can take historically different paths.[100] An analysis of the industrial process over time is the best way of understanding the changing processes of segmentation, ascription, and even choice. The structure can shed light on the poststructural contingencies without denying the latter. There is not an absolute interchangeability of categories at any given time, but the fluctuating if not flexible use of different categories of low-wage workers make us question the explanatory power of certain categories themselves. Skill, homework, the late-nineteenth-century category "sweated labor," or the new, late-twentieth-century buzzword "flexibility" are categories which are perhaps more persuasive than "immigrants" or "women" in explaining how choices are constructed and who came to work the sewing machines.

Women, Immigrants, and Skill

7

"AN INDUSTRY OF PASSAGE"[1]

The Immigrant

Waves

Old-World Traits—The Imaging of the Waves

In the course of the past 25 years the changes in mode of production are as important as the changes in nationalities, and new modes have usually accompanied new nationalities. . . . Old methods and new methods are competing together, and also the remnants of earlier nationalities, with the vanguard of later nationalities.[2]

For garment-industry observers since the turn of the century, the image of the industry has often been linked to that of the immigrants. Yet that vision has been contradictory. While the newcomers have been hailed for bringing their expertise or simple labor power to the industry, they have also been blamed for the speed-ups, low wages, and anarchic and archaic conditions. "Old-world traits," supposedly inherent and imported with the immigrants' meager baggage, have been a common way of explaining labor segmentation.

However, the synchronic explanations reverberate with echoes over time; a diachronic analysis reveals a repetitious language of blame that undermines its explanatory function. Similar epithets or accolades are attributed to different and successive immigrant groups. Have they all really brought with them such hardworking, self-exploitative, and for the most part docile traits? The discourse on immigrants is often conflicting. It has been used to explain industrial development but also its opposite, economic backwardness.

The Myth of the Jewish Tailor and Other Tales

In her thesis on women in the garment industry at the turn of the century, Mabel Willett characterized the first division of labor in the American clothing trade as "peculiar to the German people."[3] The German family system, like others after it, was used to explain the development of ready-to-wear and to blame exploitation on the new immigrants' new modes of production. Yet perhaps the most developed origins myth concerning the garment industry in general and in New York in particular has to do with the Jews. For Willett, the task system of the Russian Jews was "a form of organization as characteristic of the Jew as is the family shop of the German."[4] Three workers constituted a team—a machine operator, a baster, and a finisher—which, accompanied by two pressers per three teams, was paid by the "task," that is, per completion of a certain number of garments. For the United States Industrial Commission, investigating the trade at the turn of the century, there was also no question that the task system was a Jewish invention. The division of labor and "dexterity" of the Jews explained how the system worked. Even more recent historians have taken up the idea that the Russian Jew was "best fitted physically to the sweatshop."[5]

The imaging of the Eastern European Jews was both positive and negative. Industrial-art critic Charles Richards praised "the peculiar genius of these people for merchandising, their highly developed individualism, their artistic perception and their thorough training in the craft of tailoring." Or, as Louis Levine, early historian of the International Ladies' Garment Workers' Union (ILGWU), proudly asserted: the "Jewish needle made America the best dressed nation in the world."[6]

However, the task system (and its perpetrators) was also decried. When work was scarce, contractors took work for cheaper and cheaper prices, and, rather than reducing wages, they increased the number of coats due per task. In the 1880s, a task meant 8 to 10 coats per day, taking eight to ten hours; by 1900, the task was 20 or

"An Industry of Passage"

more coats per day for the same wages. Willett blamed the task system for driving Germans as well as women from the trade.[7]

The Industrial Commission was blatant in its racial analysis:

By this queer cooperative production in the form of team work, combined with the personal interest of piecework, the Hebrew tailors in New York have devised what is, perhaps, the most ingenious and effective engine of overexertion known to modern industry.

One reason why piecework and high speed have become the framework of the contractors' shops is probably because the Jewish people are peculiarly eager to earn a big day's wages, no matter at what sacrifice. . . . It is not for love of hard work nor because of lack of other enjoyment that the Jew is willing to work so hard, but for the sake of getting rid of work [becoming a boss]. . . . The Jewish immigrant is peculiar only in that he is not by nature a wage-earner, and he keeps before himself continually the goal of emancipation from hard work.[8]

Even a much later, more sympathetic account explained:

Much that is chaotic in the clothing industries can be traced back to the psychological peculiarities of the predominant racial group which has provided both wage-earners and manufacturers.[9]

Two theories of Jewish labor seem to coexist within the discourse on the Jewish needleworker. For some, the fact that many Jews had been tailors in the old country explained their predominance in the industry. For others, it was their prior commercial activities which had contributed to the "splendid development" of the apparel trade in New York.[10] In this version, speculation and a desire for freedom were the skills imported by the Jewish immigrants:

He wants to have freedom. This he usually has in the contractor's shop. He is very nearly "his own boss"; he can smoke, talk, run around, stay at work an hour longer, come in an hour earlier, or come later. . . . The contractor's shop is a sort of ideal worked out by this individualistic people, which holds out a fair hope to everybody of some day becoming his own boss, and, to a certain extent, of being his own boss while still at work in the shop.[11]

Indeed, remarks stressing the Jews' individualism sometimes contradicted the notion of their craft skills:

The Jew occupies a unique position in the clothing trade. His physical strength does not fit him for manual labor. His instincts lead him to speculation and trade. His individualism unsuits him for the life of a wage-earner, and especially for the discipline of a labor organization. . . . Only about 11 per cent of the Jewish immigrants were tailors in Europe. . . .[12]

In his 1913 study of the New York men's-wear industry, Harry Best spoke of the Jews' "consuming ambition" and "overmastering desire" to set up their own shops. Labor historian John Commons also considered the Jews refractory to factory discipline, preferring, as they did, "the sweatshop with its going and coming." These representations are not unique to the Russian Jew in early-twentieth-century New York. Similar characteristics have been used to explain the successes of North African Jews in contemporary Paris. But in this case *their* "commercial genius" is designated "Sephardic" and contrasted to the older generation of Ashkenazi Jews who worked their way up through the production ranks.[13]

Jews have responded to these characterizations in two ways. Some, such as Levine, proudly affirm the Jews' role in the development of the modern ready-to-wear industry. Parisian Jewish demographer Michel Roblin, writing shortly after World War II, also acknowledged their particular presence in the industry, albeit much more apologetically:

[The Yiddish emigration] has played an important role [in various sectors of the garment industry], thanks to which several positive changes have come about. However, this migration did not cast out the French from an occupation they had created several centuries earlier. On the contrary, it accelerated a tendency toward proletarianization which was already underway at the end of the nineteenth century.[14]

If some have been happy to take "blame" for the growth of the industry, no one has wanted to be held responsible for the sweatshops. Writers on both sides of the Atlantic have also offered a counterhistory of the industry, denying the tale of Jewish invention and arguing that the basic structure of the business predated the arrival of the Eastern European immigrants. Labor lawyer and economist Isaac Hourwich, in his pre–World War I general defense of the "new" immigrants, explicitly defended the Jews: "The origin of the

"An Industry of Passage"

sweating system preceded the Jewish clothing workers by more than half a century." Michel Roblin pointed out that the Germans had been in Paris before the Jews: "It is fairly certain that no essential transformation of the garment industry, however 'Jewish,' can be especially attributed to Jewish initiative."[15] Affirming or denying a group's role, ethnic stereotyping implies debate over the industry's creation story.

Italian Newcomers

Some Italian men and large numbers of Italian women then entered the New York shops and began sewing at home in the 1890s and 1900s, implying a new narrative to explain a new presence. Like the Jews, Italians were blamed for edging American women out of the trade. The Industrial Commission, for example, cast a dim eye on the Italian female finisher, "compelled to take work home, because her husband is not making enough money to support the family," and whose low wages depressed not only conditions in the clothing trade but "permitted" their husbands to work for low wages. Yet the commission pitied the American widow or married woman. She may have labored under similar circumstances, yet she was described more sympathetically as having to work due to:

the death of the breadwinner or during times when they are not fully supported by their husbands, or when they wish additional money while their husbands are being employed.[16]

Even early-twentieth-century reformer Edith Abbott, while defending women (and immigrants elsewhere) and their right to work, nonetheless contrasted "the intelligent American-born woman in the overall factories to the work of the Italian 'pants' finisher who evades the law in her insanitary [sic] tenement."[17]

Not surprisingly, however, the new group's proclivities for the trade were described in a vein similar to that of their predecessors:

The Italian, like the Jew, has a very elastic character. He can easily change habits and modes of work and adapt himself to different conditions; he is energetic and thrifty and will work hard, with little regard to the number of hours. It is quite usual for an Italian cloakmaker, like the Jew, after he has worked 10 hours in the shop with his wife to take a bundle of work home at night. . . . The Italian is able, on account of his national characteristics, artistic ability, etc., to control such work as the manufacture of clothing, silk weaving, hat making, and other trades where taste and a fine sense of touch are essential for a successful performance of the work.[18]

In Paris, Käthe Schirmacher, in her detailed study of labor specialization at the turn of the century, similarly admired the artistic imagination that the Italians brought to custom women's wear in particular, and she extended the compliment to all Latins and "Slavs" (Jews?) especially in contrast to the northern (German) foreign workers. In a language common to the period, she discussed the "natural" aptitudes of different "nationalities" and "ethnic groups."[19] A theory of labor segmentation by ethnic groups was already in the making, but the early-twentieth-century version was heavily laden with a language of racial characteristics.

Ethnic Stereotypes in Comparative Perspective

Because of their proximity in arrival to Manhattan, Jews and Italians have often been compared in ways ranging from the general to the specific. Historian Edwin Fenton, for example, in his study of Italian workers and American labor, commented that "generally the Jews were optimists, the Italians pessimists." In some cases, the comparisons made the best of a bad situation: "While mentally he is not as alert [as the Jewish worker], [the Italian worker] is sober, industrious and dexterous." In others, the comparison was odious for both parties: "The dense ignorance of the Italians make them an easy prey to the shrewd Hebrew contractors."[20]

More particularly, Italian women and Jewish women were often compared. Gendered working patterns were considered the reason for the new Italian predominance in the trade:

One point at which the Italians have an advantage is the employment of their wives and sisters. . . . There are numbers of cases where the Italian and his wife together work for the same price which the Jew receives for his labor alone, and in this way the Italian is able to crowd the Jew out of the trade.[21]

"An Industry of Passage"

Yet this causality was challenged by another image, that of the more docile Italian woman compared with the troublemaking and striking Jewish one. This was the real reason, according to some, that the Italians were gaining the edge, with even Jewish employers preferring non-Jewish workers to their more rebellious coreligionists.[22]

Ethnic comparisons sometimes reverse historical "memory" and revise earlier appraisals. One New York State factory inspector, for example, was explicit: "To say that Italian sweaters are cleaner than Jews is only a relative and comparative statement." Clearly exacerbated by the continued policy of free immigration, he went into a diatribe against the Italians, consequently embellishing, almost in spite of himself, the traits of the Jewish sweater:

And so with the new problem in "sweating." The cupidity of greedy Italians . . . is responsible for worse evils than ever existed under the Jewish phase of that problem. Comparatively speaking, the Jewish sweating is humane, and that is saying a good deal. To be sure, the Italian sweaters are not so filthy, and there are few or no padrones—but, all the same, those Italians already in the clothing business as sweaters, have graduated from the garbage heaps, the ash barrel and the rag cellar, and, having constitutions of iron, work harder than Jews, eat less, or more cheaply, for they certainly beat the Jews at cheap living. . . .[23]

The comparison, intended to explain a "new" problem, both draws upon repeated imagery ("cupidity") that undermines the contrast and leads to a rewriting of the history of the Jewish sweatshop. Two strategies seem at work by the ethnic comparativists. On the one hand, in a classic formulation, bad immigrants drive out the good and older immigrants who are valued positively in retrospect. On the other hand, the arrival of still newer groups can lead to a collapse of the representations of the older groups in contrast to subsequent generations.

Perhaps we should simply dismiss the mostly pre-1933 images as outdated, part and parcel of an old, racist language subsequently purged. A study undertaken by the Emanuel Federated Employment Service in 1931, all the while eschewing "racial characteristics" or "personality" traits as explanations for labor, revealed the continued use of a language of national characteristics:

The Italians seem to be naturally suited to the designing field, although the majority of pattern makers and designers are still Jewish. Most of the people interviewed agreed that the Italian "temperament" is unsuited for the role of employer.[24]

The repetition of these images and the use of comparative appreciations up through the latest immigrants show a continuity of language which subverts the explanation. Almost all of those who enter the trade are characterized as both "peculiarly" suited to it and as cutthroat as their predecessors.

Black and Yellow ("Travail noir et filière jaune")[25]

The Chinese in turn have been admired as well as criticized on both sides of the Atlantic. Praised as a model minority, they have also been accused of exploiting their own (like others before them).[26] The French press discovered conditions in the garment district in part due to the increasingly heated discussions over illegal workers and illegal work that have often focused rather confusedly on Asian immigrants. With estimates ranging from 5,000 to 40,000 clandestine workers in the Parisian garment sector in 1980, tales of the double-bookkeeping circuits have taken on the characteristics of a detective novel replete with a mélange of shady characters from a variety of suspicious foreign backgrounds.[27] In one version, the illegal network is run by Asians, with a Hong Kong man as the presumed brains behind the operation, working with accomplices at local French banks. In another version, a "Franco-Yugoslavian" group seems to be run by an Israeli mastermind whose mistress opens accounts all over town, including at the Lebanese Arab Bank. ("In the back-room of the Sully, a café in the Faubourg Saint-Denis quarter . . . , from 11 a.m. to 5 p.m. every day, his mistress, Eva Glab, holds court.") In yet another version, it is a Corsican who makes his appointments in a *bistrot* near the Arts et Métiers metro stop.[28]

The Chinese are represented, like others before them, as working with great speed and care, and the Chinese women are characterized as docile, like Italian women homeworkers in another time and place. Yet these characteristics take on a specific importance in the contemporary Parisian context. Compared with North Africans, for example, the Chinese are considered "acceptable" immigrants.[29] While all immigrants generally exude the image of hard work, this reputation has been closely connected, in the case of the Chinese, to notions of clandestinity: "they work like ants," they "work noiselessly, night and day, like bees in a well-enclosed hive"; "a commercial success with a mysterious scent"; "the only yellow peril to fear is that of their incommensurable facility to adapt."[30]

As an image of discretion fades into one of secrecy, the economic activity of the Chinese immigrants, like their neighborhood, has been enveloped with a certain mistrust. Like the Jews, their concentration in the industry is practically described as a conspiracy, based on family and community connections. Even the rotating credit clubs (*tontines*), which finance investments, seem suspect: they "loan money and do business during discreet card parties." As the current Minister of Justice, Jacques Toubon, once commented: "It is clear that it is an opaque community."[31]

Yet the explanations themselves seem opaque. The Chinese have been likened to the Jews and called "the Jews of Asia," with both negative and positive connotations. At the same time, they have been contrasted with the Jews, the community closeness of the latter paling in comparison with that of the Asians. The Asians' "community spirit" has thus been opposed to that other Jewish stereotype: "the extreme spirit of competition and individualism of the Jewish tradesmen."[32]

Repetitious Representations and Contradictory Causalities

The language of ethnic succession, underlaid by concerns over replacement and displacement, is most often expressed in terms of comparisons between the old and the new. From native women replacing native men to immigrants displacing natives to different immigrant groups following each other, the image is one of overlapping waves. Each new group is compared to the previous one, whose decried self-exploitation at the time of *their* arrival starts to look good as the next train- or boat-load arrives. This mechanism is of course not just true for the garment industry but describes the imaging of immigrants in general. The determination of old and new is thus as constantly in flux as the immigration waves themselves.

Three things are striking in descriptions of the garment-working waves. First, similar, if not repetitious, representations are applied from one group to the next. Groups as diverse as Italian, Puerto Rican, and African American women, Mauritian men, Chinese male contractors and female operators, have been characterized as docile. Categories such as "hardworking," "elastic," "untiring ambition," "industrious," "entrepreneurial spirit," or "group solidarity," attributed to national characteristics, have been used to explain each newcomer's attraction for the sewing machine. These traits lose their explanatory force when assigned to so many different groups over time.

But second, at any given time, the garment industry offers tales ranging from exploited immigrants to remarkable success stories, and contradictions abound in the characteristics attributed to any one group. The Jews were described as "the most helpless and inefficient immigrants that have ever entered this country," yet "gifted with a singular dexterity to many forms of lighter work."[33] German Jewish reformer Henrietta Szold commented that the Jews were "unorganizable" because of a "tradition of competitive individualism,"[34] while labor leaders pointed proudly to the ILGWU as proof of their organizing capacity. (But then the image of the Jew has often vacillated between one of evil capitalist and dangerous revolutionary.) More recently, the Chinese have been criticized as opaque and secretive but also praised as a "flexible [souple] and disciplined" labor force.[35]

Third, the reliance on national characteristics can impose a differential causality on a single phenomenon. Thus, when Jewish speed became constitutive of the task-system image, the Industrial Commission still needed to explain how Polish men (in a factory in Brooklyn) were also found to have "equal, if not greater, speed than Jews" under similar conditions.[36] In both cases speed was claimed to be inherent to the group: Jewish speed came from their organizational as well as manual skills, while Polish skill was explained by dint of their peasant origins, such robust stock engendering greater endurance and thus enormous speed. Yet if both are true, neither is entirely convincing.

Finally, however, we cannot just dismiss the multitude of images as pure artifact or discourse constructed by suspicious or critical observers. They conceal one last contradiction. They are not produced by the (malevolent?) Other alone but can emerge and be invoked by the immigrants themselves. Armenian knitwear and garment entrepreneurs have spoken with pride of their simultaneous integration into France and into the garment industry. They draw upon their own constructed cultural stereotypes in stressing the priority that Armenians give to setting up their own business, or what sociologist Martine Hovanessian has called "an ensemble of know-how rehabilitated in exile." Her informants "evoke a cultural trait resistant to repetitive work," going so far as to consider it a "chance" that, as foreigners, they were often the first fired in the interwar period: "That wasn't a bad thing for us, on the contrary. . . . When the Armenians were shown the door . . . we were as happy as kings [in setting up our own shops]." Many refer with pride to an "entrepreneurial spirit" or to the "superiority of Armenians in business" as explanation of their successes.[37]

There is a tension between explanations based on particularistic characteristics and those perceiving similarities within the immigrant condition. Even the Industrial Commission, commenting at length on the specific nature of the Jewish worker, admitted that "At the same time it is true regarding green immigrants of all races that the conditions of a strange land stimulate them to the hottest exertion of which they are capable." Jacob Riis, after a racial foray against the Jews ("he strives as hotly with his own for the profit of half a cent as he fought with his Christian competitor for the dollar"), commented that at least it can be said of the "sweater" that "he is no worse than the conditions that created him."[38]

Is it culture or structure, then, that explains immigrant labor? In most representations, culture is called upon to explain structure. Yet to what extent are ethnic explanations a posteriori justifications or myths used to support creation stories and/or to castigate newcomers? The explanations of immigrant labor often seem fortuitous if not essentialist, but their very repetition over time and their multiplicity of contradictory images within time necessarily undermines their credibility. Ethnic epithets are relative.

Geopolitical Flows: The State and Migration

If we can challenge the notion of inherent traits as we have that of imported skill as inadequate explanations for the attraction of immigrant workers to the clothing industry, how can we explain the diversity of men and women who have come to be sewers and sweaters? Unless all preexisting garment workers of the world are converging on the contemporary garment capitals, the variety of immigrants alone seems clearly to argue for the importance of opportunity rather than culture in determining labor market segmentation.

However, industrial structure is still not entirely sufficient. It does not explain *who* came nor how they got to Paris or New York. Two other major factors, classic to the study of migration movements, need to be held to account for the melting pot or salad bowl of garment workers: the push of conditions at home; and the pull not simply of the industry but of the immigration countries whose laws have turned emigration potential into an immigration reality. The presence of Jewish and Italian, Chinese and Turkish, cutters, sewers, and finishers has also been due to state intervention. Political upheavals and structural transformations sending hundreds of thousands scurrying, combined with the immigration policies of the United States and France, form what can be called geopolitical migration flows.

Jews fleeing the Czarist Empire; Armenians escaping after the genocide of 1915–17; Italians departing from economic hardship; African Americans and Puerto Ricans seeking opportunities in the more prosperous American North; Turks leaving in increasing numbers as the economic and political situation worsened in the 1960s, with political refugees fleeing after the 1980 coup d'état; North African Jews arriving in the wake of decolonization; a new generation of Armenians breaking away from troubled Lebanon, Iran, and Turkey in the 1960s and 1970s; ethnic Chinese escaping the Khmer-Rouge in 1975 and then the Vietnamese invasion of Cambodia in 1979—the kaleidoscope is frightening. Religious persecution, political repression and military conflict, population pressures, social and economic tensions, not to mention individual aspirations, family ruptures, and adventuresome lads and lasses, have all fed into the massive migrations of the nineteenth and twentieth centuries.[39] General trends punctuated by specific moments of tumult have given cause and rhythm to the migration movements.

Yet, the push is helpless without the pull, as economists and sociologists have abundantly noted. The destination imagination begins its work well before passage is booked, but the choice of landing spots is conceptualized within the realm of the plausible and the possible. In the United States and France, both major countries of immigration since the late nineteenth century, periods of industrial expansion have been accompanied by liberal immigration policies, while periods of economic closure and xenophobic contraction have led to the halting of immigration.[40] These oscillations have in many ways shaped the garment shops, just as those shops have reflected both the timing and composition of larger immigration patterns specific to each city. The immigrant story is thus another factor differentiating Seventh Avenue from the Sentier, less in the general functioning of labor within and around the garment districts than with respect to the specific groups which have ended up running the sewing machines in each city. History, geography, and politics thus explain why there have been so many Puerto Ricans, Latin Americans, and Asians in the New York shops, and so many Armenians and Turks, Serbian Yugoslavs, Tunisian Jews, and Chinese-Cambodians in the Parisian ones. Push provides the necessity, pull determines the possibilities. Colonial, neocolonial, or other geopolitical ties favor and form migration paths, while individuals decide where to go.

It would be foolhardy to suggest that the "reality" is clearer than the confounding representations. While the vision of immigrant needleworkers has been vibrant in both cities, their actual numbers remain difficult to calculate. We are stymied by the impossibility of establishing serial data over a century in two cities, where statistical categories of occupational classifications and designations of origin have changed over time and are not comparable over space.[41] The fragmentary information at our disposal is more often qualitative than quantitative. Nonetheless, by drawing together the available data, I have been able to set out some of the immigrant threads on the multicolored industrial bobbin.

To the Shores of Manhattan

First there were the English-, Scottish-, German-, and American-born custom tailors who began making up ready-made clothing in their slack time. With the tremendous growth of this new sector, many of these skilled tailors became the owners, managers, foremen, and cutters of the new establishments, recruiting German operators, Irish cutters and foremen, and French tailoresses to work in the women's cloak industry. That the Irish and Germans were among the first immigrant workers in the newly developing ready-made industry is in part due to the Irish potato famine, the Continental revolutions of 1848, economic deprivation, and political repression. In 1855, 96 percent of the 12,109 tailors in New York were foreign-born, of which 6,709 were German and 4,171 were Irish.[42] Referring to Irish predominance in the early New York garment industry, the Immigration Commission—whose report is just as chock-full of irreplaceable data as it is of racialist comments—noted somewhat snidely that "[t]he introduction of machines has made it possible to employ a less intelligent and less skilled force than when all work was done by hand."[43] Machines, technology, and de-skilling were used to explain the Irish garment workers.

Destined to have a more lasting impact on the garment-industry *imaginaire*, German and Austro-Hungarian tailors and their families began arriving in the 1840s and 1850s, followed by a few Swedes who entered the industry between 1865 and 1888. It was the Germans, with renewed migration from 1880–90, who became the most visible foreign element in the industry, and even in 1892, over ten years after the beginning of the Jewish immigration, there were still many (non-Jewish) Germans working in the industry in Manhattan.

If the Germans took over the better lines from the American, English, and Irish manufacturers for whom they had first worked, the next group along the timeline of displacement was the German Jews. According to Willett, the Jews first drove the Germans out of coats before then "encroaching" in pants. However, according to two garment-union analysts, the German Jews did not displace the English and Irish but simply entered the field as the industry grew.[44] In any case, German (along with Austrian and Hungarian) Jews entered the business from another angle. Many of them had been dealers in secondhand or new clothing in Germany, so they "slipped easily into the same business" in the United States.[45] Some were first employed by Germans before becoming contractors on their own, but many more first became peddlers before opening retail stores, then becoming wholesalers and eventually manufacturers. The German Jews came to dominate both the men's-wear and the growing women's-wear industries in the 1860s and 1870s. They were the major contractors and manufacturers of the important women's cloak

"An Industry of Passage"

sector by 1880, hiring Irish, American, and German women and girls to sew (most often at home) in the expanding trade.

The Russian "Hebrew" and the Italian Homeworker

Now came the historic event that ensured New York's dominance in women's apparel. Out of eastern Europe poured hundreds of thousands of Jews.[46]

The Russian Jews would in many ways make the biggest impact on the industry, arriving in the 1880s and 1890s as demand for ready-made women's wear took off. The myriad of Russian, Polish, and Austrian Jews who set up contractors' and small manufacturers' shops came to be known as the "moths" who, within a decade (by 1890 or 1900, depending on the account), had devoured the German Jewish "giants" of Broadway. By 1910, 75 percent of the workers in the New York coat-and-suit industry were Jewish, mostly from Eastern Europe.[47]

Russian "Hebrew" (as they were called) supremacy in the ready-to-wear industry, however important as a founding myth, was actually numerically short-lived. "The striking fact," wrote Meiklejohn in 1938, "is the displacement of the Jew by the Italian."[48] From the 1890s on, Southern Italians began migrating to New York City in large numbers, settling on the Lower East Side near the Jews in what could be called residential and industrial "cohabitation." By 1900, 15 percent of the women's cloak-and-suit workers in New York City were Italian. In 1905, perhaps some 35 percent of the workers in the New York women's-wear industry were Italian, mostly women specializing in finishing and certain hand trades, such as button making, along with a few male operators and pressers. By the 1920s, Italians were the largest single ethnic unit in the needle trades, and, by 1937, David Dubinsky estimated that some 100,000 of the 250,000 ILGWU members in the New York area were first- and second-generation Italians.[49]

Jewish and Italian women in particular formed the backbone of the growing shirtwaist trade. They became strikingly visible during the 1909–10 Uprising, when female shirtwaist makers were estimated to be about 55 percent Jewish, 35 percent Italian, and 7 percent native-born American.[50] The pervasive image then and now has often contrasted the single Jewish woman in the shop to the married Italian woman working at home. Indeed, Jewish women often discontinued working after marriage (or took in boarders rather than homework), whereas Italian women continued to do homework to increase the family wage. Nonetheless, as more detailed studies have shown, some single Italian and younger married Italian women were also factory operatives, just as some married Jewish women continued to work in the shops.[51] After 1900, Italian women came to outnumber their Jewish sisters. By then, almost all of the home finishers in New York City were Italian women, including 94 percent of the Sicilian women on Elizabeth Street. In 1920, the ILGWU estimated that some 80 percent of the 10,000 New York City hand embroiderers were Italian (women).[52]

Even more important, many of the next generation of Italian women followed their mothers into the trade, although they were the exception that confirms the rule. Edward Hutchinson, in his *Immigrants and Their Children, 1850–1950*, argued convincingly that the "immigrant trades" have generally been one-generation phenomena, the second generation being much less specialized in the trades of their parents. For the garment industry in particular, Hutchinson's tables show the continuing relative concentration of foreign-born men and women in 1950. By contrast, however, immigrant children were not only less prevalent in the garment industry than their parents, but became even less so over time. The Italian daughters were the only exception to this, especially during the period of greatest growth in the industry, up through 1910. However, as Miriam Cohen has shown, although Italian girls went into their mothers' professions as operators and finishers to a greater extent than Italian boys followed their fathers as pressers, by and large, *both* second-generation Jews and Italians went into better-paying professions.[53]

By the 1940s, then, the New York garment labor force was ready for new faces. Even before the Second World War, smaller groups from other regions had congregated within specific microsectors of the industry: about 2,000 Syrians and 700 "Spanish" workers were active in the housedress, kimono, and bathrobe trade circa 1918, a sector owned by Syrian-Turkish manufacturers who were "merciless" vis-à-vis the union, according to the latter. In the late 1920s, a

"An Industry of Passage"

(non-Jewish) Russian-Polish branch of the New York Joint Cloak Board had some 2,500 to 3,000 members. In the 1930s, Syrian, Lebanese, and Armenian women joined the New York City garment workforce. Some Spanish-speaking Sephardic Jews from Turkey and the Mediterranean area also came to New York (although far greater numbers went to Paris).[54]

By 1934, Jews had dropped to less than one-half of the ILGWU members and were only one-third by the 1940s (although they were still disproportionately male and heavily concentrated in the most skilled parts of the trade).[55] The powerful Dress Makers' Local 22, 98 percent Jewish in 1929, down to 69 percent Jewish in 1936, was only 51 percent Jewish by 1948.[56] New members to the local were more and more likely to be black or Spanish-speaking; by 1948, these two groups constituted one-half of the union's new constituents, and ten years later they comprised almost 40 percent of the Dress Makers' Local.[57]

From Close and Far: Internal Migrants and Foreigners from the Far East

The famed accents of Seventh Avenue, traditionally Yiddish and Italian, are changing, and the change is beginning to snowball. In the nation's women's wear capital, the new accents are those of San Juan and Ponce, Georgia and the Carolinas.[58]

Can African Americans and Puerto Ricans be considered immigrants? They have been called "in-migrants" and "American-born immigrants," to the objection of those who argue that they did not follow the same pattern of upward mobility as foreign-born immigrants and suffered from additional racial discrimination.[59] Yet although these United States citizens did not have to cross any formal boundaries in order to move northward, their presence in the garment industry can still be seen as part of an "immigrant" story. This is not only because they would be perceived as yet one more "other" in the industry, but also because they functioned as a substitute for those European immigrants halted at the gates by the American quota laws of 1921 and 1924. As African Americans and Puerto Ricans moved toward the industrial North in the interwar period, they palliated the halting of immigration from across the Atlantic and the "exodus" of the second generation from apparel manufacture.[60]

Already during the First World War, as the Great Migration got under way and African Americans moved northward from the American South, black women arrived in New York City as the garment trade was experiencing labor shortages. Initially employed as little-skilled cleaners, examiners, pressers, and finishers, they slowly moved into operating, while some men became pressers. With Jews and Italians still entrenched in the older and more skilled coat-and-suit branch, African Americans and soon Puerto Ricans moved primarily into the newer, and less skilled, dress trade. There were perhaps 3,000 black women in the New York City garment shops in 1925 and double that number two years later.[61] Black men formed 33.3 percent of the ILGWU's Cloak and Dress Drivers and Helpers, Local 102, and 47.5 percent of the separate (AFL) Ladies Apparel Shipping Clerks Union.[62] During the Depression, African Americans lost jobs disproportionately, as more white workers desperately sought even poorly paid jobs, but labor shortages during World War II reversed this trend again as white workers left apparel for better-paying war-industry jobs. As whites moved to the suburbs in the 1950s, African American women again got jobs in the urban garment industry in increased numbers. By 1958, some estimates calculated that 25 percent of the New York City ILGWU membership was black and Puerto Rican, with as high as 40 percent, as we have seen, in Dress Makers' Local 22 alone.[63] Four years later, the National Association for the Advancement of Colored People (NAACP) estimated that there were as many as 98,000 African Americans and Puerto Ricans—53 percent of the membership—in the New York ILGWU locals.[64]

Like Italian women before them, one of the reasons that women's work was all the more indispensable to their family economies were the low wages paid to African American and Puerto Rican men. Discrimination in hiring in other fields, active recruitment on the part of garment employers, and increased subcontracting, decentralization, and de-skilling in the dress sector also explain the growing numbers of black and Hispanic minorities in the post–World War II trade.[65] Why then did black employment in this sector decline in the 1960s? Social scientist Elaine Wrong has argued that three factors were at work: the general move of garment jobs offshore; the fact that welfare payments could be more lucrative than the low garment-industry wages; and the competition of other minorities, with the growing influx of Puerto Ricans to New York City. Roy Helfgott in the late 1950s and sociologist Roger Waldinger more recently have added that in a situation of generally declining jobs and decreasing wages, African Americans simply began to look elsewhere. Waldinger has further argued that African Americans left the trade *before* the arrival of the next wave of immigrants.[66]

Although migration from Puerto Rico to the mainland began as early as 1917, when Puerto Ricans received United States citizenship, and the ILGWU set up a Spanish department within the Dress Makers' Local 22 as early as 1933, the real mass migration to the North and to the garment industry did not occur until the 1950s.[67] Overpopulation on the island, social and economic change there, and air travel all help explain the movement northward. But so does the industry itself. After first exporting capital to Puerto Rico, New York garment firms began importing labor by sending job recruiters to the island during the economic boom of the 1950s. As casual separates became the rage and the low-skilled, low-wage skirt sector started to take over from the dress trade, these new machine operators in a new branch numerically "displaced" the older immigrants in the older cloak-and-suit specialty. Puerto Rican women made up one-half of the skirt-shop workers by the late 1950s. By the early 1960s, the Puerto Rican newcomers were even blamed for an oversupply of labor, but when many of them began returning home and only 11 percent of the second-generation women stayed on as operatives, new labor shortages appeared in the late 1960s and early 1970s.[68]

Another change in immigration law brought new faces to the garment district. The more liberal Hart-Cellar Immigration and Nationality Act of 1965 abolished national origins quotas and eased restrictions on Asian and Latin American immigration. It was dubbed the "Brothers and Sisters Law," since the family reunification provision had the unintended effect of vastly increasing immigration from those regions. The normalization of United States relations with China in the 1970s in turn facilitated immigration from the Mainland. By the 1980s, immigrants from the Dominican Republic, Taiwan and the People's Republic of China, Cuba, Haiti, Central America, Ecuador, Colombia, and Peru began to take the place of the

Ready-to-Wear and Ready-to-Work

Puerto Rican women. From 1970 to 1980, the number of foreign-born (Caribbean) blacks among New York apparel production workers increased by 69 percent, foreign-born Hispanics increased by 80 percent, and foreign-born Asians increased by some 265 percent. Latins and Asians have been called the "new-wave" immigrants.[69]

It is no real surprise, then, that Chinese, Koreans, and Dominicans have made the most recent imprint on the clothing industry and on women's sportswear.[70] The Chinese in particular have been credited with revitalizing and stabilizing women's wear in New York City. In just one decade following the 1965 law, over 300,000 Chinese entered the United States, of which one-fifth went to New York City. From 1960 to 1980, the number of Chinese living in Chinatown tripled to over 34,000 as the new immigrants moved into the old tenement apartments being vacated by older Jews and Italians.[71] In 1974, the ILGWU estimated that, although fifteen years previously there had been only 500 Chinese members in the Blouse, Skirt, and Sportswear Workers' Local 23–25, approximately 6,000 out of that local's 19,000 members now were Chinese. There were 8 garment firms in Chinatown in 1960, over 100 by 1970, and approximately 540 Chinese firms in the metropolitan area by the early 1990s; some 20,000 Chinese women workers represent more than one-sixth of the city's entire apparel labor force. Parts of Brooklyn and Queens have become new extensions of Chinatown, while over 250 Korean shops are concentrated in the garment center and Queens.[72] The garment union has been busy adding new languages to the brochures it publishes.

The Paris Cloth of Many Colors

Les étrangers qualifiés à Paris se distinguent dans leur majorité par un ensemble de qualités morales, qui commencent à se faire rare parmi les Français.[73]

At the turn of the century (before becoming a xenophobic nationalist), Käthe Schirmacher took up the immigrants' defense. She found German and Belgian tailors rivaling English ones at the top end of the men's garment industry, while Poles, Czechs, Austrians, Romanians, and Italians, in addition to the French, brought their expertise to the growing women's wear sector. As for the ready-made trade,

The unskilled foreign immigration, coming from uncultivated countries, brings its share of misery to this cursed industry: Slavs, Poles, and Russians, especially, the Jews, Romanians, and Turks are the most exploited.[74]

Counting Belgians, Germans, Italians, and Swiss only—the backbone of the border-country migrants who constituted the first major wave of foreign migration to modern France—Schirmacher found 9,410 foreigners in the 277,755-person-strong Paris garment industry, a mere 3.4 percent but undoubtedly underrepresented portion of the total garment workers. Yet, garment work constituted the third-largest activity for all foreigners in the Paris economy (after domestic service and *commerces divers*). The industry was the major activity in any single sector of Belgian immigrants (22 percent). It gave work to 10 percent of the Germans in Paris, 12.5 percent of the Italians, and 9.8 percent of the Swiss.[75] At the other end of the statistical spectrum, garment-union leader Pierre Dumas estimated in 1913 that 85 percent of the *tailleurs pour dames* in Paris were foreigners. But he may have been exaggerating, since he was unhappy with the fact.[76]

Jews, Armenians, and Italians

Dumas, occasionally writing in to the Yiddish union newspaper, *Der idisher arbayter,* was well aware of a group that Schirmacher, although noting them in passing, had failed to include in her calculations: the Eastern European Jews. Russian-Polish Jews began arriving in the 1880s and in greater numbers after 1905. According to Wolf Speiser's *Kalendar,* a Yiddish guidebook for and about them, some 8,860 Jewish immigrants were at work in the Parisian apparel industry in 1910, constituting some 29.3 percent of their working population in Paris.[77] By the interwar period, perhaps 70 percent of the Parisian ready-made garment workers were Jewish.[78] Economist Joseph Klatzmann calculated that Jews comprised 60 percent of the male garment workers in Paris in 1946 and that foreign-born Jews (Poles, Russians, and Romanians, foreigners and naturalized combined) constituted one-half of all the foreign-born working in the Parisian industry at that time. In the early 1950s, demographer Michel Roblin counted 40 percent of those listed in the Parisian telephone directory under the category "*Confection*" as Jews. Only the capmakers had an even higher percentage (60 percent).[79]

In spite of their visible concentration in the field, Eastern European Jews were not the only foreigners sewing in Paris. After the First World War, unlike in the United States, immigration remained open to France throughout the 1920s and into the early 1930s, before the Depression, and increasing xenophobia hit. The Russian-Polish Jews of the prewar period were joined by a second group of largely Polish Jewish immigrants but also by Armenians and Turkish Jews arriving in the wake of the Armenian genocide and the breakup of the Ottoman Empire.[80] Like the Jews and Italians in the Lower East Side of New York, many of the Jews and Armenians lived in the same neighborhood in Paris—Belleville—and worked in the same industries. (Some Jews gave their shops to Armenian neighbors for safekeeping during the war.) Garment work was the second most important line of work for immigrants in Paris in 1926 (after *commerce*), and 4,611 Poles, 3,115 Russians, 2,629 Italians, 2,576 Belgians, 1,328 Romanians, and 870 Armenians/Greeks were (undoubtedly under-) reported in the census.[81] In small yet nonetheless significant numbers, Italians thus also came to the garment district as Paris became a center of Italian immigration in the 1920s. In 1933, the police department estimated that of 27,978 foreigners in the Seine Department's garment industry, 8,462 were Poles, followed by 5,274 "*unités*" of Italians.[82]

While the interwar years added variety to the garment labor force, the Second World War seriously challenged that diversity. The Aryanization of Jewish firms and the deportation of 75,000 Jews from France had an impact, as we have seen, down to the garment industry where so many of them worked. While it is impossible to measure the exact numbers of Jews in the industry before and after, Klatzmann estimated that perhaps over one-half of the Jewish homeworkers had been deported.[83] Yet, ironically, at the same time, the small-scale, informal character of the industry did have one advantage. It allowed some to continue working clandestinely throughout the war.

With decolonization and the arrival of North African immigrants to France in the 1950s and 1960s, a third wave of Jews moved into the apparel business. Many Tunisian and Moroccan Jews began by plying goods at outdoor markets, as sales representatives or wholesalers, before becoming manufacturers. They gave impetus to and profited from the new economic "boom" of the 1960s and the growing expansion of sportswear in particular. A spokesman for the Sentier section of the Fédération des Juifs de France estimated in the mid-1980s that some 800 out of 1,200 firms in the area were Jewish: 90 percent owned by North African Jews (60 percent from Tunisia; 20 percent from Morocco; 10 percent from Algeria), with only 10 percent still owned by Eastern European Jews.[84]

Similarly, the Armenian garment community has been renewed as a result of a new migration and the new fad. Many of them made their way to Paris via Marseille or the silk industry in Lyon, settling in a nearby Parisian suburb, Issy-les-Moulineaux, in the early 1920s. What started out as a residential concentration became an economic fief in the 1940s as they began specializing in knitted goods. Those second-generation Armenians who stayed in the business prospered with the takeoff of sportswear, while at the same time a new generation of Armenians began to arrive from Turkey, Lebanon, and Iran in the mid-1970s. As the newcomers reinforced community and economic structures, the terms "the Armenians of Issy-les-Moulineaux" and "knitwear" have become identical.[85]

"Yugoslavs," "Turks," and "Chinese"

More recently, (mostly Serbian) Yugoslavs and Turks (often Kurds), along with large numbers of new Chinese immigrants (largely from Cambodia), have benefited from France's continued search for laborers. The government signed migration agreements with Turkey and Yugoslavia in 1965 and 1966, and even after the official halting ("suspension") of immigration to France in 1974, special dispensations were made with regard to the Lebanese and Chinese-Cambodian refugees. Those in the garment industry have for the most part taken the "Polish Jewish route," starting out as small shop- or homeworkers. With a few francs and a few machines, they hire their own and are in business. As more and more Yugoslav immigrants moved to Paris in the second half of the 1970s, many of them settled into neighborhoods near the garment industry around the rue du Faubourg Saint-Martin,[86] while Turks also began coming to the Sentier in the 1960s thanks to the bilateral labor agreement and due to worsening conditions at home.[87] The men arrived first. Many of the early ones had been tailors in Turkey. Others were recruited for the labor-needy automobile industry, for construction work, foundry labor, and the food industry. But as the automobile industry began its cycle of massive layoffs, many Turkish car workers began "migrating" from one "immigrant" job to another and from heavy industry to light. With or without prior skill, often with the help of their wives and daughters, they became ready-to-wear workers, and some set up their own firms. From the early 1980s on, a growing concentration of Turkish shops began to appear in the 10th and 11th *arrondissements* near the Sentier; restaurants and video stores specializing in Turkish delicacies and Turkish films accompanied them. When the busy season brings surplus work to the Strasbourg–Saint Denis quarter, extended families living in the nearby suburbs also help get orders filled on time. Coming full circle, some of the Turkish owners have "delocalized" part of their operations to Turkey.

The Turkish garment workers made a name for themselves in February 1980 when seventeen undocumented workers, supported by the Association des travailleurs turcs, began a hunger strike. If many Turks brought no prior sewing skill to the business, many of them did bring political skills. Backed by the CFDT, the Turkish garment workers demanded a global (not case-by-case) legalization of their situation and finally won their case; the government gave in as the *prêt-à-porter* show got under way. Within a year, 2,944 garment workers had had their status regularized, including 1,389 Turks (47.2 percent) and 755 Yugoslavs (25.6 percent). In the following two years, a more massive legalization of some 83,000 immigrants included another 9,422 garment workers. Roughly 32 percent of the latter were Turks, their high proportion again testimony to their combativity as much as to their prominence in the trade.[88]

The Chinese may have been missing from the 1980s regularization process (having entered France as refugees, they were exempt from needing a workers' permit), but they were far from absent from the industry. As large numbers of Chinese refugees (whose parents or grandparents had earlier migrated to Southeast Asia) began fleeing the Communist regimes in Vietnam, Cambodia, and Laos in 1975, some 110,000 went to France. The Chinese from Cambodia were the most numerous (40 percent), followed by refugees from Laos (30 percent) and Vietnam (27 percent).[89] More recently other Chinese immigrants have come to Paris from Hong Kong, Thailand, and Mainland China.

The French government's attempt to disperse these newcomers throughout the country failed. They settled in the new high-rises of the 13th *arrondissement* as well as in the run-down buildings of an older immigrant neighborhood: Belleville (18th and 19th *arrondissements*). Estimates of Southeast Asians in the 13th *arrondissement* alone in the late 1980s ranged widely, from 5,700 to 35,000.[90] What had originally been planned as a new, French residential area became the center of "le Chinatown," which soon became an employment and manufacturing hub for the burgeoning Chinese garment industry as well.

In one account, the concentration of the Sino-Khmer (mostly originating from Chaozhou in Southeast China) in the apparel business was almost fortuitous, a typical vision of changing immigrant groups. But, according to another version, the new Chinese contractors got help getting started by Jewish manufacturers loaning them money to rent sewing machines.[91] By one estimate, in the mid-1980s there were approximately 15,000 needleworkers in Chinatown, effecting some 70 percent of the Sentier subcontracting.[92]

Pakistanis and Mauritians

Finally, the most recent new arrivals to the garment district have been Pakistani, Sri Lankan, Mauritian (mostly of Indian origin), and African (Senegalese and Malians) men who by and large work the lowest-ranked jobs as helpers, deliverymen, and porters. They sell their labor by the half day, the day, or the hour at the place du Caire, reconstituting a veritable *chowk* (Urdu for public square, where the daily labor market congregates) in the center of Paris.[93] A sign of changing times, a minuscule hole-in-the-wall restaurant serves up an inexpensive curry dish where a Turkish lunch spot used to be.

The arrival of about two hundred Pakistani workers to the neighborhood in 1980 (some of whom had been teachers, merchants, or physical therapists at home) has been attributed to the refusal of the truckers servicing the garment district to continue to do the loading and unloading in an increasingly overcrowded and frustrating traffic situation. The wholesalers and manufacturers, not wanting to hire permanent unloaders "due to the irregularity of their needs and their undercapitalization,"[94] began to use undocumented workers. And as work in heavy industry was getting harder and harder for new immigrants to find in the general economic downturn, the garment industry's urban needs fit theirs.

In December 1982, in the wake of having gotten legal work-permits through the 1981 French government regularization program, the Pakistani workers created an Association pour une solution au problème de l'emploi clandestin dans le Sentier (ASPEC), with the support of the Confédération française démocratique du travail (CFDT). In March of the following year, they set up a porters' cooperative to function as a temporary employment agency. The state agreed to subsidize the porters' wages so that they would be above blackmarket rates. Four years later, the head of the cooperative claimed that some two hundred people had found more regular employment as a result. In 1988, the cooperative still existed, although described as "*très misérable*" and at an "*impasse*." Perhaps only 20 percent of the Sentier firms used it.[95] The informal *chowk* at the place du Caire continued to function. While the French-speaking Mauritians have had some advantage over the English-speaking Pakistani ones, members of both groups have since moved into cutting and sewing. Some have gone into business on their own.[96] Even the Pakistani owner of the curry lunch counter has apparently tried his hand at the garment trade, while Bhatti became the first important Pakistani *patron* of the Sentier.

As in New York, the figures for immigrants working in the Parisian garment industry today are difficult to establish. National industrial statistics for 1982 (only counting firms with more than ten employees) show only 6.2 percent foreigners in the combined *textile-*

habillement sector, whereas census figures for the same period indicate that there are 20 percent foreigners in that sector countrywide and 43 percent in Paris. Sociologists Mirjana Morokvasic, Annie Phizacklea, and Hedwig Rudolph have thus calculated that there were perhaps ten thousand immigrants active in the garment industry in the Paris region in the early 1980s, double the census figures yet still not taking into account nonsalaried homeworkers or undeclared home or shopworkers.[97]

Networks and Generations

As one employer recounted it:

In the 1960s my shop was mainly black and Puerto Rican, with a sprinkling of older Jews and Italians. Then one day I woke up and I found that I didn't have any more people from Puerto Rico. The only remaining black is my cutter. And the rest of my workers come from the Dominican Republic, with a bunch from Ecuador, El Salvador, and Chile.[98]

The historical formation of the garment working classes in New York and Paris has been part of the history of immigration to those cities. The history of the garment-industry labor force recapitulates much of the immigrant input to each city, just as the urban immigration story informs us about the garment workforce.

Although we can chart the century-long trend of immigrant succession and overlap as seemingly constituent to the garment industry itself, it is also a story replete with drama in the home countries, contingent upon American and French immigration policy, and upon the changing socioeconomic configurations of the late-twentieth-century city. Political scientist Saskia Sassen-Koob has powerfully argued that the continued entry of immigrants into the New York garment industry must be seen in the context of a general increase in the informal sector in the city since the early 1970s.[99] Yet, as we have seen, flexibility has been a crucial component of this industry ever since its beginnings. The explanations are thus both structural and conjunctural, individual and collective, private and public, political and economic.

But how, finally, does it work? Individuals make choices and make moves, if not within conditions wholly of their own making.

How do they decide where to go? Russian Jewish contractors went to Castle Garden and later Ellis Island to pick out tailors by their walk; Serbian *entrepreneurs* flew home to recruit workers. "I mainly hire through word of mouth," explained one Chinese contractor.[100] And news of prospective jobs travels through refugee camps. Migrants move within networks, as the migration literature has abundantly shown in the last twenty years. A Mauritian laborer helps his brother get a job at the same firm; a wholesaler gets a loan from his brother-in-law, an important jobber; another inherits a small family firm and restructures it along the lines of his own more immediate family; sisters, uncles, and in-laws all get involved. But the "family" can also be constructed. The Pakistanis in Paris, most of whom hail from the same northeast region of Pendjab and more particularly from the city of Gurjat, all call each other "cousin." The more extended community network runs concentric circles around the garment district. Networks are multiple, familial but also regional, and far from hermetic, as we will see in subsequent chapters.

If networks explain migration flows and ethnic niches, they can also help us differentiate what look like similar enclaves in Paris and New York. Two groups in particular have moved to both sides of the Atlantic: Jews and Chinese. By examining each group more closely, the "divergent comparison" reveals not linear similarity but the variety of emigration routes and destinies.[101]

Jewish emigrants from Eastern Europe moved westward in the late nineteenth century, heading first of all toward the *goldene medine* of America, but also, in appreciable numbers to England, South America, and France, and the garment industries there. In the interwar period two factors affected the composition and flow of this migration stream. The push was transformed in that the western portion of the Pale of Settlement reverted to Poland and attendant outbursts of anti-Semitism there, while the eastern, Russian, portion initially dropped restrictions on Jewish internal mobility. Polish Jews rather than Russian Jews thus dominated the interwar emigration waves. Secondly, the directional pull of immigration changed. The closing of America's gates in the 1920s occurred while France was opening its doors. Many Polish Jews, who might otherwise have gone to New York, thus ended up in Paris. This constituted a second Jewish cohort of first-generation immigrants to the Parisian garment industry, unlike the case in New York. Deportation rather than quota laws ultimately reduced the Eastern European Jewish garment force in the Parisian garment district before decolonization brought yet other Jews—and new stereotypes—from North Africa to the Sentier. Thus, under the category "Jewish tailors," Paris and New York have in fact been the destinations of different cohorts of Jewish immigrants.

By the same token, New York and Paris may both have their Chinese neighborhoods humming with sewing machines, both of which have been the focus of criticisms of the "return of the sweatshops" or the mysterious workings of the so-called *"filière asiatique."* But here, too, what look like purely structural similarities in terms of image, economic function, and migration streams are quite different in each city. The communities date to different periods and are peopled by different Chinese. The Chinese migration to the United States, facilitated through the 1965 law, has come from both Taiwan and Hong Kong as well as the People's Republic of China (with the inevitable conflicts). The Toysan dialect has been replaced by Standard Cantonese, although more Mandarin has been heard in the neighborhood since the early 1980s. The Southeast Asian Chinese migration to France is more properly placed in the context of "decolonization," as the often already French-speaking immigrants moved to the land of their prior "protectors." Wenzhou and especially Chaozhou dominate in Paris, but not only do they come from different regions and speak different dialects than the Chinese in New York but their community organizations function differently. The rotating credit associations (*tontines*) often used to explain Chinese success in Paris are much less frequent in New York, where Hong Kong capital has made a significant impact in recent years.[102]

The Parisian Chinese neighborhood has furthermore been explicitly and strenuously defended against any American comparison. Like more general French concerns adamantly challenging the idea that American urban ills or ethnic politics can be imported to France, the term "le Chinatown" has been refuted. It is contested for ignoring the rich diversity of the 13th *arrondissement* and for presuming a hermetic, ghettolike quality "à l'Américaine." Yet New York Chinatown observers have made similar provisos: that the area was much more homogeneous before the 1965 immigration, when inhabitants were principally men from the Toysan county of the Canton region, but much more demographically and ethnically mixed today: northern Chinese in addition to the southern Cantonese; wealthy immigrants from Hong Kong along with poor ones from the Mainland; some Chinese from Vietnam; and a majority of women. In short, the New York Chinatown should not be labeled an urban ghetto either.[103]

What came first, the industry or the immigrants? Each helps explain the other. The tremendous growth in women's ready-to-wear at the end of the century and the decline of the industry today have both corresponded to important periods of immigration in both New York and Paris. The industry has needed the labor; the newcomers have needed the jobs; capital and labor barriers to entry are low. Today, rising imports and a contracting market have put different pressures on garment manufacturers, while recent migration streams have brought in new workers with age-old needs of quick access to work. In times of expansion, as in times of decline, the industry has provided a particularly amenable opportunity structure, not just for owners but for workers as well.

Thus, not only have the immigrants been good for the industry, but the industry has been good for the immigrants. It provided work for over one-third of all working Jews in the United States around the turn of the century. Some 46 percent of the single Italian women (foreign-born and native-born) did garment work in New York in 1925. In a perhaps overly generous calculation, Michel Roblin estimated that sixty thousand Jews worked in one or another aspect of the Parisian garment industry in the mid-1920s, accounting for over one-half of Jewish activities in the Paris/Seine department. Already in the 1930s, 38.3 percent of the women placed by the New York City Puerto Rican Employment Service were involved in the needle trade.[104] In the early 1980s, an estimated two-thirds of all Chinese families in Chinatown had someone working in the industry, while 29.8 percent of Dominican immigrants in one survey worked in garment factories as operators, cutters, or pressmen. In Paris, perhaps 90 percent of the Chinese-Cambodian women are garment workers.[105]

Finally, the repeated renewal of the garment labor force can be seen from one last perspective. Immigrant labor in the industry is largely a single-generation phenomenon: "L'éternel processus": "Les ouvriers deviennent patron, une autre nationalité prend la relève."[106] The impact of demography on the sewing masses has been threefold. First, generational attrition occurs as the foreign-born workers get older. Second, as their sons and daughters seek better-paying jobs with better conditions elsewhere, they offer neither continuity nor succession. "It is said that the sons of cloak makers do not become cloak masters, but clerks, lawyers or business men."[107] Thus, if the first generation has been present and the second largely absent, renewal has been made possible largely thanks to a third factor and a third moment: government intervention and geopolitical migration streams. New immigrants take the place of old in an ever-repeated scenario.

Thus, what was hailed and decried at the turn of the century as a Russian Jewish specialty has turned out to be a more general immigrant one, lasting one generation or occasionally two, until education and opportunity move one group on as a next wave arrives. Immigrant waves are like generations, overlapping while replacing one another. Yet in this case each blames the next for a new set of ills. Or as some Jewish immigrants complained—with heavy accents—in the 1960s, as Yugoslavs started entering the Paris garment industry: But they are taking work away from the French!

The immigrants have been castigated by all the colors in the rainbow: green (*grine* in Yiddish, meaning greenhorns), yellow (as in strikebreakers in French, or anti-union in English), and black (as in blackmarket or *travail au noir*). Yet, as one ILGWU brochure proudly claimed: We *are* the melting pot. The Sentier, too, has been seen as "historically, traditionally, a land of welcome and of shelter for nationalities in need."[108] As long as fashions change—by whim or on purpose—and it is still necessary to have two hands to run a sewing machine, as the head of the New York Skirt and Sportswear Association stated rather bluntly, "What difference does it make if [those hands are] white, black or yellow?"[109]

Ready-to-Wear and Ready-to-Work

8

CONFLICT AND CONSENSUS ON
SEVENTH AVENUE

From one perspective, immigrant garment workers all look alike. White, black, or yellow, Buddhist, Catholic, or Jewish, they have filled the same function in the garment industry over the last century. Ready to work, usually because other options are limited, immigrants have supplied the ranks of the ready-to-wear revolution. Like native women, they have allowed the flexibility of demand to be answered with a flexibility of supply underpinned by a no-less pliant organization of labor.

Yet not all garment workers are exactly alike. If, as I have argued, the formation of the needle labor force can be explained more readily by industrial structure than by inborn or imported skill, and immigrants from around the world, like women, have ultimately had similar paths to the sewing machines, once there, what happens? The structural conclusion is incomplete without an understanding of the ways in which immigrants have related to one another within the industry. A poststructural structuralism needs to examine different perspectives and different voices, not to deny structure but to add agency to it, to explore variations on a mobile theme. One way to do this is to see how everyone, from Jews to Italians, Turks to Chinese, has interacted within the industrial patchwork. First for New York, then for Paris in the following chapter, I will show that conflict and cooperation are themselves fluctuating categories.

Two epistemological problems must be confronted. First, conflicts usually leave more traces than cooperation. The uneven stitches of the patchwork are most often revealed through the clarity if not hyperbole of conflict. Does that mean that conflicts are the more compelling "reality"?[1] The historian's task is to contemplate the silences between the shouts, those more or less extended moments of peaceful cohabitation that may be the day-to-day experience of most-of-the-time. Second, however, there is a contradictory proposition. Unions, manufacturers, as well as workers may all have a vested interest in ignoring ethnic conflict. Institutions leave more tracks than individuals, tracks that generally emphasize the positive. We know most about the New York industry thanks to the union's published records and unpublished archives, and the inter-ethnic relations most visible are those that were played out within the union context and construct. In this case, however, it is also the historian's job to understand the tensions between the lines of a repeated rhetoric of harmony. If conflicts are not the whole reality, the language of concord can be suspect as well.

In Paris, as we will see, intralabor relations were to a large extent those of a native-immigrant encounter, where a national union had to integrate foreigners into its ranks. On the contrary, for the immigrant-founded International Ladies' Garment Workers' Union (ILGWU), the first problem of integrating an "ethnic" group was that of getting Americans or American-born daughters of German and Irish immigrants to join. Although never named as such, the ILGWU was a largely Jewish immigrant organization from the outset, and its history shows the difficulties of overlapping ethnic succession, of struggles between immigrant groups for hegemony, and of challenges to the institution which questioned its very identity.

The New York story will focus on several key moments: relations between immigrants and American women in the early period of industrial growth; relations between the first immigrants, Jews and Italians; the union's later refusal to charter new language locals in 1937; Jewish-black relations in the late 1950s and early 1960s; and the Chinese strike of 1982.

An editorialist in the *Ladies' Garment Worker* of August 1914 argued that the New York dress and shirtwaist unions should be organized along gender lines. This would liberate women from the domination of male union leaders or from being "swallowed up in a sea of masculinity," as union activist Pauline Newman phrased it.[2] Already organized by ethnicity, craft, and geography, the ILGWU eventually set up women's branches within existing locals as well. They were not, however, all that successful and were largely dismantled during the interwar period.

The Jewish men organizing the ILGWU complained that "American women" (mostly second-generation Irish and German) were impervious to arguments of workers' unity. They were not alone. A growing body of literature has shown how (native) male unionists excluded women (as well as immigrants) from the labor market, often arguing that they were unorganizable. In the case of the garment and cigar trades, these struggles implicitly if not explicitly pitted male immigrants against immigrant and native-born women homeworkers.[3] Some of the early conflicts in the burgeoning ladies' ready-to-wear industry took the form of men versus women but also of Jewish immigrants complaining about American-born women for accepting lower pay and not standing up for themselves. Ethnic prejudice was mutual. If Russian Jewish labor leaders considered the American-born women too reticent, many of the latter probably considered the Russian Jews too "emotional and idealistic," as Helen Marot, leader of the Women's Trade Union League (WTUL), put it.[4] Clashes at times pitted male immigrants in workshops against American-born factory girls but also male inside shopworkers against female outside homeworkers, and Russian Jewish men against Russian Jewish female activists. The conflicts were never neat; class, ethnicity, and gender intertwined as sources of competition and contest.

If gender were paramount, as Pauline Newman argued, why were the women's branches so weak? Due to lack of interest on the part of American-born women? Due to the difficulties of coalition-building on the part of Russian Jewish women caught between middle-class gender allies (of the WTUL) and ethnic partners (Jewish working-class men)?[5] Differences among women became evident to even the most idealistic of female ILGWU organizers. Thus, while Helen Marot was complaining that efforts should be concentrated on organizing American rather than Lower East Side immigrant women, Rose Schneiderman ultimately concluded the contrary. It was American women, like Italian ones, who were just too difficult to organize, she said, the former for lack of spirit, the latter due to family pressures and traditions.[6] Jewish organizers considered *shikses* (a derogatory Yiddish term for non-Jewish women) indifferent to unionism at best, strikebreakers at worst.[7]

The salience of ethnicity or gender caused conflicting loyalties on the part of one particular, hybrid, category, the Jewish-American woman. American-born and English-speaking, a "Jewish-American Member" sent a letter to the editor of the *Message* (organ of the Ladies' Waist and Dress Makers' Union, Local 25) in 1914, complaining that she did not feel comfortable in the American Branch of the union: "Is it a question of religion, or is it a question of language?" she asked. "What about the Jewish-Americans who speak nothing but English?" Her letter revealed misunderstandings on both sides:

> I know the American Branch was organized for the purpose of unionizing the Christian girls, as they were not so quick to understand the cause as the Jewish girls. . . .
>
> I am a Jewish girl. When talking about these meetings, . . . another girl asked why I want to be butting in at their meeting, when I had a meeting of my own.[8]

A debate ensued, with the union newspaper answering that the branches had been organized by language, not by race or religion, and that the mostly Irish- and German-American branch should be opened up to (English-speaking) Jewish and Italian women. But a subsequent issue admitted that there was little response to the call, and letters to the editor complained that the American Branch was unwelcoming and in any case dull. A "Hebrew-American" suggested that a separate Jewish-American branch be set up.[9]

The demise of the women's branches, like that of the American (women's) Branch, may be understood as a result of "group loyalty remain[ing] a more compelling principle to most immigrant women than cross-ethnic gender solidarity," as Susan Glenn concluded.[10]

But we can also see these early quarrels over language and religion, and gender and ethnicity as a forerunner to the problems that union organizing would confront in this bi-gendered, multiethnic industry. The union expression of what I would call the "patchwork problem"—multiple identities in a de facto pluralist context—would be one of both exclusion and inclusion. By the 1930s, women and successive waves of immigrants would be prevented from having their own locals, but this was grounded in a construct of unity. As the Russian Jewish men structured the union in their image, they argued for the necessity of including everyone into one melting pot whole. However, tensions erupted over the way in which that whole was organized. The "structured inclusion" that resulted admitted geographic, craft, and certain ethnic distinctions. Yet even the ethnic boundaries were continually redefined.

Ultimately, perhaps, the Russian Jews continually repeated the early battle they themselves had had to fight against the Irish and German male cutters who had fought to maintain *their* hegemony against the newly arrived Russian immigrants.[11] While the cutters' conflict also had to do with competition for hegemony over craft skill, the subsequent skirmishes between American women and Russian Jews, and then between Jews and Italians, took place within the ready-made mode. As new immigrants came to town, to the factories, and to the union locals, other clashes occurred, more explicitly ethnic in nature, each time pitting new newcomers against repeatedly redefined old-timers.

Jews and Italians

In 1909, the Uprising of the 20,000 crystallized not only a powerful symbol of garment worker and working-women's combativity, but it brought to the fore an image of radical young Jewish women taking to the streets while Italian women stayed at their machines. Only 2,000 Italian women, compared to over 18,000 Jewish women, went on strike; the Italians were only 6 percent of the strikers although 35 percent of the labor force, while the Jewish women constituted 66 to 70 percent of the strikers and only 55 percent of the workforce.[12] Indeed, relations between the women were not always easy:

If they were more civilized [one Jewish organizer complained about Italian artificial-flower makers], they wouldn't take such low pay. But they go without hats and gloves and umbrellas.[13]

Stereotypes about Jewish "ringleaders" and the more "docile" Italian finishers abounded.

Much has been written trying to explain, or explain away, the Italian women who scabbed while Jewish women struck in 1909–10. Structure and culture have both been called upon: sociological differences or tradition and different worldviews. Southern Italians came from more rural, peasant backgrounds than the already more literate and urban Jews from the Russian Empire. Furthermore, visions of return (of many Italians) or settlement (of most Jews) had an impact on choices in the New World. Above all, an imported tradition of radicalism on the part of (some) Jewish women and the fact that they were allowed to go out alone at night may in and of itself explain differential strike-meeting attendance. As Miriam Cohen and Susan Glenn have pointed out, family and ethnic community support in the Jewish immigrant neighborhoods formed the setting behind Jewish women's organizing.[14]

Yet, even if cultural and sociological reasons may explain different forms of agency in a first stage, more united actions over the longer term beg for another explanation. In subsequent strikes, Italian women joined their Jewish sisters and brothers on the picket lines and rallied to the union. By the 1920s, as Roger Waldinger has pointed out, the Jewish immigrant women rabble-rousers of yore had in any case left the shops for white-collar jobs, leaving some less feisty American-born Jewish and Italian women to woman the shops and the (in any case fewer and fewer) picket lines together.[15] The union itself can be partially blamed for the early differences. Only Arturo Caroti was hired, belatedly, as an organizer in 1909. Once the ILGWU and the Women's Trade Union League found money to help organize Italian women and adapted the hours of their meetings, "tradition" or sociology were no longer real or explanational barriers to Italian organizing.

While the Uprising pointed to perceived, real, but in some cases temporary differences between Italian and Jewish women, the next stage of Jewish-Italian relations were played out largely between union men. It was only after the 1909–10 strike that the Jewish union

Ready-to-Wear and Ready-to-Work

turned to the Italian question. Italian branches (within locals) were formed after the strike, but the Italians started pressing for their own separate locals. A resolution in this sense was presented at the ILGWU convention in 1910, but to no effect. Another, more explicit, one was submitted two years later: "uneasiness prevails" between Italian and Jewish workers; "many difficulties and hardships [exist] in transacting business with [our] Jewish brothers." Furthermore, "the Italians are sensitive to pride and to self-government," and therefore needed their own local.[16] This resolution was also rejected, on the grounds that the branches already filled their needs, but Italian leaders continued to complain that they were misunderstood both in language and culture.

Why the reticence if not hostility to Italian demands on the part of the Jewish leaders? Due to a paternalistic belief that the Italians were not good organizers and needed "the friendly supervision of their more experienced brethren"?[17] Due to a fear of Italian radicalism, a stereotypical switch, but one which corresponded to the fears of the more socialist Jews with regard to the more Industrial Workers of the World–leaning Italians? Ultimately, the ILGWU, then as later, retreated to an institutional and class-based explanation, arguing that representation should be by craft or locality rather than by nationality. The rear-guard fear was that, if the Italians had their way, all of the other immigrant groups would eventually want separate locals as well.

By 1919, the Italian struggle for autonomy within the union was successful. An Italian Cloak, Suit and Skirt Makers' Union, Local 48, was set up in 1916, followed three years later by the Italian Blouse and Waist Makers' Union, Local 89. Their respective numbers were chosen explicitly to reflect their revolutionary spirit (and to counter myths of Italian docility?). Local 89's May Day parade float in 1935 was a reproduction of the Bastille; Marianne, another French revolutionary symbol, graced the cover of the local's twenty-fifth-year jubilee brochure. As the charismatic, antifascist Luigi Antonini, General Secretary of Local 89 and by then First Vice-President of the ILGWU, said at the thirtieth anniversary of the local, its mission was "to assault the industrial Bastilles" and to unite workers in fraternal bonds regardless of national or religious origins.[18]

A few jurisdictional skirmishes continued, with Local 48 complaining in 1920 that some of the other locals would not give up their Italian members![19] But by and large, an important shift had occurred. The Italians had been incorporated, albeit separately, as full-fledged members of the union fight. By 1934, Local 89 had become the largest language local in the United States, with some forty thousand members, of whom 70 percent were women.[20] The rhetoric turned rhapsodic. The term "Italian scabs" was struck from the record of a report presented to the ILGWU's convention in 1914; by 1922, the Italian locals were deemed an "integral part" of the union and pointed to with pride; in 1928 they were singled out as a "vivid example" of good unionship and praised for having remained free of Communist influence. The Italian locals had notably introduced more artistic life to the union by organizing concerts and operas, and were congratulated for having modernized the union's public relations by inaugurating radio broadcasts. Like their parent organization, they were ecumenical in their giving, sending financial aid not just (largely) to Italian and Italian-American organizations but also (a substantial contribution) to the Jewish Labor Committee as well as (more modest sums) to Jewish war veterans, the Negro Labor Committee, etc.[21] As a Jewish union manager reminisced in the Yiddish edition of *Justice* on Antonini's seventieth birthday in 1953,

even amongst those of us who did not understand a word of Italian, his words were very effective and aroused our blood. . . . Because for us his words always sounded as if we were at the Metropolitan listening to an Italian opera and not understanding a word of the text.[22]

One author went so far as to describe the Italian and Jewish cooperation in the needle-trades unions as "perhaps *the most* harmonious historic relationship ever to exist among ethnic groups in America."[23] While the shift in discourse heralded closer relations between the two groups, the evolution of this cooperation was also a sign of the newcomers becoming old-timers and consolidating their joint power within the union.

With the creation of the Italian locals, the ILGWU and the industry's ethnic identity became somewhat more clearly defined if not explicitly named. The grassroots push to establish the Italian locals, more so than the top-down efforts to create an American branch, forced the de facto Yiddish locals and Jewish leadership to recognize the "others" as the composition of the labor force shifted. Yet the ILGWU remained a basically Jewish union without ever calling itself as such. For some, the recognition of Italian locals within that construct was not enough but implied a more thorough renaming of the union's constituent parts. A resolution by an Italian local in 1932 argued that the Jewish locals should be specified; Local 22, for example, should become the Jewish Dress and Waist Makers' Union, and a separate non-Jewish, non-Italian dressmakers' union should be chartered.[24] The resolution failed, and there would never be a "Yiddish" local per se. But the issues of naming and power remained in the background, while the ILGWU maintained the firm belief that (with the exception of the Italian locals) ethnicity should not be specified, as a matter of principle, in the interest of workers' unity. This question would be at the crux of subsequent debates over the organization of other minority workers within the trade.

Structuring Difference: Language Locals and the ILGWU

New immigrants kept coming, and the Jewish male leaders and their Italian allies remained true to their own immigrant origins in the welcome they offered to other minorities. Both in its defense of immigration and immigrants ever since its founding, and in the cultural activities it sponsored, the ILGWU was in the vanguard of the labor movement. From the "new" immigrants of the turn of the century to those today, the ILGWU has gone on record—often against the AFL's restrictionist stance—for free migration. During World War II, the union, via Luigi Antonini, defended Italian-Americans from potential internment; after the war, it petitioned the government on behalf of (mostly Jewish) displaced persons and later supported the American Committee on Italian Migration's efforts to let more Italians into the country. In the 1920s as in the 1950s, the ILGWU spoke out against the quota laws and then the McCarran-Walter Act as offensive to the American tradition of haven from oppression. Since the early 1980s, the union has taken the side of the newest immigrants in urging government legislation "to help solve the dilemma of the 'undocumented' workers."[25]

Beyond defending immigration and immigrants per se, the union was caught up with the more difficult dilemma of how to organize so many peoples from around the world. It stressed the private nature of difference:

> The idea of race or religion has no place in any trade union whose members of several races and nationalities work side by side in the shops. The Union does not interfere with their racial and religious feelings and opinions. These are strictly private matters.[26]

It was a "mere evolutionary incident" that caused people to be divided into different nationalities and speak different languages. In a discourse that would be repeated again and again, the union saw its role and self-appointed task as melding all workers into "one great family."[27] Yet this accident of nature, as it were, proved to be one of the major organizational headaches of such a multiethnic union in its attempts to acknowledge private difference without creating public division.

The ILGWU was one of the few unions (along with the men's-wear union, the Amalgamated Clothing Workers of America—ACWA) to set up special programs for immigrants, in their communities and in their own languages. The Education Department, set up in 1914 ("Knowledge is power"), aimed to teach people about unionism but also to entertain and to integrate while allowing difference. Thus there were separate Yiddish, Italian, and Negro Choruses as well as the General Chorus, just as there were lectures and courses in English, Yiddish, Russian, Italian, and later Spanish and Chinese concerning the history of the trade union movement and the ILGWU. A class on "The Negro in American History" was instituted as early as the 1930s. By the 1940s, the union was offering courses in first aid (the most popular course during the war), current events, citizenship, and arts and crafts. While spreading an ideology of worker citizenship, and acting, as Steven Fraser has said with regard to the similarly structured ACWA, as "a kind of civilizing institution" or "school for socialization,"[28] the educational and cultural activities were tailored to immigrant needs and specific cultures. Antonini played Columbus in Columbus Day Parades; spaghetti was served, to their great relief, to Italian women who braved tradition and went to the union's summer resort.[29]

Language was key. The ILGWU had been founded in Yiddish, and its constitution was drawn up in that language; its early meetings were in the Eastern European mother tongue and would remain so until the younger (Jewish) members gradually forced a switch over to English, its first foreign language! As the author of an article entitled "American Branch Welcomes All English-Speaking Girls" wrote, stressing that branches were defined by language and not by race: "it was a question mostly of convenience."[30] However, the debate over language (like the refusal to name itself ethnically) was also a debate over unity and the importance of talking in one voice. The ILGWU has never been able to speak in only one language. Language was the practical stuff of organizing but also the symbolic recognition of difference.

There were sporadic, unsuccessful attempts to teach Yiddish to English-speakers. (Some of the non-Jewish union leaders learned to sprinkle Yiddish phrases in their vocabulary.) An experimental Esperanto class was tried in 1944–46. More successful were the English classes, set up for Italians circa 1918, for Spanish-speaking workers in 1948, and for Chinese workers today. There have also been "Spanish for Unionists" classes emphasizing labor and garment-industry vocabulary. But in addition to language courses, the union reached out to the immigrant neighborhoods, organizing activities for blacks in Harlem, sponsoring balls for Puerto Ricans in Spanish Harlem, setting up a Health Center in Chinatown in 1979, and establishing the Immigration Project for free counseling there in 1982.

Above all, the union has spoken out to the different language groups through its publications. In 1919, the various locals' (corresponding to crafts) newspapers were consolidated into *Justice,* one (industrial) voice albeit published in different languages.[31] The Yiddish, English, and Italian versions were not equal, however, and the Italian delegates complained at the 1920 and 1922 annual conventions that *Giustizia* needed beefing up. A Spanish edition, *Justicia,* was added in 1933, a sign of the times. By 1934, total circulation was 175,000; with 90,000 copies, English had finally become the predominant language.[32] The following year *Justice* became bimonthly, although the other language versions remained monthly. In January 1958, the Yiddish *Gerechtigkeit* was suspended; two years later the Spanish edition was enlarged.

The history of ethnic succession is writ large in the circulation history of *Justice.* So, too, is the history of the tension between

Conflict and Consensus on Seventh Ave.

difference and division. As President David Dubinsky himself justified when the Yiddish edition *Gerechtkigkeit* was discontinued,

> I am a great believer in Jewish culture, because I believe every group lives and gets inspiration from the cultural development of its own nationality. . . . [however]
>
> I believe that a union does not exist for the purpose of perpetuating cultural institutions within its own ranks.[33]

Newspapers, cultural activities, and different voices were one thing; separate locals were another. Once the Italians had their local, other groups formulating similar demands had much less success. If in 1925, subsequent to the success of the Italian locals, the General Executive Board recognized the

> necessity for chartering a lingual [*sic*] group of workers in order to facilitate organizing workers and for the sake of keeping a national group of workers close together and more efficiently organized and managed,

and if in 1928 the GEB formally recommended that the union continue to charter locals or branches on the basis of language and sex ("these methods are not offered as solutions of the tremendous problem of organization, but as steps"), these practical considerations soon paled in the face of worry over divisive factions.[34]

The ultimate banning of language locals in 1937 must be set against the ongoing fight against Communist influence that made the union wary of all forms of subdivisions. After having ousted the Communists from leadership positions and expelled their rank-and-file, shop delegate, and educational leagues in the early 1920s, the ILGWU still viewed with suspicion the clubs and groups which took their place. The latter were repeatedly disbanded in 1932, 1934, and 1937, although each such action came up against the objections that some of the groups had actually been constituted to support the union against the Communists and that, in any case, their dissolution was a threat to internal democracy. Both sides appealed to democracy; those against the clubs argued that they caused chaos and undermined democracy from within; those for the groups insisted that they were necessary so as to permit free speech and the right to organize. Dubinsky finally decided in 1937 that groups could only form for three months prior to a union election (and that others could be admitted under special conditions); he remained opposed to any change of the constitution's general limitation on groups.[35]

In the meantime, language branches had sprung up across the country. A Russian-Polish Branch of the New York Joint Cloak Board, for example, was organized in 1910, serving not only Russians and Poles but also Ukrainians and Serbs who belonged to Locals 35 (Pressers), 117 (Samplemakers), and 9 (Finishers). In 1924 and again in 1926 the branch requested a separate charter in order to become a full-fledged local. It gave the Italian locals as an example and argued that its members understood neither Yiddish nor English. Their request was initially rejected on the grounds that it was itself a multilingual branch, but a committee was set up to investigate the matter. Luigi Antonini and another, Jewish, member of the committee ultimately took the branch's side, although a third (Jewish) member of the committee demurred. In any case the branch closed down voluntarily in 1927 so as not to have anything to do with the Communist opposition, only to reopen in 1930. It remained in existence until the early 1960s, when, according to Henoch Mendelsund, General Manager of the Cloak Board, who was instrumental in its closing (over protests), the branch "[had] no more purpose."[36]

Ethnicity and politics were interwoven in the union's concerns as well as in many of the members' demands. In 1933, in the heat of the National Recovery Act strikes, a *La Prensa* article of December 23 announced that, following a meeting with a delegation of Spanish workers, Dubinsky had agreed to the idea of a Spanish local (citing the Italian example), subject to approval by the union's Executive Committee. But the announcement was premature. A Spanish Left Opposition Group soon denounced the bureaucrats of Manager Charles Zimmerman's "clique" and railed against Local 22's pronouncements boasting of its accomplishments on behalf of Spanish workers.[37] In January 1934, the union responded vigorously (in the Spanish press) to the announcement that a rival "Union Local Hispana" had been set up in East Harlem. It denounced the "so-called Spanish local" as a "shameless swindle," a "splitting scheme" that was trying to put up an "organizational wall" contrary to the union's constant efforts to "cement the ties binding the dressmakers of all nationalities and tongues."[38] The Spanish-speaking section of Dress Makers' Local 22, which had been set up in 1933, was to remain a branch.

It is not surprising then that, in 1937, the union decided that no more language sections would be chartered. Existing language locals around the country were subsequently eliminated and merged into their corresponding craft or regional local. The notable exceptions were Italian Locals 48 and 89 in New York, which remained on practical and historic grounds. But the general rule held fast, and in spite of successive immigration waves lapping at the union's doors, the non-named Jewish union and its historic Italian locals limited future expressions of ethnicity in the name of union unity. The new immigrant groups were not necessarily branded Communists, but they were perceived as threats to the established leaders' hegemony. Arguments appealing to the past and to the Italian example no longer carried any weight. By the early 1950s, the General Executive Board was adamant: "That period [of Italian, Jewish, or women's locals], we assert, is a matter of the past."[39]

Nationality or language-based local unions, progressive in their time, were not only suspect to a unifying organization such as the ILGWU. They were deemed illegal in New York under the State Anti-Discrimination Law of 1945. The Italian locals came under renewed scrutiny, but they did not give up without a fight. A *Hunter vs. Sullivan Dress Shop* case in 1946 forced them to admit Hispanics and blacks, although few ever did.[40] The United States Civil Rights Act of 1964 increased pressure to dissolve any particularistic organizations that by their nature discriminated. Responding to a complaint filed against the ILGWU concerning racial discrimination in the late 1960s, First Vice-President Molisani claimed that there were 6 to 10 "Negroes," 183 people with Spanish surnames, and 197 with other non-Italian or non-Spanish surnames (including Oriental, Greek, and Jewish) among Local 48's membership.[41] The two New York Italian locals lasted until 1977, serving older immigrants and many second- and third-generation Italian-Americans who knew little if any Italian.

It is difficult to separate the ideological from the bureaucratic, and the union has been harshly criticized on both grounds. The decision to abolish language locals was ideological both in the strictly political sense—part of the worry about the Communist threat—but also in the more general meaning. The union repeatedly insisted that there could be no divisions within one happy union. Yet, different languages, not to mention different customs, raised the same problem: How should difference be organized? Is a glee club enough, a separately chartered local too much?

Finally, language did not only differentiate garment workers from foreign lands:

The impact upon unaccustomed ears of the Puerto Rican's Spanish and the Negro's southern accent was a constant reminder that the world of the shop which they considered their own was no longer so.[42]

Race also divided the minorities within the industry and the union. Indeed, what might have been good and desirable for immigrant groups—separate sections—was seen as jim crowism with regard to African Americans. As blacks and Puerto Ricans joined Jews and Italians in the sweatshops, they sought to have their voices heard. In the context of the burgeoning civil rights movement, this led not to a demand for separate locals but to a highly publicized legal case accusing the immigrant union of discrimination.

Jews and Blacks

On April 4, 1961, Ernest Holmes, a black cutter, and the NAACP filed a formal complaint for discrimination with the New York State Commission for Human Rights against his employer and against ILGWU Cutters' Local 10.[43] After having been hired by Primrose Foundations, Inc., a corset factory, on July 29, 1960, as a general helper with a salary of fifty-two dollars per week, Holmes had started helping out with the cutting the following month. While still doing his job as general aid and being paid as such, he learned the craft and soon sought to become a full-fledged cutter. Since Primrose was a closed shop under contract with the ILGWU, Holmes needed a union card. He went to Local 10 several times, without success. In the case which ensued, the complaint against the employer was dropped, and it was the union that stood accused of acting like a closed guild. Not only was the union likened to the bosses in its regulation of the labor market, but it was accused of discriminating via that regulatory mechanism. Implicitly, the Jewish cutters were thus being protected. As Herbert Hill, then labor secretary of the NAACP, wrote:

[The ILGWU] is a trade union controlled by a rigid bureaucracy that long ago lost contact with its rank and file members. A bureaucracy that has more in common ethnically and socially with the employers than with the workers it is supposed to represent.[44]

Charles Zimmerman qualified the accusation of complicity between Jewish union leaders and employers an anti-Semitic lie.[45] In July 1962, the commission found that the union had discriminated. Holmes was eventually instated in the local.

Furthermore, a wide-ranging inquiry was instigated by Rev. Adam Clayton Powell Jr. before the House of Representatives' Committee on Education and Labor, of which he was chairman.[46] The Powell Commission took up many issues, including corruption within the industry, but it basically concentrated on two principal elements: the exclusion of blacks from skilled jobs such as cutting and pressing; and their exclusion from union leadership. In fact, the concentration of power among those leaders who had been in the union for over a third of a century (Dubinsky was seventy years old by this time) represented more than one migration wave behind. It was thus, among other things, a generational struggle, overlaid by racial and ethnic difference, that was at issue for the control of the ILGWU.

The union responded in two ways: with a multiethnic defense and with an appeal to memory. We are all minorities, said Dubinsky and Zimmerman. Zimmerman reminded the commission that his Local 22 represented thirty-two different nationalities and called itself the "League of Nations." How could a union of minorities, some of whom had fled from persecution elsewhere, be accused of discrimination? An article in *Justice* on September 1, 1962, defended the union in hurt tones:

Our ILGWU—in whose ranks hundreds of thousands of newcomers to this nation first experienced democracy—stands accused of bias. This union— which for more than six decades has been the portal through which masses of immigrants have integrated into American life—is charged with discrimination. . . . This union of ours—founded by members of minorities, built with the sacrifices of minorities, nurtured and sustained by the hopes of minorities—is accused of exploiting minorities.

The history of the union's commitment to democracy, its fights against Communism and fascism, was repeated with pride. But above all Dubinsky and Zimmerman were outraged and hurt by being called false friends of the civil rights movement. They reiterated the union's former activities and defended its honor and their own.

Indeed, the ILGWU was at the fore of the "natural alliance" between blacks and Jews. It was a prominent example of progressive liberalism and was perceived as such from the 1930s well into the 1950s, one of the rare exceptions in the AFL, along with some of the industrial unions (notably the men's-wear ACWA) of the Congress of Industrial Organization. Lester B. Granger, labor secretary (and later director) of the National Urban League, congratulated the ILGWU:

There is no union in the country which has done more for a submerged group of workers, which has offered them a truer partnership in leadership activities, and which has more consistently fought reaction in the trade union field and in politics.[47]

Already in the late 1920s, the union stood out for its help to A. Philip Randolph in his efforts to organize the first black union, the Brotherhood of Sleeping-Car Porters. During its annual convention in Chicago in 1934, in a widely publicized event, the union pulled its meeting from the Medinah Club when the hotel refused to serve the black delegates.[48] The motorcade move made nationwide news. In the same period, Frank R. Crosswaith, a black socialist and General Organizer of the ILGWU, created, with the backing of the ILGWU, the Harlem Labor Center and the Negro Labor Committee to encourage black unionization.[49] The union sought to organize African American workers in New York as of the early 1930s. In August 1933, at the time of the major New York dress strike, and thanks in large part to the National Recovery Act, which stimulated organizing across the board, some four thousand black women joined Local 22. By 1934, four black women had become delegates to the Local's executive board.[50]

The union also gave financial and moral support to the NAACP, the National Urban League, the National Committee Against Discrimination in Housing, the Bureau for Intercultural Education, etc., before such gestures were common. During the war, the union defended blacks against discrimination within the armed forces, even protesting directly to the President of the United States.[51] As

Conflict and Consensus on Seventh Ave.

early as 1944, the union took a prominent stand in favor of passage of the New York State Fair Employment Act. Within the AFL-CIO, Dubinsky fought for desegregation of the "lily-white" unions. And in 1960, during the national boycott of Woolworth restaurants, the ILGWU furnished up to eight hundred people per day on the picket lines.[52]

Yet in spite of the ILGWU's exemplary track record, certain problems became apparent as early as the late 1920s. The small Communist Needle Trades Workers' Industrial Union perceived race relations as one of the factors distinguishing it ("race prejudice has been completely abolished") from the "yellow" ILGWU.[53] During the March 1934 elections of Local 22's officers, a leaflet signed the Negro Committee of the Left Wing (NCLW) attacked Zimmerman and his co-officers:

The officials of Local 22 come to Harlem and make such beautiful speeches to the Negro dressmakers, but in the shops they permit the bosses to discriminate against us, only because we are Negroes, to pay us lower wages than the white workers.[54]

The union counterattacked through a Harlem section of Local 22, which denied the allegations and protested against political interference in the elections. Frank Crosswaith denounced the NCLW as Communists and carpetbaggers and responded in a Harlem Labor Committee leaflet that invoked the memory of Abraham Lincoln and the Emancipation Proclamation and defended "the victorious and inspiring banner of the ILGWU" in a religio-militant language. The Communists were accused of wanting to reduce the Negroes once again to slavery; however, the "New Negro" would not be duped— the era of enlightenment had arrived. The prolific and at times poetic Crosswaith wrote in *Justice* about the "happy family of the ILGWU," working to establish a "cooperative commonwealth" and a "brotherhood of all mankind." He saluted the Negro workers who joined the ILGWU as "pioneers of the New Day" and argued that the garment union's "protecting folds" gave African Americans full citizenship in the union even if they were not full citizens in the United States.[55]

Into the 1940s, however, the union was wary of Communist influence among blacks and complained that Communist opponents disguised as so-called "rank and file" and "unity" groups were stirring up racial animosities—saying to the "Spanish" and "Negroes" that the union discriminated against them, telling the Jewish members that Dubinsky was anti-Semitic and pro-Hitler—in order to damage the union.[56] Did the Harlem blacks have real griefs, or were they being influenced? Can we sort out racial disgruntlement, political manipulation, and discrimination?

By the end of the 1950s, it was no longer a question of Communists. The radicalization of the African American community in its struggle for a New Emancipation, in the North, would lead it to quarrel and eventually break with its former friends for reasons of both strategy and identity. In 1959, two years before the Holmes brief, the NAACP attacked the AFL-CIO for discrimination. This was not the first time it had done so. What was new was that it included the ILGWU in its complaint. Yesterday's allies stood accused of being incapable of eliminating discrimination in their own ranks and of having "paternalistic and missionary" attitudes vis-à-vis the African Americans.[57]

The allegations of discrimination took the form of accusations about the union structure. The ILGWU had to defend the way in which it expressed ethnic difference. Three locals came under particular scrutiny. The Powell Commission wanted to know why there were no blacks in Local 89. Because it was created for the Italians, answered Zimmerman with a touch of exasperation. Neither Irish, Poles, Jews, Chinese, nor David Dubinsky himself could belong to that local.[58] The commission also wanted to know why the Secretary-General of Puerto Rican Local 600–601 was a Jew. Because he is a labor organizer specialized in underwear, the principal garment product of the island, answered the ILGWU, adding that all of the other leaders of this local were Puerto Rican and that conditions and wages for garment workers on the island had improved markedly thanks to the union's efforts.

Finally, then, why did Local 60A, the largely black and Hispanic Shipping Clerks' union, remain a part of the mostly Jewish and Italian Pressers' Local 60? That smacked of jim crowism to the Powell Commission. A debate ensued over the notions of separation and segregation. If the Italians had their own local, why not blacks? William Schwartz, General Secretary of Local 60–60A, invoked tradition and history. He recounted the local's history, marked by a struggle between generations, the young (Jews) having had to fight (and even threaten a lawsuit) in order to have meetings and minutes in English instead of Yiddish. The old guard had countered by setting up Yiddish classes aimed not only at the American-born Jews, but for blacks and Hispanics as well. (They were not a great success.) It was not because of their race that the shipping clerks were organized separately, Schwartz argued, but because of their "craft," which placed them at the low end of the skill hierarchy. Labor segmentation, the ILGWU argued again and again, is not the union's fault. If there is discrimination and therefore segmentation, the real culprits are the factory owners.

The debate over discrimination also became a discussion over statistics and counting. The union was summoned to estimate the number of African Americans and Hispanics (or "Negroes" and "Spanish elements" or "Latin Americans") in Local 10. It claimed ignorance, arguing that it would be discriminatory to ask racial or ethnic information and that, furthermore, the union refused on principle to distinguish among its members on the basis of color. Dubinsky had already put forth the argument in 1934: "We never concern ourselves with the race, religion, nationality or color of our sisters and brothers. We know then only as garment workers," a theme repeated later by Zimmerman: there is no black problem, it is just a question of dressmakers.[59] Minorities were not to be named. In spite of this color blindness, the union nonetheless at first estimated there to be about 400 black and Hispanic cutters, a figure later dropped to 200, out of a total of 7,500.[60] Being asked to count to prove they were not discriminating, the ILGWU answered that counting was in itself discriminatory, that a worker was a worker. While ideological and defensive in its response, the union's answer was witness to the meaning of identification and counting in the early 1960s. The 1964 Civil Rights bill reinforced the union's argument, making it illegal to list membership by nationality. However, subsequent affirmative-action programs would bring classification and counting back to the fore.[61]

The union had one last argument. Dubinsky and Zimmerman blamed the women. They stressed that the high proportion of women among the rank and file—80 percent of the 443,000 nationwide members and more than 90 percent of the black and Hispanic workers—explained everything. Family responsibilities and a high turnover accounted for the women's particularly low participation in union leadership roles. As Dubinsky commented during the commission's hearings: "80 percent of our members are women, but we have only one woman vice-president. Can we be charged with discrimination against women? No!"[62]

The conflict lasted several years before subsiding, with the NAACP and the ILGWU exchanging insults ranging from Jewish racism to black anti-Semitism. (NAACP labor secretary Herbert Hill, although Jewish, was compared to Eichmann in the Yiddish daily *Forverts*.[63]) The union constructed its defense around three main themes: a de facto pluralism; its vanguard position compared to other organizations; and a historic tradition of "natural alliance." The Holmes case and the Powell Commission were witness to a period of redefinition of black identity; the history of the "natural alliance" was undergoing revision.[64] But this period was also one in which the union had to clairfy its own ethnic identity. Rejecting the implicit and explicit attacks that it was comporting itself as a "Jewish" union, the ILGWU answered by insisting on its heterocultural composition. This defense drew upon the notion that multiethnicity in and of itself was constituent of cultural pluralism, key to America's democracy.

Yet, in spite of structural similarities in the secondary labor market and a union discourse on the equality of workers, all garment workers were not alike. As each new group confronted the rigidities of industrial and union microsegmentation within the flexibility of the ready-made mode of production, they gave voice to their own demands. As the Puerto Rican women who went on a wildcat strike against their boss and against the union in 1958 painted on their placards, "We're tired of industrial peace. We want industrial justice."[65]

The Chinatown Strike and Intra-Ethnic Conflict

Women took to the streets again in 1982, taking everyone by surprise, including many of the participants themselves. The first major garment strike since 1958 was that of Chinese women insisting on a union contract. It showed how far both the Chinese women and, to a certain extent, the union had come.[66]

At the turn of the century, a San Francisco local demanded exclusion of "Asiatics" from the ILGWU in sad keeping with the restrictionist and racist times. After considerable debate, a resolution was finally adopted in 1901 accepting Chinese and Japanese members but stipulating that no charters would be issued for separate locals. However, a year later, under renewed pressure from the West Coast locals, this compromise was overruled. The constitution's preamble was amended to bar Asians from membership, a decision not overturned until a decade later.[67]

It was not until some seventy years later that a new wave of Chinese immigrants, thanks to the changed immigration law, came in large numbers to the New York industry. This time they moved quickly and massively into unionized shops and became members of the ILGWU. The 1982 strike broke out when a number of Chinese contractors refused to sign the new contracts that had been negotiated between the union and the Greater Blouse, Skirt, and Undergarment Association. The recalcitrant shop owners claimed that the contracts were discriminatory and had been drawn up without any Chinese on the negotiating team. Yet this accusation of discrimination against the Chinese masked another, intra-ethnic, conflict between the Chinese contractors and their Chinese workers that came to the fore with the women's march.

The meaning of the 1982 Chinatown strike was multiple. It was a strike in defense of wage-and-labor conditions guaranteed by a union contract, just as it was a strike for union membership itself. That being said, for many, the true meaning of union membership was medical benefits and pensions. As Peter Kwong has put it, in a highly critical view of the ILGWU, "To many Chinese, the union is nothing more than a health-insurance company."[68] Belonging to the union in health-insurance-poor America has meant the only coverage that most workers have.

According to ILGWU organizer Katie Quan, the strike was nonetheless also about class consciousness:

Class consciousness is a strange thing in the Chinese context because there's nobody who's Chinese that doesn't know that labor and management are in contradiction to each other. It's like yin and yang.[69]

Yet this interpretation flew in the face of the more prevailing image of (once again) docile women working in compatriot-run shops. Bernard Wong has stressed how Chinese owners were more than employers, that they "consciously cultivat[e] *Gam Ching* [sentimental feeling] with the workers."[70] A leaflet distributed by Chinese employers during the strike argued: "No matter if we're bosses or workers, we are one, like fingers on a hand. We're in the same boat together in this garment industry, fighting for a decent living."[71] Yet this did not prevent the women from walking out when they felt that their union privileges were being threatened.

The strike not only made the Chinese contractors take notice of their compatriot female workers but it made the union sit up as well. Given that some 90 percent of the Chinatown shops were organized, the union seems to have felt that little more of their effort was needed. Sportswear Local 23–25, whose membership was 85 percent Chinese, had been dragging its feet on a requested day care center. After the strike, the money was quickly raised through a joint union, management, and city effort, and the Garment Industry Day Care Center of Chinatown opened in late 1983.[72]

Most surprisingly to many, however, the Chinatown strike brought into question not just interethnic relations but intra-ethnic ones. The contractors had assumed that their compatriots would side with them. But

the response of the workers destroyed the myth that Chinese workers don't stand up for their rights because they work for Chinese bosses or because they're from the same part of China, or related in some way.[73]

Like Jewish strikes against Jewish bosses three-quarters of a century before, when workers refused their bosses' overtures/bribes of herring or Passover wine, the Chinese strike showed that intraethnic cleavages could supersede interethnic ones, providing a cautionary tale about automatic assumptions of ethnic bonds.[74] The union explicitly interpreted the 1982 Chinatown strike as a show of interethnic unity, based on class interests, revealing a previously hidden intra-ethnic conflict: "[W]hat has appeared as simple acquiescence to personalistic authority was often submission to coercive power."[75] The growth of the industry and rising class-consciousness had weakened the importance of ethnic bonds. In the end, Chinese workers were standing up for their own rights as workers. Community ostracism, a tactic used by employers in the past, no longer worked. After a newspaper ad denouncing a rebellious worker (complete with picture) was published in the Chinese press, the Chinese garment manufacturers' association was sued and had to print an apology.[76]

Harmony, Discord, and Memory

The ILGWU story reflects our conundrum of conflict versus consensus. There are two ways of interpreting interethnic relations within the union: by concentrating on the revealing moments of conflict or by taking the organization's proclamations of workers' unity at face value. Neither can stand alone. On the one hand, the black-Jewish dispute ultimately ended with a public making-up (between the moderate factions). As Dubinsky and Roy Wilkins, General Secretary of the NAACP, both stressed from the podium of the next ILGWU convention in 1965, the affair had merely been an unfortunate incident, a breakdown in communications between two friendly organizations. By the late 1960s, the union was appealing to black and Hispanic cutters to join Local 10 in order to block the expansion of nonunion subcontractors' "cut-up" shops.[77] On the other hand, the union's rhetoric of harmony, be it black and Jewish, or Jewish and Chinese—which need not necessarily be interpreted cynically— derives also from a certain organizational self-interest.

The expression of internationalism, drawing on the union's early commitment to socialism, has been classic and heartfelt:

In the Union we are not Irish, German, Jewish, Italian, Catholic or Protestant; we are Union people—brothers and sisters united to protect our bread and our very lives against a cruel system of wage slavery.[78]

If the language of wage slavery and a vision of class struggle later dropped out in favor of a more diffuse notion of defending workers, the themes of unity and harmony still lived on. The ILGWU has represented itself as incarnating American history, not only in its welcome of immigrants but in its functioning as a dual melting pot. The ILGWU is "the melting pot of trade unionism," a place where all immigrants are considered "citizens of the shop."[79] More generally, it serves society: "We have been proud of our role as a melting pot—

or more accurately, as a gateway to full American citizenship for successive waves of immigration."[80] As Frank Crosswaith put it more imaginatively, and long before Jesse Jackson, the union was a "human rainbow" that "represents God's concept of beauty."[81]

The language of the union's General Executive Board reports and convention proceedings have drawn on religious, familial, and historical themes. Newcomers have been likened to those of the turn of the century, coming to know the United States first of all through poor, crowded neighborhoods. The similarity of circumstances, the commonality of struggle has joined the immigrants over time, from the Jews and Italians of the past to the Chinese of today. The ILGWU has proclaimed itself and been recognized as a liberal exception within the labor movement. Union historians have consecrated this vision. The histories of Louis Levine, Will Herberg, Roy Helfgott, and more recently Gus Tyler have been proud stories of the progressive ILGWU.[82]

An alternate and often uncompromising story has described an aging oligarchy protecting itself over the years against women, minorities, African Americans, or Chinese. Alice Kessler-Harris showed the early difficulties that early-twentieth-century Russian-Jewish women had in making their voices heard. Herbert Hill, now professor of history at the University of Wisconsin-Madison, has been an outspoken, even bitter critic ever since the 1960s Holmes case. In his highly critical dissertation, Robert Laurentz argued that the ILGWU had a long history of oppressing its rank and file ever since the Protocol of 1910 made the union dependent on maintaining good relations with the employers. Peter Kwong has protested the union's indifference to the Chinese workers today.[83] Others have described the rigidities and bureaucratization of labor unions in general as leading to exclusionary policies behind an inclusive rhetoric. Frank Parkin extended Max Weber's notion of social closure to encompass apprenticeship systems, closed shops, and unions as acting as forms of exclusion in the "distributive struggle."[84]

Yet another form of self-defense has implied the opposite, a (structured) inclusion. A unified labor movement was in and of itself in the union's best interest both for political and labor reasons. As Helfgott, Research Director of the Cloak Joint Board, lucidly admitted,

Conflict and Consensus on Seventh Ave.

[Local 23] has understood that it had to establish contact with [its Puerto Rican members] if it were to keep the industry well-organized, maintain peace in the ranks, and prevent their falling prey to political foes of the present leadership. . . . Their integration can remove any threat to organized labor of their becoming a source of non-union competition.[85]

Organizing workers and defending minorities was a way of forestalling Communist influence as well as eliminating nonunion work, illegal sweatshops, and homework.

Finally, the union's self-interest has been based in one ultimate structural concern: keeping the industry in New York City. Having lost the battle against subcontracting and seen manufacturers leave the city as wages got too high or workers too feisty, the union retrenched to an industrial defense. Instead of addressing head-on the industrial limits to worker agency and worker protection, the union chose to defend its workers by defending the industry, which meant in the end defending the manufacturers. This brought it once again into sharp conflict with black and Hispanic groups in the early 1960s, for example, when it opposed a minimum-wage law and refused to support a federally funded sewing-operator training program for minorities, claiming now that skill was not a prerequisite for hiring.[86]

Beyond the union rhetoric of rainbows *and* color-blindness, the question is a comparative one. The ILGWU (like the ACWA) has often been progressive for its time, particularly compared to other unions. It has also worked hard to bring relative rationalization and "industrial peace" to a chaotic, anarchic industry. As one defender said: "It is absurd to imply that Dubinsky is no better than Mississippi's meanest bigot."[87] However, in the 1960s, while the ILGWU was still comparing itself, favorably, to the AFL and lily-white unions, black leaders had begun to compare the garment-workers' union to other criteria, those of the more militant civil rights demands. Many were all the angrier because of the union's liberal reputation and the contrast between the ILGWU's past and present.[88] The union's very stabilization policy created its own rigidities, which some workers compared unfavorably to a broader notion of industrial justice. Along a time line of arrival to the industry, new groups and their defenders, from blacks to Chinese, have repeatedly spoken up to redraw the bases of comparison. In some cases, the past has

Ready-to-Wear and Ready-to-Work

been called upon as a model to follow (the Italian example). In others, history and memory have been explicitly rejected as not good enough. As newcomers have clamored at the gates, past history has often seemed less important than immediate demands.

Who Discriminates?

While the union may thus be criticized for social closure if not worse, one of its defenses needs to be examined more closely. In answering accusations of cultural discrimination, the ILGWU responded by describing structural segmentation in a context of societal racism.[89] It argued that it did not discriminate, that employers did. While the argument was disingenuous with regard to the guildlike Local 10, and ultimately unsuccessful in the Holmes case, it was not entirely wrong. Immigrants have occupied different places within the industry (what Steven Fraser has called "ethno-occupational groups") in large part due to ethnic succession.[90] Older groups (and men compared to women) have repeatedly been concentrated in better lines and better shops. The timing of arrival in relation to economic opportunity can be as important as the cultural or economic baggage imported with the immigrants.[91] Yet ethnic succession is not only a question of timing. Each group seems to have discriminated at some point against those who followed. The question is who discriminates and why. Is it the unions, employers, or workers? Are the reasons purely cultural or simply structural, and what does this say about conflict or cohabitation within an industry?

At the turn of the century, women complained to the WTUL that manufacturers were "stir[ing] up race antagonism between Jewish and Italian girls for the purpose of retaining the cheaper labor of Italians."[92] In his 1940s study, Irving Stuart found that employers did in fact discriminate. They explained that their shop's status would be hurt if they hired blacks and Hispanics, and some expressed fear of discrimination charges in case of a dispute. Two decades later, social scientist Elaine Wrong found that, while the ILGWU and the ACWA both directly affected the placement of workers, employers too were to blame. The latter gave various reasons for at this point preferring Puerto Rican to black garment workers: the former were more willing to put up with bad conditions; they brought some skills with them. More vaguely, some employers had simply decided: "Blacks do not make good needle workers." Employers today continue to express direct hostility or more subtle criticism of minority workers.[93]

Employers have also sometimes shifted the blame onto their employees, denying that they themselves want to discriminate. They have argued that it is their workers or clients who are unfavorable to the hiring of blacks.[94] The older workers, in particular, are "displeased by the competition, both actual and potential, of any Newcomer. The high visibility of Negroes and Puerto Ricans [makes] it easy to distinguish them as Newcomers."[95] Some manufacturers and contractors have defended their position by saying that they would get better cooperation from their workers if they did not hire blacks or Hispanics. Such tacit agreement between employers and workers was reportedly widespread in the 1940s, although difficult to prove.

Ethnic conflict on the factory floor—ranging from stereotypical expressions of difference to animosity and hatreds—has existed since the beginning of the century. Competition over bundles, layoffs, or work sharing during the off-season has often caused worker antagonisms as a response to imposed flexibility. Old-timers could passively resist training newcomers. Italians were accused of being clannish and of only teaching the trade to close relatives. Some workers considered it "a social disgrace to sponsor a Negro or Puerto Rican worker in the trade. The sponsor lost social standing in the shop." After a young Jewish man started training a Puerto Rican worker and she began to pick up speed, his father advised him "Don't show her anything else, she will take the bread out of our mouths."[96]

Petty jealousies and covert hostility could also erupt over working conditions, exacerbated by age and origin. When older (probably Jewish and Italian) women going through change of life insisted on opening the windows, younger Puerto Rican women, not used to the New York climate, complained that they were freezing. Interethnic disputes have been varied. Of the 30 grievances based upon ethnic issues identified by Stuart for the 1943–49 period (9 percent of the total grievances), plaintiff and defendant were both African Americans in 13 cases, the adversaries were both Jews in 3 cases (in one case accusing one another of anti-Semitism), and 8 cases involved blacks and Jews (7 in which blacks were the plaintiff, one in which a

Jew was the plaintiff). One black woman charged that the Jews, who were speaking a foreign language, were talking about her.[97]

Workers' disputes have been explained in various ways. The first and most obvious interpretation is cultural. Racism and xenophobia account for the different places in which minorities find themselves within the industry and are a common form that ensuing conflicts take. But the overt representations of antagonisms provide an incomplete picture for two reasons. On the one hand, we must return to the structure of the industry, where flexibility fundamentally places workers in constant competition with each other. On the other, the cultural categories themselves have shifted over time.

As Gunnar Myrdal pointed out, internal class struggle among adjacent classes can be fiercer than that between top and bottom. The multiple layers of the garment industry, with its seasonal workload and cutthroat contracting atmosphere, are a fertile terrain for tension. While that tension often erupts in ethnic or racial terms, Stuart concluded, in his persuasive thesis, that economic conflict over work distribution was the major culprit: "the fear of the Newcomer as an economic competitor." Competition led to discrimination that was excused by derogatory stereotypes, which were in turn used to justify the discrimination. Inversely, as Roy Helfgott argued, when competition over scarce jobs or bundles is at a minimum, so is ethnic and generational conflict.[98]

The cultural and structural components of interethnic conflict were perhaps best combined by Will Herberg. One-time Communist and later theologian, best known for his sociological analysis of the religious structure of American life, *Protestant, Catholic, Jew,* Herberg was Education Director for the ILGWU during the 1940s. Building on Stuart's work, Herberg elaborated a more general theory of generational conflict. Competition in the workplace, like contests for power within the union, are highly affected by the changing composition of the labor force. The irony was not lost on him:

Some years ago, Jewish workers were prone to accuse the "Italians" of "taking away" their work; today, both Jews and Italians tend to look askance at the newcomers for the same reason. . . . It is perhaps ironical that the ethnic newcomers are made the object of very much the same stereotypes ("selfish," "lazy," "irresponsible," "bad union people," etc.) that were once applied to the now dominant groups of old-timers.[99]

Conflict and Consensus on Seventh Ave.

Thus, ethnic conflict takes on another dimension when examined over the long term. Newcomers are often to older immigrants what immigrants in general and women are to native (male) workers. This means that cultural antagonisms may shift; old friends can become enemies, while old foes can become allies and new competitors appear. The frontier between conflict and cooperation is redrawn over time as one group settles in and another appears.

The advantage of the generational perspective is that it is dynamic. It recognizes cultural difference while pinpointing competitive tensions. Herberg's thesis can be pushed even further by stressing the shifting nature of cultural definitions, alliances, and enmities over time.[100] The ILGWU itself, after all, sometimes found it hard to keep up with changing or multiple identities. It counted Spanish-speaking blacks as Spanish-speaking, although with an *N* (for Negro) marked by their names. In other cases, it was ecumenical: "If the name sounded Italian," that was good enough for membership in Italian Local 48; its manager's own mother, after all, was not Italian. In one later organizing drive, Local 89 sought to recruit Hispanics under the larger category "Latins." Some ethnic identities were created at work. One machine operator, from a rich Jewish family in St. Petersburg, described how she learned Yiddish only in a New York garment shop.[101] Other identities were rejected there. Just as the Jewish-American women wanted their own English-speaking—not Yiddish, not Christian—branch at the turn of the century, by 1934, English-speaking (Jewish) members of Dress Makers' Local 22 were leaving the union because they considered it "too foreign." Yet a mere decade later, Local 22 had become the symbol of integration to some third-generation Italians who wanted to switch there from the Italian dressmakers' local.[102]

Michael Walzer has written that boundaries "are vulnerable to shifts in social meaning, and we have no choice but to live with the continual problems and incursions through which these shifts are worked out."[103] A century-long history of ethnic relations in the garment industry confirms Walzer's point, but with two qualifications. First, while the long-term view illustrates the moving frontiers, this need not lead to a deconstructionist agnosticism. Boundary battles are also testimony to a dynamic process of group formation of what socioanthropologist Pierre Bouvier has called "*ensembles popula-*

tionnels cohérents."[104] At any given point in time individuals and groups know who they are (and whom they are against) and have spoken up with very definite ideas about where their ethnic or other identities lie. From Jewish-American women to Puerto Rican or Chinese ones, garment workers have stood up for their rights against their employers and against the union, as specific cultural groups within the "garment workers" construct. Their poststructural voices shed important light on the structural overview. But, second, does this mean, then, that repeated conflict is the only and inevitable story, and that cooperation is inexistent or impossible?

In the context of the garment industry, we can exclude the two extremes. Neither race riots nor absolute harmony have prevailed. While historians Gary Mormino and George Pozzetta have described how Spanish, Cuban, and Italian cigar workers in Ybor City formed a common community even while at times clashing in the labor market, Ronald Bayor has more pessimistically charted the constancy of conflict "forever lurking beneath the surface" and often erupting in American interminority relations.[105] Yet a close look at one sector over a long period can temper too gloomy an outlook.

"Memory"—or its loss—is sometimes an aid. Like the union, manufacturers and workers have often forgotten or denied conflict, on purpose or not. Jews in the 1940s, describing the good old times of group solidarity, tended to forget the bitter intra-Jewish political fights of the 1920s. Jews and Italians interviewed after World War II claimed they had always gotten along, the proud memory of the antifascist Antonini easily wiping out that of some anti-Semitic incidents which had flared in the late 1930s.[106]

As Steven Fraser has pointed out with regard to the early A C W A, different places within the industry, different cultural legacies, and different political tendencies did not ultimately inhibit peaceful coexistence. Colomba Furio argued that unions were a "tripartite force" which aided the assimilation of Italian women into American society. It gave them contacts with people from other ethnic groups, encouraged them to learn English, and gave workers common goals beyond racial tension.[107] For some black dress-ironers, their unionization was "a Cinderella tale come true." Some blacks and Hispanics said they preferred working in shops with Jewish workers or in a (Jewish) union shop, whom and which they felt would protect their rights regardless of ethnic origin. Even the paternalism of the union ("our Italian workers," "our Negro workers") was not always resented. As one Puerto Rican leader said, referring to Charles Zimmerman's activities, "it's paternalistic and so on, but it's better than anyone else."[108] There is a more cheery version of interethnic relations. Italian and Jewish women tried out their broken English on one another and exchanged food; women from all over Latin America trade customs and recipes today and join in mutual gripe sessions about husbands and children.[109]

Perhaps we can use the notion of "cohabitation" in its widest sense of getting along. Véronique de Rudder has analyzed the "functional, complementary relations" along with conflicts based on "inclusion and exclusion, rejection and cooperation, suspicion and exchange, fear and mutual aid" that make up what she has called the "banal reality" of mixed neighborhoods.[110] The same notion may apply to the workplace and the union. Life in the workshops has, as often as not, been "cordial but not close."[111]

In evaluating conflict or cooperation, the question is not only one of interpreting the silences or shouts within our sources, tempered by the optimism or pessimism of historians. Expressions of agency within the context of labor segmentation, union bureaucratization, and flexible specialization are multiple. There is no single source of blame. Workers, employers, the union, social structure, and cultural antagonisms interact. Ethnic conflict is labor competition, institutional self-defense ("bureaucratic sclerosis"[112]), and cultural difference intertwined. But while structure and culture both cause conflict, the very repetitions of the story may offer a final note of guarded optimism. The comparisons are enlightening. If yesterday's friends may be tomorrow's enemies, there may be some saving grace in the idea that today's enemies may be tomorrow's friends.

Ready-to-Wear and Ready-to-Work

9

ECONOMIC AND ETHNIC IDENTITIES IN THE PARISIAN PATCHWORK

T he similarities with New York are striking. In Paris, too, national origin and gender at times collided, especially in the early stage of the ready-made revolution. In the interwar period, the French garment-workers' unions, like the International Ladies' Garment Workers' Union (ILGWU), were confronted with foreign-language branches they wanted both to encourage yet limit. In 1937, in Paris as in New York, language sections were abolished, with institutional as well as ideological considerations leading to their demise. Finally, as across the ocean, ascribed and perceived ethnic identities have brought French and Eastern European workers, Polish and Tunisian Jews, Turks and Chinese into conflict within the Parisian garment industry.

The differences between Paris and New York are no less salient. Notions of ethnicity are different. The union has played a different role. On the one hand, ethnicity is not supposed to be a French concept, according to the universalist, egalitarian, and individualist French republican ideology.[1] On the other, the French garment-workers' unions were never as strong or as visible as the ILGWU; the labor movement was not as important a contested terrain for different immigrant groups. Where there was conflict it was within a different context than in New York. The Fédération de l'habillement was created and always construed as a French union; interethnic relations were more of a native-immigrant encounter in Paris than an immigrant-immigrant one as in New York. The political split of the French labor movement during the wars and the rise of xenophobia in France in the 1930s are also important backdrops to the Paris story. Finally, the language of conflict has been different in France. Throughout the interwar period, class and internationalism remained a more persistent part of the French labor movement's vocabulary, giving its rhetoric of harmony a different—if no less problematic—cast than the more diffuse solidarism by then prevalent in the ILGWU. Although the pertinence of class consciousness subsequently faded within the Parisian industry too, its legacy has endured even as social relations have to a certain extent been "ethnicized." Thus, while the New York story raised questions about consensus and conflict (which may also apply to Paris), the Paris tale brings to the fore the way in which garment workers have interpreted the economics of flexibility and perceptions of ethnic identity in another setting.

The Cousette *and the Immigrant* Apiéceur

The image of the famed Parisian *couturière* (dressmaker) and even the lowly *cousette* (seamstress) has been constructed differently than that of the American-born German or Irish or foreign-born female garment worker in New York. In spite of global similarities in the way in which women have been shunted into the secondary sewing-labor market on both sides of the Atlantic, the native French seamstress has retained a lingering cachet of former glory. Not only did the neighborhood *couturière* hang on longer in the face of new production methods, but the imagery of the female seamstress's *"doigts de fée"* (fairy fingers), *"goût naturel"* (inborn good taste), and *"instinct d'élégance"* carried forward into the discourse about the ready-made sector, giving women a theoretical pride of place in stark contrast to the *cousette*'s actual lot.[2]

As we have seen, 1906 was the high point of women's employment in the garment trades. The subsequent relative decline of French women in the field was due both to the general decrease in jobs from the industry's turn-of-the-century high and to the opening up of other opportunities for women. As in New York, one other factor helped contribute to this phenomenon: the arrival of immigrants. While French women continued to work in custom dressmaking and French men remained the masters of custom-tailoring for men and became *haut-couturiers* for women, native women and immigrant men became colleagues and competitors in the ready-made labor market. From the late nineteenth through the twentieth centuries, immigrant men and French women came to occupy similar yet often distinct places in the garment-industry landscape. The relationship between the two seems to be more a question of different locations than one of conflict.

First of all, foreign men did not enter just any segment of the garment industry. According to one estimate, 85 percent of the women's-wear tailors at the turn of the century were (mostly Jewish) foreigners, as compared to only 35 percent in men's wear. Eastern European immigrants also moved into fur making, the raincoat trade, and capmaking, all of which, like women's wear, were new or expanding trades during the Belle Epoque.[3] Within women's wear alone, French women and foreign men also gravitated to somewhat different sectors. Women continued to work in the dressier goods, while Jewish immigrants entered the more standardized lines. The latter became specialized in the more classic tailored outfits such as cloaks and suits, as in New York.

There was also a division in space. Women moved out of homework and into workshops and factories as the immigrants started up home and family workshops. Did the arriving immigrants thus "allow" women to move into more stable jobs? Did the immigrants "push" women out of the more flexible sector? In either case, *cousettes* and immigrant *apiéceurs* (pieceworkers) came to share the Parisian and garment space unevenly. While this seems to have occurred without too much difficulty, there were times of tension. Although the conflicts that appear were much less articulated than the debate over women's place in the pages of the New York *Message*, they are revealing nonetheless. Immigrants and women could be placed in objective competition and focus on cultural differences to explain competing interests, just as they could form alliances during certain labor actions.

For the anti-Semitic *L'Antijuif,* the major garment-workers' strike in 1901 was just a strike of French women workers against Jewish exploiters. Yet the work stoppage involving over 700 of the 800 workers employed in 55 women's-wear shops in Paris, ultimately joined foreign men (a large number of them Jewish) and some French women homeworkers along with shopworkers in a movement that aimed to change the structural conditions of the industry itself. In the walkout against piecework and homework that sought to equalize wages and prevent unfair competition, the strike initially pitted shopworkers against their bosses, but it also opposed them to homeworking and pieceworkers. To the extent that immigrants and women filled the latter role, they were both castigated. However, the strikers appealed to the immigrants and women to support their demands, and eventually an important number of Jewish and female outworkers did join the shopworkers' strike. Indeed, some of the immigrant tailors, particularly the Jewish immigrants working in family shops on Montmartre, remained intransigent in their demands to see the piecework system abolished and were unhappy when the union finally backed down.[4]

The strike's failure only pointed to the objective competition in which women and immigrants could be placed. According to one manufacturer, the only "happy result" of the labor conflict was the partial replacement of foreign workers by Parisian seamstresses, whose talent could not be surpassed: "nothing would be easier than to do without the foreign specialists."[5] Immigrant men and French women were constructed as objective competitors while represented as interchangeable outworkers. Employers used the hiring of women to threaten striking male employees with dismissal. The firm of Wormser and Boulanger menaced their three French, four Russian, two Greek, one Italian, and one Belgian workers with replacement by women when they struck in 1916. Galeries Lafayette used the same threat on other occasions.[6]

Conflicts could arise out of this objective competition just as they could emerge as the result of subjective antagonisms. Foreign workers and French women understood their differences and on occasion complained bitterly about each other. Immigrant men complained that the (French) women workers would not strike; French women objected that the foreigners' speeches were incomprehensible. The foreign male machine-operators who walked off the job at Galeries Lafayette in 1913 criticized the French female shirtwaist makers and seamstresses for not following them; only 15 to 20 French women joined the 280 striking immigrants. During a 1916 strike at Galeries Lafayette's manufacturing firm—the Société parisienne de confection—3 French skirtmakers from the rue de Provence workshop walked out of a labor meeting protesting that they could not understand the talks in Russian.[7]

Rumors and denials could feed gender and ethnic discord. They were part of both strikes and strike-breaking strategies. To help end the strike of 1913, the Galeries Lafayette management spread a rumor that the purpose of the strike, led by foreign workers, was to get the company to fire the French workers. "Groodski," the secretary of the Fédération des travailleurs de l'habillement, protested at a March 10 meeting. He expressed surprise that the (French) non-strikers could believe such a rumor and repeated, in French for their benefit, that the strikers' only purpose was to support ("*solidariser avec*") the striking female skirtworkers (their "*camarades jupières*"). Several long discussions followed, but they were again in a foreign language, as the police reporter rather frustratedly noted.[8]

In the face of objective and subjective conflicts among workers, the labor press preached male-female solidarity as a way of obviating the competition between the two. *L'Ouvrier chapelier* of November 21–December 20, 1911, wrote: "The emancipation of the workers will only be the work of the male and female workers [*travailleurs et travailleuses*] themselves." And the garment unions occasionally made specific appeals to both women and immigrants. An article in *L'Humanité* of December 27, 1923, entitled "Femmes et travailleurs étrangers se font concurrence," argued that only a "*tarif syndical*"—set prices—could combat the low wages accepted by women and foreigners. A big meeting of all garment workers was called to discuss female and immigrant labor, with talks and leaflets to be distributed in Italian, Hungarian, German, and Yiddish.[9]

Indeed, joint actions sometimes brought French women and immigrant workers together in recognition of their structural similarities rather than cultural differences, as in the 1901 strike. During the 1913 strike, *L'Humanité* celebrated the fact that Jewish immigrant garment workers had backed French women skirtmakers, causing the French employers (of Galeries Lafayette) to raise the latter's salaries too, "under the pressure of this international solidarity."[10] When a strike broke out in one of the women's-wear workshops owned by the Printemps department store in March 1916, the 30 male Russian, Romanian, Armenian, Czech, Italian, and Swiss machine operators who walked out for better conditions got 5 out of 17 female skirtmakers to join them. They also sent a special appeal in Yiddish to the Jewish homeworkers on Montmartre asking them not to accept outwork which would undercut the strike; 40 men and 30 women there voted their solidarity with the striking workers in the center of Paris. In another strike that same year, 5 French women shirtmakers joined 10 Russian male tailors in walking out of Maurice (Maladeski)'s shop.[11]

Finally, though, even the union's representations of immigrants and women were often revealingly contradictory. While preaching solidarity and stressing the similarity of women's and immigrants' roles, the pre–World War I Confédération générale du travail (CGT) sometimes viewed the (mostly Jewish) immigrant men as rabble-rousers, exasperating French union leaders by their intransigence. Women, on the other hand, were often characterized as hopeless for the cause.

The union's sometimes mixed message was mirrored by the immigrants and women themselves. Jewish immigrant leaders, while urging solidarity with the French labor movement, were in turn angry when the CGT would not hold out longer for the abolition of piecework. Female labor leaders also saw the pros and cons of different forms of labor organizing. During the 1921 Congress which debated the CGT-CGTU split, Jeanne Chevenard, who would join the more reformist CGT, warned that too revolutionary a line frightened women away. In a rather defeatist if not patronizing description of her own sex, she argued that women "come to the union for quite other things than revolutionary activity," that they don't know that much about union issues to begin with, and that

if you go before these women who already have been reticent about coming to us, and you quarrel over questions that they know nothing about and which don't interest them, you weary them and they leave.[12]

Even Adèle LeBaron, the only woman who spoke up for revolutionary action and who joined the CGTU (Confédération général du travail unitaire), said "We must not use the word 'communist' with the women, they are afraid, we are '*minoritaires*' and not communists."[13] Interestingly enough, several men defended the radical potential of

Ready-to-Wear and Ready-to-Work

women's place within the labor movement, refusing the idea that their discussions and doctrinal divisions discouraged women from organizing. They argued, with hopefully performative rhetoric, that women were perfectly capable of understanding revolutionary ideas.

Beyond the different representations of and by immigrant and female work and workers, these homeworkers and outworkers at times allied in recognition of their common, beleaguered role in the subcontracting system. At other times, however, differences of place within the industry, different attitudes toward militancy, and ethnic/cultural as well as gender identities led them down different paths. Ultimately, in a context of low unionization altogether, it seems that more women joined the CGT garment-workers' union in the interwar years, while more immigrants joined the CGTU one.[14] They chose different options for a similar cause, the betterment if not redefinition of the garment worker's role.

Immigrants and the Unions: Language Sections between Indifference and Separatism

Like the ILGWU leadership, the French unions too had a conflicting discourse toward newcomers, at times inclusive, at others exclusive. Yet the terms seem even more sharply drawn in Paris. On the one hand, a class-based rhetoric of unity and internationalism remained predominant long after the ILGWU had turned to negotiating with the manufacturers. On the other hand, a discourse of protectionism was much more transparent within the native-immigrant context in Paris. If the labor movement was to protect and better the lot of workers, the presence of immigrant workers ever since the late nineteenth century raised the question, Which workers? Defense of the working class and defense of the French working class were two different "programs" that had to be reconciled. Fundamentally, the French unions, like the ILGWU, had to decide whom they would include in their "sphere of justice," just as they sought to define the limits of labor's protective "social closure." With more or less enthusiasm, they were confronted with the necessity of organizing immigrant workers within their midst.[15] The problem, like that for the ILGWU, was how to organize class solidarity given cultural differences.

Economic and Ethnic Identities

One part of the French union's discourse was unequivocal, based on the Marxian premise that workers of all countries should unite, along with a French conceptualization that was more universalist than particularist in nature.[16] The pre–World War I CGT leadership stressed solidarity between workshop workers and homeworkers, between female and male workers, and among workers of all nationalities and religions. The union provided material and moral support for the immigrant workers' strikes and repeatedly stressed immigrant-native unity: "For us, union workers, there exist no nations . . . there exists only one nation—that of the exploited class."[17]

The immigrants mirrored this attitude in their own journals. The early Jewish workers' labor newspaper in Paris, *Der idisher arbayter*, closely allied to the CGT, stressed workers' common cause: "hand in hand with our French brothers . . . their misery is our misery. . . . [the French movement's] struggle is our struggle; its future is our future."[18] Alexander Losovsky, later head of the Profintern but an influential figure in the Jewish labor movement in Paris before the First World War, set the tone in the first and second issues of the paper: Jewish workers must join the general labor movement; they are exploited by French capital like their French comrades; to stand aside is a sin.[19]

Yet beyond theoretical and sometimes practical unity, tensions arose between the French union and the immigrant workers. Before 1914 and again in the 1930s, the "protection of national labor" became a theme parallel to that of unity in union discourse. The French socialist Jean Jaurès himself recognized the problem of workers' competition:

We protest against the invasion of foreign workers who come here to work for cheap wages [*travailleurs au rabais*]. And here there must be no misunderstanding: we do not intend, we who are internationalists, to arouse animosities of jealous chauvinism among manual workers from different countries, no; but what we do not want is that international capital seek out labor on the market where it is the most debased, humiliated, depreciated, to cast it onto the French market without control and without regulation, and to bring salaries everywhere in the world to their lowest level.[20]

While Jaurès placed the blame squarely on capital, for some union leaders and rank-and-file members, an economic analysis did not obviate the cultural differences which could also be used to explain workers' antagonisms.

In 1911, a tailor wrote to *La Guerre sociale*, the revolutionary-syndicalist paper edited by Gustave Hervé, to complain that he had lost his job due to competition from Jewish tailors. If there were an anti-Semitic movement, I would join it, he wrote. As the Jewish anarchist and writer Bernard Lazare had commented, anti-Semitism was not always aimed at the Jew but at the immigrant worker. However, the distinction was not always clear. Emile Pouget, a well-known revolutionary syndicalist, responded to the complaining tailor by commenting that "Jewish infiltration is one aspect of the issue of foreign competition," and although he went on to (try to) temper his comments with regard to the Jews, "La question des étrangers" remained one of "invasion" for him.[21]

Pierre Dumas, head of the garment-workers' union before the First World War, embodied these contradictions, for the worst as it turned out. On the one hand, Dumas defended foreign garment workers—Jews and Germans—for the "appreciable results" of their organizing efforts in 1912 and argued at the 1913 International Congress of Needle Workers in Vienna that the difficulties of organizing in Paris were not only the fault of the Jews. John Dyche gave Dumas's Vienna speech a favorable report, especially compared to the more anti-Semitic stereotypes used by the Danish and Swiss delegates.[22] On the other hand, as head of the French delegation, Dumas asked the International Congress to halt immigration to Paris for one year, and in an article he published in Yiddish in *Der idisher arbayter* of July 5, 1913, he defended this position by, among other things, blaming the immigrant workers for lowering wages and acting as strikebreakers. He insisted that his proposal did not deviate from the principle of international solidarity, but he nonetheless continued by explaining that the pluricultural (Germans, Austrians, Belgians, Russians, Poles, Bulgarians, Italians, Spaniards) character of the garment industry was soon to be transformed into a monopoly on the part of Jewish workers, particularly in the women's ready-made sector. According to him, it was the Polish (i.e., Jewish) workers who had killed the 1901 strike movement.

An *alter arbayter* (old worker) responded to Dumas in the "Free Tribune" of the next issue (August 9, 1913), castigating the delegation's proposal as "not only reactionary" but "petit bourgeois" and "utopian." The exchange did not prevent Dumas from writing in to congratulate the Jewish workers on the twenty-fifth issue (which turned out to be the last) of this Jewish-workers' newspaper. But he remained reticent on immigration, and after the war his anti-Semitism became more blatant. Dumas was finally ousted from the garment union, and after World War I he joined the Catholic fascist right.[23]

The CGT nonetheless sought to organize immigrant workers in order to effect the theoretical unity of their discourse. They began to set up language sections in Paris before World War I. Or rather, immigrant locals were created which joined the CGT and were grouped together in umbrella organizations called intersyndical committees. German workers were organized in the Deutscher Arbeiter Kartel. The best-studied intersyndical committee so far is the Intersektsionen byuro, which joined together the Yiddish-speaking sections of Jewish bakers, cobblers, locksmiths, tailors, and woodworkers, among others.[24]

While hailed as vectors of unity, the language sections and inter-syndical committees still posed problems to both the union and immigrants alike. The union's attitude toward these branches was perhaps best reflected in the immigrant press itself. The CGT sent regular greetings there to welcome the immigrants who organized. At the same time French labor leaders used that forum to warn the immigrants in their own language against cutting wages and breaking strikes. The tone was in general one of guarded warmth, urging class unity and congratulating those immigrants who joined the union, yet wary of workers' competition.

In the period before World War I, the issue of how to organize seems to have been even more of a dilemma for the immigrants themselves. Some Jewish immigrants (Bundist fur workers, for example) argued that Jewish workers should organize entirely separately, in independent unions. While the majority of organized Jewish workers were more favorable to setting up language sections within the CGT, even among them there was debate about the fragile frontier between class unity and cultural identity. *Der idisher arbayter* hailed immigrant-French unity in every one of its issues, but it also had to defend the language sections against accusations of separatism. The newspaper almost seemed to protest too much, its tone sometimes bordering on apologetics, directed, ironically, in Yiddish, to a French audience. Reflecting and responding to the latter's criticisms, *Der idisher arbayter* often urged the Jewish workers to organize and show their solidarity with the French labor movement not only as valuable in and of itself but in order to defend Jewish workers from the common complaints against immigrant labor.

Between the Wars

A double union discourse persisted into the interwar period in which calls for class unity can be found alongside worries over immigrant autonomy. After the split into the more revolutionary CGTU and the more reformist CGT, the former, even more so than the latter, was active in organizing immigrant workers. The CGTU consistently reiterated a more internationalist theme:

Workers have no homeland [*patrie*]; there are no foreign workers in France; there are workers of a single country: the Proletariat. Capitalism has created differences of language and differences of exploitation. The CGTU will struggle to make them disappear. (Applause.)[25]

During an August 1926 garment strike of Jewish workers against the jobbers and contractors of the Montmartre and La Roquette neighborhoods, the CGTU garment union called upon French workers to join their striking Jewish comrades. The now Communist newspaper *L'Humanité* even cited Jewish workers as an example for French workers to follow and celebrated the unity of "the exploited Jews and French."[26] However, native-immigrant relations still confronted three obstacles to peaceful coexistence: cultural and economic conflicts over jobs, indifference, and a fear of separatism.

Shop floor conflicts and competition for jobs persisted into the interwar period. At a 1922 meeting, one union member complained that Jewish homeworkers were hurting all garment workers. Ethnic blame doubled the structural critique against homework. Only a few months before the August 1926 strike, a delegate named Rosen complained that "race prejudice" within the labor movement needed to be eliminated "so that French and foreign workers within the trade would no longer be divided into two clans." Several months

Economic and Ethnic Identities

after the strike, Rosen and Maurice Millerat, president of the Syndicat général unitaire des travailleurs de l'habillement de la Seine, got into a verbal dispute concerning misunderstandings between French and Jewish workers within the union.[27]

French labor attitudes toward their immigrant counterparts at times focused on issues of place within the subcontracting structure. During the 1921 debate over whether the independent pieceworkers (apiéceurs) should be organized, Bellugue (soon to be head of the CGTU garment-workers' union), opposed the measure on the grounds that the union should not recruit those who exploit other workers. But he also had to insist that "race" was not an issue (in his refusal of the mostly Jewish pieceworkers), as the delegate Rottemberg had suggested.[28] When a large number of immigrants became independent contractors in the 1930s in order to avoid the effects of the 1932, 1934, and 1935 laws which limited the hiring of foreigners as employees, a similar debate concerning the class status of the façonniers was also overlaid by their foreignness.[29]

By the late 1930s, in the context of job scarcity and increasing xenophobia, another distinction emerged, including some and excluding others, separating new immigrants from old. In 1937, during the International Exhibition in Paris, a certain number of foreigners (and particularly Eastern European Jews) took advantage of their tourist visas to stay on in France and find work there. Several labor unions began to complain about unfair competition (substandard wages, poor conditions, excessive hours) from illegal refugees. Their petitions, printed in the socialist press, show that many of these were in fact in predominantly Jewish unions (leather goods, garments) seeking to protect the rights of already unionized Jewish immigrants. At a meeting of the (recently reunified) Fédération d'industrie des travailleurs de l'habillement, a delegate representing women's-wear workers in Paris complained that

there are two sorts of immigrant workers. On the one hand, there are comrades who have been in France for a certain number of years, who have worked in the shops for a certain number of years, who have struggled and militated in our unions. In late June 1936, our organization had about 600 members and at least 550 of them were immigrant comrades . . . The first question was raised by the immigrant comrades themselves. . . . After long debate, our union decided not to unionize the new immigrants.[30]

Ready-to-Wear and Ready-to-Work

Valet explained his refusal of the new immigrants by citing high unemployment in the trade and by arguing that the union had already undertaken certain measures on behalf of the older immigrants (such as petitions to the Ministère du travail to obtain work permits for them). It was the union's duty to protect those already within its sphere. By redefining its boundaries to include those class-conscious immigrants (*émigrés conscients*) who were already organized, the union—and the old-timers—agreed that the newly arrived had to be excluded.

While conflicts and protectionism could give lie to the union's internationalist rhetoric of cooperation, parallel efforts went forward to organize those immigrants who were "conscious." The main problem remained the form that immigrant sections would take. After all, for May Day in 1914, the CGT had explicitly asked the Jewish immigrants not to march separately but to join the general French parade. The Jewish immigrants had been marching in May Day celebrations ever since 1906, but they did so generally with other immigrants: Germans, Poles, Czechs.[31] Separate but within, the form of immigrant inclusion was still being negotiated during the interwar years.

At the 1921 Lille Congress of the Fédération des travailleurs de l'habillement, the union proposed reestablishing language sections like those which had existed before the war. In 1923, the CGTU (like the French Communist Party in 1925) set up a Bureau de main-d'oeuvre étrangère (MOE, committee on foreign labor) to centralize issues relating to foreign workers and to encourage and coordinate the "ethnic sections" (*sections ethniques*). That year, the Intersindikale komisie was founded, taking up where the prewar Intersektsionen byuro had left off. By 1927, thirteen intersyndical committees had been formed or were in the process thereof: Italian, Spanish, Polish, Hungarian, Jewish, Czech, Russian, Yugoslav, Romanian, Ukrainian, Bulgarian, Armenian, and Chinese.[32] A sign of the times, the Communist Party MOE changed its name to MOI (Bureau de main-d'oeuvre immigrée) in 1932, reflecting the increasing ambient xenophobia. The term *étranger* had become pejorative, and the union (and the Communist Party) henceforth preferred the term *immigré*, considered to be a more objective, economic, category.[33]

The actual number of immigrants involved was small. Out of approximately 17,000 foreigners all told in the CGTU in 1930, there were 12,000 Italians, 2,500 Poles, and 680 Hungarians nation-wide.[34] There were perhaps only 300 Jews at that time (basically in Paris), but as the depression hit and the union began organizing small-time *façonniers* (those with only one employee). Some 4,500 Jewish immigrants had joined the union by early 1936 (2,123 workers and 2,476 *façonniers*). During the Popular Front, immigrant membership, like membership in general, rose dramatically, only to drop precipitously afterward. The Communist Yiddish newspaper *Di naye prese* claimed that there were 13,000 unionized Jewish workers in the Paris area in March 1937. For the ladies' garment-workers' union, the figures vary widely, from approximately 3,000 members altogether at its peak in November 1936 to another estimate of 6,000 to 8,000 Jewish workers alone.[35]

Julien Racamond, head of the CGTU Bureau de main-d'oeuvre étrangère, attributed the low numbers of immigrant members to indifference on the part of the French union. Racamond, who pleaded the immigrants' cause energetically at every national congress, repeatedly reproached his union comrades for their lack of interest in organizing immigrant workers. He even strongly encouraged them to take up foreign languages.[36] As he argued in a somewhat last-ditch but logical appeal, French workers needed to defend the immigrants "not only out of our feelings of international brotherhood, but in our own best interest."[37] In two separate instances, the regional and central offices dealing with foreign workers complained bitterly that the national political and labor organizations were neglecting the immigrants.[38]

But while Racamond was lamenting indifference, the union was increasingly concerned over the specter of separatism, unacceptable on institutional and ideological grounds. As historians Stéphane Courtois and Denis Peschanski and former Communist activist Adam Rayski have put it, the organizational question brought the unions face-to-face with two different logics, one centripetal, the other centrifugal. The language branches were at times called *commissions de propagande*, underlining their essentially functional role of getting the message of labor unity across in different languages. But at the same time, the essential recognition of cultural difference was evident in their other designation: *sections ethniques.*[39]

In theory the intersyndical committees and foreign language sections came under the aegis of the central union (or party) organization. But in practice, they had a good deal of autonomy. Indeed this became a bone of contention between the CGT and the CGTU. The former criticized the latter's *comités intersyndicaux nationaux* as divisive, while the French Communist Party complained about poorly supervised ethnic sections in the Jewish trades and about Jewish activists in the Paris region in general:

If strong ethnic union sections exist in the Paris region, their unguided activities—poorly controlled by the union leadership, which has not sufficiently reacted against these separatist tendencies nor been sufficiently preoccupied with the immigrants' specific demands (the Jewish section in textiles, for example)—turn toward a dangerous nationalism which often leads them toward isolated actions which are for the most part doomed to failure.[40]

As the Communist Party set about centralizing its organization, it sought greater control over its language sections, although there is some question as to how effective that control was.

If in the 1920s language sections were encouraged, three things led to their ultimate demise in the 1930s: continued bureaucratic and ideological reticence over suspected separatism at worst, too great a relative autonomy at best; disappointment over results— attributed in part to their own failures at organizing the immigrants; but also, and more importantly, the shifting French political context. The rise of xenophobia in the 1930s and the passage of restrictive legislation that limited immigrant employment options as of 1932 had an effect on immigrant choices and the unions' tolerance thereof.

Language sections were abolished in the Communist Party in 1937, although some Jewish French Communists later "couldn't remember" or denied this fact. Courtois, Peschanski, and Rayski have rejected the term "dissolution," adding that, given the deteriorating political climate, it was politic for the MOI to adopt a lower profile.[41] Some of the union sections in the reunified (as of March 7, 1936) CGT seem to have continued functioning. Yet by and large, protectionism was once again on the rise. There was a decided shift in the Communist Party and in union policy against immigration. France, some labor leaders argued, "is full."[42]

After World War II, the CGT (like the CFTC and later the CFDT) again set up *groupes de langue* along the prewar model. The Jewish garment workers who had survived the war wanted to rebuild their section and were simply glad to get together again after *les années noires*. However, once again, they were seen by some others as "an abscess" contrary to union principle, and the branch "just faded out and died a natural death."[43] As other immigrants followed, the unions tried to keep up, and by the early 1970s the CGT was publishing periodicals in six foreign languages nationwide. But by then, with the exception of the Turkish garment workers, immigrant interest itself had waned.[44]

The debate over the language sections was an argument about an organizational form somewhere between international solidarity and organizational autonomy. It pointed to a disjunction between theory and practice. But the issue of *sections ethniques* was also a discussion over the role of cultural difference within a class-defined context. There were reciprocal misunderstandings and mockeries, but in the interwar period, and within the union context, the issues of cooperation or conflict between French and immigrant workers, old immigrants and new, homeworkers and shop workers, were largely conceptualized—and organized—within a discourse of class. Neither the French union leaders nor the immigrant organizers always spoke with a unified voice. Both at times expressed an ideal of solidarity alongside a practice of (modified) separatism; at other times they despaired of a working compromise. The aim of concerted labor actions was to confront the industrial structure of seasonality and subcontracting. However, the needs of immigrants and their modes of organizing challenged the union structure itself in Paris as in New York.

The predominance of class made immigrant issues in the garment trade on the whole less visible in the Sentier than on the Lower East Side during this period, even if ethnicity was not absent as a category of labor discourse and practice. More recently, however, the terms seem to have shifted. Class fades from memory, and ethnicity looms large. While class as a concept (and mobilizing mechanism) has disappeared from the vocabulary of researchers and political actors alike, the image of cultural difference has taken on larger explanatory powers in France. From a discourse where class was central, even if contested, images of the garment industry have been "ethnicized." Perhaps identities have changed less than the social construction of their importance. Cooperation and conflict, economic structure, and ethnic identities have been construed somewhat differently around the Paris sewing machines in recent times.

Jews, Turks, and Chinese

The image of the Parisian garment industry as an immigrant one has increased in the last two decades, along with greater visibility of immigrants in general. This could be a function of our sources. From CGTU meetings in the interwar period to sociological studies and magazine articles in the contemporary period, the sources available to the historian looking for information on interethnic relations within the garment industry have themselves shifted. Perhaps the Parisian garment industry simply partakes in a wider phenomenon: the decreasing importance of class as ideology and theory, leaving religion, ethnicity, and other identities in the fore. More generally, perhaps economic categories of understanding have given way, even in France, to simply ethnic ones? How have the Jews, Turks, Chinese, and others defined themselves vis-à-vis each other within the highly flexible fashion business?

As one recent sociological survey neatly summed it up: "The ideology of the Sentier affirms that there is no conflict in the Sentier: in the Sentier there is only competition."[45] Like that of the interwar unions, the contemporary language about the industry is often contradictory. There is a rhetoric of harmony and a discourse of discord; there is a language of economic competition and a recognition of ethnic networks.

In the first instance, Jews, Turks, and Chinese, *même combat*— same struggle—as the French slogan goes. Ethnicity or cultural practices do not matter. What counts is the *libéralisme sauvage,* that pure if anarchic example of free-market capitalism which characterizes the industry. Conflicts are economic, and dynamic entrepreneurs have replaced strike leaders as today's heroes. In such a view not only does ethnicity not matter, but cutthroat competition renders any other solidarity obsolete. As Pierre Aidenbaum, socialist politician of the 3d *arrondissement,* commented about his district: "Among the Sentier bosses? I don't know what solidarity means."[46] By emphasizing the economic strife that is crucial to the garment district, Aidenbaum sought to minimize the cultural character of his constituency. Indeed, it is often difficult to make the distinction between ethnic and economic conflict. A spokesman for the Sentier branch of the Fédération des Juifs de France (FJF) commented in 1985 that since the section's founding five years earlier, it had only received perhaps five or six complaints. He went on to say that, in any case, they ultimately decided that these conflicts were beyond the competence of the FJF because they were as much if not more so a problem of competition as of anti-Semitism.[47]

Yet Aidenbaum's disclaimer in fact provides a glimpse of the "ethnicization" of the Sentier. His comment, essentially denying the largely perceived Jewish character of the garment shop owners came but a month after a rash of anti-Semitic graffiti covered the neighborhood's walls.[48] But at the same time, the recent vision of the neighborhood has expanded to englobe not only the older Polish Jews and more recent North African Jews there but also the Turks and (now ex-) Yugoslavs who have come to the garment industry since the 1960s, and the Chinese working in the 13th *arrondissement* today in close collaboration with the Sentier hub. Each successive yet overlapping wave of immigrants has brought new waves of competition. Yet today, perhaps more so than yesterday, they are described more openly in terms of ethnic or cultural differences.

An article in *Le Nouvel Observateur* in early 1989 used this new language of ethnicity, beginning with a survey of the Sentier parking lot.[49] In describing the Porsches, Mercedes, and Jaguars of the new Sentier bosses, the journalist contrasted the ostentation of the North African Jews with the more discreet ways of the older Polish Jews. The article, along with similar ones elsewhere, went on to refer to a more complex cultural plurality within the garment district, in which Ashkenazic and Sephardic Jewish differences were set beside allusions to a coming Jewish-Chinese battle over the bundles.[50] In the 1980s, intra-ethnic differences among the Jews of the Sentier were thus brought into the public eye while television news programs also turned the spotlight on illegal garment workshops full of undocumented Turkish and Chinese immigrants.

The ethnic categories are themselves amalgams, the result of different immigration waves and a process of "ethnicization" through emigration as well as of journalistic ascription. Thus, while Galizianers and Litvaks from Eastern Europe became "Jews" in New

York, and Sicilians, Neapolitans, and a few Northerners became "Italians," the "Ashkenazim" and "Sephardim" in Paris have come to represent two distinct Jewish migrations, each a compound in itself. The Ashkenazim comprise the mostly Polish Jews who came to Paris before and after World War II along with the descendants of other Eastern European Jews who had come to Paris at the turn of the century and of Alsatian Jews whose families settled in Paris in the 1870s. The term "Sephardim" is widely (mis-)used to refer to North African Jews (from Tunisia, Morocco, and Algeria), although the "true" Sephardim (descendants of the Spanish Jews who, after the Inquisition, fled for the most part to Turkey or Italy), have hotly contested that usage.[51] In the Sentier, the "Jews" are now for the most part from Tunisia and Morocco, whereas the term "Turk" may refer to Turks, Kurds, or even Armenians, and the "Chinese" are largely from Cambodia. The more general terms are not mere fictions, however, that must be jettisoned as travesties of more pertinent microidentities. They are used by the individuals themselves; as Phong Tan has noted, the Sino-Khmers in Paris have become more Chinese than they ever were in Cambodia. The media message has converged with a process of ethnicization, or what Jonathan Sarna has called the formation of miniature melting pots.[52]

Jews and Jews: "Polaks" and "Tunes"

The Sentier may be Jewish (even if Aidenbaum did not want to admit it), but conflicts among Jews are certainly not new. While in the interwar period, some older Russian-Polish Jews may have tried to protect their union status against Polish Jewish newcomers, more recent antagonisms have at times strained relations between Polish Jewish old-timers and Tunisian Jewish newcomers. They not only come from different geographic and cultural areas, but they are most often of different generations and have had different itineraries within the industry.

As we have seen, according to one mid-1980s estimate, 90 percent of the Sentier firms are owned by North African Jews, of which 60 percent are Tunisian, 20 percent Moroccan, and 10 percent Algerian. The other 10 percent are held by Polish Jews.[53] While Aidenbaum spoke in measured terms of the differences between the

Polish and North African Jews (the latter having "a different nature, they express themselves much more outwardly"),[54] other Ashkenazic Jews have been more strident in criticizing the more recent Jewish immigrants, commenting disparagingly on their different style of presentation, corresponding to a new style of production and sales methods.

There are indeed differences of generation, of place in the industry, and of mobility patterns between the two groups. The Polish Jews who came to Paris in the interwar period, like the Russian Jews before them, by and large entered the industry as individual homeworkers or started small (extended) family and immigrant workshops. Many never wanted their sons to pick up a needle, as Joseph Klatzmann has recounted, and the next generation, those who survived the war, by and large went off to the university and sought more stability, more status, and less hectic occupations.[55] But some became manufacturers and, of those who were able to hold on during the war or those who survived the deportations, the industry continued to provide a livelihood.

In the 1960s, as the North African Jews came to France, many of them also gravitated to the garment industry. Some married into the industry and into the Ashkenazim. Maxi Librati, "King of the Sentier," son of Moroccan Jews, married the daughter of Polish Jews (a scandalous "mixed marriage" for its time) and initially ran his father-in-law's firm. More often the North African Jews (of modest origins, like the Polish Jews before them) started at the bottom rung of the sales hierarchy before moving into "production" as jobbers or manufacturers. Many subsequently bought businesses from the older generation of Polish Jews. Their arrival coincided with a new boom in ready-to-wear and sportswear and a reinvented, more dynamic Sentier whose success has been attributed to the newcomers' energized style.[56]

Yet beyond these different paths of social mobility, that which has struck public opinion, and been clearly expressed by all parties involved, is a difference of style, of behavior. The article in *Le Nouvel Observateur* turned the North African's Porsches into a Jewish joke, claiming that they were not really showing off: "It's first of all to show their mothers that they've made it."[57] While the Jewish mother may be called upon as a figure federating both communities, certain differences can be seen at eye level on the Sentier streets.

Ready-to-Wear and Ready-to-Work

From one storefront to another, the older Polish Jewish shops often have faded lettering and a jumble of boxes and goods visible through the window. The Tunisian Jews' facades are more often brightly lit, the attractiveness of the wholesaler's boutique reflecting the style of the clothes.[58] The differences between Sephardic and Ashkenazic Jews in the Sentier, perhaps exaggerated by the journalists, are not solely an image created from without. Polish Jews and North African Jews express their own senses of difference, which range from mutterings of misunderstanding on both sides, to real conflicts, to denial of same and expressions of solidarity.

The reciprocal visions have at times been fierce. The Polish Jews do not understand the more conspicuous consumption of the North African Jews, and the latter do not understand either "the mistrust nor the sensitivity" of the former.[59] As the Polish Jews have ceded the terrain to the newcomers, there has been sadness, bitterness, and sometimes anger. One man simply closed shop rather than sell to Moroccan Jews: "They keep going bankrupt, and they wanted to take my firm's name as well, Rosanel. I wasn't going to sell them my reputation, was I?"[60]

But there have also been other, less dramatized interpretations. One Polish Jewish manufacturer expressed the differences as a result of history and memory:

But you have to understand, we don't have the same history. We, we were sort of ashamed to be Jews, we had learned to hug the walls and lower our heads. They, they walk with their heads held high, they have not known the fear of tomorrow. They are proud to be Jews, they shout it from the rooftops, they pray with fervor and have added a lot to Judaism in the Sentier. They are entrepreneurs, gamblers, they live it up.[61]

A young North African intellectual, tired of the negative stereotypes about Sephardic Jews, stressed that the view should be turned around. She pointed out that the North African jobbers represent a newly valued image of dynamic risk-takers:

When will someone finally analyze the Sentier intelligently? See the flexibility [souplesse] there, the exemplary dynamism, the risk-taking? . . . I have never seen such a survival instinct.[62]

"Ashkenazim" and "Sephardim" have thus also become signs for contrasting types of capital, in the battle among jobbers.

Economic and Ethnic Identities

Other differences overlay the "ethnic" ones. There is an important distinction between those who manufacture dressy goods (ranging from street dresses to wedding gowns) and those who specialize in sportswear (*le sportswear*). The former disdain the latter ("I have nothing to do with sportswear"), citing their "know-how" in contrast to the more brash improvisational methods (*"bricolage"*) of the younger manufacturers. The newcomers are in turn proud of having started from scratch, scorning the old-fashioned practices of the older generation.[63]

An ethnic or cultural language can thus be used to explain difference while other modes of description are also possible: one that seeks to explain cultural differences through history and memory, another which describes the competition in terms of gowns versus sweatshirts, and another in purely economic terms—dynamic capital versus old-style business.

Turks and Chinese

The Turks, Serbian Yugoslavs, and Chinese who have entered the garment industry in the last twenty years have, like those before them, also become subcontractors in the dispersed factory of garment making. They have set up shops around Paris, filling orders for the jobbers of the Sentier, and cursing—like all garment workers and bosses before them—about the ups and downs of often unpredictable seasons. All three have been described as examples of ethnic networks in practice.[64] Like the Polish Jews, these ethnic entrepreneurs hire their compatriots right off the train or even fly home to recruit new workers. The community model explains capital accumulation for shop start-ups (the Chinese *tontine*) and especially hiring patterns. It also usually implies an internal solidarity which, in one Serbian case, led one firm's employees to work a month of August without pay in order to help their boss pay off his debts (on a hotel investment back home).[65]

The Turkish garment workers in Paris are perhaps the most interesting in their analysis of place and conflict within the industry in that they most clearly mix class and ethnicity in their understanding of differences. Thus, one Turkish contractor described his shop and workers using a language of class although displacing the pertinent fault-line. Class conflict was not, for him, a question of different interests between shop workers and their bosses. Rather the real cleavage was between contractors (*patrons d'atelier*) and their workers together against the *vrai patron*, the real boss, who is the manufacturer or jobber (*donneur d'ordre*). He stressed the contractors' ultimate dependence on the jobbers upon whom he and his workers—all, by the way, members of the Association des travailleurs turcs—relied for work.[66] The ethnic network thus shifted the class boundaries without necessarily being expressed in cultural terms. In describing contractors versus manufacturers as more problematic than the relationship between contractors and their workers, perhaps the Turkish boss was gilding the vision of his own shop. But at the same time, he was stressing one of the fundamental structural characteristics of the industry. That which he did not volunteer to the sociologist, who did not ask, was the cultural designation of those work-givers. Instead of describing the difference as one of Turkish contractors versus North African Jewish manufacturers, the "true boss" designated in this vision was economic demand.

The Turkish workers and contractors are generally more politicized than the other late-twentieth-century Paris garment workers, leading one Serbian contractor to declare that

The Yugoslavs, they're okay, although it's not like before. But as soon as you have a Turk working for you, you may as well close shop: hours, minimum wage, paid vacation, all of these demands get brought up—you can't work any more![67]

The Turkish workers led the fight for regularizing the status of undocumented workers in 1980, and they spearheaded several garment strikes in 1981. But they too can express their situation in ethnic terms, and their responses, like others, may vary in function of their interlocutors: a more classist discourse in response to the sociologist's questions, a more ethnicized one in answer to a journalist's suggestions? The cultural-ethnic vision may depend on the context.

The Turks, like the Serbs and even more recent groups, are also worried about competition from the newest comers to the field. The Chinese are seen as economic competitors as much as cultural others. In this view, economic conflict is once again displaced. The problems that contractors have with jobbers can be overshadowed by the murderous battle among contractors for work. Turks and Serbs both clearly name the Chinese as their competitors and complain that "they're undercutting prices." Exasperated, one Turkish entrepreneur exclaimed:

How do they do it?! Us, we kill ourselves working. But them, they must kill themselves even more than we do, because they manage to accept work at prices 20 to 30 percent lower than us. We really can't understand anything any longer. . . .

But he went on to say: "Be careful, it's not racism! It's a question of self-interest. Compatriots also do us dirty deals, . . . they too, they undercut prices."[68]

If "ethnic" categories (the homogeneous contractor's shop) can be interpreted in "class" categories (contractor vs. manufacturer), economic competition among contractors can also give rise to both cultural and structural explanations. "They undercut" prices or wages is a common refrain heard all along the temporal line of labor displacement: by native workers vis-à-vis foreign workers, by every immigrant group about those who follow in their footsteps. And when the newcomers are of another culture, the complaint is often translated into ethnic terms.

The price cutting of the latest workers and contractors reflects the dynamics of generational succession. Perhaps the real conflict is inter- and even microgenerational. Since cutting piece rates is the way to enter the field, each group does it in turn, only to criticize those who follow. While newcomers accept lower wages, old-timers increasingly refuse to do the same, resisting over-long hours and underpaid work no matter who their (cultural) bosses. As one Turkish shop boss admitted, "the Asian workers accept working very long days; with Turkish workers that's more and more difficult."[69] Even within immigrant cohorts, the longer they stay, as older immigrants' living and working standards rise even slightly, they become vulnerable to the cheaper prices and longer hours proposed to and accepted by those who have just come to town. Ethnic and labor distinctions are in this respect ultimately situated within the context of the contracting system.

Finally, the ethnicization of competition has been most apparent in certain speculations about the respective fortunes of the Jews of the Sentier and the Chinese of the 13th *arrondissement.* This is the fundamental ethnic conflict of the Sentier, according to one study.[70] Yet, according to some reports, if the North African Jews are now threatened on their southern flank by better quality at lower prices by the Southeast Asians, it is of their own doing. Some of the Jewish manufacturers helped the Chinese contractors get started by loaning them money to rent sewing machines.[71] Why? *"In order to block* the pressure coming from other workers who were subordinate to them."[72] The older Yugoslav and especially more politicized Turkish immigrants asking for better prices and better conditions left the Jewish manufacturers open to the next wave of garment workers who presented themselves on the market. But now that the Chinese have moved up the garment hierarchy, they have become the new contenders, with resentments expressed on both sides.[73]

Conflicts exist; they are most often described in terms of cultural differentiation. Yet at the same time, there are other discourses explicitly aimed at calming the ethnic divide. Social scientists as well as social actors in France have often insisted on harmony, denying that conflicts are "ethnic." As sociologist Jean-Pierre Hassoun has commented, it is a historical first that Jews and Chinese, the classic ethnic middlemen of the sociological literature, have actually met, in the Sentier (and New York, we hasten to add). But, he insists, the encounter has been basically trouble-free:

And although, in this neighborhood, relations between jobber-contractor have never been easy, the ambivalence which floats in the air only rarely takes the form of racism. That which is after all common interest usually wins out over tensions linked to respective place.[74]

The Chinese respect the Jewish holidays, seeing them as a sign of good health and community strength ("We too, we have our New Year"). Maxi Librati drew a parallel between the Jewish and Chinese communities in order to explain the smooth functioning of the Sentier: "Like the Jews, the Chinese have the support of a strong community. They help one another. A person's word is respected or else he'll be shut out of the community." His son reasoned in more explicitly ecumenical and economic terms:

For me, the Sentier, that's Paris. We work with everyone, Yugoslavs, Chinese. Paris, that's a mélange of cultures. Everyone plays their role. The Sentier is an industry, a gigantic supermarket.[75]

While the father spoke of community solidarities, the son perceived a de facto pluriculturalism within an essentially economic structure.

From economics to ethnicity, there are multiple modes of understanding relations in the ready-to-wear business. Everyone complains about someone else. When asked why piece rates are so low, the Turks, Armenians, and Serbs answer, because of the Chinese. The Sino-Khmers say it is because the better-paid goods are made by the Serbian Yugoslavs, while complaining that other, undocumented Chinese workers from the Mainland accept even lower rates. Two types of explanation exist. Both the ethnic network and the contracting system explain the arrival of immigrants to the labor market and their subsequent interactions. Immigrant groups continue to be perceived in terms of levels of docility ("The Pakistanis are neat and tidy, they work impeccably and put up with anything. A French person wouldn't stay more than a few days at our place."[76]) while the industry's particular structure favors a continual renewal of the labor force. Variability of demand, frantic rivalry among contractors to get work, conflictual dependencies between contractors and jobbers, and the search for the least expensive and most compliant workers explain social relationships in this business just as well as cultural characteristics. As one participant-observer put it, "When you work, you don't see the [ethnic] rivalries." When a rush is on, it does not matter who is who. Both the Jewish High Holidays and the Armenian commemoration of the 1915 massacre are observed in the Sentier. But everyone will come in if there is a big order to get out.[77]

Between class and ethnicity, the second term has come to be the focus of discord and rivalry at this end of the twentieth century. It has become a key to many multiculturalist, poststructuralist analyses. However, by insisting on the continued importance of economic structure too, I do not argue that culture does not matter. It would be ludicrous to ignore the specific identities of the different groups

Ready-to-Wear and Ready-to-Work

which have worked behind the sewing machines for the last century. Contrary to the analyses of many contemporary French social scientists, "ethnicity" in its least reified form has been a category of analysis for immigrant groups, their defenders, and their detractors throughout the century. Jews and Armenians, Turks and Chinese understand themselves within "ethnic" categories. Not to name them is to ignore their own categories of comprehension however constructed.

Nonetheless, social networks and identities are multiple and sometimes relative. A Jewish immigrant worker may essentially be a worker during a strike, an immigrant with regard to social status, a foreigner with regard to legal status, and a Jew compared to other immigrant workers. Then too, (s)he may be a Polish Jew in contrast to a Tunisian one. At the same time, contradictory examples of ethnic rivalries and alliances abound. There are those Mauritians grateful for having been "adopted" by a Jewish entrepreneur and thus able to learn the trade, while others blame their lack of success on a "Jewish mafia" limiting opportunity for the newest immigrants to the Sentier.[78] Armenians, like Jews, have been confronted with bold newcomers who have jostled older professional and ethnic identities and practices. While one study found that there was no love lost between the Jewish manufacturers and their Armenian competitors, another suggested that "Poles" and Armenians have a common cause in both feeling edged out by Tunisian Jewish and Armenian newcomers "who undercut prices, change the ways of doing business, and have an exuberant character."[79] Confronted with intra-ethnic rivalries, interethnic solidarities can be brought to the fore, the Polish Jews and older Armenians both lamenting the good old days. Finally, the Sentier has allowed some historic enmities to be reversed or ignored. Even some Armenians and Turks work together.

The language of ethnic differentiation is complex and often constructed for the needs of the moment. The usage of cultural clichés is often as important as their content.[80] As one Ashkenazic woman asserted: "No, I want to live well, that's all, I'll leave the showing off to the 'Tunes' [Tunisian Jews]. The 'Tunes,' I hate them, I avoid them." Yet her business associate, a Tunisian Jewish woman, commented wryly: "But what she's not telling you, is that she only really goes for Tunisian guys, the dog!"[81] Ethnic stereotypes are used to

Economic and Ethnic Identities

describe differences, just as they can be discarded when other factors seem more important. Groups get along just as they compete and get into conflicts, pulling out arguments of solidarity or stereotypes of difference in order to justify one or the other. On the one hand, the Sentier is seen as a (Jewish) "village"; on the other, it is described as a "jungle."[82]

The category of class is also unstable. The Turkish contractor epitomized one of the basic ambiguities of the contracting system. While a virtual employee in relation to the manufacturer or jobber, the contractor is boss to his own workers. To become a boss may be easy, but so is bankruptcy in the "rag trade." And the identification of the "real" boss is not always easy in the cascading subcontracting system.

In the end, it is not necessary to insist on a sole primacy of economic or ethnic explanations either reified or in the process of construction. Explanations can range from a harmonious utopian vision to a catastrophic stereotypical one. Most often, individuals mobilize both the economic and the cultural in order to explain profits and losses, and the multiple levels of contracting can themselves give the garment workers a multitude of identities from which to explain their lot. Jews and blacks or Jews and Italians in New York, Jews and Armenians or Turks and Serbian Yugoslavs in Paris can form "natural alliances" at given times or in an ethnic discourse of memory. Structure and culture function as nonexclusive modes of understanding. It is the use of ethnicity or economics that is important. On the one hand, the ethnicization of conflicts may minimize the industrial structure or reflect a sense of impotence in the possibility of changing it. On the other hand, to emphasize either class solidarities or cutthroat economic competition may be a way of minimizing ethnic difference.

Finally, however, it is not only the language of conflict that needs to be explained. Cultural stereotypes have been countered with a language of solidarity drawing upon both cultural and economic references. Between the wars the rhetoric of harmony was based on a solidarity of class; today it may be a solidarity of adversity within the economic system of ready-to-wear. "We believe in a mixture of races and cultures," said one Polish Jew, the business associate of a firm of Moroccan Jewish brothers.[83] As we have seen for New York, the vision of ethnic warfare can be contested by a language of appease-

Ready-to-Wear and Ready-to-Work

ment. An Armenian wholesaler can also have a Chanukah poster on his door. The Pakistani manufacturer, Bhatti, was philosophical:

To succeed in the Sentier, you have to keep your word, have a sense of humor and not interfere with anyone else's business. That's all. . . . The Sentier is one big family.[84]

Are such statements utopian or simply performative, hoping that once said, they will take effect? When a magazine investigating the Paris garment district was pleased to unearth a Frenchman from the provinces in the Sentier, the Franc-Comtois who agreed to be interviewed also had a resolutely optimistic attitude. No problem; he closed on Yom Kippur like everyone else.[85]

CONCLUSION

I s this century-long history of needles and threads, of fashion headaches and "dress stomachs," coming to an end? Will women's-garment manufacture simply leave the high-rent and relatively high-wage districts of the major urban centers and move definitively "offshore," away from the island of Manhattan and farther and farther away from the banks of the Seine? The American industry has now moved west. California recently surpassed New York in American apparel production, and Los Angeles seems to be rivaling New York City's reputation for sweatshops as well. "Paris fashions" are now made not only in the French provinces but in Romania, the Mauritius Islands, and in Southeast Asia, like everyone else's clothes.[1]

Indeed, the refrains of decline have been so central to recent writings on the garment industry that it often seems as if the Western world's history of ready-to-wear were about to vanish like Singer's sewing machines. Singer sold off its sewing-machine division in 1986. Even the ILGWU has faded, having merged with the men's-wear and textile union to form UNITE!, the Union of Needletrades, Industrial and Textile Employees. The historian's only comfort, in that case, is that the timeliest histories are often written just as the subject is about to disappear. Yet even historians like to imagine the ongoing relevance of their topic. And it looks like there may still be plenty of jobs for immigrants in the garment business in the years ahead.

In Paris as in New York, the flexibility of fashion is creating new tensions. The computer age has brought new technologies to women's wear, although not primarily to the shop floor. Even though certain tasks have been automated, no one has yet perfected a sewing machine that can feed the cloth entirely hands-free and change styles every microseason. Bar codes and computers have, however, introduced a new method of inventory control that has an effect down to the machine-operators' labor market. The *flux tendus* or tendency toward zero-inventory sales operations means that everyone from the clothing boutiques to the sales representatives to department store buyers to manufacturers and designers can know immediately whether the blues are outselling the greens, or whether bell-bottoms have indeed made a comeback. This means that reordering can occur immediately, which in turn means maintaining close-in production sites able to work the extra hours and get the clothes back on the racks before whims change or the weather turns.

The 1964 recommendations of the International Labour Office (ILO) study on the subject sound more utopian than ever:

The clothing industry should try to spread production out evenly over the entire year. To this end, every effort should be made to . . . rationalize the manufacture and distribution of clothes in order to reduce to a bare minimum the fluctuations in production and employment.

The 1995 ILO report admitted defeat. Flexibility has only "dampened the ardor of the 'all-automated' camp" and led to further offshore production and more subcontracting.[2]

We are perhaps not that far from the early-twentieth-century *veillées*, when Marguerite Audoux's heroine, Marie-Claire, and her *patronne* stayed up all night to finish a last-minute order in time for the Grand Prix at the Longchamps racetrack (only to find out that the capricious client did not wear that gown after all)![3] With the democratization of demand, there has been a democratization of blame. It is not only the fanciful bourgeoise insisting that her *couturière* work miracles. The early-twentieth-century *salons de la misère* widened the responsibility toward all of the new ready-made customers. The late-twentieth-century scandal over Thai garment workers' virtual enslavement in a Los Angeles townhouse complex has also led to a focus on the whole garment chain from supply to demand. Consumers, along with manufacturers, wholesalers, and retailers, are warned to reflect on the working conditions that often go into that bargain-basement fashion T-shirt.[4]

Toward a Poststructural Structuralism

To the majority of employers, a worker is a worker, irrespective of nationality.[5]

Turks or Asians, in the garment shops, the backaches and all-nighters are de rigueur. Only the background music is different.[6]

I am hardly suggesting that every immigrant garment worker is an indentured servant. What I have tried to show is how the constraints of extreme flexibility have created certain tendencies in labor-force recruitment and laboring conditions that have remained stubbornly recurrent over the last century. Those who have blamed the late-twentieth-century return of the sweatshop on industrial decline in the "First World" have failed to see how similar conditions have prevailed ever since the late-nineteenth-century period of growth through the height of jobber-contractor abuses in the interwar period to today. The history of the women's-wear industry in both New York and Paris over the last century is a mirror image of the fashion dialectic: industrial conditions show a constantly renewed struggle between forces of order and forces of disorder, between efforts at standardization and the siren call of fashion change. Unions have fought the bosses in order to try to stabilize working conditions, while unions, manufacturers, and their employees have at times all worked together to try to maintain the industry against runaway shops and foreign competition. At the same time, similarities in sewing have persisted, characterized by low skill needs, high seasonality, and widespread subcontracting. Flexibility, as it were, has been a constant.

This does not mean that there has been no change over space and time. Paris and New York have evolved similar ready-to-wear industries with different rhythms and different garment ideologies. They have done so in the context of specific laws and various political and labor climates. Market conditions have caused and exacerbated structural constraints in different periods, just as unions and state labor laws have tried to palliate some of the worst excesses. Industrialization has been perceived to threaten good taste in Paris; it menaces both New York and Paris with offshore production. Both markets have been hard hit by the two late-twentieth-century upstarts of apparel manufacture: sportswear and Southeast Asia, which represent the most modern expressions of increasing standardization. Both the Sentier and Seventh Avenue have been affected by a dramatic decline of their employment figures in the last few decades, along with a certain speed-up of change in the fashion core.

Indeed, the cyclical hysteria—repeatedly—seems "worse than ever before." New modes of production, consumption, and commercialization mean that the "rag trade" is described and decried today as more unstable than ever before . . . in terms reminiscent of the turn of the century. Garment-industry memory has often been short. Labor inspector Mme Letellier chastised the 1920s Parisian *cousette* for not realizing how good she had it compared to the period before World War I, just as ILGWU leaders have reminded contemporary immigrants how much worse things were before Blue Cross.[7] Over the long run, each period reinvents certain perceptions of progress and newness, with elders sometimes protesting that newcomers do not appreciate improvements won. But old-timers have also had to remind the younger generation that some apparent "new" problems are in fact old.[8]

The garment-workers' strikes in the interwar period and the "rediscovery" of the sweatshop in the last two decades are witness to a certain repetition of conditions over time. Just as manufacturers keep lamenting that the pace of production is more precarious than ever, workers and union leaders have repeatedly complained about poor hygiene and seasonal unemployment. Even if things have gotten better—and notions of hygiene and workers' rights have themselves changed over the century—what does it mean to hear such recurrent themes? It is hard to believe that they are just literary tropes. To the historian, it means that the similarity of structure surfaces even within the different narratives of garment history in Paris and New York.

How then can we conceptualize the garment worker within these specific yet analogous stories? Beyond representations of the Jewish

Conclusion

tailor, the female's "fairy fingers," or the "black"(-market) labor of the "green" workers, do garment workers form any sort of "class," and do they define themselves as such? The flexibility of production explains much about the composition of the labor force. Overwhelming numbers of immigrants and women have chosen to work the treadles and peddles of the sewing machines. From the Hudson to the Seine, Jews, Chinese, Puerto Ricans, and Pakistanis have found opportunity in the trade and have confronted similar labor conditions there. Most groups have even had the honor of being ascribed blame for the industry's poor labor record and low wages, and most— even the reputedly most docile—have refought the same battles for better conditions.

Nonetheless, the comparative method often leaves the historian talking to herself: Are all garment workers really alike? As I have suggested elsewhere, the "finding" of similarities or differences is in large part a question of the level of analysis; the closer the level of detail, the more that differences become apparent.[9] How would a Jewish machine-operator in 1930s Paris consider his or her cousin sewing across the Atlantic? Has the 1960s speed-up made life that much different for Chinese garment workers in Paris as compared to New York, or as compared to the turn of the century? The structural answer, while powerful, is not monolithic.

The immigrants of the garment labor force have come from all over the world. Social and political strife in their home countries, immigration policies in France and the United States have helped determine who has converged on the garment shops and when. By choice, yet within limited options, French women, Polish Jews, Southern Italians, American blacks, and Serbs have turned to sewing by skill or simply to survive. For the most part, they have gotten along, but not without tensions and occasional troubles, indicative of divergent expectations, perceptions, or practices behind the machines. From shop-floor conflicts over windows (open or shut, air and light) to competition over work sharing, to unequal representation within the unions, native-born women, foreign-born ones, Jews, Italians, blacks, or Turks have spoken out against their bosses and at times against union policy. They have manifested their "differences" in the labor press, on the picket lines, and in asides to sociologists, journalists, and historians. Like the Paris and New York industries themselves, the immigrants' general paths have been similar but their specific stories different. Sometimes they have protested jointly, challenging flexibility within the workplace ("down with piecework"). At other times individual groups have had specific gripes, combatting this time rigidities within the unions ("up with language branches").

The sewing operators have mobilized as immigrant or ethnic groups. They have also done so as "garment workers." The long-term, comparative perspective argues on behalf of a "poststructural structuralism" which allows for specific interests while recognizing larger categories. As Jacques Le Goff has written, comparative history is the "only one capable of providing a pertinent content to the apparently contradictory needs of historical thought: the search for a global perspective on the one hand, the respect for singularities on the other."[10] While industrial, labor, and ethnic differences exist, this does not mean that a sense of structure disappears. Poststructural voices are best heard in conjunction with the constraints that they themselves sometimes echo. The historic, transethnic, and transcontinental similarities of the fashion business are perhaps best apparent to the historian. As Le Goff has also written, "the goal of historical work is to make the historical process intelligible."[11] This may seem obvious at first glance, but it is a proposition that has been shaken by poststructuralist doubt. As we have seen, the repeated stories of subcontracting and the sweatshop do not obviate important variations on a theme in both time and space. Yet, as New York manufacturer Eli Elias once said, "To get special labor laws to get rid of sweatshops—they've got a better chance to get hit by lightning."[12]

Networks Revisited

Sewing is not the best job, but it is the only one for Chinese women. They can't stand American food. They don't speak English very much. They're afraid of the subway.[13]

She does not pay minimum wage, but she serves her workers tea.[14]

For language or for tea, the reiterated history of immigrants gathering in their compatriots' workshops raises another question, that of ethnic networks. Coming in wave after wave—according to the oceanic view of migration—or actually in family and friendship clus-

Conclusion

ters, the first circle is often familial. Jewish and Italian fathers and sons or sons-in-law, Italian, Puerto Rican, and Chinese mothers and daughters have worked side by side in the garment shops, while whole families have sewn and trimmed together in apartments laden with cloth and thread. The family or ethnic character of the shops has often meant that the only way to tell the difference between owner and employees, as the joke goes, is that the owner starts earlier and leaves later.

Networks have been justifiably hailed for explaining everything from migration routes to parish structure to language continuity to work environments. They have been an important explanatory device for immigration and ethnic history. If they still do not account for how the first emigrant ended up where he or she did, they are a powerful clue as to how others came to follow. The comfort of similarity is intuitively comprehensible. The hard part has been clarifying where, how, and when divergence subsequently occurs, how change and acculturation, however gradual or at times abrupt, happen.

Immigrant networks explain not only the churches and synagogues, mutual-aid societies and choral groups. They help us understand the dynamic of labor market segmentation and microsegmentation as well. Workers get information from kith and kin and often prefer the comradeship of a compatriot environment. The memories of migration give life to the functional paternalism of the immigrant labor market.[15] Images of Polish Jews waiting at the Gare du Nord to hire compatriots fresh off the train echo stories of those waiting for boats to arrive at Ellis Island. The Serbian contractor who half a century later flew home to recruit garment operators is but a modern variation on the same theme. A certain familial atmosphere reigns in the Armenian home-workshops in suburban Paris today.

It is thus not only employers or union closed shops which discriminate. Immigrant informational and sometimes financial networks also help "niche-ing" to occur. There exists a "dialectic between ethnic and economic complicity."[16] Alejandro Portes, Suzanne Model, and others have gone even further in arguing that immigrant networks mean a positive differentiation within the secondary labor market itself: co-ethnic employment—working for one's own—provides easier access to jobs and greater stability as compared to the higher risks of the non-co-ethnic, less-protected periphery. As

Roger Waldinger and Mirjana Morokvasic have both stressed for New York and Paris, chain migration is crucial not only for understanding economic niches and labor market segmentation in general but for the garment industry in particular.[17]

Nonetheless, networks are not the whole story, and I would suggest that three caveats must be taken into account: (1) there may be discord and dysfunctioning within the networks; (2) the multiethnic nature of many of the shops reminds us that cultural complicity is not the only framework of labor relations; and (3) network theory may imply an ipso facto ethnicization of the history of the garment trade (among others) to the detriment of the subcontracting saga.

First of all, the downside of the ethnic networks has been minimized by the optimists, if dramatized by the pessimists.[18] While homogeneity implies harmony, and paternalism can be positive, the first can mask discord and the second exploitation. Even Roger Waldinger, in his book well explaining the advantages of the ethnic entrepreneur's mobilization of resources within the community network, recognized the limits to the notion of ethnic solidarity. He heard contradictory opinions: "Hiring relatives is good," "Hiring relatives is not a good thing." While one Chinese factory owner said rather bluntly, "You don't have to pay relatives," and another explained how you can rely on them, other opinions were less sanguine: relatives could take it easy on the job, could interfere with decisions, and if they did something wrong, "it's very hard to tell them."[19] Shared ethnicity can provide

a repertoire of symbols and customs that can be invoked to underscore cultural interests and similarities so as to blunt a potentially antagonistic employer/worker relationship.[20]

But it can also be "manipulated" at worst, bypassed at best in the manufacturer's self-interest.[21] As Waldinger writes: "[E]thnic relationships are maintained but transformed under the impact of economic change." Or, as one of the Dominican owners he interviewed said, "I'm of the opinion that whoever does the work best, that's it. I don't have to see where he's from."[22]

Intracultural conflicts are evoked even more rarely than interethnic discrimination is admitted to. Yet, as one Mauritian complained, "You shouldn't count too much on your compatriots. I knew this boss in France, he was a profiteer. He took a lot of advantage of

Conclusion

me because I didn't have my legal papers."[23] In spite of the image of solidarity constructed by the Turkish contractor in Paris cited above, Turkish workers and their bosses are not exempt from conflict, just as Chinese contractors (male and female) found that *Gam Ching* was not enough when the Chinese women struck in New York in 1982. Opportunity and complicity within the immigrant milieu do not exclude competition and conflict. When a wholesaler bought the business of his Armenian friend at one-fourth its value because the latter had financial problems, a journalist exclaimed: "You swindle a friend, and he doesn't get angry?" "Of course not! It's not cheating, it's part of the game!"[24]

Second, the focus on the co-ethnic workplace has too often forgotten the truly mixed character of the garment districts. As one contractor commented, workers may get their first job through a relative, "but once they get their feet wet, zingo, they'll work anywhere."[25] I would argue that the phenomenon of ethnic networks is an ever-renewed but ever-temporary phenomenon. While family and friends clearly function as pathways to the shops in the first stage of the life cycle of each immigrant group's "wave" of arrival, in a second stage, the labor force becomes more diversified. Overlapping waves have given a multicultural cast to many of the individual shops and to the industry as a whole at any given time. Thus, while the turn-of-the-century United States Industrial Commission was able to define garment shops by the principal nationalities employed, this became more and more difficult as multiethnic shops became more and more widespread.[26] Already in the 1930s, a list of union workers in one underwear factory included a Battaglia alongside a Regina Weiss, an Elsie Sequrerar, two Santaniellos (sisters?), and a Bessie Snowhite. And although by the late 1930s the New York area dressmakers were estimated to be 51 percent Italian, 32 percent Jewish, 5 percent Negro, 2.5 percent Spanish, and 1.5 percent "old-stock" American, the other 8 percent included Britishers, Syrians, Turks, French, Hungarians, Poles, Austrians, Scandinavians, Dutch, Belgians, Russians, Irish, Chinese, Japanese, Mexicans, Bulgarians, Romanians, Czechs, Germans, Malayans, Armenians, and Hindus! The 28,000 members of the New York Dress Makers' Local 22 represented no less than 32 different national groups in the mid-1930s; there were 47 groups for 29,000 members in 1937.[27]

In the 1940s, Jewish employers were already tending to "leaven the Jewish mass with a large number of Italian workers," while Italian bosses were playing the role of the earlier Jewish "cultural intermediaries" in hiring their own above all.[28] By midcentury, workforces were often more heterogeneous in the larger contract shops, where men tended to be of the same nationality as the foreman, but women workers came from different backgrounds. Even today, in 99 percent–Chinese shops in New York City, there are often one or two Hispanic workers.

In Paris, thirty Russian, Romanian, Armenian, Czech, Italian, Swiss, and French workers were counted at one of the Printemps shops during the 1916 strike.[29] While post–World War II memory tells of more homogeneous immigrant shops during the interwar years—with Polish Jews by and large hiring Polish Jews, and Armenians hiring Armenians—the garment factories today are once again more diverse. In the early 1980s, three-quarters of the Yugoslavs in Morokvasic's sample worked for employers of the same origin, while only one-third of the Turks did; the greater homogeneity of the Yugoslav shops was undoubtedly due to the larger number of Serbian contractors in business at the time.[30] But this also means that one-quarter of the Yugoslavs and two-thirds of the Turks were working in shops of and with other nationalities. There are Turkish workers with no previous skills working alongside trained French women holding a CAP degree (*certificat d'aptitude professionnelle*) in garment making; Turks and Pakistanis sew side by side, not to mention the occasional Serbian or Turkish woman working in a Chinese shop ("but don't tell my mother").[31]

Different languages are thus heard on the shop floors, while immigrant contractors do not always hire their own. Some Jews would not hire other Jews in order to avoid conflicts (of practice and of conscience) over working on the Sabbath, or because they preferred non-Jewish operatives "for the reason that they are more docile."[32] One Armenian contractor said he explicitly avoids working for Armenian wholesalers so as not to create conflicts within the community.[33] Maxi Librati himself began with Polish Jewish and Armenian homeworkers; today he works with Turkish, Serbian, and Chinese contractors. A Moroccan Jewish firm with a Polish Jewish associate set up a factory on the outskirts of Paris with Pakistani workers. The first major Pakistani manufacturer in the Sentier, Bhatti, works with Chinese subcontractors, while Chinese-Cambodian contractors hire

Conclusion

Thai workers, Turks work for Serbian contractors, and everyone hires African and Sri Lankan porters as needed.

This does not mean that mixed shops ignore ethnic favoritism, or that a foreman will not give the best work to his relatives. But the multiethnic nature of many shops and work relations, a function of passing time and the renewal of migration streams, challenges an explanation of the garment districts based on "trust relationships" alone.[34] Cooperation, community, information sharing, and ethnic networks can explain many start-ups and hirings and a good number of hand-shaken streetcorner deals. Common origins clearly help the garment boss to hire workers and the immigrants to find jobs. But the process seems to be microgenerational, and the ethnic network often soon gives way to the "cheaper," more "docile" workforce that has just gotten off the boat, train, or plane.

Third, then, there is a final risk in "ethnicizing" relations beyond what the historical record can bear. If we look for ethnicity, we can find it. It can be as powerful an organizing principle as class or sex— and just as limiting in its monolithic pretensions.[35] The "construction" of ethnic networks presumes to a large extent that harmony is internal to the groups and conflict therefore external, that blood is thicker than water, or that tea and common customs will obviate economic strife. As we have seen, groups can define themselves in opposition to one another, assuming internal cooperation and stressing interethnic conflict. However, at the same time, ethnic identities are neither all-encompassing nor exclusive of interethnic alliance. And, above all, they are situated within the constant tensions of the subcontracting system, where contractors compete for work from jobbers, and workers compete for work from contractors. Conflicts can become most blatant when the cultural difference overlays economic antagonisms, but ethnicity is not the only expression of flexibility.

A Franco-American Perspective on Ethnicity

Workers are called arms (*bras*) in France, hands in the United States; seamstresses have been designated *petites mains* (little hands) in Paris. But "all [the garment workers] need are the fingers," commented one New York contractor.[36] The comparison among workers across the industry, and immigrant groups across the ocean and across time, still leaves one last question concerning more global differences between Paris and New York: Does this story of speedy and supple fingers allow us to draw any conclusions about the comparative fates of immigrants in both cities?

It is current comparative social-science wisdom in France (the United States rarely compares itself to anyone else) that the French do not count ethnicity and do not care about it or for it, whereas the Americans do all three. The French tend to count only two categories: citizens and noncitizens, leading Gérard Noiriel to speak of the *"tyrannie du national"* whereby the state constructs immigrants.[37] While this is to a certain extent true, the issue is more complex at the level of daily life, where identities are not determined by official documents alone. True, the American census distinguishes between foreign-born and native-born citizens, while the French one does not. Naturalized citizens are counted as French in France but also as foreign-born or "ethnic" in the United States. The two countries have thus been globally contrasted on the naming issue, the United States being into counting groups (since the 1970s), France refusing to name or recognize ethnicity in the name of a color-blind egalitarianism.[38] The meaning of ethnicity has thus been rejected in France while celebrated in the United States. The last couple of decades have seen these differences drawn even more sharply as American discourse has centered on diversity, while French discourse emphasizes universality and has slid from a wariness of "community" to a combined fear and rejection of community-ethnicity-ghettos-and-apartheid, sometimes all in one breath. Even the social-scientific language has different meaning in each place. "Interethnic relations" refer to relations among minorities in the United States; in France the term means native-immigrant relations.[39]

This does not mean, however, that the pertinence of ethnicity has always been a constant in United States history, nor that the formation of immigrant identities has been completely absent in France.[40] The garment industry is a perhaps privileged vantage point for comparing the way in which ethnic groups perceive themselves and define their boundaries against ethnic others within a common industrial setting. The finding is in fact contrary to the national stereotypes. The ILGWU argued that it was intrusive if not illegal to designate difference, while *sections ethniques* and language locals existed

Conclusion

in France. The sources in both countries range from reification to silence on the subject of ethnic difference. At different times in each city, ethnicity has taken on more or less importance. Cultural differences may exist without being named, just as conflicts may be designated as cultural when other things are (also) at stake.

Ira Katznelson posed the issue early on as to whether expressions of ethnicity or class were not a function of place: ethnicity by the hearth or in the neighborhood, politics in the workplace. This tenet of separation between home and work is much closer to the French distinction between individual, public citizenship and private (religious or other) identities.[41] To find ethnic difference in private life and class similarity on the job may almost be tautological. The question here has been, how was difference expressed not at home but at the workplace? The answer seems to be that not only does ethnicity, like flexibility, exist on both sides of the Atlantic, but it is historically variable within each city. American discourse is not uniformly ethnic, and French recognition of difference has a longer history than is usually acknowledged. In both New York and Paris, immigrant workers and contractors have identified themselves as Jews, Italians, Chinese, or Turks, and castigated the "other" over the hum of the sewing machines. At the same time, the naming and epithets have been used differently at different times, and sometimes not at all.

Is the garment industry an agent of assimilation, as the ILGWU proudly proclaimed, or a barrier to the same, "an important factor in the clannishness of the immigrant nationalities," as the early United States Industrial Commission charged the contractors?[42] In both Paris and New York, the industry has served many immigrants as the first foot in the labor market door. Garment shops have been ethnic ghettos. But they have also been mini-multinational conglomerates and one of the last vestiges of manufacturing in the modern city.

NOTES

Introduction

1 Roland Barthes, *Système de la Mode,* p. 18; see chap. 1 below.
2 Roy B. Helfgott, "Women's and Children's Apparel," in *Made in New York: Case Studies in Metropolitan Manufacturing,* ed. Max Hall, pp. 19–134; Edgar Hoover and Raymond Vernon, *Anatomy of a Metropolis;* Paul Nystrom, *The Economics of Fashion;* Larry Smith and Company, *Garment District Study,* 2 vols.; Emanuel Tobier, "Manhattan's Business District in the Industrial Age," in *Power, Culture and Place: Essays on New York City,* ed. John H. Mollenkopf, pp. 87–88; Roger D. Waldinger, *Through the Eye of the Needle: Immigrants and Enterprise in New York's Garment Trades.*
3 Edouard Debect, *L'habillement féminin en France au point de vue industriel et commercial,* p. 113.
4 Richard B. Stott, *Workers in the Metropolis: Class, Ethnicity, and Youth in Antebellum New York City,* p. 37; Georges Duveau, *La vie ouvrière en France sous le Second empire* (Paris: Gallimard, 1946), p. 211; Joan Wallach Scott, "Men and Women in the Parisian Garment Trades: Discussions of Family and Work in the 1830s and 1840s," in *The Power of the Past: Essays for Eric Hobsbawm,* ed. Pat Thane, Geoffrey Crossick, and Roderick Floud, p. 69.
5 *Occupations at the 12th Census (1900), Special Reports,* pp. 636, 638, 640; *14th Census of the United States,* vol. 4, *Population 1920, Occupations,* p. 192. Dressmakers and seamstresses (not in factory) fell from 38,850 workers in 1910, to 22,915 in 1920, to 11,633 in 1940. There were only 4,522 left in the whole New York metropolitan area in 1980. *13th Census of the United States,* vol. 4, *Population 1910, Occupation Statistics,* p. 574; *14th Census (1920),* op.

cit., p. 188; *16th Census of the United States: 1940, Population*, vol. 3: *The Labor Force*, pt. 4, pp. 364–65; *1980 Census of Population*, vol. 1: *Characteristics of the Population*, chap. D, *Detailed Population Characteristics*, pt. 34, *New York*, sec. 1: tables 194–229, p. 34-472.

6 *Census of Population: 1950*, vol. 2, *Characteristics of the Population*, pt. 32, *New York*, pp. 32-276, 32-369; *Census of Population: 1960*, vol. 1: *Characteristics of the Population*, pt. 34, *New York*, pp. 34-618, 619, 652–53; *1970 Census of Population*, vol. 1: *Characteristics of the Population*, pt. 34, *New York*, sec. 2: p. 34-917 (excluding dressmakers and seamstresses not in factory work); *1980 Census of Population*, op. cit., p. 34-473.

7 *New York Times*, Nov. 9, 1993. All of the above figures are for men's wear and women's wear combined. Abeles et al., *The Chinatown Garment Industry Study*, p. 23, estimated that women's wear alone accounted for 70,000 jobs in New York in 1975.

8 Waldinger estimated that there were 105,500 jobs in apparel manufacturing in New York in 1986, with an additional 53,000 in the wholesale end of the business (Roger Waldinger, "Tattered and Torn: The Garment Industry Hangs On," unpublished, p. 2). Cf. "Daniels on GDIC," *Justice*, May 1984; and New York State Department of Labor, "Report to the Governor and the Legislature on the Garment Manufacturing Industry and Industrial Homework" (New York, 1982), p. 9, declaring the apparel industry to be the second largest of New York's manufacturing employers (about 139,400 jobs), accounting for some 28 percent of the manufacturing jobs.

9 *Résultats statistiques du recensement général de la population (1921)*, tome II, (Paris: Imprimerie Nationale, 1925), p. 1-5 (for 1906 in recapitulative table); *Résultats statistiques (1926)*, tome III, p. 3; *Résultats statistiques (1931)*, tome II, p. 3; *Résultats statistiques (1946)*, tome V, *Tableaux pour le département de la Seine*, p. 38 (1936 and 1946 in recapitulative table; under the older classification, there were 145,971 garment industry jobs in 1936, *Résultats statistiques [1936]*, tome II, p. 3); *Recensement général de la population de 1962*, no. 75: *Seine*, p. 43.

10 Increasing their portion of nationwide French garment workers from 20.4 to 23.7 percent (44,135 people) (Guy Groux et al., "L'Atelier, l'habit et la règle: L'evolution récente des relations professionnelles et des stratégies syndicales dans les PME de l'habillement," report, Ministère du travail, de l'emploi et de la formation professionnelle, 1989, p. 17). Cf. the cautious optimism of "Le Devenir des industries du textile et de l'habillement," *Journal officiel*, Feb. 25, 1982.

11 *Le Monde*, Dec. 2, 1993. Ten years previous, Mirjana Morokvasic counted some 4,301 garment firms in Paris, of which 1,180 were listed as specializing in women's ready-to-wear (*confection*). However, as she has well pointed out, the smaller establishments are often invisible; immigrant shops, like immigrants in general, are undoubtedly vastly underreported. See Mirjana Morokvasic, "Le Recours aux immigrés dans la confection à Paris: Eléments de comparaison avec la ville de Berlin-Ouest," Ministère du travail et de la formation profes-

sionnelle: Mission de liaison interministérielle pour la lutte contre les trafics de main-d'oeuvre, 1986, pp. 3, 6, 9. Morokvasic only counted 25,700 workers in the Parisian ready-made trade, according to the 1982 census (ibid., p. 11). Other estimates range from 30,000 to 50,000: 30,000 in the Sentier: *Libération*, Feb. 16–17, 1985, cited in Guy Delorme, *Profession: Travailleur au noir* (Paris: Ouest-France, 1986), p. 106; 30,000 to 50,000 people working in 10,000 firms in the Sentier and elsewhere in Paris: *Actuel*, Apr. 1988; 45,000 people employed directly or indirectly by the Sentier: *Le Monde*, Dec. 6, 1991.

12 International Ladies' Garment Workers' Union, *General Executive Board Report and Record of the 38th Convention*, p. 2.

13 For a long time, the two New York classics were by Louis Levine and Jesse Pope, to which I would add the excellent survey by Claudia B. Kidwell and Margaret C. Christman. More recently, Roger Waldinger's important *Through the Eye of the Needle*, Steven Fraser's study of the men's-wear industry and two works focusing largely on immigrant women garment workers by Susan Glenn and Miriam Cohen have all become new classics in the field. Gus Tyler has also just published a new history of the ILGWU. See the bibliography for full references of these works. They are, however, a handful out of an impressive number of books, reports, and articles on garment manufacture in New York.

Works on the French garment industry can be more easily encapsulated within a footnote (see bibliography for full references): Daniel Roche and Philippe Perrot have made important contributions in their respective analyses of eighteenth- and nineteenth-century clothing habits and clothing makers. Henriette Vanier's older work is also quite useful. The French garment industry has been largely approached through women's history, the most impressive full-length study is Judith Coffin, *The Politics of Women's Work: The Paris Garment Trades, 1750–1915*. See also Lorraine Coons's book and articles by Christopher H. Johnson, Michelle Perrot, Jacques Rancière, Joan Wallach Scott, and Louise Tilly, cited in the bibliography.

Other French authors, such as François Faraut, Gilles Marcadet, and Jean-François Paoli; Solange Montagné-Villette; and Mirjana Morokvasic have more recently looked at the industry as an urban industry or as an employer of immigrants. See also the report by Maurizio Lazzarato, Antonio Negri, and Giancarlo Santilli, and their recent book *Des entreprises pas comme les autres: Benetton en Italie, Le Sentier à Paris*.

14 E.g., for New York: Christine Stansell, *City of Women: Sex and Class in New York, 1789–1860*; Stott, *Workers in the Metropolis*; Sean Wilentz, *Chants Democratic: New York City and the Rise of the American Working Class, 1788–1850*.

For Paris: François Faraut, *Histoire de la Belle Jardinière*; Alain Faure, "Petit atelier et modernisme économique: La production en miettes au XIXe siècle," *Histoire, économie et société* 5 (1986): 531–57; Jeanne Gaillard, "Paris, La ville, 1852–1870," doctoral thesis, Université de Paris 10, 1975. See also Stuart Bruchey, ed., *Small Business and American Life* (New York: Columbia University Press, 1980); Commission internationale d'histoire des mouvements

Notes to Pages 3–4

sociaux et des structures sociales, *Petite entreprise et croissance industrielle dans le monde aux XIXe et XXe siècles*, 2 vols.; Alain Cottereau, "Problèmes de conceptualisation comparative de l'industrialisation: L'exemple des ouvriers de la chaussure en France et en Grande Bretagne," in *Villes ouvrières, 1900–1950*, ed. Susanna Magri and Christian Topalov , pp. 41–82; and Michel Lallement, *Des PME en chambre: Travail et travailleurs à domicile d'hier et d'aujourd'hui*.

15 In his preface to Faraut, *Belle Jardinière*, p. 4.

16 Raphael Samuel, "The Workshop of the World: Steam Power and Hand Technology in Mid-Victorian Britain," *History Workshop* 3 (1977): 6–72. See also Michael Sonenscher, *Work and Wages: Natural Law, Politics and the 18th-Century French Trades;* Christine Stansell, "The Origins of the Sweatshop: Women and Early Industrialization in New York City," in *Working-Class America: Essays on Labor, Community, and American Society*, ed. Michael H. Frisch and Daniel J. Walkowitz (Urbana: University of Illinois Press, 1983), pp. 78–103; debate in *International Labor and Working-Class History (ILWCH)*: Jean H. Quartaert, "A New View of Industrialization: 'Protoindustry' or the Role of Small-Scale, Labor-Intensive Manufacture in the Capitalist Environment," *ILWCH*, no. 33 (Spring 1988), pp. 3–22, and responses by Jonathan Prude and Charles F. Sabel, pp. 23–38.

17 Charles F. Sabel and Jonathan Zeitlin, eds., *Worlds of Possibility: Flexibility and Mass Production in Western Industrialization* (Paris: Maison des Sciences de l'Homme, forthcoming); Sabel, "Response," in *ILWCH* (1988), pp. 30–38.

18 Scranton argues forcefully that by looking at batch production we can revise our "Lowell-to-General Motors by-way-of-the-railroads" vision of industrialization. See Philip Scranton, *Figured Tapestry: Production, Markets, and Power in Philadelphia Textiles, 1885–1941*, p. 3; idem, *Proprietary Capitalism: The Textile Manufacture at Philadelphia, 1800–1885;* idem, "Manufacturing Diversity: Production Systems, Markets, and an American Consumer Society, 1870–1930," *Technology and Culture* 35 (1994): 476–506.

19 On "flexible specialization," see below. On the informal economy, see e.g., Alejandro Portes, Manuel Castells, and Lauren A. Benton, eds., *The Informal Economy: Studies in Advanced and Less Developed Countries*, particularly Saskia Sassen-Koob's article, "New York City's Informal Economy," pp. 60–77; and J. J. Thomas, *Informal Economic Activity* (Ann Arbor: University of Michigan Press, 1993).

20 Karl Marx, *Capital*, 3 vols. [1887] (London: Lawrence and Wishart, 1974), pt. 4, sec. 8C, 1:442–51.

21 Alfred D. Chandler Jr., *The Visible Hand: The Managerial Revolution in American Business*, p. 246. Chandler in fact refers more often to shoes than to clothes, the former indeed industrializing earlier. As for clothes, he was wrong, however, in arguing that outwork declined with the spread of the machines (pp. 53–54, 62–63). See also David S. Landes, *The Unbound Prometheus: Technological Change and Industrial Development in Western Europe from 1750 to the Present;* Sidney Pollard, *Peaceful Conquest: The Industrialization of Eu-*

rope, 1760–1970 (New York: Oxford University Press, 1981); and the excellent analysis of the sewing machine industry in David A. Hounshell, *From the American System to Mass Production, 1800–1932.*

22 United States Industrial Commission, *Reports of the Industrial Commission*, 19 vols., 15:320–21, 368.

23 Helen Everett Meiklejohn, "Dresses—The Impact of Fashion on a Business," in *Price and Price Policies*, ed. Walton Hamilton, p. 326.

24 Larry Smith, *Garment District*, 1:16. See also Solange Montagné-Villette, "Le prêt-à-porter à Paris: de l'artisanat à l'industrie," doctoral thesis, Université de Paris 10, 1981. This image was explicitly countered with the Dec. 17, 1986–Mar. 22, 1987, exhibit at the Cité des Sciences et de l'Industrie de la Villette entitled "La Mode, une industrie de pointe."

25 Michelle Perrot, "De la nourrice à l'employée . . . Travaux de femmes dans la France du XIXe siècle," *Le Mouvement social*, no. 105 (Oct.–Dec. 1978), p. 5; Faure, "Production en miettes"; Philippe Vigier, "Rapport général," in Commission d'histoire, *Petite entreprise*, 1:105–7. See also James Schmiechen, *Sweated Industries and Sweated Labor: The London Clothing Trades, 1860–1914.*

26 Charles F. Sabel and Jonathan Zeitlin, "Historical Alternatives to Mass Production: Politics, Market, and Technology in Nineteenth-Century Industrialization," *Past and Present*, no. 108 (Aug. 1985): 133–76; Michael Piore and Charles F. Sabel, *The Second Industrial Divide* (the term "flexible specialization" is attributed to Sabel); Cottereau, "Problèmes de conceptualisation."

27 E.g., Montagné-Villette, *Le Sentier, un espace ambigu*; Georges Jollès and Jean Bounine, "Un projet pour le textile-habillement français," report, Ministère de l'industrie et de l'aménagement du territoire, 1989; similarly, see Jonathan Zeitlin and Peter Totterdill, "Markets, Technology and Local Intervention: The Case of Clothing," in *Reversing Industrial Decline? Industrial Structure and Policy in Britain and Her Competitors*, ed. Paul Hirst and Jonathan Zeitlin.

28 E. G. Ravenstein, "The Laws of Migration," *Journal of the Royal Statistical Society* 48 (1885): 167–235; 52 (1889): 241–305 (see esp. 286, 287).

29 Alejandro Portes and Robert L. Bach, *Latin Journey: Cuban and Mexican Immigrants in the United States;* Min Zhou, *Chinatown: The Socioeconomic Potential of an Urban Enclave;* Waldinger, *Through the Eye of the Needle;* Michael J. Piore, *Birds of Passage: Migrant Labor and Industrial Societies;* Mirjana Morokvasic, "Birds of Passage are also Women . . . ," *International Migration Review* 18 (Winter 1984): 886–907.

30 Morokvasic, "Immigrants in the Parisian Garment Industry," *Work, Employment and Society* 1, no. 4 (1987): pp. 443–44.

31 Two of the first to point in this direction were: Herbert Gutman, "Work, Culture, and Society in Industrializing America, 1815–1919," in *Work, Culture, and Society in Industrializing America, 1815–1919*, pp. 3–78; and Michelle Perrot, "Les rapports des ouvriers français et des étrangers (1871–1893)," *Bulletin de la Société d'histoire moderne*, 12e série, no. 12 (1960): 4–9.

32 Especially in the United States: John Bodnar, *Immigration and Industrialization: Ethnicity in an American Mill Town, 1870–1940* (Pittsburgh: University of Pittsburgh Press, 1977); Lizabeth Cohen, *Making a New Deal: Industrial Workers in Chicago, 1919–1939;* Olivier Zunz, *The Changing Face of Inequality: Urbanization, Industrial Development, and Immigrants in Detroit, 1880–1920.*

33 Only a few books, such as Gérard Noiriel, *Longwy: Immigrés et prolétaires, 1880–1980;* and Philippe I. Bourgois, *Ethnicity at Work: Divided Labor on a Central American Banana Plantation* (Baltimore: Johns Hopkins University Press, 1989), have systematically studied the change of immigrant labor over time in one economic sector.

34 Nancy L. Green, "L'histoire comparative et le champ des études migratoires," *Annales E.S.C.*, no. 6 (Nov.–Dec. 1990): 1335–50.

35 Claude Lévi-Strauss, *Anthropologie structurale* [1958] (Paris: Plon, 1974), pp. 312–13, 325; cf. Marc Bloch, "Pour une histoire comparée des sociétés européennes" [1928], *Mélanges historiques*, 1:16–40. See also Pierre Bouvier, "Différences et analogies," in *France-U.S.A.: Les crises du travail et de la production*, ed. Pierre Bouvier and Olivier Kourchid, pp. 11–17.

36 On comparative history as the closest we can get to experimentation on the past, see William H. Sewell Jr., "Marc Bloch and the Logic of Comparative History," *History and Theory* 6, no. 2 (1967): 208–18; Judith E. Vichniac, *The Management of Labor: The British and French Iron and Steel Industries, 1860–1918.*

A couple of mostly short comparative studies on the garment industry have been undertaken by Mirjana Morokvasic in collaboration with other scholars, including Annie Phizacklea, Hedwig Rudolph, and Roger Waldinger. See the bibliography for full references along with the book by Gertrude Willoughby.

37 Thomas Archdeacon, "Problems and Possibilities in the Study of American Immigration and Ethnic History," *International Migration Review* 19, no. 1 (1985): 112–34; Rudolph J. Vecoli, "European Americans: From Immigrants to Ethnics," *International Migration Review* 6, no. 4 (Winter 1972): 403–34. For a discussion of those "convergent" and "divergent" studies which have been undertaken, see Nancy L. Green, "L'histoire comparative"; and idem, "The Comparative Method and Poststructural Structuralism—New Perspectives for Migration Studies," *Journal of American Ethnic Studies* 13 (Summer 1994): 3–22. An interesting multivariate approach is Bruno Ramirez, *On the Move: French Canadian and Italian Migrants in the North Atlantic Economy.* See also Donald Horowitz and Gérard Noiriel, eds., *Immigrants in Two Democracies: French and American Experience.* For an interesting reflection on some of the problems of doing comparative immigration history, see Samuel Baily, "Cross-Cultural Comparison and the Writing of Migration History: Some Thoughts on How to Study Italians in the New World," in *Immigration Reconsidered*, ed. Virginia Yans-McLaughlin, pp. 241–53.

38 Pierre Bourdieu, *Outline of a Theory of Practice* (Cambridge: Cambridge University Press, 1977); Roger Chartier, "Le Temp des Doutes," *Le Monde,*

Supplément pour comprendre l'histoire," Mar. 1993; Herbert Gans, "Comment: Ethnic Invention and Acculturation, A Bumpy-Line Approach," *Journal of American Ethnic History* 12, no. 1 (Fall 1992): 50; Anthony Giddens, *The Constitution of Society: Outline of the Theory of Structuration* (Berkeley: University of California Press, 1984), p. 2; William H. Sewell Jr., "A Theory of Structure: Duality, Agency, and Transformation," *American Journal of Sociology* 98 (July 1992): 1–29; Sewell, "Toward a Post-materialist Rhetoric for Labor History," in *Rethinking Labor History,* ed. Lenard R. Berlanstein, pp. 15–38.

1 Fashion and Flexibility:
The Garment Industry Between Haute Couture and Jeans

1 Georg Simmel, "Fashion," [1904], *The American Journal of Sociology* 62, no. 6 (May 1957): 541–58, 558. See also Gabriel de Tarde, *Les lois de l'imitation.*

2 Roland Barthes, *Système de la mode,* p. 18.

3 Jean Dannenmuller and Jeanne E. Durand, *Comment se chauffer au temps des restrictions* (Paris: Bloud et Gay, 1940); Dominique Veillon, *La Mode sous l'Occupation,* pp. 64–73.

4 Notably by John Carl Flügel, *The Psychology of Clothes,* and, more recently, Anne Hollander, *Sex and Suits.*

5 Eve [*sic*] Merriam, *Figleaf: The Business of Being in Fashion* (Philadelphia: Lippincott, 1960).

6 Jean Berthelot, *Rapport de la classe 86B* in *Rapport du groupe XIIID: Industries accessoires du vêtement (Exposition coloniale internationale de Vincennes),* ed. René Hayem, pp. 321–22.

7 Norbert Elias, *The Civilizing Process* [1939] (New York: Urizen Books, 1978).

8 Simmel, "Fashion"; Thorstein Veblen, *The Theory of the Leisure Class;* Barthes, *Système de la Mode;* and Pierre Bourdieu, *La Distinction.* See also Paul Nystrom, *The Economics of Fashion;* Quentin Bell, *On Human Finery;* and Rosalind H. Williams, *Dream Worlds: Mass Consumption in Late 19th-Century France,* p. 107.

9 Roland Barthes, "Histoire et sociologie du vêtement," *Annales, E.S.C.* 12 (July–Sept. 1957): 430–31; and Barthes, *Système de la mode.* See Alison Lurie, *The Language of Clothes,* for a less theoretical but more amusing and choicely illustrated variation on this idea. Dictionaries distinguish clothing (*vêtement*) from garments (*habillement*), the former being the more global term, including footwear, headgear, and other accessories. Garment is the more restricted term for those items made from cloth (or perhaps knitwear) covering the body exclusive of head and toe. In common parlance, however, the terms are used interchangeably.

10 Barthes, "Histoire et sociologie du vêtement," pp. 438, 432; Bourdieu,

Distinction; Bourdieu and Yvette Delsaut, "Le Couturier et sa griffe: Contribution à une théorie de la magie," *Actes de la recherche en sciences sociales,* no. 1 (Jan. 1975): 7–36.

11 Daniel Roche, *La culture des apparences,* pp. 53, 448.

12 Gilles Lipovetsky, *L'Empire de l'éphémère,* pp. 174, 179, 13, 26, 51ff, 62–63ff. Lipovetsky admits that it is the individualism of the elite which interests him most, yet he also interprets, somewhat weakly, the jeans phenomenon as an expression of individualism. See two contrasting reviews of his book in *Le Monde,* Sept. 13, 1987, by Roland Jaccard ("Pour") and Alain Finkielkraut ("Contre"). Finkielkraut argues that "la mode consacre la déchéance de l'individu, non son apothéose." See also Elizabeth Wilson's treatment of female fashion as an artistic and political means of expression in *Adorned in Dreams: Fashion and Modernity,* in contrast to feminist critiques that see the fashion industry as repressing women's bodies.

13 Jean Baudrillard, *La société de consommation,* on the "PPDM," and more generally, Jean Baudrillard, *Le système des objets.* See also Finkielkraut, "Contre," for a (Simmelian) discussion of free choice and enslavement to group norms.

14 Stuart and Elizabeth Ewen, *Channels of Desire: Mass Images and the Shaping of American Consciousness,* p. 226, and, more generally, chaps. 11 and 12.

15 Herbert Blumer, "Fashion: From Class Differentiation to Collective Selection," *Sociological Quarterly* 10 (1969): 290.

16 *Bataille Syndicaliste,* June 1, 1913. Agnes Young argued strenuously against any notion of fashion as unpredictable. She considered that there is a "consistent orderliness" to the process to the tune of three cycles per century (Agnes Young, *Recurring Cycles of Fashion, 1760–1937*).

17 Bernard Roshco, *The Rag Race: How New York and Paris Run the Breakneck Business of Dressing American Women,* p. 65. Louis Levine, *The Women's Garment Workers,* p. 176; "Adam Smith on Seventh Avenue," *Fortune,* Jan. 1949, a spoof on how Adam Smith would have described the industry.

18 Michael J. Piore and Charles F. Sabel, *The Second Industrial Divide,* pp. 118–19, 265–66; Charles F. Sabel and Jonathan Zeitlin, "Historical Alternatives to Mass Production: Politics, Market, and Technology in Nineteenth-Century Industrialization," *Past and Present,* no. 108 (Aug. 1985): 133–76. See also Roger D. Waldinger, *Through the Eye of the Needle.*

19 Simmel, "Fashion," p. 547. Even Ford recognized the limits of standardization. See David A. Hounshell, *From the American System to Mass Production, 1800–1932,* chaps. 6 and 7.

20 Simmel, "Fashion," p. 556.

21 Bernard Smith, "Hyper-Innovation and the American Women's Clothing Trades, 1880–1930," paper presented at the Social Science History Association Meeting, Baltimore, Nov. 5, 1993.

22 Elizabeth W. Gilboy, "Demand as a Factor in the Industrial Revolution" [1932], in *The Causes of the Industrial Revolution in England,* ed. Ronald M.

Hartwell (London: Methuen, 1967), pp. 121–38; Joel Mokyr, "Demand vs. Supply in the Industrial Revolution," in *The Economics of the Industrial Revolution,* ed. idem, pp. 97–118; Neil McKendrick, "Home Demand and Economic Growth: A New View of the Role of Women and Children in the Industrial Revolution," in *Historical Perspectives: Studies in English Thought and Society,* ed. idem (London: Europa, 1974), pp. 152–210.

23 Claudia B. Kidwell and Margaret C. Christman, *Suiting Everyone;* Williams, *Dream Worlds,* on the "démocratisation de luxe" in France; and, more generally, Eugen Weber, *Peasants into Frenchmen: The Modernization of Rural France, 1870–1917* (Stanford: Stanford University Press, 1977).

24 Roche, *Culture des apparences;* Beverly Lemire, "The Theft of Clothes and Popular Consumerism in Early Modern England," *Journal of Social History* 24, no. 2 (Winter 1990): 255–76.

25 Kidwell and Christman, *Suiting Everyone,* pp. 155–64; Michael B. Miller, *The Bon Marché: Bourgeois Culture and the Department Store, 1869–1920;* Judith Coffin, "Woman's Place and Women's Work in the Paris Clothing Trades, 1830–1914," Ph.D. diss., Yale University, 1985; Williams, *Dream Worlds.* By the 1940s, the International Ladies' Garment Workers' Union commented that chain stores and mail-order houses had become the virtual employers of some sections of the industry and criticized them for lowering standards. See ILGWU, *Record of the 25th Convention* (1944), pp. 547, 577–80.

26 Randolph Starn, "Métamorphoses d'une notion: les historiens et la 'crise'," *Communications,* no. 25 (1976): 4–18.

27 Roche, *Culture des apparences.* Cf. discussion of the consumer revolution in eighteenth-century Great Britain: Neil McKendrick, "Commercialization and the Economy," in McKendrick et al., *The Birth of a Consumer Society: The Commercialization of Eighteenth-Century England* (London: Hutchinson, 1983); and critique by Ben Fine and Ellen Leopold, "Consumerism and the Industrial Revolution," *Social History* 15, no. 2 (May 1990): 151–79, making the point that historiographic interest has itself shifted globally from supply to demand, from production to consumption.

28 Philippe Perrot, "Aspects socio-culturels des débuts de la confection parisienne au 19e siècle," *Revue de l'Institut de sociologie* (Brussels), no. 2 (1977): 190. Others date this bourgeoisification to the Third Republic, e.g., Gérard Noiriel, *Les ouvriers dans la société française: XIXe–XXe siècles* (Paris: Seuil, 1986).

29 Williams, *Dream Worlds,* p. 108.

30 For a discussion of this event, see Werner Sollors, *Beyond Ethnicity: Consent and Descent in American Culture,* pp. 89–91. On the civilizing mission of clothing for the French, see Perrot, "Aspects socio-culturels," p. 192; for the U.S., see Ava Baron and Susan Klepp, "'If I Didn't Have my Sewing Machine . . .': Women and Sewing Machine Technology," in *A Needle, a Bobbin, a Strike: Women Needleworkers in America,* ed. Joan M. Jensen and Sue Davidson, p. 27; Sue Davidson, "Introduction," and Joan M. Jensen, "Needlework as

Art, Craft, and Livelihood before 1900," in ibid.; Lizabeth A. Cohen, "Embellishing a Life of Labor: An Interpretation of the Material Culture of American Working-Class Homes, 1885–1915," in *Labor Migration in the Atlantic Economies,* ed. Dirk Hoerder, pp. 321–52.

31 Perrot, "Aspects socio-culturels," p. 191; Barthes, *Système de la Mode.*

32 For readings on the notion of "taste professionals," see Leora Auslander, *Taste and Power: Furnishing Modern France.*

33 Flügel, *Psychology of Clothes,* pp. 110–13.

34 Cited by Valerie Steele, *Paris Fashion: A Cultural History,* p. 93.

35 Simmel, "Fashion," pp. 550–51. What does this say about the Queen of England's hats?

36 *American Jewess,* Jan. 1899, cited by Selma Berrol, "Class or Ethnicity: The Americanized German Jewish Woman and Her Middle Class Sisters in 1895," *Jewish Social Studies* 47 (Winter 1985): 26. On women as consumers, see Whitney Walton, *France at the Crystal Palace: Bourgeois Taste and Artisan Manufacture in the Nineteenth Century,* chap. 2.

37 The term *costume tailleur* appeared between 1879 and 1935, i.e., between the 7th and 8th editions of the *Dictionnaire de l'Académie française.* The ellipsis *tailleur* appeared between 1935 and 1958 (*Trésor de la langue française*).

38 Léon Storch, in *Classe 85—Industrie de la confection et de la couture pour hommes, femmes et enfants, Exposition universelle internationale de 1900 à Paris: Rapports du jury international,* Groupe XIII. *Fils, tissus, vêtements,* 2e partie—*Classes 85 et 86,* ed. Léon Storch, Julien Hayem, and A. Mortier, pp. 90, 79. The increasing similarity in men's and women's clothes was noted to be an infraction of a Napoleonic ordinance of 1800 forbidding women to wear men's clothes (Storch, p. 90).

39 Steele, *Paris Fashion,* p. 176.

40 Raymonde Sée, *Le Costume de la Révolution à nos jours,* cited by and commented upon by Jean Allilaire, *Les industries de l'habillement et du travail des étoffes,* p. 48; Ewens, *Channels of Desire,* p. 207. On how changing fashions reshape the female body, see, e.g., Bonnie G. Smith, *Changing Lives: Women in European History since 1700* (Lexington, Mass.: D. C. Heath and Co., 1989), pp. 196, 325ff. The corset may have been at the origin of the phrase "to die from laughing." Cf. Alain Cottereau, who dates freedom for feet to the French Revolution. "C'est la Révolution française qui aurait affranchi les pieds de la tyrannie des traditions, en permettant que le matériau se plie à la dissymétrie anatomique, donnant naissance à la distinction entre pied gauche et pied droit," in "Problèmes de conceptualisation comparative de l'industrialisation: l'exemple des ouvriers de la chaussure en France et en Grande-Bretagne," in *Villes ouvrières, 1900–1950,* ed. Susanna Magri and Christian Topalov, p. 60.

41 Roshco, *Rag Race;* Steele, *Paris Fashion;* more generally Margaret Higonnet et al., eds., *Behind the Lines: Gender and the Two World Wars* (New Haven: Yale University Press, 1987).

42 Albert Leduc, in *Classe 36: Habillement des deux sexes, Exposition univer-selle internationale de 1889 à Paris: Rapports du jury international*, ed. Alfred Picard, pp. 92, 59–60; Pierre Du Maroussem, *La petite industrie (salaires et durée du travail)*, vol. 2, *Le vêtement à Paris*, p. 135.

43 Simmel, "Fashion," p. 556, underlined in the text.

44 E.g., Hounshell, *American System;* and Merritt Roe Smith et al., *Military Enterprise and Technological Change* (Cambridge, Mass.: MIT Press, 1985).

45 On war and clothes, and especially uniforms, see, for France, Roche, *Culture des apparences*, chap. 9; Philippe Perrot, *Les dessus et les dessous de la bourgeoisie*, pp. 68, 94 and passim; Coffin, "Woman's Place," pp. 69–72. On the U.S., see, e.g., J. M. Budish and George Soule, *The New Unionism in the Clothing Industry*, p. 19. War itself can be perceived as a fashion battle. After World War II, one French commentator lamented that the prewar French uniform "étriquée ou trop vaste, faisait sourire à juste titre les étrangers" (Allilaire, *Industries de l'habillement*, p. 211).

46 Kidwell and Christman, *Suiting Everyone*, p. 103, citing Albert Bolles's *Industrial History of the United States* (1879); Du Maroussem, *Le vêtement à Paris*, p. 210.

47 United States Industrial Commission, *Reports of the Industrial Commission*, 19 vols., 15:324.

48 Organisation internationale du travail (OIT), *Réunion technique tripartite pour l'industrie du vêtement* (1964), 1:88–97; see also Nahum I. Stone, *Productivity of Labor in the Cotton-Garment Industry*.

49 Nathan Belfer, "Section Work in the Women's Garment Industry," *The Southern Economic Journal* 21, no. 2 (Oct. 1954): 191.

50 Cited in Kidwell and Christman, *Suiting Everyone*, p. 79.

51 Baron and Klepp, "If I Didn't Have"; Grace Rogers Cooper, *The Sewing Machine: Its Invention and Development*, 2d ed.; Egal Feldman, *Fit for All Men* (New York: Public Affairs Press, 1960), pp. 105–11; Frank P. Godfrey, *An International History of the Sewing Machine;* Karin Hausen, "Technical Progress and Women's Labour in the Nineteenth Century: The Social History of the Sewing Machine," in *The Social History of Politics*, ed. Georg Iggers, pp. 259–81; Hounshell, *American System*, chap. 2; Andrew B. Jack, "The Channels of Distribution for an Innovation: The Sewing-Machine Industry in America, 1860–1865," *Explorations in Entrepreneurial History* 9 (1957): 113–41; "Femmes et techniques," special issue *Pénélope*, no. 9 (Fall 1983). *Time*, Mar. 3, 1986, describes Singer's father as a German immigrant. He may have had some Jewish ancestry, but other sources have described the Singers variously as Mennonites, Protestants, or Episcopalians. Isaac Merritt seems to have been a fairly resolute atheist, except that he took communion on his deathbed. See Ruth Brandon, *A Capitalist Romance*, pp. 6–7.

52 *Time*, Mar. 3, 1986. Singer's own description of his discovery is a veritable creation story: "I worked day and night, sleeping but three or four hours out of the twenty-four and eating generally but once a day, as I knew I must get a

machine made for forty dollars, or not get it at all. The machine was completed the night of the eleventh day from the day it was commenced" (Brandon, *Capitalist Romance*, p. 47).

53 *Musée rétrospectif de la classe 79: Matériel et procédés de la couture et de la fabrication de l'habillement à l'Exposition universelle internationale de 1900, à Paris* (Saint-Cloud: Imprimerie Belin Frères, n.d.), p. 7; cf. Jeanne Bouvier, *La Lingerie et les lingères*, p. 237.

54 Marcel Doyen, *Thimonnier 1793–1857: Inventeur de la machine-à-coudre*. According to Doyen, a postage stamp in Thimonnier's honor even got his year of death wrong, and a 1957 commemorative plaque (put up on the correct centennial of his death) in his hometown of Amplepuis misspelled his name! (p. 9). (Doyen took over the business from Thimonnier's youngest son and had access to family archives.)

55 Cf. *Gazette des Tribunaux*, Feb. 23, 1831, cited by Henriette Vanier, *La mode et ses métiers*, p. 172, which reported that the National Guard prevented any damage from being done; and Doyen, *Thimonnier*, pp. 26ff, according to whom the machines were smashed. See also Coffin, "Woman's Place," pp. 54–58.

56 Bouvier, *La lingerie*, p. 237; Doyen, *Thimonnier*, p. 33.

57 Ibid., p. 31.

58 The Singer Company ultimately diversified into war matériel, and not of the uniforms sort. By 1986, when Singer sold off its sewing machine division, its major interests were in aerospace engineering, manufacturing flight simulators, electronic-warfare equipment, and guidance systems (*Time*, Mar. 3, 1986).

59 Andrew Jack, "Channels of Distribution," pp. 114–15, gives Singer three "firsts": for having combined important structural features that Jack predefines as crucial for an industrial sewing-machine; for having introduced a completely new design; and for having withstood the test of time. Can this last criterion be called a "first"?

60 Baron and Klepp, "If I Didn't Have," p. 35; Chandler, *The Visible Hand*, pp. 402–6. Costly patent infringement suits took up a good deal of the early companies' time and money, but once settled, business boomed. See Jack, "Channels of Distribution"; Judith Coffin, "Social Science Meets Sweated Labor: Reinterpreting Women's Work in Late Nineteenth-Century France," *The Journal of Modern History* 63 (June 1991): 230–70. Hounshell, *American System*, chap. 2, notes, however, that the Singer Manufacturing Company was somewhat backward in one important respect: the adoption of the "American system" of interchangeable parts; they used instead the "European method" of skilled machine workers filing hand-fitted parts into the early 1880s.

61 Feldman, *Fit for All*, p. 108; Robert Bruce Davies, *Peacefully Working to Conquer the World: Singer Machines in Foreign Markets, 1854–1920;* Coffin, "Woman's Place," chap. 3; Jacques Sylvère, "Le 'Sweating System,' Naissance de la machine à coudre," *Presse Nouvelle Hebdomadaire* (Paris), June 16, 1978.

62 See Joan Wallach Scott, "Men and Women in the Parisian Garment Trades: Discussions of Family and Work in the 1830s and 1840s," in *The Power of the*

Past: Essays for Eric Hobsbawm, ed. Pat Thane, Geoffrey Crossick, and Roderick Floud, for the gender implications of this debate; also see Karen Offen, "'Powered by a Woman's Foot': A Documentary Introduction to the Sexual Politics of the Sewing Machine in Nineteenth-century France," *Women's Studies International Forum* 11 (1988): 93–101; along with Christopher H. Johnson, "Economic Change and Artisan Discontent: The Tailors' History, 1800–48," in *Revolution and Reaction: 1848 and the 2d French Republic*, ed. Roger Price; and the debate concerning Jacques Rancière, "The Myth of the Artisan: Critical Reflections on a Category of Social History," *International Labor and Working-Class History*, no. 24 (Fall 1983): 1–16; and rejoinders, ibid., pp. 17–25, and no. 25 (Spring 1984): 37–46.

63 *Morning Post*, Feb. 14, 1848, praising a machine recently exhibited in London, quoted by Doyen, *Thimonnier*, pp. 54–55. See also Edith Abbott, *Women in Industry*, pp. 221–23; Eileen Boris, *Art and Labor: Rushkin, Morris, and the Craftsman Ideal in America* (Philadelphia: Temple University Press, 1986), passim, on the perception of machines by the arts-and-crafts movement.

64 Draft text of "Our Union's History," by Julius Hochman, ca. 1948, Joint Dress Series, Box 10, File 2, ILGWU Archives, New York.

65 Feldman, *Fit for All*, p. 109.

66 Murray Sices, *Seventh Avenue*, p. 124.

67 E.g., Pierre Dubois, *L'industrie de l'habillement: L'innovation face à la crise*, pt. 2; Kurt Hoffman and Howard Rush, *Micro-Electronics and Clothing;* Sylvie Korcarz, ed., *Les technologies nouvelles face à la mode;* Organisation International du Travail (OIT), *1ère, 2ème 3ème, et 4ème réunions techniques tripartites pour l'industrie du vêtement;* Howard Rush, "Automation and Apparel: The Impact of Technical Change," in *Technological Change and U.S./European Community Relations*, ed. Michael Smith (London: University Association for Contemporary European Studies, 1985); Emmanuel Vaillant, "Le Grand retour du sur mesure," *Science et vie*, no. 172 (Sept. 1990): 174–78; Jonathan Zeitlin and Peter Totterdill, "Markets, Technology and Local Intervention: The Case of Clothing," in *Reversing Industrial Decline? Industrial Structure and Policy in Britain and Her Competitors*, ed. Paul Hirst and Jonathan Zeitlin, pp. 170–76.

68 OIT, *Réunion tripartite* (1964), 1:10. Du Maroussem, *Le vêtement à Paris.*

69 Pierre Dubois and Giusto Barisi, *Le défi technologique dans l'industrie de l'habillement: Les stratégies des entrepreneurs français et italiens*, p. 121. OIT, *Réunion tripartite* (1964), 1:77–86.

70 OIT, *Réunion tripartite* (1964), 1:81; see also ibid (1995), 2:41; and Stone, *Productivity of Labor.*

71 Gaston Worth, *La couture et la confection des vêtements de femme;* Diana DeMarly, *The History of Haute Couture, 1850–1950;* Ed Cray, *Levi's;* and Daniel Friedmann, *Une histoire du blue-jean.* As Michel Winock has commented, "En 1970, jouant sur l'homonymie, André Clavel déclare que Lévi-Strauss est à la garde-robe ce que le structuralisme est à la pensée. C'était flatteur pour le structuralisme" ("Chanel, Courrèges et les Autres," *Le Monde*, Aug. 5, 1986).

72 Yet even underwear can go in and out of fashion, as each period seems to

rediscover. A how-to book on *lingerie*, published in France in 1917, deplored changing styles as a new phenomenon that made the prospective bride's task all the more difficult. How to constitute a trousseau that would not condemn women to wear "à un moment donné de leur vie, de la lingerie vraiment trop désuète"? (Augusta Moll-Weiss, *Le linge: Son histoire, sa confection et son entretien* [Paris: Armand Colin, 1917], p. 45). A recent report similarly announced the contemporary coming of fashion to the brassiere industry (as a way of combating the rejection of bras by the feminist movement) and the difficulties this implied for manufacturers used to longer production runs (*Libération*, July 5–6, 1986).

73 Leonard A. Drake and Carrie Glasser, *Trends in the New York Clothing Industry*, pp. 3–4.

74 In Georges Mény, *La lutte contre le sweating-system*, p. 27.

75 Pierre Bouvier, *Le travail au quotidien: Une démarche socio-anthropologique*; and idem, *Socio-anthropologie du contemporain.*

76 Cited in New York State Governor's Advisory Commission, *Cloak, Suit and Skirt Industry of New York City*, p. 22.

77 Kidwell and Christman, *Suiting Everyone*, pp. 175–77; Levine, *Women's Garment Workers*; Arsène Alexandre, *Les reines de l'aiguille: Modistes et couturières*, pp. 55–59, criticizing the "newness" theme; Françoise Vincent-Ricard, *Raison et passion: Langages de société, La Mode 1940–1990*, pp. 83–91.

78 Alexandre, *Les reines de l'aiguille*, p. 64.

79 Ibid., p. 58.

80 Complete *Oxford English Dictionary.*

81 Maurizio Lazzarato, Antonio Negri, and Giancarlo Santilli, "La confection dans le quartier du Sentier," report, Ministère du travail, de l'emploi et de la formation professionnelle, Mission recherche expérimentation (MIRE), 1990, pp. 159–60. Their report is, however, based on the false premise that the commercial activities of the Sentier can be analyzed separately from its productive structure.

82 E.g., Conseiller culturel of New York's use and definition of *prêt-à-porter*. Conseiller commercial de France à New York, *Le marché de la confection féminine aux Etats-Unis*, p. 17. The reevaluation of ready-made in France has almost been too successful. An article in *Le Monde*, Oct. 23–24, 1988, called for a redefinition of the term, complaining that it had come to include both the most commercial and the most creative items; the latter, impractical to reproduce on a large scale, can hardly be considered *prêt-à-porter* anymore.

2 Seventh Avenue

1 See Introduction, note 13 above. Also particularly thorough are Leonard A. Drake and Carrie Glasser, *Trends in the New York Clothing Industry*; Roy B. Helfgott, "Women's and Children's Apparel," in *Made in New York*, ed. Max

Hall, pp. 19–134; Ben Morris Selekman, Henriette R. Walter, and W. J. Couper, *The Clothing and Textile Industries in New York and Its Environs;* and Larry Smith and Company, *Garment District Study,* 2 vols.

2 Custom shops still remained in business, and, in 1850, the average firm size had decreased. See Richard B. Stott, *Workers in the Metropolis,* p. 39.

3 Louis Levine, *The Women's Garment Workers,* p. 6.

4 Figures rounded off from United States Immigration Commission, *Reports of the Immigration Commission,* 42 vols., 11:259.

5 Ibid. On women and men, see chap. 6 below.

6 Levine, *Women's Garment Workers,* p. 515.

7 J. B. S. Hardman, "Needle Trades in U.S.," *Social Research* 27 (Autumn 1960): 349.

8 Yet see Wendy Gamber, *The Female Economy: The Millinery and Dressmaking Trades, 1860–1930;* and Nancy Fernandez, "Women, Work and Wages in the Industrialization of American Dressmaking, 1860–1910," paper presented at the 9th Berkshire Conference on the History of Women, June 11–13, 1993.

9 Alice Kessler-Harris, "Problems of Coalition-Building: Women and Trade Unions in the 1920s," in *Women, Work and Protest,* ed. Ruth Milkman, p. 126.

10 New York State Department of Labor, *Annual Report,* 1901, 1:119; Mabel A. Magee, *Trends in Location of the Women's Clothing Industry,* p. 39. According to Helfgott, "Women's and Children's Apparel," p. 56, there were only 33 women's-wear manufacturing plants outside of New York City in 1900, but 524 by 1922. See also Selekman et al., *Clothing and Textile Industries,* p. 18.

11 It was 80 percent by 1928. International Ladies' Garment Workers' Union (ILGWU), *Record of the 19th Convention* (1928), pp. 171–72.

12 United States Industrial Commission, *Reports of the Industrial Commission,* 19 vols., 15:318. On the implication of standardization and larger plants, see Roger D. Waldinger, *Through the Eye of the Needle,* pp. 56–68. On men's wear, see Hyman H. Bookbinder and Associates, *To Promote the General Welfare: The Story of the Amalgamated* (New York: ACWA, 1950); Steven Fraser, *Labor Will Live;* Fraser, "Combined and Uneven Development in the Men's Clothing Industry," *Business History Review* 57 (1983): 522–47; Jack Hardy, *The Clothing Workers: A Study of the Conditions and Struggles in the Needle Trades;* Robert James Myers, *The Economic Aspects of the Production of Men's Clothing;* Earl D. Strong, *Amalgamated Clothing Workers of America;* and Charles Zaretz, *The Amalgamated Clothing Workers of America.* The men's-wear firms that stayed in New York City were mostly the smaller-scale shops.

13 Drake and Glasser, *Trends in New York,* pp. 50, 58, 83; Larry Smith, *Garment District;* New York City, ILGWU Archives (hereafter ILG Arch.), Dress Joint Board Series, Box 30, File 7 (hereafter 30:7), pp. 33–34.

14 Folker Fröbel, Jürgen Heinrichs, and Otto Kreye, *The New International Division of Labor,* pp. 87, 104, passim; Waldinger, *Through the Eye of the Needle,* pp. 54–56, 68–71.

15 Larry Smith, *Garment District,* passim; Waldinger, *Through the Eye of the Needle,* esp. pp. 97–103.

16 In 1939, almost one-half (48.5 percent) of the New York garment industry was devoted to unit-priced silk dresses. See Gertrud B. Greig, *Seasonal Fluctuations in Employment in the Women's Clothing Industry in New York*, p. 60.

17 See, e.g., ILG Arch., David Dubinsky Series, 280:1A and 1B for comparative earnings information.

18 New York State Department of Labor, *Annual Report*, 1904, 1:68.

19 Florence S. Richards, *The Ready-to-Wear Industry, 1900–1950*, p. 14. For the most complete history of union activity in women's wear, see Levine, *Women's Garment Workers;* and Gus Tyler, *Look for the Union Label: A History of the International Ladies' Garment Workers' Union;* as well as Melech Epstein, *Jewish Labor in U.S.A. (1882–1952)* 2 vols. "It is a saying on the East Side that there is always a strike going on somewhere" (*Industrial Commission*, 15:327–28).

20 David Montgomery, *The Fall of the House of Labor: The Workplace, the State and American Labor Activism, 1865–1924*, p. 121.

21 Ibid., pp. 120–22.

22 Levine, *Women's Garment Workers*, p. 80. On the early strikes, see ibid., chaps. 6 and 7; Joel Seidman, *The Needle Trades*, p. 116.

23 Hardy, *Clothing Workers*, passim.

24 Joseph Brandes, "From Sweatshop to Stability: Jewish Labor Between Two World Wars," *YIVO Annual* 16 (1976): 21.

25 See note 12 above, along with Steven Fraser, "*Landslayt* and *Paesani:* Ethnic Conflict and Cooperation in the Amalgamated Clothing Workers of America," in *"Struggle a Hard Battle": Essays on Working-Class Immigrants*, ed. Dirk Hoerder, pp. 280–303.

26 *Industrial Commission*, 15:332–34; more generally, see Levine, *Women's Garment Workers;* J. M. Budish and George Soule, *The New Unionism in the Clothing Industry.*

27 E.g., Lazar Teper, "A Union View of Automation and Technological Advancement," p. 3, in Louis Stulberg Series 4:8, ILG Arch.; cf. ILGWU, *Report of the General Executive Board* (hereafter GEB; 30th Convention, 1959), p. 421.

28 ILGWU, *Report of the GEB and Record of the 38th Convention* (1983), p. 37; *Immigration Commission*, 11:388.

29 Levine, *Women's Garment Workers*, p. 154, and chap. 21; see also Leon Stein, ed., *Out of the Sweatshop*, p. 70; Irving Howe, *World of Our Fathers* (New York: Simon and Schuster, 1976), pp. 298–300; Epstein, *Jewish Labor*, 1: chap. 22; Theresa Serber Malkiel, *The Diary of a Shirtwaist Striker*, ed. Françoise Basch; Susan Glenn, *Daughters of the Shtetl;* Edwin Fenton, *Immigrants and the Union, A Case Study: Italians and American Labor, 1870–1920*, pp. 487–99.

30 Although usually depicted as a simple worker ("a wisp of a girl," Levine, *Women's Garment Workers*, p. 154), which embellishes the story of rank-and-file female determinism against both employer tactics and union bureaucracy, Lemlich was a member of the executive board of Local 25 (Stein, *Out of the Sweatshop*, p. 66).

31 Levine, *Women's Garment Workers*, p. 149; cf. Charlotte Baum, Paula Hyman, and Sonya Michel, *The Jewish Woman in America*, p. 141, estimating 65 percent of the women to be Jewish, 26 percent Italian, and 8 percent native-born American. Hardman, "Needle Trades," p. 326, undoubtedly exaggerated when he named the latter (10 percent rather than 8) "pure Yankee stock."

32 Maxine Schwartz Seller, "The Uprising of the Twenty Thousand: Sex, Class, and Ethnicity in the Shirtwaist Makers' Strike of 1909," in *"Struggle a Hard Battle,"* ed. Dirk Hoerder, p. 267.

33 Amalgamated Ladies' Garment Cutters' Local 10, *Cutters' Almanac, 1902–1962*, p. 86.

34 Levine, *Women's Garment Workers*, p. 176, and chap. 22.

35 Ibid., pp. 198, 542–45; Richards, *Ready-to-Wear*, pp. 15–16.

36 Jesse Thomas Carpenter, *Competition and Collective Bargaining in the Needle Trades, 1910–1967*, p. 297. Justice Louis D. Brandeis, one of its architects, hoped the Protocol would "lift industrial relations out of the jungle to a civilized plane" (Hardman, "Needle Trades," p. 347). See also Julius Henry Cohen, counsel for the manufacturers' union, *Law and Order in Industry* (New York: Macmillan, 1916).

37 Brandes, "Sweatshop to Stability," p. 20; and Fraser, *Labor Will Live.*

38 Hardy, *Clothing Workers*, esp. chaps. 2 and 3.

39 Levine, *Women's Garment Workers*, pp. 312–16. Carpenter, *Competition*, writing half a century later, was more positive in his evaluation of the Protocol, just as he was more optimistic about the advantages of collective bargaining in general.

40 New York State Factory Investigating Commission, *Reports*, 13 vols. (1912–15); the classic account is Leon Stein, *The Triangle Fire.*

41 ILGWU, *Report of the GEB and Record of the 38th Convention* (1983), p. 37.

42 Cf. New York City Board of Education Vocational Survey Commission, "A Survey of the Garment Trades in New York City," typescript, 1930, held at ILG Arch; and ibid., Joint Dress Series 10:2, 1948 version of "Our Union's History."

43 He also notes how the changing composition of the labor force—which we will examine below—was also a factor in the rise and decline of union activities. Roger Waldinger, "Another Look at the International Ladies' Garment Workers' Union: Women, Industry Structure and Collective Action," in *Women, Work, and Protest*, ed. Ruth Milkman; Montgomery, *The Fall of the House of Labor*, pp. 118–22.

44 See esp. New York State Governor's Advisory Commission, *Cloak, Suit and Skirt Industry of New York City*, for a good overview of the 1880–1920 situation.

45 Richards, *Ready-to-Wear*, p. 23.

46 *Message*, Sept. 17, 1915.

47 Magee, *Trends in Location*, p. 68.

48 The terms are used by Carpenter, *Competition*, pp. 297–301, and passim.

49 Hardman, "Needle Trades," p. 348.

50 Levine, *Women's Garment Workers*, pp. 360–81.

51 ILGWU, *Report of the GEB* (23rd Convention, 1937), p. 10.

52 A language which continued to be used. See, e.g., National Coat and Suit Industry Recovery Board, *Reports and Resolutions, 14th and 18th Annual Meetings* (New York: National Executive Board, 1950, 1954), forewords (p. 3).

53 Quoted in Myers, *Economic Aspects*, p. 54; see Hadassa Kosak, "The Rise of the Jewish Working Class, New York, 1881–1905," Ph.D. diss., City University of New York, 1987, pp. 181–85, on the union's attitudes toward some of the early, nonapproved, "undisciplined" strikes.

54 Seidman, *Needle Trades*, chap. 9; Levine, *Women's Garment Workers;* Stanley Nadel, "Reds versus Pinks: A Civil War in the International Ladies' Garment Workers' Union," *New York History* 66, no. 1 (Jan. 1985): 48–72.

55 Philip S. Foner, *The Fur and Leather Workers' Union* (Newark: Nordan Press, 1950); Hardy, *Clothing Workers*, pp. 116–48.

56 Levine, *Women's Garment Workers*, p. 353.

57 Hardman, "Needle Trades," p. 342.

58 Hardy speaks, with quotation marks, of the "pogrom of 1926" (*Clothing Workers*, p. 67). The Communists influential in the needle trades were part of a faction opposed to Foster's leadership (Nadel, "Reds vs. Pinks").

59 See Seidman, *Needle Trades*, chap. 9; Hardy, *Clothing Workers*, chaps. 2 and 3.

60 Although the ILGWU consistently announced that it had finished off the Communist opposition, there were still such opposition groups into the 1940s. See chap. 8 below.

61 "The story of his life is part immigrant saga, part success story. It is the chronicle of a crusade and the realization of a visionary dream" (ILGWU, *Report of the GEB and Record of the 38th Convention* [1983], p. 8).

62 In response to a personal, handwritten appeal from Léon Blum in 1948, David Dubinsky sent funds for Blum's *Le Populaire*. The ILGWU also sent money regularly to trade unionists in Italy, Israel, and France through the 1950s and helped support the Yiddish socialist newspaper in Paris, *Unser Shtime*, until the 1960s. See Léon Blum to David Dubinsky, June 16, 1948, Dubinsky 249:4A, ILG Arch.; Irwin Wall, *L'influence américaine sur la politique française, 1945–1954*, pp. 163–64.

63 Brandes, "Sweatshop to Stability," p. 21. Myers, *Economic Aspects;* Fraser, *Labor Will Live*, chap. 12. The fact that the ACWA ultimately merged with the textile workers can be seen as another telling symbol of its more industrial nature.

64 For the union's account of the AFL/CIO conflict, see ILGWU, *Report of the GEB* (23d Convention, 1937), pp. 194–219, and idem, *GEB* (29th Convention, 1956), pp. 26–40.

65 Brandes, "Sweatshop to Stability," pp. 88–89.

66 New York State Department of Labor, "Report to the Governor and the Legislature on the Garment Manufacturing Industry and Industrial Homework" (New York, 1982), p. 7. On the 1920s, see also Waldinger, "Another Look."

67 Stein, *Out of the Sweatshop*, p. 222.

68 ILGWU, *Report of the GEB* (22d Convention, 1934), p. 42.

69 *New York Times,* Aug. 12, 1934, cited in Carpenter, *Competition,* p. 597, note 9; Carpenter, among others, sees the origins of the 1933 codes in the garment industry Protocols of 1910, p. 592, note 2. See also Eileen Boris, *Home to Work: Motherhood and the Politics of Industrial Homework in the United States.*

70 Contractor limitation had been written into the 1924 and 1926–27 collective-bargaining contracts in the higher-skilled women's coats-and-suits sector, but it was not really effective until the NRA codes. See also Drake and Glasser, *Trends in New York,* pp. 124, 130. Carpenter, the optimist, is forced to admit that without the government codes, the prior collective bargaining agreements had often not been very effective. Furthermore, he also acknowledges that after the NRA codes were declared unconstitutional, the industry reverted to its bad habits (*Competition,* pp. 716–17, 818–20).

71 Lazare Teper and Nathan Weinberg, *Aspects of Industrial Homework in the Apparel Trades,* p. 36.

72 Ibid., p. 34.

73 Richards, *Ready-to-Wear,* p. 27.

74 Teper and Weinberg, *Industrial Homework,* pp. 34–37.

75 Albeit forty years after the same had occurred in men's wear, as Richards commented, *Ready-to-Wear,* p. 27.

76 New York State, "Report to the Governor," p. 71.

77 Max Danish, *The World of David Dubinsky,* pp. 129–31.

78 Ibid., p. 130.

79 Richards, *Ready-to-Wear,* p. 29.

80 Greig, *Seasonal Fluctuations,* pp. 33–35.

81 Bernard Roshco, *The Rag Race,* pp. 40–41.

82 ILGWU, *Report of the GEB* (30th Convention, 1959), p. 122.

83 Hardman, "Needle Trades," p. 351; Brandes, "Sweatshop to Stability," p. 133.

84 Roshco, *Rag Race,* p. 112.

85 New York State Department of Labor, "Report on the Garment Industry in New York State" (New York, 1982), pp. 18, 25, 32 (this report was also incorporated into New York State, "Report to the Governor," as appendix D); Organisation internationale du travail (OIT), *3e réunion technique tripartite pour l'industrie du vêtement,* 3:60; Charles S. Goodman, *The Location of Fashion Industries, with Special Reference to the California Apparel Market.*

86 For the labor figures, I have used the "Industry" tables: *Census of Population: 1950,* vol. 2: *Characteristics of the Population,* pt. 32, *New York* (Washington, D.C.: GPO, 1952), p. 32-369; *1970 Census of Population,* vol. 1: *Characteristics of the Population,* pt. 34, *New York,* sec. 2, p. 34-1147; on the firms, see Sharon Zukin, *Loft Living* (Baltimore: Johns Hopkins University Press, 1982), pp. 24, 27; cf. Introduction above for figures on operatives alone.

87 *New York Times,* Sept. 6, 1987.

88 Magee, *Trends in Location,* pp. 12–13.

89 Drake and Glasser, *Trends in New York;* Glasser was somewhat more optimistic than Drake, however, p. iv.

90 Helfgott, "Women's and Children's Apparel," pp. 72–73.

91 In absolute numbers, these figures are much less dramatic: New York's small growth represented an increase of over 6,400 workers, not that far from the more than 7,800 new employees added to the Los Angeles workforce (Larry Smith, *Garment District*, 1:10; cf. Goodman, *Location of Fashion*).

92 Richards, *Ready-to-Wear*, p. 27.

93 Roshco, *Rag Race*, p. 126.

94 Although, as Drake and Glasser pointed out, rent costs may be as little as 2 percent of the average dress firm's total costs (*Trends in New York*, pp. 113–14).

95 However, those coat-and-suit makers who had survived the "major shake-out" of the 1970s were doing well (*New York Times*, Sept. 25, 1987).

96 S. Frank Baily, Principal, High School of Fashion Industries, interview, July 25, 1984; Waldinger, *Through the Eye of the Needle*, pp. 71–78.

97 ILGWU, *Record of the 22d Convention* (1934), pp. 173, 410; New York State, "Report on the Garment Industry," pp. 25, 47; Abeles et al., *Chinatown Study*, p. 17. For comparison with the United Kingdom, see Swasti Mitter, "Industrial Restructuring and Manufacturing Homework: Immigrant Women in the UK Clothing Industry," *Capital and Class* 27 (Winter 1986): 50; and Annie Phizacklea, *Unpacking the Fashion Industry*, who point out that many imports come from high-wage countries, and that Britain has its own sweatshops. Similarly, a study by Anne Krueger, quoted in the OIT, *2e réunion tripartite* (1980), 3: table 10 (p. 34), showed that labor displacement in the American garment industry from 1970–76 was, in some sectors, attributable to increased productivity rather than imports.

98 OIT, *2e réunion tripartite* (1980), 1:93. Young female Japanese blouse-makers were getting 7 cents an hour compared to $1.50 for ILGWU members. Danish, *Dubinsky*, pp. 237–38. See, for example, ILGWU, *Report of the GEB* (29th Convention, 1956), p. 14; idem, *GEB* (30th Convention, 1959), p. 113; *GEB* (31st Convention, 1962), pp. 9–24. Japan's share of imports declined as its wages grew relative to its neighbors. José R. De La Torre et al., *Corporate Responses to Import Competition in the U.S. Apparel Industry*, pp. 57–58.

99 De La Torre, *Corporate Responses*, pp. 13, 59–60.

100 New York State, "Report on the Garment Industry," p. 47.

101 Zukin, *Loft Living*, p. 27.

102 New York State, "Report to the Governor," Submission "A."

3 The Sentier

1 Philippe Perrot, *Les dessus et les dessous de la bourgeoisie*, pp. 57–58, 61, 156–57. See also Nicole Pellegrin, *Les vêtements de la liberté: Abécédaire des pratiques vestimentaires françaises de 1780 à 1800;* Aileen Ribeiro, *Fashion in the French Revolution;* and Daniel Roche, *La culture des apparences*, p. 299.

2 Which is not to say that there is not a very rich national and international history to be written from the ILGWU archives, from antifascism in the 1930s (the Antonini files) to free-trade unionism after World War II (the Dubinsky files). But these are issues which have less to do with the industry per se.

3 Lynn Hunt, *Politics, Culture and Class in the French Revolution* (Berkeley: University of California Press, 1984).

4 Roche, *La culture des apparences;* Steele, *Paris Fashion,* has also argued that sartorial change occurred *before* the Revolution.

5 Ribeiro, *Fashion in the French Revolution,* p. 46; Roche, *La culture des apparences,* p. 62; Ribeiro, *Fashion in the French Revolution,* pp. 88–90.

6 Hunt, *Politics, Culture,* pp. 52–53.

7 François Faraut, "La confection masculine à Paris depuis le 19ème siècle: Le cas de la Belle Jardinière," doctoral thesis, Ecole des Hautes Etudes en Sciences Sociales, 1983, p. 10. For this early period, see also Judith G. Coffin, "Gender and the Guild Order: The Garment Trades in 18th-Century Paris," *Journal of Economic History* 54 (Dec. 1994): 768–93; Steven Kaplan, "Les corporations, les 'faux ouvriers' et le faubourg Saint-Antoine au XVIIIe siècle," *Annales, E.S.C.* 43 (Mar.–Apr. 1988): 353–78; Michael Sonenscher, *Work and Wages;* and Cynthia M. Truant, "The Guildswomen of Paris: Gender, Power and Sociability in the Old Regime," *Proceedings of the Annual Meeting of the Western Society for French History* 15 (1988): 130–38.

8 Roche, *La culture des apparences,* p. 482.

9 Both cited in Henriette Vanier, *La mode et ses métiers,* p. 100.

10 Perrot, *Dessus et dessous,* p. 128; Eugen Weber, *Peasants into Frenchmen* (Stanford: Stanford University Press, 1976).

11 Lémann, *De l'industrie des vêtements confectionnés en France,* pp. 34–35, 37.

12 Ibid., pp. 27, 35; cf. Perrot, *Dessus et dessous,* pp. 125–35; Philippe Perrot, "Aspects socio-culturels des débuts de la confection parisienne au 19e siècle," *Revue de l'Institut de sociologie* (Brussels), no. 2 (1977): 185–202, 191; Rosalind H. Williams, *Dream Worlds.*

13 Albert Leduc, in *Classe 36: Habillement des deux sexes,* pp. 92, 59–60; Pierre Du Maroussem, *La petite industrie (Salaires et durée du travail),* vol. 2: *Le vêtement à Paris,* p. 135; Jean Allilaire, *Les industries de l'habillement et du travail des étoffes,* p. 45.

14 Du Maroussem, *Le vêtement à Paris,* p. 395. On Du Maroussem's method of investigation, see Judith Coffin, "Social Science Meets Sweated Labor: Reinterpreting Women's Work in Late Nineteenth-Century France," *Journal of Modern History* 63 (June 1991): 230–70.

15 Perrot, *Dessus et Dessous,* pp. 95–96; Christopher H. Johnson, "Economic Change and Artisan Discontent: The Tailors' History, 1800–48," in *Revolution and Reaction,* p. 93; Joan Wallach Scott, "Men and Women in the Parisian Garment Trades: Discussions of Family and Work in the 1830s and 1840s," in *The Power of the Past,* ed. Thane, Crossick, and Floud, p. 72; François Faraut, *Histoire de la Belle Jardinière,* p. 9. See also Christopher H. Johnson, "Patterns of Proletarianization: Parisian Tailors and Lodève Woolens Workers," in *Consciousness and Class Experience in Nineteenth-Century Europe,* ed. John Merri-

man; A. Focillon, "Tailleur d'habits de Paris," in *Les ouvriers des deux mondes*, vol. 2; Chambre de Commerce de Paris, *Statistique de l'industrie à Paris résultant de l'enquête faite par la Chambre de Commerce pour les années 1847–48* (Paris: 1864), passim; and Joan Scott's important analysis of the latter, "Statistical Representations of Work," in Steven Laurence Kaplan and Cynthia J. Koepp, eds., *Work in France*, pp. 335–63.

16 Including the large provincial market. M.D. Hubert de Vautier, *Exposition internationale de Saint-Louis (1904), Rapport du groupe 59*, p. 85.

17 Faraut, *Belle Jardinière*, pp. 83–93, 102–8.

18 Yves Lequin, *Les ouvriers de la région lyonnaise, 1848–1914*, 2 vols. (Lyon: Presses de l'Université de Lyon, 1977).

19 Perrot, *Dessus et dessous*, pp. 95–96.

20 Scott, "Men and Women."

21 Yvonne Moustiers, *Le Sentier: Histoire d'un quartier célèbre*, p. 9.

22 Jeanne Gaillard, "Paris, La ville, 1852–1870," doctoral thesis, Université de Paris 10, 1975, p. 199. On the Sentier, see also pp. 197–200, 378, 404.

23 David Montgomery, *The Fall of the House of Labor*, p. 117; on the origins of the department stores in Paris compared to the United States, see Michael B. Miller, *The Bon Marché*, pp. 30–31; he stresses the similarities in patterns of development rather than attributing a "first," although he allows that most accounts credit Paris with having invented the department store. On the Bon Marché as manufacturer, see ibid., pp. 57–58. See also Faraut, *Belle Jardinière;* Judith Coffin, "Woman's Place and Women's Work in the Paris Clothing Trades, 1830–1914," Ph.D. diss., Yale University, 1985, pp. 60–69; and, of course, Emile Zola's great classic, *Au Bonheur des Dames.*

24 Gaillard, *Paris*, p. 537.

25 Philippe Simon, *Monographie d'une industrie de luxe, la haute couture*, pp. 99–110; Germaine Deschamps, *La crise dans les industries du vêtement et de la mode à Paris pendant la période de 1930 à 1937*, pp. 51–54 and passim; Léon Storch, in *Classe 85—Industrie de la confection et de la couture pour hommes, femmes et enfants, Exposition universelle internationale de 1900 à Paris: Rapports du jury international*, Groupe XIII, *Fils, tissus, vêtements*, 2e partie—*Classes 85 et 86*, ed. Léon Storch, Julien Hayem, and Auguste Mortier, p. 40. Counterfeiting remains a pervasive problem to this day. René Lacoste, tennis champion and inventor of the alligator shirt (whose wife remarked skeptically at the time, Who would want to buy a shirt with an alligator on it?), has spent much of his later years fighting counterfeit alligator emblems the world over (interview, Paris, April 27, 1984).

26 Henri Hauser and Henri Hitier, eds., *Enquête sur la production française et la concurrence étrangère*, vol. 2 of *Industries textiles—Industries du vêtement*, pp. 311–13, 418–21. The latter figures are not broken down for *modèles* and *confection.* See Simon, *Monographie . . . la haute couture*, p. 99; Deschamps, *La crise*, pp. 1–2, 68.

27 E.g., Hauser and Hitier, *Enquête;* confidential report, "Situation de l'indus-

trie de la flanelle manufacturée et des sous-vêtements en France avant les hostilités; modifications qui pourraient être apportées au régime de cette industrie dans l'intérêt de la production nationale et de notre exportation," n.d., $F^{12}8054$ (1917–18): Comité consultatif des arts et manufacture, Transformation de textiles, Archives Nationales, Paris (hereafter AN).

28 Coquet, "La Couture," in Hauser and Hitier, *Enquête*, p. 319. See also "Rapport général au Comité consultatif des arts et manufactures, ch. 20: Les Industries textiles, les industries utilisant les tissus, vêtements, etc.," p. 304, $F^{12}8054$ (1917–18), AN.

29 Letellier thus involuntarily admitted that her optimism was not shared by everyone. It was also undoubtedly colored by the fact that she was writing in a period of relative prosperity and labor scarcity. See "Le travail féminin à Paris, avant et depuis la guerre, dans les industries du vêtement," *Bulletin du Ministère du Travail*, a series of fifteen articles written by Gabrielle Letellier and collaborators, published from October 1925 through September 1929.

30 *Comptes rendus des séances de la Commission départementale du travail (1903–4)*, $F^{22}471$: Commission départementale du travail (Seine), AN.

31 Camille Doublot, *La protection légale des travailleurs de l'industrie du vêtement*, p. 135; Léon de Seilhac, *L'industrie de la couture et de la confection à Paris*, pp. 97–106; Jacqueline Contant, *L'industrie à domicile salariée*, pp. 72ff; Michelle Zancarini-Fournel, "Genèse de la loi de 1892," paper presented at the conference "Le genre de la production" at the Université de Paris-8, June 24–25, 1993; Vincent Viet, *Les Voltigeurs de la République: L'inspection du travail en France jusqu'en 1914*, 2 vols., 2:489–93.

32 Cover letter, Aug. 5, 1909, $F^{22}443$: Travail des femmes et des enfants, File 32, AN; see also AN, $F^{22}439$: Travail des femmes et des enfants; and Viet, *Voltigeurs*, 2:423–24.

33 Mary Lynn Stewart, *Women, Work and the French State: Labour Protection and Social Patriarchy, 1879–1919*, p. 67; Deschamps, *La crise*, p. 77.

34 The 1917 law prompted a detailed debate on the working woman's week and, in effect, her biorhythms. With the English week, women had won their half-day off all the better to cook and clean, as many of the law's proponents intended. On the fight for the eight-hour day, cf. Gary Cross, *A Quest for Time: The Reduction of Work in Britain and France, 1840–1940* (Berkeley: University of California Press, 1989); and Benjamin Hunnicutt, *Abandoning Shorter Hours for the Right to Work* (Philadelphia: Temple University Press, 1988).

35 The clothing industry alone accounted for between 39 percent and 54 percent of all of the summonses for night work and overtime violations from 1896 to 1908 (Stewart, *Women, Work*, p. 142).

36 Jeanne Bouvier, *Mes Mémoires*, pp. 102, 106–20; see also Bouvier, *La lingerie et les lingères*.

37 Contant, *Industrie à domicile*, p. 44.

38 Catherine Rhein, "Jeunes femmes au travail dans le Paris de l'Entre-deux-guerres," doctoral thesis, Université de Paris 7, 1977, p. 423.

39 Deschamps, *La crise*, p. 48. See, more generally, for this period, Mary Louise Roberts, "Samson and Delilah Revisited: The Politics of Women's Fashion in 1920s France," *American Historical Review* 98 (June 1993): 657–84.

40 Cf. "Le travail féminin," *Bulletin* 32:10–12 (Oct.–Dec. 1925): 346, and 35:1–3 (Jan.–Mar. 1928): 16; and see Deschamps, *La crise*, pp. 12–13.

41 Deschamps, *La crise*, pp. 14, 21–22, 26, 30–31.

42 Nancy L. Green, *The Pletzl of Paris: Jewish Immigrant Workers in the Belle Epoque*, pp. 128–30.

43 Françoise Blum, "Féminisme et syndicalisme: Les femmes dans la Fédération de l'habillement," master's thesis, Université de Paris 1, 1977, p. 143. Cf. M. Colin, *Ce n'est pas d'aujourd'hui* (Paris: Editions sociales, 1975). The following account of the strikes draws on "Le travail féminin," *Bulletin* 34:4–6 (Apr.–June 1927): 162–69; *Le peuple français* (Paris), Apr.–June 1980, 25–28; AN, F⁷13882: Grèves—Habillement, File "Grève générale de l'habillement 1923"; and Blum, "Femmes et syndicalisme," pp. 140–49. See also Laura Lee Downs, "Women's Strikes and the Politics of Popular Egalitarianism in France, 1916–1918," in *Rethinking Labor History*, ed. Lenard R. Berlanstein.

44 Blum, "Femmes et syndicalisme," pp. 184–99. On the repertory of strike actions, see "La vie collective des grévistes" in Michelle Perrot, *Les ouvriers en grève*, 2 vols., 2:547–644.

45 Jean-Louis Robert, "Ouvriers et mouvements ouvriers parisiens pendant la grande guerre et l'immédiat après-guerre," *thèse d'état*, Université de Paris 1, 1989; Blum, "Femmes et syndicalisme."

46 Suzanne Lion, *Le Peuple* (Paris), Apr. 22, 1923. See AN, F⁷13882, File "Grève générale de l'habillement 1923."

47 Blum, "Femmes et syndicalisme," pp. 150–60. See Henri Boisgontier, *Les syndicats professionnels féminins de l'Abbaye et l'Union centrale des syndicats professionnels féminins* (Paris: Jouve, 1927).

48 Blum, "Femmes et syndicalisme," p. 52. Fédération des travailleurs de l'habillement, *Compte rendu, 11e Congrès national* (Lyon, 1919), p. 15; Jean Bruhat and Marc Piolot, *Esquisse d'une histoire de la CGT* (Paris: CGT, 1966), p. 87. Nonetheless, due to the fragmented nature of the industry, the overall percentage of unionization in *habillement* remained quite low, only 6.7 percent in the 1914 to 1921 period, making it twenty-fourth among the CGT federations. See Blum, "Femmes et syndicalisme," p. 64; Michel Dreyfus, *Histoire de la CGT*, pp. 125, 139.

49 Blum, "Femmes et syndicalisme," p. 63.

50 Fédération de l'habillement, *11e Congrès* (Lyon, 1919); and idem, *12e Congrès* (Lille, 1921).

51 On the CSR, see *La Couture* (Paris), June 1921; and *Le Peuple*, June 14, 1921.

52 *Le Peuple*, Jan. 18, 1923.

53 *Le Peuple*, June 14 and Aug. 3, 1921; report, July 4, 1923, F⁷13741: Habillement, 1920–29, AN.

54 Report, Mar. 24, 1929, F⁷13741, AN.

55 Fédération de l'habillement, *20e Congrès* (Paris, 1937), p. 23.

56 Michel Monikowski, "1936–1986, Des Juifs dans le Front Populaire," *La presse nouvelle* (Paris), June 1986; Paul Chaupin, interview, Paris, Aug. 7, 1986.

57 Antoine Prost, *La CGT à l'époque du Front populaire, 1934–1939* (Paris: Armand Colin, 1964), pp. 193–94.

58 Fédération nationale des fabricants français de confection pour hommes et garçonnets, *Compte rendu du Congrès de Paris* (1937), p. 11. Emphasis in the original.

59 Ibid., p. 35.

60 Fédération de l'habillement, *20e Congrès* (Paris, 1937), pp. 92–95.

61 "Ne travailler que huit heures, c'est diminuer le chômage . . . ne faire que huit heures en atelier, c'est enrayer le surmenage" (*L'Ouvrier de l'habillement* [Paris], July 1906, pp. 2, 4).

62 Gertrude Willoughby, *La Situation des ouvrières du vêtement en France et en Angleterre*, pp. 150–51.

63 Bouvier, *Mémoires*, p. 102.

64 The typescript of the Fédération de l'habillement, *23e Congrès* (Lyon, 1948), located at the Confédération Général du Travail (CGT) Archives in Montreuil, seems to indicate that Matline's critique was not only officially revised but indeed reversed. Matline's words were changed (by whom?) as follows: "La première loi [celle de 1915], ~~il faut le dire~~, a été adopté et votée ~~non pas~~ sur l'initiative de la CGT, ~~il faut le dire, mais sur l'initiative des chrétiens parce qu'ils ont considéré que la femme tout en restant au foyer, doit pouvoir apporter un petit salaire par un petit travail exécuté à la maison.~~" p. 99. See ibid., p. 97, on Matline's appeal to memory concerning prewar conditions.

65 For a discussion of the difficult problem of defining *façonniers*, see Joseph Klatzmann, *Le travail à domicile dans l'industrie parisienne du vêtement*, pp. 99–108; and Steven Zdatny, *The Politics of Survival: Artisans in Twentieth-Century France*, passim, for the similar problem of the *artisanat*. For a more legalistic debate on whether homeworkers were salaried employees or really independent workers, see: Fédération de l'habillement, *12e Congrès* (Lille, 1921); ibid., *20e Congrès* (Paris, 1937), p. 76; *L'Habillement* (Paris), no. 12 (Oct.–Nov. 1938), pp. 3–4. For the nineteenth century, see Alain Faure, "Petit atelier et modernisme économique: La production en miettes au XIXe siècle," *Histoire, économie et société* 5, no. 4 (1986): 531–57. This problem was not unknown in New York, where, for example, after the wage-and-hours law was enacted, jobbers "sold" yarn to independent homeworkers who then "resold" it back to them. A legal debate took place as to whether or not an employer-employee relationship still existed. See New York, ILGWU Archives, Dubinsky Series, Box 304, File 4A; Boris, *Home to Work*.

66 A quota law of Aug. 1932, "protégeant la main-d'oeuvre nationale," restricted the percentage of immigrants who could work as salaried employees

in certain industries. This led many to go to work for themselves, although two decree-laws of Aug. and Oct. 1935 placed further restrictions on the right of foreigners to be artisans or pedlers. See Vicki Caron, "Loyalties in Conflict: French Jewry and the Refugee Crisis, 1933–1935," *Leo Baeck Institute Yearbook* 36 (1991): 305–37; and Caron, *Uneasy Asylum* (1977). In an astonishing reversal of memory, these same laws which were qualified as "décret-scélérats de Laval" in 1948 ("Laval-gzirus," see Patrick Altman, "Les conséquences de la crise économique des années 30 sur la population juive immigrée de Paris," unpublished, 1985, p. 33) have been reinterpreted by some with hindsight as an opportunity for the Polish Jews—"Grâce à Laval nous avons tous pu sortir de la clandestinité. Oui, le même Laval qui va couvrir les lois anti-juives sous l'Occupation" (*Actuel,* Paris, Apr. 1988)—and even as the origin of the entrepreneurial takeoff of the Sentier! (*Regards,* Brussels, no. 219 [Dec. 22, 1988–Jan. 11, 1989]: 21.) Two overviews of this legislation are Marcel Livian, *Le régime juridique des étrangers en France;* and Jean-Charles Bonnet, *Les pouvoirs publics et l'immigration dans l'entre-deux guerres.*

67 Report, June 7–13, 1922, F⁷13882: Grèves—Habillement, File "1922," AN.

68 Fédération de l'habillement, *12e Congrès* (Lille, 1921); report, Jan. 30, 1921, F⁷13741: Habillement et chapellerie, File "Habillement, 1920–21," AN; *La Couture,* May 1921, in the same file; Fédération de l'habillement, *20e Congrès* (Paris, 1937), p. 76.

69 Dominique Veillon, *La mode sous l'Occupation: Débrouillardise et coquetterie dans la France en guerre (1939–1945),* and particularly pp. 58–61, 71, 222.

70 Faraut, *Belle Jardinière,* pp. 127–30.

71 Henry Rousso, "L'Aryanisation économique: Vichy, l'occupant et la spoliation des Juifs," *Yod,* no. 15–16 (1982): 51–79; Rousso, "L'organisation industrielle de Vichy (perspectives de recherches)," *Revue d'histoire de la deuxième Guerre Mondiale,* no. 116 (1979): 27–44; Michel Margairaz and Henry Rousso, "Vichy, la guerre et les entreprises," *Histoire, économie et société* 11 (3d trimester 1992): 337–67; and Alain Beltran, Robert Frank, and Henry Rousso, eds., *La vie des entreprises sous l'Occupation.* Concentration was also contemplated in the United States. See strictly confidential memorandum, Nov. 16, 1942, "Concentration of Industry and its Possible Application in the Women's Garment Industry," Zimmerman Series, Box 16, File 9, Research Department, ILGWU Archives.

72 E.g., letter, Jan. 8, 1944, F¹²10483: Vêtement, correspondance générale, 1943–44, AN.

73 "[La] disparition des éléments israélites a permis dans la période de crise actuelle de réapprovisionnement de conserver une activité réduite des maisons aryennes" (Ministry to Comité d'organisation du vêtement, with reference to Group III [women's ready-made], Mar. 25, 1942, F¹²10479: Vêtement, correspondance générale 1942, AN). See also below. The modalities of Aryanization were spelled out, among other things, in the legal manual prepared for the

profession by R.-M. Etienne, P. Bucaille, and R. Deffains, *Guide professionnel du textile et du vêtement et de leurs accessoires*, pp. 73–82.

74 See, e.g., letters, Feb. 25 and 26, 1943, F^{12}10480: Vêtement, correspondance générale 1943, AN.

75 Rousso, "L'aryanisation économique," pp. 54–55. See also Joseph Billig, *Le Commissariat général aux questions juives (1941–1944)*, 3 vols., 1:167–98, 309–27; 3:259–87, 326–29; Michael R. Marrus and Robert O. Paxton, *Vichy France and the Jews*, pp. 152–60.

76 Many became *administrateurs provisoires* for personal gain, but some volunteered on behalf of Jewish owners in order to protect the property. Those who acquired Jewish firms were worried about the legal validity of the purchase. Dr. Elmar Michel, head of the economic section of the Militärbefehlshaber, tried to reassure them, but in 1943 an association of owners of former Jewish enterprises was formed nervously to protect their interests (Raul Hilberg, *The Destruction of the European Jews* [New York: Holmes and Meier, 1985]), 2:619–20). The *administrateurs provisoires* were described by the director of the SCAP as ranging from timid to clumsy to negligent to unconscientious to unscrupulous, i.e., those who colluded with the Jews (Marrus and Paxton, *Vichy and the Jews*, p. 157).

77 E.g., letter, Oct. 12, 1942, F^{12}10479: Vêtement, correspondance générale 1942, AN.

78 Officially called the Comité générale d'organisation de l'habillement et du travail des etoffes, headed by J. Deligny and located at 8, rue de Richelieu. The number of firms in each sector is indicated in parentheses: haute couture and custom-made (70,000); men's ready-made (1,702); women's ready-made (2,365); white goods (4,381); furs (not indicated); accessories (5,902); textile trade (2,918). Report, p. 4, Dec. 1, 1944, F^{12}10497: Vêtement, organisation de l'habillement, AN. The 70,000 figure in the first group is an estimate; the others come from the censuses undertaken by the COV as one of its first tasks.

79 Henri Rousso, "Les Comités d'organisation, Aspects structurels et économiques, 1940–1944," master's thesis, Université de Paris 1 and Ecole Normale Supérieure de St. Cloud, 1976, pp. 194–98.

80 Billig, *Commissariat général*. Shortly after he had received the order to proceed with the mass arrest of (ultimately 12,884) Jews in Paris on July 16–17, 1942, André Tulard, Sous-directeur des étrangers et des affaires juives of the Police Department and holder of the card file of registered Jews, advised the Commissariat général aux questions juives that it should arrange to recuperate the tools and other goods that were going to be left behind. A month later, M. Charbonneaux of the Sous-direction du vêtement was still urging the CGQJ to act in order to keep approximately 4,000 sewing machines in French, rather than German, hands. The matter was entrusted to a Monsieur Boue at the CGQJ, and it was eventually planned to sell or rent the machines through the women's ready-made section of the COV (letters, Aug. 12 and Sept. 1, 1942, F^{12}10479, Vêtement, correspondance générale 1942, AN).

81 Jean Allilaire says as much in his 1944 report. See Report, Dec. 1, 1944,

Notes to Pages 96–98

under cover letter of Mar. 15, 1945, F¹²10497; Vêtement, organisation de l'habillement, AN. In this end-of-the-war report—a post-facto justification?—Allilaire also defended the *comités d'organisation* by implying that they voluntarily dragged their feet with regard to German and ministerial requests for lists of firms to "concentrate" and also that they tried to keep garment workers from being drafted to Germany for the Service du travail obligatoire. (The relatively low number of male workers in the garment industry meant that in any case fewer people were affected by the STO.) See also Allilaire, *Industries de l'habillement.*

82 Note pour le Cabinet du directeur, Jan. 8, 1944, F¹²10483: Vêtement, correspondance générale 1943–44, AN.

83 Note statistique, ibid.

84 Letter, Mar. 3, 1943, F¹²10480: Vêtement, correspondance générale 1943, AN (this earlier report lists the same number—1,223—of concentrated firms as of *Mar. 1,* 1943); letter, Feb. 24, 1944, F¹²10484: Vêtement, correspondance générale 1944. Compare Billig's table for June 1944, *Commissariat général,* 3:328.

85 Report, p. 4, Dec. 1, 1944, under cover letter of Mar. 15, 1945, F¹²10497: Vêtement, organisation de l'habillement, AN.

86 Jacques Adler, *Face à la persécution,* pp. 174, 180, 196, 199. On specific instances of protection, see Jan. 7, 1944, on the Novelty firm, F¹²10483: Vêtement, correspondance générale 1943–44, AN; and the feather import firm of Maurice Gluck, July 29, 1943, F¹²10481: Vêtement, correspondance générale 1943, AN.

87 Adler, *Face à la persécution,* pp. 179–80; David Diamant, *Les Juifs dans la Résistance* (Paris: Le Pavillon, 1971), pp. 150–52; *In kamf far freiheit (Combattants de la liberté)* (Paris: Farlag Oyfsnay, Commission intersyndicale juive auprès de la CGT, 1948), pp. 33–54; Jacques Ravine, *La résistance organisée des Juifs en France, 1940–1944* (Paris: Julliard, 1973), pp. 80–82; and, more generally, Adam Rayski, *Le choix des Juifs sous Vichy* (Paris: La Découverte, 1992); and Renée Poznanski, *Etre juif en France pendant la seconde Guerre Mondiale* (Paris: Hachette, 1994). Annette Wieviorka, *Ils étaient juifs, résistants, communistes* (Paris: Denoel, 1986), is very critical of the sabotage successes described by Communist writers and harshly condemns what she calls a "suicide social" (p. 121). Adler, *Face à la persécution,* p. 179, however, describes these actions as part of an "insoluble dilemma": to work for the German war effort or die of hunger.

88 On other conflicts, see, e.g., letter, Nov. 10, 1941, F¹²10478: Vêtement, correspondance générale 1941, AN; report, Dec. 1, 1944, under cover letter of Mar. 15, 1945, F¹²10497: Vêtement, organisation de l'habillement, AN; Billig, *Commissariat général,* 3:265–66; Marrus and Paxton, *Vichy and the Jews,* p. 158; Rousso, "Les comités d'organisation," pp. 194–98; and Margairaz and Rousso, "Vichy."

89 Robert O. Paxton, *Vichy France* (New York: Norton, 1975), on bureaucratic and other continuities from the Vichy to the postwar period.

90 Letter, Mar. 25, 1942, F¹²10479: Vêtement, correspondance générale 1942, AN.

91 Allilaire, *Industries de l'habillement*, p. 88. See also Jacques Desmyttere, *Les grandes industries modernes: Les industries textiles et celles de l'habillement*, p. 165. In 1962, Paris still produced 40 percent of garments in France but 65.9 percent of women's clothes. See D. Guizien, "L'industrie textile et de l'habillement en région parisienne," Institut d'aménagement et d'urbanisme de la région parisienne (1973), p. 9; cf. Brigitte Delacourt, *Mouvement du capital et emploi dans l'habillement* (Paris: Institut syndical d'études et de recherches économiques et sociales, 1980), pp. 19, 21.

92 E.g., Léon Laborde (M. le Comte), *De l'union des arts et de l'industrie*, 2 vols.; Gaston Worth, *La couture et la confection des vêtements de femme*, p. 95; Marius Vachon, *Nos industries d'art en péril* (Paris: L. Baschet, 1882); Siegfried Bing, *La culture artistique en Amérique* (Paris: N.p., 1896); and, more recently, Patrick Fridenson, "Un tournant taylorien de la société française (1904–1918)," *Annales E.S.C.* no. 42 (Sept.–Oct. 1987): 1031–60. See also Debora L. Silverman, *Art Nouveau in Fin-de-Siècle France*, chap. 3; Williams, *Dream Worlds*, chap. 5; and Whitney Walton, *France at the Crystal Palace*.

93 Jarillot proposed the creation of a bureau d'études. Letter, with reference to Group III (women's ready-made), Mar. 25, 1942, F¹²10479: Vêtement, correspondance générale 1942, AN.

94 Report, Dec. 1, 1944, under cover letter of Mar. 15, 1945, pp. 11–14, F¹²10497: Vêtement, organisation de l'habillement, AN; Allilaire, *Industries de l'habillement*, pp. 385–95. See also Jean Giry, *Projet d'organisation d'une usine moderne de confection de vêtements féminins (en grande série)* (Paris: Centre de perfectionnement technique des industries de l'habillement, [1945]); and J. Laurent, *La fabrication des chemises aux Etats-Unis* (Paris: Centre d'études techniques des industries de l'habillement, [1948]).

95 Desmyttere, *Les grandes industries modernes*, pp. 174–75.

96 Françoise Vincent-Ricard, *Raison et passion*, p. 84. On the productivity missions, see Richard Kuisel, "L'American Way of Life' et les missions françaises de productivité," *Vingtième Siècle*, no. 17 (Jan.–Mar. 1988): 21–38; and the publications of the Association française pour l'accroissement de la productivité.

97 Fédération de l'habillement, *23e Congrès* (Lyon, 1948), typescript, CGT Archives.

98 Fédération de l'habillement, *24e Congrès* (1950), typescript, Sept. 29, 1950, CGT Archives. "Irwin Braun" is, of course, Irving Brown, who reigned over postwar free trade unionism in France for several decades. See Irwin Wall, *The United States and the Making of Postwar France, 1945–1954*; Annie Lacroix-Riz, "Autour d'Irving Brown: L'A.F.L., le Free Trade Union Committee, le Département d'Etat et la scission syndicale française (1944–1947)," *Le Mouvement social*, no. 151 (Apr.–June 1990): 79–118.

99 The term "le New Look" or "le 'new-look'" (with or without quotation marks) referred to Dior's Corolle and En huit lines. The phrase apparently came

from fashion reporter Carmel Snow, who said to Dior, "Your dresses have such a new look." The term stuck, but as Dior later wrote: "Si j'ose citer la mode de 1947, qu'on a appelé le New Look, elle n'a eu de succès que parce qu'elle allait dans le sens d'une époque qui cherchait à sortir de l'inhumain pour retrouver la tradition" (*Hommage à Christian Dior* [Paris: Musée des arts de la mode, 1987], p. 27; see also pp. 14–15).

100 Solange Montagné-Villette, "Le prêt-à-porter à Paris: De l'artisanat à l'industrie," doctoral thesis, Université de Paris 10, 1981, p. 52. Another term which posed a problem was "sportswear." As the Conseiller commercial de France in New York commented, the term could not be translated as *vêtement de sport* because it was not just worn for active sports, but was more *habillé*. (Everything is relative.) Thus "sportswear" could only be classified as a *vêtement de ville*. This difficulty explains the term's importation without translation. Conseiller commercial de France in New York, p. 15. In the other direction, the English language imported the term *couturier*, without quotation marks, to designate dressmaking. The earliest example given in the *Oxford English Dictionary* is from 1899.

101 Gisèle Joannes, interview, Bourse du Travail, Paris, Mar. 7, 1985; Vincent-Ricard, *Raison et passion*, p. 86.

102 *Actuel*, April 1988.

103 Bernard Roshco, *The Rag Race*, p. 123.

104 *Le Monde* (Paris), Jan. 22, 1985, p. 23.

105 As a friend remarked, who chooses to remain anonymous.

106 Montagné-Villette, "Le prêt-à-porter," p. 11.

107 Allilaire, *Industries de l'habillement*, pp. 340, 228, 70, 325. Allilaire did not recognize the postwar baby boom under way.

108 Commissariat général du [VIe] plan, *Rapports des comités: Industrie de l'habillement, Industrie du cuir et de la chaussure*, pp. 25, 27.

4 Bermuda Shorts in Comparative Perspective

1 John Stuart Mill, "Two Methods of Comparison" (excerpt from *A System of Logic*, 1888), in *Comparative Perspectives: Theories and Methods*, ed. Amitai Etzioni and Frederic L. DuBow, pp. 205–13; Nancy L. Green, "L'histoire comparative et le champ des études migratoires," *Annales E.S.C.*, no. 6 (Nov.–Dec. 1990): 1335–50.

2 Writing after the World Exhibition of 1851 in London. Léon Laborde (M. le Comte), *De l'union des arts et de l'industrie*, 2 vols., 1:317; see also 1:382–83, 397. For an interesting analysis of De Laborde, see Whitney Walton, *France at the Crystal Palace*.

3 Nancy L. Green, "Art and Industry: The Language of Modernization in the Production of Fashion," *French Historical Studies* 18 (Spring 1994): 722–48.

4 The classic expression of this dilemma is Walter Benjamin, "The Work of Art

in the Age of Mechanical Reproduction," in *Illuminations* [1955] (New York: Harcourt, Brace and World, 1968), pp. 219–53.

5 Jean Allilaire, *Les industries de l'habillement et du travail des étoffes*, pp. 54, 395, 155ff; see discussion of Allilaire's postwar report in chap. 3 above. For earlier examples, see Léon Storch, *Classe 85—Industrie de la confection et de la couture*, in *Classes 85 et 86*, ed. Léon Storch, Julien Hayem, and Auguste Mortier, p. 39; Gaston Worth, *La couture et la confection des vêtements de femme*, p. xv; Pierre Du Maroussem, *La petite industrie (salaires et durée du travail)*, vol. 2: *Le vêtement à Paris*, p. 294.

6 The term "taste professionals" comes from Leora Auslander, *Taste and Power: Furnishing Modern France* (Berkeley: University of California Press, 1996.)

7 Philippe Simon, *Monographie . . . la haute couture*, p. 135.

8 Roger Catin, "Les industries textiles et celles de l'habillement," course lectures, Institut d'etudes politiques, 1951–52, p. 95.

9 Arsène Alexandre, *Les reines de l'aiguille*, p. 54.

10 Edouard Debect, *L'habillement féminin en France au point de vue industriel et commercial*, pp. 111–12. Cf. Gertrude Willoughby, *La situation des ouvrières du vêtement en France et en Angleterre*, p. 45, on the harsh English climate and the need for sturdy ready-to-wear garments in England.

11 Lucien Romier, *La confection*, p. 11; Worth, *Couture*, p. 95. Cf. more contemporary versions of the French view of German apparel in Centre national du commerce extérieur, *Le marché du prêt-à-porter en Allemagne fédérale* (Paris: CNCE, Service d'étude des débouchés, 1963), and, more recently, in *Le Monde*, September 12, 1987.

12 Romier, *Confection*, p. 12.

13 Emile Levasseur, *L'ouvrier américain*, 2 vols., 1:50–51; 2:32–40.

14 Ibid., 1:116; cf. 1:46, 113–18.

15 Allilaire, *Industries de l'habillement*, p. 73.

16 See Richard Kuisel, "L'"American Way of Life' et les missions françaises de productivité," *Vingtième Siècle*, no. 17 (Jan.–Mar. 1988): 21–38; and the publications of the Association française pour l'accroissement de la productivité.

17 Catin, "Industries textiles," p. 91.

18 Allilaire, *Industries de l'habillement*, p. 56.

19 Conseiller commercial de France à New York, *Le marché de la confection féminine aux Etats-Unis*, p. 15. Imagine what he must think of 1990s Parisian styles.

20 Ibid., p. 32. Cf. Union des industries textiles, *L'exportation vers les Etats-Unis* (Paris: UIT, September 1971): "Il est absolument *exclu que ce soient les acheteurs qui s'adaptent*, même marginalement, aux normes du vendeur" (p. 5, emphasis in the original). See also Centre français du commerce extérieur, *Guide pratique de l'exportation du textile et de l'habillement aux Etats-Unis* (Paris: CFCE, 1985).

21 More generally, on changing French views of Americans, see Jacques

Portes, *Une fascination réticente: Les Etats-Unis dans l'opinion française* (Nancy: Presses universitaires de Nancy, 1990); Denis Lacorne, Jacques Rupnik, and Marie-France Toinet, *The Rise and Fall of Anti-Americanism* (New York: St. Martin's Press, 1990); Christine Faure and Tom Bishop, *L'Amérique des Français* (Paris: François Bourin, 1992).

22 Françoise Vincent-Ricard, *Raison et passion*, esp. pp. 84–94.

23 E.g., Bernard Roshco, *The Rag Race: How New York and Paris Run the Breakneck Business of Dressing American Women*, p. 125.

24 Charles Russell Richards, *Art in Industry*.

25 E.g., Paul Nystrom, *The Economics of Fashion*, pp. 174–75; Jeanette Jarnow and Beatrice Judelle, *Inside the Fashion Business*, 2d ed., pp. 176–78, 188; Richards, *Art in Industry*, p. 13.

26 Richards, *Art in Industry*, p. 473; cf. pp. 2–13.

27 In an interesting twist on reciprocal visions, while the French nervously went abroad to study at art schools and trade schools elsewhere, the Americans looked to France. Marius Vachon, author of *Nos industries d'art en péril* (Paris: L. Baschet, 1882), undertook a series of studies on art schools and trade schools in other countries, e.g., *Pour la défense de nos industries d'art: L'instruction artistique des ouvriers en France, en Angleterre, en Allemagne et en Autriche* (Paris: A. Lahure, 1899), parts of which were in turn translated into English and subtitled as "lessons for the United States" (Washington, D.C.: GPO, 1923).

28 Claudia B. Kidwell and Margaret C. Christman, *Suiting Everyone*, p. 15; Richards, *Art in Industry*, pp. 29, 474.

29 Roshco, *Rag Race*, p. 9.

30 Richards, *Art in Industry*, p. 474. See also Jarnow and Judelle, *Fashion Business*, p. 178.

31 Roshco, *Rag Race*, p. 130; Kidwell and Christman, *Suiting Everyone*, pp. 173–75.

32 Roshco, *Rag Race*, p. 153.

33 Kidwell and Christman, *Suiting Everyone*, p. 15. Yet see Lizabeth Cohen, "Embellishing a Life of Labor: An Interpretation of the Material Culture of American Working-Class Homes, 1885–1915," in *Labor Migration in the Atlantic Economies*, ed. Dirk Hoerder, pp. 321–52; and Cohen, *Making a New Deal*, chaps. 2 and 3, on consumers' own choices.

34 Murray Sices, *Seventh Avenue*, p. 83. On the American design offensive, see Valerie Steele, *Paris Fashion: A Cultural History*, p. 233; Richards, *Art in Industry*, passim; Wendy Gamber, "A 'Feminine' Skill: Gender, Technology, and Power in the Dressmaking Trade, 1860–1910," paper presented at the 9th Berkshire Conference, June 11–13, 1993, pp. 13–14, 32; Nystrom, *Economics of Fashion*, p. 180; Roshco, *Rag Race*, p. 109. This trend was not limited to clothing. E.g., see Jeffrey L. Meikle, *Twentieth-Century Limited: Industrial Design in America, 1925–1939*; Arthur J. Pulos, *The American Design Adventure, 1940–1975*.

35 Nystrom, *Economics of Fashion*, p. 379.

36 *Women's Wear Daily*, Jan. 9, 1925, cited in Bernard Smith, "Hyper-Innovation and the American Women's Clothing Trades, 1880–1930," paper presented at the Social Science History Association Meeting, Baltimore, Nov. 5, 1993, p. 11.

37 During World War II. International Ladies' Garment Workers' Union, *Report of the General Executive Board* (25th Convention, 1944), p. 44.

38 Roshco, *Rag Race*, p. 144.

39 Nystrom, *Economics of Fashion*, pp. 379–96.

40 Roshco, *Rag Race*, p. 144; Jarnow and Judelle, *Fashion Business*, p. 176.

41 See Gilles Lipovetsky's most ardent exposition of this concept in *The Empire of Fashion*.

42 OECD figures cited in Organisation internationale du travail, *Réunion technique tripartite pour l'industrie du vêtement*, 3 vols., 1964, 1:158, table XXV.

43 Emile Levasseur, *L'ouvrier américain*, 2 vols., 1:423–25; Catin, p. 91.

44 Walton, *France at the Crystal Palace*.

45 Jeanne Gaillard, "France," in Commission internationale d'histoire des mouvements sociaux et des structures sociales, *Petite entreprise et croissance industrielle dans le monde aux XIXe et XXe siècles*, 2 vols., 1:139. See also Philippe Vigier, "Conclusions générales," and "Rapport général, 3e partie" pp. 11–38 and 105–26, ibid.; Louis Bergeron and Patrice Bourdelais, eds., *La France est-elle douée pour l'industrie?*, forthcoming; François Crouzet, *De la supériorité de l'Angleterre sur la France: L'économisme et l'imaginaire, 17e–20e siècles* (Paris: Perrin, 1985); Alain Faure, "Petit atelier et modernisme économique: La production en miettes au XIXe siècle," *Histoire, économie et société* 5 (1986): 531–57; Patrick Fridenson and André Straus, eds., *Le capitalisme français, Blocages et dynamismes d'une croissance;* Tom Kemp, *Industrialization in Nineteenth-Century Europe* (New York: Humanities Press, Inc., 1969); Charles Kindleberger, *Economic Growth in France and Britain, 1851–1950* (Cambridge, Mass.: Harvard University Press, 1964); David Landes, *The Unbound Prometheus;* Maurice Lévy-Leboyer, "Les processus d'industrialisation: Le cas de l'Angleterre et de la France," *Revue historique* 239 (1968): 281–98; Patrick O'Brien and Calgar Keyder, *Economic Growth in Britain and France, 1780–1914: Two Paths to the Twentieth Century.*

46 Simon, *Haute couture*, p. 69, and more generally, pp. 65–75.

47 Leonard A. Drake and Carrie Glasser, *Trends in the New York Clothing Industry*, p. 29.

48 Margaret Higonnet et al., eds., *Behind the Lines: Gender and the Two World Wars* (New Haven: Yale University Press, 1987); Jean-Jacques Becker et al., *14–18, La Très grande guerre* (Paris: Le Monde Editions, 1994); Robert Laurentz, "Racial/Ethnic Conflict in the New York City Garment Industry, 1933–1980," Ph.D. diss., SUNY-Binghamton, 1980, pp. 182–92.

49 Reported in *L'ouvrier de l'habillement* (Paris), no. 105, Aug. 1913.

50 Ibid. At the International meeting, the delegate Martschouk explained the

Notes to Pages 115–122

French union's poor showing on: (1) the French workers' character (lacking in organizing spirit); and (2) foreign workers being attracted to Paris but refractory to mobilizing there.

51 Jacques Julliard, *Autonomie ouvrière: Etudes sur le syndicalisme d'action directe*, p. 120. Other recent comparisons among working classes and labor movements include: Richard Biernacki, *The Fabrication of Labor: Germany and Britain, 1640–1914* (Berkeley: University of California Press, 1995); James E. Cronin, "Neither Exceptional nor Peculiar: Towards the Comparative Study of Labor in Advanced Societies," *International Review of Social History* 38 (1993): pp. 59–75; Laura Lee Downs, *Manufacturing Inequality;* Jeffrey Haydu, *Between Craft and Class: Skilled Workers and Factory Politics in the United States and Britain, 1890–1922* (Berkeley: University of California Press, 1988); Ira Katznelson and Aristide Zolberg, eds., *Working-Class Formation: Nineteenth-Century Patterns in Western Europe and the United States;* Scott Lash, *The Militant Worker: Class and Radicalism in France and America* (London: Heinemann Educational Books, 1984); Gary Marks, *Unions in Politics: Britain, Germany, and the United States in the Nineteenth and Early Twentieth Centuries* (Princeton: Princeton University Press, 1989); Louise Tilly and Joan Scott, *Women, Work and Family;* and Judith E. Vichniac, *The Management of Labor.*

52 William H. Sewell Jr., *Work and Revolution in France: The Language of Labor from the Old Regime to 1848* (New York: Cambridge University Press, 1980); idem, "Artisans, Factory Workers, and the Formation of the French Working Class, 1789–1848," in Katznelson and Zolberg, eds., *Working-Class Formation*, pp. 45–70; and Katznelson, "Working-Class Formation: Constructing Cases and Comparisons," in ibid., p. 39.

53 Werner Sombart, *Why Is There No Socialism in the United States?* [1906] (White Plains, NY: International Arts and Sciences Press, 1976); Aristide Zolberg, "How Many Exceptionalisms?" in Katznelson and Zolberg, eds., *Working-Class Formation*, pp. 397–455.

54 Georges Sorel, *Reflections on Violence* [1906] (New York: Collier Books, 1961). The main proponent of this thesis was Peter Stearns, *Revolutionary Syndicalism and French Labor: A Cause without Rebels* (New Brunswick: Rutgers University Press, 1971), contested, however, by Michelle Perrot, *Les ouvriers en grève, France 1871–1890*, 2 vols.; and Edward Shorter and Charles Tilly, *Strikes in France, 1830–1968* (Cambridge, Eng.: Cambridge University Press, 1974). Sorel himself, of course, argued that the general strike functioned as a mobilizing myth.

55 Vichniac, *Management of Labor*, esp. introduction, for a good analysis of the comparative problem.

56 Fédération des travailleurs de l'habillement, *Compte rendu, 1er Congrès national* (Nîmes, 1893), pp. 9–10.

57 Reutlinger suggested this distinction in comparing England and the United States. See Andrew S. Reutlinger, "Reflections on the Anglo-American Jewish Experience: Immigrants, Workers, and Entrepreneurs in New York and Lon-

don, 1870–1914," *American Jewish Historical Quarterly* 66 (June 1977): 473–84. See also Roy B. Helfgott, "Trade Unionism among the Jewish Garment Workers of Britain and the United States," *Labor History* 2, no. 2 (1961): 202–14; and Karin Hofmeester, *Van Talmoed tot Statuut: Joodse Arbeiders en Arbeiders-bewegingen in Amsterdam, London en Parijs, 1880–1914* (Amsterdam: Stichting beheer IISG, 1990).

58 Roger Waldinger, "Another Look at the International Ladies' Garment Workers' Union: Women, Industry Structure and Collective Action," in *Women, Work, and Protest,* ed. Ruth Milkman.

59 See, e.g., Michel Dreyfus, *Histoire de la CGT,* introduction.

60 Theda Skocpol, *Protecting Soldiers and Mothers: The Political Origins of Social Policy in the United States.* Skocpol argues that while the European countries were putting into place "paternalist" benefits largely for male wage-earners, the United States pioneered a distinctively "maternalist" welfare state. For some critical appraisals of Skocpol's argument, see Alex Keyssar's review in *The Nation* 256, no. 16 (1993): 566–70; Felicia Kornbluh, "Some Are More Equal," *Radical History Review* 57 (1993): 250–57; and Susan Pedersen, *Family, Dependence, and the Origins of the Welfare State: Britain and France, 1914–1945.*

61 Cf. François Ewald, *L'Etat providence* (Paris: Grasset, 1986); and Elinor Accampo, Rachel Fuchs, and Mary Lynn Stewart, *Gender and the Politics of Social Reform in France, 1870–1914;* Sanford Elwitt, *The Third Republic Defended: Bourgeois Reform in France, 1880–1914* (Baton Rouge: Louisiana State University Press, 1986); and Judith Stone, *The Search for Social Peace: Reform Legislation in France, 1890–1914.* The historiography of turn-of-the-century welfare legislation in the United States has most recently turned around an analysis of women's role in the creation of the American reforms, taking off from Paula Baker's seminal article, "The Domestication of Politics: Women and American Political Society, 1780–1920," *American Historical Review* 89, no. 3 (1984): 620–47.

62 Allan Mitchell, *The Divided Path: The German Influence on Social Reform in France after 1870.* See also his other Franco-German comparisons: *The German Influence in France after 1870: The Formation of the French Republic* (Chapel Hill: University of North Carolina Press, 1979); *Victors and Vanquished: The German Influence on Army and Church in France after 1870* (Chapel Hill: University of North Carolina Press, 1984). Philp Nord has criticized Ewald, Mitchell, and the feminist perspective in his review article, "The Welfare State in France, 1870–1914," *French Historical Studies* 18, no. 3 (Spring 1994): 821–38. Nord remains an optimist, though, countering the pessimistic perspectives with his emphasis on a "republican vision [helping to] power welfare-state construction" in France. See Nord, *The Republican Moment: The Struggle for Democracy in 19th-Century France* (Cambridge, Mass.: Harvard University Press, 1995).

63 Just as Skocpol focuses on soldiers' and mothers' pensions, with opposite results. See Skocpol, *Protecting Soldiers and Mothers;* Susan Pedersen, *Family,*

Dependence, and the Origins of the Welfare State. See also John Weiss, "Origins of the French Welfare State: Poor Relief in the Third Republic, 1871–1914," *Journal of Social History* 13 (Spring 1983): 75–76.

64 However, women had more input over policy decisions in the latter countries. See Seth Koven and Sonya Michel, "Womanly Duties: Maternalist Politics and the Origins of Welfare States in France, Germany, Great Britain, and the United States, 1880–1920," *American Historical Review* 95, no. 4 (Oct. 1990): 1076–1108; and idem, eds., *Maternalist Policies and the Origins of Welfare States* (New York: Routledge, 1993).

65 Alisa Klaus, *Every Child a Lion: The Origins of Infant Health Policy in the United States and France, 1890–1920*, p. 289; Jane Jensen, "Representations of Gender: Policies to 'Protect' Women Workers and Infants in France and the United States before 1914," in *Women, the State, and Welfare*, ed. Linda Gordon, pp. 152–72.

66 Mary Lynn Stewart, *Women, Work and the French State.* See also Leora Auslander and Michelle Zancarini-Fournel, eds., *Différences des sexes et protection sociale, XIXe–XXe siècles;* Marilyn Boxer, "Protective Legislation and Home Industry: The Marginalization of Women Workers in Late Nineteenth–Early Twentieth-Century France," *Journal of Social History* 20, no. 1 (Fall 1986): 45–65; and Lorraine Coons, *Women Home Workers in the Parisian Garment Industry, 1860–1915*, p. 271.

67 Alice Kessler-Harris, *Out to Work: A History of Wage-Earning Women in the United States*, chap. 7; Judith Baer, *The Chains of Protection: The Judicial Response to Women's Labor Legislation* (Westport, Conn.: Greenwood Press, 1978).

68 Eileen Boris, "Regulating Industrial Homework: The Triumph of 'Sacred Motherhood'," *Journal of American History* 71 (Mar. 1985): 745–63; and idem, *Home to Work*, chap. 1. For France, see, e.g., report, June 26, 1903 (concerning family workshops, not homework per se), F²²471: Commission départementale du travail (Seine), Archives Nationales, Paris; and Joan Wallach Scott, "Men and Women in the Parisian Garment Trades: Discussions of Family and Work in the 1830s and 1840s," in *The Power of the Past: Essays for Eric Hobsbawm*, ed. Thane, Crossick, and Floud, pp. 70, 74–75; and Willoughby, *Ouvrières en France et Angleterre*, p. 39, on the "femme au foyer."

69 E.g., *Le minimum de salaire dans l'industrie à domicile* (Paris: Félix Alcan and Marcel Rivière, 1912), p. 89; Judith Coffin, "Social Science Meets Sweated Labor: Reinterpreting Women's Work in Late Nineteenth-Century France," *Journal of Modern History* 63, no. 2 (June 1991), p. 255; Fédération de l'habillement, *Compte rendu, 9e congrès* (Bordeaux, 1912), p. 55; Jean-Pierre Durand, "Le travail à domicile en France aujourd'hui," *Travail et Emploi*, no. 23 (Mar. 1985), pp. 33–48; Boris, " 'Sacred Motherhood,' " p. 751.

70 The issue was described as one of "liberté individuelle," respecting "les affaires personnelles des ouvriers," which, according to one critic, "va jusqu'à l'indifférence [où] il faut voir une des principales causes des nombreuses misères qui pèsent sur l'ouvrière à domicile." See Camille Doublot, *La protec-*

tion légale des travailleurs de l'industrie du vêtement, p. 122; Scott, "Men and Women"; Coons, *Women Home Workers*, chaps. 5 and 6 on the legislative debates concerning homework.

71 My choice of comparative units here is a voluntary departure from purely symmetrical national-level comparisons. Due to the differences between the decentralized American system and the more centralized French one, it makes more sense to compare those laws which most directly affected the Parisian and New York industries, i.e., French law and New York State law.

72 Stewart, *Women, Work*, explicitly sees these provisions as a powerful example of the legislating of a dual labor market.

73 Boris, *Home to Work*, pp. 158–61, 214.

74 Jenson, "Representations of Gender," pp. 156, 158. See also Miriam Cohen and Michael Hanagan, "The Politics of Gender and the Making of the Welfare State, 1900–1940: A Comparative Perspective," *Journal of Social History* 24 (Spring 1991): 469–84, looking at social feminists' language rather than that of the state; and Klaus, *Every Child a Lion*, pp. 289–90. Only the *Muller vs. Oregon* Supreme Court decision of 1908 allowed hours regulations specifically for women (as an explicit exception to the notion of freedom of contract), but none were passed at the state level. Minimum-wage laws for women were, however, passed in different states between 1912 and 1923. See Alice Kessler-Harris, *Out to Work*, p. 12; idem, "Women and Welfare: Public Interventions in Private Lives," *Radical History Review* 56 (1993): 127–36.

75 Boris, *Home to Work*, passim; Miriam Cohen and Michael Hanagan, "The Political Economy of Social Reform: The Case of Homework in New York and Paris, 1900–1940," *French Politics and Society* 6, no. 4 (Oct. 1988): 31–38. See Coons, *Women Home Workers*, chap. 6, on the debates leading up to the ultimately ineffectual 1915 French law.

76 Lazare Teper and Nathan Weinberg, *Aspects of Industrial Homework in the Apparel Trades*, p. 37.

77 On the discourse of rights and freedom used by homework defenders in the 1980s, see Boris, *Home to Work*, pp. 358–61.

5 The Sweatshop as Workplace and Metaphor

1 Emile Levasseur, *L'ouvrier américain*, 2 vols., 1:431. He adds, however, that these immigrants were probably better off in New York than they had been in their home countries. Madeleine Guilbert and Viviane Isambert-Jamati, *Travail féminin et travail à domicile*, imagined the spelling as "sweatschop," p. 23.

2 Judith Coffin, "Social Science Meets Sweated Labor: Reinterpreting Women's Work in Late Nineteenth-Century France," *Journal of Modern History* 63, no. 2 (June 1991): 230–70; William Reddy, *The Rise of Market Culture: The Textile Trade and French Society, 1750–1900*, pp. 180–82.

3 Jonathan Zeitlin and Peter Totterdill, "Markets, Technology and Local Inter-

vention: The Case of Clothing," in *Reversing Industrial Decline? Industrial Structure and Policy in Britain and Her Competitors*, ed. Paul Hirst and Jonathan Zeitlin; cf. Michael J. Piore and Charles F. Sabel, *The Second Industrial Divide;* Charles F. Sabel and Jonathan Zeitlin, "Historical Alternatives to Mass Production: Politics, Market, and Technology in Nineteenth-Century Industrialization," *Past and Present*, no. 108 (Aug. 1985): 133–76; idem, eds. *Worlds of Possibility: Flexibility and Mass Production in Western Industrialization;* Roger Waldinger, *Through the Eye of the Needle;* and Mirjana Morokvasic, Roger Waldinger, and Annie Phizacklea, "Business on the Ragged Edge: Immigrant and Minority Business in the Garment Industries of Paris, London, and New York," in *Ethnic Entrepreneurs: Immigrant Business in Industrial Societies*, ed. Roger Waldinger, Howard Aldrich, and Robin Ward, pp. 157–76.

4 That is, the Piore of *Birds of Passage*, rather than the Piore of *The Second Industrial Divide.*

5 Elizabeth Hasanovitz, *One of Them* (Boston: Houghton Mifflin, 1918), p. 272; *The Paris Metro*, Mar. 30, 1977.

6 Organisation internationale du travail (OIT), *Réunion technique tripartite pour l'industrie du vêtement* (1964), report 3, *Les problèmes résultant des fluctuations de l'emploi dans l'industrie du vêtement;* Carol Joan Smith, "Women, Work, and Use of Government Benefits: A Case Study of Hispanic Women Workers in New York's Garment Industry," Ph.D. diss., Adelphi University, 1980, pp. 71ff.

7 Alexander Keyssar, *Out of Work: The First Century of Unemployment in Massachusetts*, chap. 3; Sidney Webb and Arnold Freeman, eds. *Seasonal Trades;* and Gareth Stedman Jones, *Outcast London: A Study in the Relationship between Classes in Victorian Society* (Harmondsworth, Eng.: Penguin, 1984). See also, for New York, Gertrud Greig, *Seasonal Fluctuations in Employment in the Women's Clothing Industry in New York;* Christine Stansell, *City of Women: Sex and Class in New York, 1789–1860;* and cf. Richard B. Stott, *Workers in the Metropolis*, pp. 24–25, 118–19, and passim; and Sean Wilentz, *Chants Democratic.* For France, see Michael Sonenscher, *Work and Wages*, on the instability and fluidity of the earlier period.

8 New York State Governor's Advisory Commission, *Cloak, Suit and Skirt Industry of New York City*, p. 22.

9 OIT, *Réunion tripartite* (1964), *Compte rendu sommaire*, p. 36; ibid., report 3: *Fluctuations de l'emploi;* OIT, *2ème réunion tripartite* (1980), *Note sur les travaux*, p. 65; idem, *4ème réunion* (1995), 2:41.

10 Webb and Freeman, *Seasonal Trades*, p. 59; Jeanne Bouvier, *La lingerie et les lingères*, pp. 300–301; Mary Lynn Stewart, *Women, Work and the French State*, p. 144; Coffin, "Social Science Meets Sweated Labor," pp. 257, 262–63; and Lorraine Coons, *Women Home Workers in the Parisian Garment Industry, 1860–1915*, pp. 198–209. The American consumers' leagues in particular often urged the use of a standards-approved label to increase buyer awareness. Consumers' leagues on both sides of the Atlantic also sought to bring pressure on the state and employers to better working conditions.

11 Karl Marx, *Capital*, 3 vols. (London: Lawrence and Wishart, 1974), 1:450.

Notes to Pages 138–142

12 Alfred Picard, gen. ed., *Exposition universelle internationale de 1889 à Paris: Rapports du jury international*, Classe 36: *Habillement des deux sexes*, by Albert Leduc, p. 58; Pierre Du Maroussem, *La petite industrie (salaires et durée du travail)*, vol. 2, *Le vêtement à Paris*, p. 306.

13 *Justice*, May 15, 1946, cited by Robert Laurentz, "Racial/Ethnic Conflict in the New York City Garment Industry, 1933–1980," Ph.D. diss., SUNY-Binghamton, 1980, p. 192.

14 International Ladies' Garment Workers' Union (ILGWU), *Record of the 16th Convention* (1922), pp. 93, 124. Jesse Thomas Carpenter, *Competition and Collective Bargaining in the Needle Trades, 1910–1967*, pp. 125–37, on the union's attempts to limit contracting; Benjamin K. Hunnicutt, *Abandoning Shorter Hours for the Right to Work* (Philadelphia: Temple University Press, 1988), pp. 71–75, on work sharing.

15 ILGWU, *Record of the 17th Convention* (1924), p. 229.

16 ILGWU, *Report of the General Executive Board* (23d Convention, 1937), pp. 10–11.

17 *Der idisher arbayter* (Paris), Apr. 5, 1913.

18 "Le travail féminin à Paris, avant et depuis la guerre, dans les industries du vêtement," *Bulletin du Ministère du travail* 33, no. 7–9 (July–Sept. 1926): 252. Cf. "many people connected with the industry are disgusted with conditions as they are at present, yet accept them as inevitable." Emanuel Federated Employment Service, "An Industrial Survey of the Needle Trades to Determine a Vocational Guidance Policy for Young Men of Jewish Descent with Regard to the Industry," p. 34.

19 City College Oral History Research Project, "New York City Immigrant Labor Oral History Collection," Tamiment Library (New York City, n.d.), I-105. For some contemporary evidence from Hispanic women garment workers in New York City, see Smith, "Women, Work."

20 Hadassa Kosak, "The Rise of the Jewish Working Class, New York, 1881–1905," City University of New York, Ph.D. diss., 1987, p. 206; see also p. 120.

21 OIT, *Réunion tripartite* (1964), 3: chaps. 4 and 5; and ibid., *Compte rendu sommaire*, pp. 40–45.

22 See, e.g., New York State Department of Labor, *The Women's Clothing Worker and Unemployment Insurance*. In 1956, 24 percent of New York City's unemployment compensation was paid out to women's-wear garment workers (*New York Herald Tribune*, Sept. 29, 1958). On unemployment insurance as a means of regulating the effect of fluctuating demand, see also Steven Fraser, *Labor Will Live*, pp. 215–18.

23 What Sandrine Tasmadjian has called "une maison évolutive," in Nancy L. Green et al., "Les rapports habitat/travail dans l'industrie de l'habillement à Paris et dans sa banlieue," p. 100. Contractors' shops have also been called "kitchen and bedroom" shops (Kosak, "Jewish Working Class," p. 205). See also Waldinger, *Through the Eye of the Needle*.

24 Marx, *Capital*, 1:445–46.

25 Sometimes called *petits grossistes* in French. However, the French version of

the OIT report did not translate the term when referring to the American industry (OIT, *Réunion tripartite* [1964], 1:42).

26 Helen Everett Meiklejohn, "Dresses—The Impact of Fashion on a Business," in *Price and Price Policies*, ed. Walton Hamilton, p. 322. The State Governor's Commission also admitted to the difficulty of making a clear distinction between the pre–World War I manufacturer-contractor system and the interwar jobber-submanufacture system (New York State Governor's Advisory Commission, *Cloak, Suit*, pp. 1–8 and passim, and p. 24 on "worms").

27 *Le Monde Affaires*, Mar. 7, 1987. Manoukian subcontracts everything from production to design, using designers on a freelance basis for a season or two, after which they lose their creativity.

28 New York State Governor's Advisory Commission, *Cloak, Suit*, p. 14.

29 *Fortune* magazine, cited in Roger Waldinger, "Another Look at the International Ladies' Garment Workers' Union: Women, Industry Structure and Collective Action," in *Women, Work, and Protest*, ed. Ruth Milkman, p. 103.

30 In New York City, for example, the average number of workers per establishment in women's wear fell from 27.8 in 1899 to 17.9 in 1921 (Louis Levine, *The Women's Garment Workers*, p. 521). On the "semi-artisans" and "small hands" in other subcontracted Parisian trades, see Leora Auslander, *Taste and Power: Furnishing Modern France*; Lenard R. Berlanstein, *The Working People of Paris, 1871–1914*, pp. 84–91; and Alain Faure, "Petit atelier et modernisme économique: La production en miettes au XIXe siècle," *Histoire, économie et société* 5, no. 4 (1986): 531–57.

31 Cited in OIT, *Réunion tripartite* (1964), 1: table XII, p. 42.

32 New York State Governor's Advisory Commission, *Cloak, Suit*, p. 43; ILGWU, *The Story of the ILGWU*, p. 25.

33 Levasseur, *L'ouvrier américain*, 1: chap. 7; Mirjana Morokvasic, "Immigrants in the Parisian Garment Industry," *Work, Employment and Society* 1, no. 4 (1987): 450; ILGWU, *Report of the General Executive Board* (26th Convention, 1947), p. 93; Abeles et al., *The Chinatown Garment Industry Study*, p. 4; on the early *apiéceurs*, see Joan Wallach Scott, "Men and Women in the Parisian Garment Trades: Discussions of Family and Work in the 1830s and 1840s," in *The Power of the Past*, ed. Thane, Crossick, and Floud, p. 73.

34 Maurizio Lazzarato, Antonio Negri, and Giancarlo Santilli, "La confection dans le quartier du Sentier," report, Ministère du travail, de l'emploi et de la formation professionnelle, MIRE, 1990, p. 186; Pierre Dubois, *L'industrie de l'habillement: L'innovation face à la crise*, pp. 55–58. Abeles et al., *Chinatown Study*, pp. 4, 69, found that contractors work for an average of 4.6 jobbers, and manufacturers give out work to some 27 different contractors.

35 Levine, *Women's Garment Workers*, pp. viii, 15; Roy Helfgott, "Women's and Children's Apparel," in *Made in New York*, ed. Max Hall, p. 30; Waldinger, *Through the Eye of the Needle*, pp. 137–38, and chap. 6 in general. By comparison, it costs 500,000 francs to start a restaurant. See Yinh Phong Tan, "Restaurants et ateliers: Le travail des Sino-khmers à Paris," *ASEMI* 15, no. 1–

4 (1984):288. José R. De La Torre et al., *Corporate Responses to Import Competition in the U.S. Apparel Industry*, p. 37, calculated that the average plant and equipment in the garment industry was $2,335 per production worker, compared to $24,245 for all manufacturing.

36 ILGWU, *Report of the General Executive Board* (27th Convention, 1950), p. 93; Helfgott, "Women's and Children's Apparel," p. 31; Joel Seidman, *The Needle Trades*, p. 42; Commission internationale d'histoire des mouvements sociaux et des structures sociales, *Petite entreprise et croissance industrielle dans le monde aux XIXe et XXe siècles*, 2 vols., 1:6, 20; Cathy Pappas, accountant in the New York garment district, interview, June 11, 1984. See also Elaine Wrong, *The Negro in the Apparel Industry*, table 7, p. 18, showing employment turnover in the apparel industry to be higher than that of all manufacturing sectors as a whole.

37 Meiklejohn, "Dresses," pp. 329, 334, 324, 343; Senator Franz S. Leichter, "The Return of the Sweatshop," unpublished report, 3 vols. (1979–1982), 2:28, cf. Peter Kwong, *The New Chinatown*, p. 68. Often firms close for legal reasons, only to reopen under another name, with or without their former employees. Roshco estimated the turnover of manufacturers as running about 20 percent per year before 1932 (Bernard Roshco, *The Rag Race*, p. 109. Some ILGWU statistics showed the turnover of jobbers and manufacturers from 1937 to 1942 to range from 16.2 to 25.7 percent; these figures dipped during the prosperous war years, ranging from 4.6 to 9.2 percent from 1943 to 1946, to return to prewar levels of about 15 percent in 1947 and 1948 (Report, Dress Industry Data, February 8, 1949, Dress Joint Series, Box 3, File 11, ILGWU Archives, New York). The State Governor's Commission estimated that one-third close per year (New York State Governor's Advisory Commission, *Cloak, Suit*, p. 45). See also Florence S. Richards, *The Ready-to-Wear Industry, 1900–1950*, pp. 32, 26.

38 Lazzarato et al., "Confection dans le Sentier," p. 77; *Le Nouvel Observateur*, Feb. 9–15, 1989.

39 Käthe Schirmacher, *La spécialisation du travail—Par nationalités, à Paris*, p. 70.

40 ILGWU, *Story*, p. 22; "Der khazer mark in 'Hester' Park," *Forverts*, Sept. 29, 1907, in Nancy L. Green, ed. *Jewish Workers in the Diaspora* (Berkeley: University of California Press, forthcoming).

41 ILGWU, *The Outside System of Production in the Women's Garment Industry in the New York Market*, p. 14; ILGWU, *Report of the General Executive Board* (19th Convention, 1928), pp. 7–8; Carpenter, *Competition*, pp. 116, 132.

42 Cited in Carpenter, *Competition*, p. 109. See Susan Glenn's view of the oppressive paternalistic immigrant shop in *Daughters of the Shtetl*, passim. In one case, women called an "orphan strike" to protest their boss's "fatherly affection." See Nancy Schrom Dye, *As Equals and Sisters: The Labor Movement and the Women's Trade Union League of New York*, p. 67.

43 Cited in Kosak, "Jewish Working Class," p. 141.

44 Cited in Carpenter, *Competition*, p. 107.

45 Jacob Loft, "Jewish Workers in the New York City Men's Clothing Industry," *Jewish Social Studies* 2, no. 1 (Jan. 1940): 76.

46 U.S. Industrial Commission, *Reports of the Industrial Commission*, 19 vols., 15:379.

47 Meiklejohn, "Dresses," p. 347.

48 Cited in OIT, *Réunion tripartite* (1964), 2:20–21.

49 William M. Reddy, *Money and Liberty in Modern Europe.*

50 Alejandro Portes and Manuel Castells, "World Underneath: The Origins, Dynamics, and Effects of the Informal Economy," in *The Informal Economy*, ed. Portes, Castells, and Benton, p. 13. For a contrasting view, stressing continuity, see Annie Phizacklea, *Unpacking the Fashion Industry.*

51 Sabel and Zeitlin, "Historical Alternatives"; Zeitlin, "Industrial Districts and Local Economic Regeneration: Overview and Comment," in *Industrial Districts and Local Economic Regeneration*, ed. F. Pyke and W. Sengenberger (Geneva: International Institute for Labour Studies, 1992); and Zeitlin and Totterdill, "Markets, Technology."

52 Cited in Jonathan Boyarin, *Polish Jews in Paris* (Bloomington: Indiana University Press, 1991), p. 52.

53 Abe S. Weiss, "Garment Workers of Other Lands," typed manuscript in ILGWU Archives, F. Cohn, 11:1, n.d. [written during World War II], p. 22.

54 OIT, *2e réunion tripartite* (1980), report 2.

55 Klatzmann, *Travail à domicile*, p. 99.

56 On the notion of *bloc socio-technologique*, see Pierre Bouvier, *Le travail au quotidien;* and idem, *Socio-anthropologie du contemporain.* On continuity in homework in France, see Michel Lallement, *Des PME en chambre.*

57 Faraut, *Belle Jardinière;* Marx, *Capital* 1:443.

58 New York State Department of Labor, *1st Annual Report* (1901), 1:126–27; *13th Annual Report* (1913), pp. 49–52; *28th Annual Report* (1928), p. 175; *31st Annual Report* (1931), p. 18.

59 New York State, Factory Investigating Commission, *2d Report*, 4 vols. (New York: 1913), 2:729; Eileen Boris, "Regulating Industrial Homework: The Triumph of 'Sacred Motherhood,'" *Journal of American History* 71 (Mar. 1985):746, 760; and Boris, *Home to Work*, p. 168.

60 Jean Lupiac, *La loi du 10 juillet 1915 pour la protection des ouvrières dans l'industrie du vêtement*, p. 3; Valentine Paulin, "Le travail à domicile en France, ses origines, son évolution, son avenir," *Revue internationale du travail* 37, no. 2 (Feb. 1938): 231; Joseph Klatzmann, *Le Travail à domicile;* cf. Michelle Perrot, "Femmes et machines au XIXe siècle," *Romantisme*, no. 41 (1983), p. 14.

61 Fédération de l'habillement et de la chapellerie, *24e Congrès national* (1950), typescript, CGT Archives, Montreuil.

62 New York State Department of Labor, "Report to the Governor and the Legislature on the Garment Manufacturing Industry and Industrial Homework" (New York, 1982), p. 13.

63 Solange Montagné-Villette, "Le prêt-à-porter à Paris: de l'artisanat à l'in-

dustrie," doctoral thesis, Université de Paris 10, 1981, p. 103; D. Guizien, "L'industrie textile et de l'habillement en région parisienne," Institut d'aménagement et d'urbanisme de la région parisienne (1973), p. 43.

64 The 20 percent figure comes from Roger Waldinger and Michael Lapp, skeptically quoting two union officials in "Back to the Sweatshop or Ahead to the Informal Sector?" *International Journal of Urban and Regional Research* 17, no. 1 (1993): 24; "New York Is Fighting Spread of Sweatshops," *New York Times*, Nov. 16, 1987.

65 Ruth Shallcross, *Industrial Homework*, see esp. pp. 2, 209.

66 If tailors and dressmakers can be counted as homeworkers, homeworkers can also be counted as independent workers. By counting homeworkers as entrepreneurs, the 1848 *Statistique de l'industrie à Paris*, for example, significantly lowered the number of workers. See Joan Scott, "Statistical Representations of Work: The Politics of the Chamber of Commerce's *Statistique de l'industrie à Paris, 1847–48*" in *Work in France*, ed. Steven Kaplan and Cynthia J. Koepp, p. 347.

67 Paulin, "Travail à domicile," p. 206.

68 Jamie Faricellia Dangler, "Industrial Homework in the Modern World Economy," paper presented at the 2d International Forum on the History of the Labor Movement and of the Working Class, Paris, June 26–28, 1985, Unesco. On the domestic economy, see Marx, *Capital*, 1:434–51. Marx therefore consistently used the term "so-called" domestic system to describe the more modern variant, which, in any case, he expected to disappear. Eileen Boris and Cynthia Daniels, eds., *Homework: Historical and Contemporary Perspectives on Paid Labor at Home* (Urbana: University of Illinois Press, 1989); Boris, *Home to Work;* Judith Coffin, "Woman's Place and Women's Work in the Paris Clothing Trades, 1830–1914," Ph.D. diss., Yale University, 1985, chap. 4; Mirjana Morokvasic, Annie Phizacklea, and Hedwig Rudolph, "Small Firms and Minority Groups: Contradictory Trends in the French, German and British Clothing Industries," *International Sociology* 1, no. 4 (Dec. 1986): 397–419; and Stansell, *City of Women*, all argue that outwork was not marginal but central to production.

69 As even Joan Scott mentioned in her article on the importance of understanding gender relations in the Parisian garment trades of the 1830s–1840s, "References to the family serve rather as a foil for considerations of the conditions of work" (Scott, "Men and Women," p. 76).

70 See Alain Cottereau, "Problèmes de conceptualisation comparative de l'industrialisation: L'exemple des ouvriers de la chaussure en France et en Grande Bretagne," in *Villes ouvrières, 1900–1950*, ed. Susanna Magri and Christian Topalov, pp. 54, 69, on the fluid boundaries between homework and the factory system in the late nineteenth-century shoe industry. For the eighteenth century, see Sonenscher, *Work and Wages.*

71 The Homework Protective League argued that homework was part of the "constitutional" right to work. See Boris, " 'Sacred Motherhood,' " p. 754; *Home to Work;* Coons, *Women Home Workers*, chaps. 5 and 6. Some French

regulators seeking to set a minimum wage for women's homework (men were considered able to take care of themselves) warned that too much regulation would cause it to disappear, thereby depriving women of an important opportunity for work (*Le minimum de salaire dans l'industrie à domicile* [Paris: Félix Alcan and Marcel Rivière, 1912], p. 89). See also Lallement, *Des PME en chambre.*

72 Marilyn Boxer, "Protective Legislation and Home Industry: The Marginalization of Women Workers in Late Nineteenth–Early Twentieth-Century France," *Journal of Social History* 20, no. 1 (Fall 1986): 51.

73 New York State, Bureau of Factory Inspectors, *12th Annual Report* (1897), p. 760; see also New York State Department of Labor, *13th Annual Report* (1913), pp. 50–51; and idem, *18th Annual Report* (1918), pp. 39–42; and Paris, Archives Nationales, F^{22}571 (1911): Inspection du travail, Maisons de couture.

74 Guilbert and Isambert-Jamati, *Travail féminim,* pp. 163–64; Emmanuel Ma Mung, "Logiques du travail clandestin des Chinois," in *Espaces et travail clandestins,* ed. Solange Montagné-Villette, p. 103; Coons, *Women Home Workers,* pp. 292–93.

75 Fédération des travailleurs de l'habillement, *Compte rendu du 9e congrès* (Bordeaux, 1912), pp. 56–57; see also, e.g., New York State Department of Labor, *11th Annual Report* (1911), p. 27; idem, 1912, p. 58.

76 Virginia Yans-McLaughlin, "Metaphors of Self in History: Subjectivity, Oral Narrative, and Immigration Studies," in *Immigration Reconsidered,* ed. idem, p. 276.

77 Meiklejohn, "Dresses," pp. 352–53. The point of Meiklejohn's description (in 1938), however, was to show how conditions had improved thanks to the union's efforts.

78 A 1904 amendment to the New York Factory Law explicitly attempted to enforce better lighting of workrooms, halls, and stairways, "deemed necessary in the interest of public morality" (New York State Department of Labor, *4th Annual Report* [1904], 1:68). Cf. another recent image of a garment shop: *Actuel,* April 1988.

79 Coffin, "Social Science Meets Sweated Labor"; Boris, *Home to Work.*

80 Charles Booth, "Sweating," in *Labour and Life of the People,* ed. idem, 3 vols. (London: Williams and Norgate, 1889–91), 1:481–500; Beatrice Webb, "How to do away with the Sweating System," in Sidney and Beatrice Webb, *Problems of Modern Industry,* pp. 139–40; James Schmiechen, *Sweated Industries and Sweated Labor.* For the United States, see *Industrial Commission,* 15:320; and United States House of Representatives, *Report on the Sweating System,* H. Rept. 3309, 52d Cong, 2d sess, 1893. For France, see Théodore Cotelle, *Le "sweating-system," Etude sociale;* Pierre Du Maroussem, *La question ouvrière,* 4 vols., vols. 2 and 3; and Georges Mény, *La lutte contre le sweating-system.* On the reformers' literature, see also Christian Topalov, *Naissance du chômeur: 1880–1910* (Paris: Albin Michel, 1994).

81 Cotelle felt that the term "system" was too precise in French (and overused in English) and that sweating was too chaotic to be called a system. See Cotelle, "Sweating-system," pp. v–vi; Levasseur, *L'ouvrier américain*, 1:431; New York State Bureau of Factory Inspectors, *12th Annual Report* (1897), p. 47.

82 Jack Hardy, *The Clothing Workers*, p. 218.

83 Leichter, "Return of the Sweatshop," 1:4. The New York Department of Labor measured carbon-dioxide levels in factories in 1908, while the French Ministry of Labor conducted an extensive survey of the cubic meters of air per worker in Parisian garment shops in 1911, in order to implement a 1904 law on proper ventilation. See New York State Department of Labor, *8th Annual Report* (1908), 1:19–20; Paris, Archives Nationales, F^{22}571 (1911): Inspection du travail; Leon Stein, *The Triangle Fire*. See also OIT, *Réunion tripartite* (1964), 2:chap. 5, on hygiene and safety in the garment industry; and idem, *2e réunion* (1987), 1: pt. 1, pp. 73–74, on the use of chemicals in the industry.

84 Coffin, "Social Science Meets Sweated Labor," pp. 255–60.

85 Jo-Ann Mort, "Return of the Sweatshop," *Dissent* (Summer 1988): 364; "Despite Tough Laws, Sweatshops Flourish," *New York Times*, Feb. 6, 1995; "Week in Sweatshop Reveals Grim Conspiracy of the Poor," *New York Times*, Mar. 12, 1995; "Sweatshop instead of Paradise," *Washington Post*, Sept. 10, 1995. With thanks to Joan Grimbert for this reference.

86 *Le Monde*, July 20, 1985; *Libération*, Apr. 22, 1987.

87 Leichter, "Return of the Sweatshop," 2:3–4. "The New Sweatshops," *Newsweek*, Sept. 10, 1990; *New York Times*, Mar. 6, 1994. See also Barbara Koeppel, "The New Sweatshops," *The Progressive* 5 (Nov. 1978): 22–26; *New York Times*, Oct. 12–13, 1983, and Sept. 6, 1987; Mort, "Return." Leichter also investigated organized crime and the links of truckers to contractors and jobbers in his three-part report.

88 Levine, *Women's Garment Workers*, p. x.

89 Pauline Newman, "We Kept the Faith," quoted in Leon Stein, ed., *Out of the Sweatshop*, p. 342. Cf., however, the 1958 newspaper series in the *New York Herald Tribune*, exposing conditions in the industry.

90 ILGWU, *General Executive Board Report and Record of the 38th Convention* (1983) p. 346; *New York Times*, Mar. 6, 1994.

91 Waldinger and Lapp, "Back to the Sweatshop"; Leichter, "Return of the Sweatshop"; Morrison G. Wong, "Chinese Sweatshops in the United States: A Look at the Garment Industry," in *Research in the Sociology of Work*, ed. Ida Simpson and Richard Simpson, pp. 357–79. For France, see different definitions of "travail au noir": Rosine Klatzmann, *Le travail noir* (Paris: PUF, Que sais-je, 1982); Roxanne Silberman, Jean-Pierre Garson, and Yann Moulier-Boutang, *Economie politique des migrations clandestines de main-d'oeuvre* (Paris: Publisud, 1986).

92 Piore and Sabel, *Second Industrial Divide*, p. 264.

93 "The New Sweatshops," *Newsweek*, Sept. 10, 1990; "New York's Terror Taxis, Explained," *New York Times*, Aug. 21, 1994. Not to mention the "aca-

demic sweatshop": see special issue of *Anthropology of Work Review,* "Demystifying the Changing Structure of Academic Work," 15, no. 1 (Spring 1994); and, on flexibility in the academy, *Perspectives* 33, no. 5 (May–June 1995): 9–18.

6 Women, Immigrants, and Skill in the Garment Shops

1 The major contemporary works on the garment industry tend to treat primarily either women or immigrants. E.g., the two otherwise excellent, Judith Coffin, "Woman's Place and Women's Work in the Paris Clothing Trades, 1830–1914," Ph.D. diss., Yale University, 1985 (although see pp. 149–55); and Roger D. Waldinger, *Through the Eye of the Needle.* See, however, James Schmiechen, *Sweated Industries and Sweated Labor,* on immigrants and women in the London garment industry and two recent books which focus on immigrant women garment workers: Susan Glenn, *Daughters of the Shtetl;* and Miriam Cohen, *Workshop to Office.* For a perceptive approach to some of the methodological problems in analytical dualisms, see Lourdes Benería and Martha Roldán, *The Crossroads of Class and Gender;* and Joy Parr, *The Gender of Breadwinners,* pp. 7–9. See also Kathie Friedman Kasaba, "'A Tailor Is Nothing without a Wife, and Very Often a Child': Gender and Labor-Force Formation in the New York Garment Industry, 1880–1920," in *Racism, Sexism, and the World-System,* ed. Joan Smith et al. (Westport, Conn.: Greenwood Press, 1988).
2 Mabel Hurd Willett, *The Employment of Women in the Clothing Trade,* p. 49.
3 Sally Hillsman, "Entry into the Labor Market: The Preparation and Job Placement of Negro and White Vocational High School Graduates," Ph.D. diss., Columbia University, 1970, p. 36.
4 The classic analysis is that of Heidi Hartmann, "Capitalism, Patriarchy and Job Segregation by Sex," in *Women and the Workplace: The Implications of Occupational Segregation,* ed. Martha Blaxall and Barbara Reagan, pp. 137–69.
5 Judith G. Coffin, "Credit, Consumption, and Images of Women's Desires: Selling the Sewing Machine in Late Nineteenth-Century France," *French Historical Studies* 18, no. 3 (Spring 1994): 749–83; Lorraine Coons, *Women Home Workers in the Parisian Garment Industry, 1860–1915;* Diane Elson, "Nimble Fingers and Other Fables," in *Of Common Cloth: Women in the Global Textile Industry,* ed. Wendy Chapkis and Cynthia Enloe (Amsterdam: Transnational Institute, 1983), pp. 5–14; Debora L. Silverman, *Art Nouveau in Fin-de-Siècle France,* chap. 11.
6 In addition to Hartmann, "Capitalism, Patriarchy"; see e.g., Anne Phillips and Barbara Taylor, "Sex and Skill: Notes towards a Feminist Economics," *Feminist Review,* no. 6 (1980): 79–88; and Christine Stansell, "The Origins of the Sweatshop: Women and Early Industrialization in New York City," in *Working-Class America: Essays on Labor, Community, and American Society,* ed. Michael H. Frisch and Daniel J. Walkowitz (Urbana: University of Illinois Press, 1983), p. 91.

7 Ava Baron, ed., *Work Engendered: Toward a New History of American Labor;* Mary H. Blewett, *Men, Women and Work: Class, Gender, and Protest in the New England Shoe Industry, 1780–1910* (Urbana: University of Illinois Press, 1988); Margery W. Davies, *Woman's Place Is at the Typewriter: Office Work and Office Workers, 1870–1930* (Philadelphia: Temple University Press, 1982); Laura Lee Downs, *Manufacturing Inequality;* Ruth Milkman, *Gender at Work: The Dynamics of Job Segregation by Sex During World War II* (Urbana: University of Illinois Press, 1987); Sonya O. Rose, *Limited Livelihoods: Gender and Class in Nineteenth-Century England* (Berkeley: University of California Press, 1991); Joan Wallach Scott, *Gender and the Politics of History.*

8 Although some production stayed in the home, especially in rural areas. See Nancy Page Fernandez, "'If a Woman Had Taste . . .': Home Sewing and the Making of Fashion, 1850–1910," Ph.D. diss., University of California-Irvine, 1987. For France, see Christopher H. Johnson, "Economic Change and Artisan Discontent: The Tailors' History, 1800–48," in *Revolution and Reaction: 1848 and the 2d French Republic,* ed. Roger Price; Judith Coffin, *The Politics of Work: The Paris Garment Trades, 1750–1915,* chapter 1; Joan Wallach Scott, "Men and Women in the Parisian Garment Trades: Discussions of Family and Work in the 1830s and 1840s," in *The Power of the Past,* ed. Thane, Crossick, and Floud; and Louise A. Tilly, "Paths of Proletarianization: Organization of Production, Sexual Division of Labor, and Women's Collective Action," *Signs* 7, no. 2 (Winter 1981): 400–417.

9 Wendy Gamber, *The Female Economy;* Coffin, *Politics of Work.*

10 Christine Stansell, *City of Women,* p. 91.

11 Coffin, "Woman's Place," p. 212.

12 New York State Department of Labor, *11th Annual Report,* 1911, p. 27.

13 Karen Offen, "'Powered by a Woman's Foot': A Documentary Introduction to the Sexual Politics of the Sewing Machine in Nineteenth-century France," *Women's Studies International Forum* 11, no. 2 (1988): 93–101; Coffin, "Woman's Place," pp. 114–18; Karin Hausen, "Technical Progress and Women's Labour in the Nineteenth Century: The Social History of the Sewing Machine," in *The Social History of Politics,* ed. Georg Iggers, pp. 259–81; Michelle Perrot, "Femmes et machines au XIXe siècle," *Romantisme,* no. 41 (1983): 5–17; Leon Stein, ed., *Out of the Sweatshop,* chap. 8.

14 E.g., Coffin, "Woman's Place," p. 213; and idem, "Credit, Consumption." As Michelle Perrot has pointed out, the Singer ultimately became a "rêve subverti," "l'instrument de leur servitude: l'usine à domicile" (Michelle Perrot, "La femme populaire rebelle," in *L'Histoire sans qualités,* ed. Christiane Dufrancatel et al. (Paris: Galilée, 1979), p. 140).

15 Concerning the waist and dress trade. See Ab. Baroff, "Our Union and its Problems," *Message,* Apr. 17, 1914.

16 New York State Office of Factory Inspectors, *13th Annual Report* (1898), p. 790.

17 Edith Abbott, *Women in Industry,* pp. 242–45. The report is well known for

its racist bias. Abbott herself criticized what she saw as a "racial" prejudice among Jews which discouraged Jewish women from working outside the home. The process of substitution was, for her, not just that of immigrants replacing natives, but more specifically of Jewish men (in the shops) edging out American (or even Jewish) women in their homes (ibid., pp. 228–31). On the Abbott sisters' defense of immigrant women, see Wendy Sarvasy, "Beyond the Difference versus Equality Policy Debate: Postsuffrage Feminism, Citizenship and the Quest for a Feminist Welfare State," *Signs* 17, no. 2 (Winter 1992): 329–62. Cf. Willett, *Employment of Women*, pp. 33, 55, 72.

18 Sholom Asch, *The Mother* [1930], trans. Nathan Ausübel (New York: Ams Press, 1970), p. 121; cf. p. 160. See also Charlotte Baum, Paula Hyman, and Sonya Michel, *The Jewish Woman in America*, p. 197.

19 Referring to cutting and pressing. See International Ladies' Garment Workers' Union (ILGWU), Educational Department, *The Story of the ILGWU*, p. 21.

20 *Résultats statistiques du recensement des industries et professions* (1896), tome I (Paris: Imprimerie nationale, 1899), pp. 232, 246.

21 *Résultats statistiques du recensement général de la population* (1921), tome II (Paris: Imprimerie Nationale, 1925), p. 1-5 (recapitulating 1906); idem (1926), tome III (Imprimerie Nationale, 1929), p. 3; idem (1936), tome II (Imprimerie Nationale, 1941), p. 3; idem (1962), no. 75: Seine (Imprimerie Nationale, 1966), p. 43; idem (1946), tome V, Tableaux pour le département de la Seine, p. 38; *Recensement de l'industrie 1963* (Résultats pour 1962), Série Structures, vol. 1, pp. 10–11 (Paris: Imprimerie Nationale, 1965). Cf. Joseph Klatzmann, *Le travail à domicile*, pp. 26–27.

22 Abbott, *Women in Industry*, p. 241; cf. p. 231; David Montgomery, *The Fall of the House of Labor*, p. 118; ILGWU, *Story*, pp. 21–23; Louis Levine, *The Women's Garment Workers*, p. 395; J. M. Budish and George Soule, *The New Unionism in the Clothing Industry*, pp. 25–27. For New York, derived from *Report of Manufacturing Industries in the United States, At the 11th Census, 1890*, pt. 2: *Statistics of Cities*, pp. 395–96.

23 Derived from *13th Census of the United States, vol. IV, Population 1910— Occupational Statistics*, pp. 572, 574; ibid., *14th Census* (1920), p. 192; ibid., *15th Census* (1930), pp. 1088, 1090. For ready-made dressmakers alone, men were as much as 45.2 percent of the workforce in 1930, although again, women's share increased sharply in the subsequent years of depression. See "Distribution of Male and Female Workers, Metropolitan Area, 1922, 1925, 1930, 1934," Dress Joint Board, 30:7, ILGWU Archives. In 1934, when women became a high 77.9 percent of the dressworkers in the New York City area, men remained 100 percent of the cutters and 80.1 percent of the pressers, but only 17.9 percent of the operators ("Distribution of Male and Female Workers in Metropolitan Area, by Crafts, 1934," ibid).

24 Florence S. Richards, *The Ready-to-Wear Industry, 1900–1950*, p. 19; Abbott, *Women in Industry*, p. 242; Levine, *Women's Garment Workers*, p. 396.

25 Madeleine Guilbert, cited in Louise A. Tilly and Joan W. Scott, *Women, Work and Family*, p. 197, see also pp. 152–53; Catherine Rhein, "Jeunes femmes au

travail dans le Paris de l'entre-deux-guerres," doctoral thesis, Université de Paris 7, 1977. See also Sylvie Zerner, "De la couture aux presses: L'emploi féminin entre les deux guerres," *Le Mouvement social*, no. 140 (July–Sept. 1987): 9–25, who, however, discounts garment work as not being industrial.

26 Baum, Hyman, and Michel, *Jewish Woman*, p. 146. The cutting knife, which permitted the cutting of several layers of cloth, replaced scissors, which could only cut through one thickness at a time.

27 Levine, *Women's Garment Workers*, app. I, table X, p. 521.

28 Klatzmann, *Travail à domicile*, pp. 29, 81. Although some 60 percent of the total garment industry *patrons* were women in 1946, 77.6 percent of the foreign-born *patrons* in Paris were men. Similarly, whereas 83.5 percent of the total Parisian garment workers (*employés, ouvriers* and *cadres inférieurs*) were women, only 52.6 percent of the foreign-born workers were; there were approximately 5,500 foreign male garment workers (ibid., p. 80). Note that Klatzmann was more concerned about homeworking among male breadwinners than among women, for whom he sees it, classically, as a "travail d'appoint" (p. 99). He also debunks the notion of liberty and independence, however (passim).

29 Nathan Belfer, "Section Work in the Women's Garment Industry," *The Southern Economic Journal* 21, no. 2 (Oct. 1954): 192–93; Larry Smith and Company, *Garment District Study*, 2 vols., 2:33.

30 In 1970, 20.6 percent of the cutting operatives and 34.7 percent of the pressers in the New York metropolitan area were women. See *1970 Census of Population*, vol. 1, *Characteristics of the Population*, pt. 34, *New York*, sec. 2, p. 34–917; Kenan Ozturk, "Les Turcs dans la confection à Paris," *Hommes et migrations*, no. 1116 (Nov. 1988): 22–28. By one estimate, there may be up to 40 percent men working in the Los Angeles garment industry today. See James Loucky et al., "Immigrant Enterprise and Labor in the Los Angeles Garment Industry," in *Global Production*, ed. Edna Bonacich et al., p. 352.

31 Solange Montagné-Villette, *Le Sentier, Un espace ambigu*, p. 74. Mirjana Morokvasic found that 91.1 percent of the Turkish, 82.9 percent of the Tunisian, and 46.9 percent of the Yugoslavian garment workers whose situations were regularized in 1981–83 were men. She notes, however, that women were surely seriously underrepresented in the procedure. See Mirjana Morokvasic, "Le Recours aux immigrés dans la confection à Paris: Eléments de comparaison avec la ville de Berlin-Ouest," report, Ministère du travail et de la formation professionnelle: Mission de liaison interministérielle pour la lutte contre les trafics de main-d'oeuvre, 1986, pp. 14, 16, 30–31; Riva Kastoryano, *Etre turc en France*, p. 132.

32 Willett, *Employment of Women*, pp. 53, 65–67. One American unionist was surprised to find that in the English dress industry there were many more female cutters (4,477) than male (2,452), whereas in the United States all cutters were men (Abe Weiss, "Garment Workers of Other Lands," typescript, p. 15, Fania Cohn Series, 11:1, ILGWU Archives).

33 *Rapports sur l'application pendant l'année 1907 des lois réglementant le travail* (Paris: Imprimerie nationale, 1908), p. 3.

34 Montagné-Villette, *Le Sentier,* p. 91.

35 New York State Department of Labor, *2d Annual Report* (1902), 2:88.

36 *New York Times,* February 6, 1995; e.g., Aristide Zolberg, "International Migrations in Political Perspective," in *Global Trends in Migration: Theory and Research on International Population Movements,* ed. Mary M. Kritz et al., pp. 3–27.

37 Michael J. Piore, *Birds of Passage: Migrant Labor and Industrial Societies;* Waldinger, *Through the Eye of the Needle,* pp. 5–9; Mirjana Morokvasic, Roger Waldinger, and Annie Phizacklea, "Business on the Ragged Edge: Immigrant and Minority Business in the Garment Industries of Paris, London, and New York," in *Ethnic Entrepreneurs,* ed. Waldinger, Aldrich, and Ward, pp. 157–76.

38 United States Immigration Commission, *Reports of the Immigration Commission,* 42 vols., vol. 11, pt. 6, comparing New York City, Chicago, and Baltimore; Robert Parmet, *Labor and Immigration in Industrial America* (New York: Twayne, 1981), p. 215, note 51; Robert Wechsler, "The Jewish Garment Trade in East London 1875–1914," Ph.D. diss., Columbia University, 1979; Schmiechen, *Sweated Industries;* Annie Phizacklea, *Unpacking the Fashion Industry;* Anne Kershen, *Uniting the Tailors;* Loucky, "Los Angeles Garment Industry."

39 Donna Gabaccia, "Immigrant Women: Nowhere at Home?" *Journal of American Ethnic History* 10 (Summer 1991): 61–87; Mirjana Morokvasic, "Birds of Passage Are Also Women. . . . ," *International Migration Review* 18, no. 4 (Winter 1984): 886–907; Annie Phizacklea, ed., *One Way Ticket: Migration and Female Labour.* Several recent monographs include Hasia R. Diner, *Erin's Daughters in America: Irish Immigrant Women in the Nineteenth Century* (Baltimore: Johns Hopkins University Press, 1983); Elizabeth Ewen, *Immigrant Women in the Land of Dollars: Life and Culture on the Lower East Side, 1890–1925;* Glenn, *Daughters of the Shtetl;* Cohen, *Workshop to Office.* For the importance of women in the international migration streams, see Marion F. Houston, Roger G. Kramer, and Joan M. Barrett, "Female Predominance of Immigration to the United States Since 1930: A First Look," *International Migration Review* 18, no. 4 (Winter 1984): 908–63; Donna Gabaccia, *From the Other Side: Women, Gender and Immigrant Life in the U.S., 1820–1990.*

40 Morokvasic, Phizacklea, and Rudolph have even postulated that it is gender oppression within the ethnic group which has permitted the ethnic businessman to be successful. See Mirjana Morokvasic, Annie Phizacklea, and Hedwig Rudolph, "Small Firms and Minority Groups: Contradictory Trends in the French, German and British Clothing Industries," *International Sociology* 1, no. 4 (Dec. 1986): 407.

41 Phizacklea, ed., *One Way Ticket,* p. 108; idem, *Unpacking.*

42 Morokvasic, "Birds of Passage"; idem, "Immigrants in Garment Production in Paris and in Berlin," in *Immigration and Entrepreneurship,* ed. Ivan Light and Parminder Bhachu, p. 88; idem, "Immigrants in the Parisian Garment Industry," *Work, Employment and Society* 1, no. 4 (1987): 452–53 (on the different meanings of homework for men and women); Benería and Roldán, *Crossroads.*

43 Alice Kessler-Harris, "Organizing the Unorganizable: Three Jewish Women and Their Union," in *Class, Sex, and the Woman Worker,* ed. Milton Cantor and Bruce Laurie, pp. 144–65; and idem, "Problems of Coalition-Building: Women and Trade Unions in the 1920s," in *Women, Work and Protest,* ed. Ruth Milkman, pp. 110–38. See also Rose Pesotta's memoirs, *Bread upon the Waters;* Annelise Orelick, *Common Sense and a Little Fire: Women and Working-Class Politics in the United States, 1900–1965;* and Ann Schofield, *"To Do and to Be": Ladies, Immigrants, and Workers, 1893–1986.*

44 Glenn, *Daughters of the Shtetl.*

45 Thomas Kessner and Betty Boyd Caroli, "New Immigrant Women at Work: Italians and Jews in New York City, 1880–1905," *Journal of Ethnic Studies* 5, no. 4 (Winter 1978): 19–31.

46 Whether this is a "traditional" cultural concept is debatable. Both in Eastern Europe and in Southern Italy, married women had important roles within the family economy. Is it possible that emigration raised the global family wage, permitting a new "cultural tradition" to emerge? Cf., for example, Virginia Yans-McLaughlin, *Family and Community: Italian Immigrants in Buffalo, 1880–1930;* and John W. Briggs' critique, "Fertility and Cultural Change among Families in Italy and America," *American Historical Review* 91 (Dec. 1986): 1129–45; and Cohen, *Workshop to Office,* esp. pp. 7, 53, 68, 80.

47 Ewen, *Immigrant Women.* See my discussion of different comparative strategies in Nancy L. Green, "L'histoire comparative et le champ des études migratoires," *Annales E.S.C.,* no. 6 (Nov.–Dec. 1990): 1335–50.

48 Cohen, *Workshop to Office,* p. 93. And she has made an important methodological point: the citywide differences analyzed by Kessner and others look more similar at the neighborhood level (Miriam Cohen, "From Workshop to Office: Italian Women and Family Strategies in New York City, 1900–1950," Ph.D. diss., University of Michigan, 1978, pp. 91, 96).

49 Jesse Pope, *The Clothing Industry in New York,* p. 66; Anna Bezanson, "Skill," *Quarterly Journal of Economics* 36, no. 4 (Aug. 1922): 626–45; Phillips and Taylor, "Sex and Skill," p. 79.

50 Office du Travail, *Associations professionnelles ouvrières,* vol. 2: *Cuirs et peaux, Industries textiles, habillement, ameublement, travail du bois,* p. 658. On the notion of "bloc socio-technologique" see Pierre Bouvier, *Le Travail au quotidien: Une démarche socio-anthropologique.*

51 Scott, "Men and Women"; Johnson, "Economic Change"; Coffin, "Woman's Place"; Joan Jensen and Sue Davidson, eds., *A Needle, a Bobbin, a Strike: Women Needleworkers in America;* cf. Jacques Rancière, "The Myth of the Artisan: Critical Reflections on a Category of Social History," *International Labor and Working-Class History,* no. 24 (Fall 1983): 1–16, and subsequent debate in ibid., 17–25, and no. 25 (Spring 1984): 37–46.

52 United States Industrial Commission, *Reports of the Industrial Commission,* 19 vols., 15:318.

53 Especially because the dressmakers were less skilled, mostly women, and the target of Communist influence. Most male cloakmakers who shifted to

dresses at that time saw the move as only temporary. ILGWU, *Report of the General Executive Board* (19th Convention, 1928), pp. 258–60; ILGWU, *Record of the 19th Convention* (1928), pp. 171–72. See also Jesse Thomas Carpenter, *Competition and Collective Bargaining in the Needle Trades, 1910–1967,* p. 125.

54 Louise Odencrantz, *Italian Women in Industry: A Study of Conditions in New York City,* p. 62; Levine, *Women's Garment Workers,* p. 528.

55 Irving R. Stuart, "A Study of Factors Associated with Inter-Group Conflict in the Ladies' Garment Industry in New York City," Ph.D. diss., New York University, 1951, pp. 113–15, citing U.S. Department of Labor, *Earning in the Women and Children's Apparel Industry.*

56 Cited in Organisation internationale du travail, *Réunion technique tripartite pour l'industrie du vêtement* (1964), 1:70. Of the total, 89.5 percent of the workers were women, although men were over-represented in the more skilled categories.

57 "Jewish DPs in the Occupied Territories," memo from Lazare Teper to David Dubinsky, Sept. 29, 1947, Dubinsky Series, 151:2a and 2b, ILGWU Archives; Emil Schlesinger (ILGWU lawyer) to Allen Devaney, Esq., (U.S. Immigration Office), Oct. 15, 1947, ibid.; Umhey 8:4, ibid. Only in 1955 did the most highly skilled, almost entirely white, Jewish and Italian cutters' Local 10 (finally) set up grading classes "to replenish losses from death or retirement." See draft memo under cover letter, Dec. 27, 1966, Local 10 Series 32/10/11, 7:2; "Local 10 Summary of Conditions and Activities, May–Oct. 1958," cover letter, July 29, 1959, ibid.

58 On the need for skilled workers, see Charles S. Goodman, *The Location of Fashion Industries, with Special Reference to the California Apparel Market,* pp. 72–73; *New York Times,* Aug. 2, 1953, reporting on the continuing skill crisis in custom men's wear; and Clothing Manufacturers' Association of the U.S.A., *A Statement, Indicating the Economic Status of Our Industry and Its Importance in Times of Peace and in National Emergency,* dealing specifically with men's wear.

59 *Daily News Record,* Aug. 3, 1953.

60 Thomas Bailey and Roger Waldinger, "Primary, Secondary, and Enclave Labor Markets: A Training Systems Approach," *American Sociological Review* 56 (Aug. 1991): 432–45 (listed jobs are necessarily more skilled ones); Waldinger, *Through the Eye of the Needle,* pp. 151–53; Waldinger and Michael Lapp, "Immigrants and Their Impact on the New York Garment Industry," unpublished, Nov. 1988; Waldinger and Lapp, "Back to the Sweatshop or Ahead to the Informal Sector?" *International Journal of Urban and Regional Research* 17, no. 1 (1993): 6–29; Mrs. Eisner, New York State Apparel Employment Service, interview, Aug. 6, 1984.

61 Harold Siegel, Greater Blouse, Skirt and Undergarment (contractors') Association, interview, New York, Aug. 22, 1984.

62 Angela Coyle, "Sex and Skill in the Organization of the Clothing Industry," in *Work, Women and the Labour Market,* ed. Jackie West, p. 15. Elaine Wrong

commented, "What is considered craft work in this industry would be categorized semiskilled in many others" (*The Negro in the Apparel Industry*, p. 73).

63 Laura Lee Downs, *Manufacturing Inequality*, chap. 3 and 6. Stuart's 1940s study showed that vocational training did not have that much effect on black and Puerto Rican hiring in the dress industry; they were still only hired at the semiskilled level and only got into higher-skilled crafts if they had friends or relatives (Stuart, "Inter-Group Conflict," p. 170; cf. Wrong, *Negro in Apparel*, pp. 107–15 on on-the-job training).

64 Nathan Brown (Principal, HSFI) to Luigi Antonini (Local 89), Mar. 12, 1957, Antonini Series 24:15, ILGWU Archives; for Local 22, see ILGWU, Zimmerman 7:6. Children whose parents were in the industry got special consideration (Michael Katzoff [HSFI] to Gus Tyler [ILGWU], Nov. 16, 1962, Tyler 11:12, ibid).

65 Hillsman, "Entry into the Labor Market," p. 102.

66 Agenda for Annual Meeting of Fashion Crafts Educational Commission, June 24, 1969, Tyler 11:12, ILGWU Archives. On "defecting" see Hillsman, "Entry into the Labor Market," pp. 174, 241, 298. This was especially true for those (more white than black or Hispanic) students in the better tracks ("elite" Fashion Design students).

67 Saul F. Baily (Principal, HSFI) to Henoch Mendelsund (ILGWU), Mar. 27, 1973, Cloak Joint 10:6, ILGWU; interview with Mr. Halperin and Mr. Baily, HSFI, New York, July 25, 1984; telephone interview, Mr. Halperin, Nov. 3, 1995. Originally set up to train machine operatives, HSFI now trains more skilled samplemakers, cutters, and salespeople.

68 Mr. Halperin, interview, HSFI, New York, July 25, 1984; cf. Hillsman, "Entry into the Labor Market," p. 51.

69 Typed note on the history of the HSFI, Nov. 23, 1956, Cloak Joint 10:6, ILGWU Archives; Patrick Hennessey, telephone interview, June 30, 1995.

70 Organisation internationale du travail, *Réunion tripartite* (1964), 1:107–40.

71 Cited in Odencrantz, *Italian Women*, p. 41. See also Glenn, *Daughters of the Shtetl*, pp. 98–103.

72 Roger Ikor, *Les fils d'Avrom: Les eaux mêlées* (Paris: Albin Michel, 1955), pp. 159, 161.

73 James Oneal, *A History of the Amalgamated Ladies' Garment Cutters' Union Local 10*, p. 149. Cf. Odencrantz, *Italian Women*, pp. 61–62, 37. Virginia Yans-McLaughlin, "Italian Women and Work: Experience and Perception," in *Class, Sex, and the Woman Worker*, ed. Milton Cantor and Bruce Laurie, pp. 101–19; Ana Juarbe, "'Nosotras Trabajamos en la costura. . . .' Puerto Rican Women in the Garment Industry," *Newsletter of the Centro de Estudio Puertorriquenos* (Feb. 1984): 3–6.

74 John Bodnar, "Immigration, Kinship, and the Rise of Working-Class Realism in Industrial America," *Journal of Social History* 14 (Fall 1980): 50–51. Immigrant historians such as John Briggs, *An Italian Passage: Immigrants to Three American Cities, 1890–1930* (New Haven: Yale University Press, 1978),

and Josef Barton, *Peasants and Strangers: Italians, Rumanians and Slovaks in an American City, 1890–1950* (Cambridge: Harvard University Press, 1975), have debated how immigrants' prior occupational experiences influenced the kinds of jobs they took. See also Edward P. Hutchinson, *Immigrants and their Children, 1850–1950*, pp. 64–65.

75 Glenn, *Daughters of the Shtetl*, p. 49.

76 These figures are for Baltimore, Chicago, and New York City combined. For New York alone, the only figures given are for male employees: 63.3 percent of the Russian Hebrew and 66.8 percent of the Southern Italian men (more than in the other cities) were previously engaged in clothing manufacture before migrating (*Immigration Commission*, 11:375–76, 286–87).

77 U.S. Department of Labor, Bulletin of the Bureau of Labor Statistics, no. 147, *Wages and Regularity of Employment in the Cloak, Suit, and Skirt Industry* (Washington: GPO, 1915), p. 159.

78 New York State Bureau of Factory Inspectors, *7th Annual Report* (1892), p. 10.

79 Samuel Joseph, *Jewish Immigration to the United States from 1880 to 1910* [1914] (New York: Arno, 1969), pp. 140–42.

80 Odencrantz, *Italian Women*, pp. 314, 60; Kastoryano, *Etre turc en France*, p. 182.

81 If Dubinsky's cutters' skills were thus acquired in the U.S., one could argue that his union skills were imported. See also City College Oral History Research Project, "New York City Immigrant Labor Oral History Collection," Tamiment Library, I-105.

82 Foerster, *Italian Emigration of Our Times*, pp. 347–49.

83 Odencrantz, *Italian Women*, p. 44.

84 Mirjana Morokvasic, "Le Comportement économique des immigrés dans le secteur de la confection," paper given at GRECO conference on "Mutations économiques et travailleurs immigrés dans des pays industriels," Vaucresson, Jan. 28–30, 1988.

85 Actually a French Jew of Moroccan origin (*Actuel*, April 1988). See also Edwin Fenton, *Immigrants and the Union, A Case Study*, pp. 467–68; Nancy L. Green et al., "Les quartiers parisiens de l'industrie de l'habillement et les relations pluri-ethniques," report, Ministère de la culture, MIRE, 1987, p. 174; Martine Hovanessian, *Le lien communautaire: Trois générations d'Arméniens*, pp. 152–54; Roy Helfgott, "Puerto Rican Integration in the Skirt Industry in New York City," in *Discrimination and Low Incomes*, ed. Aaron Antonovsky and Lewis Lorwin, pp. 272–73.

86 Abraham Bisno, *Abraham Bisno: Union Pioneer* (Madison: University of Wisconsin Press, 1967), p. 37; Odencrantz, *Italian Women*, pp. 265–67; Yinh Phong Tan, "Restaurants et ateliers: Le travail des Sino-khmers à Paris," *ASEMI* 15 (1984): 283.

87 Anahide Ter Minassian, "Les Arméniens de France," *Les Temps modernes* 43 (July–Sept. 1988): 207; Tan, "Restaurants," pp. 282–83; Morokvasic, "Paris and Berlin," pp. 86–87.

88 Willett, *Employment of Women*, p. 110; Stuart, "Inter-Group Conflict," pp. 168–71; Michel K., interview, Bourse du Travail, Paris, May 15, 1986.

89 Mrs. Eisner, interview, Aug. 6, 1984.

90 E.g., L. Delpon De Vissec, "De la distribution du travail à domicile dans l'industrie de la confection parisienne," *Mémoires et documents du Musée social* 5 (Mar. 1908): 93; Eileen Boris, *Home to Work;* Carol Joan Smith, "Women, Work, and Use of Government Benefits: A Case Study of Hispanic Women Workers in New York's Garment Industry," Ph.D. diss., Adelphi University, 1980.

91 Madeleine Guilbert and Viviane Isambert-Jamati, *Travail féminin et travail à domicile*, chap. 7; see also pp. 119–24, 127; and Perrot, "Femmes et machines."

92 Guilbert and Isambert-Jamati, *Travail féminin*, p. 199.

93 *Libération*, Apr. 22, 1987.

94 Waldinger, *Through the Eye of the Needle*, pp. 169–79.

95 Patricia Pessar, "The Dominicans: Women in the Household and the Garment Industry," in *New Immigrants in New York*, ed. Nancy Foner, pp. 103–29; Morrison G. Wong, "Chinese Sweatshops in the United States: A Look at the Garment Industry," in *Research in the Sociology of Work*, ed. Ida Simpson and Richard Simpson, p. 368.

96 Morokvasic, Phizacklea, and Rudolph, "Small Firms."

97 John R. Commons, *Races and Immigrants in America* (New York: Macmillan, 1907), p. 133; Beatrice Webb, "How to Do Away with the Sweating System," in *Problems of Modern Industry*, ed. Sidney and Beatrice Webb, p. 143, note 1. Cf. Schmiechen, *Sweated Industries*.

98 Abbott, *Women in Industry*, p. 216.

99 Ruth Milkman, "Gender and Trade Unionism in Historical Perspective," in *Women, Politics, and Change*, ed. Louise Tilly and Patricia Gurin, pp. 87–107.

100 Joy Parr, "Disaggregating the Sexual Division of Labour: A Transatlantic Case Study," *Comparative Studies in Society and History* 30 (July 1988): 532; Parr, *The Gender of Breadwinners*.

7 "An Industry of Passage": *The Immigrant Waves*

1 Henoch Mendelsund, ILGWU, interview, New York, Sept. 4, 1984.

2 United States Industrial Commission, *Reports of the Industrial Commission*, 19 vols., 15:343.

3 Mabel Hurd Willett, *The Employment of Women in the Clothing Trade*, p. 33.

4 Ibid., p. 35.

5 *Industrial Commission*, 15:345; Judith Greenfeld, "The Role of the Jews in the Development of the Clothing Industry in the United States," *YIVO Annual of Jewish Social Sciences* 2–3 (1947–48): 193.

6 Charles Russell Richards, *Art in Industry*, p. 11; Louis Levine, *The Women's Garment Workers*, p. 170.

Notes to Pages 182–189

7 Willett, *Employment of Women*, p. 35; see also pp. 36–37, 75; Emile Levasseur, *L'ouvrier américain*, 2 vols., 1:430.

8 *Industrial Commission*, 15:346–47; see also 19:326–27.

9 Ben Morris Selekman, Henriette R. Walter, and W. J. Couper, *The Clothing and Textile Industries in New York and Its Environs*, p. 19.

10 Jesse Pope, *The Clothing Industry in New York*, pp. 45, 6–7; Florence S. Richards, *The Ready-to-Wear Industry, 1900–1950*, p. 7; Robert Wechsler, "The Jewish Garment Trade in East London, 1875–1914," Ph.D. diss., Columbia University, 1979.

11 *Industrial Commission*, 15:346–47.

12 *Industrial Commission*, 15:325; see also United States Immigration Commission, *Reports of the Immigration Commission*, 42 vols., 11:370.

13 Henry Best, *The Men's Garment Industry of New York and the Strike of 1913* (New York: University Settlement Society, [1914]), pp. 5, 6; John R. Commons, *Races and Immigrants*, p. 133; Maurizio Lazzarato, Antonio Negri, and Giancarlo Santilli, "La confection dans le quartier du Sentier," report, Ministère du travail, de l'emploi et de la formation professionnelle, MIRE, 1990, p. 166. See also Maurizio Lazzarato et al., *Des entreprises pas comme les autres*.

14 Michel Roblin, *Les Juifs de Paris*, p. 115.

15 Isaac Hourwich, *Immigration and Labor*, p. 25; adding that conditions had even improved compared to those of earlier women workers, ibid., pp. 363ff; Roblin, *Juifs de Paris*, p. 114.

16 *Industrial Commission*, 15:370–71.

17 Edith Abbott, *Women in Industry*, p. 217. On Abbott, cf. Wendy Sarvasy, "Beyond the Difference versus Equality Policy Debate: Postsuffrage Feminism, Citizenship and the Quest for a Feminist Welfare State," *Signs* 17, no. 2 (Winter 1992): 329–62.

18 *Industrial Commission*, 19:326–27.

19 The English and German were more skilled in men's wear. See Käthe Schirmacher, *La spécialisation du travail . . . Par nationalités, à Paris*, pp. 67, 142, 150–55.

20 Edwin Fenton, *Immigrants and the Union, A Case Study*, p. 466, an appraisal recently reaffirmed by Virginia Yans-McLaughlin, "Metaphors of Self in History: Subjectivity, Oral Narrative, and Immigration Studies," in *Immigration Reconsidered*, ed. Virginia Yans-McLaughlin, pp. 254–90; Pope, *Clothing Industry*, p. 54; New York State Bureau of Factory Inspectors, *14th Annual Report* (1899), p. 42.

21 *Industrial Commission*, 15:326.

22 E.g., Emanuel Federated Employment Service, "An Industrial Survey of the Needle Trades to Determine a Vocational Guidance Policy for Young Men of Jewish Descent with Regard to the Industry," p. 33. On Jewish and Italian women, see e.g., Miriam Cohen, *Workshop to Office*; Elizabeth Ewen, *Immigrant Women in the Land of Dollars*; Susan Glenn, *Daughters of the Shtetl*; Thomas Kessner and Betty Boyd Caroli, "New Immigrant Women at Work:

Italians and Jews in New York City, 1880–1905," *Journal of Ethnic Studies* 5 (Winter 1978): 19–31.

23 New York State Bureau of Factory Inspectors, *12th Annual Report* (1897), p. 759; cf. *13th Annual Report* (1898), p. 789.

24 Emanuel Federated, "Industrial Survey," pp. 32, 15.

25 *Le Monde* subtitle, June 11, 1985. *Travail noir* is the term for illegal work in French; the *filière jaune* or literally yellow network has been used somewhat pejoratively to describe the Chinese contractors.

26 Min Zhou, *Chinatown;* Peter Kwong, *The New Chinatown;* Michelle Guillon and Isabel Taboada-Leonetti, *Le Triangle de Choisy: Un quartier chinois à Paris,* pp. 170–92. See also Jacqueline Costa-Lascoux and Live Yu-Sion, *Paris-XIIIe, Lumières d'Asie,* pp. 138–55; and Live Yu-Sion, "La Diaspora chinoise en France," doctoral thesis, Ecole des Hautes Etudes en Sciences Sociales, 1991.

27 Solange Montagné-Villette, *Le Sentier, Un espace ambigu,* p. 96. On the "taxi" companies which issue false invoices and facilitate an elaborate system of fake pay slips and tax evasion, see ibid., pt. 2; Mission de liaison inter-ministérielle pour la lutte contre les trafics de main-d'oeuvre, *Bilan de la lutte contre le trafic de main-d'oeuvre 1984–1985,* pp. 147–63; Guy Delorme, *Profession: Travailleur au noir* (Paris: Ouest-France, 1986), pp. 107–9; Mirjana Morokvasic, "Immigrants in the Parisian Garment Industry," *Work, Employment and Society* 1 (1987): 456–59.

28 For these different stories, see: *Le Monde,* June 11, and Oct. 3, 1985, and Jan. 29, 1986; *Actuel* (Paris), Apr. 1988.

29 Paul White, Hilary Winchester, and Michelle Guillon, "South-East Asian Refugees in Paris," *Ethnic and Racial Relations* 10, no. 1 (Jan. 1987): 51.

30 All cited in Catherine Flé, "L'insertion professionelle des réfugiés du Sud-est asiatique," Diplôme d'études approfondies, Université de Paris 7, 1985, p. 28; *Magazine Hebdo,* Nov. 30, 1984; *Le Monde,* Jan. 8–9, 1984; *Le Figaro,* Dec. 30, 1983; *La fureur du rat,* roman policier par A. Gautie, 1984.

31 *Le Monde,* June 11, 1985, and Oct. 5–6, 1986.

32 Lazzaratto et al., "Confection dans le Sentier," p. 171, see also pp. 168–69.

33 Pope, *Clothing Industry,* pp. 47–48.

34 Cited in J. M. Budish and George Soule, *The New Unionism in the Clothing Industry,* p. 61.

35 *Libération,* Apr. 22, 1987.

36 *Industrial Commission,* 15:357.

37 Martine Hovanessian, *Le lien communautaire: Trois générations d'Arméniens,* pp. 141–44, 213.

38 *Industrial Commission,* 15:346–47. This sentence is the second ellipsis in the quote on "queer cooperative production" above. See also Jacob Riis, *How the Other Half Lives* (New York: Charles Scribner's Sons, 1890), p. 80.

39 On macromigration waves, see e.g., Aristide R. Zolberg, "International Migration Policies in a Changing World System," in *Human Migration,* ed.

Notes to Pages 194–199

William H. McNeill and Ruth S. Adams, pp. 241–86; idem, "International Migrations in Political Perspective," in *Global Trends in Migration: Theory and Research on International Population Movements*, ed. Mary M. Kritz et al., pp. 3–27; Leslie Page Moch, *Moving Europeans: Migration in Western Europe since 1650* (Bloomington: Indiana University Press, 1992); Michael R. Marrus, *The Unwanted: European Refugees in the Twentieth Century* (New York: Oxford University Press, 1985). See also Ellen Percy Kraly, "U.S. Immigration Policy and the Immigrant Populations of New York," in *New Immigrants in New York*, ed. Nancy Foner, pp. 35–78.

40 For some recent overviews of immigration to the United States, see Thomas Archdeacon, "Problems and Possibilities in the Study of American Immigration and Ethnic History," *International Migration Review* 19 (1985): 112–34; John Bodnar, *The Transplanted: A History of Immigrants in Urban America;* Roger Daniels, *Coming to America: A History of Immigration and Ethnicity in American Life;* Nancy L. Green, *Et ils peuplèrent l'Amérique: L'odyssée des émigrants* (Paris: Gallimard, 1994). France was the only European country after 1850 to import instead of export labor. By 1931, France had more immigrants percentage-wise than the United States. See Gary S. Cross, *Immigrant Workers in Industrial France;* Yves Lequin, ed., *La mosaïque France: Histoire des étrangers et de l'immigration;* Gérard Noiriel, *Le creuset français: Histoire de l'immigration XIXe–XXe siècles.* For some comparative approaches, see Donald Horowitz and Gérard Noiriel, eds. *Immigrants in Two Democracies;* and Nancy L. Green, "L'immigration en France et aux Etats-Unis, Historiographie comparée," *Vingtième siècle,* no. 29 (Jan.–Mar. 1991), pp. 67–82.

41 Cf. Patrick Simon, "Nommer pour Agir," *Le Monde,* Apr. 28, 1993, and Dominique Schnapper, *La communauté des citoyens.* See E. P. Hutchinson's lament and critique of the statistics problem, *Immigrants and Their Children, 1850–1950,* pp. 70–77.

42 Egal Feldman, *Fit for All Men* (New York: Public Affairs Press, 1960), p. 95; cf. Richard B. Stott, *Workers in the Metropolis,* p. 92.

43 *Immigration Commission,* 11:271; Joel Seidman, *The Needle Trades,* p. 31; Pope, *Clothing Industry,* p. 27.

44 Willett, *Employment of Women,* p. 69; Budish and Soule, *New Unionism,* p. 48. Pope argued that the better class of Irish and Germans were pushed "up" (into department stores, offices) rather than "out" by Jews (Pope, *Clothing Industry,* pp. 51–53). On German Jews in the United States, see, e.g., Naomi W. Cohen, *Encounter with Emancipation: The German Jews in the United States, 1830–1914* (Philadelphia: Jewish Publication Society, 1984); and Avraham Barkai, *Branching Out: German-Jewish Immigration to the United States, 1820–1914* (New York: Holmes and Meier, 1994).

45 Levine, *Women's Garment Workers,* p. 9.

46 Roy B. Helfgott, "Women's and Children's Apparel," in *Made in New York,* ed. Hall, p. 48.

47 Ibid., p. 93; Greenfeld, "Role of the Jews," p. 203; Levine, *Women's Garment Workers,* pp. 169–70; Arthur Liebman, *Jews and the Left.* There has been

Notes to Pages 199–202

a flourishing of literature on Eastern European Jews in New York City ever since Irving Howe, *World of Our Fathers* (New York: Simon and Schuster, 1976). But see also Moses Rischin's earlier *The Promised City: New York's Jews, 1870–1914.*

48 Helen Everett Meiklejohn, "Dresses—The Impact of Fashion on a Business," in *Price and Price Policies,* ed. Walton Hamilton, p. 354. On Italians in New York City, see, e.g.: Miriam Cohen, *Workshop to Office;* Robert F. Foerster, *The Italian Emigration of our Times;* Donna Gabaccia, *From Sicily to Elizabeth Street: Housing and Social Change among Italian Immigrants, 1880–1930;* Robert Orsi, *The Madonna of 115th St.: Faith and Community in Italian Harlem, 1880–1950* (New Haven: Yale University Press, 1985).

49 Fenton, *Italians and American Labor,* p. 467; Levine, *Women's Garment Workers,* pp. 99, 172; Irving R. Stuart, "A Study of Factors Associated with Inter-Group Conflict in the Ladies' Garment Industry in New York City," Ph.D. diss., New York University, 1951, p. 103; Pope, *Clothing Industry,* p. 54; John Stuart Crawford, *Luigi Antonini: His Influence on Italian-American Relations,* p. 15; J. B. S. Hardman, "Needle Trades in U.S.," *Social Research* 27 (Autumn 1960): 333; Dubinsky estimate is cited by Humbert S. Nelli, "The Economic Activities of Italian Americans," in *Ethnicity and the Work Force,* ed. Winston Van Horne (Madison: University of Wisconsin System, 1985), p. 203.

50 Levine, *Women's Garment Workers,* p. 149; Theresa Serber Malkiel, *The Diary of a Shirtwaist Striker,* ed. Françoise Basch. In addition to works on Jewish and Italian women in New York City mentioned above, see, more generally, Ronald H. Bayor, *Neighbors in Conflict: The Irish, Germans, Jews, and Italians of New York City, 1929–1941;* Rudolf Glanz, *Jew and Italian: Historic Group Relations and the New Immigration, 1881–1924* (New York: Shulsinger Bros., Inc., 1971); Nathan Glazer and Daniel Patrick Moynihan, *Beyond the Melting Pot: The Negroes, Puerto Ricans, Jews, Italians and Irish of New York City;* Thomas Kessner, *The Golden Door: Italian and Jewish Immigrant Mobility in New York City, 1880–1915.*

51 See esp. Miriam Cohen, *Workshop to Office;* and Gabaccia, *Elizabeth Street;* along with Robert Laurentz, "Racial/Ethnic Conflict in the New York City Garment Industry, 1933–1980," Ph.D. diss., SUNY-Binghamton, 1980, p. 133; and Fenton, *Italians and American Labor,* p. 501.

52 Of the 20,000 licenses for homework granted by the City of New York in 1900, approximately 95 percent were held by Italians, mostly home finishers. See *Industrial Commission,* 15:369; Gabaccia, *Elizabeth Street,* pp. 63–64; Fenton, *Italians and American Labor,* p. 468; Ruth Shallcross, *Industrial Homework,* pp. 27–28; International Ladies' Garment Workers' Union (ILGWU), *Record of the 15th Convention* (1920), p. 39.

53 Hutchinson, *Immigrants and their Children,* pp. 84, 103–5, 128–31, 139–49, 163, 172–75, 178–96, 226–27, 230–31, 234–35, 238–39; Miriam Cohen, "From Workshop to Office: Italian Women and Family Strategies in New York City, 1900–1950," Ph.D. diss., University of Michigan, 1978, p. 80; idem, *Workshop to Office.*

54 ILGWU, *Record of the 12th Convention* (1914), p. 195; ibid., *14th Convention* (1918), p. 97; ILGWU, *Report of the General Executive Board* (19th Convention, 1928), p. 251; Max Danish, *The World of David Dubinsky*, p. 298; Seidman, *Needle Trades*, p. 32; Budish and Soule, *New Unionism*, p. 47; Anthony Sciuto, ILGWU manager, interview, New York, Sept. 10, 1984.

55 Certain locals—9 (hand finishers), 35 (pressers), and 117 (children's-wear machine operators)—remained predominantly Jewish into the late 1950s (Seidman, *Needle Trades*, p. 43; Helfgott, "Women's and Children's Apparel," p. 94).

56 Joseph Brandes, "From Sweatshop to Stability: Jewish Labor between Two World Wars," *YIVO Annual* 16 (1976): 105; cf. Stuart, "Inter-Group Conflict," p. 139; and Will Herberg, "The Old-timers and the Newcomers: Ethnic Group Relations in a Needle Trades Union," *Journal of Social Issues* 9 (1953): 13.

57 Stuart, "Inter-Group Conflict," p. 140; Danish, *Dubinsky*, p. 298; *New York Herald Tribune*, Oct. 3, 1958.

58 Peter Braestrup, "Life Among Today's Garment Workers," *New York Herald Tribune*, Sept. 29, 1958. On the Great Migration of blacks from the South, and African American workers in New York City, see e.g.: Charles Lionel Franklin, *The Negro Labor Unionist of New York;* Florette Henri, *Black Migration Movement North, 1900–1920;* Daniel M. Johnson and Rex R. Campbell, *Black Migration in America: A Social Demographic History;* Carole Marks, *Farewell— We're Good and Gone: The Great Black Migration;* Sterling D. Spero and Abram L. Harris, *The Black Worker: The Negro and the Labor Movement;* and Charles Wesley, *Negro Labor in the United States, 1850–1925* (New York: Russell and Russell, 1927).

59 Cf. Roy Helfgott, "Puerto Rican Integration in the Skirt Industry in New York City," in *Discrimination and Low Incomes*, ed. Aaron Antonovsky and Lewis Lorwin, p. 269; and Stuart, "Inter-Group Conflict," p. 56; with Laurentz, "Racial/Ethnic Conflict." More generally, see e.g., Stanley Lieberson, *A Piece of the Pie: Blacks and White Immigrants since 1880;* Andrés Torres, *Between Melting Pot and Mosaic;* and Roger Waldinger, *Still the Promised City? New Immigrants and African-Americans in Post-Industrial New York.*

60 Waldinger, *Through the Eye of the Needle*, chap. 5.

61 Elaine Gale Wrong, *The Negro in the Apparel Industry*, p. 31, citing Greene and Woodson; see also Laurentz, "Racial/Ethnic Conflict," p. 92; Seidman, *Needle Trades*, p. 38; and Jack Hardy, *The Clothing Workers*, pp. 12, 20.

62 Franklin, *Negro Labor Unionist*, pp. 160–66.

63 *New York Herald Tribune*, Sept. 29, 1958. ILGWU officials estimated there to be approximately 30 to 40,000 Negroes and Puerto Ricans in the New York City locals, comprising about one-quarter of the membership (evaluated however at 200,000); blacks alone were estimated to be about 10,000; cf. ibid., Oct. 3, 1958; Brandes, "Sweatshop to Stability," p. 107; Danish, *Dubinsky*, p. 299. An earlier confidential ILGWU memo in 1952 estimated there to be 26,422 Puerto Ricans (13.4 percent) and 19,878 blacks (10.1 percent) among the New York City membership. Yet Puerto Ricans represented 53.7 percent of the skirtmakers; and Puerto Ricans and blacks constituted 42.6 and 32.5 percent respectively of the beltmakers (memorandum, Lazare Teper to President Dubinsky, Dec. 30, 1952, Dubinsky Series, Box 280, File 1C, ILGWU Archives, New York). In the early 1960s, Dubinsky counted 60,000 to 70,000 African Americans and Puerto Ricans (United States House of Representatives Committee on Education and Labor, *Investigation of Labor Irregularities and Discrimination in the Garment Industry*, p. 250).

64 NAACP Report, "Racial Discrimination and the ILGWU in New York City," Nov. 1962, pp. 3–4, 6–7, 9, 11, Zimmerman series, Box 26, File 9, ILGWU Archives. By comparison, there had only been 4.9 percent blacks in the union in 1935 (6,260 out of 128,275) (Franklin, *Negro Labor Unionist*, p. 162).

65 Laurentz, "Racial/Ethnic Conflict," pp. 187–88, and passim.

66 Wrong, *Negro in Apparel*, pp. 63–64; Helfgott, "Puerto Rican Integration"; Waldinger, *Through the Eye of the Needle*, pp. 109–22; and Waldinger, *Promised City?* chap. 5.

67 In addition to Helfgott, "Puerto Rican Integration," see: Lawrence Chenault, *The Puerto Rican Migrant in New York City;* Rose Goldsen, *The Puerto Rican Journey: New York's Newest Migrants;* Oscar Handlin, *The Newcomers: Negroes and Puerto Ricans in a Changing Metropolis;* Abram J. Jaffe, ed., *Puerto Rican Population of New York City* [1954] (New York: Arno Press, 1975); Virginia Sanchez Korrol, *From Colonia to Community: The History of Puerto Ricans in New York City, 1917–1948.*

68 Helfgott, "Puerto Rican Integration." By the end of 1955, there were some 45,000 Puerto Ricans (nearly all women) in the unionized New York women's wear garment shops (Danish, *Dubinsky*, p. 298). See also ILGWU, *Record of the 30th Convention* (1959), p. 478; "Study of Population Characteristics and Hospitalization Experience 1965," Cloak Joint Series, Box 37, File 2, table 5, ILGWU Archives; Carol Joan Smith, "Women, Work, and Use of Government Benefits: A Case Study of Hispanic Women Workers in New York's Garment Industry," Ph.D. diss., Adelphi University, 1980, pp. 55–56.

69 Roger Waldinger and Michael Lapp, "Immigrants and Their Impact on the New York Garment Industry," unpublished, 1988, pp. 5, 48; Waldinger, *Through the Eye of the Needle*, p. 167; Adriana Marshall, "New Immigrants in New York's Economy," in *New Immigrants in New York*, ed. Nancy Foner, pp. 79–101. See also New York State Department of Labor, "Report to the Governor and the Legislature on the Garment Manufacturing Industry and Industrial Homework," New York, 1982; and Patricia Pessar, "The Dominicans: Women in the Household and the Garment Industry," in Foner, ed., *New Immigrants*, pp. 103–29.

70 On Dominicans and Koreans in New York City, see, e.g.: Foner, ed., *New Immigrants;* Glenn Hendricks, *The Dominican Diaspora: From the Dominican Republic to New York City, Villagers in Transition;* Sherri Grasmuck and Patricia R. Pessar, *Between Two Islands: Dominican International Migration;* Illsoo Kim, *The New Urban Immigrants: Korean Immigrants in New York City.*

71 Abeles et al., *The Chinatown Garment Industry Study*, pp. 84–85; see also

pp. 22–25, 29. By 1980, there were 138,309 Chinese in the New York metropolitan area (ibid., p. 239). New York has thus superseded San Francisco as the largest Chinese community in the United States. See, e.g., Kwong, *New Chinatown;* Chalsa Loo and Paul Ong, "Slaying Demons with a Sewing Needle: Feminist Issues for Chinatown's Women," *Berkeley Journal of Sociology* 27 (1982): 77–87. Bernard Wong, *Chinatown: Economic Adaptation and Ethnic Identity of the Chinese;* Zhou, *Chinatown.*

72 Written statement submitted to the U.S. Commission on Civil Rights, cover letter, June 7, 1974, Louis Stulberg Series, Box 22, File 8, ILGWU Archives; Waldinger, *Through the Eye of the Needle,* pp. 3, 117, 148, 200; idem, "Tattered and Torn," p. 16; Abeles et al., *Chinatown Study,* pp. 1, 55; Bernard Wong, "New Immigrants in New York's Chinatown," in Nancy Foner, ed. *New Immigrants,* p. 266; *New York Times,* Nov. 9, 1993.

73 Schirmacher, *Spécialisation du travail,* p. 155. Her general point was to insist that immigrant workers were not competing unfairly with French workers. On Schirmacher's subsequent ideological itinerary, see Liliane Krips, "Comment passer du libéralisme au nationalisme *volkish* tout en restant féministe," in *Femmes, Nations, Europe,* ed. Marie-Claire Hoock-Demarle (Paris: Université de Paris 7, 1995), pp. 62–77.

74 Schirmacher, *Spécialisation du travail,* p. 71; cf. pp. 92, 67.

75 Ibid., pp. 15, 171–74. On these border migrants, see also Nancy L. Green, " 'Filling the Void': Immigration to France before World War I," in *Labor Migration in the Atlantic Economies,* ed. Dirk Hoerder; Hervé Le Bras, "Lieux et métiers des étrangers en France depuis 1851," *Vingtième siècle,* no. 7 (July– Sept. 1985): pp. 19–35. In the 1840s, approximately two-fifths of all tailors in Paris were immigrants (from Germany, Hungary, and Poland), although almost all of their workers were French women. See Louis Chevalier, *La formation de la population parisienne au XIXe siècle,* INED—Travaux et Documents 10 (Paris: PUF, 1950), p. 182; Christopher H. Johnson, "Economic Change and Artisan Discontent: The Tailors' History, 1800–48," in *Revolution and Reaction,* ed. Roger Price, p. 92. Faraut says those of foreign origin were two-thirds of the *ouvriers tailleurs* in 1848 (François Faraut, *Histoire de la Belle Jardinière,* pp. 28–29). See Daniel Roche, *La culture des apparences,* pp. 300–301, on provincial migrants who came to work for Parisian masters in the eighteenth century.

76 *L'Humanité* (Paris), July 22, 1913.

77 Speiser, *Kalendar* (Paris: n.p., 1910), pp. 78–80. For a comparative table of Jewish, Belgian, German, Italian, Swiss, and French occupations circa 1900, see Nancy L. Green, *The Pletzl of Paris,* p. 122. On immigrant Jews in Paris during this period, see also Paula Hyman, *From Dreyfus to Vichy: The Remaking of French Jewry;* and David Weinberg, *A Community on Trial: The Jews of Paris in the 1930s.*

78 *Passages* (Paris), Dec. 1988.

79 Joseph Klatzmann, *Le travail à domicile dans l'industrie parisienne du vêtement,* pp. 81–82; Michel Roblin, *Les Juifs de Paris,* pp. 99–100. On the Jew-

ish specialty in capmaking, see Green, *Pletzl of Paris,* pp. 134–36, 155–65; and Maurice Lauzel, *Ouvriers juifs de Paris: Les casquettiers* (Paris: Edouard Cornély et Cie., 1912).

80 Many more of the Sephardic Jews went into wholesaling and retailing of cloth and linens. However, some 11 to 12 percent of the women worked in *confection* in the interwar years (Annie Benveniste, *Le Bosphore à la Roquette: La communauté judéo-espagnole à Paris, 1914–1940,* pp. 111, 115, 117). On Spanish Jews and Armenians in Paris, see also Edgar Morin, *Vidal et les siens* (Paris: Seuil, 1989); Martine Hovanessian, *Le lien communautaire: Trois générations d'Arméniens;* and Nancy L. Green et al., "Les quartiers parisiens de l'industrie de l'habillement et les relations pluri-ethniques," report, Ministère de la culture, MIRE, 1987, chaps. 5 (by Annie Benveniste) and 6 (by Sandrine Tasmadjian). For a warm depiction of Jewish-Armenian solidarity, see Clément Lépidis' novel *L'Arménien* (Paris: Seuil, 1973).

81 Georges Mauco, *Les étrangers en France,* p. 300. Cf. Laurent Couder's calculation of 3,425 Italians (mostly women): Laurent Couder, "Les Italiens dans la région parisienne dans les années 1920," in *Les Italiens en France de 1914 à 1940,* ed. Pierre Milza, p. 508.

82 Reported in *L'Habillement* (Paris), no. 16 (1939). On Italians in Paris, see Marie-Claude Blanc-Chaléard, "Immigration et implantation des Italiens dans l'espace parisien," *La Trace,* no. 6 (Sept. 1992), p. 23; idem, "Les Italiens dans l'Est parisien des années 1880 aux années 1960," doctoral thesis, Institut d'Etudes Politiques, 1995; and Laurent Couder, "Les immigrés italiens dans la région parisienne pendant les années 1920," doctoral thesis, Institut d'Etudes Politiques, Paris, 1987.

83 Klatzmann, *Le travail à domicile,* p. 86.

84 Yet the Institut national de la statistique et des études économiques counted 2,700 firms in the neighborhood for 1986 (Green et al., "Quartiers parisiens," p. 107).

85 Armenians in nearby suburbs such as Alfortville specialize in ready-made cloth goods. See Hovanessian, *Lien communautaire,* esp. pp. 152–60, 208–13, 220–30; Green et al., "Quartiers parisiens," p. 172 and chap. 6 (by Sandrine Tasmadjian); and Nancy L. Green et al., "Les rapports habitat/travail dans l'industrie de l'habillement à Paris et dans sa banlieue," report, Ministère de l'équipement, du Logement, de l'aménagement du territoire et des transports (MELATT), 1988, chap. 5 (by Tasmadjian).

86 The Serbs constituted almost half of the Yugoslavs in France, whereas the majority of those who went to Germany were Croatians (Mladen Friganovic, Mirjana Morokvasic, Ivo Bauic, *Iz Jugoslavije na rad u Francusku* [Zagreb: Institut de Géographie de l'Université de Zagreb, 1972], pp. 75, 106). On the Yugoslavs, see Montagné-Villette, *Le Sentier,* p. 118; and Mirjana Morokvasic, "Le Recours aux immigrés dans la confection à Paris: Eléments de comparaison avec la ville de Berlin-Ouest," Ministère du travail et de la formation professionnelle: Mission de liaison interministérielle pour la lutte contre les trafics de main-d'oeuvre, 1986.

Notes to Pages 209–211

87 The French Office Nationale d'Immigration set up an office in Turkey in 1969. See Kenan Ozturk, "Les Turcs dans la confection à Paris," *Hommes et Migrations,* no. 1116 (Nov. 1988): 22–8; Green et al., "Habitat/travail," chap. 3 (by Ozturk); Riva Kastoryano, *Etre turc en France;* idem, "Paris-Berlin: Politiques d'immigration et modèles d'intégration," in *Les musulmans dans la société française,* ed. Rémy Leveau and Gilles Kepel (Paris: Presses de la Fondation Nationale des Sciences Politiques, 1988), pp. 141–69; Montagné-Villette, *Le Sentier,* pp. 117–18; Maryse Tripier, *L'Immigration dans la classe ouvrière française.*

88 Rosine Klatzmann, *Le travail noir* (Paris: PUF, 1982), pp. 29–30; *Le Monde,* Feb. 11, 1981; Kastoryano, *Etre turc en France,* pp. 128–32. Ultimately 207 Pakistanis were regularized (*Le Monde,* Aug. 5–6, 1984). Cf. Montagné-Villette, *Le Sentier,* p. 96; and Morokvasic, "Recours aux immigrés"; Roxanne Silberman, Jean-Pierre Garson, and Yann Moulier-Boutang, *Economie politique des migrations clandestines de main-d'oeuvre* (Paris: Publisud, 1986).

89 Guillon and Taboada, *Triangle de Choisy,* p. 133. See also Costa-Lascoux and Live, *Paris-XIIIe;* Emmanuel Ma Mung, "Logiques du travail clandestin des Chinois," in *Espaces et travail clandestins,* ed. Solange Montagné-Villette, pp. 99–106; Yinh Phong Tan, "Restaurants et ateliers: Le travail des Sinokhmers à Paris," *ASEMI* 15 (1984): 277–91; Green et al., "Habitat/travail," chap. 4 (by Tan); Michelle Guillon and Isabel Taboada-Leonetti, *Le Triangle de Choisy;* Anne Raulin, "Espaces marchands et concentrations urbaines minoritaires—La petite Asie de Paris," *Cahiers internationaux de sociologie* 85 (1988): 225–42; Jean-Pierre Hassoun and Y.-P. Tan, "Les Chinois de Paris, Minorité culturelle ou constellation ethnique," *Terrain,* no. 7 (Oct. 1986), pp. 34–44; White, Winchester, and Guillon, "South East Asian Refugees," p. 48.

90 White, Winchester, and Guillon, "South East Asian Refugees," p. 50, estimated in 1987 that there were 10,000 to 15,000. On the development of this neighborhood and its attraction for Chinese immigrants, see ibid., p. 52; and Guillon and Taboada, *Triangle de Choisy.* Costa-Lascoux and Live, *Paris-XIIIe,* pp. 27–30, stress that there are less than 6,000 Southeast Asian nationals living in the 13th *arrondissement* today but admit that this does not count naturalized citizens, who are numerous among the Chinese newcomers. Another recent study thus concludes that there are 35,000 Asians living in the 13th *arrondissement* today (*Le Monde,* June 7, 1995).

91 Lazzarato et al., "Confection dans le Sentier," pp. 168–69. See chap. 9 below.

92 Delorme, *Travailleur au noir,* pp. 100, 107.

93 *Le Monde,* Feb. 22, and Feb. 24–25, 1983; Aug. 5–6, 1984; Sept. 11–12, 1988; Green et al., "Quartiers parisiens," pp. 108–13, 130–33 (by Annie Benveniste and Vasoo Vuddamalay); Montagné-Villette, *Le Sentier,* pp. 118–20.

94 Chantal Beltz, "Une solution originale au problème de l'emploi clandestin:

la coopérative des débardeurs pakistanais du quartier du Sentier," in Mission de liaison interministérielle pour la lutte contre les trafics de main-d'oeuvre, *Bilan de la lutte contre les trafics de main-d'oeuvre* (Paris: Documentation Française, 1983), p. 121.

95 Lazzaratto et al., "Confection dans le Sentier," p. 173; Montagné-Villette, *Le Sentier,* p. 120.

96 On Mauritians in the Sentier, see Vasoodevan Vuddamalay, "Les mécanismes de structuration du mouvement migratoire mauricien en France," doctoral thesis, Ecole des Hautes Etudes en Sciences Sociales, 1993, pp. 334–55.

97 Morokvasic, "Recours aux immigrés," pp. 3, 6, 9, 11; Mirjana Morokvasic, Annie Phizacklea, and Hedwig Rudolph, "Small Firms and Minority Groups: Contradictory Trends in the French, German and British Clothing Industries," *International Sociology* 1 (Dec. 1986): 413; André Lebon, *Immigration et 7e Plan, Analyse économique* (Paris: Documentation Française, 1977), p. 79; Mirjana Morokvasic, "Le Comportement économique des immigrés dans le secteur de la confection," paper presented at G R E C O 13 conference, "Mutations économiques et travailleurs immigrés dans des pays industriels," January 28–30, 1988, Vaucresson. Cf. *Libération,* Apr. 12, 1996.

98 Waldinger, *Through the Eye of the Needle,* p. 116.

99 Saskia Sassen-Koob, "New York's Informal Economy," in *The Informal Economy: Studies in Advanced and Less Developed Countries,* ed. Alejandro Portes et al.; Saskia Sassen, *The Mobility of Labor and Capital.*

100 Abeles et al., *Chinatown Study,* p. 60. See also Green et al., "Quartiers parisiens," pp. 134–38.

101 Nancy L. Green, "L'histoire comparative et le champ des études migratoires," *Annales E.S.C.,* no. 6 (Nov.–Dec. 1990), pp. 1335–50.

102 Liang Tsong-Heng and Marie Holzman, *Chinois de Paris* (Paris: Editions Seghers, 1989), pp. 258–62; Abeles et al., *Chinatown Study,* pp. 53–54. The French term is actually named after a Lombard banker; the Chinese term *hui* for association is more often used elsewhere (Hassoun and Tan, "Les Chinois de Paris").

103 Tsong-Heng and Holzman, *Chinois de Paris,* pp. 242–45; Costa-Lascoux and Live, *Paris-XIIIe,* pp. 113, 148–49; Abeles et al., *Chinatown Study,* pp. 103–12; Kwong, *New Chinatown,* pp. 7, 13–14, 22–23; Bernard Wong, *Chinatown;* Zhou, *Chinatown,* p. xvii. On the more general debate over ghettos in France, see Sophie Body-Gendrot, *Ville et violence* (Paris: PUF, 1993); Véronique de Rudder, "Immigrant Housing and Integration in French Cities," in *Immigrants in Two Democracies: French and American Experience,* ed. Horowitz and Noiriel, pp. 247–67; Véronique de Rudder and Michèle Guillon, *Autochtones et immigrés en quartier populaire* (Paris: CIEMI L'Harmattan, 1987); and Loïc J. D. Wacquant, "Pour en finir avec le mythe des 'cité-ghettos': Les différences entre la France et les Etats-Unis," *Annales de la recherche urbaine* 52 (Sept. 1992): 20–30.

104 Liebman Hersch, *Le Juif errant d'aujourd'hui* (Paris: M. Giard et E. Brière, 1913), pp. 140–45; Miriam Cohen, "From Workshop to Office," p. 80; Roblin,

Juifs de Paris, pp. 110–12; derived from Chenault, *Puerto Rican Migrant,* p. 74.

105 Abeles et al., *Chinatown Study,* p. ii; cf. Morrison G. Wong, "Chinese Sweatshops in the United States: A Look at the Garment Industry," in *Research in the Sociology of Work,* ed. Ida Simpson and Richard Simpson, p. 364; Hendricks, *Dominican Diaspora,* p. 76; Tan, "Restaurants et ateliers," p. 283. Tan adds that this new wage work in France has not fundamentally challenged the male authority structure.

106 *Actuel,* Apr. 1988. See Hans Jaeger, "Generations in History," *History and Theory* 24 (1985): 273–92; and special issue of *Vingtième Siècle,* no. 22 (Apr.–June 1989) on "Les générations."

107 Selekman et al., *Clothing and Textile Industries,* p. 58. See also Melech Epstein, *Jewish Labor in U.S.A. (1882–1952),* 2 vols., 2:422–24. As one owner said: "My kids going into this business? . . . I told my daughter that if she ever went into this business, I'd break her leg" (Waldinger, *Through the Eye of the Needle,* p. 129).

108 "The ILGWU is a great melting pot" (ILGWU, *Equal Opportunity Union Made,* p. 7); on the Sentier: *Passages,* Dec. 1988.

109 Eli Elias, President of the New York Skirt and Sportswear Association, interview, New York City, Mar. 2, 1984.

8 Conflict and Consensus on Seventh Avenue

1 John Higham also makes this point in the preface to the 2d edition of *Strangers in the Land: Patterns of American Nativism, 1860–1925.*

2 Susan Glenn, *Daughters of the Shtetl,* pp. 230–31.

3 Eileen Boris, *Home to Work;* Catherine Collomp, "Syndicats ouvriers et immigration aux Etats-Unis, 1881–1900," thèse d'état, Université de Paris-8, 1985; Heidi Hartmann, "Capitalism, Patriarchy and Job Segregation by Sex," in *Women and the Workplace,* ed. Blaxall and Reagan, pp. 137–69; Alice Kessler-Harris, "Problems of Coalition-Building: Women and Trade Unions in the 1920s," in *Women, Work and Protest,* ed. Ruth Milkman, pp. 110–38; Kessler-Harris, *Out to Work,* pp. 136–41; Ruth Milkman, "Organizing the Sexual Division of Labor: Historical Perspectives on 'Women's Work' and the American Labor Movement," *Socialist Review* 10 (Jan.–Feb. 1980): 95–150; Gwendolyn Mink, *Old Labor and New Immigrants in American Political Development: Union, Party, and State, 1875–1920;* Michelle Perrot, "La femme populaire rebelle," in *L'histoire sans qualités,* ed. Christiane Dufrancatel (Paris: Galilée, 1979), pp. 152–54.

4 Carolyn D. McCreesh, *Women in the Campaign to Organize Garment Workers, 1880–1917,* p. 166; Pauline Newman, "Our Women Workers," *Ladies' Garment Worker* (New York), Nov. 1913; *Message* (New York), Nov. 26, 1915, and Feb. 4, 1916; Kessler-Harris, "Organizing the Unorganizable," pp. 150–

51; Françoise Basch, intro., Theresa Malkiel, *Journal d'une gréviste*, ed. Françoise Basch (Paris: Payot, 1980).

5 Kessler-Harris, "Coalition-building"; idem, "Organizing the Unorganizable." See also Hanita Blumfeld, "Jewish Women Sew the Union Label: A Study of Sexism and Feminism in the Emerging Unionization of the Garment Industry, New York City," *Humanity and Society* 6 (Feb. 1982): 33–45; Glenn, *Daughters of the Shtetl*, chap. 6; Nancy Schrom Dye, *As Equals and Sisters*, pp. 97, 115–16; John H. M. Laslett, "Gender, Class, or Ethnocultural Struggle? The Problematic Relationship between Rose Pesotta and the Los Angeles ILGWU," *California History* 72 (Spring 1993): 20–39; Annelise Orelick, *Common Sense and a Little Fire;* and Ann Schofield, *"To Do and to Be": Ladies, Immigrants, and Workers, 1893–1986*.

6 McCreesh, *Women Organize*, p. 183.

7 Kessler-Harris, "Organizing the Unorganizable," p. 150. Susan Glenn has explained the Jewish women's image of their own radicalism as part fact, part "rhetorical romanticism," a powerful ethnic myth Jews constructed about themselves" (*Daughters of the Shtetl*, p. 192).

8 "A Question of Importance," letter to the editor, *Message*, Mar. 27, 1914. The issue was already raised in ibid., Feb. 13, 1914.

9 Ibid., July 24, 1914; Mar. 19 and May 28, 1915.

10 Glenn, *Daughters of the Shtetl*, p. 236.

11 Amalgamated Ladies' Garment Cutters' Local 10, *Cutters' Almanac, 1902–1962;* Robert Parmet, *Labor and Immigration in Industrial America* (Boston: Twayne, 1981), pp. 109–10. Louis Levine, *The Women's Garment Workers*, pp. 135–42.

12 Levine, *Women's Garment Workers*, p. 149; Glenn, *Daughters of the Shtetl*, pp. 191–92, citing an estimate by Helen Marot. Maxine Schwartz Seller, "The Uprising of the Twenty Thousand: Sex, Class, and Ethnicity in the Shirtwaist Makers' Strike of 1909," in *"Struggle a Hard Battle,"* ed. Dirk Hoerder, p. 267, estimated as many as 21,000 Jewish women strikers. See chap. 2 above.

13 Van Kleeck, *Artificial Flower Makers*, cited in Kessner and Caroli, p. 28.

14 For the more cultural interpretation, see Virginia Yans-McLaughlin, *Family and Community*, and idem, "Metaphors of Self in History: Subjectivity, Oral Narrative, and Immigration Studies," in *Immigration Reconsidered*, ed. idem, pp. 254–90; for a more sociological view, see Miriam Cohen, *Workshop to Office*, pp. 79–82; and Glenn, *Daughters of the Shtetl*, pp. 188–206.

15 Roger Waldinger, "Another Look at the International Ladies' Garment Workers' Union: Women, Industry Structure and Collective Action," in *Women, Work, and Protest*, ed. Ruth Milkman. Waldinger has stressed some of the structural reasons—growth of the industry and increasing factory concentration in the period up until 1910—rather than Jewish women's radicalism, as accounting for the rise and later decline in strike activity. Donna Gabaccia has pointed out more generally: "Within fifteen years of migration to the United States, Switzerland, and Germany, organization had commenced among the

unskilled [Italians]—and scabbing was no longer a serious problem" (Donna Gabaccia, " 'For Us There are no Frontiers': Italian Labor Migrants and Internationalism, 1876–1914," paper presented at the American Italian Historical Association Conference, Nov. 2, 1990, p. 11).

16 ILGWU, *Record of the 11th Convention* (1912), pp. 89–90. See also pp. 5, 79–81, 91, 100–101, 104. Ibid., *10th Convention* (1910), p. 83; see also pp. 49, 57, 74, 81, 89. Some of the very same language was used to argue for the setting up of the second Italian local, Local 89, adding that the "great success" of Local 48 "surprised the Jewish sisters and brothers" and was a precedent to be followed (ibid., *14th Convention* [1918], p. 110).

17 Edwin Fenton, *Immigrants and the Union, A Case Study*, p. 542.

18 Luigi Antonini, "The '89" (1949), Dress Joint Series, Box 1, File 12 (hereafter 1:12), ILGWU Archives, New York (hereafter ILG Arch.). On early Italian-Jewish relations in the ILGWU, see Ronald Bayor, *Neighbors in Conflict*, pp. 5, 20–21, 85; Fenton, *Italians and American Labor*, pp. 499, 504–8, 538–45; Colomba Marie Furio, "Immigrant Women and Industry: A Case Study. The Italian Immigrant Women and the Garment Industry, 1880–1950," Ph.D. diss., New York University, 1979, pp. 221, 243–44; Rudolf Glanz, *Jew and Italian: Historic Group Relations and the New Immigration, 1881–1924* (New York: Shulsinger Bros., Inc., 1971), pp. 168–69; Parmet, *Labor and Immigration*, pp. 65, 111–13, 116–17. On more general treatments of Italian radicalism in the United States, see, e.g., Donna Gabaccia, *Militants and Migrants: Rural Sicilians Become American Workers* (New Brunswick: Rutgers University Press, 1988); Gary R. Mormino and George E. Pozzetta, *The Immigrant World of Ybor City: Italians and their Latin Neighbors in Tampa, 1885–1985;* Rudolph Vecoli, ed., *Italian American "Radicalism": Old World Origins and New World Developments* (Staten Island: American Italian Historical Association, 1962).

19 ILGWU, *Record of the 15th Convention* (1920), p. 39.

20 ILGWU Educational Department, *The Story of the ILGWU*, p. 18; "Census of Membership—Local 89," Antonini 40:1, ILG Arch.

21 ILGWU, *Record of the 12th Convention* (1914), p. 207; idem, *Report of the General Executive Board (GEB)* (16th Convention, 1922), p. 77; idem, *Report of the GEB* (19th Convention, 1928), p. 265. ILGWU Local 89, *Ultra: Strenna Commemorativa del XV anniversario della fondazione della Italian Dressmakers Union* (New York: Italian Labor Education Bureau, [1934]). For various donations, see, e.g., Luigi Antonini to David Dubinsky, Dec. 5, 1945, pp. 2–3, Antonini 40:1, ILG Arch.; ibid., Annual Report, Italian Dress Makers' Union, 1946, Schedule 3.

22 Joseph Breslow, *Gerechtigkeit*, Nov. 1953, English translation, pp. 1, 3–4, ILG Arch., Dress Joint 1:12; see also *Jewish Daily Forward* editorial, Sept. 15, 1953, in ibid.

23 Glanz, *Jew and Italian*, p. 38. His emphasis.

24 ILGWU, *Record of the 21st Convention* (1932), pp. 104, 247.

25 Confidential memorandum, Luigi Antonini to Lieutenant Governor Charles

Poletti, Governor Herbert Lehman, and Mayor Fiorello H. Laguardia, May 4, 1942, Antonini 1:6: Aliens 1942, ILG Arch. American Committee on Italian Migration to David Dubinsky, Nov. 12, 1959, Dubinsky 371:3, ILG Arch. ILGWU, *GEB Report and Record of the 30th Convention* (1959), p. 366. Ibid., *38th Convention* (1983), pp. 135, 327, 337.

26 *Message*, Mar. 19, 1915.

27 *Message*, Aug. 18, 1916.

28 Steven Fraser, "*Landslayt* and *Paesani*," in "*Struggle a Hard Battle*," ed. Dirk Hoerder, pp. 296–97; idem, *Labor Will Live;* Catherine Collomp, "Ethnic Identity, Americanization and Internationalism in the Jewish Labor Movement in the 1920s," in *Ethnic Cultures in the 1920s in North America*, ed. Wolfgang Binder, pp. 157–73.

29 Expecting "dishes of Russian and German concoction," the Italian women were thrilled to find pasta at Unity House. "We are internationalists in these [union] matters, but fierce nationalists as regards our appetites" (Annie and Fannie Cassia, "Let Us Trample upon Prejudice," *Message*, Aug. 4, 1916).

30 *Message*, Mar. 19, 1915. The early convention reports attest to the perceived need of holding meetings and publishing minutes in English, yet at the 1910 convention it was merely decided that this was up to the discretion of the individual locals (ILGWU, *Record of the 10th Convention* [1910], p. 91).

31 The earlier papers included the *New Post* (in English and Yiddish), *Gleicheit*, the *Message*, the *Ladies' Garment Worker, La Operaia, Lotta de Classe*, a Russian monthly bulletin, and a raincoat-makers' newsletter, "a sample of illiteracy rarely equalled in our press" (ILGWU, *Record of the 13th Convention* [1916], p. 54).

32 ILGWU, *Report of the GEB* (22d Convention, 1934), p. 174. A French-language monthly was ultimately edited in Montreal.

33 ILGWU, *Record of the 30th Convention* (1959), p. 320. Some of the older members were incensed at the abandonment of the Yiddish edition. Dubinsky himself responded to this "very difficult question" by taking responsibility for the decision and adding "and I declare to you that I am not an anti-Semite. (Laughter.) I am as good a Jew as anyone. (Applause.)" He continued, however, with a requiem for the Yiddish language, spoken but no longer read by his daughter, not even spoken by his granddaughter (ibid.).

34 ILGWU, *Report of the GEB* (18th Convention, 1925), p. 137; idem, *GEB* (19th Convention, 1928), p. 265.

35 On the clubs and groups, see especially ILG Arch., Dubinsky 13:2–4, 5A; issues of the *Dress Presser* in ibid., 13:3, and the minutes of the third quarterly meeting of the GEB, May 1938, in ibid., 13:5A, pp. 42–45; along with e.g., ILGWU, *Report of the GEB* (21st Convention, 1932), p. 73; ibid., *GEB* (1934), passim; idem, *Record of the 23d Convention* (1937), pp. 405–12; and ibid., *25th Convention* (1944), pp. 414f. Of course, at the same time, in the period prior to breaking off with the CIO, Dubinsky was defending the right of unions to organize in a group within the AFL for the purpose of propagating change.

Notes to Pages 227–231

See, e.g., ILGWU, *Report of the GEB* (23d Convention, 1937), pp. 197–98. For a discussion of language locals in the ACWA, see Fraser, "Landslayt," pp. 294–95; and idem, *Labor Will Live.*

36 Henoch Mendelsund, interview, New York, June 11, 1984. In 1950, the Branch had some 1,000 members. "Russian-Polish Branch 40th Anniversary" (1950), Joint Cloak 20:9, ILG Arch. For the Branch's history, see ibid., 31:2A: Russian-Polish Branch; ILGWU, *Record of the 12th Convention* (1914), p. 187; ibid., *17th Convention* (1924), pp. 69, 269–70; and idem, *Report of the GEB* (19th Convention, 1928), pp. 250–52. A memorandum of Apr. 20, 1961, addressed by the Branch to Dubinsky, vigorously protested Mendelsund's decision to close them.

37 English translation of *La Prensa* article and leaflet addressed to "Spanish Dressmakers" in ILG Arch., Zimmerman 33:11.

38 The typescript of this statement, signed by the Spanish Section of Dress Makers' Union, Local 22, is in ILG Arch., Zimmerman 8:4: Educational Activities. The draft letter to the Spanish press is dated Jan. 2, 1934. See also handwritten undated memorandum on Puerto Rican workers in ibid., Tyler 53:6.

39 ILGWU, *Report of the GEB* (28th Convention, 1953), p. 17.

40 A black ILGWU dressmaker filed a complaint to the New York State Commission Against Discrimination, complaining that she could not work in shops organized by the Italian local. See Herbert Hill, "Race and Ethnicity in Organized Labor: The Historical Sources of Resistance to Affirmative Action," in *Ethnicity and the Work Force*, ed. Winston A. Van Horne (Madison: University of Wisconsin System, 1985), pp. 19–64.

41 Memorandum, Emil Schlesinger to President Louis Stulberg, July 25, 1968, p. 3, Stulberg 22:8, ILG Arch. Herbert Hill refuted this assertion, claiming that twenty years after *Hunter vs. Sullivan* "not a single Negro or Spanish-speaking person holds membership in the two Italian locals." See Herbert Hill, "Guardians of the Sweatshops: The Trade Unions, Racism, and the Garment Industry," in *Puerto Rico and Puerto Ricans*, ed. Adalberto Lopez and James Petras, p. 404.

42 Irving R. Stuart, "Minorities vs. Minorities," *Journal of Social Psychology* 59 (1963): 94.

43 For the Holmes case and the Powell Commission inquiry, see: ILG Arch., Zimmerman 26:8–9, Tyler 17:2, Falikman 8:2a–2c, and newspaper clippings in file entitled "Powell Commission" (not classified in 1984); *Justice*, Sept. 1 and 15 and Oct. 1 and 15, 1962; and the exchange between Herbert Hill (NAACP) and Gus Tyler (ILGWU): Hill's attack in ILG Arch., Zimmerman 26:8, published in *New Politics*, Summer 1962; Tyler's response, "The Truth about the ILGWU," *New Politics*, Autumn 1962; and Hill's answer, "The ILGWU—Fact and Fiction—A Reply to Gus Tyler," *New Politics*, Winter 1963. See also United States House of Representatives, *Investigation of Labor Irregularities and Discrimination in the Garment Industry*, p. 95.

44 Hill deposition, p. 1, in ILG Arch., Zimmerman 26:8.

45 In a draft letter (sent?) to Roy Wilkins after the N A A C P brief supporting Hill (I L G Arch., Zimmerman 26:8).

46 Herbert Zelenko was chairman of the Ad Hoc Subcommittee set up to conduct the investigation. The I L G W U had already crossed paths with Powell in 1944, when he headed a People's Committee which formed an opposition Rank and File Group within Local 22 at the time of its elections. See Powell to "Dear Sisters," Feb. 9, 1944; and Zimmerman's response in *Justice,* Mar. 1, 1944, and Crosswaith to Zimmerman, Mar. 6, 1944, all in I L G Arch., Zimmerman 26:9 and 28:3. See also Charles V. Hamilton, *Adam Clayton Powell, Jr.: The Political Biography of an American Dilemma* (New York: Atheneum, 1991); and Murray Friedman, *What Went Wrong? The Creation and Collapse of the Black-Jewish Alliance* (New York: Free Press, 1995), pp. 93–95, 100, 103.

47 Granger to Zimmerman, Apr. 6, 1937, and Sept. 20, 1948, Zimmerman 27:4, I L G Arch.; Zimmerman to Hubert, May 29, 1933, Zimmerman 27:4, ibid. Robert Laurentz, "Racial/Ethnic Conflict in the New York City Garment Industry, 1933–1980," Ph.D. diss., SUNY-Binghamton, 1980, had a much more negative assessment of the union: "The fact that the I L G W U was considered during these years [1930s–1940s] to be among the more progressive labor unions in the United States was more a reflection of how racist other labor unions were. . . ." (p. 225); see also pp. 304–12. However, Charles Franklin, *The Negro Labor Unionist of New York,* like Sterling D. Spero and Abram Harris, *The Black Worker: The Negro and the Labor Movement,* insisted on the exemplary nature of the I L G W U in this period. See also Hasia Diner, *In the Almost Promised Land: American Jews and Blacks, 1915–1935* (Westport, Conn.: Greenwood Press, 1977), pp. 199–203; Philip S. Foner, *Organized Labor and the Black Workers, 1619–1981;* Philip S. Foner and Ronald L. Lewis, eds., *The Black Worker: A Documentary History,* 8 vols., cf. vols. 6 and 7 with 8 (also edited by Robert Cvornyek); Cheryl Lynn Greenberg, *Or Does it Explode? Black Harlem in the Great Depression;* Charles H. Wesley, *Negro Labor in the United States, 1850–1925* (New York: Vanguard, 1927); and Elaine Wrong, *The Negro in the Apparel Industry.* On some of the C I O efforts with regard to race relations in other industries, see, e.g., Lizabeth Cohen, *Making a New Deal,* pp. 333–49; Fraser, *Labor Will Live;* and August Meier and Elliott Rudwick, *Black Detroit and the Rise of the UAW* (New York: Oxford University Press, 1979).

48 For a cynical interpretation of this move, see Laurentz, "Racial/Ethnic Conflict," pp. 167–68.

49 Frank Crosswaith and Alfred Lewis, *Negro and White Labor Unite for True Freedom* (New York: Negro Labor News Service, [193?]); John Howard Seabrook, "Black and White: The Career of Frank R. Crosswaith," Ph.D. diss., Rutgers University, 1980.

50 I L G W U, *Record of the 22d Convention* (1934), p. 124; Edith Kine, "Garment Union Comes to Negro Worker," *Justice,* May–June 1935 (first published in *Opportunity* 12 (Apr. 1934), pp. 107–10, and reprinted in Foner and Lewis, eds., *Black Worker,* 6:179–82).

Notes to Pages 234–235

51 Local 155 to the President of the United States, Sept. 21, 1943, Local 155 Series 9:4, ILG Arch. The ILGWU's donations were fairly ecumenical, ranging from Jewish organizations to Arab refugee relief to black causes. See Max Danish, *The World of David Dubinsky*, p. 186; ILG Arch., Local 155, 5:5, Dubinsky 353:2a. However, by the early 1960s, the fact that ultimately much more money was given to Jewish and Italian organizations than to black or Puerto Rican ones was criticized. See Dorothy Rabinowitz, "The Case of the ILGWU," *Dissent* 19 (1972): 88–89.

52 For a fairly complete list of the union's civil rights activities, see report, Jewish Labor Committee, pp. 7–8, Zimmerman 26:8, ILG Arch.; see ibid., Zimmerman 27:4 for his activities in Cleveland.

53 Henry Rosemond, "No Race Prejudice in Needle Trades Union," *Daily Worker*, Mar. 1, 1929 (reprinted in Foner and Lewis, eds., *Black Worker*, 6:174–75).

54 ILG Arch., Zimmerman 28:2. See also Zimmerman 4:7 with regard to this 1934 dispute.

55 HLC leaflet in ILG Arch., Zimmerman 4:7; Frank R. Crosswaith, "The True Path for Negro Labor," *Justice*, Nov. 1934; idem, "May Day Is Our Day," *Justice*, May 1, 1935; and idem, "Fay—An Examiner," *Justice*, Jan. 15, 1936.

56 *Dress Presser*, Mar. 1940; letter from Dubinsky to all locals and Joint Boards, Aug. 19, 1940, Zimmerman 4:7, ILG Arch.; ILGWU, *Report of the GEB* (26th Convention, 1947), p. 84; Danish, *Dubinsky*, pp. 247–48. See also Mark Naison, *Communists in Harlem during the Depression.*

57 *Pittsburgh Courier* article of Dec. 12, 1959 ("Will Negro, Jewish Labor Leaders War over Civil Rights?") and the more conciliatory issue of Jan. 2, 1960 ("Randolph, Wilkins Deny 'War' but Cite 'Differences' "). See ILG Arch., Zimmerman 4:10 and Dress Joint Board 1:9.

58 House of Representatives, *Investigation*, p. 95.

59 Dubinsky's remark was cited in a pamphlet of the Harlem Labor Committee. See ILG Arch., Zimmerman 4:7. Zimmerman's comment was picked up by the Communist newspaper, the *Daily Worker*, Mar. 6, 1952, which then editorialized that a black dressmaker still could not buy a house by insisting that she was a dressmaker.

60 House of Representatives, *Investigation*, p. 55. The statistical skirmish mirrored the legal one, with Hill charging that there were "virtually no" black or Spanish-speaking cutters, while Zimmerman initially responded that there were hundreds of them. See Zimmerman's resignation speech (from the NAACP Legal Defense Fund) in Zimmerman 26:7, ILG Arch. See also Fleischman to Hill, Oct. 26, 1962, p. 3, Zimmerman 26:8, ibid. There are two lists in ILG Arch., Falikman 8:2a–2b, one comprising 199, the other 236, names of black or Hispanic cutters. An estimate of 75 to 100 Puerto Ricans and 100 Negroes was reported in the *New York Herald Tribune*, Oct. 2, 1958. If there were 200 minority cutters out of 7,500, i.e., 2.7 percent, this figure can be compared to the more general estimate of from 30 to 50 percent black and Hispanic ILGWU members in the New York locals in 1962. See NAACP report, pp. 3–4, 6–7, 9,

11, Zimmerman 26:9, ILG Arch. The ILGWU was also at pains to prove that there were minority members among the leadership. See Jewish Labor Committee memorandum, Nov. 16, 1962, Zimmerman 26:8, and Shane to Dubinsky, p. 3, Nov. 20, 1962, Zimmerman 26:9, ILG Arch.

61 Henoch Mendelsund, ILGWU, interview, New York, Sept. 4, 1984; Friedman, *What Went Wrong?* pp. 310–13.

62 *New York Herald Tribune*, Aug. 25, 1962. Cf. ILG Arch., Zimmerman 26:8 and 26:9, passim.

63 ILG Arch., Zimmerman, 26:8. A reference to Hitler had already been used in 1934 (ibid., Zimmerman 28:2). Hill refuted the accusation of anti-Semitism in his article "The ILGWU—Fact and Fiction," pp. 26–27.

64 For a fuller treatment of this issue, see Paul Berman, ed., *Blacks and Jews: Alliances and Arguments* (New York: Delacorte Press, 1994); Claybourne Carson, "Blacks and Jews in the Civil Rights Movement," in *Jews in Black Perspectives*, ed. Joseph Washington, pp. 113–31; and, ibid., more generally; Lenwood G. Davis, *Black-Jewish Relations in the United States, 1752–1984: A Selected Bibliography* (Westport, Conn.: Greenwood Press, 1984); Diner, *Almost Promised Land;* Friedman, *What Went Wrong?;* Jonathan Kaufman, *Broken Alliance: The Turbulent Times between Blacks and Jews in America* (New York: Charles Scribner's Sons, 1988); Jack Salzman, ed., *Bridges and Boundaries: Blacks and Jews.*

65 "Puerto Ricans Rebel against Boss—and Union," *New York Herald Tribune*, Oct. 8, 1958.

66 Different versions of this strike may be found in Abeles et al., *The Chinatown Garment Industry Study*, pp. 77–81; Peter Kwong, *The New Chinatown*, pp. 147–58; Ruth Milkman, "Organizing Immigrant Women in New York's Chinatown: An Interview with Katie Quan," in *Women and Unions*, ed. Dorothy Sue Cobble, pp. 281–98. The Abeles report, written for the union, obviously gives credit to the ILGWU for mobilizing the strike; Milkman gives agency to the immigrant women, although in conjunction with the union; Kwong is the most critical of the union, attributing it the least role.

67 ILGWU, *Record of the 2d Convention* (1901), p. 7; Levine, *Women's Garment Workers*, p. 111.

68 Kwong, *New Chinatown*, p. 151.

69 Milkman, "Interview with Quan," p. 287.

70 Cited in Waldinger, *Through the Eye of the Needle*, p. 160.

71 Mirjana Morokvasic, Roger Waldinger, and Annie Phizacklea, "Business on the Ragged Edge," in *Ethnic Entrepreneurs*, ed. Waldinger, Aldrich, and Ward, p. 172.

72 Milkman, "Interview with Quan," p. 284; Kwong, *New Chinatown*, pp. 148–50.

73 Milkman, "Interview with Quan," p. 291.

74 For other examples of intra-ethnic differentiation and conflict, see, e.g., essays on Brighton Beach and Chinatown in Nancy Foner, ed., *New Immigrants in New York;* Illsoo Kim, *The New Urban Immigrants;* Nancy L. Green, "Les

juifs étrangers à Paris," in *Le Paris des étrangers,* ed. André Kaspi and Antoine Marès (Paris: Imprimerie Nationale, 1989), pp. 106–18.

75 Abeles et al., *Chinatown Study,* p. 79. See also pp. 80, 83.

76 Ibid., pp. 79–80.

77 ILGWU, *Report of the GEB and Record of the 32d Convention* (1965), p. 369; Local 10, 3:7, ILG Arch.

78 *Message,* Mar. 19, 1915.

79 ILGWU, *Report of the GEB* (28th Convention, 1953), p. 17; written statement submitted to the U.S. Commission on Civil Rights, cover letter, June 7, 1974, Stulberg 22:8, ILG Arch.

80 Talk at the National Urban League, Sept. 9, 1959, Dress Joint Board 2:3, ILG Arch.

81 ILGWU, *Record of the 25th Convention* (1944), p. 334.

82 Levine, *Women's Garment Workers;* Roy Helfgott, "Puerto Rican Integration in the Skirt Industry in New York City," in *Discrimination and Low Incomes,* ed. Aaron Antonovsky and Lewis Lorwin [pseud. Louis Levine], pp. 249–79; Will Herberg, "The Old-timers and the Newcomers: Ethnic Group Relations in a Needle Trades Union," *Journal of Social Issues* 9, no. 1 (1953): 12–19; Gus Tyler, *Look for the Union Label;* Moses Rischin, "The Jewish Labor Movement in America: A Social Interpretation," *Labor History* 4, no. 3 (Fall 1963): 227–47.

83 Kessler-Harris, "Problems of Coalition-Building." Hill's dispute with the union became news again in 1992 when the Jewish Museum in New York organized an exhibit entitled "Bridges and Boundaries: African-Americans and American Jews" (Salzman, ed., *Bridges and Boundaries*). The ILGWU criticized that part of the exhibit that referred to what it deemed "30-year-old discredited charges by an official of the NAACP" and convinced museum officials to pull those references from the show. Hill sent a letter to the *New York Times* castigating the museum for its pusillanimity (*New York Times,* Apr. 20, and Hill's letter, May 9, 1992). (I thank Roger Waldinger for bringing this to my attention.) Laurentz, "Racial/Ethnic Conflict," in his strident critique of the union, argued that union bureaucracy was by nature discriminatory. His structural analysis of the ILGWU's behavior is interesting but marred by what seems to be an unequivocal hatred of the union, to which he imputes the blackest motives at every juncture. Peter Kwong has also harshly criticized the union's centralization and its being more dependent on manufacturers than on its rank and file (Kwong, *New Chinatown,* pp. 149–50).

84 Frank Parkin, *Marxism and Class Theory: A Bourgeois Critique* (London: Tavistock, 1979), pp. 44–47, 56–57; Max Weber, *The Theory of Social and Economic Organization* (New York: Free Press, 1964), pp. 139–43; Kessler-Harris, "Problems of Coalition-building," pp. 120–21; Robert Michels, *Les partis politiques: Essai sur les tendances oligarchiques des démocraties* (Paris: Flammarion, 1971). An obvious comparison is the long-time Irish-run Transport Workers' Union in New York City. See Joshua Freeman, *In Transit: The Transport Workers' Union in New York City, 1933–1966* (New York: Oxford

University Press, 1989); and Pierre Bouvier, *Le travail au quotidien: Une dé-marche socio-anthropologique*, pp. 99–107.

85 Roy B. Helfgott, "Puerto Rican Integration in a Garment Union Local," in *Proceedings of the 10th Annual Meeting*, ed. Edwin Young (N.p.: Industrial Relations Research Association, 1948), pp. 274–75. Cf. pp. 276–77 in the later and longer version of this article in *Discrimination and Low Incomes*, ed. Antonovsky and Lorwin; and a shorter, earlier (?) version in Dress Joint 3:5, ILG Arch.

86 Hill, "Guardians of the Sweatshop," pp. 388–400; Wrong, *Negro in Apparel*, pp. 19, 107–9, 120.

87 J. C. Rich, "The NAACP vs. Labor," *The New Leader*, Nov. 26, 1962 (reprinted in Foner, Lewis, and Cvornyek, eds., *Black Worker*, 8:170).

88 Kenneth B. Clark, *Ghetto noir* (Paris: Robert Laffont, 1966), p. 58. Hill, "Guardians of the Sweatshop," p. 393.

89 A follow-up study of High School of Fashion Industries graduates showed that discrimination or segmentation even began at the high school level, with black women disproportionately concentrated in the lowest track. See Sally Hillsman, "Entry into the Labor Market: The Preparation and Job Placement of Negro and White Vocational High School Graduates," Ph.D. diss., Columbia University, 1970.

90 Fraser, "Landslayt," p. 282.

91 E.g., John Bodnar, *Immigration and Industrialization: Ethnicity in an American Mill Town, 1870–1940* (Pittsburgh: University of Pittsburgh Press, 1977); Stephen Steinberg, *The Ethnic Myth;* Olivier Zunz, *The Changing Face of Inequality.*

92 Cited in Glenn, *Daughters of the Shtetl*, p. 188.

93 Irving R. Stuart, "A Study of Factors Associated with Inter-Group Conflict in the Ladies' Garment Industry in New York City," Ph.D. diss., New York University, 1951; Wrong, *Negro in Apparel*, pp. 50, 97, and more generally, pp. 66–75 (from interviews in 1968 and 1973); Waldinger, *Through the Eye of the Needle*, p. 156.

94 Harold Siegel, Greater Blouse, Skirt and Undergarment (contractors') Association, interview, New York, Aug. 22, 1984.

95 Stuart, "Inter-group Conflict," p. 185. Stuart consistently capitalizes "Newcomer."

96 Ibid., pp. 200, 183, see also pp. 174, 182; idem, "Minorities," p. 93.

97 Stuart, "Inter-group Conflict," pp. 162–63. Another three cases involved Jews vs. "miscellaneous," one case involved an Italian plaintiff and a Jewish defendant, another a black plaintiff and a Puerto Rican defendant, and one was listed as Negro vs. "miscellaneous." On the windows wars, see Stuart, "Minorities," p. 98.

98 Gunnar Myrdal, *An American Dilemma* (New York: Harper and Bros., 1944), pp. 67–73; Stuart, "Inter-group Conflict," p. 115; Helfgott, "Puerto Rican Integration," in Antonovsky and Lorwin, eds., *Discrimination and Low Incomes*, esp. p. 271. Helfgott goes so far as to argue that "the shortage of labor

prevents discrimination" (p. 270). Cf. Stanley Lieberson, *A Piece of the Pie,* p. 382.

99 Herberg, "Old-timers," p. 15. Herberg's thesis was in many ways a defense of the union against "the familiar stereotype of union leaders hoarding a monopoly of power" (ibid., p. 19). In 1953, he viewed the newcomers as simply accepting the lag of leadership representation and "show[ing] no particular resentment" toward the Jewish and Italian leadership (ibid., p. 19).

100 See the classic article by Barth on the social constructedness of ethnicity, in Fredrik Barth, ed., *Ethnic Groups and Boundaries: The Social Organization of Culture Difference.* For a good historians' view, see Kathleen Conzen et al., "The Invention of Ethnicity: A Perspective from the U.S.A.," *Journal of American Ethnic History* 12, no. 1 (Fall 1992): 3–41.

101 See "Ethnic composition of membership" (ca. 1962) in partial lists of chairladies in Local 105, 3:9, ILG Arch.; Memorandum, Emil Schlesinger to President Louis Stulberg, July 25, 1968, p. 3, Stulberg 22:8, ILG Arch.; Manuel Gonzalez, ILGWU, interview, Sept. 6, 1984; City College Oral History Research Project, New York City Immigrant Labor Oral History Collection, Tamiment Library, I-105.

102 Stuart, "Inter-group Conflict," p. 174.

103 Michael Walzer, *Spheres of Justice* (Oxford: Blackwell, 1983), p. 319.

104 Pierre Bouvier, *Socio-anthropologie du contemporain.*

105 Mormino and Pozzetta, *Ybor City;* Bayor, *Neighbors in Conflict,* p. 1; and Ronald H. Bayor, "Historical Encounters: Intergroup Relations in a 'Nation of Nations,'" *Annals AAPSS* 530 (Nov. 1993): 14–27. In another context, see Maryse Tripier, "L'immigration dans la classe ouvrière en France," doctorat d'état, Université de Nantes, 1987, chaps. 11–12.

106 Stuart, "Inter-group Conflict," p. 173; City College Oral History Collection, e.g., I-104, I-105, I-108. Cf. Bayor, *Neighbors in Conflict,* pp. 84–85, who stresses how international politics could impinge on local relations. See also John Stack, *International Conflict in an American City: Boston's Irish, Italians, and Jews, 1935–1944;* and Susan Olzak, *The Dynamics of Ethnic Competition and Conflict.*

107 Fraser, "Landslayt," discussing Jews and Italians within the men's garment-workers' union; Furio, "Italian Immigrant Women," p. 335.

108 Kine, "Garment Union Comes to Negro Worker"; Stuart, "Inter-group Conflict," p. 173; *New York Herald Tribune,* Oct. 3, 1958.

109 E.g., Glenn, *Daughters of the Shtetl,* p. 188; Elizabeth Weiner and Hardy Green, "A Stitch in Our Time: New York's Hispanic Garment Workers in the 1980s," in *A Needle, a Bobbin, a Strike: Women Needleworkers in America,* ed. Joan Jensen and Sue Davidson, pp. 284–85.

110 My translation from the French original, cf. Véronique de Rudder, "Immigrant Housing and Integration in French Cities," in *Immigrants in Two Democracies,* ed. Donald Horowitz and Gérard Noiriel, pp. 247–67. See also Maryse Tripier, *L'Immigration dans la classe ouvrière française,* esp. pp. 267–72; and Véronique de Rudder and Michèle Guillon, *Autochtones et immigrés en quar-*

tier populaire: Du marché d'Aligre à l'îlot Châlon (Paris: CIEMI L'Harmattan, 1987).

111 Glenn, *Daughters of the Shtetl*, p. 188.

112 Fraser, *Labor Will Live*, p. 205.

9 Economic and Ethnic Identities in the Parisian Patchwork

1 Dominique Schnapper, *La communauté des citoyens;* Rogers Brubaker, *Citizenship and Nationhood in France and Germany* (Cambridge: Harvard University Press, 1992); Gérard Noiriel, *La Tyrannie du national: Le droit d'asile en Europe 1793–1993.*

2 E.g., Jean Berthelot, in *Rapport de la classe 86B, Rapport du Groupe XIIID: Industries accessoires du vêtement (Exposition coloniale internationale de Vincennes),* ed. René Hayem, pp. 339, 350; Albert Leduc, in *Classe 36: Habillement des deux sexes, Exposition universelle internationale de 1889 à Paris: Rapports du jury international,* ed. Alfred Picard, p. 89; Arsène Alexandre, *Les reines de l'aiguille: modistes et couturières;* Edouard Debect, *L'habillement féminin en France au point de vue industriel et commercial;* Judith Coffin, *The Politics of Women's Work: The Paris Garment Trades, 1750–1915.*

3 Nancy L. Green, *The Pletzl of Paris,* pp. 38–41; 85 percent estimate by Pierre Dumas in *Der idisher arbayter* (Paris), July 5, 1913. See chap. 7 above.

4 *L'Antijuif,* 1900 (n.d.) in Marguerite Durand dossier DOS/331/GRE, file Grèves 1901, p. 21; Préfecture de Police Archives (hereafter APP), BA1394: Tailleurs, Grèves des ouvriers, File "Grève des tailleurs pour dames chez Paquin, Doucet, King, Doeuillet, Raudnitz, Bechoff et Berr, février 1901"; Office du travail, *Bulletin de l'Office du travail* (1901), pp. 174–75, reporting the number of strikers as 2,000; *Archives israélites* (Paris), Feb. 14, 1901; *La Libre Parole* (Paris), Feb. 5, 7, and 11, 1901; Léon Storch, in *Classe 85—Industrie de la confection et de la couture pour hommes, femmes et enfants, Exposition universelle internationale de 1900 à Paris: Rapports du jury international, Groupe XIII. Fils, tissus, vêtements, 2e partie—Classes 85 et 86,* ed. Léon Storch, Julien Hayem and Auguste Mortier, p. 42; Green, *Pletzl of Paris,* pp. 128–30.

5 Storch et al., *Exposition universelle, 1900,* pp. 41–42.

6 APP, BA1394, "Grève . . . Wormser et Boulanger, février 1916," and APP, BA1394, "Grève . . . Galeries Lafayette, avril 1915."

7 E.g., APP, BA1394, "Grève . . . Galeries Lafayette, février 1913"; *Der idisher arbayter,* Jan. 4 and Feb. 8, 1913; APP, BA1394, "Grève . . . Galeries Lafayette, septembre 1916." On this strike, see also Jean-Louis Robert, "Ouvriers et mouvements ouvriers parisiens pendant la grande guerre et l'immédiat après-guerre," Université de Paris 1, thèse d'Etat, 1989, 2:401–4, 441–43, and, more generally, on gender conflicts in the labor movement, tome 2, chap. 12.

8 Report, Mar. 10, 1913, F⁷13881: File "Galeries Lafayette," Archives Nationales, Paris (hereafter AN).

Notes to Pages 250–255

9 See AN: F⁷13741: Habillement, 1920–29.

10 Simon Cukier et al., *Juifs révolutionnaires* (Paris: Messidor, 1987), pp. 23–24.

11 APP, BA1394, "Grève . . . Printemps, mars 1916"; APP, BA1394, "Grève . . . Maurice, février 1916."

12 Fédération des travailleurs de l'habillement, *Compte rendu, 12e Congrès national* (Lille, 1921), p. 27. See Françoise Blum's excellent master's thesis, "Féminisme et syndicalisme: Les femmes dans la Fédération de l'habillement," Université de Paris 1, 1977, p. 116.

13 Fédération de l'habillement, *12e Congrès* (Lille, 1921), p. 39; Blum, "Féminisme et syndicalisme," p. 118.

14 Almost all of the Jewish immigrants joined the CGTU. See David Weinberg, *A Community on Trial*, pp. 58–61, 172–83; Paula Hyman, *From Dreyfus to Vichy: The Remaking of French Jewry*, pp. 102–8; Cukier et al., *Juifs révolutionnaires*, pp. 38–41, 60–63, 86–87, 94–95. On women in the CGT, see Blum, "Féminisme et syndicalisme"; and Michel Dreyfus, *Histoire de la CGT*, pp. 125, 139.

15 Léon Gani, *Syndicats et travailleurs immigrés;* René Gallissot and Nadir Boumaza, *Ces Migrants qui font le prolétariat* (Paris: Méridiens-Klincksieck, 1994); Maryse Tripier, *L'Immigration dans la classe ouvrière française.* The CGT and then the CGTU attempted to encourage migration regulation at the international level. E.g., Fédération de l'habillement, *12e Congrès* (Lille, 1921); Stéphane Courtois, Denis Peschanski, and Adam Rayski, *Le Sang de l'étranger* (Paris: Fayard, 1989), p. 23. More generally, on the issue of international socialism and the immigration question, see Claudie Weill, *L'Internationale et l'autre* (Paris: Arcantère, 1987).

16 Maryse Tripier, "L'immigration dans la classe ouvrière en France," thèse d'état, Université de Nantes, 1987, p. 568.

17 Julien Racamond, secretary of the French bakers' union and later CGTU official in charge of immigrant labor, writing in to *Der idisher arbayter*, Feb. 8, 1913.

18 *Der idisher arbayter*, Nov. 17, 1911, and Oct. 5, 1912.

19 *Der idisher arbayter*, Oct. 9 and Nov. 17, 1911. On Losovsky, see Green, *Pletzl of Paris*, pp. 155–67, 183–85; Georges Haupt and Jean-Jacques Marie, *Les Bolsheviks par eux-mêmes* (Paris: Maspero, 1969), p. 280.

20 Cited in Maurice Hollande, *La défense ouvrière contre le travail étranger* (Paris: Bloud et Cie., 1913), p. 200. See also Harvey Goldberg, "Jean Jaurès and the Jewish Question: The Evolution of a Position," *Jewish Social Studies* 20 (Apr. 1958): 70–93.

21 *La Guerre sociale* (Paris), Dec. 20–26, 1911; Bernard-Lazare, *Antisémitisme, son histoire et ses causes* (Paris: Léon Chailley, 1894), pp. 384–86; see also his comment in *Tribune libre* (Paris), May 24, 1896; *La Guerre sociale*, Jan. 3–9, 1912.

22 *L'Ouvrier de l'habillement* (Paris), Oct. 1912 and July 1913; John Dyche, "My Tour in Europe," *Ladies' Garment Worker*, Dec. 1913.

23 *Der idisher arbayter,* July 4, 1914; Zosa Szajkowski, *Di profesyonele bave-gung tsvishn di yidishe arbeter in Frankraykh biz 1914* (Paris: Fridman, 1937), p. 181; Robert, "Ouvriers," pp. 442, 1477. Dumas explained his joining Georges Valois' movement as a return to his conservative family origins and a search for the old France of a "vie des métiers": "Ce n'est pas moi qui ai abandonné les idées révolutionnaires, mais bien plutôt celles-ci qui se sont dérobées." See "Pierre Dumas, dit Diogène," in *Dictionnaire biographique du mouvement ouvrier français,* ed. Jean Maitron, tome 12, pp. 101–2.

24 Green, *Pletzl of Paris;* Hyman, *Dreyfus to Vichy;* and Weinberg, *Community on Trial.* The Deutscher Arbeiter Kartel awaits its historian. On the functioning of intersyndical committees in general, see Robert, "Ouvriers," 4:962.

25 Confédération Générale du Travail Unitaire (CGTU), *Compte rendu, 3ème Congrès national* (Paris, 1925), p. 400. See also Gani, *Syndicats et immigrés;* Ralph Schor, *L'opinion française et les étrangers, 1919–1939,* pp. 257–73, 570–75; Yves Lequin, "Métissages imprudents?" in *La Mosaïque France,* pp. 407–10; Gallissot and Boumaza, *Ces migrants,* pp. 41–46.

26 *L'Humanité* (Paris), Aug. 26, 1926; see AN: F⁷13741: Habillement, 1920–29; and AN: F⁷13883: Habillement.

27 Report, Sept. 13, 1922, F⁷13741, AN; report, May 6, 1926, "Habillement 1920–29;" F⁷13741, AN; report, Nov. 27, 1926, ibid.

28 *La Couture* (Paris), May 1921; see AN: F⁷13741. At one point Bellugue seemed to argue that all *apiéceurs* were exploiters; at another, he suggested that the union was only against those who exploited others. Fédération de l'habille-ment, *12e Congrès* (Lille, 1921); Cf. report, Jan. 30, 1921, F⁷13741, AN, and *La Couture,* May 1921, in same file. See chap. 3 above.

29 E.g., Vicki Caron, "Loyalties in Conflict: French Jewry and the Refugee Crisis, 1933–1935," *Leo Baeck Institute Yearbook* 36 (1991): 305–37; Hyman, *Dreyfus to Vichy,* pp. 106–7; Joseph Klatzmann, *Le Travail à domicile dans l'industrie parisienne du vêtement;* Marcel Livian, *Le régime juridique des étrangers en France;* Michael R. Marrus and Robert O. Paxton, *Vichy France and the Jews;* Weinberg, *Community on Trial,* pp. 60, 163–64.

30 Fédération de l'habillement, *20e Congrès* (Paris, 1937), p. 99. See also ibid., pp. 80, 96–98; and Vicki Caron, "The Politics of Frustration: French Jewry and the Refugee Crisis in the 1930s," *Journal of Modern History* 65 (June 1993): 338, note 92; and idem, *Uneasy Asylum* (forthcoming), citing *Le Populaire,* Sept. 29 and Dec. 29, 1937, and Mar. 14, 1938.

31 New York, Bund Archives, Kemfer file; Szajkowski, *Profesyonele bavegung,* pp. 27, 74, 102.

32 Fédération de l'habillement, *12e Congrès* (Lille, 1921), pp. 79–81; CGTU, *3ème Congrès* (Paris, 1925), pp. 411–12; ibid., *5e Congrès* (1929), p. 14; Raca-mond, "Le problème de la main-d'oeuvre étrangère," *L'Humanité,* Sept. 12, 1927; Gani, *Syndicats et immigrés,* pp. 117–19; Hyman, *Dreyfus to Vichy,* pp. 103 and 271, note 74.

33 Courtois, Peschanski, and Rayski, *Sang de l'étranger,* pp. 16, 29; Cukier et al., *Juifs révolutionnaires,* pp. 38–41. The question had already been raised by

the CGT in 1925. See Schor, *Opinion française*, p. 247. On the transformation of the notion of "étranger" within French society, see Gérard Noiriel, *Le creuset français*, chap. 2; and Nancy L. Green, "L'immigration en France et aux Etats-Unis, Historiographie comparée," *Vingtième siècle*, no. 29 (Jan.–Mar. 1991), pp. 67–82.

34 Lequin, *Mosaïque*, p. 409.

35 Hyman, *Dreyfus to Vichy*, pp. 106–7. Paul Chaupin, interview, Paris, Aug. 7, 1986; Cukier et al., *Juifs révolutionnaires*, pp. 95–96; Weinberg, *Community on Trial*, p. 35.

36 Racamond, "Le problème de la main-d'oeuvre étrangère," *L'Humanité*, Sept. 12, 1927. See the very complete entry on Racamond in *Dictionnaire biographique du mouvement ouvrier français*, ed. Jean Maitron and Claude Pennetier, 39:323–34.

37 CGTU, *3e Congrès* (1925), pp. 395–96.

38 Rapport du Bureau régional [de la Seine] de la main-d'oeuvre étrangère [à la CGTU], Mar. 21, 1925, F⁷13975: Surveillance des menées communistes, "France: organisations étrangères," AN; rapport de la section centrale de la MOE [au PCF], n.d. [ca. Jan. 1929], F⁷13250: Antifascisme, 1929, AN.

39 Courtois, Peschanski, and Rayski, *Sang de l'étranger*, p. 23. The term "sections ethniques" was used at the 1925 Congress and continued to be used in the similarly worded resolutions on behalf of immigrant workers proposed (by Racamond) again in 1931 and 1933.

40 Parti communiste, "L'importance de la MOE et les diverses immigrations," in *Bulletin spécial d'information de la section centrale de la MOE* (Paris, 1930), cited in Cukier et al., *Juifs révolutionnaires*, p. 62. See also Weinberg, *Community on Trial*, pp. 58–60; Hyman, *Dreyfus to Vichy*, pp. 104–5; and Schor, *Opinion française*, pp. 246–56, 273.

41 Weinberg, *Community on Trial*, p. 180, note 3; Hyman, *Dreyfus to Vichy*, p. 272, note 99. Jacques Kergoat, "Immigrés: Brefs Espoirs," *Le Monde aujourd'hui*, May 25–26, 1986. Weinberg suggests that dissolution of the Jewish intersyndical was particularly motivated by two factors: the Jewish section was considered too "Jewish," defending particularist Jewish interests; and their continued defense of *façonniers* was by now considered petit-bourgeois deviationism. This may be true, but the Jewish language sections were not the only ones disbanded. Castellani argues that that which was presented as a technical question of reorganization was also, in the general context of bolshevization of the PCF, an attempt to eliminate a Bordiguiste opposition from forming in France. See Loris Castellani, "La bolchévisation des groupes de langue italienne au sein du PCF," *La Trace*, no. 4 (Oct. 1990), pp. 7–13; Courtois, Peschanski, and Rayski, *Sang de l'étranger*, pp. 46, 429, note 13.

42 See Hyman, *Dreyfus to Vichy*, pp. 106–7.

43 Interview, Michel K., Bourse du Travail, Paris, May 15, 1986.

44 In Arabic, Portuguese, Spanish, Italian, Serbo-Croatian, and Turkish: *Manbar al Khâdim al Gazaïri* (52,600 copies), *O Trabalhador* (38,200 copies), *Unidad* (37,100 copies), *Lavoro* (21,200 copies), *Yu Radnik* (6,000 copies), and

Türk Işçilèri (2,500 copies). Gani, *Syndicats et immigrés,* pp. 227–31. See Juliette Minces, *Les travailleurs étrangers en France* (Paris: Seuil, 1973), chap. 11; Gallissot and Boumaza, *Ces migrants,* chap. 5.

45 Maurizio Lazzarato, Antonio Negri, and Giancarlo Santilli, "La confection dans le quartier du Sentier," report, Ministère du travail, de l'emploi et de la formation professionnelle, MIRE, 1990, p. 172; see also pp. 158, 175.

46 Interview in *Passages,* Dec. 1988. Aidenbaum was subsequently elected mayor of that district in 1995.

47 Nancy L. Green et al., "Les quartiers parisiens de l'industrie de l'habillement et les relations pluri-ethniques," report, Ministère de la Culture, MIRE, 1987, p. 107.

48 *Le Monde,* Nov. 13–14, 1988; *L'Express,* Jan. 20, 1989.

49 *Le Nouvel Observateur,* Feb. 9–15, 1989.

50 E.g., *Libération,* Apr. 22, 1987; *Actuel,* Apr. 1988; *Passages,* Dec. 1988.

51 Haim Vidal Sephiha, *L'agonie des Judéo-espagnols* (Paris: Edition Entente, 1977). As one Sephardic Turkish Jew commented bitterly about the new "Sephardim" in the Sentier: They are "mal élevés," with "pratiques de voyous. Un petit vieux s'est fait casser la figure parce qu'il n'avait pas payé ses traites en temps et en heure . . . De mon temps, tout se passait sur parole" (*Passages,* Dec. 1988).

52 Yinh Phong Tan, "Restaurants et ateliers: Le travail des Sino-khmers à Paris," *ASEMI* 15 (1984): 277–91; Jonathan D. Sarna, "From Immigrants to Ethnics: Toward a New Theory of 'Ethnicization,'" *Ethnicity* 5 (1978): 370–78; and Joshua A. Fishman, ed., *The Rise and Fall of the Ethnic Revival.*

53 See chap. 11; and Green et al., "Quartiers parisiens," p. 107.

54 Interview, *Passages,* Dec. 1988.

55 Joseph Klatzmann, interview, Paris, June 22, 1979.

56 Green et al., "Quartiers parisiens," pp. 123–26.

57 *Le Nouvel Observateur,* Feb. 9–15, 1989.

58 Green et al., "Quartiers parisiens," pp. 122–27.

59 *Le Nouvel Observateur,* Feb. 9–15, 1989.

60 *Actuel,* Apr. 1988.

61 *Passages,* Dec. 1988.

62 Ibid., Dec. 1988.

63 Ironically, perhaps, while the Ashkenazim appeal to tradition in manufacturing and commercial methods, the Sephardim are better known for their more traditional religious practices (Green et al., "Quartiers parisiens," pp. 93, 125–26). The newer Armenians have also brought a heightened sense of cultural identity to Issy-les-Moulineaux (Martine Hovanessian, *Le lien communautaire: Trois générations d'Arméniens*).

64 Mirjana Morokvasic, "Le Recours aux immigrés dans la confection à Paris: Eléments de comparaison avec la ville de Berlin-Ouest," Ministère du travail et de la formation professionnelle: Mission de liaison interministérielle pour la lutte contre les trafics de main-d'oeuvre, Paris, 1986; Tan, "Restaurants et ateliers"; Nancy L. Green et al., "Les Rapports habitat/travail dans l'industrie

de l'habillement à Paris et dans sa banlieue," report, Ministère de l'équipement, du logement, de l'aménagement du territoire et des transports (MELATT), 1988; Kenan Ozturk, "Les Turcs dans la confection à Paris," *Hommes et migrations*, no. 1116 (Nov. 1988), pp. 22–28.

65 Mirjana Morokvasic, "Le comportement économique des immigrés dans le secteur de la confection," Colloque du GRECO 13 "Mutations économiques et travailleurs immigrés dans des pays industriels," Vaucresson, January 28–30, 1988, p. 8; idem, "Recours aux immigrés," p. 29.

66 Guy Groux et al., "L'Atelier, l'habit et la règle: L'évolution récente des relations professionnelles et des stratégies syndicales dans les PME de l'habillement," report, Ministère du travail, de l'emploi et de la formation professionnelle, 1989, esp. pp. 229–34.

67 Morokvasic, "Recours aux immigrés," p. 29. A Jewish labor leader put it differently. Commenting that not one Yugoslav joined the union, he characterized them by their *"esprit de loucre"* in contrast to the Turkish immigrants' *"esprit de classe"* (interview, Michel K., May 15, 1986).

68 *Libération*, Apr. 22, 1987. Cf. Green et al., "Quartiers parisiens," p. 123; and a Mauritian decrying "l'invasion chinoise . . . [qui] a cassé les marchés et les prix." See Vasoodevan Vuddamalay, "Les mécanismes de structuration du mouvement migratoire mauricien en France," doctoral thesis, Ecole des Hautes Etudes en Sciences Sociales, 1993, p. 357. Another labor leader was also careful to contradict his initial cultural critique. When speaking of the Yugoslavs who entered the trade in the late 1950s and early 1960s, he remarked: "Ils ont fait beaucoup de mal." But he added just as quickly, "Ce n'était pas exprès" (interview, Michel K., May 15, 1986).

69 Groux et al., "L'Atelier," p. 239.

70 Lazzarato et al., "Confection dans le Sentier," p. 181.

71 The major mode of Chinese garment shop financing, though, is the *tontine*. See chap. 7; and Jean-Pierre Hassoun and Y.-P. Tan, "Les Chinois de Paris, Minorité culturelle ou constellation ethnique," *Terrain*, no. 7 (Oct. 1986), pp. 34–44.

72 Lazzarato et al., "Confection dans le Sentier," pp. 168–69, underlined in the original.

73 See, e.g., Solange Montagné-Villette, *Le Sentier, Un espace ambigu*, p. 122.

74 *Passages*, Dec. 1988; Hassoun and Tan, "Chinois de Paris."

75 *Actuel*, Apr. 1988.

76 Ibid.

77 Sandrine Tasmadjian, interview, Aug. 4, 1987; Green et al., "Quartiers parisiens," p. 89.

78 Vuddamalay, "Mauriciens en France," pp. 357, 340, note 1.

79 Hovanessian, *Trois générations d'Arméniens*, pp. 156, 158, 178, 210–11, 220–30; Lazzarato et al., "Confection dans le Sentier," p. 183; Green et al., "Quartiers parisiens," pp. 189, 192, 126, and chap. 5 (written by Tasmadjian); Green et al., "Habitat/travail," chap. 5 (written by Tasmadjian); and Sandrine Tasmadjian, interviews, Paris, Aug. 4, 1987, and Dec. 19, 1995.

80 Jocelyne Dakhlia, "La question des lieux communs," in *Les formes de l'expérience: Une autre histoire sociale,* ed. Bernard Lepetit (Paris: Albin Michel, 1995), pp. 39–61.

81 *Passages,* Dec. 1988.

82 Ibid.

83 *Actuel,* Apr. 1988.

84 Ibid.

85 *Passages,* Dec. 1988.

Conclusion

1 In 1995, a townhouse complex in Los Angeles was raided, where some seventy Thais were working in sweatshop conditions and being held against their will. The employers (the owner was called "Auntie") had confiscated their passports and let no one out of the compound; money was deducted from wages to pay back the passage money and cost of false documents (*Washington Post,* Sept. 10, 1995). On deindustrialization and globalization, see Folker Fröbel, Jürgen Heinrichs, and Otto Kreye, *The New International Division of Labor;* Saskia Sassen, *The Global City: New York, London, Tokyo* (Princeton: Princeton University Press, 1991).

2 Organisation internationale du travail, *Réunion technique tripartite pour l'industrie du vêtement, Compte rendu sommaire,* 1964, p. 42; idem, *4ème réunion* (1995), 2:41.

3 Marguerite Audoux, *L'Atelier de Marie-Claire* [1920] (Paris: Grasset, 1987), pp. 96–107. When the dressmakers' shop converted to making ready-made goods for a department store, they still ended up working Christmas Eve to get out a rush order (pp. 136–38, 147–48).

4 For the *salons de la misère,* see chap. 5 above. Also see "A Stain on Fashion," *Washington Post,* Sept. 12, 1995.

5 Louise C. Odencrantz, *Italian Women in Industry,* p. 63.

6 *Libération* (Paris), Apr. 22, 1987.

7 Letellier is the main author of the articles on "Le travail féminin à Paris, avant et depuis la guerre, dans les industries du vêtement," which appeared from Oct. 1925 through Sept. 1929 in the *Bulletin du Ministère du travail.* See especially the first article; and Leon Stein, ed., *Out of the Sweatshop,* p. 326.

8 See chap. 3, note 64 above.

9 Nancy L. Green, "L'histoire comparative et le champ des études migratoires," *Annales E.S.C.,* no. 6 (Nov.–Dec. 1990): 1335–50.

10 Preface to the French edition, Jacques Le Goff, *Histoire et mémoire* (Paris: Gallimard, 1988), p. 13.

11 LeGoff, *History and Memory* (New York: Columbia University Press, 1992), p. 124.

12 Eli Elias, interview, New York, Mar. 2, 1984.

13 Mrs. Chin, in Stein, ed., *Out of the Sweatshop,* p. 326.

14 *New York Times,* Mar. 12, 1995. See e.g., Bernard Wong, *Chinatown,* on the functioning of the Chinese immigrant network.

15 On paternalism, see, e.g., Donald Reid, "Industrial Paternalism: Discourse and Practice in 19th-Century French Mining and Metallurgy," *Comparative Studies in Society and History* 27 (1985): 579–607; idem, "In the Name of the Father—A Language of Labor-Relations in Nineteenth-Century France," *History Workshop,* no. 38 (1994): 1–22.

16 Martine Hovanessian, *Le lien communautaire,* p. 212.

17 Alejandro Portes and Robert L. Bach, *Latin Journey;* Suzanne Model, "Ethnic Bonds in the Work Place: Blacks, Italians, and Jews in New York City," Ph.D. diss., University of Michigan, 1985, e.g., pp. 361–62, 375–76, 407; Roger D. Waldinger, *Through the Eye of the Needle;* and Mirjana Morokvasic, "Immigrants in the Parisian Garment Industry," *Work, Employment and Society* 1 (1987): 441–62.

18 E.g., the debate between Bonacich and Waldinger in *International Migration Review* 27 (1993): 685–701.

19 Waldinger, *Through the Eye of the Needle,* pp. 157, 163, and more generally, pp. 160–66. Cf. Waldinger, "The Ethnic Enclave Debate Revisited," *The International Journal of Urban and Regional Research* 17, no. 3 (1993): 428–36.

20 Waldinger in Abeles et al., *Chinatown Study,* p. 61.

21 Cf. "ethnic commonalities also provide a repertoire of symbols and customs that can be invoked or manipulated to underline the cultural interests and similarities that owners share with their work forces" (Mirjana Morokvasic, Roger Waldinger, and Annie Phizacklea, "Business on the Ragged Edge: Immigrant and Minority Business in the Garment Industries of Paris, London, and New York," in *Ethnic Entrepreneurs,* ed. Waldinger, Aldrich and Ward, p. 172.

22 Waldinger, *Through the Eye of the Needle,* pp. 165, 161. This Dominican owner had a mixed Hispanic workforce.

23 Vasoodevan Vuddamalay, "Les mécanismes de structuration du mouvement migratoire mauricien en France," doctoral thesis, Ecole des Hautes Etudes en Sciences Sociales, 1993, p. 361.

24 *Actuel* (Paris), Apr. 1988.

25 Harold Siegel, Greater Blouse, Skirt and Undergarment (contractors') Association, interview, New York, Aug. 22, 1984.

26 Irving R. Stuart, "A Study of Factors Associated with Inter-Group Conflict in the Ladies' Garment Industry in New York City," Ph.D. diss., New York University, 1951, p. 102; United States Industrial Commission, *Reports of the Industrial Commission,* 19 vols., 15: 325–27, 343–44.

27 "Members in Union Two or More Years," 1934, S. Cohen shop, Local 62 Series, Box 11, File 2, ILGWU Archives; Helen Everett Meiklejohn, "Dresses— The Impact of Fashion on a Business," in *Price and Price Policies,* ed. Walton Hamilton, p. 354; ILGWU, *The Story of the ILGWU,* p. 28; Max Danish, *The World of David Dubinsky,* p. 298.

28 Jacob Loft, "Jewish Workers in the New York City Men's Clothing Industry," *Jewish Social Studies* 2 (Jan. 1940): 77, discussing men's wear.

29 Préfecture de Police Archives, BA1394: Tailleurs, grèves des ouvriers, file "Grève . . . Printemps, mars 1916."

30 Mirjana Morokvasic, "Le Recours aux immigrés dans la confection à Paris: Eléments de comparaison avec la ville de Berlin-Ouest," Ministère du travail et de la formation professionnelle: Mission de liaison interministérielle pour la lutte contre les trafics de main-d'oeuvre, Paris, 1986, p. 28. The sample consisted of undocumented immigrant garment workers whose status was legalized in 1981–83.

31 Guy Groux et al., "L'Atelier, l'habit et la règle: L'Evolution récente des relations professionnelles et des stratégies syndicales dans les PME de l'habillement," report, Ministère du travail, de l'emploi et de la formation professionnelle, 1989; *Hommes et migrations*, Sept. 1993; *Libération*, Apr. 22, 1987. See also Nancy L. Green et al., "Les quartiers parisiens de l'industrie de l'habillement et les relations pluri-ethniques," report, Ministère de la culture, MIRE, 1987, pp. 126–29.

32 Emanuel Federated Employment Service, "An Industrial Survey of the Needle Trades to Determine a Vocational Guidance Policy for Young Men of Jewish Descent with regard to the Industry," p. 33.

33 Green et al., "Quartiers parisiens," p. 188.

34 See introduction, along with Jonathan Zeitlin, "Industrial Districts and Local Economic Regeneration," in *Industrial Districts and Local Economic Regeneration*, ed. Frank Pyke and Werner Sengenberger (Geneva: International Institute for Labour Studies, 1992). Alfred Marshall first developed the idea of industrial districts in 1890. See Alfred Marshall, *Principles of Economics* [1890] (London: Macmillan, 8th ed., 1922), pp. 267–90. Cf. Waldinger, *Through the Eye of the Needle*, p. 143, on the "low-trust" environment.

35 Maryse Tripier, "L'immigration dans la classe ouvrière en France," thèse d'état, Université de Nantes, 1987, pp. 362–63; Caroline B. Brettell, "Is the Ethnic Community Inevitable? A Comparison of the Settlement Patterns of Portuguese Immigrants in Toronto and Paris," *The Journal of Ethnic Studies* 9 (Fall 1981): 1–17; Gans, "Comment: Ethnic Invention and Acculturation," *Journal of American Ethnic History* 12, no. 1 (Fall 1992): p. 45, arguing that ethnicity has been used as a surrogate for class in the United States.

36 Harold Siegel, interview, Aug. 22, 1984.

37 Cf. Gérard Noiriel, *La Tyrannie du national;* and Dominique Schnapper, *La communauté des citoyens;* Donald Horowitz and Gérard Noiriel, eds., *Immigrants in Two Democracies.*

38 Cf. Schnapper, *Communauté des citoyens;* and Patrick Simon, "Nommer pour agir," *Le Monde* (Paris), Apr. 28, 1993.

39 David Hollinger has contrasted the "particularist enthusiasms of the last three decades with the universalist initiatives that preceded them" in the United States. See David A. Hollinger, "How Wide the Circle of the 'We'?

American Intellectuals and the Problem of the Ethnos since World War II," *American Historical Review* 98 (Apr. 1993): 322; idem, *Postethnic America: Beyond Multiculturalism* (New York: Basic Books, 1995); John Higham, "Multiculturalism and Universalism: A History and Critique," *American Quarterly* 45 (June 1993): 195–256. As Marco Martiniello has noted in *L'ethnicité dans les sciences sociales contemporaines* (Paris: PUF, Que-Sais-je, 1995), p. 5, the term ethnic has become used in France as "régulièrement associé à des aspects dégradants et rétrogrades de l'humanité."

40 For a historicization of this issue, see Nancy L. Green, "L'immigration en France et aux Etats-Unis, Historiographie comparée," *Vingtième siècle*, no. 29 (Jan.–Mar. 1991), pp. 67–82; and François Weil, "Migrations, migrants et ethnicité," in *Chantiers d'histoire américaine*, ed. Jean Heffer and François Weil, pp. 407–432.

41 Katznelson, *City Trenches* (Chicago: University of Chicago Press, 1981), p. 18. Richard Oestreicher challenged this dichotomy, speaking of multiple cultural systems, in "Urban Working-Class Political Behavior and Theories of American Electoral Politics, 1870–1940," *The Journal of American History* 74 (Mar. 1988): 1257–86.

42 *Industrial Commission,* 15:321.

BIBLIOGRAPHY

Archival Material

New York

Center for Migration Studies. Staten Island.
  001, 027, 028: American Committee on Italian Migration.
City College Oral History Research Project. "New York City Immigrant Labor
  Oral History Collection." Tamiment Library.
International Ladies' Garment Workers' Union Archives.
  (I consulted the Archives when they were still in New York City. They have
  since been transferred to the New York State School of Industrial and Labor
  Relations at Cornell University. *ILGWU* box and file numbers are indicated
  in the notes as, e.g., Dubinsky 30:2.)
  Presidents' Correspondence:
    Benjamin Schlesinger. 1914–23, 1928–32.
    Morris Sigman. 1923–28.
    David Dubinsky. 1932–66.
    Louis Stulberg. 1966–75.
  Local Managers' Correspondence:
    Local 9—Cloak and Suit Finishers, NYC. Isidore Sorkin, 1933–41; Louis
      Hyman, 1942–51.
    Local 10—Cutters, NYC. Isidore Nagler, 1939–52; Moe Falikman, 1952–
      68.
    Local 22—Dressmakers' Union. Collection 32/22/15; Collection 32/22/
      57 (Education Dept.); also, see Zimmerman below.

Local 48—Italian Cloakmakers. 1916–72.

Local 62—Underwear and Negligee, NYC. Samuel Shore, 1930–46; Louis Stulberg, 1947–56.

Local 89—Italian Dressmakers, NYC. See Antonini below.

Local 105—1939–70.

Local 155—Knit Goods, NYC. Louis Nelson, 1932–68.

Antonini, Luigi. General Secretary, Italian Dressmakers' Union. 1919–68.

Cohn, Fannia. Executive Secretary, Education Dept., 1918–62.

Tyler, Gus. Assistant President, 1963–80.

Umhey, Frederick F. Executive Secretary, 1934–55.

Zimmerman, Charles S. (Collection 32/22/14). Secretary-Manager, Dressmakers' Union, 1933–58.

New York Cloak Joint Board.

New York Dress and Waistmakers' Joint Board. Julius Hochman, 1928–58; Charles S. Zimmerman, 1958–72.

Research Department Collection.

Paris

Archives Nationales, Paris (AN).

F^{7}12767: Textile.

F^{7}12768: Tailleurs d'habits.

F^{7}13250: Anti-fascisme 1929 (re foreign labor).

F^{7}13518–19: Etrangers en France, 1881–1935.

F^{7}13740–41: Habillement, 1920–1929.

F^{7}13880–81: Chapeliers, tailleurs, grèves.

F^{7}13882–83: Habillement, grèves.

F^{7}13975: Surveillance des menées communistes.

F^{12}8054: Transformation de textiles.

F^{12}10477–84: Vêtement, correspondance générale, 1941–1944.

F^{12}10497: Vêtement, organisation de l'habillement.

F^{22}376: Repos hebdomadaire, tailleurs, et al.

F^{22}439: Travail des femmes et enfants.

F^{22}441: Travail des femmes et enfants.

F^{22}443: Travail des femmes et enfants.

F^{22}471: Travail des femmes et enfants.

F^{22}571: Ateliers de couture.

Archives de la Seine, Paris.

D.P.—Patentes:

Rue de Cléry, 1925, 1931, 1934.

Rue du Sentier, 1925, 1931, 1934.

Manuscript census:

Rue de Cléry, 1926, 1931, 1936.

Rue du Sentier, 1926, 1931, 1936.

Confédération générale du travail Archives, Montreuil.

Fédération de l'habillement et de la chapellerie, *Congrès national*, 1948 and 1950, typescripts.

Préfecture de Police Archives, Paris (APP).

BA1376: Habillement, grèves 1917–1918.

BA1393–94: Tailleurs, grèves des ouvriers.

BA1423: Habillement, chambre syndicale.

BA1444: Tailleurs, chambre syndicale.

Printed Primary and Secondary Sources

Abbott, Edith. *Women in Industry.* 1910. Reprint, New York: Arno Press, 1969.

Abeles, Schwartz, Haeckel, Silverblatt, Inc. *The Chinatown Garment Industry Study.* New York: ILGWU Local 23–25 and New York Skirt and Sportswear Assn., 1983.

Accampo, Elinor A.; Rachel G. Fuchs; and Mary Lynn Stewart. *Gender and the Politics of Social Reform in France, 1870–1914.* Baltimore: Johns Hopkins University Press, 1995.

Adler, Jacques. *Face à la persécution.* Paris: Calmann-Lévy, 1985. Eng. ed. *The Jews of Paris and the Final Solution.* New York: Oxford University Press, 1987.

Aftalion, Albert. *Le développement de la fabrique et le travail à domicile dans les industries de l'habillement.* Paris: J.-B. Sirey and Journal du Palais, 1906.

Aine. *Les patronnes, employeés et ouvrières de l'habillement à Paris, leur situation morale et matérielle.* Paris: Société d'économie sociale, 1897.

Alexandre, Arsène. *Les reines de l'aiguille: Modistes et couturières.* Paris: Théophile Belin, 1902.

Allilaire, Jean. *Les industries de l'habillement et du travail des étoffes.* Paris: Société d'éditions françaises et internationales, 1947.

Amalgamated Ladies' Garment Cutters' Local 10. *Cutters' Almanac, 1902–1962.* New York: ILGWU, 1962.

Antonini, Luigi. *Dynamic Democracy.* New York: Eloquent Press Corp., [1944?].

Archdeacon, Thomas J. *Becoming American: An Ethnic History.* New York: Free Press, 1983.

Atsma, Hartmut, and André Burguière, eds. *Marc Bloch aujourd'hui: Histoire comparée et sciences sociales.* Paris: Editions de l'EHESS, 1990.

Auslander, Leora. *Taste and Power: Furnishing Modern France.* Berkeley: University of California Press.

Auslander, Leora, and Michelle Zancarini-Fournel. *Différences des sexes et protection sociale, XIXe–XXe siècles.* Saint-Denis: Presses Universitaires de Vincennes, 1995.

Bailey, Thomas, and Roger Waldinger. "Primary, Secondary, and Enclave Labor Markets: A Training Systems Approach." *American Sociological Review* 56 (Aug. 1991): 432–45.

Baily, Samuel L. "The Italians and the Development of Organized Labor in Argentine, Brazil and the United States, 1880–1914." *Journal of Social History* 3 (Winter 1969): 123–34.

——. "The Adjustment of Italian Immigrants in Buenos Aires and New York, 1870–1914." *American Historical Review* 88, no. 2 (Apr. 1983): 281–305.

Baker, Paula. "The Domestication of Politics: Women and American Political Society, 1780–1920." *American Historical Review* 89, no. 3 (1984): 620–47.

Baron, Ava, ed. *Work Engendered: Toward a New History of American Labor.* Ithaca: Cornell University Press, 1991.

Baron, Ava, and Susan Klepp. "'If I Didn't Have My Sewing Machine . . .': Women and Sewing Machine Technology." In *A Needle, a Bobbin, a Strike: Women Needleworkers in America,* edited by Joan M. Jensen and Sue Davidson. Philadelphia: Temple University Press, 1984, pp. 20–59.

Barth, Fredrik, ed. *Ethnic Groups and Boundaries: The Social Organization of Culture Difference.* Boston: Little, Brown, 1969.

Barthes, Roland. "Histoire et sociologie du vêtement." *Annales, E.S.C.* 12, no. 3 (July–Sept. 1957): 430–31.

——. *Système de la mode.* Paris: Seuil, 1967.

Baudrillard, Jean. *Le système des objets.* Paris: Gallimard, 1968.

——. *La société de consommation.* Paris: Gallimard, 1970.

Baum, Charlotte; Paula Hyman; and Sonya Michel. *The Jewish Woman in America.* New York: New American Library, 1975.

Bayor, Ronald H. *Neighbors in Conflict: The Irish, Germans, Jews, and Italians of New York City, 1929–1941.* Baltimore: Johns Hopkins University Press, 1978.

Belfer, Nathan. "Section Work in the Women's Garment Industry." *The Southern Economic Journal* 21, no. 2 (Oct. 1954): 188–200.

Bell, Quentin. *On Human Finery.* New York: Schocken Press, 1976.

Beltran, Alain; Robert Frank; and Henry Rousso, eds. *La vie des entreprises sous l'Occupation.* Paris: Belin, 1994.

Benería, Lourdes, and Martha Roldán. *The Crossroads of Class and Gender: Industrial Homework, Subcontracting, and Household Dynamics in Mexico City.* Chicago: University of Chicago Press, 1987.

Benoist, Charles. *Les ouvrières de l'aiguille à Paris.* Paris: L. Chailley, 1895.

Benveniste, Annie. *Le Bosphore à la Roquette: La communauté judéo-espagnole à Paris, 1914–1940.* Paris: L'Harmattan, 1989.

Berlanstein, Lenard R., ed. *Rethinking Labor History.* Urbana: University of Illinois Press, 1993.

——. *The Working People of Paris, 1871–1914.* Baltimore: Johns Hopkins University Press, 1984.

Berthelot, Jean. *Rapport de la classe 86B, Rapport du groupe XIIID: Industries accessoires du vêtement (Exposition coloniale internationale de Vincennes).* Edited by René Hayem. Paris: Ministère des Colonies, [1931].

Bezanson, Anna. "Skill." *Quarterly Journal of Economics* 36, no. 4 (Aug. 1922): 626–45.

Billig, Joseph. *Le Commissariat général aux questions juives (1941–1944).* 3 vols. Paris: CDJC, 1955–60.

Binder, Frederick M., and David M. Reimers. *All the Nations under Heaven: An Ethnic and Racial History of New York City.* New York: Columbia University Press, 1995.

Blanc-Chaléard, Marie-Claude. "Les Italiens dans l'Est parisien des années 1880 aux années 1960." Doctoral thesis. Institut d'Etudes Politiques, 1995.

Bloch, Marc. "Pour une histoire comparée des sociétés européennes." 1928. *Mélanges historiques,* vol. 1, pp. 16–40. Paris: Editions de l'EHESS, 1983.

Blum, Françoise. "Féminisme et syndicalisme: Les femmes dans la Fédération de l'habillement." Master's thesis, Université de Paris I, 1977.

Blumer, Herbert. "Fashion: From Class Differentiation to Collective Selection." *Sociological Quarterly* 10 (1969): 275–91.

Bodnar, John. *The Transplanted: A History of Immigrants in Urban America.* Bloomington: Indiana University Press, 1987.

Bollore, M. "Les activités textiles dans le quartier du Sentier." Paris: Atelier parisien d'urbanisme, 1972.

Bonacich, Edna. "A Theory of Middleman Minorities." *American Sociological Review* 38 (Oct. 1973): 583–95.

——. "A Theory of Ethnic Antagonism: The Split Labor Market." *American Sociological Review* 37, no. 5 (Oct. 1972): 547–59.

Bonacich, Edna, and Roger Waldinger. "The Other Side of Ethnic Entrepreneurship" and "The Two Sides of Ethnic Entrepreneurship." *International Migration Review* 27, no. 3 (1993): 685–701.

Bonnet, Jean-Charles. *Les pouvoirs publics et l'immigration dans l'entre-deux guerres.* Lyon: Université de Lyon–2, 1976.

Bookbinder, Hyman H., Associates. *To Promote the General Welfare: The Story of the Amalgamated.* New York: ACWA, 1950.

Boris, Eileen. *Home to Work: Motherhood and the Politics of Industrial Homework in the United States.* Cambridge: Cambridge University Press, 1994.

Bourdieu, Pierre. *La distinction.* Paris: Editions de Minuit, 1979.

Bourdieu, Pierre, and Yvette Delsaut. "Le couturier et sa griffe: Contribution à une théorie de la magie." *Actes de la recherche en sciences sociales,* no. 1 (Jan. 1975): 7–36.

Bouvier, Jeanne. *La lingerie et les lingères.* Paris: Gaston Doin et Cie., 1928.

——. *Mes mémoires.* Vienna: L'Action intellectuelle, 1936.

Bouvier, Pierre. *Socio-anthropologie du contemporain.* Paris: Galilée, 1995.

——. *Le travail au quotidien: Une démarche socio-anthropologique.* Paris: PUF, 1989.

Bouvier, Pierre, and Olivier Kourchid, eds. *France-U.S.A.: Les crises du travail et de la production*. Paris: Meridiens Klincksieck, 1988.

Boxer, Marilyn. "Women in Industrial Homework: The Flowermakers of Paris in the Belle Epoque." *French Historical Studies* 12, no. 3 (Spring 1982): 401–23.

——. "Protective Legislation and Home Industry: The Marginalization of Women Workers in Late-Nineteenth–Early-Twentieth Century France." *Journal of Social History* 20, no. 1 (Fall 1986): 45–65.

Brandes, Joseph. "From Sweatshop to Stability: Jewish Labor between Two World Wars." *YIVO Annual* 16 (1976): 1–149.

Brandon, Ruth. *A Capitalist Romance*. Philadelphia: J. B. Lippincott Co., 1977.

Budish, J. M., and George Soule. *The New Unionism in the Clothing Industry*. New York: Harcourt, Brace and Howe, 1920.

Bythell, Duncan. *The Sweated Trades: Outwork in 19th-century Britain*. New York: St. Martin's Press, 1978.

Cannistraro, Philip V. "Luigi Antonini and the Italian Anti-Fascist Movement in the U.S., 1940–1943." *Journal of American Ethnic History* 5, no. 1 (Fall 1985): 21–40.

Caron, Vicki. "Loyalties in Conflict: French Jewry and the Refugee Crisis, 1933–1935." *Leo Baeck Institute Yearbook* 36 (1991): 305–37.

——. *Uneasy Asylum: France and the Jewish Refugee Crisis of the 1930s*. Stanford: Stanford University Press, forthcoming.

Carpenter, Jesse Thomas. *Competition and Collective Bargaining in the Needle Trades, 1910–1967*. Ithaca: New York State School of Industrial and Labor Relations, 1972.

Carson, Claybourne. "Blacks and Jews in the Civil Rights Movement." In *Jews in Black Perspectives*, edited by Joseph Washington. London: Fairleigh Dickinson, 1985, pp. 113–31.

Castellani, Loris. "La bolchévisation des groupes de langue italienne au sein du PCF." *La Trace*, no. 4 (Oct. 1990): 7–13.

Catin, Roger. "Les industries textiles et celles de l'habillement." Course lectures. Paris: Institut d'Etudes Politiques, 1951–52.

Centre d'études et de documentation sur l'immigration italienne. *L'immigration italienne en France dans les années 1920*. Paris: CEDEI, 1987.

Chan, Sucheng. *Asian Americans: An Interpretive History*. Boston: Twayne, 1991.

Chandler, Alfred D., Jr. *The Visible Hand: The Managerial Revolution in American Business*. Cambridge: Harvard University Press, 1977.

Chapkis, Wendy, and Cynthia Enloe, eds. *Of Common Cloth: Women and the Global Textile Industry*. Amsterdam: Transnational Institute, 1983.

Chenault, Lawrence. *The Puerto Rican Migrant in New York City*. New York: Columbia University Press, 1938.

Clothing Manufacturers' Association of the U.S.A. *A Statement, Indicating the Economic Status of Our Industry and Its Importance in Times of Peace and in National Emergency*. N.p., 1961.

Bibliography

Coffin, Judith G. "Credit, Consumption, and Images of Women's Desires: Selling the Sewing Machine in Late Nineteenth-Century France." *French Historical Studies* 18, no. 3 (Spring 1994): 749–83.

———. "Gender and the Guild Order: The Garment Trades in 18th-Century Paris." *Journal of Economic History* 54, no. 4 (Dec. 1994): 768–93.

———. *The Politics of Women's Work: The Paris Garment Trades, 1750–1915.* Princeton: Princeton University Press, 1996.

———. "Social Science Meets Sweated Labor: Reinterpreting Women's Work in Late Nineteenth-Century France." *Journal of Modern History* 63, no. 2 (June 1991): 230–70.

———. "Woman's Place and Women's Work in the Paris Clothing Trades, 1830–1914." Ph.D. diss., Yale University, 1985.

Cohen, Lizabeth A. "Embellishing a Life of Labor: An Interpretation of the Material Culture of American Working-Class Homes, 1885–1915." In *Labor Migration in the Atlantic Economies,* edited by Dirk Hoerder. Westport, Conn.: Greenwood Press, 1985, pp. 321–52.

———. *Making a New Deal: Industrial Workers in Chicago, 1919–1939.* New York: Cambridge University Press, 1990.

Cohen, Miriam. *Workshop to Office: Two Generations of Italian Women in New York City, 1900–1950.* Ithaca: Cornell University Press, 1992.

Cohen, Miriam, and Michael Hanagan. "The Political Economy of Social Reform: The Case of Homework in New York and Paris, 1900–1940." *French Politics and Society* 6, no. 4 (Oct. 1988): 31–38.

———. "The Politics of Gender and the Making of the Welfare State, 1900–1940: A Comparative Perspective." *Journal of Social History* 24 (Spring 1991): 469–84.

Collomp, Catherine. "Syndicats ouvriers et immigration aux Etats-Unis, 1881–1900." Thèse d'état, Université de Paris-8, 2 vols., 1985.

———. "Ethnic Identity, Americanization and Internationalism in the Jewish Labor Movement in the 1920s." In *Ethnic Cultures in the 1920s in North America,* edited by Wolfgang Binder. Frankfurt am Main: Peter Lang, 1993, pp. 157–73.

Commissariat général du [VIe] plan, *Rapports des comités: Industrie de l'habillement, Industrie du cuir et de la chaussure.* Paris: La Documentation française, 1971.

Commission internationale d'histoire des mouvements sociaux et des structures sociales. *Les migrations internationales de la fin du XVIIIe siècle à nos jours.* Paris: Editions du CNRS, 1980.

———. *Petite entreprise et croissance industrielle dans le monde aux XIXe et XXe siècles.* 2 vols. Paris: Editions du CNRS, 1981.

Conseiller commercial de France à New York. *Le marché de la confection féminine aux Etats-Unis.* N.p., 1960.

Contant, Jacqueline. *L'industrie à domicile salariée.* Paris: Librairie technique et économique, 1937.

Bibliography

Conzen, Kathleen, et al. "The Invention of Ethnicity: A Perspective from the U.S.A." *Journal of American Ethnic History* 12, no. 1 (Fall 1992): 3–41.

Coons, Lorraine. *Women Home Workers in the Parisian Garment Industry, 1860–1915.* New York: Garland Publishing, 1987.

Cooper, Grace Rogers. *The Sewing Machine: Its Invention and Development.* Washington, D.C.: GPO, 1976.

Costa-Lascoux, Jacqueline, and Live Yu-Sion. *Paris-XIIIe, Lumières d'Asie.* Paris: Autrement, 1995.

Cotelle, Théodore. *Le "sweating-system," Etude sociale.* 2d ed. Angers: J. Siraudeau, 1904.

Cottereau, Alain. "Problèmes de conceptualisation comparative de l'industrialisation: L'exemple des ouvriers de la chaussure en France et en Grande Bretagne." In *Villes ouvrières, 1900–1950,* edited by Susanna Magri and Christian Topalov. Paris: L'Harmattan, 1989, pp. 41–82.

Couder, Laurent. "Les immigrés italiens dans la région parisienne dans les années 1920." Doctoral thesis, Institut d'Etudes Politiques, 1987.

Coyle, Angela. "Sex and Skill in the Organization of the Clothing Industry." In *Work, Women and the Labour Market,* edited by Jackie West. London: Routledge and Kegan Paul, 1982, pp. 10–26.

Crawford, John Stuart. *Luigi Antonini: His Influence on Italian-American Relations.* New York: Local 89 ILGWU, 1950.

Cray, Ed. *Levi's.* Boston: Houghton Mifflin, 1978.

Cross, Gary S. *Immigrant Workers in Industrial France.* Philadelphia: Temple University Press, 1983.

Daniels, Roger. *Coming to America: A History of Immigration and Ethnicity in American Life.* New York: Harper, 1990.

Danish, Max. *The World of David Dubinsky.* Cleveland and New York: World Publishing Co., 1957.

Daulatly, Georges. *La main-d'oeuvre étrangère en France et la crise économique.* Paris: Domat-Montchrestien, 1933.

Davies, Robert Bruce. *Peacefully Working to Conquer the World: Singer Machines in Foreign Markets, 1854–1920.* New York: Arno Press, 1976.

Debect, Edouard. *L'habillement féminin en France au point de vue industriel et commercial.* Poitiers: Imprimerie Maurice Bousrez, 1908.

De Certeau, Michel. *La culture au pluriel.* 1974. Reprint, Paris: Christian Bourgois, 1980.

De La Torre, José R., et al. *Corporate Responses to Import Competition in the U.S. Apparel Industry.* Atlanta: Georgia State University College of Business Administration, 1978.

DeMarly, Diana. *The History of Haute Couture, 1850–1950.* New York: Holmes and Meier, 1986.

Deschamps, Germaine. *La crise dans les industries du vêtement et de la mode à Paris pendant la période de 1930 à 1937.* Paris: Librairie technique et économique, 1937.

Desmyttere, Jacques. *Les grandes industries modernes: Les industries textiles et celles de l'habillement.* Paris: Les cours de droit, 1955–56.

"Le devenir des industries du textile et de l'habillement." *Journal officiel,* Feb. 25, 1982.

De Vissec, L. Delpon. "De la distribution du travail à domicile dans l'industrie de la confection parisienne." *Mémoires et documents du Musée social* 5 (Mar. 1908): 81–95.

Dinnerstein, Leonard; Roger L. Nichols; and David M. Reimers. *Natives and Strangers.* New York: Oxford University Press, 1979.

Divine, Robert A. *American Immigration Policy, 1924–1952.* New Haven: Yale University Press, 1957.

Doublot, Camille. *La protection légale des travailleurs de l'industrie du vêtement.* Paris: Société du Recueil général des lois et des arrêts et du Journal du Palais, 1899.

Downs, Laura Lee. *Manufacturing Inequality: Gender Division in the French and British Metalworking Industries, 1914–1939.* Ithaca: Cornell University Press, 1995.

———. "Women's Strikes and the Politics of Popular Egalitarianism in France, 1916–1918." In *Rethinking Labor History,* edited by Lenard Berlanstein. Urbana: University of Illinois Press, 1993, pp. 114–48.

Doyen, Marcel. *Thimonnier 1793–1857: Inventeur de la machine-à-coudre.* Lyon: Imprimerie Lescuyer, 1968.

Drake, Leonard A., and Carrie Glasser. *Trends in the New York Clothing Industry.* New York: Institute of Public Administration, 1942.

Dreyfus, Michel. *Histoire de la CGT.* Brussels: Complexe, 1995.

Dubinsky, David, and A. H. Raskin. *David Dubinsky: A Life with Labor.* New York: Simon and Schuster, 1977.

Dubofsky, Melvyn. *When Workers Organize: New York City in the Progressive Era.* Amherst: University of Massachusetts Press, 1968.

Dubois, Pierre. *L'industrie de l'habillement: L'innovation face à la crise.* Paris: Documentation française, 1988.

Dubois, Pierre, and Giusto Barisi. *Le défi technologique dans l'industrie de l'habillement: Les stratégies des entrepreneurs français et italiens.* Paris: CNRS, Groupe de Sociologie du travail, 1982.

Du Maroussem, Pierre. *La question ouvrière.* 4 vols. Paris: Arthur Rousseau, 1892.

———. *La petite industrie (salaires et durée du travail).* Vol. 2: *Le vêtement à Paris.* Paris: Imprimerie nationale, 1896.

Du Roselle, Bruno. *La crise de la mode.* Paris: Fayard, 1973.

Dyche, John. *Bolchevism in American Labor Unions: A Plea for Constructive Unionism.* New York: Boni and Liveright, 1926.

Dye, Nancy Schrom. *As Equals and Sisters: The Labor Movement and the Women's Trade Union League of New York.* Columbia: University of Missouri Press, 1980.

Bibliography

Emanuel Federated Employment Service. "An Industrial Survey of the Needle Trades to Determine a Vocational Guidance Policy for Young Men of Jewish Descent with Regard to the Industry." New York: n.p., 1931.

Epstein, Melech. *Jewish Labor in U.S.A. (1882–1952)*. 2 vols. New York: Trade Union Sponsoring Committee, 1950–53.

Etienne, R.-M.; P. Bucaille; and R. Deffains. *Guide professionnel du textile et du vêtement et de leurs accessoires*. Rouen: R.-M. Etienne, 1942.

Ewen, Elizabeth. *Immigrant Women in the Land of Dollars: Life and Culture on the Lower East Side, 1890–1925*. New York: Monthly Review Press, 1985.

Ewen, Stuart, and Elizabeth Ewen. *Channels of Desire: Mass Images and the Shaping of American Culture*. New York: McGraw-Hill, 1982.

Faraut, François. *Histoire de la Belle Jardinière*. Paris: Belin, 1987.

Faraut, François; Gilles Marcadet; and Jean-François Paoli. *Industries urbaines à Paris*. Paris: IDRASS, 1982.

Faure, Alain. "Note sur la petite entreprise en France au XIXe siècle: Représentations d'Etat et réalités." In *Entreprises et entrepreneurs XIX–XXe siècles*. Paris: Presses de l'Université de Paris Sorbonne, 1983, pp. 199–228.

——. "Petit atelier et modernisme économique: La production en miettes au XIXe siècle." *Histoire, économie et société* 5, no. 4 (1986): 531–57.

Fédération des travailleurs de l'habillement. *Comptes rendus des 1e* (Nîmes, 1893), *2e* (Lyon, 1894), *3e* (Toulouse, 1897), *6e* (Limoges, 1906), *7e* (Avignon, 1908), *8e* (Paris, 1910), *9e* (Bordeaux, 1912), *11e* (Lyon, 1919), et *12e* (Lille, 1921) *Congrès nationaux*.

Fédération unitaire des travailleurs du textile-vêtement (CGTU). *Comptes rendus des Congrès nationaux*. 1923 (Congrès de fusion), 1924, 1926.

Fédération des travailleurs de l'habillement (CGT réunifié). *Comptes rendus des Congrès nationaux*. Paris, 1935, 1937.

Fédération des travailleurs de l'habillement et de la chapellerie. *Comptes rendus des Congrès nationaux*. 1954, 1955. (For 1948 and 1950, see CGT Archives above.)

Fenton, Edwin. *Immigrants and the Union, A Case Study: Italians and American Labor, 1870–1920*. New York: Arno Press, 1975.

Fernandez, Nancy. "Women, Work and Wages in the Industrialization of American Dressmaking, 1860–1910." Paper presented at the 9th Berkshire conference on the History of Women, June 11–13, 1993.

Fine, Ben, and Ellen Leopold. "Consumerism and the Industrial Revolution." *Social History* 15, no. 2 (May 1990): 151–79.

Fishman, Joshua A., ed. *The Rise and Fall of the Ethnic Revival*. Berlin: Mouton Publishers, 1985.

Flé, Catherine. "L'insertion professionelle des réfugiés du Sud-est asiatique." Diplôme d'études approfondies, Université de Paris-7, 1985.

Flügel, John Carl. *The Psychology of Clothes*. 1930. Reprint, New York: AMS Press, 1976.

Focillon, A. "Tailleur d'habits de Paris." In *Les ouvriers des deux mondes,* vol. 2. Paris: Société internationale des études pratiques d'économie sociale, 1858.

Foerster, Robert F. *The Italian Emigration of our Times.* 2d ed. Cambridge: Harvard University Press, 1924.

Foner, Nancy, ed. *New Immigrants in New York.* New York: Columbia University Press, 1987.

Foner, Philip S. *Organized Labor and the Black Worker.* 1974. Reprint, New York: International Publishers, 1982.

Foner, Philip S., and Ronald L. Lewis, eds. *The Black Worker: A Documentary History.* 8 vols. Philadelphia: Temple University Press, 1978–84.

Frader, Laura. "Engendering Work and Wages: The French Labor Movement and the Family Wage." In *Gender and Class in Modern Europe*, edited by Laura L. Frader and Sonya O. Rose. Ithaca: Cornell University Press, 1996, pp. 142–64.

Frager, Ruth. *Sweatshop Strife: Class, Ethnicity, and Gender in the Jewish Labor Movement of Toronto, 1900–1939.* Toronto: University of Toronto Press, 1992.

Franklin, Charles Lionel. *The Negro Labor Unionist of New York.* New York: Columbia University Press, 1936.

Fraser, Steven. *Labor Will Live: Sidney Hillman and the Rise of American Labor.* New York: Free Press, 1991.

——. "*Landslayt* and *Paesani*: Ethnic Conflict and Cooperation in the Amalgamated Clothing Workers of America." In *"Struggle a Hard Battle": Essays on Working-Class Immigrants*, edited by Dirk Hoerder. DeKalb: Northern Illinois University Press, 1986, pp. 280–303.

Freeman, Gary P. *Immigrant Labor and Racial Conflict in Industrial Societies: The French and British Experience, 1945–1975.* Princeton: Princeton University Press, 1979.

Fridenson, Patrick. "Un tournant taylorien de la société française (1904–1918)." *Annales, E.S.C.* 42, no. 5 (Sept.–Oct. 1987): 1031–60.

Fridenson, Patrick, and André Straus, eds. *Le capitalisme français: Blocages et dynamismes d'une croissance.* Paris: Fayard, 1987.

Friedman-Kasaba, Kathie. *Memories of Migration: Gender, Ethnicity and Work in the Lives of Jewish and Italian Women in New York, 1870–1924.* Albany: SUNY Press, 1995.

Friedmann, Daniel. *Une histoire du blue-jean.* Paris: Ramsay, 1987.

Fröbel, Folker; Jürgen Heinrichs; and Otto Kreye. *The New International Division of Labor.* Cambridge and Paris: Cambridge University Press and Maison des Sciences de l'Homme, 1981.

Furio, Colomba Marie. "Immigrant Women and Industry: A Case Study. The Italian Immigrant Women and the Garment Industry, 1880–1950." Ph.D. diss., New York University, 1979.

Gabaccia, Donna. *From the Other Side: Women, Gender and Immigrant Life in the U.S., 1820–1990.* Bloomington: Indiana University Press, 1994.

——. *From Sicily to Elizabeth Street: Housing and Social Change among Italian Immigrants, 1880–1930.* Albany: SUNY Press, 1984.

Bibliography

Gaillard, Jeanne. "Paris, la ville, 1852–1870." Doctoral thesis, Université de Paris-10, 1975.

Gamber, Wendy. *The Female Economy: The Millinery and Dressmaking Trades, 1860–1930.* Urbana: University of Illinois Press, forthcoming.

Gani. Léon. *Syndicats et travailleurs immigrés.* Paris: Editions sociales, 1972.

Gans, Herbert. "Comment: Ethnic Invention and Acculturation, A Bumpy-Line Approach." *Journal of American Ethnic History* 12, no. 1 (Fall 1992): 42–52.

——. "Symbolic Ethnicity: The Future of Ethnic Groups and Cultures in America." *Ethnic and Racial Studies* 2 (1979): 1–20.

Geertz, Clifford. "The Uses of Diversity." *Michigan Quarterly Review* 25, no. 1 (Winter 1986): 105–23.

Gemähling, Paul. *Travailleurs au rabais, La lutte syndicale contre les sous-concurrences ouvrières.* Paris: Bloud et Cie., 1910.

Girard, Alain, and Jean Stoetzel. *Français et immigrés.* Travaux et Documents, vol. 19–20. Paris: INED, 1953–54.

Glazer, Nathan, and Daniel Patrick Moynihan. *Beyond the Melting Pot: The Negroes, Puerto Ricans, Jews, Italians and Irish of New York City.* Cambridge: MIT Press, 1963.

Gleason, Philip. "The Melting Pot: Symbol of Fusion or Confusion?" *American Quarterly* 16 (Spring 1964): 20–46.

Glenn, Susan. *Daughters of the Shtetl: Life and Labor in the Immigrant Generation.* Ithaca: Cornell University Press, 1990.

Godfrey, Frank P. *An International History of the Sewing Machine.* London: R. Hale, 1982.

Goldsen, Rose. *The Puerto Rican Journey: New York's Newest Migrants.* New York: Russell and Russell, 1967.

Goodman, Charles S. *The Location of Fashion Industries, with Special Reference to the California Apparel Market.* Ann Arbor: University of Michigan Press, 1948.

Gordon, David M.; Richard Edwards; and Michael Reich. *Segmented Work, Divided Workers: The Historical Transformation of Labor in the United States.* Cambridge, Eng.: Cambridge University Press, 1982.

Grasmuck, Sherri, and Patricia R. Pessar. *Between Two Islands: Dominican International Migration.* Berkeley: University of California Press, 1991.

Green, Nancy L. "Art and Industry: The Language of Modernization in the Production of Fashion." *French Historical Studies* 18, no. 3 (Spring 1994): 722–48.

——. "L'histoire comparative et le champ des études migratoires." *Annales E.S.C.*, no. 6 (Nov.–Dec. 1990): 1335–50.

——. "L'immigration en France et aux Etats-Unis, Historiographie comparée." *Vingtième siècle*, no. 29 (Jan.–Mar. 1991): 67–82.

——. *The Pletzl of Paris: Jewish Immigrant Workers in the Belle Epoque.* New York: Holmes and Meier, 1986.

Green, Nancy L.; Annie Benveniste; Jeanne Brody; and Sandrine Tasmadjian.

"Les quartiers parisiens de l'industrie de l'habillement et les relations pluri-ethniques." Report, Ministère de la culture, Mission recherche expérimentation (MIRE), 1987.

Green, Nancy L.; Kenan Ozturk; Yinh Phong Tan; Sandrine Tasmadjian; and Agnès Vince. "Les rapports habitat/travail dans l'industrie de l'habillement à Paris et dans sa banlieue." Report, Ministère de l'equipement, du logement, de l'aménagement du territoire et des transports, 1988.

Greenberg, Cheryl Lynn. *Or Does it Explode? Black Harlem in the Great Depression.* New York: Oxford University Press, 1991.

Greenfeld, Judith. "The Role of the Jews in the Development of the Clothing Industry in the United States." *YIVO Annual of Jewish Social Sciences* 2–3 (1947–48): 180–204.

Greig, Gertrud B. *Seasonal Fluctuations in Employment in the Women's Clothing Industry in New York.* New York: Columbia University Press, 1949.

Grew, Raymond. "The Case for Comparing Histories." *American Historical Review* 85, no. 4 (Oct. 1980): 763–78.

Groux, Guy; Eliane Le Dantec; Robert Linhart; and Giancarlo Santilli. "L'atelier, l'habit et la règle: L'évolution récente des relations professionnelles et des stratégies syndicales dans les PME de l'habillement." Report, Ministère du travail, de l'emploi et de la formation professionnelle, 1989.

Guilbert, Madeleine, and Viviane Isambert-Jamati. *Travail féminin et travail à domicile.* Paris: CNRS, 1956.

Guillon, Michelle, and Isabel Taboada-Leonetti. *Le triangle de Choisy: Un quartier chinois à Paris.* Paris: L'Harmattan, 1986.

Guizien, D. "L'industrie textile et de l'habillement en région parisienne." Paris: Institut d'aménagement et d'urbanisme de la région parisienne, 1973.

Gutman, Herbert. "Work, Culture, and Society in Industrializing America, 1815–1919." In *Work, Culture, and Society in Industrializing America, 1815–1919,* edited by Herbert Gutman. New York: Alfred A. Knopf, 1976, pp. 3–78.

Handlin, Oscar. *The Newcomers: Negroes and Puerto Ricans in a Changing Metropolis.* Cambridge, Mass.: Harvard University Press, 1959.

———. *The Uprooted.* 2d ed. 1951. Reprint, Boston: Little, Brown and Co., 1973.

Hardman, J. B. S. "Needle Trades in U.S." *Social Research* 27, no. 3 (Autumn 1960): 321–58.

Hardy, Jack. *The Clothing Workers: A Study of the Conditions and Struggles in the Needle Trades.* New York: International Publishers, 1935.

Hartmann, Heidi. "Capitalism, Patriarchy and Job Segregation by Sex." In *Women and the Workplace: The Implications of Occupational Segregation,* edited by Martha Blaxall and Barbara Reagan. Chicago: University of Chicago Press, 1976, pp. 137–69.

Hassoun, Jean-Pierre, and Y.-P. Tan. "Les Chinois de Paris, Minorité culturelle ou constellation ethnique." *Terrain,* no. 7 (Oct. 1986): 34–44.

Hausen, Karin. "Technical Progress and Women's Labour in the Nineteenth Century: The Social History of the Sewing Machine." In *The Social History of Politics*, edited by Georg Iggers. New York: St. Martin's Press, 1985, pp. 259–81.

Hauser, Henri, and Henri Hitier, eds. *Enquête sur la production française et la concurrence étrangère*. Vol. 2 of *Industries textiles—Industries du vêtement*. Paris: Association nationale d'expansion économique, 1917.

Helfgott, Roy B. "Trade Unionism among the Jewish Garment Workers of Britain and the United States." *Labor History* 2, no. 2 (1961): 202–14.

———. "Women's and Children's Apparel." In *Made in New York: Case Studies in Metropolitan Manufacturing*, edited by Max Hall. Cambridge, Mass.: Harvard University Press, 1959, pp. 19–134.

———. "Puerto Rican Integration in the Skirt Industry in New York City." In *Discrimination and Low Incomes*, edited by Aaron Antonovsky and Lewis Lorwin (pseud. Louis Levine). New York: New York State Commission Against Discrimination, 1959, pp. 249–79.

Hendricks, Glenn. *The Dominican Diaspora: From the Dominican Republic to New York City, Villagers in Transition*. New York: Teachers College Press, 1974.

Henri, Florette. *Black Migration: Movement North, 1900–1920*. Garden City, N.Y.: Anchor Books, 1975.

Herberg, Will. "The Old-Timers and the Newcomers: Ethnic Group Relations in a Needle Trades Union." *Journal of Social Issues* 9, no. 1 (1953): 12–19.

Higham, John. *Strangers in the Land: Patterns of American Nativism, 1860–1925*. 1955. Reprint, New York: Atheneum, 1985.

Hill, Herbert. "Guardians of the Sweatshops: The Trade Unions, Racism, and the Garment Industry." In *Puerto Rico and Puerto Ricans*, edited by Adalberto Lopez and James Petras. New York: Schenkman, 1974, pp. 384–416.

Hillsman, Sally. "Entry into the Labor Market: The Preparation and Job Placement of Negro and White Vocational High School Graduates." Ph.D. diss., Columbia University, 1970.

Hoffman, Kurt, and Howard Rush. *Micro-Electronics and Clothing: The Impact of Technical Change on a Global Industry*. New York: Praeger, 1988.

Hollander, Anne. *Sex and Suits: The Evolution of Modern Dress*. New York: Kodansha International, 1995.

Hoover, Edgar, and Raymond Vernon. *Anatomy of a Metropolis*. New York: Doubleday, 1959.

Horowitz, Donald L. "Europe and America: A Comparative Analysis of 'Ethnicity.'" *Revue européenne des migrations internationales* 5, no. 1 (2d trimester 1989): 47–61.

Horowitz, Donald L., and Gérard Noiriel, eds. *Immigrants in Two Democracies: French and American Experience*. New York: New York University Press, 1992.

Hounshell, David A. *From the American System to Mass Production, 1800–1932*. Baltimore: Johns Hopkins University Press, 1984.

Hourwich, Isaac. *Immigration and Labor*. New York: G. P. Putnam's Sons, 1912.

Hovanessian, Martine. *Le lien communautaire: Trois générations d'Arméniens.* Paris: Armand Colin, 1992.

Hutchinson, Edward P. *Immigrants and Their Children, 1850–1950.* New York: John Wiley and Sons, 1956.

——. *Legislative History of American Immigration Policy, 1798–1965.* Philadelphia: University of Pennsylvania Press, 1981.

Hyman, Paula. *From Dreyfus to Vichy: The Remaking of French Jewry.* New York: Columbia University Press, 1979.

Institut d'aménagement et d'urbanisme de la région d'Ile-de-France. *L'emploi dans le textile et l'habillement de l'Ile-de-France.* Paris: IAURIF, 1983.

International Ladies' Garment Workers' Union (ILGWU). "The Outside System of Production in the Women's Garment Industry in the New York Market: The Problems Which It Has Created, Their Adverse Effect upon the Workers, and the Provisions of the Existing Labor Agreements Which Have Aided in Their Solution." New York, 1951.

——. *Report of the General Executive Board and Record of the Proceedings of the Convention.* From the *1st Convention* (1900) through the *38th Convention* (1983).

ILGWU, Educational Department. *Equal Opportunity, Union Made.* New York: ILGWU, 1962.

——. *The Story of the ILGWU.* New York: ILGWU, 1935.

ILGWU, Local 89. *We, the Italian Dressmakers Speak.* New York: Eloquent Press Corp., 1944.

Jack, Andrew B. "The Channels of Distribution for an Innovation: The Sewing-Machine Industry in America, 1860–1865." *Explorations in Entrepreneurial History* 9, no. 3 (1957): 113–41.

Jacomet, Dominique. *Le textile-habillement: Une industrie de pointe!* Paris: Economica, 1987.

Jarnow, Jeanette, and Beatrice Judelle. *Inside the Fashion Business.* 2d ed. New York: John Wiley and Sons, 1974.

Jay, Raoul. *La semaine anglaise dans l'industrie du vêtement.* Paris: Félix Alcan and Marcel Rivière, 1917.

Jensen, Joan, and Sue Davidson, eds. *A Needle, a Bobbin, a Strike: Women Needleworkers in America.* Philadelphia: Temple University Press, 1984.

Jenson, Jane. "Representations of Gender: Policies to 'Protect' Women Workers and Infants in France and the United States before 1914." In *Women, the State, and Welfare,* edited by Linda Gordon. Madison: University of Wisconsin Press, 1990, pp. 152–77.

Johnson, Christopher H. "Economic Change and Artisan Discontent: The Tailors' History, 1800–48." In *Revolution and Reaction: 1848 and the 2d French Republic,* edited by Roger Price. London: Croom Helm, 1975, pp. 87–114.

——. "Patterns of Proletarianization: Parisian Tailors and Lodève Woolens Workers." In *Consciousness and Class Experience in Nineteenth-Century*

Bibliography

Europe, edited by John Merriman. New York: Holmes and Meier, 1979, pp. 65–84.

Johnson, Daniel M., and Rex R. Campbell. *Black Migration in America: A Social Demographic History.* Durham: Duke University Press, 1981.

Jollès, Georges, and Jean Bounine. "Un projet pour le textile-habillement français." Report, Ministère de l'industrie et de l'aménagement du territoire, 1989.

Juarbe, Ana. " 'Nosotras trabajamos en la costura . . .' Puerto Rican Women in the Garment Industry." *Newsletter of the Centro de Estudio Puertorriquenos* (Feb. 1984): 3–6.

Julliard, Jacques. *Autonomie ouvrière: Etudes sur le syndicalisme d'action directe.* Paris: Seuil, 1988.

Kaplan, Steven Laurence, and Cynthia J. Koepp, eds. *Work in France.* Ithaca: Cornell University Press, 1986.

Kastoryano, Riva. *Etre Turc en France.* Paris: L'Harmattan, 1986.

Katznelson, Ira. *Black Men, White Cities: Race, Politics and Migration in the United States, 1900–30, and Britain, 1948–68.* London: Oxford University Press, 1973.

Katznelson, Ira, and Aristide Zolberg, eds. *Working-Class Formation: Nineteenth-Century Patterns in Western Europe and the United States.* Princeton: Princeton University Press, 1986.

Kershen, Anne. *Uniting the Tailors.* Ilford, Essex: Frank Cass, 1995.

Kessler-Harris, Alice. "Organizing the Unorganizable: Three Jewish Women and Their Union." In *Class, Sex, and the Woman Worker,* edited by Milton Cantor and Bruce Laurie. Westport, Conn.: Greenwood Press, 1977, pp. 144–65.

——. *Out to Work: A History of Wage-Earning Women in the United States.* New York: Oxford University Press, 1982.

——. "Problems of Coalition-Building: Women and Trade Unions in the 1920s." In *Women, Work and Protest,* edited by Ruth Milkman. Boston: Routledge and Kegan Paul, 1985, pp. 110–38.

Kessner, Thomas. *The Golden Door: Italian and Jewish Immigrant Mobility in New York City, 1880–1915.* New York: Oxford University Press, 1977.

Kessner, Thomas, and Betty Boyd Caroli. "New Immigrant Women at Work: Italians and Jews in New York City, 1880–1905." *Journal of Ethnic Studies* 5, no. 4 (Winter 1978): 19–31.

Keyserling, Leon Hirsch. *The New York Dress Industry: Problems and Prospects.* N.p., 1963.

Keyssar, Alexander. *Out of Work: The First Century of Unemployment in Massachusetts.* New York: Cambridge University Press, 1986.

Kidwell, Claudia B., and Margaret C. Christman. *Suiting Everyone: The Democratization of Clothing in America.* Washington, D.C.: Smithsonian Institution Press for the National Museum of History and Technology, 1974.

Kim, Illsoo. *The New Urban Immigrants: Korean Immigrants in New York City.* Princeton: Princeton University Press, 1981.

Bibliography

Klatzmann, Joseph. *Le travail à domicile dans l'industrie parisienne du vête-ment.* Paris: Armand Colin, 1957.

Klaus, Alisa. *Every Child a Lion: The Origins of Infant Health Policy in the United States and France, 1890–1920.* Ithaca: Cornell University Press, 1993.

Kleiner, Harry. *The Garment Jungle.* Screenplay. 1956.

Korcarz, Sylvie, ed. *Les technologies nouvelles face à la mode.* Paris: Centre d'études des systèmes et des technologies avancées, 1986.

Koven, Seth, and Sonya Michel. "Womanly Duties: Maternalist Politics and the Origins of Welfare States in France, Germany, Great Britain, and the United States, 1880–1920." *American Historical Review* 95, no. 4 (Oct. 1990): 1076–1108.

Kuisel, Richard. "L'American Way of Life' et les missions françaises de pro-ductivité." *Vingtième siècle,* no. 17 (Jan.–Mar. 1988): 21–38.

Kwong, Peter. *Chinatown, N.Y.: Labor and Politics, 1930–1950.* New York: Monthly Review Press, 1979.

——. *The New Chinatown.* New York: Noonday Press, 1987.

Laborde (M. le Comte de), Léon. *De l'union des arts et de l'industrie.* 2 vols. Paris: Imprimerie impériale, 1857.

Lacroix-Riz, Annie. "Autour d'Irving Brown: L'A.F.L., le Free Trade Union Committee, le Département d'Etat et la scission syndicale française (1944–1947)." *Le Mouvement social,* no. 151 (Apr.–June 1990): 79–118.

Lallement, Michel. *Des PME en chambre: Travail et travailleurs à domicile d'hier et d'aujourd'hui.* Paris: L'Harmattan, 1990.

Landes, David S. *The Unbound Prometheus: Technological Change and Indus-trial Development in Western Europe from 1750 to the Present.* Cambridge, Eng.: Cambridge University Press, 1969.

Larry Smith and Company. *Garment District Study.* 2 vols. New York: Larry Smith and Co., 1957.

Laurentz, Robert. "Racial/Ethnic Conflict in the New York City Garment In-dustry, 1933–1980." Ph.D. diss., SUNY-Binghamton, 1980.

Lazzarato, Maurizio; Yann Moulier-Boutang; Antonio Negri; and Giancarlo Santilli. *Des entreprises pas comme les autres: Benetton en Italie, Le Sentier à Paris.* Paris: Publisud, 1993.

Lazzarato, Maurizio; Antonio Negri; and Giancarlo Santilli. "La confection dans le quartier du Sentier." Report, Ministère du travail, de l'emploi et de la formation professionnelle, MIRE, 1990.

Leduc, Albert. *Classe 36: Habillement des deux sexes, Exposition universelle internationale de 1889 à Paris: Rapports du jury international.* Edited by Alfred Picard. Paris: Imprimerie nationale for the Ministère du commerce, de l'industrie et des colonies, 1891.

Leeder, Elaine J. *The Gentle General: Rose Pesotta, Anarchist and Labor Orga-nizer.* Albany: SUNY Press, 1993.

Le Febvre, Yves. *L'ouvrier étranger et la protection du travail national.* Paris: C. Jacques et Cie., 1901.

Bibliography

Leichter, Senator Franz S. "The Return of the Sweatshop." Unpublished. 3 vols. 1979–82.

Lémann. *De l'industrie des vêtements confectionnés en France.* Paris: Paul Dupont, 1857.

Lemire, Beverly. "The Theft of Clothes and Popular Consumerism in Early Modern England." *Journal of Social History* 24, no. 2 (Winter 1990): 255–76.

Lequin, Yves, ed. *La mosaïque France: Histoire des étrangers et de l'immigration.* Paris: Larousse, 1988.

Levasseur, Emile. *L'ouvrier américain.* 2 vols. Paris: L. Larose, 1898.

——. *Questions ouvrières et industrielles en France sous la 3e République.* Paris: Arthur Rousseau, 1907.

Levine, Louis. *The Women's Garment Workers: A History of the International Ladies' Garment Workers' Union.* New York: B. W. Huebsch Inc., 1924.

Lieberson, Stanley. *A Piece of the Pie: Blacks and White Immigrants since 1880.* Berkeley: University of California Press, 1980.

Liebman, Arthur. *Jews and the Left.* New York: John Wiley and Sons, 1979.

Light, Ivan. *Ethnic Enterprise in America: Business and Welfare among Chinese, Japanese and Blacks.* Berkeley: University of California Press, 1972.

Lipovetsky, Gilles. *L'Empire de l'éphémère.* Paris: Gallimard, 1991. English trans: *The Empire of Fashion.* Princeton: Princeton University Press, 1994.

Live, Yu-Sion. "La diaspora chinoise en France." Doctoral thesis, Ecole des Hautes Etudes en Sciences Sociales, 1991.

Livian, Marcel. *Le régime juridique des étrangers en France.* Paris: Librairie générale de droit et de jurisprudence, 1936.

Loft, Jacob. "Jewish Workers in the New York City Men's Clothing Industry." *Jewish Social Studies* 2, no. 1 (Jan. 1940): 61–78.

Loo, Chalsa, and Paul Ong. "Slaying Demons with a Sewing Needle: Feminist Issues for Chinatown's Women." *Berkeley Journal of Sociology* 27 (1982): 77–87.

Loucky, James, et al. "Immigrant Enterprise and Labor in the Los Angeles Garment Industry." In *Global Production: The Apparel Industry in the Pacific Rim,* edited by Edna Bonacich et al. Philadelphia: Temple University Press, 1994, pp. 345–61.

Lupiac, Jean. *La loi du 10 juillet 1915 pour la protection des ouvrières dans l'industrie du vêtement.* Paris: Librairie Arthur Rousseau, 1918.

Lurie, Alison. *The Language of Clothes.* New York: Random House, 1981.

Magee, Mabel A. *Trends in Location of the Women's Clothing Industry.* Chicago: University of Chicago Press, 1930.

Malkiel, Theresa Serber. *The Diary of a Shirtwaist Striker.* Edited by Françoise Basch. Ithaca: ILR Press, 1990.

Ma Mung, Emmanuel. "Logiques du travail clandestin des Chinois." In *Espaces et travail clandestins,* edited by Solange Montagné-Villette. Paris: Masson, 1991, pp. 99–106.

Margairaz, Michel, and Henry Rousso. "Vichy, la guerre et les entreprises." *Histoire, économie et société* 11 (3d trimester 1992): 337–67.

Marks, Carole. *Farewell—We're Good and Gone: The Great Black Migration.* Bloomington: Indiana University Press, 1989.

Marrus, Michael, and Robert O. Paxton. *Vichy France and the Jews.* New York: Basic Books, 1981.

Marshall, Ray. *The Negro and Organized Labor.* New York: John Wiley, 1965.

Mauco, Georges. *Les étrangers en France.* Paris: Armand Colin, 1932.

McCreesh, Carolyn D. *Women in the Campaign to Organize Garment Workers, 1880–1917.* New York: Garland Publishing, 1985.

Meikle, Jeffrey L. *Twentieth-Century Limited: Industrial Design in America, 1925–1939.* Philadelphia: Temple University Press, 1979.

Meiklejohn, Helen Everett. "Dresses—The Impact of Fashion on a Business." In *Price and Price Policies,* edited by Walton Hamilton. New York: McGraw-Hill, 1938, pp. 299–393.

Mellinger, Pierre; Marie-Annick Oury; and Haude Salomon De Saint Severin. *Guide pratique de l'exportation du textile et de l'habillement aux Etats-Unis.* Paris: Centre français du commerce extérieur, 1985.

Mény, Georges. *La lutte contre le sweating-system.* Paris: M. Rivière, 1910.

Mesnaud de Saint-Paul, Jean. *De l'immigration étrangère en France considérée au point de vue économique.* Paris: Arthur Rousseau, 1902.

Meyers, Robert James. *The Economic Aspects of the Production of Men's Clothing.* Chicago: University of Chicago Libraries, 1937.

Milkman, Ruth. "Gender and Trade Unionism in Historical Perspective." In *Women, Politics, and Change,* edited by Louise Tilly and Patricia Gurin. New York: Russell Sage Foundation, 1990, pp. 87–107.

——. "Organizing Immigrant Women in New York's Chinatown: An Interview with Katie Quan." In *Women and Unions: Forging a Partnership,* edited by Dorothy Sue Cobble. Ithaca: ILR Press, 1993, pp. 281–98.

——. "Organizing the Sexual Division of Labor: Historical Perspectives on 'Women's Work' and the American Labor Movement." *Socialist Review* 10 (Jan.–Feb. 1980): 95–150.

Mill, John Stuart. "Two Methods of Comparison." In *Comparative Perspectives: Theories and Methods,* edited by Amitai Etzioni and Frederic DuBow. Boston: Little, Brown, 1970, pp. 205–13. (Excerpt from *A System of Logic,* 1888).

Miller, Michael B. *The Bon Marché: Bourgeois Culture and the Department Store, 1869–1920.* Princeton: Princeton University Press, 1981.

Milza, Pierre, ed. *Les Italiens en France de 1914 à 1940.* Paris: Boccard, 1987.

Mink, Gwendolyn. *Old Labor and New Immigrants in American Political Development: Union, Party, and State, 1875–1920.* Ithaca: Cornell University Press, 1986.

Mission de liaison interministérielle pour la lutte contre les trafics de main-d'oeuvre. *Bilans de la lutte contre le trafic de main-d'oeuvre 1983, 1984–85.* Paris: Documentation française, 1983, 1986.

Mitchell, Allan. *The Divided Path: The German Influence on Social Reform in France after 1870.* Chapel Hill: University of North Carolina Press, 1991.

Moch, Leslie. *Moving Europeans: Migration in Western Europe Since 1650.* Bloomington: Indiana University Press, 1992.

Model, Suzanne. "Ethnic Bonds in the Work Place: Blacks, Italians, and Jews in New York City." Ph.D. diss., University of Michigan, 1985.

Mokyr, Joel. "Demand vs. Supply in the Industrial Revolution." In *The Economics of the Industrial Revolution,* edited by Joel Mokyr. London: Allen and Unwin, 1985, pp. 97–118.

Montagné-Villette, Solange. *Le Sentier, Un espace ambigu.* Paris: Masson, 1990.

Montgomery, David. *The Fall of the House of Labor: The Workplace, the State and American Labor Activism, 1865–1924.* Cambridge and Paris: Cambridge University Press and Maison des Sciences de l'Homme, 1987.

Mormino, Gary R., and George E. Pozzetta. *The Immigrant World of Ybor City: Italians and their Latin Neighbors in Tampa, 1885–1985.* Urbana: University of Illinois Press, 1987.

Morokvasic, Mirjana. "Birds of Passage Are Also Women . . ." *International Migration Review* 18, no. 4 (Winter 1984): 886–907.

——. "Immigrants in Garment Production in Paris and in Berlin." In *Immigration and Entrepreneurship: Culture, Capital, and Ethnic Networks,* edited by Ivan Light and Parminder Bhachu. New Brunswick: Transaction Publishers, 1993, pp. 75–95.

——. "Immigrants in the Parisian Garment Industry." *Work, Employment and Society* 1, no. 4 (1987): 441–62.

——. "Le recours aux immigrés dans la confection à Paris: Eléments de comparaison avec la ville de Berlin-Ouest." Report, Ministère du travail et de la formation professionnelle: Mission de liaison interministérielle pour la lutte contre les trafics de main-d'oeuvre, Feb. 1986.

Morokvasic, Mirjana; Annie Phizacklea; and Hedwig Rudolph. "Small Firms and Minority Groups: Contradictory Trends in the French, German and British Clothing Industries." *International Sociology* 1, no. 4 (Dec. 1986): 397–419.

Morokvasic, Mirjana; Roger Waldinger; and Annie Phizacklea. "Business on the Ragged Edge: Immigrant and Minority Business in the Garment Industries of Paris, London, and New York." In *Ethnic Entrepreneurs: Immigrant Business in Industrial Societies,* edited by Roger Waldinger, Howard Aldrich, and Robin Ward. Newbury Park, Calif.: Sage Press, 1990, pp. 157–76.

Moustiers, Yvonne. *Le Sentier: Histoire d'un quartier célèbre.* Paris: Imprimerie du Palais, n.d.

Nadel, Stanley. "Reds versus Pinks: A Civil War in the International Ladies' Garment Workers' Union." *New York History* 66, no. 1 (Jan. 1985): 48–72.

Naison, Mark. *Communists in Harlem during the Depression.* Urbana: University of Illinois Press, 1983.

Nelli, Humbert S. *From Immigrants to Ethnics: The Italian-Americans*. New York: Oxford University Press, 1983.

New York City Board of Education. Vocational Survey Commission. "A Survey of the Garment Trades in New York City." N.p., 1930.

New York State Board of Mediation and Arbitration. *Annual Reports*. 1887–1900. (Then merged into Dept. of Labor reports.)

New York State Bureau of Factory Inspectors. *Annual Reports*. 1886–1900. (Then merged into Dept. of Labor reports.)

New York State Bureau of Industries and Immigration. *Annual Reports*. 1910–1921. (Then merged into Dept. of Labor reports.)

New York State Bureau of Labor Statistics. *Annual Reports*. 1883–1900. (Then merged into Dept. of Labor reports.)

New York State Department of Labor. *Annual Reports*. 1901–81.

——. "Report to the Governor and the Legislature on the Garment Manufacturing Industry and Industrial Homework." New York, 1982.

New York State Department of Labor Division of Employment. *The Women's Clothing Worker and Unemployment Insurance*. New York: Bureau of Research and Statistics, 1953.

New York State Department of Labor Homework Inspection Bureau. *Bulletin Relating to Tenement House Manufacture*. 1923–34.

New York State Governor's Advisory Commission. *Cloak, Suit and Skirt Industry of New York City*. New York: Evening Post Job Printing Office, 1925.

Noiriel, Gérard. *Le creuset français: Histoire de l'immigration XIXe–XXe siècles*. Paris: Seuil, 1988.

——. *Longwy: Immigrés et prolétaires, 1880–1980*. Paris: Presses Universitaires de France, 1984.

——. *La tyrannie du national: Le droit d'asile en Europe 1793–1993*. Paris: Calmann-Lévy, 1991.

Nord, Philip. "The Welfare State in France, 1870–1914." *French Historical Studies* 18, no. 3 (Spring 1994): 821–38.

Nugent, Walter. *Crossings: The Great Transatlantic Migrations, 1870–1914*. Bloomington: Indiana University Press, 1992.

Nystrom, Paul. *The Economics of Fashion*. New York: Ronald Press, 1928.

O'Brien, Patrick, and Calgar Keyder. *Economic Growth in Britain and France, 1780–1914: Two Paths to the Twentieth Century*. London: Allen and Unwin, 1978.

Odencrantz, Louise C. *Italian Women in Industry: A Study of Conditions in New York City*. New York: Russell Sage Foundation, 1919.

Offen, Karen. " 'Powered by a Woman's Foot': A Documentary Introduction to the Sexual Politics of the Sewing Machine in Nineteenth-century France." *Women's Studies International Forum* 11, no. 2 (1988): 93–101.

Office du Travail. *Associations professionnelles ouvrières*. Vol. 2: *Cuirs et peaux, industries textiles, habillement, ameublement, travail du bois*. Paris: Imprimerie nationale, 1901.

——. *Enquête sur le travail à domicile dans l'industrie de la lingerie.* 5 vols. Paris: Imprimerie nationale, 1907–11.

Olzak, Susan. *The Dynamics of Ethnic Competition and Conflict.* Stanford: Stanford University Press, 1992.

Oneal, James. *A History of the Amalgamated Ladies' Garment Cutters' Union Local 10.* New York: Local 10, 1927.

Orelick, Annelise. *Common Sense and a Little Fire: Women and Working-Class Politics in the United States, 1900–1965.* Chapel Hill: University of North Carolina Press, 1995.

Organisation internationale du travail. *1e, 2e, 3e et 4ème réunions techniques tripartites pour l'industrie du vêtement.* Geneva: Bureau International du Travail, 1964, 1980, 1987, 1995.

Ozturk, Kenan. "Les Turcs dans la confection à Paris." *Hommes et migrations,* no. 1116 (Nov. 1988): 22–28.

Pairault, André. *L'immigration organisée et l'emploi de la main-d'oeuvre étrangère en France.* Paris: PUF, 1926.

Parr, Joy. *The Gender of Breadwinners: Women, Men, and Change in Two Industrial Towns, 1880–1950.* Toronto: University of Toronto Press, 1990.

Paulin, Valentine. "Le travail à domicile en France, ses origines, son évolution, son avenir." *Revue internationale du travail* 37, no. 2 (Feb. 1938): 205–40.

Pedersen, Susan. *Family, Dependence, and the Origins of the Welfare State: Britain and France, 1914–1945.* New York: Cambridge University Press, 1993.

Pellegrin, Nicole. *Les vêtements de la liberté: Abécédaire des pratiques vestimentaires françaises de 1780 à 1800.* Paris: Alinéa, 1989.

Perlman, Selig. "Jewish-American Unionism, Its Birth Pangs and Contribution to the General American Labor Movement." *Publications of the American Jewish Historical Society* 41, no. 4 (June 1952): 297–337.

Perrot, Michelle. "Femmes et machines au XIXe siècle." *Romantisme,* no. 41 (1983): 5–17.

——. *Les ouvriers en grève, France 1871–1890.* 2 vols. Aix-en-Provence: Mouton and Ecole Pratique des Hautes Etudes, 1974.

——. "Les rapports des ouvriers français et des étrangers (1871–1893)." *Bulletin de la Société d'histoire moderne* 12e série, no. 12 (1960): 4–9.

Perrot, Philippe. *Les dessus et les dessous de la bourgeoisie.* Paris: Fayard, 1981. English trans: *Fashioning the Bourgeoisie: A History of Clothing in the 19th Century.* Princeton: Princeton University Press, 1994.

——. "Aspects socio-culturels des débuts de la confection parisienne au 19e siècle." *Revue de l'Institut de sociologie* (Brussels), no. 2 (1977): 185–202.

Pesotta, Rose. *Bread upon the Waters.* Ithaca: ILR Press, 1987.

Pessar, Patricia. "The Dominicans: Women in the Household and the Garment Industry." In *New Immigrants in New York,* edited by Nancy Foner. New York: Columbia University Press, 1987, pp. 103–129.

Phillips, Anne, and Barbara Taylor. "Sex and Skill: Notes towards a Feminist Economics." *Feminist Review,* no. 6 (1980): 79–88.

Bibliography

Phizacklea, Annie, ed. *One Way Ticket: Migration and Female Labour.* London: Routledge and Kegan Paul, 1983.

———. *Unpacking the Fashion Industry.* London: Routledge, 1990.

Piore, Michael J. *Birds of Passage: Migrant Labor and Industrial Societies.* Cambridge, Eng.: Cambridge University Press, 1979.

Piore, Michael J., and Charles F. Sabel. *The Second Industrial Divide.* New York: Basic Books, 1984.

Pope, Jesse. *The Clothing Industry in New York.* Columbia, Mo.: E. W. Stephens Publishing Co., 1905.

Portes, Alejandro, and Robert L. Bach. *Latin Journey: Cuban and Mexican Immigrants in the United States.* Berkeley: University of California Press, 1985.

Portes, Alejandro; Manuel Castells; and Lauren A. Benton, eds. *The Informal Economy: Studies in Advanced and Less Developed Countries.* Baltimore: Johns Hopkins University Press, 1989.

Prato, Giuseppe. *Le protectionnisme ouvrier.* Translated by Georges Bourgin. Paris: Marcel Rivière, 1912.

Prost, Antoine. "L'immigration en France depuis cent ans." *Esprit,* no. 348 (Apr. 1966): 532–45.

Przeworski, Adam, and Henry Teune. *Logic of Comparative Social Inquiry.* New York: John Wiley and Sons, 1970.

Pulos, Arthur J. *American Design Ethic: A History of Industrial Design to 1940.* Cambridge, Mass.: MIT Press, 1983.

———. *The American Design Adventure, 1940–1975.* Cambridge, Mass.: MIT Press, 1988.

Quartaert, Jean H. "A New View of Industrialization: 'Protoindustry' or the Role of Small-Scale, Labor-Intensive Manufacture in the Capitalist Environment." *International Labor and Working-Class History,* no. 33 (Spring 1988): 3–22.

Ramirez, Bruno. *On the Move: French Canadian and Italian Migrants in the North Atlantic Economy, 1860–1914.* Toronto: McClelland and Stewart, 1990.

Rancière, Jacques. "The Myth of the Artisan: Critical Reflections on a Category of Social History." *International Labor and Working-Class History,* no. 24 (Fall 1983): 1–16.

Raulin, Anne. "Espaces marchands et concentrations urbaines minoritaires— La petite Asie de Paris." *Cahiers internationaux de sociologie* 85 (1988): 225–42.

Ravenstein, E. G. "The Laws of Migration." *Journal of the Royal Statistical Society* 48, no. 2 (1885): 167–235; 52, no. 2 (1889): 241–305.

Reddy, William M. *Money and Liberty in Modern Europe.* Cambridge: Cambridge University Press, 1987.

———. *The Rise of Market Culture: The Textile Trade and French Society, 1750–1900.* Cambridge and Paris: Cambridge University Press and Maison des Sciences de L'Homme, 1984.

Reid, Donald. "In the Name of the Father—A Language of Labor-Relations in Nineteenth-Century France." *History Workshop,* no. 38 (1994): 1–22.

Reutlinger, Andrew S. "Reflections on the Anglo-American Jewish Experience: Immigrants, Workers, and Entrepreneurs in New York and London, 1870–1914." *American Jewish Historical Quarterly* 66, no. 4 (June 1977): 473–84.

Rhein, Catherine. "Jeunes femmes au travail dans le Paris de l'entre-deux-guerres." Doctoral thesis, Université de Paris-7, 1977.

Ribeiro, Aileen. *Fashion in the French Revolution.* New York: Holmes and Meier, 1988.

Richards, Charles Russell. *Art in Industry.* New York: Macmillan Co., 1922.

Richards, Florence S. *The Ready-to-Wear Industry, 1900–1950.* New York: Fairchild Publishers, Inc., 1951.

Rischin, Moses. *The Promised City: New York's Jews, 1870–1914.* New York: Corinth Books, 1962.

Robert, Jean-Louis. *Les ouvriers, la patrie, et la Révolution: Paris, 1914–1919.* Besançon: Presses universitaires de Besançon, 1995.

Roberts, Mary Louise. *Civilization without Sexes: Reconstructing Gender in Postwar France, 1917–1927.* Chicago: University of Chicago Press, 1994.

Roblin, Michel. *Les Juifs de Paris.* Paris: A. et J. Picard, 1952.

Roche, Daniel. *La culture des apparences: Une histoire du vêtement XVIIe–XVIIIe siècle.* Paris: Fayard, 1989. Eng. trans: *The Culture of Clothing: Dress and Fashion in the Ancien Régime.* New York: Cambridge University Press, 1994.

Romier, Lucien. *La confection.* Paris: Association nationale d'expansion économique, 1917.

Rosenwaike, Ira. *Population History of New York City.* Syracuse: Syracuse University Press, 1972.

Roshco, Bernard. *The Rag Race: How New York and Paris Run the Breakneck Business of Dressing American Women.* New York: Funk and Wagnalls, 1963.

Rousso, Henry. "L'aryanisation économique: Vichy, l'occupant et la spoliation des Juifs." *Yod,* no. 15–16 (1982): 51–79.

———. "Les comités d'organisation, Aspects structurels et économiques, 1940–1944." Master's thesis, Université de Paris-1 and Ecole Normale Supérieure de St. Cloud, 1976.

Rudder, Véronique de. "Immigrant Housing and Integration in French Cities." In *Immigrants in Two Democracies: French and American Experience,* edited by Donald Horowitz and Gérard Noiriel. New York: New York University Press, 1992, pp. 247–67.

Sabel, Charles F. and Jonathan Zeitlin. "Historical Alternatives to Mass Production: Politics, Market, and Technology in Nineteenth-Century Industrialization." *Past and Present,* no. 108 (Aug. 1985): 133–76.

———, eds. *Worlds of Possibility: Flexibility and Mass Production in Western Industrialization.* Paris: Maison des Sciences de l'Homme, forthcoming.

Bibliography

Salzman, Jack, ed. *Bridges and Boundaries: Blacks and Jews.* New York: Braziller, 1992.

Samuel, Raphael. "The Workshop of the World: Steam Power and Hand Technology in Mid-Victorian Britain." *History Workshop* 3 (1977): 6–72.

Sanchez Korrol, Virginia. *From Colonia to Community: The History of Puerto Ricans in New York City, 1917–1948.* Westport, Conn.: Greenwood Press, 1983.

Sassen, Saskia. *The Mobility of Labor and Capital.* Cambridge: Cambridge University Press, 1988.

Sassen-Koob, Saskia. "New York's Informal Economy." In *The Informal Economy,* edited by Alejandro Portes, Manuel Castells, and Lauren A. Benton. Baltimore: Johns Hopkins University Press, 1989, pp. 60–77.

Sauvy, Alfred. *Le travail noir et l'économie de demain.* Paris: Calmann-Lévy, 1984.

Sayad, Abdelmalek. "Les trois âges de l'émigration algérienne." *Actes de la recherche en sciences sociales* 15 (June 1977): 59–79.

Schirmacher, Mlle (Käthe). *La spécialisation du travail—Par nationalités, à Paris.* Paris: Arthur Rousseau, 1908.

Schmiechen, James. *Sweated Industries and Sweated Labor: The London Clothing Trades, 1860–1914.* Urbana: University of Illinois Press, 1984.

Schnapper, Dominique. "Centralisme et fédéralisme culturels: Les émigrés italiens en France et aux Etats-Unis." *Annales, E.S.C.* 29, no. 5 (Sept.–Oct. 1974): 1141–59.

——. *La communauté des citoyens.* Paris: Gallimard, 1994.

——. "Quelques réflexions sur l'assimilation comparée des travailleurs émigrés italiens et des Juifs en France." *Bulletin de la Société française de sociologie* 3, no. 7 (July 1976): 11–18.

Schofield, Ann. *"To Do and to Be": Ladies, Immigrants, and Workers, 1893–1986.* Boston: Northeastern University Press, forthcoming.

Schor, Ralph. *L'opinion française et les étrangers, 1919–1939.* Paris: Publications de la Sorbonne, 1985.

Scott, Joan Wallach. *Gender and the Politics of History.* New York: Columbia University Press, 1988.

——. "Men and Women in the Parisian Garment Trades: Discussions of Family and Work in the 1830s and 1840s." In *The Power of the Past: Essays for Eric Hobsbawm,* edited by Pat Thane, Geoffrey Crossick, and Roderick Floud. Cambridge and Paris: Cambridge University Press and Maison des Sciences de l'Homme, 1984, pp. 67–93.

——. "Statistical Representations of Work: The Politics of the Chamber of Commerce's *Statistique de l'Industrie à Paris, 1847–1848.*" In *Work in France,* edited by Steven Laurence Kaplan and Cynthia J. Koepp. Ithaca: Cornell University Press, 1984, pp. 335–63.

Scranton, Philip. *Figured Tapestry: Production, Markets, and Power in Philadelphia Textiles, 1885–1941.* Cambridge: Cambridge University Press, 1989.

Bibliography

———. "Manufacturing Diversity: Production Systems, Markets, and an American Consumer Society, 1870–1930." *Technology and Culture* 35 (1994): 476–506.

———. *Proprietary Capitalism: The Textile Manufacture at Philadelphia, 1800–1885.* Cambridge: Cambridge University Press, 1983.

Sée, Raymonde. *Le costume de la Révolution à nos jours.* Paris: Editions de la Gazette des Beaux-Arts, 1929.

Seidman, Joel. *The Needle Trades.* New York: Farrar and Rinehart, 1942.

Seilhac, Léon de. *L'industrie de la couture et de la confection à Paris.* Paris: Firmin-Didot, 1897.

Selekman, Ben Morris; Henriette R. Walter; and W. J. Couper. *The Clothing and Textile Industries in New York and Its Environs.* New York: Regional Plan of New York and Its Environs, 1925.

Seller, Maxine Schwartz. "The Uprising of the Twenty Thousand: Sex, Class, and Ethnicity in the Shirtwaist Makers' Strike of 1909." In *"Struggle a Hard Battle": Essays on Working-Class Immigrants,* edited by Dirk Hoerder. DeKalb: Northern Illinois University Press, 1986, pp. 254–79.

Sewell, Jr., William H. "Marc Bloch and the Logic of Comparative History." *History and Theory* 6, no. 2 (1967): 208–18.

Shallcross, Ruth. *Industrial Homework.* New York: Industrial Affairs Publishing Co., 1939.

Sices, Murray. *Seventh Avenue.* New York: Fairchild Publications, 1953.

Silverman, Debora L. *Art Nouveau in Fin-de-Siècle France.* Berkeley: University of California Press, 1989.

Simmel, Georg. "Fashion." 1904. *The American Journal of Sociology* 62, no. 6 (May 1957): 541–58.

Simon, Julian L. *The Economic Consequences of Immigration.* Oxford: Basil Blackwell, 1989.

Simon, Philippe. *Monographie d'une industrie de luxe, la haute couture.* Paris: Presses Universitaires de France, 1931.

Singer-Kerel, Jeanne. "Foreign Workers in France, 1891–1936." *Ethnic and Racial Studies* 14, no. 3 (July 1991): 279–93.

———. "'Protection' de la main-d'oeuvre nationale en temps de crise: Le précédent des années trente." *Revue européenne des migrations internationales* 5, no. 2 (1989): 7–27.

Skocpol, Theda. *Protecting Soldiers and Mothers: The Political Origins of Social Policy in the United States.* Cambridge, Mass.: Harvard University Press, 1992.

———, ed. *Vision and Method in Historical Sociology.* Cambridge, Eng.: Cambridge University Press, 1984.

Smelser, Neil J., ed. *Comparative Methods in the Social Sciences.* Englewood Cliffs, N.J.: Prentice Hall, 1976.

Smith, Bernard. "Hyper-Innovation and the American Women's Clothing Trades, 1880–1930." Paper presented at the Social Science History Association Meeting, Baltimore, November 5, 1993.

Smith, Carol Joan. "Women, Work, and Use of Government Benefits: A Case Study of Hispanic Women Workers in New York's Garment Industry." Ph.D. diss., Adelphi University, 1980.

Sollors, Werner. *Beyond Ethnicity: Consent and Descent in American Culture.* New York: Oxford University Press, 1986.

Sonenscher, Michael. *Work and Wages: Natural Law, Politics and the 18th-Century French Trades.* Cambridge: Cambridge University Press, 1989.

Spero, Sterling D., and Abram L. Harris. *The Black Worker: The Negro and the Labor Movement.* New York: Columbia University Press, 1931.

Stack, John. *International Conflict in an American City: Boston's Irish, Italians, and Jews, 1935–1944.* Westport, Conn.: Greenwood Press, 1979.

Stansell, Christine. *City of Women: Sex and Class in New York, 1789–1860.* Urbana: University of Illinois Press, 1987.

Steele, Valerie. *Paris Fashion: A Cultural History.* New York: Oxford University Press, 1988.

Steinberg, Stephen. *The Ethnic Myth.* Boston: Beacon Press, 1981.

Stein, Leon. *The Triangle Fire.* Philadelphia: J. B. Lippincott Co., 1962.

———, ed. *Out of the Sweatshop.* New York: Quadrangle, 1977.

Stewart, Mary Lynn. *Women, Work and the French State: Labour Protection and Social Patriarchy, 1879–1919.* Kingston: McGill-Queen's University Press, 1989.

Stone, Judith. *The Search for Social Peace: Reform Legislation in France, 1890–1914.* Albany: SUNY Press, 1985.

Stone, Nahum I. *Productivity of Labor in the Cotton-Garment Industry.* Washington, D.C.: Government Printing Office, 1939.

Storch, Léon (Classe 85); Julien Hayem; and Auguste Mortier (Classe 86). *Industrie de la confection et de la couture pour hommes, femmes et enfants. Exposition universelle internationale de 1900 à Paris: Rapports du jury international, Groupe XIII. Fils, tissus, vêtements, 2e partie—Classes 85 et 86.* Paris: Imprimerie nationale, 1902.

Stott, Richard B. *Workers in the Metropolis: Class, Ethnicity, and Youth in Antebellum New York City.* Ithaca: Cornell University Press, 1990.

Strong, Earl D. *Amalgamated Clothing Workers of America.* Grinnell, Iowa: Herald-Register Publishing Co., 1940.

Stuart, Irving R. "A Study of Factors Associated with Inter-Group Conflict in the Ladies' Garment Industry in New York City." Ph.D. diss., New York University, 1951.

———. "Minorities vs. Minorities." *Journal of Social Psychology* 59 (1963): 93–99.

Takaki, Ronald. *Strangers from a Different Shore.* New York: Penguin, 1989.

Tan, Yinh Phong. "Restaurants et ateliers: Le travail des Sino-khmers à Paris." *ASEMI* 15, no. 1–4 (1984): 277–91.

Tapinos, Georges. *L'immigration étrangère en France.* Paris: PUF, 1975.

Tarde, Gabriel de. *Les lois de l'imitation.* 1895. Reprint, Geneva: Slatkine Reprints, 1979.

Bibliography

Teper, Lazare, and Nathan Weinberg. *Aspects of Industrial Homework in the Apparel Trades.* New York: ILGWU Research Dept., 1941.

Ter Minassian, Anahide. "Les Arméniens de France." *Les Temps modernes* 43, no. 504–506 (July–Sept. 1988): 189–234.

Tilly, Louise A. "Paths of Proletarianization: Organization of Production, Sexual Division of Labor, and Women's Collective Action." *Signs* 7, no. 2 (Winter 1981): 400–417.

Tilly, Louise A., and Joan W. Scott. *Women, Work and Family.* New York: Holt, Rinehart and Winston, 1978.

Tobier, Emanuel. "Manhattan's Business District in the Industrial Age." In *Power, Culture, and Place: Essays on New York City,* edited by John Mollenkopf. New York: Russell Sage Foundation, 1988, pp. 77–105.

Torres, Andrés. *Between Melting Pot and Mosaic: African Americans and Puerto Ricans in the New York Political Economy.* Philadelphia: Temple University Press, 1995.

"Le travail féminin à Paris, avant et depuis la guerre, dans les industries du vêtement." *Bulletin du Ministère du travail,* 15 articles running from 32, no. 10–12 (Oct.–Dec. 1925): 345–61 through 36, no. 7–9 (July–Sept. 1929): 209–26.

Tribalat, Michèle, ed. *Cent ans d'immigration: Etrangers d'hier, Français d'aujourd'hui.* Paris: PUF and INED, Travaux et Documents, 1991.

Tripier, Maryse. *L'Immigration dans la classe ouvrière française.* Paris: CIEMI L'Harmattan, 1990.

——. "Travailleurs immigrés, Pour l'analyse des générations migratoires." In *Les communautés pertinentes de l'action collective,* edited by Denis Segrestin. Paris: CNAM, Copedith, 1981, pp. 5–19.

Truant, Cynthia M. "The Guildswomen of Paris: Gender, Power and Sociability in the Old Regime." *Proceedings of the Annual Meeting of the Western Society for French History* 15 (Western Society for French History, 1988): 130–38.

Tyler, Gus. *Look for the Union Label: A History of the International Ladies' Garment Workers' Union.* Armonk, N.Y.: M. E. Sharpe, 1995.

United States House of Representatives, Committee on Education and Labor. *Investigation of Labor Irregularities and Discrimination in the Garment Industry.* Washington, D.C.: Government Printing Office, 1962.

United States Immigration Commission. *Reports of the Immigration Commission.* 42 vols. Washington, D.C.: Government Printing Office, 1911.

United States Industrial Commission. *Reports of the Industrial Commission.* 19 vols. Washington, D.C.: Government Printing Office, 1900–1902.

Vanier, Henriette. *La mode et ses métiers: Frivolités et luttes des classes, 1830–1870.* Paris: Armand Colin, 1960.

Vautier, M.D. Hubert de. *Exposition internationale de Saint-Louis (1904), Rapport du groupe 59.* Paris: Comité français des expositions à l'étranger, 1906.

Veblen, Thorstein. *The Theory of the Leisure Class.* New York: Macmillan, 1899.

Bibliography

Vecoli, Rudolph J. "European Americans: From Immigrants to Ethnics." *International Migration Review* 6, no. 4 (Winter 1972): 403–34.

Veillon, Dominique. *La mode sous l'Occupation: Débrouillardise et coquetterie dans la France en guerre (1939–1945)*. Paris: Payot, 1990.

Vichniac, Judith E. *The Management of Labor: The British and French Iron and Steel Industries, 1860–1918*. Greenwich, Conn.: JAI Press, 1990.

Viet, Vincent. *Les voltigeurs de la République: L'inspection du travail en France jusqu'en 1914*. 2 vols. Paris: CNRS Editions, 1994.

Vincent-Ricard, Françoise. *Raison et passion: Langages de société, La mode 1940–1990*. Paris: Textile/Art/Langage, 1983.

Wacquant, Loïc. "Banlieues françaises et ghetto noir américain: De l'amalgame à la comparaison." *French Politics and Society* 10, no. 4 (Fall 1992): 81–103.

Waldinger, Roger. "Another Look at the International Ladies' Garment Workers' Union: Women, Industry Structure and Collective Action." In *Women, Work, and Protest*, edited by Ruth Milkman. Boston: Routledge and Kegan Paul, 1985, pp. 86–109.

——. *Still the Promised City? New Immigrants and African-Americans in Post-Industrial New York*. Cambridge: Harvard University Press, 1996.

——. *Through the Eye of the Needle: Immigrants and Enterprise in New York's Garment Trades*. New York: New York University Press, 1986.

Waldinger, Roger; Howard Aldrich; and Robin Ward, eds. *Ethnic Entrepreneurs: Immigrant Business in Industrial Societies*. Newbury Park, Calif.: Sage Press, 1990.

Waldinger, Roger, and Michael Lapp. "Back to the Sweatshop or Ahead to the Informal Sector?" *International Journal of Urban and Regional Research* 17, no. 1 (1993): 6–29.

Wall, Irwin. *The United States and the Making of Postwar France, 1945–1954*. Cambridge: Cambridge University Press, 1991.

Walton, Whitney. *France at the Crystal Palace: Bourgeois Taste and Artisan Manufacture in the Nineteenth Century*. Berkeley: University of California Press, 1992.

Ward, David, and Olivier Zunz, eds. *The Landscape of Modernity: Essays on New York City, 1900–1940*. New York: Russell Sage Foundation, 1992.

Washington, Joseph R., ed. *Jews in Black Perspectives: A Dialogue*. London: Fairleigh Dickinson, 1985.

Webb, Beatrice. "How to Do away with the Sweating System." In *Problems of Modern Industry*, edited by Sidney and Beatrice Webb. New York: Longmans, Green and Co., 1902, pp. 139–55.

Webb, Sidney, and Arnold Freeman, eds. *Seasonal Trades*. London: Constable and Co., Ltd., 1912.

Wechsler, Robert. "The Jewish Garment Trade in East London, 1875–1914." Ph.D. diss., Columbia University, 1979.

Weil, François. "Migrations, migrants, ethnicité." In *Chantiers d'histoire américaine*, edited by Jean Heffer and François Weil. Paris: Belin, pp. 407–32.

Bibliography

Weinberg, David. *Les Juifs à Paris de 1933 à 1939*. Paris: Calmann-Lévy, 1974. Eng. ed.: *A Community on Trial: The Jews of Paris in the 1930s*. Chicago: University of Chicago Press, 1977.

Weiner, Elizabeth, and Hardy Green. "A Stitch in Our Time: New York's Hispanic Garment Workers in the 1980s." In *A Needle, a Bobbin, a Strike: Women Needleworkers in America*, edited by Joan Jensen and Sue Davidson. Philadelphia: Temple University Press, 1984, pp. 278–96.

Wertheimer, Barbara, and Anne Nelson. *Trade Union Women: A Study of Their Participation in New York City Locals*. New York: Praeger, 1975.

White, Paul; Hilary Winchester; and Michelle Guillon. "South-East Asian Refugees in Paris." *Ethnic and Racial Relations* 10, no. 1 (Jan. 1987): 48–61.

Wilentz, Sean. *Chants Democratic: New York City and the Rise of the American Working Class, 1788–1850*. New York: Oxford University Press, 1984.

Willett, Mabel Hurd. *The Employment of Women in the Clothing Trade*. New York: Columbia University Press, 1902.

Williams, Rosalind H. *Dream Worlds: Mass Consumption in Late 19th-Century France*. Berkeley: University of California Press, 1982.

Willoughby, Gertrude. *La situation des ouvrières du vêtement en France et en Angleterre*. Paris: Presses Universitaires de France, 1926.

Wilson, Elizabeth. *Adorned in Dreams: Fashion and Modernity*. Berkeley: University of California Press, 1987.

Wong, Bernard. *Chinatown: Economic Adaptation and Ethnic Identity of the Chinese*. New York: Holt, Rinehart and Winston, 1982.

——. "New Immigrants in New York's Chinatown." In *New Immigrants in New York*, edited by Nancy Foner. New York: Columbia University Press, 1987, pp. 243–71.

Wong, Morrison G. "Chinese Sweatshops in the United States: A Look at the Garment Industry." In *Research in the Sociology of Work*, edited by Ida Simpson and Richard Simpson. Greenwich, Conn.: JAI Press, 1983, pp. 357–79.

Woodward, C. Vann, ed. *The Comparative Approach to American History*. New York: Basic Books, 1968.

Worth, Gaston. *La couture et la confection des vêtements de femme*. Paris: Imprimerie Chaix, 1895.

Wrong, Elaine Gale. *The Negro in the Apparel Industry*. Philadelphia: Wharton School Industrial Research Unit, 1974.

Yans-McLaughlin, Virginia. *Family and Community: Italian Immigrants in Buffalo, 1880–1930*. Ithaca: Cornell University Press, 1977.

——. "Metaphors of Self in History: Subjectivity, Oral Narrative, and Immigration Studies." In *Immigration Reconsidered*, edited by Virginia Yans-McLaughlin. New York: Oxford University Press, 1990, pp. 254–90.

Young, Agnes. *Recurring Cycles of Fashion, 1760–1937*. New York: Harper and Bros., 1937.

Zappia, Charles A. "Unionism and the Italian American Worker: A History of the New York City 'Italian Locals' in the ILGWU, 1900–1934." Ph.D. diss., University of California, Berkeley, 1994.

Zaretz, Charles. *The Amalgamated Clothing Workers of America.* New York: Ancon Publishing Co., 1934.

Zdatny, Steven. *The Politics of Survival: Artisans in Twentieth-Century France.* New York: Oxford University Press, 1990.

Zeitlin, Jonathan, and Peter Totterdill. "Markets, Technology and Local Intervention: The Case of Clothing." In *Reversing Industrial Decline? Industrial Structure and Policy in Britain and Her Competitors,* edited by Paul Hirst and Jonathan Zeitlin. Oxford: Berg, 1989, pp. 155–90.

Zhou, Min. *Chinatown: The Socioeconomic Potential of an Urban Enclave.* Philadelphia: Temple University Press, 1992.

Zolberg, Aristide R. "International Migration Policies in a Changing World System." In *Human Migration,* edited by William H. McNeill and Ruth S. Adams. Bloomington: Indiana University Press, 1978, pp. 241–86.

——. "International Migrations in Political Perspective." In *Global Trends in Migration: Theory and Research on International Population Movements,* edited by Mary M. Kritz et al. New York: Center for Migration Studies, 1983, pp. 3–27.

——. "The Next Waves: Migration Theory for a Changing World." *International Migration Review* 23, no. 3 (Fall 1989): 403–30.

Zunz, Olivier. *The Changing Face of Inequality: Urbanization, Industrial Development, and Immigrants in Detroit, 1880–1920.* Chicago: University of Chicago Press, 1982.

Interviews

New York

Andrade, Kathy. ILGWU, Local 23–25. Oct. 4, 1984.

Baily, Saul F. Principal, High School of Fashion Industries (HSFI). July 25, 1984.

Chishti, Muzzafar. Director, Immigration Project, ILGWU. May 30 and Aug. 6, 1984.

Eisner, Mrs. New York State Apparel Employment Service. Aug. 6, 1984.

Elias, Eli. President, New York Skirt and Sportswear Association. Mar. 2, 1984.

Gonzalez, Manuel. Manager and Vice-President, ILGWU. Sept. 6, 1984.

Goodman, Shirley. Fashion Institute of Technology (FIT). Aug. 28, 1984.

Halperin, Mr. Assistant Principal, HSFI. July 25, 1984; and telephone interview, Nov. 3, 1995.

Kozinn, Andrew (President) and Schmidt, Stanley (Fashion Directory). Saint Laurie Ltd. July 12, 1984.

Meagher, Richard J. Dean, Continuing Education Program, FIT. Sept. 6, 1984.

Bibliography

Mendelsund, Henoch. ILGWU. Sept. 4, 1984.

Pappas, Cathy. Accountant in the Garment District. June 11, 1984.

Sciuto, Anthony. Manager, ILGWU Local 62–32. Sept. 10, 1984.

Siegel, Harold. Greater Blouse, Skirt and Undergarment (contractors') Association. Aug. 22, 1984.

Tyler, Gus. Former head of ILGWU Education Department and Assistant President. Sept. 17, 1984.

Wisoff, Lloyd. Former worker in Bonnaz embroidery pocketbooks. Mar. 5, 1984.

Paris

Chaupin, Paul. Labor leader. Aug. 7, 1986.

Flom, Paul. Garment manufacturer. Sept. 25, 1986.

Fogel, Michèle. Family works in the Sentier. May 10, 1987.

Gronovski, Ludwik. Jewish immigrant labor leader. Sept. 19, 1977.

Joannes, Gisèle. Former secretary-general of the Fédération de l'Habillement. Mar. 7, 1985.

Klatzmann, Joseph. Directeur d'Etudes à l'Ecole des Hautes Etudes en Sciences Sociales. Author of *Le travail à domicile.* May 25 and June 22, 1979.

Lacoste, René. Former tennis star; clothing industrialist; inventor of the "alligator shirt." Apr. 27, 1984.

Lederman, Jacques. Secretary of the Leather Workers' Union. Oct. 12, 1977.

"Michel K." Labor leader, Bourse du Travail. May 15, 1986.

Rayski, Adam. Resistance hero. Oct. 5, 1985.

Tasmadjian, Sandrine. Researcher; worked in the Sentier. Aug. 4, 1987; Dec. 19, 1995.

Tollet, André. Former Communist leader. Telephone interview, May 4, 1987.

INDEX

Austrians: in New York, 201, 288; in
   Paris, 207, 259

Balmain, Pierre, 101
Balzac, 76
Barondess, Joseph, 52
Barthes, Roland, 16–17
Baudelaire, 76
Baudrillard, Jean, 18, 41
Baum, Charlotte, 167
Bayor, Ronald, 249
Belgians: in New York, 288; in Paris,
   207–9, 254, 259
Belle Jardinière, 40, 78, 80, 95, 151
Belleville, 209, 212
Bellugue, Fernand, 90–91, 262, 371
   n.28
Benefits, 126–27, 138. *See also*
   ILGWU
Benetton, 6
Benoist, Charles, 153
Bergdorf Goodman, 47
Bergeron, Louis, 4
Bhatti, 213, 279, 289
Billig, Joseph, 98
Bisno, Abraham, 182
Blacks. *See* African Americans
Bloc socio-techologique, 40, 151, 175
Bloomer, Betty, 27
Bodnar, John, 180
Bohemians, 169
Bon Marché, 80
Booth, Charles, 156
Boris, Eileen, 131, 156
Boston, 32, 35, 52
Bourdieu, Pierre, 17–18
Boussac, 101
Bouvier, Jeanne, 84, 93
Bouvier, Pierre, 40, 248
Bradley and Carey's Hoop Skirt
   Works, 45
Brandeis, Louis D., 54, 309 n.36
"Braun, Irwin," 101, 321 n.98
British garment industry, 109, 115,
   138, 156, 215, 312 n.97

Bronx, South, 158
Brooklyn, 52, 197, 207
Brooks Brothers, 45
Brown, Irving. *See* "Braun, Irwin"
Bulgarians, 259, 263, 288
Bund, 55, 98, 260

Cacharel, 101
California, 67, 68, 280. *See also* Los
   Angeles
Capmakers, 93, 209, 253
Cardin, Pierre, 101–2
Caroli, Betty Boyd, 173
Caroti, Arturo, 224
Carpenter, Jesse, 148
Castells, Manuel, 149
Centre d'études techniques des in-
   dustries de l'habillement (CETIH),
   100, 178
Chandler, Alfred, 4
Chanel, Coco, 28, 101
Chevenard, Jeanne, 256
Chicago, 48, 52, 69, 169, 172, 173
Child labor, 46–47, 153, 155
Children's wear, 70, 109, 147
Chile, immigrants from, 214
Chinatown. *See* Chinese, in New
   York; Chinese, in Paris
Chinese, 1, 9–11, 155, 170, 175,
   195–199, 215, 284, 292; com-
   pared in New York and Paris, 216–
   17, 284; compared with Jews, 196,
   212, 275–76; in New York, 7, 40,
   147–49, 158, 169, 178, 185, 206–
   7, 216–17, 220, 229, 237, 243–
   44, 284, 287–89 (*see also* Strikes,
   New York, 1982); in Paris, 7, 11,
   147, 157, 169, 182, 184, 195–96,
   199–200, 210–12, 216–17, 251,
   263, 267–77, 282, 289, 356 n.90;
   Turks and, 273–74; women, 172,
   185, 195, 197, 207, 216–17, 239–
   42, 249, 286
Chinese-Cambodians. *See* Chinese,
   in Paris

Index

Chinese Garment Makers' Association, 148

Christman, Margaret, 21, 113–14

Civilizing function of clothing, 16–17, 25, 76–77, 103, 114, 118–19

Civil Rights Bill. *See* Legislation, U.S.

Clark, Edward, 36

Cloak, Suit, and Skirt Manufacturers' Protective Association, 54

Cloak-makers. *See* Coat and suit industry

Cloakmakers' Joint Board. *See* ILGWU Joint Board

Coat and suit industry, 23, 27, 32, 45–47, 57, 59, 62–64, 67, 166–67, 175–76, 180, 192, 201–2, 205–6, 253. *See also* ILGWU, New York Joint Board; ILGWU, Locals 2 and 9

Coffin, Judith, 156–57

Cohen, Miriam, 131–32, 174, 203, 224

Collective bargaining, 150; France, 87, 91, 126; United States, 50, 55, 59, 61, 63, 86, 122–23, 125, 142, 148

Colombians, 206

Colonial clothing. *See* Exports

Comité de défense des chambres syndicales de la couture, des dentelles et des broderies, 81

Comité d'organisation du vêtement (COV), 95–99

Comités syndicalistes révolutionnaires (CSR), 90

Commissariat général aux questions juives (CGQJ), 97

Committee for, then Congress of Industrial Organization (CIO), 60–62, 235. *See also* AFL-CIO

Commons, John, 185, 191

Communists: New York, 58–61, 125, 156, 226, 230–37, 244, 247, 310 n.60 (*see also* NTWIU; TUEL);

Paris, 74, 89–92, 125, 256, 261–65; split with French socialists, 85, 89–92, 125, 252 (*see also* Confédération générale du travail unitaire)

Comparative history, 8–9, 298 n.36–37; level of analysis, 123–24, 174, 284, 343 n.48; methods, 105–6, 126–27, 133, 139, 160, 284–285, 329 n.71; spatial comparisons, 73, 106, 123–24, 127, 133, 169, 186; temporal comparisons, 41–43, 73, 106, 186

Confédération française démocratique du travail (CFDT), 125, 211, 213, 265

Confédération générale du travail (CGT), 101, 125, 256; homework and, 84; language sections and, 256–66, 372 n.41; merger with CGTU, 122, 265; split in 1920, 89–91, 256, 261; split in 1947, 101, 125; women and, 256–57. *See also* CGTU; Fédération de l'habillement

Confédération générale du travail–Force ouvrière (CGT-FO), 101, 125

Confédération générale du travail unitaire (CGTU), 267; language sections and, 261–65; merger with CGT, 122, 265; women and, 256–57

Connecticut, 69, 168

Consumers' leagues, 141, 330 n.10

Consumption, 17–18, 24, 71, 102. *See also* Demand; Department stores

Contracting, 10, 20, 92, 124, 133, 139, 144–50, 152, 155–56, 160, 176, 205, 244, 246, 257, 262, 266, 274, 278, 281, 285, 287, 290; compared to homework, 133, 150–51; definitions, 6; efforts to regulate, 51, 63, 72–73, 144; model

Index

413

Index

Index

ILGWU branches (cont.)
nese (refused), 240; Italian, 224–
27, 248 (see also Locals 48 and
89); Italian locals as examples for
others, 230–32, 237, 245; "Jewish
union," 220, 226–27, 229, 232,
239; Russian-Polish, 204, 231;
Spanish, 206, 231; women's, 221–
23, 232
ILGWU Joint Board and Locals: New
York Joint Board of Cloak, Suit,
and Skirt Makers' Unions, 47, 55,
62, 177, 204, 231, 243; Local 2
(Cloak operators), 60; Local 9
(Cloak finishers), 60, 231; Local 10
(Cutters), 180, 233, 238, 242, 245;
Local 22 (Dress Makers), 47, 60–
61, 204–6, 227, 231, 234–36,
248, 288; Local 23-25 (Blouse,
Skirt, and Sportswear Workers),
207, 241, 244; Local 25 (Ladies'
Waist and Dress Makers), 47, 53,
60, 222; Local 35 (Pressers), 231;
Local 48 (Italian Cloak, Suit, and
Skirt Makers), 225–26, 232, 248;
Local 60-60A (Pressers and Ship-
ping Clerks), 237; Local 89 (Italian
Blouse and Waist Makers), 225–
26, 232, 237, 248; Local 102
(Cloak and Dress Drivers and
Helpers), 205; Local 117 (Sample-
makers), 231; Local 600-601
(Puerto Rico), 237
International Tailors' Congress. See
International Congress of Nee-
dleworkers
International Union Bank, 64
Intersektsionen byuro, 260, 263
Intersindikal komisie, 263
Irish, 201–2, 223, 237, 242, 288
Isambert-Jamati, Viviane, 183–84
Issy-les-Moulineaux, 210
Italians: in New York, 1, 7, 10, 11,
58, 170–71, 174, 180, 192–95,
199, 202–9, 214, 243, 246–48,

269, 278, 284, 286, 288, 289, 292
(see also ILGWU, Locals 48 and
89); in Paris, 193, 207–9, 254–56,
259, 263–64, 289; Jews and, 192–
95, 202, 220, 223–27, 247, 250
Italians, women, 54, 155, 172–74,
192–97, 202–5, 217, 222–26,
249, 286; American-born, 203,
234; skill, 179–82. See also
Women, Italian and Jewish,
compared

Jacobs, In re, 129
Japan, 31, 70; Japanese immigrants,
288
Jarillot, 100
Jaurès, Jean, 258
Jeans, 21, 23, 28, 39–40, 117
Jenson, Jane, 127, 131
Jewish Labor Committee, 226
Jews (general), 1, 9, 10, 170–71, 199,
218, 268–69, 284, 286, 289, 292;
compared in New York and Paris,
215–16, 284; compared with Chinese, 196, 212, 275–76; as tailors,
7, 170, 189–92, 216, 283–84
Jews in New York (general):
American-born, 222, 224;
Austrian-Hungarian, 201; German,
197, 201–2; Jewish-American
women, 11, 248–49; Turkish, 204
Jews in New York, Eastern European
(Polish, Russian), 33, 52, 54, 58,
60, 168, 173–75, 180–81, 186,
189–94, 197–98, 201–5, 207,
209, 214–15, 217, 243, 246, 248–
49, 268–69, 278, 284, 288–89;
African Americans and, 220, 233–
39, 242, 244–50; American
women and, 221–23; Italians and,
192–95, 202, 220, 223–27, 247,
250. See also ILGWU
Jews in Paris (general), 3, 191, 267,
268, 275, 277–78; Alsatian, 269;
Turkish, 7, 204, 209

Index

Index

Index

Index

Index

Index

Index

Women garment workers (*cont.*) 243; immigrants and, 168, 190, 221–23 (in New York), 253–57 (in Paris); Italian and Jewish, compared, 173–74, 193–94, 202–3, 223–25, 250, 359 n.15; strikers in New York, 53–54 (*see also* "Uprising of the 20,000"); strikers in Paris, 86–88; union activist, 62, 256. *See also* Division of labor, gendered; Employment statistics; Homework; Secondary labor market; Skill

Women's Bureau, U.S., 130

Women's Trade Union League (WTUL), 53–54, 173, 221, 224, 245

Wong, Bernard, 240–41

Work clothes, 39, 48, 52, 78, 97

Work sharing, 63, 142–44, 246, 284

World War I, 10, 27, 31, 67; France, 81–82, 85, 90, 104; United States, 56, 205

World War II, 10, 31, 67, 120–21; France, 74, 95–100, 104, 121; United States, 65–66, 67–68, 121, 205, 227

Wormser and Boulanger, 254

Worth, Charles Frederick, 116

Wrong, Elaine, 205, 245

Yiddish, 228–29, 231, 238, 248, 255, 256, 264, 361 n.33. See also *Idisher arbayter, Der*

Yugoslavs, 7, 11, 170, 195, 200, 210–11, 215, 218, 263, 268, 272–78, 284, 286, 289–90

Zeitlin, Jonathan, 5, 138, 150

Zimmerman, Charles (Sacha), 61, 231, 234–35, 237–38, 250. *See also* ILGWU, Local 22

Zolberg, Aristide, 123

Nancy L. Green is Director d'Etudes (Professor) at the Ecole des Hautes Etudes en Sciences Sociales, and Visiting Professor at the Overseas Studies Program in Paris, Stanford University. She is the author of *The Pletzl of Paris: Jewish Immigrant Workers in the Belle Epoque* and *Et ils peuplèrent l'Amérique: L'odyssée des émigrants.*

Library of Congress Cataloging-in-Publication Data

Green, Nancy L.
Ready-to-wear and ready-to-work : a century of industry and immigrants in
Paris and New York / Nancy L. Green.
  p.   cm. — (Comparative and international working-class history)
Includes bibliographical references and index.
ISBN 0-8223-1884-9 (cloth : alk. paper). — ISBN 0-8223-1874-1 (paper :
alk. paper)
1. Immigrant clothing workers—France—Paris—History.   2. Immigrant
clothing workers—New York (State)—New York—History.   3. Immigrants—
Employment—France—Paris—History.   4.   Immigrants—Employment—
New York (State)—New York—History.   I. Title.   II. Series.
HD6073.C62F734   1997
331.4′887′094436—dc20   96-24659
                                                                  CIP